PROCLAIMING REVOLUTION: BOLIVIA IN COMPARATIVE PERSPECTIVE

Proclaiming Revolution:
Bolivia in Comparative Perspective

Edited by
Merilee Grindle and Pilar Domingo

A Joint Publication of
Institute of Latin American Studies, University of London
and
David Rockefeller Center for Latin American Studies,
Harvard University

Distributed by
Harvard University Press
Cambridge, Massachusetts
London, England

First printed in Great Britain.

A joint publication of the Institute of Latin American Studies, University of London, and the David Rockefeller Center for Latin American Studies, Harvard University.

Institute of Latin American Studies
31 Tavistock Square, London WC1H 9HA, UK

David Rockefeller Center for Latin American Studies
Harvard University, 61 Kirkland St, Cambridge, Mass., USA

ISBN 0–674–01141–4

Library of Congress Cataloging-in-Publication Data
Proclaiming revolution : Bolivia in comparative perspective / edited by Merilee Grindle and Pilar Domingo.
p. cm. — (David Rockefeller Center series on Latin American studies, Harvard University ; 10)
Includes bibliographical references.
ISBN 0-674-01141-4
1.Bolivia— History—Revolution, 1952. 2. Bolivia—History—1938—1982. 3. Bolivia—History—1982- 4. Revolutions—Latin America—History—20th century. 5. Social change—Bolivia—History—20th century. 6. Political participation—History—20th century. I. Grindle, Merilee Serrill. II. Domingo, Pilar. III. Series.

F3326.P76 2003
984.05'2–dc21

2003005161

British Library Cataloguing-in-Publication Data
A catalogue record for this book is available from the British Library

Table of Contents

Acknowledgements vii
List of Contributors ix
List of Tables xi
List of Figures xii
List of Acronyms xiii

INTRODUCTION

Chapter 1 **1952 and All That: The Bolivian Revolution in Comparative Perspective**
Merilee S. Grindle 1

HOW REVOLUTIONARY THE REVOLUTION?

Chapter 2 **The Bolivian National Revolution: A Comparison**
Laurence Whitehead 25

Chapter 3 **The Domestic Dynamics of the Mexican and Bolivian Revolutions**
Alan Knight 54

Chapter 4 **Braked but not Broken: The United States and Revolutionaries in Mexico and Bolivia**
Ken Lehman 91

REVOLUTIONARY VISIONS AND ACTORS

Chapter 5 **Revolutionary Memory in Bolivia: Anticolonial and National Projects from 1781 to 1952**
Sinclair Thomson 117

Chapter 6 **The Origins of the Bolivian Revolution in the Twentieth Century: Some Reflections**
James Dunkerley 135

Chapter 7 **Revisiting the Rural Roots of the Revolution**
Laura Gotkowitz 164

Chapter 8 **Capturing Indian Bodies, Hearths and Minds: 'El hogar campesino' and Rural School Reform in Bolivia, 1920s–1940s**
Brooke Larson 183

REVOLUTIONARY CONSEQUENCES

Chapter 9 **The National Revolution and its Legacy**
Juan Antonio Morales 213

Chapter 10 **Social Change in Bolivia since 1952**
Herbert S. Klein 232

Chapter 11 **A Comparative Perspective on Education Reforms in Bolivia: 1950–2000**
Manuel E. Contreras 259

UNFINISHED AGENDAS AND NEW INITIATIVES

Chapter 12 **Political Parties Since 1964: The Construction of Bolivia's Multiparty System**
Eduardo Gamarra 289

Chapter 13 **Shadowing the Past? Policy Reform in Bolivia, 1985–2002**
Merilee S. Grindle 318

Chapter 14 **The Offspring of 1952: Poverty, Exclusion and the Promise of Popular Participation**
George Gray Molina 345

CONCLUSION

Chapter 15 **Revolution and the Unfinished Business of Nation- and State-Building**
Pilar Domingo 364

Bibliography 381

ACKNOWLEDGEMENTS

This volume is the result of collaboration between the David Rockefeller Center for Latin American Studies (DRCLAS) at Harvard University and the Institute for Latin American Studies (ILAS) at the University of London; it is testimony to the spirit of inquiry that animates both organizations. At the suggestion of James Dunkerley, director of ILAS and one of the editors, both centers agreed to co-sponsor a conference, convened at Harvard in early May 2002, on 'The Bolivian Revolution at 50: Comparative Views on Social, Economic and Political Change'. The purpose of this conference was to present current research as a retrospective on the Revolution of 1952 and to compare its social, economic and political causes and consequences with those of other major national revolutions. We were gratified by how eager scholars in Bolivia, the USA and the UK were to participate in this event and were excited by the new insights and careful analysis found in the papers presented there.

The directors of DRCLAS and ILAS, John Coatsworth and James Dunkerley, encouraged and shaped the conference and this volume with their advice and support. We are deeply grateful to them for their interest and the assistance of the centers they lead. In addition, the authors benefited from the helpful critiques by Olivia Harris and Pilar Domingo of the University of London, John Coatsworth, Jane Mangan, Jorge Dominguez and Mary Hilderbrand of Harvard University and Susan Eckstein of Boston University. As the volume took shape, we also received helpful advice from two anonymous reviewers. The insights of these scholars were critical to the revised versions of the papers that appear here.

The conference could not have occurred without the dedication and spirit of the staff at the David Rockefeller Center at Harvard. In particular, Marcela Rentería and Neida Jiménez marshaled their many talents to ensure that the conference proceeded without logistical or culinary hitches. After the conference, June Erlick took charge of the publications process until a revised manuscript was delivered to John Maher at ILAS. Here, we can only celebrate their professionalism and advice, but they also know how much of the resulting volume rested in their capable hands. Also at Harvard, Aaron Jette and Helen Hawkins worked ably on the manuscript against very tight deadlines. We are very grateful to all who contributed their time, effort and advice to this volume. While they deserve credit for its appearance, the editors and authors, of course, take responsibility for its intellectual content.

List of Contributors

Manuel E. Contreras is a Social Development Specialist-Lecturer at the Inter-American Institute for Social Development (INDES) at the Inter-American Development Bank in Washington, DC. He has written extensively on Bolivian economic history and current social and educational policy issues. He is currently working on a monograph to commemorate the tenth anniversary of Bolivia's 1994 education reform and a history of education in that country in the twentieth century.

Pilar Domingo is a Researcher at the Instituto de Estudios de Iberoamérica y Portugal at the University of Salamanca, Spain. Her research focuses on democratic government, rule of law and judicial politics in Latin America, with particular interest in Bolivia and Mexico. Recent publications include 'Party Politics, Intermediation and Representation,' in Crabtree and Whitehead (eds.), *Towards Democratic Viability: The Bolivian Experience* (2001) and *Rule of Law in Latin America* (2001), co-edited with Rachel Sieder.

James Dunkerley is Director of the Institute for Latin American Studies and Professor of Politics at Queen Mary, University of London. His books include *Rebellion in the Veins: Political Struggles in Bolivia,* 1952–82 (1984) and *Americana: The Americas in the World, Around 1850* (2000).

Eduardo Gamarra is Director of the Latin American and Caribbean Center and Professor of Political Science at Florida International University. He is co-author with James Malloy of *Revolution and Reaction: Bolivia, 1964–1985* (1988) and co-editor of two books on political and policy reform. He has written extensively on political parties in Bolivia and other Latin American countries.

Laura Gotkowitz is Assistant Professor of History at the University of Iowa. Her work on race and gender in twentieth-century Bolivia has appeared in collections published in Bolivia and the United States. She is the author of the forthcoming book, *Within the Boundaries of Equality: Citizenship, Race, and Nation. Bolivia, 1880–1952.*

George Gray Molina is Director of the Unidad de Análisis de Política Económica (UDAPE) in the Bolivian government and was Director of the Maestrías para el Desarrollo Program of the Universidad Católica Boliviana. He has written on the Popular Participation program in Bolivia and on issues of inclusion and exclusion in the country.

Merilee Grindle is Edward S. Mason Professor of International Development at the Kennedy School of Government at Harvard University and faculty chair of the MPA programs. Her two most recent books are *Audacious Reforms: Institutional Invention and Democracy in Latin America* (2000) and *Despite the Odds: The Contentious Politics of Education Reform* (forthcoming).

Herbert S. Klein is Professor of Latin American History at Columbia University. He is the author of three books on Bolivian history: *Parties and Political Change in Bolivia (1880–1952)* (1969), *Haciendas and Ayllus: Rural Society in the Bolivian Andes in the 18th and 19th Centuries* (1993) and *A Concise History of Bolivia* (2002). He has also published extensively on Brazil, the comparative history of slavery in Latin America and colonial fiscal history.

Alan Knight holds the Chair of Latin American History at Oxford University. He is the author of *The Mexican Revolution* (2 volumes, 1986) and numerous articles on Mexican history and politics. He has just published two volumes of a planned three-volume history of Mexico (*From the Beginning to the Spanish Conquest* and *The Colonial Era*) and is currently working on study of Mexico in the 1930s.

Brooke Larson is Professor of History at Stony Brook University. Her books include *Cochabamba, 1550–1900. Colonialism and Agrarian Transformation in Bolivia* (2nd edition, 1998) and, more recently, I*ndígenas, élites y estado en la formación de las repúblicas andinas* (2002). She is currently writing a book on the contentious cultural politics and social practice of rural Indian schooling in early twentieth-century Bolivia.

Ken Lehman is Associate Professor of History at Hampden-Sydney College in Virginia. He lived and taught in Bolivia and is the author of *Bolivia and the United States: A Limited Partnership*. He is currently working on a study of the United States and the Bolivian revolutionary regime, 1952–64.

Juan Antonio Morales obtained his MA and PhD in Economics at the Catholic University of Louvain, Belgium and is the author of over 40 books and articles. He is currently President of the Central Bank of Bolivia. Prior to this, he was a professor at the Universidad Católica Boliviana and lectured in several European, American and Latin American universities.

Sinclair Thomson is Associate Professor of Latin American History at New York University and the author of *We Alone Will Rule: Native Andean Politics in the Age of Insurgency* (2002). His chapter in this volume is part of his current work on the meaning of great Andean insurrection in contemporary historical consciousness.

Laurence Whitehead is an Official Fellow in Politics at Nuffield College, Oxford and Director of Oxford University's newly established Centre for Mexican Studies. He is editor of *Oxford Studies in Democratization* and was co-editor of the *Journal of Latin American Studies* until 2002. His most recent publication on Bolivia is a volume edited with John Crabtree, *Towards Democratic Viability: The Bolivian Experience* (2001).

List of Tables

Table 6.1:	Tin Exports, 1900–30	141
Table 6.2:	World Production of Tin, by country, 1900–52 (000 tons)	142
Table 6.3:	Tax Burden of Patiño Mines, 1924–49	149
Table 6.4:	Mining Taxes and State Revenue	150
Table 6.5:	Foreign Exchange Policies, 1932–52	151
Table 6.6:	Tin Production by Firm (annual average; metric tonnes)	152
Table 6.7:	US and UK Tin Stocks, 1942–45 (long tons, metal content)	154
Table 9.1:	The Human Development Index and its Components for Selected Latin American Countries	221
Table 9.2:	Per capita Gross Domestic Product in Bolivia and Latin America	222
Table 9.3:	Infant Mortality Rates (per thousand) in Bolivia and Latin America	223
Table 10.1:	Distribution of Land in Bolivia in 1950	233
Table 10.2:	Land Ownership by Type of Unit, Bolivia 1950	234
Table 10.3:	Capital Cities According to the National Census, 1846-2001	235
Table 10.4:	Bolivia in Comparative Perspective — Life Expectancy and Mortality	246
Table 10.5:	Bolivia in Comparative Perspective — Adult Illiteracy	249
Table 11.1:	Annual Growth Rates for Enrollment in Primary Education in Bolivia and Cuba for Selected Periods	264
Table 11.2:	Level of Achievement in Mathematics and Language by Third Grade Students in Urban and Rural Areas, 2000 (percentage of students at a given level)	281
Table 11.3:	Level of Achievement in Language and Mathematics by Third Grade Students with and without Education Reform (percentage of students at a given level)	281
Table 13.1:	Policy Reform in Bolivia 1985–2002	320
Table 14.1:	Population Growth 1950–2001	347
Table 14.2:	Schooling by Age Cohorts	348
Table 14.3:	Poverty Exit Time	349
Table 14.4:	Municipal Election Results 1987–99	354

List of Figures

Figure 10.1:	Age Pyramid by Sex, Bolivia 1950	237
Figure 10.2:	Changing Life Expectancy in Bolivia by Sex and by Decade 1949-2000	239
Figure 10.3:	Total Fertility and Infant Mortality in Bolivia, 1950-1995	240
Figure 10.4:	Crude Birth, Death, Out-Migration and Growth Rates of the Bolivian Population, 1950-2005 (per 1,000 resident population)	240
Figure 10.5:	Ratio of Population Surviving by Given Age, Bolivia 1950-55 and 2000-05	242
Figure 10.6:	Life Expectancy in Bolivia and Haiti, 1950-95 – Males	244
Figure 10.7:	Life Expectancy in Bolivia and Haiti, 1950-95 – Females	244
Figure 10.8:	Infant Mortality in Bolivia, Haiti and All Latin America, 1950-2000	245
Figure 10.9:	Percentage who attended Primary School for the Age Cohort Born in that Year (from Household Surveys 1999-2000)	247
Figure 10.10:	Average Years of Schooling Completed in 2000	247
Figure 10.11:	Level of Adult Illiteracy in Bolivia and Latin America in 2000	248
Figure 10.12:	Percentage Illiteracy by Age and Sex, Bolivia, 1976 Census	250
Figure 10.13:	Difference in Net Rates of Participation in Primary Education in Latin America in 2000	251
Figure 11.1:	Primary School Enrollment in Bolivia and Cuba, 1942–69	263
Figure 11.2:	Number of Rural Education Núcleos, 1935-68	265
Figure 11.3:	Bolivia, Mexico and Latin America: Average Years of Education by Birth Cohort, 1920–75	267
Figure 11.4.	Education Expenditure as a Percentage of GDP	279

List of Acronyms

AD	Acción Democrática (Venezuela)
ADN	Acción Democrática Nacionalista
AF of L	American Federation of Labor
CEPB	Confederación de Empresarios Privados de Bolivia
CIO	Congress of Industrial Organizations
CNE	National Electoral Court
COB	Central Obrera Boliviana
COMIBOL	Corporación Minera de Bolivia
CONDEPA	Conciencia de Patria
CROM	Confederación Regional Obrera Mexicana
CSUTCB	Confederación Sindical Unica de Trabajadores Campesinos de Bolivia
CTM	Confederación de Trabajadores de Mexico
ENVP	Effective number of parties
ETARE	Technical Support Team for Education Reform
FAOSTAT	Statistical Database of the Food and Agriculture Organization of the United Nations
FOF	Federación Obrera Feminina
FSB	Falange Socialista Boliviano
FSTMB	Federación Sindical de Trabajadores Mineros de Bolivia
FTAA	Free Trade Area of the Americas
GMD	Guomindang (China)
IIAA	Institute of Inter-American Affairs
ILDIS	Instituto Latinoamericano de Investigaciones Sociales
ILO	International Labor Office
INE	Instituto Nacional de Estadísticas de Bolivia
KMT	Kuomintang (China)
LNDR	Liga Nacional para la Defensa Religiosa (Mexico)
MAC	Ministerio de Asuntos Campesinos
MAS	Movimiento al Socialismo
MBL	Movimiento Bolivia Libre
MECOVI	Programa para el Mejoramiento de las Encuestas y la Medición de las Condiciones de Vida en América Latina
MIR	Movimiento de la Iquierda Revolucionaria
MNR	Movimiento Nacional Revolucionario
MNRA	Movimiento Nacionalista Revolucionario Auténtico
MNRI	MNR Izquierda

MRTK-L	Movimiento Revolucionario Túpac Katari de Liberación
NFR	Nueva Fuerza Republicana
NPE	Nueva Política Económica
OCIA	Office of the Coordinator of Inter-American Affairs
ORIT	Organización Regional Interamericano de Trabajadores
OTBs	Organizaciones Territoriales de Base
PAN	Partido Acción Nacional (Mexico)
PCB	Partido Comunista de Bolivia
PCM	Partido Comunista de México
PIR	Partido de la Izquierda Revolucionaria
PMEC	Patiño Mines and Enterprises Consolidated
PNR	Partido Nacional Revolucionario (Mexico)
POR	Partido Obrero Revolucionario
PPL	Popular Participation Law
PPS	Partido Popular Socialista (Mexico)
PRI	Partido Revolucionario Institucional (Mexico)
PRIN	Partido Revolucionario de la Izquierda Nacionalista
PRM	Partido de la Revolución Mexicana
PRUN	National Unification Revolutionary Party (Mexico)
PSOB	Partido Socialista Obrero Boliviano
RADEPA	Razón de Patria
RFC	Reconstruction Finance Corporation
SCIDE	Servicio Cooperativa Inter-Americano de Educación
SIMECAL	Sistema de Medición de Calidad (Education)
UCS	Unión Cívica de Solidaridad
UDAPE	Economic Policy Analysis Unit
UNS	Unión Nacional Sinarquista
YPFB	Yacimientos Petrolíferos Fiscales Bolivianos

INTRODUCTION

Chapter 1

1952 and All That: The Bolivian Revolution in Comparative Perspective

Merilee S. Grindle

9 April 2002, the fiftieth anniversary of the Revolution of 1952, passed quietly in Bolivia. In the Plaza Murillo in La Paz, the Movimiento Nacionalista Revolucionario (MNR) celebrated the occasion with a rally and speeches by its presidential candidates, Gonzalo Sánchez de Lozada and Carlos Diego Mesa Gisbert. Mesa Gisbert, the candidate for vice president, extolled the importance of the popular insurrection that toppled the old order — the *Rosca*, the *latifundia* and an army that was then in the service of the oligarchy.[1] He invoked the names of revolutionary heroes — Víctor Paz Estenssoro, Hernán Siles Zuazo, Walter Guevara Arze, Juan Lechín Oquendo and others — and insisted that the events of April 1952 were 'to change the destiny of an entire country and to begin a revolution that would stand alongside the Mexican and Cuban revolutions as one of the most important in the history of Latin America'.[2] MNR presidential candidate Sánchez de Lozada followed with a speech in which he railed against the corruption and ineptitude of the government currently in power.[3]

These events were reported on national television and newspapers produced dutiful editorials about the events of 1952. *La Razón* published a special section on the revolution, detailing the importance of its legacy — the nationalization of the mines, the agrarian reform, universal suffrage and the diversification of the economy.[4] In a few cities campaign events invoked the country's revolutionary past. Opposition parties used the occasion to denounce the MNR and the 'new oligarchy' that had emerged when Bolivian industries were privatized and sold to transnational businesses.[5] One editorial commented dispiritedly that Bolivians needed to think about whether the country 'is capable of beginning processes of great regional importance without having the strength and continuity to achieve them successfully'.[6]

Beyond these few events, 9 April was like most other days in the country. There were no parades, it was not a national holiday, the government made no official announcement about the event and most Bolivians seemed to take little notice of the anniversary of their revolution. The flags most in evidence at celebrations were not those of the nation but those of the MNR. More generally, Bolivians are not often reminded of the revolution. No major street in La Paz is named Avenida 9 de Abril or Avenida de la Revolución. No important public park or plaza is named after a revolutionary hero. Major figures of the revolution remain controversial and enigmatic in the popular mind.

The tepid observance of the anniversary of Bolivia's revolution in 2002 stands in considerable contrast to how other Latin American countries remember their revolutionary upheavals. In Mexico, a country often emulated by Bolivia's revolutionaries, the events, heroes, villains and consequences of 1910 are celebrated in public murals, national colors, statues, street names and vivid political rhetoric. In Cuba, the iconography of the 1959 Revolution cannot be overlooked, the names of Che, Fidel and Camilo are universally invoked, the *Granma* has been encased in glass and hoisted into public prominence, great public spaces are named for the event and the language of revolution is everywhere. Even in Nicaragua, whose revolution left a country bitterly divided and impoverished, there are statues and places that commemorate the vision and nationalism of the Sandinistas.

It is easy, of course, to find reasons to explain the lack of celebratory hoopla in Bolivia in 2002. The revolution is deeply associated with the MNR; its marking by a government led by Acción Democrática Nacionalista would not have seemed a good idea to that government. More broadly, 50 years after the revolution, disappointment shaded much scholarship and commentary on the country's condition. Critics pointed to its continued poverty; the failure of agrarian reform to create productive agriculture among the peasant population of the highlands; the failure of universal suffrage and education reform to emancipate Aymara, Quechua, Guaraní and other indigenous peoples from poverty and powerlessness; the emergence of a middle class dependent on state largesse; the development of a corrupt and patronage-ridden state; the ubiquity of clientelism; the continuation of a tradition of racism and injustice; an economy resisting growth and prone to crisis; and a host of other problems.

Moreover, the events of April 1952 were brief compared to revolutionary struggles in other countries. Three days of confrontations primarily in La Paz, Cochabamba and Oruro contrast with almost a decade of widespread violence in Mexico, over two tumultuous years in Cuba and the better part of a year in Nicaragua. The number of Bolivian martyrs pales in comparison with these other countries — about 550 dead in Bolivia, but over a million in Mexico and many thousands in Cuba and Nicaragua. Perhaps as important, radical measures were taken quickly — most within the first 18 months of the new government — and then the revolutionary dynamic gave way to its Thermidor in 1956. Mexico, Cuba and Nicaragua took more time to construct their revolutions.

From other perspectives, however, the Bolivian Revolution was not so different from others in Latin America. It is certainly not alone in having fallen short of its transformative purpose. In Mexico, the radical vision of the *agraristas* and workers who fought for a new day gave way to an authoritarian party regime skilled in the arts of political control. The Cuban Revolution also spawned a party that was quick to build a country in its own image. And the Nicaraguan Revolution fell as prey to authoritarian and centralizing tendencies as did those in Mexico and Cuba. There are other similarities. While Mexico had its *soldaderas* and revolutions in Cuba and Nicaragua had their heroines, Bolivia had its Barzolas who staunchly defended the party in the wake of the revolution. While it was primarily workers who were at the barricades in April 1952, peasants were as important to the accomplishment of agrarian reform as were those in Mexico, Cuba and Nicaragua. These countries also shared the same revolutionary goals — nationalization of important industries, redistribution of land, radical expansion of education, empowerment of subordinate groups.

Indeed, the Bolivian Revolution of 1952 was important. It introduced changes that, for their time and place, were transformative. The army was destroyed in a mere three days of fighting. Workers and peasants took up arms to claim the country as their own. Overnight, an electorate of 200,000 was expanded to over one million through the introduction of universal suffrage. Industries that had placed most of the economic power of the country in a very few hands were nationalized and turned over to worker organizations to manage. Land concentrated in feudal haciendas was distributed to peasant communities. Education was declared to be universal and free. The MNR and its allies among worker and peasant organizations promoted a new vision of nationalism that redefined the nature of citizenship and politics in the country. Certainly these accomplishments were significant.

Yet questions remain about events and processes surrounding 1952. Bolivia's revolution is less studied than the twentieth century's other social revolutions; its causes and consequences are less often the subject of debate and new scholarship. The 50th anniversary of the revolution offered an opportunity to explore contrasting visions about change in this oft forgotten country and to put its experience in historical and comparative perspective. In May 2002, a conference on the Bolivian Revolution was organized by the David Rockefeller Center for Latin American Studies (DRCLAS) of Harvard University and the Institute of Latin American Studies (ILAS) at the University of London. Researchers from Bolivia, the UK and the USA met at Harvard to present current scholarship on the revolution and to compare it with other major national revolutions.

This volume presents the results of that inquiry. Several chapters explore the extent to which 1952 can be considered a revolution in the tradition of those great social transformations that occurred in France, Mexico, Russia, China and Cuba. Other contributors address the question of historical memory and the extent to which the revolution shaped new interpretations of Bolivia's place in the world and assess perspectives that place rural and indigenous protest at the margin of the events that led up to the events of 1952. Some chapters consider the consequences of the revolution in the political and economic development of the country since 1952. And some contributors write of Bolivia 50 years after the revolution, assessing the parties, structures and policies currently shaping economic, political and social conditions in the country. Contributors do not speak with one voice on these issues, but they consistently conclude that the revolution added up to much more than its 50th anniversary suggested.

A Skeletal History of the Revolution

Contributions to this volume address a wide variety of events related to the antecedents to the revolution, what occurred during the 12 years that the MNR held power between 1952 and 1964, the enduring consequences of revolution and the unfinished work of economic, political and social transformation. They make reference to historical events and discuss their meaning in the broader sweep of Bolivian and Latin American history. This section provides a brief chronology of important events from the 1940s to the 1990s to serve as a background for those discussions. Its purpose is not to interpret the revolution, but simply to present a skeleton on which subsequent chapters can drape their interpretations.

The party that led and inherited the revolution, the Movimiento Nacionalista Revolucionario, was formally organized in 1941 around a core of urban intellectuals, students and middle class professionals. Its initial orientation was nationalist, corporatist and socialist, and it was not initially a party that sought a broad base of electoral support. In 1943, the party joined the government of Gualberto Villarroel, helped introduce a series of reforms and encouraged the political organization of workers and peasants. Nevertheless, mounting opposition and miscalculations by the government led to a popular uprising and Villarroel was killed, later to be remembered as a martyr to the revolution in formation. Subsequent governments, along with the military, reinforced the power of the country's oligarchy of tin barons and landholders. Repression of the MNR and radical workers' groups followed and in 1949 the MNR led an insurrection against the government; a brief civil war ensued. On the losing side, with its leaders driven into exile or jailed, the party nevertheless became convinced that it had a growing base of support in the country.

With this support, the MNR emerged the winner from elections in 1951. Such was the volatility and polarization of politics, however, that the elections were annulled and the military again assumed power. Throughout its first decade, then, the MNR found itself in a highly unstable, deeply factionalized and often violent political environment. In a context of extraordinary social and political inequality, radical and armed workers, an indigenous population increasingly conscious of its subordination, a weak and ineffective state and an economy in deep crisis, the next step was revolution.

On the evening 8 April 1952, 2,000 national policemen under the command of General Antonio Seleme joined MNR party leaders under Hernán Siles Zuazo in La Paz to set in motion an uprising that had been in the planning for some time. During the night, the police, workers and party loyalists occupied the city; at dawn, Radio Illimani announced — prematurely — that a revolution had triumphed. The army assembled 8,000 soldiers above and below the city and began counter-attacks. Seleme, certain the army would win, handed leadership over to the MNR and ran off to the Chilean Embassy. The insurrection took on renewed life, however, when miners north of the city moved against the army, captured their air base and routed them. Elsewhere, miners and MNR loyalists prevented the military from aiding beleaguered regiments in La Paz. The end was swift. The military virtually disintegrated and on Good Friday, 11 April, Siles Zuazo accepted a formal surrender. The city of La Paz was left in the control of armed workers and MNR activists; Siles Zuazo was sworn in as provisional president on 13 April. Víctor Paz Estenssoro, the party's leader and winner of the 1951 elections, returned from exile in Argentina on 15 April to assume the presidency.

The MNR emerged as the leader of the revolution, but workers and peasants were essential to its triumph and survival. On 17 April the Central Obrera Boliviana (COB) brought the armed and powerful workers' organizations together under the leadership of Juan Lechín, head of the Federación Sindical de Trabajadores de Bolivia, the strongest and largest of these organizations. The power of the COB and the insistence on its demands underpinned the speed and radical nature of many of the new government's policies. Similarly, in rural areas inhabited by indigenous populations, armed peasant syndicates and villages began turning hacienda owners off the land and taking control of the countryside.[7] With power clearly in the hands of the MNR and its worker and peasant allies, the major initiatives of the revolution were put in place in short order. Universal suffrage was declared on 21 July; on 31 October the country's major mining enterprises were nationalized; on 2 August 1953, the agrarian reform was announced; and in 1955, the education reform became law.

Before long, however, economic disorder disrupted the plans of the government. In 1956, US foreign aid and a US-inspired IMF stabilization plan brought an end to the most radical phase of the revolution, a result not unwelcome to more conservative elements within the MNR. In the period between 1956 and 1964, militant workers who formed the left wing of the party were increasingly marginalized and the MNR government came to depend on a coalition of middle class, military and peasant adherents. Indeed, under the pressure of divergent interests, the party split and split again during the late 1950s and early 1960s. An increasingly factionalized government turned ever more to the military to maintain order and particularly to suppress the demands of radical mine workers. Shortly after Paz Estenssoro was elected to his third term in office, on November 3, 1964, the military overthrew the MNR government.

Between 1964 and 1978 the military ruled in a series of populist and authoritarian governments joined by alternating factions of the MNR. During this period, the eastern part of the country, with its center in Santa Cruz, grew rapidly in economic power and its claims for political voice increased. This region, distant from the issues and passions of the revolution, represented the non-indigenous, non-mining economy of the country. It also developed as an alternative base of power where the MNR was weak.

Along with other political parties, the MNR was banned in 1974. With the return of democratic elections in 1978, it re-emerged with Paz Estenssoro as its presidential candidate and captured a distant third place in fraudulent elections. Contention over the outcome resulted in a coup, a countercoup, new elections in 1979, an interim president, a coup, another interim president, another election and then a violent and corrupt military interregnum between 1980 and 1982. Finally, in October 1982, the winner of the 1980 elections, Hernán Siles Zuazo, now of the Unidad Democrática Popular party, was confirmed president. Three very turbulent years later, the MNR under Paz Estenssoro was returned to the presidency to oversee the introduction of a wide range of neoliberal policy reforms in the context of a severe economic crisis. The MNR lost the elections of 1989, but reemerged in the presidency in 1993 and, during the next four years, introduced a series of innovative economic, political and social policies that made the government a darling of international development assistance agencies. The MNR had come a long way from its beginning in 1941. But did it make a revolution?

The Revolutionary Experience: New Scholarship, New Findings

After 50 years, the Revolution of 1952 remains a vital topic in historiography and social, economic and political analysis. As subsequent chapters indicate, when historians revisit the revolution, they find important parallels with the Mexican Revolution and explanations for why the United States turned a less aggressive eye on Bolivia and Mexico than it did on Cuba and Nicaragua. They also find deep changes in the social conditions of the country that parallel changes found in other Latin American countries, revolutionary or not. They find parallels in previous periods of Bolivian history and an old regime that sought to reconstruct indigenous culture to accord with its own values and behaviors. They find groups previously considered not to have contributed much to the revolution active protagonists in bringing it about.

When political scientists revisit the revolution, they find policy improvisation along with predictable political dynamics and new generations of Bolivians who interpret the challenge of political representation in distinct ways. They find that policy changes of the late twentieth century owe something to the political forms devised by the revolution to hold a broad coalition of interests together but much more to new dynamics of policy formation and implementation. They find that parties spawned before and after the revolution are a weak link in the continued political development of the country. And, when economists revisit the revolution, they find cause to criticize the defects of the development policies it adopted.

Taken together, these findings are suggestive of new interpretations of revolutionary processes, emphasizing new antecedents and new actors. This volume presents these interpretations in four sections. First, a series of chapters addresses the issue of the scope of revolutionary change ushered in though the events of 1952. Second, several chapters deal with the meaning of revolution in Bolivia over time and the actors that shaped the meaning of that event. Then, a series of chapters considers the economic and political consequences of the revolution in the period after 1952. A fourth set of chapters considers contemporary political and social issues in Bolivia and explores the extent to which the revolution remains to be accomplished. A concluding chapter takes a look at the accumulation of unfinished agendas that are critical to the future social, political and economic development of the country.

How Revolutionary the Revolution?

Does the Bolivian Revolution of 1952 belong on the list of great social upheavals, side by side with the French, Mexican, Russian, Chinese and Cuban revolutions? This is the question central to the analyses provided by Laurence Whitehead, Alan Knight and Ken Lehman. In separate chapters, they consider the actions of the Bolivian government between 1952 and 1964 and assess the major challenges it confronted domestically and internationally. They assess the major accomplishments and failures of the MNR government and compare this revolutionary 'moment' to the accomplishments of other major revolutions. Central to all these chapters is an explicit comparison with other countries that have experienced major social transformations.

In Chapter 2, Laurence Whitehead argues that the Bolivian experience was indeed a thoroughgoing social revolution. He is clear that the policies put in place in the early years of the MNR government were radical, intentional and far-reaching and that they destroyed critically important components of the old order — the military, the landowners, the big mining companies. The revolution came about because previous governments failed to respond to mounting internal demands for reform. Moreover, the

MNR experience in the Villarroel government destroyed the party's belief in reformism; if the old order would not permit reform, the only option was to sweep it away. Radical policies in the initial months of the new government were a clear and perhaps inevitable response to pent-up demands for change. But Whitehead argues that redistribution was also a way to hold the center while reaching agreement with the agendas of different revolutionary groups made strong by their control over arms and constituencies. In this context, universal suffrage, which Whitehead sees as a deeply revolutionary innovation at the time, was a clear policy to institutionalize radical policies and undermine the power of the right.

By the mid-1950s, however, the weakness of the state had become apparent and Whitehead demonstrates that its inability to manage and implement many of its initial policies stood in stark contrast to the increasing strength of local pressures and political dynamics. Just as important, competing factions emerged within the party and within the COB. In a context of deep economic crisis, the government did what it deemed necessary to reconstitute central authority — it appealed for US economic support even though this meant supporting counter-insurgency as a national policy, marginalizing the COB and the radical workers and making alliances with new groups of entrepreneurs, the military, the Church and other conservative forces. Domestically, holding the center increasingly meant not policy but a division of spoils of office — public positions, projects and jobs. Together, these strategies ended the revolution and made Paz complicit in its demise even before the military coup of 1964. Despite this faltering, Whitehead places Bolivia in the pantheon of great revolutions. That it failed to live up to its initial radical promises was a result of the weakness of the state and the lack of alternatives available to a small and dependent country. But its accomplishment set a benchmark against which later events would be measured.

In the subsequent chapter, historian Alan Knight agrees that Bolivia experienced a significant social revolution. Yet his comparison of Bolivia and Mexico indicates how distinct revolutionary processes can be. Moreover, great revolutions can achieve common social objectives but differ radically in their political legacies. Although both were centered in the urban middle class and made through alliances with workers and peasants, Knight demonstrates a series of important distinctions between the Bolivian and Mexican revolutionary experiences. Prior to revolution, Mexico had experienced 30 years of 'order and progress' under the Porfiriato, while Bolivia could look back on two decades of weak, unstable and vacillating governments and corresponding economic turmoil. He considers the factors that explain why Mexico's workers were less revolutionary than Bolivia's, its peasants more radical and its anti-US sentiments more moderate. Moreover, the revolution in Mexico was protracted and reaped a high toll of death and destruction; Bolivia's was rapid and much less violent. Mexico's radical policies took decades to be realized; Bolivia's were consummated in a very short period. Mexico kept control over its new military; Bolivia nurtured the forces that swept it from power. The role of the revolutionary parties differed also — the MNR led the forces of change in Bolivia, the PRI emerged in the aftermath of the violent phase of the revolution in Mexico.

Yet Bolivian revolutionaries sought to emulate the Mexican experience and, as both revolutions moved to the right, both relied on the support of the beneficiaries of agrarian reform to enable them to break with more radical elements. Even here, the relative success of Mexico in building a strong and centralized state and the continued failure to create such an institution in Bolivia meant that the countryside related distinctly to government: in Mexico through caciques and clientelism that looked to the center; in Bolivia through caciques who retained considerable autonomy and a clientelist system that was never fully captured by the MNR. Knight also notes the more democratic nature of the revolutionary experience in Bolivia with the dramatic extension of the franchise and the broader base of electoral possibilities. He contrasts these with the degree of control and authoritarianism wrought by the PRI. The paths to and from revolution differed in these two countries, he argues, yet both survived in part because the United States was inclined to tolerate the changes they introduced.

The issue of the relationship with the United States is further addressed by Ken Lehman in Chapter 4. He focuses on a central comparative insight — the USA came to terms with the Mexican and Bolivian revolutions, both supporting and constraining them, while it committed itself to opposing and breaking the Guatemalan, Cuban and Nicaraguan revolutions. Lehman considers the extent to which Mexican and Bolivian leaders were able to find room to challenge the USA and to seek accommodation with it, permitting both revolutions and their redistributive policies to survive. In the case of Mexico, he argues that rivalries among revolutionary leaders often caught the US government off guard, creating ambiguities that led different officials to distinct interpretations of events. This provided the country with opportunities for confronting US interests and reaching accommodations that were supported and opposed by distinct interests in the US. At the same time, rivalries among powers engaged in World War I provided additional openings for Mexican leaders to pursue their goals vis-à-vis Washington. The extensive nature of US interests in Mexico, as well as a shared border, limited the extent to which Washington was willing to sustain confrontations with the revolutionary government. Eventually, a lasting rapprochement was possible because power struggles within the regime were settled in favor of the Sonoran dynasty, ensuring a revolutionary path that would be sympathetic to capital and foreign investment.

Bolivia was less advantaged in its relationship with the USA. Its revolution occurred at a time of deep American hostility to communist influences in the world and when its dependence on tin made it particularly vulnerable to US power. Without much delay, however, Washington recognized the new regime in the belief that the revolution was of a homegrown and popular variety and that Paz Estenssoro represented the moderates among many more radical groups. Nationalization of the mines was certainly on the cards from the outset, but as US interests lost little through this event, Washington was satisfied with Bolivian promises to recognize private property rights and international obligations. A stalemate over tin exports provided the revolutionary government with additional space for survival; support from other countries in Latin America, American labor sympathy for the plight of Bolivian miners, as well as innuendoes of impending sales of tin to communist countries encouraged the USA to consider an aid package for the country. Thus, in Washington's view, supporting the revolution — or at least supporting Paz — became a way of supporting democracy and economic development. The Bolivian government was able to accomplish important policy changes, but it did so in pragmatic recognition of the limits to which it could go in confronting the USA and its international and economic interests.

Revolutionary Visions and Actors

Central to the concerns of Sinclair Thomson and James Dunkerley are questions about the meaning of nationalism in Bolivia, a concept fraught with ambiguities in a society of deep ethnic tensions whose history is testimony to the power of internal colonialism. In Chapter 5, Thomson shows how, at distinct moments, images of the indigenous past were reinterpreted to accord with different understandings of nationalism. The Túpaj Katari insurrection of 1781 was at one point reviled as a brutal racial war and at another, as the stirrings of independence and at yet another, as a foundational moment for Bolivian nationalism. In the first decades of the twentieth century, national memory painted the eighteenth century uprising as a moment of divisive and fearful racial war that threatened the basis of emerging nationalism in the country. Túpaj Katari, who led the insurrection, was 'fearsome, crude and violent, if not downright barbarous' in this memory.[8] The 'barbarous' Katari is contrasted with the historical perspective on Túpac Amaru in the northern Andes, who was remembered as 'civilized' and representative of a desire for a united and independent country no longer under the yoke of 'foreigners'.

Yet, in the years leading up to the 1952 Revolution, 1781 was reinterpreted as a movement whose primary claim was anti-colonial. Nevertheless, the indigenous insurgency came up short in comparison with the independence movement in mid-century historiography precisely because it was difficult to see it as a multi-class or multiethnic struggle. In developing their own understanding of nationalism, then, the revolutionary leaders of 1952 were left with a difficult historical legacy. They could claim to embrace the indigenous past and the current leadership of Aymara and Quechua revolutionaries, but at the same time they were unable to come to terms with claims for indigenous distinction and autonomy. To celebrate the 1952 Revolution as a major accomplishment of both nation-building and state-building, where races and classes came together in struggle, it was necessary to ignore evidence of Indian subordination within the new Bolivia. Only at the end of the century did *katarismo* re-emerge as a statement about internal colonialism and a struggle for cultural and political assertion.

In Chapter 6 James Dunkerley seeks to distinguish the origins of the revolution from the same sort of time-distorting historical memory. The somnolent observance of the 50th anniversary was, he argues, only a reflection of what many Bolivians had come to believe about their revolution. The adulation that usually surrounds leaders of great revolutions was compromised, in the case of Bolivia, by popular awareness that the post-revolutionary lives of these heroes were simultaneously all-too-human and all-too-visible. Similarly, the MNR's post-revolutionary life, and particularly its actions in 1964 and 1985, obscured the ability to read the party in its revolutionary and pre-revolutionary guises. Revolution, Dunkerley argues, is properly understood as both a set of actions and a process that generates a vision of a new order. In Bolivia, an important part of the process of revolution was the emergence of a vision about the nation and the meaning of belonging to that nation. From this perspective, then, the Chaco war can be understood as an event that, by revealing the weakness and incompetence of the state, contributed to an emergent vision of a unitary nation and a strong and effective state. These kinds of historical roots to revolution are difficult to pin down, but they are no less important in considering the antecedents to such events.

Dunkerley lays to rest another frequent misunderstanding of the causes of revolution. He argues that it is difficult to sustain the perception that a major contributor to the events of 1952 was a ponderous and resistant old order whose sole purpose was to serve the interests of the *Rosca.* He presents evidence of considerable political change in the years after the Chaco War and shows that class conflict in the mining regions predated this period. Analysis of the tin industry, the vicissitudes of its international price, the actions of the tin barons, a catalogue of protests, strikes and repression, along with the partisan battles of incipient political parties, indicate the often chaotic nature of the processes and events that led up to the 9 April insurrection. Processes such as these are important in the breakdown of the old order, but so, too, are contingent events. Dunkerley reminds us that had 15,000 new army recruits been training to shoot guns and follow orders rather than learning to march so they could participate in an imminent diplomatic ceremony, the military might have had a better chance to resist the uprising in La Paz. Of such factors, the fabric of history is partially woven. This leads Dunkerley to argue that viewing the revolution in simple terms of nationalist, anti-imperialist, or anti-oligarchical commonalities tends to erase the significance of much of the process and the events leading up to it. With Thomson, then, he warns us to take care how we read the events of the past.

This is particularly true in assessing the rural roots of the revolution. A common view is that the indigenous population played little role in the event or in the unstable political and economic interactions that led up to it. Laura Gotkowitz and Brooke Larson, however, demonstrate that rural areas were both a site of considerable protest prior to the revolution and a site of repeated efforts by elites and government to colonize the hearts and minds of the Indian majority. They coincide in demonstrating the extent to which rural areas were arenas for state action and indigenous claims for justice and autonomy. Far from the view that the rural population was largely absent in making the revolution, becoming active only in the wake of its violent phase, both demonstrate that a long tradition of protest characterized indigenous political action and an equally long tradition of repression and fear characterized elite and state response to such mobilization.

Gotkowitz tells a story of indigenous mobilization focused on rights to land and justice. She analyzes the Indigenous Congress of 1945 and widespread rural unrest in 1947 to make her case. The congress was a critical event in the political life of indigenous groups because it brought together leaders from across the country and strengthened and expanded politically important networks that had initially been formed before the Chaco War. In addition, the congress gave indigenous communities a national forum, it produced a series of decrees by the Villarroel government that went to the heart of many of the most important rural demands and it provided an opportunity to forge links with workers' organizations and to become more familiar with the legal intricacies of making claims against the state. According to Gotkowitz, Villarroel wanted to expand the reach of the state into what was considered, at the time, to be a stateless rural society. The MNR was a reluctant supporter of the congress and the indigenous interests it espoused and understood clearly the threat of widespread rural mobilization. Protest and demands on the one side, concern about order and control on the other, thus conspired to bring about this historic congress. At the event, indigenous leaders promised to conform to the norms of the urban and 'civilized' world in response to their petitions to end *pongueaje* and *mitanaje*, to return land to rural communities, to establish rural schools and to reign in the power of the landlords.

After Villarroel's demise in 1946, a series of rural uprisings demonstrated the extent to which indigenous communities were mobilized around implementation of the decrees that emerged from the congress. In the protests, strikes and violence of 1947, Gotkowitz demonstrates how the aggrieved communities invoked law as a solution to their problems. Indeed, her analysis presents consistent evidence of active indigenous communities that were networked with workers' organizations and other communities, focused on their rights, using the courts and other institutions of the state to make their demands known. Moreover, in case studies of four instances of rural unrest, Gotkowitz details the extent to which the traditional alliance between local authorities and landlords was breaking down. The most consistent outcome of protest and rebellion was, of course, repression. But after 1947, protests, strikes and resistance continued up to the eve of the revolution.

In Chapter 8, Larson indicates the extent to which the pre-revolutionary state attempted to 'bring Indians into the ambit of the state and remake them into a docile, moral and productive workforce'.[9] Rural education policy thus sought to maintain control over a culturally distinct majority population, while also ensuring that the economy of the country could be developed with a labor force that was both available and appropriate for productive enterprises. Clearly, any education policies affected only a tiny portion of the rural population, but Larson investigates the meaning behind the various projects designed for the rural masses from the 1920s to the early 1950s. In the 1920s, the educational vision was primarily that of keeping indigenous people in rural areas and focused on the work 'best suited' to their cultures and physiques — agricultural labor. With this and subsequent notions of rural education, however, educators were faced with a dilemma: how to keep the Indian in his place but alter the customs that interfered with the productivity of his labor. For policy planners of the time, such values as 'temperance, thrift, cleanliness and hard work', might best be inculcated in rural boarding schools, a plan that was expanded in the 1930s and 1940s to include rural normal schools.[10]

But counter-elites also had visions for the development of rural Bolivia. In the 1930s and 1940s, leftist and syndicalist organizations began to see the new rural normal schools as sites for education that taught relevant knowledge and that inspired a sense of cultural pride along with better hygiene. In the 1930s, the famed Warisata experiment became a model of how the rural schools could foster indigenous protest, demands for rights and recognition of cultural distinctiveness. But by 1940, this vision of the rural school was replaced by a new and much more conservative project in which social stability became the goal of pedagogy. Indeed, as Larson shows, there was a shift in the idea of education from issues of social, economic and political justice toward efforts to transform the

Indian home into a source of stability and conformity. Late in the decade, and with the active involvement of US development assistance, schools were expected to promote 'highly ritualized regimes to regulate and reform child rearing, food, clothing and fashion, sleeping arrangements, architecture and spatial layouts and modes of sociability in the interior of the peasant school and family'.[11] In the 1940s, it was to be the peasant home that would curtail the possibility of social revolution emerging from the countryside. Again, the implementation of this vision was always highly constricted — at the outset of the revolution, only a small portion of rural children had access to school — but the way in which rural education was imagined and planned said much about the political purposes it was expected to serve.

Revolutionary Consequences

The Bolivian Revolution left behind important legacies in a series of major policy innovations — the nationalization of the mines, the agrarian reform and universal suffrage — and a deeper sense of nationalist identity. It also left behind a legacy of institutional weakness, low growth and unstable politics. Three chapters directly address the question of the economic and political consequences of the revolution. They explore how the revolution shaped the institutions and the policies of the post-revolutionary period and what issues it left behind for subsequent governments to grapple with.

Juan Antonio Morales pays tribute to the accomplishments of the revolution — new structures of landholding in the countryside, new structures of power providing more scope for peasants, women and the middle class, the development of dynamic new regions in the country. Yet his view of the revolution is a sobering one; its most important failure was the inability to create the bases for economic growth in the country. He holds the revolution to account for a range of policies that did little to advance and much to harm national economic development. The revolutionary government was unable to deal effectively with inflation or fiscal deficits and did not respond to the famine created in the wake of the agrarian reform. For Morales, the weakness of the state-led growth model it adopted was demonstrated in the performance of the state mining company and the mining unions; they exploited the mines only to milk them dry. Low agricultural productivity, a large foreign debt, inflation, fiscal deficits and economic dislocation forced a partial reversal of state policies in 1956 through a US supported stabilization program. Then, the state-led model gave way to a state capitalist approach in 1960 when the MNR adopted this developmentalist strategy. All together, however, these policies left behind a public sector of exaggerated size and weak institutions for economic development. Such factors consistently discouraged private investment.

Indeed, Morales speaks of the failure of the state as a significant factor in the poor economic performance of the Bolivian economy. Most strikingly, he argues, the policies of the revolution and the post-revolutionary period contributed to the creation of a private sector that was weak, averse to risk and with little incentive to invest in technology or physical or human capital improvements. Only in the eastern part of the country, where the reach of the government was weak, did a more vibrant form of capitalist development occur. This is a stinging indictment of the Bolivian Revolution and its consequences for economic development. Yet Morales tempers his criticism to some degree by posing the counterfactual. If the revolution had not happened, he suspects that the narrow oligarchy of the pre-revolutionary period would have adopted policies that would have made the state less intrusive and that would have resulted in institutions more friendly to property rights and markets. On the other hand, it is unlikely, he believes, that such a government would have adopted policies to lessen the degree of poverty and exclusion of the poor majority in the country.

Morales' conclusion is questioned in Chapter 10, written by Herbert Klein. He provides a social profile of Bolivia on the eve of revolution and an assessment of how that profile changed in the subsequent 50 years. He also compares the social accomplishments of this period with those of other countries, thus providing a lens for assessing how much change can be credited to the revolution. Klein demonstrates the extent to which Bolivia was rural, underdeveloped and inequitable at mid-century. Most of the population was engaged in agriculture and most people were outside the small wage economy. Six per cent of landowners controlled 92 per cent of the agricultural land and they had few incentives to use their land productively. Less than a quarter of the population lived in population centers with 2,000 or more inhabitants. Largely illiterate, most of the rural population did not speak Spanish. Life expectancy was very low, infant mortality very high and population growth only modest.

With the revolution, these conditions began to change. Migration to urban areas and the development of rural infrastructure brought major changes in health, life expectancy, population growth and access to education. Literacy expanded to all but about 15 per cent of the population and Spanish became the dominant language. Klein notes the problems attendant upon rapidly growing urban areas in poor countries, but also the impact of migration on access to health, education, social mobility and the political importance of the poor majority. Bolivia in 2002 was still poor and underdeveloped, but it was a dramatically different country than it had been in 1952. Klein does not credit much of this change to revolution, however. Social conditions in other countries in the region, including the majority that did not experience revolution, also show impressive gains over the same 50-year period. While the gap between Bolivia and other countries in terms of many social indicators has narrowed, it remains second only to Haiti at the bottom of the list of Latin American countries in terms of many social welfare measures. While little can be directly tied to the revolution, Klein contends that the engagement of the poor in national political life is an important achievement and that persistently low economic growth rates diminished the impact of the inclusionary policies of the revolution. It was, he argues, the revolution that unleashed the capacity of poor Bolivians to demand access to education and a voice in national policy.

Manuel Contreras, in Chapter 11, takes up the issue of the impact of revolution on education in Bolivia. Education reform, although much less studied than the nationalization of the mines or the agrarian reform, was a central revolutionary act. Based on the notion of universal, free and obligatory public education carried out in the Spanish language and similar across regions, classes and ethnic groups, the 1955 reform embodied the nationalist objectives of the revolution. Cultural unity and national identity were the expected outcomes of the new system. Moreover, the revolutionary government considered that expanded and unified education would be the basis for the future economic and social progress of the country. Contreras agrees with Klein that considerable progress in education occurred after 1952, but he faults the revolution for not going further in promoting change. He finds that the revolution did not introduce a major disjuncture in school enrollments; rather, there was a relatively smooth progress of pre-revolutionary dynamics in expanding access and increasing years of education through the end of the century. When compared to Cuban advances, Contreras argues that Bolivia's experience can hardly be termed revolutionary. Moreover, the reform's goals were often subverted by poorly trained and paid teachers, a curriculum that was not relevant to the life situation of most students, systematic under-funding of educational services and budget allocations skewed toward tertiary rather than primary education. Indeed, when he compares the country's three major education reforms in the twentieth century, he finds the education reform of 1994 far more revolutionary in content and intent than the pre-revolutionary liberal reform or the 1955 project. This new law recognized the educational importance of cultural diversity and the difficulties of effective learning when children are introduced to school in a 'foreign' language. It sought to rectify limitations of teacher training and it decentralized control over important education decisions to departments and municipalities. And, the newer reform focused much more on the importance of the quality of education while the earlier reform was primarily about access to education. Contreras is hopeful that this reform will deliver more and better education than its revolutionary predecessor did.

Unfinished Agendas and New Initiatives

In the three chapters forming this section of the volume, the central issues relate not just to revolutionary consequences, but also to changes that are not so easily linked to the events of 1952 and the challenges facing Bolivia 50 years after the revolution — the agenda for economic, political and social development. In Chapter 12, Eduardo Gamarra is critical of the political legacy of the revolution. In assessing the role of political parties in Bolivia's post-revolutionary politics, he takes them to task for not being more responsive to the concerns of civil society and, because of that, for becoming irrelevant to the political dynamics of the country. Part of the problem, he contends, is that political parties followed the model of the MNR in attempting to capture corporate interests within the structure of the party and to claim the exclusive prerogative of representing societal interests. Because parties were unsuccessful in fully incorporating these interests, their support could only be attracted and maintained through the distribution of patronage. Similarly, the development of parties in Bolivia after the revolution was broken by long periods of authoritarian rule, when their structures atrophied. Political parties were further implicated in the extensive turmoil of the transition to democracy between 1982 and 1985, leaving a residue of public skepticism about the ends and means of these organizations. The emergence of government based on party coalitions in the 1980s and 1990s did much to make policy innovation possible, but it also spawned an image of parties that were not much different from each other and that were compromised through congressional deals after elections. To add to their problems, the neoliberal reforms of the 1980s and 1990s, by diminishing the size and functions of the state, limited the extent to which parties could use state resources to hold themselves together and attract partisan support. Parties dependent on patronage and state largesse were unable to find new bases for popular support and thus found themselves vulnerable to claims that they were unresponsive and unrepresentative.

For these reasons, the traditional parties declined in importance and new parties emerged to take on the tasks of representing popular demands to government. In addition, new forms of organizations, primarily NGOs, but also popular and community organizations, emerged to assume the task of representing interests in the political sphere. What also emerged was mobilization of social protest and political demand making around particular issues of concern — water, rights of coca growers, anti-privatization. These organizations did not seek to form coalitions with parties or to advance electoral interests. Rather, their strategies included direct protests, marches, roadblocks and resistance to government policies. For Gamarra, these demand-making strategies 'do little to promote civic mindedness' in the country.[12] Yet Gamarra also maintains that, to some degree, the traditional political parties are getting a bad rap. Through a series of creative governing coalitions, they provided support to successive presidents to introduce important policy changes. The protest against the parties was to some extent a protest against the policies that were introduced as well as against the participatory limitations of a pacted democracy. Gamarra questions how these parties can develop enough legitimacy and representative capacity to respond to major conflicts characterizing politics 50 years after the revolution.

In the following chapter, Merilee Grindle also addresses the question of the role of political parties in post-revolutionary Bolivia, but focuses more specifically on the role of the MNR in the major policy changes introduced in the 1980s and 1990s. The scope of the changes was indeed large, she argues in a review of the Nueva Política Económica in 1985 at the hands of Paz Estenssoro's government, and the changes introduced by the government of Gonzalo Sánchez de Lozada between 1993 and 1997. Together, these reforms represent a neoliberal policy revolution — stabilization, liberalization, deregulation, privatization, fiscal reform, state downsizing, decentralization. Indeed, Bolivia led other countries in Latin American in the timing and the depth of its policy changes. How was it that the MNR, a party of revolution, nationalism and statism could design and promote liberal, internationalist and market-oriented policies, she asks?

In fact, Grindle asserts, the MNR as a party was little engaged in the definition of the neoliberal revolution or in developing the policies that gave it substance, even though it was the party in power when the most important of the new policies were introduced. She shows that the NPE, the capitalization program, Popular Participation and the 1994 education reform were all designed with minimal input from party headquarters and with great reliance on independent technocrats, academics and entrepreneurs. Thus, the reforms could stray so far from the rhetoric of the MNR because MNR operatives were largely absent at their creation. But this does not mean that the party was irrelevant to the fate of the policy changes. The big tent nature of the party and its ability to forge governing coalitions based on the distribution of state patronage were critical to the adoption of the reforms and helped maintain a precarious political peace around their introduction. Gamarra and Grindle agree on the importance of the ability of the party to form coalitions, but Grindle is somewhat more optimistic about the capacity of the traditional political parties to find ways to remain relevant to politics, if not to policy.

In Chapter 14, George Gray Molina explores different processes of political mobilization and inclusion that have occurred in the past 50 years and finds a series of interesting changes in everyday definitions of social mobility, nationalism and political participation. The generation of Bolivians who experienced the revolution first hand was brought into national political and social dynamics through the laws relating to suffrage, agrarian reform and state ownership, as well as through collective demand making on the state. For those born after the revolution, but before 1972, the predominant experience was one of the disintegration of collective and corporatist forms of political representation and their replacement by clientelist relationships in mediating the interaction between the state and its citizens. For an even more recent generation, mobility and inclusion were sought through individualized vehicles of education, urbanization and jobs in the formal labor market. At the same time, and with the introduction of Popular Participation in 1993, efforts to manage political demand making from the center gave way to local negotiation and conflict over power and resources. Gray Molina demonstrates the extent to which political participation grew in local elections, the increase in the number of political parties that contested elections and the greater volatility in electoral outcomes. As a consequence, the nationalism of the revolution, emphasizing unity and glossing over obvious differences in class, ethnicity and power, was replaced by more locally diverse bases of identity and more fragmented politics.

In this context, the discussion of nationalism changed. No longer a concept about national sameness, nationalism came to incorporate more elements of cultural diversity and ethnic distinctions. The constitutional changes introduced in the 1990s stated that Bolivia was 'free, independent, sovereign, multi-ethnic and pluri-cultural'. In this new notion of nationalism, identity with the whole was based on an explicit recognition of differences within it. Paradoxically, Gray Molina notes, Bolivians were becoming more conscious about diversity at the same time that the linguistic bases of ethnicity were diminishing. Inclusion thus became understood more as a consequence of individual choice — through education and incorporation into an urban and modern economy — and more focused on local levels of political participation and contestation over resources and patronage and more organized around political parties than unions. These latter two factors, Gray Molina argues, began to revive some earlier collectivist ideas about inclusion.

Weakness and Resiliance

In the final and concluding chapter of this volume, Pilar Domingo returns to a theme raised by virtually all contributors to this volume, that of the weakness of the Bolivian state, which predated the revolution, and the constraints that this poses for the pursuit of any policies, revolutionary or otherwise. Taking the historical weakness of state structures in Bolivia as a starting point, Domingo argues that the Bolivian Revolution facilitated the evolution of the political system from oligarchic rule, through an era of nationalist *movimientismo* and zero-sum politics, to a period of electoral politics and more fluid expressions of political pluralism. At the same time, however, the revolutionary experience in Bolivia did not serve to consolidate a clear and socially embedded political and economic project that would endure over time. Nonetheless, its development, social and political impacts were far from negligible. In hindsight, it is clear that contemporary channels of political contestation and articulation of social demands are rooted in important ways in the experience of revolution.

Despite these accomplishments, Domingo points to the weakness of state structures, combined with the complex dynamics of political and social conflict and demand articulation at the local, rural and sectoral level — which often were at odds with power struggles within central government — and shows how they ultimately undermined the various political and developmental options as these unfolded. Moreover, neither the post-revolutionary years of nationalist rhetoric and state-led growth, nor the incomplete and fragile incursion into democratic government and liberal economics of the recent decades, have been able to shift the logic of patronage politics characteristic of Bolivia's political heritage. Domingo concludes that despite unresolved issues of governance and state capacity, poverty and exclusion, Bolivia's current political resilience, in comparison to recent developments in neighboring countries, is rooted in its revolutionary legacy.

A Future for the Bolivian Revolution?

The chapters in this volume provide testimony to the historical importance of the Bolivian Revolution of 1952. Among its consequences were a major agrarian reform, an economy guided by state participation, government by a party wedded to nationalist goals, a strong and radical labor movement, a modernized military and a state that was more centralized and that penetrated further into national territory than had ever been the case in the past. After the revolution, and for the first time in the country's history, indigenous groups were incorporated into national economic and political life and a sense of national identity extended to a much larger portion of the population.

But contributors to this volume are also clear that the gains of the Bolivian Revolution were limited, in part because of the Thermidorian reversal in 1956, in part because it lost control of the military, in part because authoritarianism and clientelism wove conservative biases into structures of political contestation in the country, in part because the MNR became a party of neoliberal policy reform in 1985, in part because the parties that emerged from the revolution and its aftermath lost their capacity to represent social demands. Even accepting these limitations, however, social change was significant after 1952 and social mobility previously denied to the indigenous population became more possible. Moreover, the country continued to demonstrate a capacity for institutional innovation. Along with neoliberal economic reforms, for example, came imaginative new efforts to link the periphery to the center within the country and to increase the relevance of education to the country's poor. These changes are not trivial and while many cannot be directly tied to the revolution, they can be linked to the capacity of old revolutionaries to adapt to economic and political exigencies and to call on loyalties and legacies of the revolution to establish a modicum of political order after the country returned to democratic rule in 1982.

NOTES

1 The *Rosca* (small kernel) was the popular term for the small oligarchy composed primarily of three tin mining companies that largely dictated state policy in the years prior to the revolution.
2 http://www.boliviasipuede.com/actualidad/discurso.html, author's translation.
3 Diario Correo del Sur, Sucre, 10 April 2002. http//www.correodelsur.com/20020410/w_nacional5.shtml.
4 http://ea.gmesa.net/2002/04-Abril/20020409/Especial/Abril/esp020409a.html.
5 http://www.correodelsur.com/20020409/w_noticia1.shtml
6 http://ea.el-nuevodia.com/2002/04-Abril/09Abril2002/Editorial/April/editorial020409.html, author's translation.
7 The Santa Cruz region, and a few other areas with little or no indigenous populations, were largely unaffected by the violence or the agrarian reform.
8 See chapter 5, p. 121.
9 See chapter 8, p. 185.
10 See chapter 8, p. 189.
11 See chapter 8, p. 195
12 See chapter 12, p. 302.

HOW REVOLUTIONARY THE REVOLUTION?

CHAPTER 2

The Bolivian National Revolution: A Twenty-First Century Perspective

Laurence Whitehead

It was impossible, maintained *La Nación*, to measure the magnitude of any social revolution merely by the degree of its violence: the Bolivian National Revolution got underway in 1952 with only about 600 casualties whereas hundreds of thousands of deaths in *la violencia* of Colombia after 1948 had not insured social change there. On the contrary, maintained *La Nación*, a social revolution could be determined only by advances in all of a country's aspects of development — political, social and economic — and therefore 'we cannot assert with any certainty at this time that the Cuban Revolution can be considered as such.[1]

This chapter deals with the twelve years of government by the MNR that was inaugurated by the National Revolution of April 1952 and that came to an end with the military coup of November 1964. On one view, this was essentially a political revolution, the inauguration of a dominant party regime, followed by its eventual decomposition. The chapter will indeed pay attention to the national dynamics of this political regime. But on a second view, one particularly prevalent in Bolivia at that time, this was more than just a political change of guard — it was a *social* revolution.

This chapter draws on the by now reasonably well-established narrative history of those 12 years,[2] but it has a more comparative and theoretical focus. It draws on that history to construct a synthetic interpretation of the Bolivian Revolution, one that can be compared with other social revolutions. This synthetic interpretation is constructed from the perspective of the ensuing half-century, and more especially in the light of our changing perceptions of social revolutions in general. This involves revisiting some very old questions from a new perspective. Was 1952–64 really a *social* revolution as claimed in the 1950s, or — knowing what we do about the subsequent trajectory of the MNR and its leaders — should we reclassify it as another relatively banal instance of merely political change reflecting elite opportunism and manipulation? Even if we regard it as more than just a change of guard in the government, did it clear the way to some kind of 'progressive' reconstruction of Bolivian society that would not have been attainable through more consensual means? Or did it impose disruption and sacrifice in the name of a utopian future that was either illusory or, to the extent that it was genuine, could better have been pursued through persuasion and negotiation with those it in fact defeated? Was the revolution 'betrayed' from within or blockaded by its enemies? In what sense did it 'succeed' or 'fail'?

As indicated in this and the following two chapters, these discussions about comparative experiences of social revolution raise big issues of historical method (notably because of the strong counter-factuals they invoke); and of social theory. For example, can we identify and bracket for comparison large-scale structures and processes, with the latter periodically breaking through the former? Are there discontinuous periods of accelerated historical change, and if so do they have any determinate direction? Similar questions have been asked about the Mexican, Cuban and Nicaraguan revolutions, not to mention their French, Russian and Chinese forerunners and counterparts. After the collapse of the Soviet bloc, these are questions that look different from the way they seemed during the Cold War.

Looking back at the National Revolution after half a century, and with these comparative and theoretical preoccupations in mind, involves taking the Bolivian Revolution as seriously as all these other counterparts. The main aim of this chapter is to demonstrate that the Bolivian case can extend and refine the general analysis of revolutionary change and equally that comparative analysis can add value to the interpretation of Bolivia's historical experience.

Other contributors to this volume consider some major aspects of the pre-revolutionary regime and social structure and offer assessments of aspects of the post-revolutionary outcome. This chapter deals with the political and social dynamics of the relatively short period of the National Revolution itself. The following section looks 'inside' the 1952–64 MNR regime and offers an overall interpretation of its revolutionary trajectory. Three critical issues are selected for this purpose: i) the sources of the initial radicalism; ii) the interplay between local and national dynamics; and iii) the means by which the MNR leadership attempted to reconstitute its national authority once the initial pressures from below had been released. Rather than viewing the first MNR regime as a predictable project, this framework draws attention to the improvisation and contingency of the revolutionary period. However, it also assumes that there was a structure underlying the contingency: in theoretical terms this chapter rests on the assumption that social revolutions can be analysed as 'dialectical' processes with limited time spans and a constrained range of possible outcomes.[3] If so, this framework can not only be used to reinterpret the Bolivian experience of 1952–64, it can also be used to compare the National Revolution with similar experiences in the light of more general theories of revolution. The third and final section of this chapter reverts to such analytical issues.

1952–64: A Synthetic Interpretation

Initial Radicalism

Fifty years later it is easy to underestimate the boldness and radicalism of the experiment launched in April 1952. The only precedents then available were the Mexican, Russian and Chinese revolutions, all very violent and protracted. After six years Bolivia would be overshadowed by Cuba and its sequels but none of that was foreseeable in the early 1950s. On the contrary, 1952 was at the height of the Korean War and witnessing the rise of McCarthyism. Just when Bolivia nationalized its mines, the Mossadeq government in Iran was overthrown for threatening to control its oil companies. No sooner had Bolivia decreed a sweeping land reform than the CIA overthrew Arbenz in Guatemala. (He was accused of communism in part for promoting a milder land reform law.) In Cuba, 1952 was the year of the Batista coup. In South America, this was an era of Washington-approved military dictatorships in Venezuela, Colombia and Peru. The more compatible regimes of Vargas and Perón were both heading for a fall. The only significant sources of external sympathy for a revolutionary project in Bolivia were distant Mexico and perhaps (to a degree) neighboring Chile under Carlos Ibañez. For public consumption the Peronists might express verbal solidarity with the Bolivian Revolution, but MNR leaders knew better than to count on any real help from Buenos Aires.[4] As for the USA, Washington might eventually be reconciled to a *fait accompli* in La Paz, but it was certainly no promoter of revolutionary radicalism in Bolivia and Patiño Mines was registered in Delaware.

So the initial radicalism was clearly generated from within. Some of its sources are well covered elsewhere in this volume: the rural struggles over land and education and against internal colonialism; the Chaco War and its consequences for nationalism and state building, most notably during the Villarroel regime. There is also a now unfashionable but not-to-be forgotten literature on the mining sector and the labor radicalism it generated through the Miners Federation, and later the COB, under the leadership of Juan Lechín.[5] In addition to these Bolivia-specific sources of radicalism, the comparativist will search for more standardized precursors of revolution, for example, in the state apparatus, the military establishment, within the leadership of the insurgent forces and in the system of political representation.

Since this chapter is about developments *after* April 1952 there is only space here for a very summary mention of these issues. A standard interpretation would be that the *status quo ante* (it hardly merits the designation *ancien régime*) was too narrow, too rigid and too precarious to manage the pressures outlined above. The 'military socialist' experiments of Busch and Villarroel were failed attempts at a proactive response, but when they fell (and the way they fell) this fractured not only the army, but the state as a whole and it bequeathed a legacy of frustrated hopes that would have overwhelmed any subsequent reformist administration. After the artificial economic stimulus of the Second World War, post-1945 Bolivia faced fiscal, monetary and investment bottlenecks that left almost no margin for class compromise. The party system was in any case both incipient and highly polarized. After the violence of the 1946 showdown. representative politics became unviable because (as the 1951 election confirmed) any opening of political space would be filled by outlawed figures from the deposed regime. So, with a disorganized state, a demoralized and fractured military and a dysfunctional party system, pre-revolutionary Bolivia was in no condition to absorb discontent either from below, or from the 'outs'. The result was a classic 'reactionary' interlude between 1947 and 1952, one in which those with something to lose relied on repression and played for time, without being able to formulate any hegemonic project. On this interpretation, the radicalism of 1952–55 arose largely from the pent-up demands of all those disparate forces that had been united by exclusion over most of the preceding *sexenio.*[6]

They were united by the MNR, a movement with a record for verbal radicalism, combined with great tactical flexibility (critics would say 'opportunism') and an impressive ability to co-opt or outmanoeuvre its rivals. In opposition, the MNR rallied very diverse tendencies, some steeped in social radicalism (in the mining camps, sectors of the peasantry and certain urban popular groupings), but also conservative nationalists and, of course, a leavening of careerists. Once back in power, the MNR had broad mass appeal, but was also a centralized and hierarchical structure with an authoritarian *jefe.* It could win democratic elections (even under Bolivia's restricted suffrage), but was not known for accepting electoral defeats graciously. Oligarchs associated it with the murder of prominent opponents under Villarroel and the PIR (the Partido de la Izquierda Revolucionaria, the main Marxist party of the 1940s) had dogmatically portrayed it as a fascist party. Those who entered into alliance with the MNR risked being outmaneuvred by it (as many RADEPistas felt they had been in 1946 — this may help explain why the Falange backed out of its partnership with the conspirators on the very eve of the revolution).[7] The aggressive and intolerant style of the MNR forced its opponents into a corner: either they accepted its leadership or they joined the reactionaries. So when the MNR returned to power in triumph, in April 1952 (with the twin mandates of a democratic majority and a popular urban insurrection) neither right nor traditional left were in a position to exercise countervailing power. The right migrated to the Falange Socialista Boliviano — FSB (or fled) and the PIR dissolved itself as an organized alternative. Any restraint on radicalism in the early years would therefore have to be generated from *within* the MNR.

As with other revolutions, it was not immediately clear who would inherit power, nor on what basis, nor to what ends. The La Paz conspirators did not intend to precipitate a head on confrontation with the armed forces and they seem to have envisaged a number of quickly discarded possibilities — co-government with a military president, new elections for both president and congress, perhaps the marginalization of exiled party leaders in Buenos Aires. It took strong pressure from the labor movement (quickly organized into the Central Obrera Boliviano — the COB) to precipitate the nationalization of the mines and to accelerate and radicalize the agrarian reform. Returning from exile without a renewed electoral mandate, or a congress, or even a cabinet of his choice, President Paz Estenssoro had to maneuvre constantly between the COB, the surviving armed forces, his party rivals and the US Embassy. The radicalism of his initial policies was a product of this vulnerability as much as of any prior pragmatic decisions.

So the incoming president and *jefe* de la revolución tried to play for time before defining his course. Two failed coups from the right helped to crystallize the radical course that soon emerged. In synthesis, there were two compelling reasons for this, but it is hard to apportion the weight between them. The initial radicalism of the revolution was 'over-determined' by, on the one hand, the balance of forces within the victorious movement and, on the other, by the 'objective' need to dismantle the *status quo ante* and to secure the regime against a counter-revolution, before attempting to rein in revolutionary excesses.

For the schematic purposes of this section it may suffice to classify April 1952 until around early 1956 as the period of initial radicalism.[8] Then Paz Estenssoro began preparing to hand leadership of the revolution (and the poisoned chalice of an IMF stabilization plan) to his vice-president, and long-term rival, Hernán Siles Zuazo. The interplay between strong local and weak national power dynamics (to be discussed below) occupied most of the period from the mid-1950s to the early 1960s. And the efforts to reconstitute national authority and to subordinate pressures from below (also discussed below) became much more central once Víctor Paz returned to the presidency for a second term in 1960.

The radical tilt to the balance of forces after April 1952 can be tracked from a number of angles. The very fact that urban insurrectionaries in La Paz had secured a capitulation by the forces of order resulted in a shift of power that was by no means foreseen, let alone desired, by many backers and even leaders of the new government. The initial plan had been a military coup, backed by popular support.[9] But once the military had crumbled the armed leaders of the insurrection (with Juan Lechín and his *sindicato* supporters at the forefront) controlled power on the streets. Thus they would only relinquish that leverage if offered extensive co-government and opportunities for autonomous organisation. In return for the ministries of mines, labor and peasant affairs, and the legitimation of the COB, the MNR secured acceptance of the outcome of the 1951 presidential election. The exiled *jefe* returned from Buenos Aires to occupy what was termed the *constitutional* presidency to which he had been elected in 1951 (with the head of the insurrection, Hernán Siles, as his vice-president). But the congress of 1951 was not called into being and no local elections were held. The cabinet over which Victor Paz Estenssoro presided was the one already nominated in his absence by the victors in the street fighting. And local power was exercised by party militants who exercised *de facto* rather than *de jure* control. For the first couple of years press freedom was not protected.[10] But this meant institutionalizing a degree of power sharing that prolonged and in some ways even intensified the administrative paralysis of the pre-revolutionary period.[11] It also created two options for all those claimants who had been either genuinely persecuted or could at least present themselves as worthy of favours from the new regime. They could seek satisfaction through the MNR, or through its equal partner in directing the revolution, the trade union confederation headed by Juan Lechín, the COB. This made controlling and absorbing the return of the 'outs' far more problematic than before. ('Las peras no alcanzan para todos' was the famous phrase of Victor Paz on this point.) It prompted radicalisation, because one of the most effective ways to accommodate all these demands was to redistribute property and to expand state employment.

At a more basic level, radicalization was driven by the distribution of weapons (a 'correlation of forces' in the most literal sense). Even before the revolution, the Chaco veterans had often retained their firearms and thus transformed the balance of power in their communities. The miners had had their own access to dynamite. Many Indian communities had possessed the numerical strength, organization and basic implements needed periodically to impose their wills on their localities (except when contested by detachments of security forces). This was why the pre-revolutionary Bolivian state was so vulnerable and why the insurrection of April 1952 was militarily capable of prevailing. After the insurrection, the COB secured a commitment that one third of all subsequently imported weapons would be distributed via its channels. For a while it even seemed possible that *sindicato* militias might permanently displace the security forces of the state. In due course, by purging and reorganising the military, and by enlisting US support, Víctor Paz contrived to roll back this situation.[12] But it was not until 1956 that rival militias began to divide the mining camps and that a wedge was driven between the worker and peasant wings of the COB.

During the early years such repressive force as remained at the government's disposal (essentially the *Control Político* forces under Colonel Claudio San Román) were directed principally against the threat of counter-revolution from the right. Until then, therefore, the MNR government was in no position to rein in radicalism on its left. In fact, failed attempts by the right wing of the MNR to break free from *co-gobierno* and block the COB provoked successive waves of further radicalisation in 1953 and 1954 as the dissidents were purged and the *sindicatos* pressed ahead with their social demands. The crucial political victories that Paz secured during this period were to secure left-wing acceptance of a system of representation that could later be deployed against them and to construct a 'nationalist' project (actually dependent on US aid) with wide enough appeal to stabilize the regime until the initial wave of radical demands had abated.

So much for the internal balance of forces within the MNR as an explanation for the revolution's initial radicalism. But we must not underestimate the importance of a second, parallel and overlapping consideration. If, as key elements in the MNR leadership apparently believed, the *status quo ante* had proved itself too narrow and rigid to accommodate any degree of reformism, then it would have to be dismantled and replaced. The purge of the armed forces was bound to be far-reaching, even in the absence of the COB, given all that the military hierarchy had done to block reform since 1946. It is true that the MNR hoped to return to power via a military coup, but it was also known that Villarroel's attempts to coexist with the mining *Rosca* and the semi-feudal oligarchy were seen to have failed, so that when the party did regain power, much more drastic measures would be required, at least in the *altiplano.* Nationalization of the mines, a sweeping land reform and universal suffrage were already on the agenda, however the conspiracy unfolded, because that is what Bolivia's previous history had led many in the opposition to expect, and to demand.

This is not the place to rehearse the well-known arguments for and against the MNR's most distinctive revolutionary measures of the 1950s. Víctor Paz, as president responsible for enacting these measures, himself acknowledged their deficiencies. (In the 1980s he initiated a comprehensive overhaul and — in key respects — reversal of the statist and distributivist policies he had implemented in the 1950s). The question at issue here is slightly different. Why were so many radical (and in many respects untried) measures enacted so rapidly immediately after April 1952? This was not the orderly implementation of a sequence of developmental strategies by a coherent administration with a long-term planning horizon. It was a chaotic and revolutionary upheaval driven by a sense of immediate necessity and by the desire to create irreversible outcomes before it was too late.

This may be easier to understand when one recalls that for its supporters, the failure of the Villarroel administration was a cathartic experience. After six years in opposition, uncertain whether they would ever get a second chance, or what terrible price they might have to pay in order to return, the authors of the revolution did not think they could afford to risk a second reversal. In this, they may have resembled other revolutionary leaders, such as the Cubans in 1959 who could not risk another 1933, or Lenin's determination to avoid another 1905. The Bolivians' sense of urgency and danger would have been reinforced by the intransigence of their opponents, who had already suppressed one major MNR-led rebellion in 1949 and who showed no compunction about cancelling the 1951 election after they had lost it. To the disappointment of the La Paz revolutionary committee, their opponents had also proved resilient enough to thwart General Seleme's initial coup of 9 April 1952.

Admittedly the radicalism of 1952–55 was somewhat out of line with the more calculated practices of the MNR in government both before and since. It reflected the unexpected loss of control and the consequent risk of being outbid by disorderly pressures from below (shades of the *bogotazo*?). But it was not purely an opportunistic reflection of the balance of internal forces. Reading the MNR's proclamations and self-justifications before the insurrection confirm that their return to power was theorized as a revolutionary discontinuity in Bolivian history, as a step change from one system of domination and socioeconomic organization to another. Such a reading can be defended notwithstanding the accompanying evidence of ambiguity and disagreement about the specific content of the measures envisaged and of the coalition required to put them into operation. If this contention is correct, then Bolivia belongs in a specific cluster of historical experiences that deserve the designation of 'social revolutions' and that require comparative analysis as a distinctive category of processes.

To pursue this argument with specific application to the radicalism of 1952–55 requires careful study of the measures then adopted. Most analysis concentrates on the land reform,[13] the nationalization of the mines or the reform of education. But it is also worth emphasising the far-reaching implications of establishing universal suffrage in the wake of the 9 April insurrection.

Bolivia's registered electorate rose from 205,000 (6.6 per cent of the estimated population) in 1951 to 1,127,000 (33.8 per cent) in 1956, and the number of valid votes recorded rose almost eightfold — from 126,000 (61.6 per cent of those registered) to 958,000 (85 per cent).[14] It is worth recalling the regional context at this time. Although Argentina had enjoyed universal manhood suffrage since 1916 it was not until 1951 that women voted for the first time, and similarly it was not until 1952 that Chile extended the vote to both sexes. Although women gained the vote in Peru in 1956, it was not until 1980 that illiterates were enfranchized there. In Brazil, women gained the vote in 1932, but illiterates were excluded until 1989. In Mexico, the principle of universal manhood suffrage (i.e. including illiterates) extended right back before the revolution, but females only obtained the vote in 1955. In Guatemala after 1945 the vote was theoretically obligatory for all literates and voluntary for illiterate men. Illiterate women could not vote until 1966. In Ecuador, illiterates did not gain the vote until 1978. In summary, when the Bolivian Revolution granted the vote both to women and to illiterates, by regional standards this was a bold innovation.[15]

In post-revolutionary Bolivia, universal suffrage was not just an isolated measure. It was an integral component of the whole package of early radical legislation. This involved extending the vote to illiterates in a society where over half the urban population and more than three quarters of the rural population were truly unable to read and write, and indeed where a majority of the population lacked basic schooling and perhaps even verbal fluency in the language of state administration. It involved granting the right to choose both national and local political representatives to communities that had often recently obtained their own supplies of armaments and had organized their first *sindicato* assemblies (which constituted a form of direct democracy in many localities). It meant giving a say on public policy to hundreds of thousands of land reform beneficiaries and organized workers who could be counted on to vote against any reversal of asset redistributing measures.

In some circumstances, the granting of votes to women can be a technique for strengthening conservative values (for example, where the Catholic Church has a strong following amongst them). In others, the enfranchizement of illiterates can reinforce the political leverage of local landowners (an argument against universal suffrage used by some on the Brazilian left at this time). But in Bolivia, as in post-revolutionary Mexico, the effect of universal suffrage was to signal to those opposed to the revolution that its policies were here to stay and that the MNR would remain in office for the indefinite future.[16] In this context the promise of universal suffrage both boosted the initial radicalism of the regime and increased its chances of reconstituting state authority on a different basis over the longer run. But the experience of successive elections under the MNR was disillusionary. Either open electoral contests generated local factionalism and perhaps even violence, or centrally controlled elections alienated those they excluded. A more genuinely competitive party system would be needed eventually to generate a post-revolutionary source of popular legitimacy.

Interplay between the National and the Local

This section is mainly concerned with the dynamics of the MNR regime once the initial wave of radical measures had been absorbed and before administrative centralization had taken hold (i.e., between the mid-1950s and the early 1960s).[17] In Malloy's questionable terminology 'a deflation of national power took place, and the country reverted to "lower" forms of organisation. Effective decision-making power became localized and/or segmented.'[18] But it should be noted from the outset that similar patterns were apparent from the earliest days of the revolution (and indeed even before 9 April), and that they were never completely overridden either by the numerous *intervenciones* decreed by the National Policy Committee of the MNR, or by the Pacto Militar-Campesino, or indeed by the subsequent

Barrientos dictatorship. Still, they were most visible, and perhaps most constraining, during the administration of Hernán Siles Zuazo (1956–60). This was the period when the central government seemed at its weakest and most vulnerable. The military were still keeping a low profile, with the police and the militias mainly responsible for public order; the ruling party was divided into factions, most of which looked to the absent *jefe* as the ultimate arbiter; the major revolutionary changes had been enacted and the problem now was how to make them work effectively; the economy was at its low point, with strict IMF disciplines reinforced by heavy dependence on a US aid program that was becoming increasingly intrusive; the FSB was conspiring to overturn the regime by direct action, knowing that despite its electoral strength in key cities and some small towns it could never break the MNR's hold on power by any other means; and President Siles was resorting to hunger strikes to offset his administration's lack of authority and manoeuvrability. Even if he had spent twelve hours a day signing land reform decrees, the backlog would still have continued to mount up.[19]

In short, during this period the aspirations aroused by the National Revolution came into conflict with its real possibilities. All revolutions have to contend with this disjuncture, and typically revolutions can draw on sources of legitimation, hope and fear, that carry them through the early setbacks. In Bolivia too, the revolution had accumulated a reserve of strength that sustained the national government until Paz Estenssoro could return with a new project (the Washington-financed Triangular Plan) and at the head of a new coalition (with Lechín as his vice-president and a revived military providing backbone to the *jefe's* control of the party). But in the interim the national authorities looked weak and directionless. President Siles (1956–60) attempted to rule by constitutional means. He was elected concurrently with the Congress and he sought institutional legitimacy to offset his relatively weak position in the MNR. He divided the CSTCB from the COB and he did his best to face down the Comité Pro-Santa Cruz. It was his bad luck that the Cuban Revolution eclipsed Bolivia's claims to vanguard status and that economic events conspired to discredit his national leadership. However, at least for external observers, the re-emergence of Bolivia's chronic problems of administrative incapacity and political paralysis at the national level has one beneficial side effect. It enables them to inspect the interplay between local and national initiatives with an unimpeded view from below. This view highlights the extreme heterogeneity of the revolutionary process as experienced by the various groups, interests and regions that it engulfed.

Few if any parts of Bolivian society were unaffected by the cascade of measures enacted in La Paz, yet the impacts were strongly filtered through diverse local experiences. The Land Tenure Centre at Madison Wisconsin has generated a rich array of local studies that can be mined to document this assertion for much of the *altiplano* and valley regions. For example, Charles Erasmus portrayed a pattern of delayed mobilization and partial landlord accommodation to the new order in traditional Quechua areas of Chuquisaca that differs drastically from most of the conventional stereotypes.[20] The Nor Yungas coffee and cocoa zone studied by Madeline Barbara Leons is a world apart from the Norte de Potosí as portrayed by Tristan Platt, or the lakeside conflict zone of Achacachi, or the dense peri-urban agriculture of Cliza and Ucureña;[21] not to mention the high pastoralists, or the new settlers who followed the highways that began opening up to the Oriente. A similar multiplicity of local realities opens up once we explore the mining sector beyond the stereotypical but unrepresentative cases of Catavi/Siglo XX. The wolfram co-operative at Kami was at times one of the most productive and best organized of units within the Miners Federation, but wolfram followed a quite different economic rhythm from that of tin and Kami's relationship with the MNR regime was accordingly desynchronized.[22] If we look beyond highland agricultural and mining the picture becomes yet more varied. What most mattered at the border posts was whether the customs regime favoured opportunities for smuggling, and if so in which direction. What particularly mattered to large landowners in Santa Cruz was whether they could gain access to heavily subsidized credit in order to import agricultural machinery. Meanwhile, the lowland city's urban elite was mostly interested in the oil royalties that they hoped to ring fence beyond the reach of grasping fiscal authorities in the capital. Ordinary lowlanders feared the competition for work from the migrant army of highlanders who followed the opening of the Santa Cruz–Cochabamba highway. In vineyards of San Pedro (Ciniti province), the revolution threatened the market for *singani* and the investments from the Patiño interest; in Tarija the biggest worry was that a nationalist project would leave the needs of remote provincial capitals unattended; and so on.

So how did the big themes on the revolutionary agenda filter down to all this myriad of specific local and provincial interests? Only a few rough approximations of an answer are possible here. One is that somehow or other almost all the groups and interests mentioned above were reached and affected by what the Revolution did (or failed to do). Its success, its meaning, its presence has to be deciphered through all these indirect and mediated effects, and not just by some summary reading of official intentions or aggregate indicators. Much of the literature contains a tendency to over-schematize, to take very partial viewpoints or counter-verities as more representative of the whole than they can possibly be. We need to attend to the part played by intermediaries, brokers and political entrepreneurs who assisted the process of reconciling national agendas with extremely varied and specific local interests. (Think, for example, of the La Paz policeman whose response to 9 April was to take off his uniform, walk back to his hometown in the *altiplano* and turn himself into the leader of its peasant *sindicato*, while always maintaining contact with his former colleagues in the capital's police force so that he was alert to opportunity and to danger as national politics lurched one way or the other.) A second, rather obvious, point is that — at least in the absence of strong centralized discipline — the process of adjusting parochial interests in line with a new national revolutionary discourse generates a spectrum of excuses for relaunching local conflicts under a new guise. No doubt the rivalry between Cliza and Ucureña had deep historical roots, but before the revolution it remained mostly latent. Once one side had the opportunity to secure weapons and encouragement from say the COB, the other side would be sure to line up with the rival revolutionary faction, and as the two became proxies for a national power struggle the local rivalry degenerated into virtual trench warfare. Similar conflicts arose between the mining *sindicato* of Catavi/Siglo XX and the smaller but strategically located *sindicato* of Huanuni. The urban land invasions orchestrated in Santa Cruz by Luis Sandoval Morón reflected a parallel struggle for power within that city's MNR *comando* (which, in turn, was weighty enough to attract powerful patrons and equally powerful enemies within the national structure of the party).[23]

In summary, while there was always a two-way interplay between national and local political dynamics, in Bolivia the local components were characteristically strong and diverse. What seem at first sight to be national divisions motivated by questions of high politics or even ideology were often tributary to lower level conflicts which often had much more specific and parochial motivations.[24] From the mid-1950s to the early 1960s this type of political struggle became increasingly visible and intractable, as the initial impulse of the revolution lost momentum. If a national revolutionary government was to maintain its cohesion and to steer the country towards a coherent developmental path, it would have to reconstitute its authority on a more centralized and disciplined basis.

The Reconstitution of State Authority[25]

To some extent this third theme dates right back to 9 April 1952, and in fairness to the Siles administration it also constituted a priority between 1956 and 1960, although not one where he achieved much success either then or subsequently.[26] Malloy overstates the case when he describes the position of the national authorities in 1960 as 'absurd', but there is enough truth in his characterisation to reveal something of the psychology of the time:

> It is not too much of an exaggeration to say that national authority was roughly coterminous with the city limits of La Paz. Sandoval Morón and Ruben Julio effectively ruled almost half the existing territory of the

> country between them. The bulk of the *altiplano* was under the thumb of Toribio Salas. José Rojas held sway in the Valley … Northern Potosí was in a state of anarchic inter-tribal warfare. The major mining camps were indisputably controlled by local sindicatos. The overall situation had deteriorated to such a point that national officials, including the president, could not safely travel throughout large sections of the country without the express permission and protection of local bosses.[27]

The reconstitution of state authority emerges most clearly as a dominant preoccupation after the return of Paz Estenssoro to the presidency for a second term (which he eventually, and unsuccessfully, sought to extend into a third successive period of personalized control). His return coincided with the election of Kennedy to the White House and the subsequent launch of the Alliance for Progress, so one element in the analysis concerns an attempt to position post-revolutionary Bolivia as a beneficiary, and perhaps even a 'showcase', of Washington's new policy. But there was also a downside to this international strategy. The Alliance for Progress may have offered aid to reformist governments, and it looked forgivingly on pro-US regimes that also engaged in land reform and economic interventionism. But it was also a counter-insurgency alliance. Within this framework the only kind of national authority that could be built up and consolidated with US support was a reliably anti-communist regime with a firm commitment to the suppression of pro-Cuban tendencies. It was doubtful whether Washington would ever overlook Juan Lechín's role in building up the Bolivian Miners' Federation by mobilizing workers against American mine managers, or could forget his flirtations with various forms of Marxism. In any case, beyond the personal profile of Paz's vice-president (and presumptive successor in the presidency in 1964) the miners federation and the COB remained full of class warriors and anti-imperialist activists, who rejoiced over the Bay of Pigs. If they had a complaint against the Cuban Revolution it was that it was showing up the timidity of its Bolivian counterpart. In short, if Paz proposed to reinvigorate the Bolivian Revolution by making it a showcase of the Alliance for Progress, his new project would involve breaking the coalition he had forged to bring him back to office.

Turning therefore to the domestic balance of power, if the COB and the FSTMB were to be marginalized (they eventually broke away to form the PRIN, Partido Revolucionario de la Izquierda Nacionalista, with Lechín as its chief) Paz's project for the reconstitution of a national revolutionary authority would have to rest on alternative sources of support. The Bolivian case can be fitted into a comparative framework that would also accommodate such analogous episodes as the institutionalization of the Mexican Revolution after 1928. Within such a framework the main areas for consideration would be: i) the formulation of an overall diagnosis and prescription ('project') that may unify disparate forces in pursuit of a common goal; ii) the organisation of a system of consultations, and if necessary side payments, aimed at strategic groups where co-operation would be needed and who could not simply be rallied to this official project; iii) the structuring of a system of intelligence, discipline and control aimed at those who may otherwise have the capacity and inclination to resist the resurgent authorities; and finally, iv) some process of feedback, perhaps based on an electoral calendar or some other pre-fixed timetable of party congresses or cabinet reshuffles, that could institutionalize project monitoring and that may provide the flexibility needed to protect the authority from the possible failure or discredit of its initial project.

The Project

The 'project' of the second Paz administration was a long-term plan for economic development. After the revolutionary legislation of the early 1950s, it had been necessary to stabilize the economy, under IMF direction. Now that the economic and political foundations of the new regime were in place, the next stage would be a state co-ordinated drive from a sustained growth 'take off' backed by loans and technical assistance from the Washington-based development agencies. Under this project the disparate and conflicting power groups within Bolivia could be directed to refocus their energies on this long-term collective objective from which they could also stand to benefit in the end. Within this logic, the MNR would monopolize the national interest, and would be justified in imposing discipline on dissenters. This pursuit of national unity could also be invoked to justify a policy of reconciliation with elite groups that had formerly been identified with opposition to the revolution.

Coalition Strategy

Consequently the second Paz administration also required a *coalition strategy*. It aimed to establish working relations with such strategic groups as the medium-scale mine owners, the Pro-Santa Cruz Committee, the Catholic Church and even the conservative press, all of which had felt under threat during the first years of the revolution, but which would now need to be reassured and, if possible, enlisted in the national development project. When considering how to reconstitute state authority it was critical to assess which elements of the *status quo ante* remained intact after the disorder of the revolutionary period, and what it would take to neutralize their opposition, or better still to secure their co-operation. For example, the *latifundistas* of the *altiplano* had been eclipsed, but the large landowners of the Oriente were on the rise.[28] Likewise the 'big three' mine owners were expropriated, but other privately owned mines remained in existence, and some had considerable geological potential. Paz was still the *jefe* of a revolutionary movement and knew better than to expect an easy spontaneous reconciliation with the propertied classes. But if the MNR could convince these key actors that they would have something to gain from co-operation and much to lose from die-hard opposition, this would broaden the base of the new strategy and improve its chances of success. Side payments, personal appointments and a judicious distribution of the resources generated from Washington would be required. The more Paz asserted his authority within the MNR, and the more he used it to curb the pro-Castro left, the easier his relations with these conservative groups should become.

Reasserting Social Discipline

So the reconstitution of state authority also required a strategy for reorganising the ruling party and for reasserting social discipline through the restored forces of order. Hunger strikes had no part in Paz Estenssoro's political repertoire, but more successfully than Siles, he had long specialized in cultivating support within the military, and in linking the party he had founded with the security agencies. Evidently the Alliance for Progress would not welcome the restoration of the so called *campos de concentracíon* that had characterized his first term, but perhaps there was no need for that. Within the MNR he had encouraged the formation of military cells within the party, initially to ensure the loyalty of the reformed military.[29] This instrument could now be used to control factionalism and stiffen discipline inside the ruling party. Although the *sindicatos* still had their old guns, the state could issue its regular forces with new calibre weapons requiring a different type of ammunition.[30] The president could ensure control over the National Political Committee of the MNR and then use that instrument to 'intervene' and suspend disorderly elements of the ruling party at local level.[31]

It is difficult to know whether a strategy of this kind guaranteed a conflict between Paz and the left from the outset. As it turned out, however, the Bay of Pigs was followed by the Missile Crisis, the assassination of Kennedy and the rise of the Mann Doctrine in Washington. Under such circumstances. Paz was increasingly forced into making an explicit choice between protecting his ties with the USA (which increasingly bypassed the ruling party in its dealings with the resurgent military) and seeking to conciliate Lechín and his followers. In this context he was almost bound to choose the military, and his strategy for the reconstitution of state authority became detached from the consolidation of a broadly based ruling revolutionary party.[32] The MNR cycle therefore came to a demoralising close.

Constitutional and Democratic Structures

Thus far this synthetic interpretation of the 1952–64 experience has highlighted the 'revolutionary' dynamics of the period. This may facilitate comparison between Bolivia and subsequent Latin American revolutionary processes, for example in Cuba and Nicaragua. But from the perspective of subsequent Bolivian history, and taking into account the currently prevailing negative assessment of revolutions as little more than false utopias and excuses for authoritarianism, this section cannot close without at least a brief mention of the *constitutional* and indeed *democratic* components of the Bolivian National Revolution.

The MNR derived part of its legitimacy from its conquest of power via a popular insurrection in April 1952. It also generated support as the only available embodiment of popular nationalist aspirations, a source of legitimation that was raised to a higher level by the revolutionary laws of the first Paz administration. But in addition to these powerful national-populist credentials, the MNR could also claim a democratic and constitutional legitimacy. Despite the absence of trustworthy rules of the electoral game, it won a succession of electoral victories in the 1940s, culminating in the success of the Paz–Siles ticket in the 1951 presidential elections. Following the revolution, Siles and Lechín chose (after some hesitation) to allow Paz to return from exile and serve his constitutionally mandated four-year term (at a time when their leadership of the insurrection might well have enabled them to disregard that constraint). Thereafter, Paz handed over to his vice-president at the appointed moment, and he withdrew from direct involvement in national politics when Siles took office. Universal suffrage may have created a very lopsided electoral balance, but between 1956 and 1962, elections were held on schedule and democratic procedures were more or less respected.[33]

Within this framework it would have been perfectly possible for Paz to complete his second term and then hand over to an elected successor. This raises an intriguing counter-factual issue. Had he done so, the latent conflicts within his party and in Bolivian society concerning the outcome of the post-revolutionary settlement might well have proved unmanageable. He may have been particularly swayed by the thought that his most obvious successor, Juan Lechín, was a divisive figure and perhaps incapable of running a responsible government. But there is also an alternative argument, and it was one that his former party comrades found increasingly convincing. By imposing himself on the presidency for a third term in opposition to Siles and Lechín and without a credible democratic mandate, Paz assumed responsibility for destroying the institutional foundations of the MNR regime. Twenty years were to elapse before reliably fixed electoral calendars were re-established and formal democratic legitimation was restored. This constitutional thread runs through the dynamics of the 1952–64 process quite as much as the 'revolutionary' thread. Both are integral to any 'dialectical' interpretation of the Bolivian National Revolution.

1952–64 in Comparative and Theoretical Perspective

The previous section drew on fairly well-established analyses of Bolivian political history, but the narrative was pruned with the aim of highlighting aspects of the Bolivian Revolution that facilitate comparison with analogous processes and underscoring the themes of most theoretical interest.

Bolivian revolutionaries were home grown, but they were not completely insulated from parallel experiences elsewhere. Images (possibly distorted) of the Mexican and Soviet revolutions were present in Bolivia as examples and influences, and some rather traditional variants of Marxism (mostly filtered through the Chile of the 1930s) provided an important intellectual reference point. There was also a nationalist tradition sharpened by the Chaco War, which seems to have incorporated some influences from European fascism. The Falange owed a debt to Franco, and the liberal constitutional tradition received some succour from parts of Latin America (for example Uruguay and Chile) and intermittently also from Europe and North America. So it is not ahistorical to compare Bolivia with other parallel experiences and external sources of influence. After 1959 the Bolivian Revolution was eclipsed by the more spectacular and outward looking Cuban, Chilean and Nicaraguan processes, and it exerted almost no external influence of its own. Nevertheless, from the perspective of 2002 it is legitimate to compare the Bolivian Revolution both with relevant predecessors and with analogous successors. The Bolivian experience provides a reality check on general theories of social revolution that can be used to supplement the more classical exemplars. So this section explores that terrain.

There are various 'stage' or 'sequence' theories of revolution. The simplest framework is to distinguish between causes, course and consequences. But that takes the revolution itself as a sharply demarcated event or set of events that can be clearly segregated from what went before and came after. However, the Bolivian case confirms the comparative generalisation that a revolution is an extended process, with deep historical roots and long-term repercussions. It would be very artificial to argue the revolution began in, say, April 1952 and ended in, say, November 1964. We can date a political regime in that way, but as a *social process* the Bolivian Revolution built up from the Chaco War, through military socialism and accelerated after the failure of the Villarroel regime. In some respects it had lost impetus by about 1955, in other respects it was still alive in the Asamblea del Pueblo of 1971, or indeed in the road blockades of recent years. It was, therefore, a *social* revolution and not just a *political* regime change. This is because of its impact and the hold it developed on the popular imagination of an entire society, and because of the way it reordered Bolivia's collective understanding of relations of power and of social purpose.

From this perspective it seems appropriate to explore a 'dialectical' interpretation of the Bolivian Revolution. On this view, the revolution expressed a clash of ideas about fundamental issues of national identity and collective direction. The ideas motivating the revolution gained early expression in the 1938 Constitutional Convention and extended their popular appeal through the 1940s. After 1952, prior constraints on the application of these ideas were abruptly lifted and a variety of rival interpretations of the meaning of the revolution competed for ascendancy. Within a few years its initial consequences were visible and many illusions had been shattered. But the debate continued and indeed continues to some extent right down to this day (for example when the MNR, the MIR — Movimiento de la Izquierda Revolucionaria — and the *indigenistas* clash over the legacy of 1952). Some of the competing ideas that had been pushed to margin during the radical phase of the revolution (constitutionalism, rule of law) have staged a remarkable comeback. Other ideas that were once thought to express the genius of the revolution have fallen into desuetude and perhaps even been disowned by those who invented them (*control obrero,* union assemblies, *co-gobierno*). But this revolutionary ferment of proposals, ideas and experiments needs to be understood as a continuous *dialectical process.* These powerful collective experiences remain available for reincorporation into ongoing debates, they are all generated by a shared exposure to a revolutionary political and social transformation, and the lessons of the 1950s remain present in all subsequent political debate.

More concretely, this chapter has focussed on 1952–64, and on the political dynamics of the revolutionary period. What this procedure is intended to highlight is that the 'revolution' cannot be treated as a black box, neatly separated from what caused it and from what it caused. It was an *extended process* characterized by a great deal of contingency and uncertainty. Within that general framework it is, however, possible to distinguish an underlying structure of initial radicalism, leading to localism and dispersion, followed by the attempted re-establishment of hierarchical authority constructed on an alternative basis. Looking at the Bolivian Revolution from this perspective serves to improve its comparability with social revolutions more generally and to link it up with wider debates in comparative historical analysis.[34]

However, Latin American and comparative history is full of episodes and indeed processes that are characterized by contingency, abrupt policy lurches, localism and recentralization. If 1952 Bolivia is to be distinguished from most of these and bracketed instead with the more celebrated upheavals of Mexico, Cuba and Nicaragua (not to mention such 'classical' revolutions as those of France, Russia and China) then we need to specify some high threshold characteristics of a 'social revolution' to distinguish this period from more general episodes of turmoil. The claim here is that Bolivia went through a *national* revolution in the following vital aspects: i) its far reaching social changes affected the national population as a whole, extending more or less comprehensively (albeit unevenly) throughout the population; ii) these changes generated a new sense of national identity and gave rise to a qualitatively distinct form of state-building; iii) although in many respects initially disorderly and incoherent, these changes were cumulatively irreversible and created a new baseline for all subsequent developments.

If this characterisation is accepted, then 1952 Bolivia *does* belong in a relatively select class of historical experiences, which requires separate comparative and theoretical examination. Reverting to an issue raised in the introduction, this involves the claim that in certain circumstances we can identify either an *ancien regime*, or at least a *status quo ante*, that is sufficiently resilient and coherent to obstruct necessary change, but that is unable to absorb it. A revolution is then the moment of breakthrough when this old structure is swept away and — in a short period of time — a concentration of delayed innovations and untested experiments takes its place. Clearly, if an *ancien regime* is to be 'swept away' by political action, this will involve a degree of violence. But the essential criterion is the extent of the resulting social change, rather than the magnitude of the violence involved in securing it. Bolivia was far less violent than any of the other cases mentioned.[35] But it has been argued that the social impact of 1952 was sufficiently far-reaching to raise Bolivia above the threshold for inclusion in this universe of transformative processes. The resulting policy innovations and untested social experiments may work badly, but in the absence of counter-revolution (for example Guatemala in 1954 or Chile in 1973) they become the benchmark for all subsequent national politics.

Since the disintegration of the Soviet bloc, all social revolutions have tended to lose their mystique, and this context of disenchantment tends to define prevailing assumptions about what revolutions involve even among academics. Revolutionary rhetoric is hard to re-read and take seriously in such a setting. The debates that fired the imagination of participants who believed they had the opportunity to create a better society now seem unrealistic or even incomprehensible. It is tacitly or even explicitly assumed that all such radical attempts at utopian social engineering were either utterly fanciful, or more probably cynical deceptions. (Reformist and market friendly utopians are typically exempted from this anathenization, however.) There is indeed plentiful evidence that those recent exponents of revolutionary change often used their advantages to shore up authoritarian elites, to monopolize privileges and to suppress criticism. Cuba and Nicaragua are increasingly viewed from this optic even by those who used to defend these two revolutions.

The Bolivian Revolution provides an interesting counterpart to all this. Unlike Castro, Allende or the Sandinista leadership, the MNR leaders made few bids for international support. Domestically, they generated a legitimizing discourse that envisioned a big expansion of the state and what might be called social engineering to bring about a better future. But neither Paz nor Siles embraced any form of utopianism, and Lechín improvized according to whoever happened to be his current policy adviser.[36] This is not to underestimate the intellectual content of the debates between the various Bolivian contenders for power at the national level. Ideas mattered in revolutionary Bolivia. But the ideas in question were mostly quite practical and the main debates were known to be over tactics and factional interests.[37] Bolivian nationalism was mostly defensive — an expression of the fear that without a big collective effort Bolivia's fragile institutions and national identity would be in peril — rather than optimistic, let alone aggressive. It was not until the second Paz administration that serious social engineering was proposed, and at that point the discourse was already highly technocratic.[38] The radical rhetoric of the COB or the Asamblea del Pueblo had a narrow domestic audience and was often not intended all that seriously. There *were* radical movements on the streets and in the communities, but what drove them were overwhelmingly immediate and local demands. The recent mass mobilization in Cochabamba in 2000 against the water companies provides a contemporary illustration of this general pattern. When Che Guevara raised the banner of continental socialist revolution in Bolivia, only a small cadre of students and left-wing activists understood the terms of his proposal. His death, and what was often viewed as his noble example, may perhaps have struck a chord in the hearts of many Bolivians. But his revolutionary theory came from another planet.

This observation connects with the earlier discussion in this chapter of the interplay between local and national perspectives. Revolutionary elites may decree sweeping changes from the balconies of presidential palaces in capital cities. But if society is affected, it is because of the way local actors respond to these signals in their villages, neighborhoods and mining camps. That was true in April 1952, and it remains true whoever currently occupies the Palacio Quemado. In Bolivia the presence of the parochial, and the precariousness of the presidential, is palpable. This is a contrast with most countries that have undergone a social revolution and then constructed a persuasive edifice of rationalizers and defenders of the post-revolutionary order.

Revolutions are sometimes presented as 'integrating' or even homogenising previously fragmented societies, but at least in the Bolivian case that image vastly exaggerates the scope for remolding a nation from the top downwards. After all, even the decrees enacting the most radical measures were legalistic documents in written Spanish. This in a society where the law hardly reached the bulk of the population, where sophisticated literacy was known to no more than a very small minority and where a majority was not even fluent in the language of administration. The *indigenistas* of today anathemize the MNR for attempting to impose a false mestizo uniformity on communities of *indios* ruled by a white elite. But this critique both exaggerates and at the same time underestimates the 1952 Revolution. It also essentializes 'Indian' identities that were actually more fluid, even then. It exaggerates the MNR's capacity to remold society from above, but it simultaneously underestimates the assault on symbolic hierarchies that flowed from the April insurrection.

President Paz chaired many cabinet meetings and engaged in a lifetime of political intrigues, but one of the greatest shocks to his entourage came shortly after his return from exile, in April 1952, when he instructed his ministers to dance with the *cholas* who had been invited into the presidential palace from the nearby central market. The revolution was partly about breaking down caste-like barriers of social distance inherited from colonial times. These days all right-thinking radicals scorn the way the MNR redescribed the *indios* as *campesinos*. But this is because they fail to grasp the symbolic breakthrough that this represented at the time. At the local level, to recognize all Bolivians as sharing some common identity (however fictitious) was literally to turn the world upside down.

Theorists of revolution working from the classical Marxist tradition used to argue that a genuine revolution needed to express the ascendancy of the proletariat over the propertied classes (preferably a working class led by an enlightened vanguard party). The MNR always rejected this language, asserting that it was a 'nationalist' movement uniting Bolivians of all classes (other than the *Rosca* and those leftist intellectuals who had fallen captive to anti-national ideologies — and even the latter might be subject to recuperation). The reality is that the Bolivian system of social stratification was neither so horizontal as in the Marxist model, nor so vertically segmented (between 'nationalists' and the 'anti-patria') as in the alternative account. As Malloy noted in 1970, most cleavages were localized and identities were often defined by markers other than property-ownership and dependence on wage labor. There were big opportunities for social mobility within the revolutionary process, with new settlement and truckers' networks springing up in the countryside in the wake of the organic reform. Even the proletarian COB drew its strength as much from neighbors, housewives and the unemployed as from its unionized workforce. There was plenty of revolutionary conflict over property entitlements, access to the state and more local issues of power and symbolic ascendancy. During the radical phase of the land reform it was not uncommon for rural activists to slaughter the livestock on the basis that at least they would enjoy a fiesta before the inevitable landlord revenge. There was said to be a risk of famine in some of the larger cities after 1953, as peasants withheld supplies that would have been purchased with worthless currency.[39] Neither a class theory of revolution, nor its 'populist poly-class' antithesis takes us anywhere close to mapping such interactions.

Another comparative and theoretical issue concerns the nature of the post-revolutionary order. According to a classical argument, the destructive phase of the revolution is likely to be followed by a ruthless recentralization of power, a Thermidorean reaction. However, the post-revolutionary order may also be capable of mobilising sources of support that are broader and deeper than anything available to the pre-revolutionary regime. So the question is not just *how much* centralisation of power can occur, but *where* the new order's strength comes from and *what* it is used for. The classic argument is that after the trauma of revolution the society craves order and rallies to whoever can provide it. (The Bolivian Armed Forces relied on this reflex when they took power in 1964, but they only generated their own variants of disorder.) An alternative view is that a successful revolution generates stability precisely because it removes all the expectation of future revolution, although this is not true of Bolivia. A third consideration is that social revolution opens up opportunities for social ascent that were previously blocked off. The stability arises from the desire of the 'new class' or the stratum of revolutionary activists to cling to the advantages gained by their cohort, regardless of the broader vicissitudes of the economy or the society. In Bolivia, however, the opportunities for ascent were limited and precarious. Finally, there is a literature suggesting that revolution clears the way for more accelerated capitalist accumulation and the enrichment of a 'political bourgeoisie', although capital accumulation has been quite anaemic in Bolivia since 1952.

All these discussions revolve around the new basis on which post-revolutionary authority may be constituted. This chapter has sketched a synthetic interpretation of this issue, as it applies to Bolivia in the early 1960s. The two main points to highlight here are: i) even at this stage there is a great deal of contingency, with no guarantee that power will be successfully reconstituted and monopolized by the heirs of revolution (hence the 'revolution betrayed' issue); and ii) given the destructive potential of infighting within the revolutionary elite (each faction will be tempted to use the same voluntarist methods as before, this time directed against his comrades, until 'the revolution devours its children'), some kind of impersonal structure of rules may be required. This was how the PRI arose in Mexico. In Bolivia the constitutional and even democratic framework of the revolution created a possibility of elite circulation and power sharing. But as it turned out — for reasons I consider to be quite contingent — this proved insufficient to perpetuate the MNR in power.[40]

Mao Zedong famously asserted that 'power grows from the barrel of a gun', and it is widely argued that successful revolutions create their own legitimacy through imposition. The 'dialectical' perspective of this chapter cautions against any such mechanical translation of force into durable power. Collectivities have to be *persuaded* to accept revolutionary outcomes, and too much indiscriminate use of force without accompanying justification is likely to prove delegitimizing. In the Bolivian case *electoral* legitimacy preceded the *insurrectional* variety, and when Paz sought to have himself re-elected through an act of imposition his party was ousted from office for a generation. This experience underlines the need to attend to the multi-dimensionality of power and authority. Nowadays, both the MNR and the PRI tend to re-imagine their historical trajectories in terms of democratic legitimation. Such reinterpretations are as false and unbalanced as earlier triumphalist assertions of the conquerors' right to rule.

This chapter has treated revolutions as discrete processes of national transformation. Of course there is also a 'world systems' or 'dependency' school of interpretation, which draws attention to the role of external dependency and intrusion. Others in this volume have focused on the undeniably important role of external influences on the Bolivian Revolution.[41] The Cuban and Nicaraguan processes are other contemporary experiences that can profitably be evaluated from this perspective. Although this brief account of Bolivia between 1952 and 1964 has made some reference to the role of US aid, and to the intrusions of Washington's associated political conditionality, this has not been placed at the centre of the analysis. Here it may suffice to note that the invocation of a 'nationalist' justification for seizing power is not necessarily incompatible with a heavy resort to external support and protection.

Finally, in counter-revolutionary times intellectuals may propagate the theory that revolutions have become impossible just as at other times they may be presented as 'inevitable.' This was the tenor of the 'end of history' analysis that received wide currency after the fall of the Berlin Wall. What this discussion, and the Bolivian case study, both indicate is that real revolutions are relatively rare and troubling experiences. But when they do happen they constitute a class of processes with a distinctive rhythm and logic that can profitably be studied as a cluster. Perhaps this is an observation of purely historical interest. Or perhaps there are lessons from such experiences as the Bolivian National Revolution that still have some relevance, even in the twenty-first century.

Notes

1 The MNR's official newspaper, *La Nación*, 3 February 1959, as quoted in Knudson (1986), p. 347.

2 For my bibliography of the period see the Bethell (ed.) (1995), pp. 806–10. A more narrative approach to the history of the revolution is contained in my chapter on Bolivia since 1930 in Bethell (ed.) (1992).

3 Orthodox Marxism sought to monopolize 'dialectical' analysis, with the result that when communist ideology was discredited this language was out of fashion. However, all revolutionary processes contain inner tensions which make them unstable and which unfold through conflict (including conflict of ideas) over time. In this sense (which is not to be confused with the old orthodoxy) the comparative historical analyses of revolutions would be mis-specified in the absence of a dialectical perspective.

4 Indeed, in the May 1951 election Perón supported Gariel Gosálves in his failed presidential bid against Víctor Paz. For more detail see Antezana E. (1988), p. 1752.

5 See, for example, Rodríguez Ostria (1991a) and Ora (1977) (by the trotskyist veteran).

6 The failings of pre-revolutionary administration and government were charted in some detail in the report of the Keenleyside Mission, a technical assistance document prepared for the economic and social council of the United Nations in 1951 (reporting on a three month visit in 1950). For a 'fiscal crisis' approach to the revolution see Gallo (1991).

7 RADEPA (Razón de Patria), a nationalist military organization, emerged out of the Chaco War.

8 Actually it is possible to identify some critical first steps towards restraining revolutionary radicalism from a very early point (e.g. the reopening of the Colegio Militar in 1953), but that is with the benefit of hindsight.

9 Antezana (1988) reconstructs the tortuous course of the revolution day-by-day through the first half of April 1952. His account highlights the many misjudgements and opportunistic maneuvres that separated the original plan from the eventual outcome. But the focus on individual ambitions fails to explain the scope of the resulting revolution. For that a larger focus and a longer time frame are required.

10 'There was censorship during the first two years of MNR rule when the government feared counter-revolution by the *Falange Socialista Boliviana* and others … *La Razón* … was prevented from reopening not by government action but rather popular wrath … circumstances surrounding the assault on *Los Tiempos* of Cochabamba on 9 November 1953 are more confused … but a careful study of both newspapers reveals reasons why they fell victim to a social revolution which neither understood.' Knudson (1986), p. 380.

11 René Zavaleta Mercado went so far as to describe this as a situation of 'dual power', analogous to Kerensky and the Soviets in 1917. However, the leader of the COB, Juan Lechín, was certainly no Lenin. According to his *Memorias* he had agreed to stand down in favour of Siles in the MNR's vice-presidential slot for 1951. He also

ceded the presidency to Siles in 1956 and declined an apparent offer of the presidency (by Paz) in 1960. In all these cases he indicates that a presumed US veto was the cause of his withdrawal, although other sources suggest that he also lacked the patience for office work. According to his memoirs, during the first Paz government his supporters believed he could bring down the president at will, by means of a telephone call. Why did he never use this supposed power? 'No lo derrocamos en esta época porque pensábamos que sus vacilaciones eran para evitar que los Estados Unidos nos estragulen. Yo pensaba que Paz jugaba ese complicado ajedrez, pero pensaba que lo hacía a favor del país.' Lechín Oquendo (2000), p. 287. See also p. 260.

12 For an exceptionally thoughtful and well-researched analysis from within the armed forces see General Prado Salmon (1984). Two months after the revolution the COB decided to organize its own armed militias, an initiative that was viewed as both humiliating and threatening to the regular armed forces. But in a shrewd maneuvre the military establishment responded by offering training and support. 'A nivel reservado, en acuerdo con el Presidente Paz, el Mando decidió destinar, además de oficiales subalternos instructores, oficiales superiores para que en la práctica ejerzan el comando de los regimientos de milicianos organizados … De esta manera … El Comando Nacional de las milicias nunca llegó a funcionar … y poco a poco las unidades de milicianos se fueron convirtiendo en grupos de presión zonal … Como elementos de sostén político al régimen, en funciones de seguridad interna, de represión política … liberando a las fuezas militares de cualquier participación en tareas represivas' (p. 54). Thus, at the very outset the foundations were laid for an eventual subordination of the party to the state and of an eventual displacement of the militias by the regular military. This clarifies points left unclear by Lechín's account (2000, pp. 294–9).

13 The Land Tenure Center at Madison Wisconsin undertook a series of detailed studies of different aspects of Bolivia's land reform, which still provide a large data bank for subsequent evaluation. The contemporary debate in Bolivia tends to undervalue the import of what was achieved then, either because so much rural poverty persisted thereafter, or on the grounds that this was a mestizo reform undertaken to the detriment of the Aymara and Quechua nations. While there can be no denying the uneven impact of the land reform and the acute problems of development that still afflict nearly all of the Bolivian *campo*, in the context of its time the Bolivian land reform remains a remarkably revolutionary transformation. The old Andean landlord class was effectively dispossessed, *sindicators campesinos* spread far and wide (often serving as fronts for more traditional *ayllu* struc-

tures) and the Bolivian state established a much stronger presence in the countryside. (The education reform was also relevant here). The contrast with highland Peru demonstrates the difference made by the land reform, which also paved the way for more recent experiments with 'popular participation'.

14 In the first unambiguously democratic elections of 1985 there were 2.1 million registered voters, of whom a little over 1.7 million actually voted.

15 Gloria Ardaya is justified in arguing that despite the best efforts of such dedicated woman revolutionaries neither the MNR's rise to power nor the enfranchizement of women did much to break the patriarchal structure of Bolivian society, at least during the period under review. For her instructive account of the Comandos Femeninas and the María Barzola Movement in the 1950s see Ardaya (1992). Rural women were represented within the party via the (male-dominated) *sindicatos*. The party's Comandos Femeninas only operated in the urban centers.

16 In fact the MNR won 84.4% of the valid votes cast in 1956, 85.0% in 1958, 76.1% in 1960, 84.8% in 1962 and finally — ominously in fact — it claimed 97.9% in 1964 (a contest with no opposition and a big increase in spoilt ballots). Universal suffrage swamped the parties of the traditional left, as well as those of the counter-revolutionary right. But it was not until the ruling party turned its machinery of electoral control against those who the Mexicans would call members of the 'revolutionary family' (first Walter Guevara Arze, later Lechín and finally Hernán Siles himself) that the regimes electoral legitimacy was squandered. Lechín claims that in the 1960 election Paz was determined to so control the vote that he obtained a 50% majority in the cities and 70% in the countryside, Lechín's argument was that this was unnecessary, since the MNR would win a free vote (Lechín, 2000, pp. 371–2).

17 James Malloy has analysed the MNR's various early efforts to recentralize power and in particular to concentrate public spending in the 'caja unica' of the public treasury, but he also notes that the immediate effect of these measures was centrifugal — rather than producing a 'seizure' of state power, the insurrection tended to destroy it (Malloy, 1970, pp. 246–7). By the late 1950s the IMF and USAID had established severe financial disciplines, but inflation control left the Bolivian state with virtually no margin of maneuvre in response to demands from below. Not until the Alliance for Progress reached Bolivia did administrative centralisation become a viable option.

18 *Ibid.*, pp. 246–7.

19 MNR militants advocated direct action to redistribute land on the grounds that otherwise all initiative would be lost in the fog of 'alto-

Peruvian' bureaucracy. A legal dossier prepared by a local *sindicato* would be sent to La Paz, where the Consejo Nacional de Reforma Agraria was besieged by interminable deputations of *campesino* petitionaries. The next step would be to seek the endorsement of the Ministry of Peasant Affairs, after which the dossier would pass to the presidency for the chief executive's personal signature of each title. Even then the document had to pass back through the whole chain, down to the departmental and then the provincial *juzgados* before returning to the original *sindicato*. Juan Carlos Camacho Romero quotes the example of one petition dated December 1954, which finally secured presidential authorization in 1971. For this reason reformism was not seen as an option by many MNR activists. Social change could only come about by revolutionary means. Camacho Romero (1989), p. 75.

20 In Heath, Erasmus and Buechler (1969).

21 Leons (1984); Platt (1982) (esp. chapter 5); Albó (1979); Dandler (1969). For an overview see Calderón and Dandler (eds.) (1986).

22 Dorris Widerkehr's doctoral dissertation on the miners of Kami Cooperative is available from university microfilms (Ann Arbor, Michigan).

23 I attempted to trace this process in Whitehead (1973). This elicited an as yet unpublished riposte from the Sandoval Morón family, *Bolivia: revolución y contrarevolución en el Oriente* (1952–64), a two hundred page manuscript which contains much valuable material, as well as some special pleading.

24 Much the fullest treatment of these issues (strongly focussed on the Oriente, but a nationwide interpretation) is Roca (1979). Compare Malloy (1970), pp. 249–51.

25 'A successful revolutionary insurrection usually leads to a thorough destruction of state-level authority, control and order. evolutionary elites thereby are faced not simply with the task of reordering the society in particular images and the pursuit of particular concrete goals, but, more immediately, they are faced with the problem of achieving order per se.' *Ibid.*, p. 245.

26 He returned to office as a democratic president 1982–85.

27 Malloy (1970), p. 291. What this portrayal does not reveal is the reciprocal nature of the state–local interdependencies. Unlike Mexico, or China or Afghanistan during their periods of warlordism, the national government was quickly able to re-establish increased central control without that must resort to violence.

28 The central argument of the Sandoval Moron group in Santa Cruz was that the national leadership of their party was building up what it fondly hoped would be a 'national bourgeoisie' in the Oriente, but which in practice would be a counter-revolutionary oligarchy. The

Comando Departamental of the MNR therefore felt justified in making its own popular revolution (mainly based on the forced distribution of urban land) in defiance of the authorities in La Paz.

29 The first Célula Militar was established in La Paz on 31 October 1953 (Prado, 1984, p. 57). By the end of the 1950s the armed forces were in the process of recovering their prestige and their capacity for action in all parts of the national territory. At this point the top officers in the hierarchy were also the leaders of the Célula Militar. Consequently this component of the governing party did not split into factions when the rest of the MNR became divided. As a united block with the armed forces behind them, during the 1960–64 period this cell gradually came to dominate the host party (*Ibid.*, pp 101–44).

30 Until 1958 the army was equipped with German Mausers. Starting in 1959 it witched to MI semi-automatic rifles from the USA. This involved a change of calibre, so that imported ammunition for the new weapons could not be used in the (more widely available) old ones (*Ibid.*, pp. 99–100).

31 General Barrientos began his rise to political prominence as an *interventor* sent to impose order on the battling factions in the Cochabamba Valley, where his fluency in Quechua proved a powerful asset.

32 As late as February 1964 President Paz still thought he might retain control of his party and escape dependence on General Barrientos, but the tactics of his civilian rivals undercut that endeavour. On a longer view this failure was probably inherent in the 1961 Constitutional provision allowing the re-election of the incumbent president.

33 The 'more or less' in this sentence may need to be contextualized. The electoral calendar was respected. There was little electoral violence. The Falange contested these elections across the nation and secured some important local victories. Elections were more effectively contested than in, say, Mexico at the same time. There was substantial press freedom. Not many Latin American countries consistently observed higher democratic standards than those then prevailing in Bolivia.

34 There is a fairly exhaustive bibliography in Goodwin (2001). For the wider debates see Mahoney and Rueschemeyer (eds.)(2003).

35 Although if the Chaco War is taken into account this assertion would have to be modified.

36 This is the clue to his career that is missing from his *Memorias*, which do however reveal something of his easy-going nature and his lack of confidence in his own grasp of ideological issues.

37 Knudson's (1986) account of the ideas debated in the party newspa-

per *La Nación* in the late 1950s illustrates this point. The writers included such noted intellectuals and polemicists as Augusto Céspedes, José Cuadros Quiroga and René Zavaleta Mercado.

38 In the *Cambridge History* I described Victor Paz as 'Bolivia's first technocrat' on the basis of an article he wrote in *El Diario* in 1930 (Whitehead, 1991, p. 512, footnote 1).

39 US food aid may have averted that danger, but the political economy of its distribution requires further research. There is a suggestive starting point in Ardaya (1992).

40 Malloy stresses the intense competition for public employment among the politicized urban middle classes and its destabilizing consequences in post-revolutionary Bolivia. See Malloy (1970), especially Chapter 12 on the 'structure and process' of post-insurrectionary politics.

41 In 1964 Paz Estenssoro concluded that he could not discuss oil policy in his cabinet, since half his ministers were what he called 'Gulfmen' (i.e. aligned with Gulf Oil).

CHAPTER 3

The Domestic Dynamics of the Mexican and Bolivian Revolutions Compared

Alan Knight

In August 1964, less than three months before the MNR government was toppled by military coup, a British diplomat ventured an interesting, optimistic, but not altogether novel, comparison:

> Bolivia is 'on the move' and with an average amount of good luck and help from its friends there seems no reason why the Bolivian Revolution — the second in Latin America — should not eventually attain the same sort of stability and prosperity as has at last been achieved by the first — Mexican — revolution. Much of the long drawn out history of the Mexican Revolution is echoed in Bolivia and the short-term 'ups and downs' of Bolivian politics should not distract us from doing what we can to help Bolivia follow the Mexican example'.[1]

A high-minded purpose (perhaps); but a hopeless prediction. In November the MNR was overthrown and its potential emulation of the PNR/PRM/PRI came to a sudden end. In this chapter I return to the same question. However, I am concerned not just with the question of why the MNR did not emulate the PRI; I will also address the broader, and intimately related, question, of how the Bolivian Revolution resembled, or differed from, the Mexican from the outset. To this end, I begin with the causes of the revolutions, analyze their respective courses and conclude with the 1964 divergence.

By way of initial clarification, I would make two points. First, this sequential analysis implied, in my view, a shift from structural to conjunctural factors (both of which are important). Thus, in the first part of the chapter I give priority to the broad features of pre-revolutionary Mexico and Bolivia which made them both potentially revolutionary, in ways that were sometimes similar, sometimes different. Later, however, I shift to conjunctural factors — that is to say, the dynamics (or 'logics')[2] of the two revolutions. Here, comparison becomes more difficult, because conjunctural dynamics are more fluid and fast moving. For example, the long-term structure of mining or *latifundismo* implies certain clear-cut relationships, tensions and possibilities; in contrast, the short-term political processes, which gave rise to the insurrections of 1910 and 1952, were more stochastic, subject to individual decisions and 'random' accidents. Similar decisions and accidents helped determine the two revolutionary trajectories after 1910 and 1952. Over time, the conjunctural dynamics of revolution overlaid and obscured some (not all) of the original structural factors.

Second, this raises the question of the purpose of comparison. I am very skeptical about general theories of 'revolution': I do not believe that 'revolutions' — or, to narrow the sample drastically — 'great' or 'social' revolutions display clearly patterned common features (except inasmuch as such features are tautologically implied by the concept 'revolution').[3] In particular, I have little time for generic theories which posit either common stages of revolution or common etiology (e.g., the 'J-curve').[4] In short, the term 'revolution' may be useful as a descriptive label (like 'war' or 'hole in the ground'), but this does not mean that a meaningful theory of 'revolutions' (or wars or holes in the ground) can be usefully fashioned.[5] The comparison presented here obeys a different rationale. First, it confines itself to two cases (though I hazard some references to other revolutions in passing). Second, it proceeds from the assumption that some revolutions share common characteristics, especially when we consider the collective actors involved (less so the plots in which they are involved). Actors have certain interests and goals; their relationships with other actors may follow a common pattern.[6] Well-chosen cases — and I think Mexico and Bolivia are well chosen — will therefore reveal common patterns. In the process, the comparison should illuminate both cases. It will not advance our formulation of a general theory of revolution; but it should advance our knowledge of Mexico, or Bolivia, or both.

Structural Comparisons

The choice of this pairing is partly arbitrary (I know about Mexico, the volume focuses on Bolivia),[7] but it also has a less random rationale, which derives from the similarities which the two cases exhibit. Of course, there is nothing to stop us comparing the Bolivian with the French or Chinese revolutions; or the MNR with the CPSU or CCP. However, there are advantages in comparing cases that display some demonstrable similarities. Mexico and Bolivia are the two Latin American countries which, in the course of the twentieth-century,[8] experienced 'great' or 'social' revolutions that were successful, in the sense of substantially transforming their societies, but which did not result in socialism.[9] More positively — and riskily — we might say they were also 'bourgeois' and, certainly, 'nationalist' revolutions.[10]

Nor is this historical kinship confined to the common revolutionary experience. As we enter the 'structural' analysis, we could note some common antecedent features (as well as differences). Mexico and Bolivia both belonged to the Spanish colonial heartland — the heavily populated highlands of Andean America and Mesoamerica, where the Spaniards capitalized on the triple advantages of an imperial state that they could hi-jack, a dense Indian population that they could dominate and mineral resources that they could exploit. Conquered at the outset, Mexico and Upper Peru were among the last of Spain's mainland colonies to achieve independence. Thereafter, Mexican and Bolivian history continued to display some common features: political stability was hard to achieve; as mining declined, the (money) economy languished; military interventions vitiated republican rule; foreign invasions occurred; and rapacious neighbors made off with outlying territory. Not until the last quarter of the nineteenth century did a semblance of stability loom, thanks in large measure to the onset of railways and the revival of mining. Both Mexico and Bolivia thus entered the twentieth century under the aegis of authoritarian 'oligarchic' government, which presided over a largely peasant population and relied on a crucial export sector, in which mining predominated. Both also possessed highland capitals, whose authority was resented in outlying (lowland) regions — regions which in the case of the Mexican north and the Bolivian east, were less Indian, which abutted a powerful and somewhat predatory neighbor and which were destined to prosper in the course of the twentieth century.

As I shall suggest, these broad similarities engendered certain common tensions and problems. But, similarities aside, there were some significant differences that should also be flagged at the outset.[11] Three in particular demand brief attention. First, the ethnic balance in the two countries was substantially different: Mexico, to put it crudely, was a mestizo nation, Bolivia an Indian nation governed by a mestizo/*criollo* minority. In 1910, about 15 per cent of the Mexican population was reckoned to be Indian; in Bolivia in 1952 the figure was over 60 per cent — making it the most Indian of the Spanish-American republics.[12] Bolivia was therefore more sharply ethnically polarized (it might be compared to the Mexican south: Yucatán and Chiapas).[13] Second, the Mexican economy, colonial and national, had achieved a greater degree of integration and market activity than the Bolivian. Mining, though crucial, was less dominant; and mining had, since the colonial period, depended on free labor rather than extra-economic coercion.[14] Mexican haciendas too (as I shall note shortly) were more developed, market-oriented and reliant on free labor than Bolivian ones. Third, Mexican 'cultural' integration was also greater. In part, cultural integration reflected economic trends — the market served to integrate and 'acculturate' — in part it derived from the more successful proselytization of the Catholic Church. To a greater degree than Bolivia, Mexico was a Catholic society, possessed of a powerful Catholic Church and a ubiquitous national patroness, the Virgin of Guadalupe. Mexican miners, for example, did not revere the Pachamama or pay tribute to *el tío*.[15] On the contrary, for all their rowdy behavior and contestation of state power, miners often showed profound respect for the Catholic Church.[16] Catholic hegemony carried important consequences, both 'positive' and 'negative'. Coupled with economic integration, Catholic hegemony probably fostered a precocious sense of nationhood and of Mexican providentialism: creole 'proto-patriotism' in the colonial period, liberal and conservative nationalism after Independence.[17] Bolivian notions of nationhood, fatally compromised by sharp ethnic polarization, were correspondingly weaker. On the other hand, the Bolivian Revolution, as I shall note, lacked the shrill anticlericalism of its Mexican counterpart: the Church simply did not matter so much.

Whatever the causes — and I have suggested three interlocking factors: ethnicity, the market and Catholicism — Mexico displays a historical record of broad popular mobilization in the name of national causes.[18] While the insurgency of 1810 may be a controversial case, it is clear that by the 1860s Mexicans were prepared to rally en masse to a liberal-patriotic cause led by a Zapotec president, Benito Juárez (compare Bolivia's roughly contemporaneous liberal caudillo: the egregious and ethnocidal Mariano Melgarejo).[19] The Mexican Revolution of 1910 again involved a multiplicity of ethnic groups, loosely united in national and regional coalitions: *Maderismo*, *Zapatismo*, *Villismo*, *Carrancismo*. Ethnicity counted, but — for better or worse — it was subsumed in broader politico-social-clientelist alliances. With the partial and peripheral exceptions of the Yaqui and the Quintana Roo Maya insurrections, Porfirian Mexico produced nothing to compare with Bolivia's autonomous Indian rebellions of 1898–99 (which were bigger, more threatening and located in the country's heartland).[20] Nor, save for some minor exceptions in the deep south, did the Mexican Revolution generate that querulous fear of caste war which — with good reason — affected Bolivian cities and landed estates after 1952.[21] Florencia Mallon's contrast of Mexico and Peru — suggestive rather than definitive though it may be — could as well be applied to Mexico and Bolivia.[22]

If valid, this contrast implies that any major revolution which affected 1910 Mexico or 1952 Bolivia was likely to assume somewhat contrasting forms: the former could count on generations of greater social, economic and cultural integration; the latter would be prey to local, regional and, above all, ethnic particularisms. Any twentieth-century Mexican revolution occurred in a *patria forjada* (at least to some extent); in Bolivia, a lot of forging remained to be done. This difference would affect both the character of the revolution and the historical mission assumed by the victorious revolutionaries.

If we shift the focus from the *longue durée* to the conjunctural crises of the respective old regimes, differences are again apparent.[23] To simplify the analysis, I will focus on the major collective actors, the two political regimes and the immediate causes of revolution. The social structure of both the Mexican and Bolivian *anciens regimes* can be analyzed in terms of: a politico-economic oligarchy (which implies an 'agent' state, pretty faithfully responsive to the interests of the economic oligarchy);[24] a massive majoritarian peasantry; a much smaller urban/industrial working class; and a small but growing (and largely urban) middle class. In both cases, revolution occurred when a political movement loosely led by urban middle-class reformists challenged the old regime and, in the process, struck a de facto alliance with peasant and working-class groups. However, the character of these (roughly comparable) collective actors varied, as did their relationships, and thus the way the subsequent plot unfolded.

In both countries the peasants constituted a majority (70–80 per cent) of the population.[25] In Bolivia, the peasantry was largely Indian, in Mexico, largely mestizo. For reasons already mentioned, the Mexican peasantry had a record of engagement in national mobilization, in alliance with other classes (under the banner not only of *Juarismo*, but also of early *Porfirismo*). In Bolivia, such cross-class alliances came rather later, in part under the stimulus of the Chaco War, and they tended to be more fragile. Perhaps even more important, the agrarian structures and tensions that provided the crucible of peasant insurrection were different. In Mexico market signals and economic integration were stronger; and, especially once the Porfirian regime had built the required infrastructure and bolstered business confidence, commercial *hacendados* responded by increasing resources, output and profits.[26] The chief victims were neighboring peasant communities which now faced a severe threat to land and autonomy.[27] Meanwhile, the Porfirian state, apart from acting as an 'agent' of the landed oligarchy, imposed its own fiscal, political and military burdens, chiefly to the disgust of more remote *serrano* communities.[28] The agrarian tensions of the revolution therefore tended to pit villagers (the 'external' peasantry) against expansionist haciendas. The 'internal' peasantry (resident hacienda peons and day laborers) tended to be less 'revolutionary': they faced tighter hacienda control (especially in the deep south); they may have felt some lingering deference towards paternalist landlords; and they had less to gain, much more to lose, by supporting the revolutionary cause.[29] Outside the deep south (where, of course, Indians predominated), Mexican haciendas tended not to be heavily coercive; in a labor-surplus society, landlords could usually get and retain labor by means of economic rewards (sometimes cash wages; often by means of sharecropping rentals or labor tenancies). Yucatán had its whipping posts and barracoons, Chiapas its notorious lumber camps; but the haciendas of Morelos, the Bajío or the sprawling, socially mobile north, did not have to rely on coercion. The economic resources of the landlord class, backed by the power of the Porfirian state, kept the internal peasantry in check. Even as the agrarian reform got under way, first violently and chaotically during the 1910s, then more systematically and officially after 1920 (and especially after 1934), so the free villagers made the running and the resident peons and *jornaleros* followed at a distance — if they did not actively side with the embattled hacienda.[30]

In Bolivia, village clashes with expansionist haciendas were common enough; and they had provoked protests and rebellions in the past.[31] But this conflict does not appear to have been as powerful and pervasive in Bolivia as a whole as in Mexico: thus, the closest counterpart to, say, Morelos, was Cochabamba, an arable farming region where market demand coexisted with a combative independent peasantry.[32] On the *altiplano*, haciendas were more sluggish, backward, even 'feudal.' They clashed with 'external' peasants (especially over the question of pasture and livestock, which was a lesser consideration in Mexico); but, more important, they depended on the labor of tied 'internal peasants' (colonos), whose numbers had grown through the nineteenth century, as haciendas had grown and free villages had been expropriated.[33] Not only were Bolivian *colonos* relatively more numerous than Mexican peones: they were also subject to a more coercive and serflike exploitation (hence the ubiquity and, I think, the validity of the 'feudal' label).[34] Lacking vigorous markets, Bolivian haciendas relied on squeezing a surplus from a poor and dependent peasantry.[35] Landlords extracted cheap or free labor, in the form not only of labor services, but also of the hated domestic services *pongueaje*.[36] Demesne production tended to be less significant in Bolivia than Mexico (where, for example, the sugar haciendas of Moreos, the cotton estates of La Laguna, or the pulque *latifundia* of Hidalgo resembled commercial plantations); many highland Bolivian haciendas appear to have comprised a patchwork of peasant plots *sayañas*.[37] Hacienda control was pervasive: *colonos* were bought and sold with properties like Russian serfs; *colonos* were (in some cases, not all) denied access to markets; women had to serve in the big house; and dissidents suffered corporal punishment.[38] Though there were 'good' landlords, whose paternalism, rooted in old Andean reciprocal practices, moderated oppression and even earned them a measure of deferential respect, the norm was clearly more coercive, exploitative and primitive than its Mexican counterpart (outside the Mexican south, where comparable coercive relationships prevailed).[39] It seems clear that this contrast derived in part from contrasting patterns of economic development, in part from the ethnic polarization which, in Bolivia, justified and maintained such 'feudal' forms of labor. Thus, although it is fair to say (as I just did) that both revolutions involved a shotgun marriage between insurgent peasants and middle-class reformists, the peasants in question were different and displayed different grievances. Mexico's villagers looked to recover lost land and autonomy; Bolivia's *colonos* sought to throw over the traces of an oppressive feudalism. The first — which involved a confrontation with dynamic and productive haciendas (e.g., the haciendas of Morelos of La Laguna) — tended to be more radical than the second, which implied the overthrow of a parasitic and unproductive elite. Thus, by the 1930s, the Mexican agrarian reform began to transcend 'bourgeois' limits and to create collective *ejidos*.[40]

If we switch the comparison to the Mexican and Bolivian working classes, the contrasts are less striking but they remain significant. In both cases, the working class was a minority. Given the greater development of the Mexican economy, the Mexican working class was somewhat larger and more diversified. Yet, as the unfolding plot makes clear, Mexican workers played a less salient and autonomous role in the armed revolution than their Bolivian counterparts. (Thus, to put it crudely, the Mexican Revolution was more of a 'peasant war' than the Bolivian.) In part, this may have again reflected old traditions of popular mobilization: Rodney Anderson has convincingly shown that the dominant ideology of the Porfirian working class was patriotic liberalism, rather than radical anarcho-syndicalism;[41] Mexico produced no equivalent of the insurgent Trotskyist miners of the 'red fortress' of Catavi or the maximalist Tesis de Pulacayo.[42] In this, I suspect, it was Bolivia rather than Mexico that was unusual. Without rehearsing old debates about 'revolutionary' and 'non-revolutionary' workers,[43] we can nevertheless concede that Latin American working class movements have usually eschewed armed revolution in favor of reformism, urban politicking and instrumental lobbying.[44] (So, of course, did many peasants; however, in Mexico peasants appear to have been more disposed to revolutionary action than their working-class counterparts, in part because the [external] peasant/hacienda conflict was a zero-sum game, in which one side's gains — historically, the hacienda's — were the other side's losses. The worker/capitalist relationship could be mitigated by mutual benefits, so long as production, productivity and profits increased; however, since the 1920s, this was not the case in the majority of Bolivia's tin mines.)[45] In Bolivia, too, many working class groups adopted moderate, 'economistic' and reformist strategies — and the MNR capitalized on these differences with their 'divide-and-rule' strategy.[46] The big exception were the miners. Absent the miners, the Bolivian 'proletarian revolution' would look a lot more like the Mexican, in which workers actively joined political parties, voted in elections (when allowed), formed trade unions and struck tactical alliances with congenial *políticos*.

Why were the miners different? Several reasons — all pretty familiar — can be advanced. It is a commonplace that mining camps and communities tend to breed strong sentiments of solidarity, which combine both occupational and residential ties.[47] The work, in particular, fosters a kind of fraternity born of risk and confinement,[48] to which might be added the machismo of mining and the access to de facto weaponry (e.g., dynamite) which it affords. Isolation reinforces a sense of community, which can turn mining camps into electoral, syndical or military bastions. Nevertheless, these factors by no means guarantee effective collective militancy. There have been 'paternalist' mining communities (and Patiño at least among the Big Three acquired something of a paternalist reputation);[49] and in Mexico, notwithstanding the famous clash at Cananea in 1907, mining camps did not become nests of revolutionary activity after 1910. Even during the radical 1930s, the record of Mexico's miners was mixed: though the miners union, SITMMSRM, became one of the major industrial unions with which government and business had to reckon,[50] it did not display the sustained militancy of say, the oil-workers union (STPRM) or even the railwaymen (STFRM). There was no wholesale expropriation, no workers' control, in the Mexican mining sector, as there was in the oil and railway industries. Government restraint, coupled with rising wages (and other perks), kept the miners in line during the militant years of Cardenismo.[51]

Three possible factors help to explain this partial discrepancy. The most obvious and important is the strategic salience of the Bolivian miners. Minerals comprised some 95 per cent of Bolivian exports (tin, some 60 per cent), and mining generated around 15 per cent of GDP. Mexico was not a 'monoculture' of this kind: the comparable figures (c.1910) would be 75 per cent and nine per cent.[52] Furthermore, Bolivian production was relatively concentrated: the mining workforce numbered 27,000, compared to Mexico's 97,000 (thus, it took about 11,000 Mexican miners to produce one per cent of GDP, but only 1,800 Bolivians, a contrast that reflects, of course, Mexico's greater economic diversification). Bolivian production was also spatially concentrated: Llallagua, with a labor force of some 4,000, generated about 30 per cent of Bolivian tin, thus about 20 per cent of the country's foreign exchange. Cananea, a comparable Mexican mining town, had a workforce of about 3,500 (2,300 of them Mexicans), who produced around half of the country's copper, or four per cent of Mexican foreign exchange.[53] In fact, the closest parallels to the Bolivian mining centers, at least in terms of economic muscle, were Mexican oil camps and oil towns, for example, Poza Rica, Doña Cecilia (Ciudad Madero) and Minatitlán, during the petroleum boom of the late 1910s and early 1920s. We should note, however, that the oil boom began *after* the revolution was under way and while the working class in these communities was still in formation. By the time syndical organization had set in, the boom was over and the oil workers' economic muscle — though far from negligible — had atrophied.

Secondly, it has been suggested that Bolivian miners' solidarity was fostered both by the way work was organized and by a peculiar cosmology-cum-worldview.[54] I am not sure if, in respect of the work process, Bolivia differed significantly from Mexico. But worldviews certainly differed, as I have already suggested. Since the days of the *mita*, Bolivia's mines had relied on Indian labor drafts, drawn from the massive Andean peasant population, while Mexico's mines had largely relied on free wage labor, chiefly migrants from the south who trekked north in search of income and livelihood. Northern colonial Mexican mining towns, like Chihuahua, tended to be fluid, mobile and mestizo.[55] By the twentieth century border towns like Cananea drew in southern migrants, Chinese and Americans. Bolivian mining communities tended to be more homogeneous, replicating Indian/peasant practices in a harsh, isolated setting: the cult of the *tío* and Pachamama, 'pagan' practices, anthropomorphic visions of the mine.[56] Now it does not follow that such a hybrid culture should necessarily fuel militancy; nor is it easy to measure how far such diffuse cultural practices contribute to political activism (they could, after all, generate quietism, with religion figuring, one might say, as the coca of the people). Nevertheless, it seems likely that such beliefs and practices colored miners' attitudes — perhaps fostering a more militant anti-capitalism — and also reinforced sentiments of solidarity, which may have derived from other sources (work, residence and shared historical experience). After all, nonconformity *per se* did not make Welsh miners militant; but the chapel certainly helped encourage solidarity and organization.

A crucial factor must be historical experience. Mining, especially tin mining, was crucial for the Bolivian economy, hence governments took a close interest in production (they depended on tin not only for foreign exchange but also for a significant slice of government revenue).[57] At the same time, mining was an aleatory activity, subject to the vicissitudes of both below-ground production and international demand. Hence the arbitrary, ludic, cynical temper of *el tío*. Bolivian mining rode a roller-coaster of international booms and busts in the 40 years prior to the revolution.[58] These vicissitudes depended crucially on factors beyond Bolivia's control: first, cycles of demand generated by international war and recession; second, the growth of formidable overseas competition. War boosted demand and stoked the fires of militancy; recession produced lay-offs — 'white massacres' — and hardship. (Compare Mexican oil and mining, where the vicissitudes were less marked and where, it could be argued, even the Porfirian old regime showed some disposition to conciliate working class grievances and to channel organized labor into peaceful, mutualist channels. I suspect the urban/mestizo character of Mexican labor helped: the authorities were more ready to establish a dialogue with fellow-city dwellers who looked and sounded like them, than with primitive pyjama-clad Indians out in the sticks).

A final important point of comparison must be made: somewhat paradoxically, Bolivia's miners (who worked in Bolivian-owned enterprises) appear to have been rather more militantly nationalist than Mexico's miners, who labored for foreigners. (Again, nationalism was more apparent in the Mexican oil camps.) In Mexico, despite well-known clashes like Cananea, revolutionary anti-Americanism or anti-imperialism was sporadic; it was often triggered by US government policy rather than a deeply-dyed antipathy to US business in Mexico.[59] Of the foreign communities resident in revolutionary Mexico, Chinese and Spaniards suffered a good deal more from popular reprisals than Americans (or Britons). Popular nationalism — or 'xenophobia' — appears to have derived less from (perceived) economic exploitation than from resentment at US policy and gringo slights. At Cananea it was wage differentials between Mexican and US employees, rather than the fact of American ownership of the mine, which stirred resentment. Even the celebrated oil expropriation of 1938 — which came after some 25 years of revolutionary mobilization and 'acculturation' and which therefore cannot be regarded as an expression of spontaneous revolutionary nationalism — occurred because the oil companies, intransigent to the last, thought they could defy the authority of President Cárdenas and the sovereignty of the Mexican state.[60]

Bolivian workers did not, by and large, groan under the yoke of US imperialism: the mines were owned by (quasi-) Bolivians; the railways were partly British; total US investment in Bolivia in 1952 was substantially less than it had been in Mexico in 1910.[61] Bolivian resentment towards the USA was directed against a regional hegemon and principal customer (for tin) — a customer which, by virtue of being a hegemon, could, so it appeared, play fast and loose with the market when it chose. Mexico, too, depended heavily on the US market: but it was less reliant on a single (not very competitive) export; it had other markets (note how Cárdenas beat the oil company boycott after March 1938); and it could exploit its geopolitical position to extract better terms from the *coloso del norte*.[62] Indeed, Mexican bargaining power vis-à-vis the United States was enhanced by the large US stake in the Mexican economy: US bankers, for example, did not want the oil companies to drive Mexico into bankruptcy; US manufacturers (exporters and investors) wanted a prosperous, pro-American Mexico. In comparison, Bolivia had little geopolitical or economic *palanca*. We have, then, an interesting conclusion: the presence of large foreign investments did not, of itself, provoke popular nationalism; but the capricious policy-making of a regional hegemon did.[63]

Though peasants and miners were crucial allies of the MNR in 1952 and after, they did not found or control the party. It is, of course, risky to attribute class or origins to a relatively small political elite and riskier still to infer political stance from class origins (after all, Cuba's 26 July Movement tended to be urban and middle-class, much like the MNR).[64] Nevertheless, it seems clear that the founders and early protagonists of the MNR were largely urban, educated, middle-class professionals. Despite the influx of worker and peasant leaders after 1952, MNR ministers during the 1950s and 1960s continued this trend. In this, the MNR resembled Mexico's *Maderistas* of 1908–13, who were often drawn from the burgeoning middle class of Mexico's swelling cities;[65] they also resembled, in terms of both social background and ideological persuasion, the *Apristas* of contemporary Peru. While Bolivian middle-class mobilization was clearly subject to conjunctural pressures — economic vicissitudes, international events and, perhaps most important of all, relations with other classes and ethnic groups —[66] some kind of substratum of goals and interests, the bedrock of middle-class/MNR activism, endured, even if, over time, it was overlaid with fresh strata and thus subjected to confusing slippage and distortion.

In both Porfirian Mexico and 'oligarchic' Bolivia, the urban middle class was a small but growing sector, who, while they did not suffer the extreme disenfranchizement of Indian peasants, were well aware of their political exclusion.[67] They were also aware of their growing numbers and of international benchmarks against which they measured their own marginality. Mexican middle-class liberals looked to the United States, France and Argentina; their Bolivian counterparts looked, *inter alia*, to Mexico. It was particularly galling for them when partial political opening was followed by renewed closure (with Mexico's Creelman interview or the Convergencia in Bolivia), especially when closure coincided — as it did in Bolivia — with inflation and declining real income.[68] It seems reasonable, if unoriginal, therefore, to regard the MNR, like the *Maderistas*, as protagonists of those rising 'middle sectors' who were once so popular in Latin American political science.[69]

But we should note three important and related considerations. First, the Bolivian Revolution — and its enemies — embodied a significant student element, which might be regarded as the organizational vanguard of the (usually disorganized) middle class.[70] The student element was much weaker in the Mexican case. Individual students, of course, participated in the revolution; but collective organization was weak and numbers were small. Furthermore, during the armed revolution most students appear to have been relatively conservative (the university reform movement, which began in Córdoba, Argentina, in 1918, was yet to make its presence felt).[71] It was not until the 1950s and 1960s that Mexican students — now giving voice to progressive middle-class critiques of the incumbent PRI — became a major force in Mexican politics. Bolivian students, in contrast, played a disproportionate role from the start.

Second, as the specific case of the students suggests, the ideology of middle-class protest — of the middle-class claim to a place in the political sun — varied a good deal from time to time and place to place. *Maderismo* was quintessentially liberal, harking back to Juárez and the 1857 Constitution, seeking to emulate US progressivism.[72] The MNR, born in the dark shadows of the 1940s, blended nationalism with fascism, or so its critics alleged. To some extent, this was illusory: 'fascism' was an easy imputation and it derived its logic in part from the odd political concatenations of the 1930s and 1940s, when, in Bolivia as in Argentina, the Stalinist left joined in alliance with the pro-Ally (*ergo* 'democratic') oligarchy, thus encouraging its opponents to flirt with fascism (or, at least, with 'nationalism', which might carry democratic or authoritarian connotations). To put it crudely: a middle-class bid for political access was more likely to assume nationalist and illiberal tones in 1940s Bolivia than it had in 1900s Mexico. 'World-time' had moved on and created new ideological constraints and opportunities.

More important still, I think, middle-class activism depended crucially on the activism of other classes. It was reactive and fungible. Scholars once used to talk of the peasantry as a class of 'low classness.' The middle class, I suggest, was a class of even lower classness.[73] It was not just that the middle class spanned a range of occupations and interests and, for this and other reasons, lacked any coherent solidarity. It was also that middle-class political attitudes were highly fluid and dependent on relationships to other classes/ethnicities — and on the enveloping political context. In 1908–11, confronting Díaz's oligarchic dictatorship, Mexico's middle class espoused an upbeat, optimistic, inclusionary political liberalism; thereafter, facing peasant insurrection, working-class mobilization and praetorian intervention, many of them recanted and retreated into conservatism, if not reaction. (Similar stories are well known in interwar Europe — or, more recently, in Central America).[74] By the 1930s, the urban middle class was strongly anti-*Cardenista.* So, too, in Bolivia: middle-class activists sought political power and a measure of sociopolitical reform; but once the *Rosca* was removed, and more radical popular demands surfaced, the middle-class divided. Some stuck with the MNR (not least for reasons of jobs and political preferment); many veered towards the FSB, the MNRA and the military, their denunciations of MNR demagogy and corruption echoing those of Cárdenas's critics in 1930s Mexico.[75] (Indeed, their denunciations were probably more severe, stimulated by levels of inflation which postrevolutionary Mexico had never suffered.) Like Madero in 1911–13, Paz Estenssoro found — especially in 1960–64 — that the middle class were fickle and that the middle-class constituency was a shifting sand on which to build a stable revolutionary regime.

Conjunctural Comparisons

As the collective career of the middle class strongly suggests, 'structural' explanations, based on the enduring interests and related attitudes of social groups, are only a part, and, over time, a diminishing part of revolutionary history. (True, the middle class, being a 'class of low classness' may be particularly politically fickle; the miners, in contrast, displayed more consistent attitudes, based on their more clearcut material interests: jobs, unions and communities). So I now turn to the plot, which could be conventionally summarized in three acts: the background to the revolutionary outbreak (pre-1910 in Mexico, pre-1952 in Bolivia); the 'processes' of the revolutionary regimes (1920–40 in Mexico, 1952–64 in Bolivia); and the revolutionary collapse in Bolivia (1964), which contrasts with the slow transmogrification of the PRM/PRI after 1940. Acts two and three crucially involve the question I posed at the outset: why the MNR could not emulate the PNR/PRM/PRI. However, any answer to that question must embrace both the structural factors already sketched and the early etiology of the respective revolutions.

The revolutions of 1910 and 1952 were both directed against narrow, unrepresentative, oligarchic regimes (indeed, that would seem to be true of almost all 'great' revolutions: no such revolution has toppled a representative democracy). Like Charles I, Louis XVII, the Emperor Nicholas II, the Manchu Dowager Empress, Fulgencio Batista and Anastasio Somoza, both Díaz and Ballivián headed authoritarian regimes which lacked broad legitimacy. Beyond that banal statement, which highlights simply the vulnerability of authoritarian regimes, no clearcut common etiology can be found. As I have argued elsewhere, Theda Skocpol's emphasis on great power rivalry, leading to defeat and bankruptcy, has some merit in the case of Bolivia, but not Mexico.[76] Economic vicissitudes, linked to swings in the business cycle, no doubt counted but the Mexican and Bolivian experiences were significantly different.[77] The political pre-histories of the two countries also differed. Díaz had presided over some 30 years of 'order and progress'. He was adulated by foreign observers, who, like most Mexican pundits, had no sense that a revolution was imminent: 'I consider general revolution out of the question', reported a German diplomat in 1910, 'as does public opinion and the press'.[78] The Bolivian Revolution, in contrast, culminated some 20 years of economic and political turmoil: the depression (particularly severe for a mineral monoculture like Bolivia); the Chaco War; military socialism; the suicide of Germán Busch and the revival of the oligarchic regime; the Second World War (which boosted demand for tin, while imposing its own extraneous logic on Bolivian politics); the revolution of 1943 and the Villarroel regime; Villarroel's traumatic fall from power; and the final, discordant swansong of the *Rosca* after 1946.[79] Without entering into this complex narative — which contrasts with the relative blandness of the late Porfiriato (say, 1890–1910) — let me tease out some salient and contrasting features.

The most obvious, which is central to any comparative analysis of the two revolutions, is that in Bolivia the MNR preceded and, to some degree, engendered the revolution; while in Mexico the revolution preceded and engendered the PNR/PRM/PRI. In this respect, the Bolivian Revolution followed the 'normal' twentieth-century — Communist, or occasionally fascist — pattern, while the Mexican is *sui generis* (comparable 'bourgeois' revolutions either fail to produce a party at all [e.g., France, 1789]; or, as in the Communist or Italian fascist model, the party precedes the revolution [e.g., China's KMT/GMD]). Given this contrasting relationship between party and revolution, one might have expected the MNR — as author of the revolution — to display more cohesion and longevity than the 'postrevolutionary' PNR/PRM/PRI. In fact, of course, it is the other way around.

The genesis of the MNR is well known. It began as a nationalist and reformist party, hostile to the *Rosca*, ambivalent about democracy and carrying the ideological imprint of its 1940s origins. Prior to 1952, it had enjoyed a share of power under Villarroel; it had survived severe repression and exile after 1946; and it displayed its continuing popularity in the abortive elections of 1951. Thus, by 1952 it was a seasoned party, which had, albeit briefly, enjoyed power and office and which presented the biggest party-political challenge to the floundering *Rosca.* (As such, it bears comparison with the contemporary Cuban Ortodoxos). Just as it had relied on army bayonets to achieve power in 1943, so it needed the support of police, dissident military and, above all, the armed miners to seize power by insurrection in 1952. Forty years earlier, Madero's revolutionaries faced a somewhat similar, sclerotic regime (though the regime's sclerosis became apparent only with hindsight). Both revolutionary groups favored a swift, insurrectionary strike: the MNR succeeded (the uprising was over in three days with perhaps 600 casualties);[80] Madero, however, initiated a six-month civil war, which was followed by nearly a decade of intense fighting, during which over a million Mexicans died.[81]

'As of marriages,' Womack writes, 'so of revolutions: the best take years to turn out well.'[82] True for the *Maderista* revolt of 1910–11 — a 'victory won too soon' — Womack's aphorism also fits the Bolivian Revolution of 1952.[83] The speed of success carried several crucial implications. As regards the revolutionary movement itself, it had not been tried by fire; it came to power swiftly and relatively painlessly; and it did so in loose partnership with popular forces — notably the miners and peasants — who were independent allies rather than loyal subordinates. Common interests had brought this disparate alliance together in 1952; particular interests could easily drive them apart thereafter. It was as if Madero had taken power in 1910–11 and retained it beyond 1913 (that is, as if the Huerta coup had never happened, or had been defeated, as was entirely possible).[84] Madero, too, had enjoyed a loose alliance with peasant and working class elements, without remotely dominating either.[85] And even the revolutionary victors — Carranza in 1915–20 and Obregón and Calles in 1920–28 — only gradually imposed the authority of the revolutionary state upon their fractious popular allies. They were eventually able to do so — without necessarily attaining the untrammeled hegemony which 'statolatrist' interpretations of the Mexican Revolution wrongly suppose — because the prolonged social revolution (a) eliminated or severely weakened the social forces supportive of the old regime; (b) brought to power a revolutionary army which could not be ousted (except by means of a schism within its own ranks, as in 1923); (c) obliged the revolutionary leadership to embrace popular demands; (d) empowered popular forces, not least by giving them guns, organization and experience; (e) created a rich discursive repertoire of revolutionary heroes, myths and exploits; and (f) thoroughly exhausted the country, so that the post-1915 process of reconstruction counted on broad, if not always enthusiastic, support.[86]

Crucial in this process was the 'neo-Porfirian' coup against Madero in 1913, which ensured that the revolution would enter a second, prolonged and polarized struggle. The Huerta coup (1913) bears some resemblance to 1964: it was spearheaded by the army and, in the short term, was successful. But the resemblance is also misleading. First, the Madero government had been in power for less than two years and had failed to embark upon genuine social reform (compare the MNR's 12 years and the substantial reform which it promoted, especially at the outset). Thus the Mexican Revolution remained unconsummated, expectations of reform still ran high and — in contrast to the peasants of Cochabamba, who backed Barrientos — Zapata and most other popular rebels, readily resisted Huerta and the army. Second, Huerta and his cronies attempted a thorough counterrevolution (Huerta resembled Kornilov much more than Barrientos). As a result his regime polarized Mexico and pushed the revolution forward (subjectively counter-revolutionary, it proved objectively revolutionary: such is the Hegelian Cunning of Reason). Third, of course, it failed — and, in failing, it opened the way to a more durable, ruthless, but reformist regime (compare, as exponents of revolutionary statecraft, Calles and Madero). That regime, furthermore, was dominated by the army — a 'societal army', in Rouquié's terms,[87] which had grown up piecemeal amid the turmoil of revolution, which was self-made, somewhat meritocratic, distinctly populist, proud of its annihilation of Díaz's Federals and jealous of its politico-military power. There would therefore be no recreation of the old army; rather, over two generations, at the instigation of the revolutionary leadership (Obregón, Calles, Amaro, Cárdenas, Ávila Camacho), the (societal) army born of the armed revolution would gradually transmute into the more professional, politically docile army of the 1950s.

Of course, the 1952 Revolution also resulted in the partial elimination of the old Bolivian army and the creation of rival centers of armed power (the various militia forces maintained by the MNR, the miners and the peasant *sindicatos*). Both processes were messy and, at times, bloody. Thus, Bolivia in the 1950s and '60s, like Mexico in the 1920s and '30s, lived in a condition of endemic violence, characterized by political and personal vendettas, sporadic attempts at assassination, widespread access to weaponry and promising careers for *pistoleros*.[88] 'No Bolivians need to be reminded,' an observer commented, 'that armed labor groups exist or that, when armed, they have been known to behave with drunken irresponsibility.'[89] The big difference was that, in Mexico, violence was gradually displaced from the top to the bottom ('the soldiers die and the generals live', as one hard-bitten cacique put it);[90] and, after 1924, no armed challenge to the incumbent regime ever looked like succeeding. The *Cristeros* could create a good deal of local mayhem, but they could not march in triumph on Mexico City. And the revolutionary generals themselves — who during 1915–25 were the biggest threat to stability and regime-consolidation — suffered a Darwinian process of recurrent culling, which, by the later 1920s, convinced most of them that it made more sense to support the regime and die with their boots on, at home, on their profitable new haciendas or in their smart Colonia Roma town houses. In Bolivia, of course, no revolutionary army emerged from the — brief — armed struggle; there was no praetorian hero like Obregón to seize control and crack the whip over his fellow generals; rather, coercive power was diffused among a range of actors, with none exercising dominance, until the rebuilt army proved capable of ousting the MNR and crushing rival challenges after 1964. In that the Bolivian army had internalized elements of the revolution — and did not therefore attempt a thorough counter-revolution (compare Huerta, Kornilov, Pinochet) — there were distant echoes of the Mexican ('societal army') syndrome.[91] Nevertheless, the contrast is clear: the Mexican Revolution produced its own army, which was tamed by its own generals (notably Obregón, Calles and Amaro); the brief Bolivian Revolution, while spawning a good deal of violence, had no such *ultima ratio* at its disposal; instead, like Madero or Allende, it made the great mistake of fostering the instrument of its own destruction.

That it did so was not just a matter of bad luck or bad judgment. The MNR's nurturing of the army reflected a broader set of political pressures, which, again, differed from those faced by Mexico's revolutionaries. Let me address this complex question by returning to the cast of collective actors previously analyzed. It is perfectly reasonable to see both the Mexican and the Bolivian revolutions as coalitions of middle-class, peasant and working-class forces, directed against a constellation of old regime interests (which in Bolivia carry the succinct label of *La Rosca*; there is no Mexican equivalent).[92] Of course, the same could be said of most 'social' revolutions; the different outcomes — radical or moderate, successful or abortive —[93] depend on the balance of these forces, their interaction and the global context in which these processes occur. In 1910–13, Madero's relationship to his working-class and — *a fortiori* — his peasant allies was tenuous, his control over them highly imperfect. (In Bolivia, I would suggest the balance was reversed: the MNR found it easier to control the peasantry than the workers, especially the miners: the difference relates to the structural characteristics of peasant and working-class mobilization already mentioned.) Even Carranza, for all his crafty Realpolitik, was a reactive president, bobbing on the agitated waves of a social revolution — and, of course, he did not make it to port.

During the 1920s the balance shifted, as the infant revolutionary state achieved a measure of stability and security. It did so in part by accommodating popular demands and promoting popular leaders: hence the swathe of plebeian generals, demagogic labor leaders and upstart peasant caciques who so appalled foreign observers, and who gave the Mexican regime a genuinely populist character unique in Latin America at the time. Popular forces could not be *systematically* repressed (though there was a good deal of *selective* repression); nor could they be blandly co-opted (because they were not entirely stupid, and they expected pay-offs, individual and collective, in return for their support). Thus, as historians of the revolutionary state now routinely incant, the process of state-building was both 'top-down' (an assertion of control) and 'bottom-up' (an expression of popular agency).[94] The balance varied by region ('revolutionary' states like Morelos accommodated more successfully to the new regime than Catholic *mocho* states like Jalisco) and also by period (the Maximato [1928–34] was a time of retrenchment and repression, prior to the renewed reformism of the Cárdenas years). Violence, as I have said, was endemic; and political mobilization, though extensive and ebullient, did not usually take the form of decorous electoral politics. However, the social reform of these years was genuine and substantial: the widespread distribution of land (thus, the destruction of the old Porfirian *hacendado* class); the establishment of labor laws, industrial courts and powerful *sindicatos* and *centrales*; federal (especially rural) education; *indigenismo*; anticlericalism; cultural nationalism; and economic nationalism — which reached its apogee in the oil expropriation of 1938. Official policy aside, these were years of social effervescence, when, as already mentioned, new social and political elites came to the fore and old systems of deference, based on class or caste distinctions, were decisively weakened. The revolutionary leadership did not so much create this new dispensation, as creatively take advantage of it.

It seems to me that, despite its premature demise, the regime of the MNR witnessed several similar trends. Like the Mexican, the Bolivian Revolution was — and was seen to be — a successful social revolution, even though its official progenitor lost power and, in this sense, did not 'succeed' in the manner of the PNR/PRM/PRI.[95] In terms of social change, the two revolutions are roughly comparable; in terms of political outcome, they sharply differ. In the final part of this chapter I shall address this contrast.

Even though the insurrection of April 1952 was brief and (by Mexican standards) relatively bloodless, it formed part of a longer process of social and political mobilization, which had radical results. The reforms of the MNR (land and labor reform, economic nationalism and democratization, broadly defined) had already been anticipated, at least rhetorically, by the Villarroel administration, whose ouster, it is clear, had provoked a kind of counter-revolution not only at national level, but also in the provinces.[96] For this reason it seems wrong to regard the peasantry as politically quiescent or indifferent to the appeal of revolution; if peace prevailed in the countryside — especially in the Cochabamba Valley and around Lake

Titicaca — it was in part a Roman peace.[97] When the revolution occurred — and, as I mentioned, it did not come like a bolt from the blue — the reformist agenda resumed. As in Mexico, reform affected land tenure, labor organization and national resources. Bolivia's land reform was the second most radical ('bourgeois') reform after the Mexican.[98] It was different from — perhaps less radical than — the Mexican reform not just in quantitative terms, but also because, qualitatively, it did not expropriate productive capitalist estates or establish large collective farms.[99] Rather, it dismounted a parasitic feudal class, thus emancipating the *colonato*, who now escaped *pongueaje* and corporal punishment, realized the marginal product of their labor and could market their produce without hindrance. The domestic market expanded, and the peasants, newly empowered, broke out of the 'cellular confinement' which the hacienda system had imposed on them; in Bolivia, as in Mexico, the peasant political constituency suddenly counted.[100] The landlords, meanwhile, went off to sulk, grumble, plot and wait tables.[101]

With regard to labor, on the other hand, the Bolivian Revolution was distinctly *more* radical than the Mexican. It depended for its success on working-class mobilization, and its triumph signaled an explosion of unionization. Ten years later there were 390 unions in Bolivia, including *sindicatos* of the unemployed and the busy *contrabandistas* of Beni and Santa Cruz.[102] The miners federation, in particular, acquired a degree of autonomy and political access which went beyond anything achieved by Mexican *sindicatos* — a fair reflection of the different balance of forces evident in the two (armed) revolutions. While the CROM and the CTM ultimately served to stabilize and centralize Mexican state power (in return for rewards), the FSTMB and the COB escaped the control of the MNR and proceeded on a path of confrontation and fragmentation. This outcome reflected not only the dynamics of the initial revolutions, but also the potentials of the two political economies. Any revolution in a less than high-mass-consumption society — which means every social revolution to date — faces an acute dilemma between the demand for redistribution and consumption and the need for investment and growth. Stalin 'solved' the dilemma brutally by means of collectivization, centralized planning and other unsavory methods, which the tsarist legacy made possible. In Mexico and Bolivia the revolutionary leadership — to their credit — avoided Stalinism. But they were caught in the classic dilemma. The Mexican regime took redistribution seriously, especially in the 1930s, until Cárdenas hit 'the limits of state autonomy' around 1938.[103] Thereafter, the regime switched tacks. The MNR, too, tried to redistribute and then — with Siles' stabilization plan and Paz's Triangular Plan — to retrench. But the MNR lacked not only the political power to enforce its decisions (after all, the chief victims of stabilization and the Triangular Plan were their erstwhile militant allies, the miners), but also the economic resources which might moderate the dilemma. The Mexican economy grew robustly, with moderate inflation, as the *Cardenista* reforms went ahead.[104] The MNR reforms coincided with rampant inflation, which eroded gains, alienated opinion (both middle- and working-class) and opened the door to US-mentored structural adjustment *avant la lettre.*

Thus, the Mexican and Bolivian revolutionaries adopted comparable goals — we might say the typical goals of a nationalist, reformist but far from socialist blueprint. The chief difference, in respect of land and labor, was that the balance differed (the Mexican Revolution was more of a peasant revolution; the Bolivian Revolution had a more militant labor component); and, for reasons both structural and conjunctural, the Mexican regime was better placed, politically and economically, to maintain control of the process.[105] Before turning to the final comparative component — nationalism — let me address two interesting differences.

First, though both revolutions were democratic in conception, the Bolivian was more democratic in practice, especially in terms of procedural practice. Both revolutions 'empowered': social mobility increased; plebeians rose to become top *políticos*; mass publics counted as they had not under the old regime. Some of this transformation, as I have said, was messy and violent: plebeians rose by virtue of their skills with the pistol; and mass publics did not necessarily exert their influence through the ballot box. In both countries, for example, it became common practice to bring truckloads of peasants into town to demonstrate support and browbeat opponents.[106] In both countries, too, elections were less than transparent; and the revolutionary parties peddled jobs for the boys on a grand scale.[107] Power was certainly more broadly diffused; however, in Bolivia the extension of the franchise was more dramatic, the electoral process counted for more and the MNR — more out of necessity than choice, I suspect — failed to attain that incremental political control, leading to monopoly, that the PNR/PRM/PRI achieved. Political pluralism continued in Bolivia, as it was progressively closed down in Mexico.[108] Mexican oppositionists like Jorge Prieto Laurens complained of the hated official 'steamroller' which flattened their aspirations and organizations; though similar metaphors were to be heard in Bolivia, Prieto Laurens' lament was more pertinent and lasting.[109]

The second, more striking, difference concerns the Church. The MNR — and the Bolivian Revolution more generally — was relatively untainted by anticlericalism, while in Mexico anticlericalism was probably the most salient and consistent policy of the Calles years, and its influence spilled over into education, land reform, labor organization, art and culture. In Bolivia, we find snippets of anticlericalism (e.g., radical miners confronting the Oblate Fathers);[110] but in general it is the *absence* of this defining characteristic of Mexican revolutionary culture that is striking. Indeed, we find the Archbishop of La Paz being called upon to mediate on behalf of the (Paz) government — an outcome that would have been unthinkable in the Mexico of Calles and Cárdenas.[111] Of course, explaining an absence — the dog that did not bark in the night — is a tricky and perhaps odd historical exercise. Why *should* the MNR have been anticlerical anyway? The only presumption in favor of anticlericalism is that progressive and popular revolutions in Catholic countries often are: Mexico aside, compare France after 1789 or Spain in the 1930s.[112]

Mexican anticlericalism, which of course built on a long history of prior Church–State conflict, derived from three principal causes that were either absent, or much weaker, in Bolivia. First, anticlericalism presupposed a strong Church and a strong State that competed for the hearts and minds of their people. In Bolivia, we may hypothesize, the state was weak (both historically and in its fledgling MNR form after 1952); but the Church, too, was much weaker than its Mexican counterpart. Priests were thin on the ground (Mexico in 1910 had about 50 per cent more priests per capita than Bolivia in 1952) and popular religious heterodoxy was rampant — in the twentieth century as it had been in the seventeenth.[113] Neither party saw the point of a battle for hearts and minds. Second, Mexican anticlericalism was premised on a positivistic and scientific world view, which held the Catholic Church to be an obstacle to the rational, productive and patriotic organization of society. There is scant evidence that such a worldview prevailed in Bolivia; again, this may reflect the weakness of the Church; or it may suggest that positivism (which, for all their political differences, linked Porfirian and revolutionary *pensadores* and policy-makers in Mexico) was at a discount. Thirdly, the Mexican revolutionaries complained, with some justice, that the Catholic Church resisted progress and allied with their enemies: at national level, in its sympathy for Huerta; and locally, where *curas* preached against land reform and atheistic 'socialist' education. Again, the Bolivian revolutionaries seem not to have seen the Church as a major enemy, nor were revolutionary policies — in the fields of education or 'cultural politics' more generally — overtly hostile to the Church.

Anticlericalism aside, the ideologies of the MNR and the Mexican Revolution were often strikingly similar. Bolivia looked for inspiration to the Mexican Revolution and the MNR employed Mexican experts in the field of agrarian reform.[114] The big difference was not ideological but practical: the MNR could not match the PNR/PRM/PRI for organizational success. A major factor, as I have noted, was the brevity of the April 1952 insurrection, which failed to create either shared camaraderie on the part of the victorious revolutionaries, or shared sentiments of war-weariness on the part of the population as a whole. The MNR remained stuck in Madero's dilemma: they had unleashed a tiger — or, we should say, several tigers — and they now had to ride them.[115] Like Madero, they found their early middle-class leaching away, some to the dissident MNRA, some to the FSB. President Siles sought to reassure the right and counter the right's fears of both popular radicalism and runaway inflation, but in doing so he inevitably antagonized the left. Paz and Lechín then came together in a fragile center-left coalition; but Lechín constantly had to watch rivals (like Sanjinés) who threatened his working class base;[116] while Paz had to call upon peasant power to offset that of the workers, especially the miners; and, fearful of both, he rebuilt the national army and, by 1963–64, was acting in close cahoots with Barrientos and (even more) Ovando.[117] An additional factor, analyzed by Lehman in this volume, was US aid, which was clearly deployed as a weapon to defang the revolution, to impose market discipline and to bolster the MNR right.

Again, we can detect clear Mexican equivalents of these collective actors and their coalitions and collisions; but the balance of forces and the outcome were different. Though the middle class had bolted *Maderismo* in 1911–13, they had nowhere to go after 1920. Catholics could flock to LNDR, Acción Católica, the Unión Nacional de Padres de Famila, even the UNS (the strength and variety of these organizations attested to the power of the Catholic constituency and their alienation from the revolution). But as the Cristiada showed, armed Catholic insurrection could not succeed; and the Constitution banned confessional parties. A huge slice of the political nation was thus disenfranchized — and there was no Falange Socialista Mexicano to which Mexican middle-class conservatives could turn.[118] Ultimately, the middle-class came to terms with the PRM/PRI as the latter moderated after 1940, making its peace with the church, coddling business and ditching its more radical social policies. Thus, Mexico's Thermidor came like a thief in the night, not by way of a sudden bloody coup like 1964. On the left, a much smaller slice of the political nation — the old anarchists, the new PCM — were also marginalized; but many on the left decided they could find a comfortable niche in the PNR/PRM's capacious bosom. The PCM, for example, became an ardent supporter of Cárdenas after 1935; Lombardo made an art of intellectually rationalizing his support for the PRM/PRI and CTM. Dissident labor unions sometimes resisted the party and its official labor confederation (Morones' CROM in the 1920s, Lombardo's CTM in the 1930s), but they lacked the autonomous power of Bolivia's miners. Mexico's miners were scattered; the oil workers faced industrial decline after 1921; and from the late 1920s, the railways similarly shed quantities of labor. Furthermore, Mexico's workers had never constituted a truly autonomous military force: at best, they had been recruited as dependent allies of revolutionary armies; and when, in the 1930s, Lombardo talked of establishing a workers' militia, the army balked and the project never prospered.[119] Again, the fact of a prolonged armed revolution ensured the revolutionary state, if not a complete monopoly of the means of violence, at least a dominant share of the market.

The position of the peasantry in the two post-revolutionary societies was more closely comparable. In both cases, the peasantry figured as tactical allies of national revolutionary leaders. Under Magaña, even the *Zapatistas* — quintessential peasant revolutionaries, who profoundly disdained corrupt political *cabrones* — cut a deal with the presidential heir-apparent Obregón. Once elected, Obregón could also count on peasant support in order to defeat praetorian insurrection, notably with the dangerous de la Huerta rebellion of 1923–24. Peasants (*agraristas*) marched against the Cristeros. And in the mid-1930s, Cárdenas mobilized peasants and deployed land reform in order to defeat his (*Callista*) enemies and further legitimize the revolutionary state (in the eyes of some — by no means all). In Mexico, as in Bolivia, land reform could lead to political involution, as newly endowed *agraristas* concentrated on cultivating their gardens.[120] *Agrarista* caciques — some of them veterans of the armed revolution — became key local and regional figures: Cedillo in San Luis or Ernesto Prado in the Once Pueblos of Michoacán performed roles not unlike those of Toribio Salas and José Rojas.[121] They distributed land, mobilized their clients, resisted rivals and brokered deals with the 'center.' However, the dynamics of rural *caciquismo* seem to have moved in different directions in (centripetal) Mexico and (centrifugal) Bolivia. In the latter, peasant leaders acquired increasing autonomy; they spurned the authority of the center; in Cochabamba they backed Barrientos' bid for national power, thus dooming the MNR.[122] In Mexico, the trend favored the center: caciques realized that their own survival and prosperity depended on enlisting the center's support — by way of *ejidos*, roads, schools, arms and political back-up. Caciques who overtly resisted the center were winkled out (as Barrios was, from the Sierra Norte de Puebla), or, if they were foolish enough to rebel, like Cedillo in 1938, they were crushed.[123]

So too with provincial governors (who were not necessarily peasant leaders). In Bolivia regional bosses like Salvador Morón in Santa Cruz and Rubén Julio Castro in Beni grew in stature, especially if — as in the case of Santa Cruz — their department prospered and exhibited sentiments of anti-La Paz provincial patriotism which they could build on.[124] In this, Santa Cruz resembled Nuevo León or Sonora. But the *neoleonés* bourgeoisie never sought to colonize the PNR/PRM; while Sonora enjoyed a privileged niche within the revolution in the 1920s and, even when Cárdenas confronted Governor Yocupicio in the 1930s, the Sonorenses defended their provincial interests without resorting to overt defiance.[125] Centrifugal provincialism remained within bounds; the center held.

Why did regional leaders — both peasant caciques and state/department bosses — generally toe the line in Mexico, while bucking the center in

Bolivia? Their contrasting responses were rational reflections of the balance of power. Historically, Mexico was used to greater centralization: Bolivia had had no counterpart of the 35-year Díaz dictatorship; its transport and communication networks were skeletal; in discursive terms, Bolivia lacked the old nationalist myths and memories which underpinned *mexicanidad* and which the revolution could appropriate to is own advantage. After the extreme fragmentation of the 1910s, the Mexican revolutionary state renewed the battle for centralization with increasing success (as revisionist historians like to point out, this is a classic Tocquevillean sequence). It is difficult to measure the extent to which the new schools and mass media fostered sentiments of national cohesion. What is clear — for example, in the patriotic jamboree of March 1938 — is that the revolutionary state gradually acquired mechanisms of political control and cajolery: the *ejido*, the federal school, the *sindicato*, the labor arbitration tribunals and, after 1929, the new national party. The latter, as I noted earlier, postdated the revolution by nearly 20 years: it served to agglutinate the surviving revolutionaries (some of whom clearly displayed a rough camaraderie born of revolutionary soldiering).[126] The PNR/PRM came to provide a broad church outside which there was no political salvation. Thus, while the MNR maintained a hierarchical, cellular and paramilitary character (the legacy of its clandestine and insurrectionary origins), the PNR/PRM was, from the outset, a loosely assembled confederation, a loyal arm of government, a deep reservoir of patronage and a broad tent that accommodated, and did not challenge, the — increasingly professionalized — revolutionary army. The PNR, unlike the MNR, was built to exercise state power, not to challenge it. While Mexico's patriotic and revolutionary culture may have helped maintain a loose unity (at the same time excluding a mass of disaffected Catholics and middle-class liberals), a highly pragmatic system of rewards and punishments — Díaz's old *pan o palo*, bolstered by economic growth and updated to suit the populist politics of post-1920 — kept political elites and their clienteles broadly in line. (Compare the dogged self-defeating loyalty of Lombardo with Lechín's wayward opportunism.) In Mexico, therefore, the centripetal forces exerted by burgeoning mass organizations successfully countered the centrifugal forces of *caciquismo* and provincialism, which, in Bolivia, went from strength to strength.

Finally — and somewhat counter-intuitively — the USA played a lesser role in determining the outcome of the Mexican Revolution than it did the Bolivian. Although I do not propose to cover the foreign relations of the two revolutions, which Lehman ably analyses in the next chapter, it is impossible to detach foreign relations from the internal dynamics of the two regimes, especially in the Bolivian case. I have suggested that the Bolivian Revolution embodied nationalist and anti-imperialist elements, even though US interests in Bolivia were far smaller than those in Mexico; and that Mexican anti-Americanism often tended to be political (spurred by slights to Mexican sovereignty) rather than economic (stimulated by the US economic presence). US investment in Mexico increased between the late *Porfiriato* and the 1920s; and the Sonoran administrations were not inherently hostile to that trend. Given this rough starting point, why did the USA come to play a more purposive, significant and (I would say) negative role in Bolivian politics, rather than Mexican (without, in either case, resorting to direct coercive intervention)?

First, though Mexico was close, it was big and unmanageable. During the armed revolution direct US interventions (Veracruz, the Punitive Expedition) had proved counter-productive;[127] even indirect manipulation had to reckon with Mexico's size, complexity and historic suspicion of the Yankees, even when they came bearing gifts. Attempts to use Mexico's food shortage as leverage against Carranza failed;[128] ten years later, Dwight Morrow showed that more subtle means might get results, so long as the Americans also made concessions; and Josephus Daniels, another ten years on, adopted a similar strategy of conciliation and cajolery. Bolivia was in a weaker position: poorer, dependent on foreign food imports and shackled to a declining tin industry. Tin, food and aid provided the triple means for US manipulation of Bolivia's political economy. Food aid rapidly mounted after 1952;[129] and the modernization of the tin mines became a central tenet of both US and MNR policy. 'Modernization', of course, meant layoffs and diversification, hence a weakening of the militant miners unions. It also meant coercive interventions in the mines, hence the deployment of the refurbished Bolivian army and the armed peasant militia in opposition to the miners. It does not require a conspiracy theorist to see how US policy, apart from aligning with the center/right of the MNR in its quest for capitalist modernization, helped prise apart the fragile coalition of 1952 and nudge the regular army to the center of the political stage.

Nothing of the kind happened in Mexico. Mexico did not need US food and, since Huerta's default, had had no recourse to foreign loans. The Mexican economy was also reassuringly diversified. US markets were crucial; but US business interests valued Mexican custom and, of course, did not speak with one voice. The oil companies' shrill cries for retribution — in the early 1920s and again after 1938 — fell on largely deaf ears. Sixty years before NAFTA, Cárdenas showed that a measure of economic integration — fortuitously complemented by the geopolitical logic of the time — afforded Mexico some protection against arbitrary aggression on the part of the USA. Bolivia had no such advantages. While its geopolitical remoteness perhaps protected it from the fate of Guatemala, its economic irrelevance meant that the USA could, to coin a phrase, 'squeeze it until the pips squeaked'. Squeezing was particularly attractive, since the likely political consequences would be a turn to the right, not to the left.

The relative success of the USA thus depended crucially on domestic Bolivian factors: the bastion of the left was in decline; the right-right of the

MNR readily aligned with US policy; the army lapped up US aid; and, of course, there was no rival superpower on whom the MNR would call to redress the balance.[130] Thus, of the three Latin American social revolutions which the USA confronted in the 1950s, the Bolivian, like the Guatemalan, was eventually subverted from within, with a good deal of American connivance; Cuba avoided subversion, but at the cost of becoming a Soviet client. Compared to Guatemala, however, the Bolivian Revolution had at least had a run for its money: the reforms of the 1950s could not be undone; and the military that ousted the MNR (with US connivance) did not embark upon a thorough and immediate counter-revolution. This alignment of US and Bolivian interests in turn reflects a key — perhaps obvious — point. The Bolivian Revolution, like the Mexican, remained essentially bourgeois-nationalist. That is to say, while it promised and enacted substantial reforms — abolishing agrarian 'feudalism,' democratizing society, nationalizing economic assets — it did not trespass beyond the pale of capitalism. Of course, it favored a more responsible, managed capitalism (no rarity in the post-1945 world). And some Bolivian — like some Mexican — revolutionaries sought to go further, calling for *una sociedad sin clases* or 'a workers' parliament which will transcend the democratic bourgeois judicial framework and open the road to a government of workers and peasants.'[131] But the anti-capitalist radicals were a minority and they were defeated more by domestic machinations than by foreign manipulation (compare Cuba, where the balance differed and the radicals triumphed). In both Mexico and Bolivia, therefore, the United States enjoyed the benefit of going with the flow, of paddling in the mainstream. In Cuba, in contrast, the USA faced a graver threat, both geopolitically and ideologically; it responded aggressively and helped push a radical revolution in a yet more radical direction. The Mexican and Bolivian revolutions, though undoubtedly radical in terms of domestic criteria, were geopolitically and ideologically less threatening. Democracy and land reform might appall Bolivia's feudal landlords or the Casta Divina of Porfirian Yucatán (as, of course, they had appalled the planters of the American South in the previous century). But they hardly posed a profound threat to American values. Even if the USA had never existed — a much more demanding counter-factual in the Mexican than the Bolivian case! — it seems very unlikely that the Mexican or Bolivian revolutions would have debouched into socialism.

The United States thus contributed to the denouement of 1964, but in partnership with powerful Bolivian interests. In cracking down on the left, deploying the army against the miners and expelling Lechín from the MNR, Paz came to rely increasingly on the army and on US aid.[132] The peasants, endowed with land, and fragmented into a host of cacical machines, saw no reason to defend the MNR; many, indeed, supported Barrientos. The PRI, in contrast, had never been beholden to a separate regular army and had kept the USA at arm's length; it retained peasant support, loosely controlled labor and made provincial bosses see the wisdom of collaboration rather than confrontation. Long-term national loyalties, coupled with superior resources (hence more ample patronage) and a certain camaraderie of the revolution, maintained the cohesion of the Mexican revolutionary elite. Their Bolivian counterpart, for all their ideological kinship, faced a different situation and, by 1964, it had fatefully reverted to its role of 20 years earlier (1943–46): a civilian party that depended for power on the consent and collaboration of the military.

NOTES

1 Bullock to Foreign Office, 19 Aug. 1964, FO 371/174429, AX 1015/53. President Víctor Paz Estenssoro seems to have labored under the same misapprehension in 1964: See Whitehead (1991), p. 342.

2 See Knight (1986), p. 302.

3 See Knight (1990a), pp. 178–9.

4 See Davies (1969), pp. 671–709.

5 See McIntyre (1971), p. 260.

6 See Paige (1978).

7 I have therefore focused rather more on Bolivia — in both my research for and writing of this chapter; and I use Mexico as a kind of backdrop for the Bolivian analysis. Some Mexicanists might well object to my version of the backdrop.

8 A thoroughly arbitrary periodization — which appears even more starkly in the common description of the Mexican Revolution as 'the first of the twentieth century'. The important point is that — arbitrary 'hectohistory' aside — the two revolutions were just over a generation apart, hence more potentially comparable than, say, the English and the Chinese revolutions.

9 I mean 'socialism' in the practical sense of a Communist regime and a command economy (Russia, Eastern Europe, Cuba); I am not claiming that these regimes/economies represented 'real' socialism, as advocated by, for example, Marx or Rosa Luxemburg.

10 Knight (1985), pp. 1–37.

11 I mean 'outset' not just of this chapter, but of the historical processes; which begs the question of when the respective 'outsets' — the beginnings of the revolutions — should be dated. I take Mexico c. 1910 and Bolivia c. 1950 as the starting points; so I am not comparing contemporaneous societies.

12 See Kelley and Klein (1981), p. 49.

13 On Bolivia's enduring and entrenched ethnic divide, see Taussig, (1980), p. 190; Lehman, (1999), p. 58; Ashe to Foreign Office, 20 March 1953, FO 371/103626, AX1015/4: 'Bolivian politicians always go in fear of Indian mobs descending upon the fat and comparatively wealthy towns with fire and sword' (a statement which, even if it was a somewhat exaggerated response to the tense conditions of 1952–53, contained a kernel of truth and for which it would be difficult to find a Mexican counterpart, at least outside the deep south).

14 Brading and Cross (1972), pp. 557–9 ; on the deficiencies of Bolivia's rail network, see Lehman, Bolivia and the United States, p. 54.

15 Taussig (1980), pp. 143–54; Nash (1979), chap. 5.

16 Ladd (1988), pp. 98, 100.

17 See Brading (1985).

18 See Katz (1988), p. 16.

19 See Pearse (1975), pp. 120–1.

20 *Ibid.*, pp. 130–9; Dunkerley (1984), pp. 22–5.

21 'Unless the (Agrarian Reform) Decree satisfies the greed and hatred of the Indians for the Whites, there will be an uproar': Lomax to Foreign Office, 31 March 1953, FO371/103626, AX 1015/5; see also note 13 above.

22 See Mallon (1995).

23 I am (I think) using 'conjuncture' in the Braudelian sense, which implies a broader sweep of time — in this case, roughly the generation preceding the revolutionary outbreak, rather than a short, sharp, critical moment (as 'conjuncture' has come to mean).

24 'Agency' is clearly a relative concept: even weak states enjoy some measure of autonomy vis-à-vis dominant classes. However, oligarchic Bolivia displayed a high degree of 'agency', that is, of state compliance with dominant class interests.

25 As mentioned above (note 11), I am comparing c. 1910 Mexico with c. 1950 Bolivia: see Knight (1986), vol. 1, p. 79; and C.C. Finch, 'A Labor Report on Bolivia (Oct. 1959–Dec. 1960),' US Embassy, La Paz, 3 February 1961, enclosed in Holliday to Foreign Office, 22 March 1961, FO 371/156638, AX 2181/2, pp. 3, 11, which gives figures of 2.5 million peasants (*campesinos*) in a population of 3.8 million (i.e., 66 per cent), eight years after the revolution; in contrast, there were 52,000 (unionized) miners.

26 See Knight (1986), vol. 1, p. 79ff.

27 This 'traditional' view has been contested by 'revisionist' scholarship. My reasons for adhering (broadly) to the traditional view are put forward in Knight (1986), vol. 1, chap. 3 and Knight (forthcoming).

28 See Knight (1986), vol. 1, pp. 115–27.

29 *Ibid.*, vol. 1, pp. 85–9, 170.

30 See Knight (1991), pp. 73–104.

31 See, for example, Langer, (1989), pp. 77–87, 200, on the Yamparaez rebellion, which climaxed in 1927. The same decade witnessed the rebellion of Jesús de Machaca, a community which engaged in aggressive land seizures on the eve of the 1952 Revolution: Alfredo Ríos to Gobernación, 8 January 1951, from Hacienda Lacoyo, complaining of armed incursions by the *indios de Jesús de Machaca*, who were *haciendo disparos de armas de fuego, poniendo en fuga a los colonos de la finca*: Archivo de la Paz, 1951(4), 2291715.

32 Pearse (1975), pp. 141–3; on the long-term evolution of Cochabamba, see Larson, (1998), especially chapter 10. Cochabamba certainly resembled Morelos by virtue of its dynamic economy and vigorous peasant movement; however, the fairly clearcut conflict between Morelos sugar plantations and peasant villages was absent; Cochabamba witnessed a more complex struggle between prosperous peasants, assertive *colonos* and embattled landlords.

33 Pearse (1975), pp. 120, 123, which suggests that the ratio of *colonos* to *comuneros* shifted from 1:2 to 2:1 during the nineteenth century.

34 Pearse (1975), p. 124, refers to 'serfs' toiling on 'manors'; more recently, Lehman (1999), p. 100, terms pre-revolutionary Bolivian agrarian society 'near feudal'. Foreign observers concurred that 'the former land tenure system was virtual serfdom': Lomax to Foreign Office, 4 September 1953, FO 371/103638, AX 1281/3. Needless to say, 'feudal' does not denote a carbon copy of medieval Europe, complete with fiefs, vassalage and manorial courts; but it does imply weak demand, very limited markets, a substantial degree of labor coercion, primitive technology and a politico-economically dominant landed class.

35 Langer (1989), pp. 76–6, 173. A good example of such a squeeze is that of the Hacienda San Jacinto, Coroico, Nor Yungas, where, in return for access to their *sayañas*, *colonos*, both men and women, were obliged to perform two days a week of unpaid work for the hacienda (these duties included both field work and household services). In January 1952, however, the *mayordomo* arbitrarily raised the work quota to three days, alleging that the rising output of the peasant plots justified a higher labor rent. The *colonos*' ensuing protest embodied several key points: that they had hitherto performed their duties 'religiously'; that their *sayañas* were not so lush and profitable; that 'humiliating [household] services' were banned by law; that the *mayordomo*'s decision contravened Article 2 of Decree 321 of May 1945 (of the Villarroel administration). They also looked forward to 'the day that will come when Bolivia decrees the agrarian law' (which, of course, happened the following year). The landlord's response was also illustrative: 'only Communists can repudiate property rights …

and in Bolivia Communist norms are prohibited and have been outlawed'. See the correspondence of José Palli and *colonos*, and Máximo Pereira (*mayordomo*), with Gobernación, December 1951–February 1952, Archivo de la Paz, 1951(4), 752921.

36 Pearse (1975), pp. 125–6; Dandler and Torrico A. (1987), pp. 338, 353; Heath (1969), p. 181.

37 Pearse (1975), pp. 149, 161, note 1, suggests that hacienda demesne production was much smaller than peasant *minifundista* production. See also Leons and Leons (1971), pp. 272–3.

38 See Pearse (1975), p. 127; Heath (1969), p. 182.

39 Langer (1989), p. 196; Pearse (1975), p. 129, questions the scale and significance of paternalism. Carranza Fernández (1972) similarly suggests that coercion and intimidation tended to outweigh paternalism. For the Mexican comparison, see Wells (1985), chap. 6; and Benjamin (1989), pp. 2–30.

40 See Hamilton (1982), pp. 164–9.

41 See Anderson (1976), pp. 254–72.

42 Quote from Holliday to Foreign Office, 3 July 1961, FO371/156588, AX 1015/22. On the Pulacayo Thesis, see Lora (1977), pp. 243–8.

43 See Landsberger (1967), chap. 8, which notes that Bolivia, where labor 'was a genuinely revolutionary actor' (pp. 280–1) diverges from the Latin American norm — of reformist, economistic labor mobilization.

44 Collier and Collier (1991) roughly confirms the rule; and Bolivia does not figure in their paired comparisons.

45 Fox (1970) charts fluctuating production and declining productivity since the late 1920s.

46 On Paz Estenssoro's careful cultivation of unions (such as the factory workers), in opposition to the miners, see Holliday to Foreign Office, 20 June and 30 October 1961, AX 1015/21, /40, FO 371/156588. The 'divide-and-rule' strategy went beyond labor politics; some have seen it as an integral feature of Paz Estenssoro's political style, even personal character (Fellman Velarde, cited by Whitehead, 1991, p. 544, n. 29). I would tend to see it more as a response to structural circumstances (as well as a recurrent feature in all politics).

47 See Hobsbawm (1998), p. 124; Klubock (1998), p. 3.

48 See Bernstein (1964), pp. 156, 194.

49 See Nash (1979), pp. 54, 91, 96–7, 159–60.

50 See Bernstein (1965), p. 192.

51 *Ibid.,* pp. 196–8

52 Solís (1971), pp. 90, 104; Nash (1979), pp. 214–5; Malloy and Thorn (1971) (appendices), pp. 370–1; Finch, 'Labor Report on Bolivia' (see note 25), p. 3.

53 Fox (1970), p. 6; Bernstein (1965), p. 58.
54 See Nash (1979), chap.5.
55 See Brading and Cross (1972); Martin (1996), chapter 3..
56 See Taussig (1980), chap. 8.
57 On the eve of the revolution, about 50 per cent of Bolivian government revenue derived from tin: Thorn (1971), p. 175; Morales and Pacheco (1999), pp. 160–1. Bernstein's figures (1965, pp. 30–1) suggest that, in the late *Porfiriato*, mining taxes yielded only 5–10 per cent of Mexican government income. Of course, the taxation of minerals could take various forms (e.g., taxes on production, legal documents, concessions, exports), hence it is not clear if these figures compare like with like.
58 See Contreras (1993), pp. 41, 44.
59 Knight (1987), pp. 32–9. Note that by 1917–18 Cananea, the supposed hotbed of militant nationalism, was working 'at full capacity': Bernstein (1965), p. 118.
60 Knight (1992), chapter 4.
61 '[Quasi]-Bolivians' because the big three — Patiño in particular — had progressively 'transnationalized' themselves. Hence there was a US stake in Patiño's enterprise, perhaps to the tune of 20 per cent (roughly $500,000): Blasier (1971), p. 71. US investment in Mexico in 1910 stood at about $1 billion, or about 80 per cent of Mexican GNP. US investment therefore bulked larger in the Mexican economy (even in relative terms); and it bulked larger within the United States' overseas investment portfolio.
62 Hence FDR's kid-gloved treatment of Mexico in 1938: Niblo (1995), pp. 38–41.
63 On Bolivian resentment at seemingly capricious US tin-purchasing policy, see Lehman (1999), pp. 79–80, 84–6, 97. A British Foreign Office analyst, reviewing the events of April 1952, concluded that 'the principal architect of the present coup d'état was Mr Stuart Symington of the US Reconstruction Finance Corporation': minute on Lomax to Foreign Office, 10 April 1952, FO 371/97702, AX 1015/5.
64 Thomas (1967); and Farber (1976), p. 189.
65 See Knight (1986), vol. 1, pp. 43–4, 62. As I go on to note, however, students played a lesser role in the Mexican Revolution and its aftermath; indeed, the role of the Mexican academy tended to be conservative rather than radical: Garciadiego Dantan (1996), pp. 65–70.
66 It is worth stressing that class attitudes and alignments are not immutable givens but 'relational' and dynamic. Thus, they change over time and react to other class attitudes and alignments. As a result, middle-class liberalism and progressivism can easily relapse into middle-class conservatism, even reaction — when, for example,

property rights, political privileges or notion of respectability are seen to be threatened by plebeian uppishness (consider Europe after 1918). Ethnic differences — which often shadow and accentuate class differences — may compound such processes, as they did in both Mexico and (*a fortiori*) Bolivia. It is something of a mystery why, over the last generation or so, the quite reasonable recognition that classes do not follow a simple script (bourgeoisie=liberal, workers=socialist) seems to have led to a wholesale repudiation of class analysis and its replacement by an equally reductionist — but more flaccid — form of 'cultural' explanation.

67 Knight (1986), vol. 1, pp. 41–4, 62;. Malloy (1970), pp. 61–2, 107–9, 159.

68 See Klein (1971), pp. 40, 43–4. This political sequence — partial opening followed by renewed closure — would seem to fit the pattern of Davies' 'J-curve' (see note 4 above). However, the J-curve is too vague and malleable to be of much use as an explanatory tool; it is also one of those 'explanations' which — not surprisingly, given its vagueness and malleability — can easily be found in *some* revolutionary preambles, but not all; but which can almost certainly be found in a great many more *non*-revolutionary preambles, which no-one has bothered to examine (with this model in mind).

69 See Johnson (1958).

70 Students — of both left and right — played a role in the fall of both Villarroel in 1946 (as the MNR leadership well remembered: Lomax to Foreign Office, 6 August 1953, FO 371/103625, AX 1015/16) and Paz in 1964: Gamble to Foreign Office, 23 November 1964, FO 371/174431, AX1015/89.

71 Garciadiego Dantan (1996), which, p. 63, gives a (surprisingly low) figure of only 1,000 university students in Mexico in 1910: thus, only one student for every 15,000 Mexicans. Klein (1982) pp. 227–8, gives a (surprisingly high) figure of 12,000 university students in 1951: thus, one student for every 250 Bolivians.

72 See Knight (1986), vol. 1, pp. 68–70.

73 By using the past tense ('was') I am limiting this generalization to the Bolivian case; although I think it would have some validity — as a tendency, not a cast-iron law — at the global level.

74 See Booth and Seligson (1993), pp. 115–24.

75 On middle-class disenchantment with the MNR and defection to the FSB, see Whitehead (1991), p. 551. Even at a time (1961) when President Paz was cracking down on the miners and the left, the British Ambassador reported that 'the professional and middle classes are too embittered by what has happened to them since 1952 to rally to Dr Paz's support on the Communist issue': Holliday to Foreign Office, 3 July 1961, FO 371/156588, AX1015/22.

76 See Knight (1990a).

77 The Mexican Revolution of 1910 was preceded by the country's conversion to the Gold Standard and the recession of 1907–8. The cumulative effects of these events, and their relationship to both the political opposition of 1908–10 and the armed insurrection of 1910 (which were different movements, often involving different actors), have often been asserted, but have not been adequately clarified. It is, however, significant that the recession was over by 1910. In Bolivia, in contrast, the Korean War further exacerbated inflationary tendencies that dated back to the Chaco War; while the ending of the Korean conflict, coupled with US manipulation of tin prices, hit Bolivian export earnings hard. Both countries, therefore, suffered 'external shocks' in the years before their revolutions; but so did many other Latin American economies, which did not experience revolutions. The external shock of 1930 was systemically much more severe; but it provoked no social revolutions.

78 Karl Bünz, German envoy to Mexico, quoted in Katz (1981), p. 1.

79 In light of this 20-year cycle, another coup hardly seems surprising. However, Dunkerley (1984), p. 2, states that there was little expectation of a coup/revolt in early 1952. British Foreign Office opinion differed: 'it has been evident for some time,' G.H.S. Jackson minuted, after the news of the insurrection reached London, 'that the junta's days were numbered [and that] social unrest and the MNR's clandestine activism have steadily increased': minute on Lomax to Foreign Office, 10 April 1952, FO 371/97702, AX1015/5. I do not think Jackson was just being wise after the event; his conclusion was based on information flowing to London during 1951–52.

80 Dunkerley (1984), pp. 1–4, offers a good account.

81 McCaa (forthcoming) offers an important reevaluation, stressing the demographic costs of the revolution.

82 See Womack (1969), p. 67

83 *Ibid.* Of course, it may be misleading to talk of 'the Bolivian Revolution of 1952', as if all the diagnostic features of ('great', 'social') revolutions were evident between April and December 1952; the same objection could be made to 'the Mexican Revolution of 1910–11'. In both cases, the initial insurrectionary episodes were key parts of longer processes; and it is the processes that merit the 'social revolutionary' label.

84 Knight (2000), vol. 1, pp. 46–9.

85 Though Madero's labor policy did achieve some success in mediating industrial disputes and, to some degree, appealing to — some would say 'co-opting' — organized labor: Knight (1986), vol. 1, pp. 424–43.

86 See Knight (1986), vol. 2.

87 See Rouquié (1987), p. 42.

88 Knight (1997), pp. 107–30. Bolivia's civilian armed militia was 'a political fact of the first magnitude', which, union leaders liked to boast, possessed as much weaponry as the regular army. A more sober estimate reckoned there were 16,000 armed militiamen — about half peasants, the rest mostly workers, especially miners. However, some 85 per cent of their arms were of Chaco war vintage — useful for prosecuting local feuds, inadequate for a frontal assault on the state, especially as the armed forces revived and rearmed: see Finch, 'Labor Report on Bolivia' (see note 25), p. 6. (This imbalance in weaponry helps explains the rapid success of the 1964 coup: see Gamble to Foreign Office, 23 Nov. 1964, FO 371/174431, AX1015/89.) Thus, in 1930s Mexico, as in 1950s–60s Bolivia, violence tended to be low-level, decentralized and endemic: every cacique/boss/*político* needed his armed back up (Barrientos, after all, was the victim of five assassination attempts prior to 1964 — although some were quite likely of his own making.) Lechín, for example, was protected by 'a permanent squad of armed militia who live[d] at his house'; an American neighbor noted that 'the garage [of the house] cannot be used for cars as it is very well stocked with submachine guns and cases of ammunition': A.J. Pick (Canadian ambassador to Peru, then in Bolivia) to Foreign Office, 21 July 1961, FO 371/156588, AX1015/36.

90 See Friedrich (1986), p. 11.

91 Parallels may also be sought with the Peruvian military which, though it was not 'societal' in the same sense as the Mexican revolutionary army, did display nationalist, populist and reformist tendencies, like the Bolivian.

92 'Científico' became a loose term of abuse for Díaz's inner coterie of political and financial collaborators, headed by Limantour; but they were among the first to fall in 1910–11, along with their leader; other elements of the 'Mexican *Rosca*' — landlords, generals, provincial elites, local caciques — survived longer (and did not acquire a pejorative collective label: *la reacción* was, perhaps, the closest, but that lacked the direct, demotic flavor of '*la Rosca*').

93 The implications of revolutionary 'success' or 'failure' require some clarification (and the Mexican and Bolivian cases are good examples). In the most profound sense, a (great, major, social) revolution 'succeeds' by virtue of a substantial, rapid and radical transformation of sociopolitical structures (that's what makes it a [great, major, social] revolution rather than a coup, rebellion or failed revolution). In this sense, both Mexico and Bolivia qualify, Mexico rather more convincingly, perhaps. In a narrower sense, 'success' attaches to the victorious revolutionaries who, in Mexico, consolidated a new regime

(hence were doubly successful), but who in Bolivia lost power after 12 years (hence were 'unsuccessful', at least compared to their Mexican, Russian, Chinese and Cuban counterparts). Unlike the Guatemalans after 1954, however, the Bolivians did not witness the destruction of many of the revolutionary gains (a counter-revolution, in effect); hence, the eventual failure of the MNR did not mean the failure of the revolution *in toto.*

94 See Joseph and Nugent (eds.) (1994), p. 13.

95 Criteria of 'success' are explained above, note 93. Foreign observers had no doubt that a revolution was occurring, or had occurred: as a Canadian diplomat observed, correctly if inelegantly, in 1961: 'perhaps only like Mexico and unlike most other Latin American countries, Bolivia underwent and is still undergoing a deep social revolution in which the illiterate Indian masses are playing a major part': A.J. Pick report, 26 July 1961, enclosed in FO 371/156588, AX 1015/33.

96 Pearse (1975), pp. 145–6; Dandler and Torrico (1987), pp. 361–70; see also Rivera Cusicanqui (1984), chap. 4.

97 Both Klein (1982), p. 234, and Malloy (1970), p. 188, strongly imply that peasant mobilization was primarily a *response* to the 1952 Revolution (which was overwhelmingly an urban/syndical affair), not a major contributing factor. Other sources (see notes 35, 96 above) suggest rising discontent and activism in the countryside. Carranza Fernández (1972), p. 27, writes of a 'latent situation of insurgency' on the hacienda Parotani, Cochabamba, in the late 1940s.

98 Kelley and Klein (1981), p. 62

99 See Pearse (1975), pp. 146–51.

100 *Ibid.*, pp. 151–61. McEwen (1975) offers contrasting case studies.

101 McEwen (1975), p. 152, cites 'a once important *hacendado* (who) now waits on customers in his dingy bar' in Coroico.

102 Finch, 'Labor Report on Bolivia' (see note 25), pp. 2–3. Smuggling boomed because of the government's attempts to manage the exchange rate, which created shortages and a flourishing black market.

103 Hamilton (1982), chapters 7 and 8.

104 See Cárdenas (1987).

105 I should stress that I am *not* resuscitating the battered corpse of the all-powerful regime of the PNR/PRM/PRI (to whose demise I hope that I made some modest contribution). The Mexican revolutionary regime was never as strong as such 'statolatrist' interpretations suggested. But it *was* stronger than its Bolivian counterpart. A further clarification: the 'strength' of the Mexican regime was most marked in terms of its stamina and survival (like the Duracell rabbit, it kept going and going — at least until 2000). Such strength-as-endurance depended on constant deals, negotiations, minor repressions, extensive clientelism and endem-

ic corruption (all of which the MNR also tried during its 12 year tenure). However, particularly after 1940, the 'strength' of the Mexican regime in terms of its capacity to transform society — its strength-as-power — was rather less, certainly less than many sweeping analysts have asserted. There is an obvious complimentarity here: the avoidance of radical transformation (real or attempted) made deals more feasible; while the prevalence of deals tended to blunt the thrust of radical reform.

106 Thus, during the June 1961 crisis, when the government faced student demonstrations, miners' protests and a possible general strike, President Paz 'rounded up most of his support from the campesino union headed by his old friend José Rojas who immediately marched 5 –10,000 armed Indians to La Paz in order to protect the government against the threat from the mine workers. Indians from all over the hills could be seen in and out of La Paz, hiding a gun under their ponchos': A.J. Pick report, 26 July 1961, enclosed in FO 371/156588, AX 1015/33. Many similar stories could be cited.

107 MNR clientelism and ballot rigging — strongly reminiscent of similar activities in PNR/PRM/PRIísta Mexico — seem to be somewhat underestimated in the secondary literature. For a detailed critique of MNR *caciquismo*, bribery and browbeating of opponents, see Gamble to Foreign Office, 23 November 1964, FO 371/174431, AX1015/89.

108 The breakaway of Guervara Arze's MNRA could be compared to similar Mexican schisms (such as Almazán's PRUN in 1940) and Lechín's shortlived PRIN perhaps resembled Lombardo's PPS. But, in addition, Bolivia boasted a vigorous right-wing party, the FSB, which was much more effective than the pre-1980 PAN, as well as several small but strident leftwing parties.

109 Knight (1994), p. 78; Holliday to Foreign Office, 2 January 1961, FO 371/156586, AX 1011/1 (on Paz's 'steamroller tactics').

110 Holliday to Foreign Office, 14 July 1961, FO 371/156588, AX 1015/23. Nash (1979), pp. 28–9, notes a modicum of miner anticlericalism.

111 The occasion was the taking of 19 foreign hostages by militant miners in Catavi in December 1963 — a tense situation that Lechín, among others, wanted to resolve rapidly and peacefully. A journalist on the spot recalled how 'he had happened to be with the Oblate Fathers in Catavi when Sr Lechín rushed in and called out: "I need a Bishop. Any bishop. What can you offer?"': Holliday to Foreign Office, 20 December 1963, FO 371/174427, AX 1015/1. Ten years before, Lechín had denounced the Church — and the Jews — for colluding with the FSB (Lomax to Foreign Office, July 1953, FO 371/103625, AX 1015/10); by the 1960s he had mellowed and, it appears, had a working relationship with the papal nuncio (Pick to Foreign Office, 21 July 1961, FO 371/156588, AX1015/36).

112 Even Italian fascism carried some of the genes of anticlericalism, evident first in its radical origins, later in its totalitarian strivings after 1930. Perón, too, was ambivalent towards the Church; after a cloying, if insincere, embrace, Justicialismo and Catholicism parted company in 1955. Thus, the generalization might be framed in broader terms: in strongly Catholic countries, ambitious, mass-mobilizing political movements (not solely those on the left) are quite likely to display anticlericalism.
113 Lynch (date??), p. 533, gives figures of one priest for every 3,331 Mexicans in 1910; Lloyd Mecham (1966), p. 186, suggests one priest for every 4,755 Bolivians in 1960.
114 On the Mexican influence, see Malloy (1970), pp. 197, 234–5; Whitehead (1991), p. 532.
115 Attributed to Porfirio Díaz: Garner (2001), p. 220.
116 See the report of F.E. Sharples, British Labour Attaché, October 1961, FO 371/156638, AX2181/3.
117 Paz's increasingly close relations with the military, especially Ovando (who had been his commanding officer during the Chaco War), are amply documented in the British records: see, for example, the report of Military Attaché J.F.C. Melrose, 21 March 1964, FO 371/174428, AX1015/31.
118 The PAN (1939–c.1968) could not perform this role: it was too staid, too limited in appeal, constitutionally debarred from proclaiming a Catholic affiliation and too closely tied to conservative business interests who did not want to antagonize the ruling party. Things changed in the 1970s and '80s, especially following the bank nationalization of 1982, which offended and alarmed the private sector.
119 Basurto (1983), pp. 78–9. To my knowledge, this topic has never been thoroughly investigated.
120 Pearse (1975), p. 157. Finkler (1974) contrasts two post-reform communities in the Valle del Mezquital, Hidalgo: one ('Nalcan' = Caltimacan?), a landless community of migrant workers, was — necessarily — highly mobile, open and extrovert; the other ('Itel' = Tezontepec de Aldama?), endowed with good irrigated land, became relatively isolated and involuted. Scott (1976), p. 222, refers to this process — whereby successful reform breeds involution — as 'encapsulation'.
121 Pearse (1975), pp. 159–60; Kohl (1982), pp. 607–28; Ankerson (1984); Boyer (1994).
122 Albó (1987), pp. 384–5; Holliday to Foreign Office, 8 January 1964, FO 371/174427, AX 1015/5.
123 Brewster (1996), pp. 105–28; Ankerson (1984) chapter 8.
124 Holliday to Foreign Office, 13 March 1961, FO 371/156587, AX 1015/10; Bullock to Foreign Office, 5 February 1964, FO 371/174427, AX 1015/14.

125 Saragoza (1988); Bantjes (1998).
126 Santos (1984) is replete with examples of revolutionary gunslinging and camaraderie.
127 Katz (1981), pp. 564–5, 568–9, 576–7, which sums up US interventionism.
128 Knight (1986), vol. 2, p. 413.
129 Lehman (1999), pp. 118–19.
130 The Soviet Union made overtures — Khruschev offered Bolivia a tin smelter as part of a $150 million aid package in 1960 — but these were declined, not least because they would have jeopardized the crucial flow of US aid: Holliday to Foreign Office, 2 January 1961, FO 371/156568, AX 1011/1.
131 The first was the slogan of the CTM at the time of its foundation in the 1930s; the second derives from Dunkerley (1984), p. 47.
132 As early as 1955 the British Ambassador had concluded that US aid was the crucial economic factor: 'the future now depends less upon this or that trade factor than upon US aid — now taken as a matter of course': Lomax to Foreign Office, 7 January 1955, FO 371/114507, AX 1015/1. Paz's reliance on the regular armed forces — rather than the party militia — was explicit: Holliday to Foreign Office, 2 January 1961, FO 371/156568, AX 1011/1.

CHAPTER 4

Braked but not Broken: Mexico and Bolivia — Factoring the United States into the Revolutionary Equation

Ken Lehman

A month after the April 1952 Revolution, Robert Alexander, economist at Rutgers University and Latin American troubleshooter for the American Federation of Labor, wrote the State Department to advocate recognizing Bolivia's new revolutionary regime. Contrasting the delay in recognizing Paz with 'the rather hasty recognition of Batista', Alexander placed events in Bolivia within a larger context of revolutionary tensions in Latin America. Bolivia's revolution was long overdue, he argued, and the MNR had shown its commitment to 'take steps in the direction of a basic social change'. 'This revolution is not something we can stop,' he concluded. 'We can ride with it and try to guide it, but we will be foolhardy indeed if we try to brake it or break it.'[1]

Nearly another month passed before the United States recognized the MNR. Then, over the next 12 years, US officials decided not only to 'ride with' Bolivia's revolution, but also to give it unusual support. Alan Knight and Laurence Whitehead have developed in greater detail the significant and irreversible structural changes the 1952 Revolution brought to Bolivia. As Alexander foresaw, it was a social revolution that altered the class base of power, mobilized new political actors and redistributed wealth. In only a few cases, Bolivia being one, has the United States supported social revolutions and perhaps in no other case has it committed itself so fully to a revolutionary regime as in Bolivia. As Whitehead observes in Chapter 2, the current orthodoxy is that revolutions provide 'little more than false utopias and excesses for authoritarianism'.[2] This chapter argues from earlier orthodoxies. Revolutions are sometimes the only way to loosen a privileged minority's grip on power and they provide the powerless an important sense of their ability to shape history. Beginning from these premises, the role the United States played in supporting, directing and channeling Bolivia's unfolding revolutionary process — of braking but not breaking it — is one of the revolution's most significant legacies.

As the regional Great Power, the United States normally plays a conservative role in the hemisphere. It is a powerful nation-state and an economic center that profits from a stable capitalist system and, for security purposes, prefers an orderly hemisphere that is friendly to US interests.

Armed with the economic and political leverage that accompanies its power, the USA has often resisted revolutionary change. It played a central role in breaking other revolutions in the hemisphere and, on occasion, has supported the overthrow of democratically elected reform governments. Therefore, the conservative interests and considerable leverage of the United States become important conditioning influences for Latin American regimes that wish to alter existing conditions significantly.

But there are other aspects of US relations with its neighbors. Suffice it here to mention only two. First, US national 'interest' is the product of competing interests within a Smithian marketplace and a pluralistic Madisonian state. Competing interests perceive possibilities as well as dangers in an occasional disruption of the status quo and this opens spaces for revolutionaries to gain support. Second, the United States shows a second face to the world — one that elsewhere I refer to as 'America'.[3] 'America' is a more nebulous cultural entity than is the 'United States' — a *Weltanschauung* built on dreams, hopes, myths and a missionary ideology of developmental liberalism. America believes in itself and its place in history and seeks to export the benefits of its system. This makes America both imperialistic and profoundly revolutionary. The clash between 'national interest', the various more parochial interests of US citizens and the ideals of America creates a central conflict in American foreign policy. The fact that the three exist in symbiosis confuses those who analyze US foreign policy, but it opens additional spaces within which revolutionaries can maneuver for support.

By definition, revolutions disturb the status quo and by their nature they both destroy and create. By what strategies then, did revolutionaries in Bolivia successfully disturb, destroy and create beneath the watchful hegemony of the United States? This chapter uses Mexico for comparative purposes, in part because Alan Knight has provided an excellent analytical comparison of the two revolutions, in part because these are the only two social revolutions in the hemisphere that the United States did not try to break. More specifically, the chapter asks how in each case revolutionary leaders factored the influence of the regional Great Power into their revolutionary strategies. Then, in closing, the chapter briefly addresses a second question: to what degree did US influence brake revolutionary developments in both countries and to what effect? The United States played a much more direct role in shaping and braking revolutionary outcomes in Bolivia than in Mexico. All attempts to evaluate such outcomes, as do the chapters in this volume, must factor in the United States, just as revolutionaries themselves had to do.

Not Broken — Mexico

In *Hovering Giant*, Cole Blasier contrasts Mexico and Bolivia, where revolutionary regimes reached accommodation with the United States, to

Guatemala and Cuba, where they did not. In all four cases, the United States gave at least indirect support to the rebels, but when they seized power and introduced reforms that threatened US economic interests or seemed to endanger regional stability, indirect support turned quickly to open hostility. In both Mexico (1913) and Bolivia (1946), the USA helped remove reform governments. However, in all four cases US opposition gave rise to governments that took an even more independent line. Reform turned revolutionary, targeted entrenched US interests and threatened regional stability. Social and political reforms increased participation of previously disenfranchized social sectors and destabilized traditional politics. Blasier observes that in the revolutionary stage, US policy tended to polarize into support or resistance on strategic grounds. Two key factors determined whether the USA opted for conciliation or repression: first, was it possible to work out mutually acceptable solutions to conflicts and second, could improved relations reduce the dangers of interference by a hostile Great Power? [4]

Blasier's arguments, more subtle than this brief summary can convey, provide a useful framework for comparative analysis, with the additional merit of including several counter cases. But Blasier notes at the outset that his analysis 'unfolds in terms of Latin American actions and corresponding US reactions'.[5] This suits Blasier's purpose, which is to examine US policy. But here, it seems useful to flip the terms and examine the reaction of revolutionaries to the interests and actions of the United States. In short, how did the United States factor into the revolutionary calculus, and does flipping the terms corroborate Blasier's essential arguments or call them into question?

Actually, neither of Blasier's key arguments — flexibility on both sides or the threat of Great Power rivalries — seems particularly pertinent to Mexico. Venustiano Carranza, the key figure through much of the crucial period (1911–24), was notorious for *not* seeking accommodation with the United States and final accommodation did not occur until the 1920s when Great Power rivalries were largely a non-issue. The primary reason that Mexico's revolution survived possible US opposition was because it was too fluid and multifaceted to be easily broken. The revolution was not just a single revolution, but many, each with a different leader, a different class base, different objectives, centered in a different region of the country and each unfolding over time. Each revolution incorporated the United States into its strategies and calculations in a different way.

Francisco Madero saw the USA as a model, but underestimated its power and the conservative impact of its interests. He illustrates both the opportunities and dangers posed to revolutionaries by the United States. Madero based his revolt in the United States, armed his forces there, drew inspiration from US progressive reforms and benefited from broad American sympathy for his objectives and Taft's narrow interpretation of neutrality laws.[6] But, once in power, Madero felt the limitations imposed by the United States. His mildly nationalist policies quickly clashed with US interests and the man who championed them, Ambassador Henry Lane Wilson.[7] Madero failed to capture the American imagination or to enlist powerful US interests in his support. But perhaps his greatest failure was to rely on Diaz's army to maintain order in an essentially unchanged economic and social system.[8] The results were tragic for Madero and deeply significant to the Mexican Revolution. Future revolutionary leaders would more carefully address each of the issues that made Madero so vulnerable.

Emiliano Zapata gave little attention to the United States, and it played minimally into his calculations or objectives.[9] Pancho Villa understood US power and, for a time, took advantage of its interests and ideals, but ultimately he was disillusioned. Both Villa and Zapata helped to convince officials in Washington that this was a revolution that could not be rolled back and that land reform would be an essential ingredient. Crucial initial support for Villa came from US consuls in Durango and Torreón who were impressed by the way the northern strongman protected US property from his victorious army.[10] Their favorable comments reached Washington just as difficulties with Carranza, the titular head of the revolutionary forces, began to mount in the aftermath of the Veracruz landing. Villa also captured the American imagination in a way no other revolutionary leader yet had. The mythmakers of Hollywood signed a deal with Villa in early 1914 for some of the first wartime newsreels. The newsreel footage was later mixed into a fictional film, *The Life of General Villa* in which Villa, transformed by Hollywood into a champion of the yeomanry, pursued the federal officer who had debauched his sister.[11] It was an image that built on existing stereotypes while at the same time transcending them.

At a more sophisticated level, the image of Villa conveyed by radical journalist John Reed did the same. Reed spent four months in Mexico in late 1913, covering Villa's campaign. Reed's image of Villa tapped a deep American counter-cultural critique of modernism and dominating economic interests and appealed to a latent American sympathy for the downtrodden. President Wilson apparently read Reed's articles closely and the two men met in the White House to discuss Mexico.[12] Ironically, Villa also became the favorite of US business interests. They considered him a strong man who better protected foreign business interests than other revolutionary leaders. Until the end of 1914, Villa imposed no forced loans on US-owned businesses and the taxes he demanded were lower than those demanded by Carranza.[13] Villa effectively maneuvered the spaces opened to him. He was, Alan Knight notes, the 'man on horseback' and 'the champion of democracy; … Napoleon and Lincoln rolled into one', with a dollop of Wyatt Earp and Robin Hood thrown in for good measure.[14]

But relations between the United States and Villa deteriorated rapidly after his defeat at Celaya in early April 1915. To that point, a large part of

Villa's attraction to Americans had been his respect for US property. He had not needed to seize or tax US properties because of the income he received from estates he had confiscated from the old Porfirian elite. As his US support increased, Villa printed fiat money backed by the confidence of American companies that he would win, their faith that the US government was backing him and their hope that the paper would someday be worth even more. It was a confidence game and after Celaya, Villa no longer commanded the necessary confidence.[15] No longer did he seem so invincible yet simple, so strong yet friendly; no longer was he the reformer who left US interests untouched and his relations with the USA steadily deteriorated towards the confrontations at Santa Ysabel and Columbus. After the Columbus raid, the Torreón consul who had earlier championed Villa's cause now said of him: 'This is a different man than we knew. All the brutality of his nature has come to the front and he should be killed like a dog.'[16]

Relations between the United States and Venustiano Carranza were not subject to such vicissitudes because they were never close. Carranza feared the power of the United States and kept it at arms length but sought accommodation with its interests. At every step, he consistently asserted Mexican autonomy at the same time he worked to rein in the revolution. His policies before and during World War I displayed his shrewdness. Carranza resisted Pershing's punitive raid until Wilson was forced to withdraw; enlisted German support while offering them little; discouraged the Germans from sabotaging the oil fields at the same time he effectively staved off the threats of Northern intervention.[17] Blasier observes that the Great Power rivalries that accompanied World War I opened negotiating space to Carranza that he effectively used. But after the war, Mexico was more dependent on the United States than ever and the dangers of intervention were as high as before the war. After Carranza fell in 1920 and a government even less sympathetic to the revolution than Wilson's came to power in Washington in 1921, Carranza's successor, Alvaro Obregón, finally made peace with the United States as a step towards institutionalizing the revolution.

The amorphous nature of Mexico's revolution made it hard to control from the outside, even if the United States had been clear on its objectives and resolute in its response. It was neither. Katz observes that if there was a pattern to US policy toward Mexico, it was one of 'consistent American inconsistency'.[18] At the outset, there was a disjuncture between Taft and his man in Mexico, Henry Lane Wilson. Then the election of Woodrow Wilson brought a significant shift in policies and objectives. The debate on Wilson continues. To Kenneth Grieb, Wilson resembled 'a crusader who, convinced of his own righteousness and expecting violent opposition from the forces of evil, closes his mind to everything and presses forward with grim determination, certain that his cause will triumph'. In a more balanced evaluation, Alan Knight observes that: 'Wilson believed that liberal government was the best guarantor of political order, which in the Latin American context, was good for American trade and investment, and good for the maintenance of the Monroe Doctrine and the Roosevelt Corollary. Moralism and *Realpolitik* were not polar opposites.' Mark Gilderhus argues that for Wilson, ideology, material interests and security concerns assumed different weights in different circumstances and that Wilson's policy can only be evaluated within a situational framework.[19]

Whatever Wilson's views, his policies remained inconsistent. Magnifying the confusion was his dependence on personal agents with little experience in Mexico. A French diplomat commented that Wilson's agents 'were constantly fighting among themselves in order to further the interests of one of the revolutionary leaders whose fortunes they have personally embraced'. After sending his former student, David Lawrence, to Mexico in 1916 to negotiate with Carranza, Wilson himself became exasperated: 'The usual thing has happened: a man is sent down to explain our exact position and purpose and within a day or two sends a comprehensive plan of his own.'[20] Wilson's conflicting purposes and inconsistent policies again opened spaces within which Mexico's revolutionary leaders effectively maneuvered. While he is justifiably criticized for his ethnocentrism and naiveté, Wilson consistently refused to break Mexico's revolution and thus he deserves some of the responsibility (or credit) for its survival.

Another factor also explains why Mexico's revolution was not broken. Because Mexico is so near and important to both the United States and America — so significant to US security and to US interests — a multiplicity of voices competed and confused matters still further. Historian Fred Rippy makes the following observation about the final accommodation with Obregón. 'The chambers of commerce in the Southwest and elsewhere were primarily interested in Mexican trade … [and] humanitarians and plain people thought more of equity and the future of the oppressed masses of Mexico than of the international rules of capitalistic nations and vested interests of United States captains of industry. It was the old story repeating itself. Mexico was finding protection in the rivalries and diverse views of the several groups which constituted the American nation.'[21] In the final analysis, Mexico's revolution survived, in part because it was too complex to be as easily simplified or attributed as later revolutions would be.[22]

Five (and more) revolutions with five (and more) leaders and five (and more) sets of objectives complicated Mexico's revolution. Finally, however, through a process of elimination and what Knight calls the 'logic' of this particular revolution, the five (and more) revolutions became one revolution and each leader and faction played a role in protecting it from the United States. Madero gave the revolution legitimacy. Zapata made it a revolution. Villa briefly captured the American imagination and guaranteed a certain degree of sympathy among some influential Americans. Carranza fiercely resisted US attempts to direct or control it and Obregón began to institutionalize its gains while reconciling with the United States. Together Mexico's revolutionary leaders took maximum advantage of the spaces opened by the clash between US strategic and economic interests and the distinctly American *Weltanschauung* of Wilson.

Not Broken — Bolivia

Bolivia and Mexico provide useful comparisons as made clear in Alan Knight's contribution to this volume. In terms of external relations, the key similarity, of course, is that in those countries — and only these countries — revolutions received US support. But the differences are also striking. The Mexican Revolution began in the waning days of classic imperialism, when the right of 'superior' nations to intervene in the affairs of 'lesser' peoples was widely assumed. The revolution in Mexico spanned the period when the US definitively moved from regional to a global power and when the imperialist system, centered in Europe, began to crumble. By 1952, US power had increased substantially, but so had the influence of ideologies like nationalism, anti-imperialism and communism, and the costs of intervening in the affairs of other nations. In the early 1950s, Guatemala, Iran and Bolivia became testing grounds for new forms of intervention.

A more significant difference is the relative importance of Mexico and Bolivia to the United States. Mexico is the southern neighbor of the United States; subtly lurking in the American consciousness even if in stereotyped ways. Mexico is near, influential and potentially wealthy. In Mexico, overlapping US interests led to greater public awareness of the revolution and created significant competing pressures within the pluralistic political system of the United States. And because Mexico was so important to the United States, it took on added importance to other powers as well, giving Mexico a leverage that Bolivia never enjoyed. Finally, because of Mexico's proximity to the United States, America invades the Mexican consciousness, making anti-Americanism and *pochismo* blend in infinite shades.

On the other hand, Bolivia lurks, even today, at the fringes of the American consciousness. It is the place where the other guys lose your package in the airfreight commercial. In 1952, not many Americans knew much about Bolivia and US economic interests were few. Not even Bolivia's over-priced, low-grade tin held much attraction by 1952. In Bolivia, negotiations between MNR leaders and their US counterparts took place outside the public eye and this created wholly different dynamics. Because there were fewer US interests in Bolivia, the relative influence of those interests was much greater. Then too, Bolivia's revolution occurred at a time in the early Cold War when nations were forced into rather clearly defined camps. There was no international competition over Bolivia to provide it leverage. The USA did not have a significant rival in the hemisphere until later in the decade, when Khrushchev brought a more adventurous foreign policy to the Soviet Union and Cuba exposed fissures in the bipolar world.

But, with these differences in mind, accommodation between the United States and the Bolivian revolutionaries was no simpler than in Mexico. Bolivia's National Revolution came with a speed and finality that worried US officials and placed it immediately in a Cold War framework. Immediately after the April revolt, contacts inside the MNR told US officials that the sudden, complete collapse of the government and army frightened them. The State Department asked its embassy in La Paz to monitor the situation closely to determine who was in charge, the degree of communist influence and whether MNR nationalization plans might 'develop into another Iran'. It did not reassure the department that Guatemala was the first country to recognize the new regime or that Guatemala's governing party exulted 'that we are no longer alone in the hemisphere'.[23]

Bolivia's pre-revolution poverty, its political alienation and deep class and ethnic divisions made the old order weak and building an opposition coalition around a unifying core of vaguely defined nationalism relatively easy. But once the old order collapsed, these same features posed a formidable challenge to the political moderates who headed the MNR. According to revolutionary theory, the reign of moderates under such conditions is necessarily short, because the very traits that make them moderate also make them easy prey for the superior fervor and discipline of extremists. The economic difficulties confronting the new government further jeopardized the moderates. Tin contract negotiations with the United States were suspended and world prices for tin, the source of 60 per cent of Bolivia's foreign exchange, were in free fall.

The United States had used its commercial tin stocks to burst a speculative price bubble during the Korean War. The conflict this policy engendered had undermined Bolivia's military government, but now it also threatened the fragile coalition that came to power after the revolution. Workers, especially the tin miners, demanded nationalization of the mines, but the only market for Bolivia's tin was the United States government and European smelters, where the private tin owners were major shareholders. The dilemma exposed Bolivia's dependency, but rather than leading to a collapse of the revolutionary coalition, it contributed instead to a basic understanding between President Víctor Paz Estenssoro, who headed the traditional, nationalist, middle class core of the MNR, and Juan Lechín Oquendo, who headed the mine workers and the Central Obrera Boliviana (COB). The two men rarely saw eye-to-eye, but they shared a willingness to negotiate. Paz preferred co-optive reform and balancing of forces to confronting the powerful unionists head-on, and the MNR Central Committee, despite occasional right-wing challenges, broadly supported his position. And though Trotskyite union leaders were critical, Lechín won general labor support for his *entrista* policies calling labor to enter the government, to cooperate but constantly to push union demands.

Co-optive reform and *entrismo* created areas of common agreement within which Paz and Lechín constantly bargained. Together they balanced the imperative to reform with the demands of survival; the unifying appeal of nationalism with the reality of Bolivia's economic dependency on world tin markets; the pressures of competing demands with the pragmatic quest for concessions. Without going into detail, their bargaining usually went something like this. The labor-left would push Lechín to make radical demands and Paz and party moderates would counter-argue that reforms must remain sufficiently circumscribed so as not to expose the revolution to counter-revolutionary pressures from inside or outside the country. Taking advantage of the fact that Washington perceived him as a moderate, and Lechín as a dangerous radical, Paz would then press US officials for concessions and understanding that would allow him to stay in the driver's seat. Then, he and Lechín would hammer out a final compromise that would be minimally acceptable to all factions and Lechín would promote it to his followers as the best that could be done without endangering the revolution. This process produced rapid and far-reaching reform, but of an ad hoc and compromised nature. [24]

After six months of intense bargaining, the final nationalization decree was such a compromise. The degree to which the United States was party to the bargaining becomes apparent when Paz spoke to celebrating miners on the day the decree was announced. In a speech punctuated by dynamite blasts, Paz told them that this was neither socialism nor a blow against private enterprise. Rather, he argued, in words clearly designed more for Washington than for his dynamite-wielding audience, 'breaking the barons' stranglehold on Bolivia's economy would now open vast new fields of private investment'.[25] Even the date the decree was announced, October 31, may have been chosen with an eye to the United States. The MNR's public relations firm in the United States, Selvage and Lee, recommended that the decree be issued during the heavy news days just prior to US elections on 4 November to reduce negative publicity.[26]

Those elections brought an economizing, pro-business, Cold Warrior, Dwight D. Eisenhower, to office. The change of administrations and philosophies, as well as the continuing decline in tin prices, compounded the MNR's difficulties. As rumors of an international boycott of Bolivia's newly nationalized tin spread, Bolivia's foreign minister, Walter Guevara Arze, visited Guatemala and Mexico to rally support. Then, in December, in perhaps its most vigorous effort to avoid being isolated, Bolivia jointly sponsored a resolution in the United Nations General Assembly that asserted the right of UN members to nationalize resources of vital national interest. Vice President Hernán Siles Zuazo headed Bolivia's delegation, and the measure passed overwhelmingly, with the United States casting one of only four dissenting votes.[27]

Independent of this diplomatic triumph, economic conditions worsened. At the end of 1952, 70 per cent of Bolivia's normal mineral export trade was suspended due to nationalization. Foreign exchange reserves evaporated, hampering the importation of food and exacerbating Bolivia's chronic inflation.[28] Rising peasant unrest, work stoppages and land seizures further disrupted food supplies; the rural unrest raised the threat of counter-revolution on the right. Then in early March of 1953, the newly inaugurated Eisenhower administration announced that current tin contracts would fill both strategic and commercial stockpiles by the end of the year and that the US government had no further interest in a tin contract with Bolivia.[29]

To this point, the depth, speed and potential of Bolivia's revolution, its instability, it's policies of economic nationalism, even the putative influence of communists, were all less important to US officials than was the obvious willingness of MNR leaders to incorporate the United States into their internal bargaining process. But without at least the hope of a tin contract, there was no US leverage, and without US leverage, there was no reason to orient policy to satisfy the United States. Pressed from all sides, Bolivia's revolutionary leaders began to espouse a much more independent line. At the first anniversary of the revolution in April, the MNR rallied the support of progressive forces throughout the hemisphere. Former and future Venezuelan president, Rómulo Betancourt, and former Guatemalan foreign minister, Manuel Galich, attended and spoke of joint Latin American action to curb the 'tremendous economic power' of the United States. At the anniversary rally, President Paz compared Bolivia to Iran and warned of the dangers that imperialist interests posed to revolutions.[30]

Later that month, the MNR opened full relations with Guatemala and accepted the credentials of Galich to stay in La Paz as Guatemala's permanent emissary. Paz expressed personal interest in Guatemala's land reform and invited Guatemalan Vice President Julio Estrada de la Hoz to visit Bolivia to share information on the program. At the same time, a Guatemalan military officer provided special revolutionary training to the Bolivian general staff.[31] Then, at a 1 May rally, with no tin contract yet in sight, President Paz told workers that he had established relations with Czechoslovakia and was prepared to sell tin behind the Iron Curtain. Lechín followed with an angry denunciation of US economic aggression and demanded immediate mineral sales to the socialist nations.[32]

On the surface, relations between the United States and the MNR appeared to be deteriorating rapidly, but there were other layers to the process. Víctor Andrade, Bolivia's ambassador to the United States, commented in his memoir that he counted upon an underlying American sympathy with the underdog that he first observed in the missionaries at the Methodist school he attended in La Paz. 'In the United States ... admitting an error awakens much more sympathy than strong assertions of opinion. The United States is a country which always favors the weak, the underdog. To take advantage of this trait for one's cause is the wisest course.'[33] He counseled his superiors in La Paz to explain carefully the objectives of the revolution in such terms and to build links to progressive forces inside the USA. In order to gain this sort of sympathetic understanding of the task facing their regime, the MNR invited several sympathetic journalists and labor officials to the anniversary celebrations, and Gardner Jackson of the CIO and Ernesto Galarza of the AF of L attended.[34]

Galarza first became interested in Bolivia in late 1942 after the Catavi 'massacre'. While he was chief of the Division of Labor and Social Information of the Pan American Union, Galarza wrote a background piece on the attack against striking miners for *The Nation* in which he criticized US tin-procurement policies and their impact on workers. The article was among the factors that prompted the State Department to send a North American team that included several labor representatives to study worker conditions in Bolivia's mines. The commission report was cautiously worded but nonetheless highly critical of labor conditions, not only in the mines but also on surrounding haciendas. The Catavi Massacre and the commission report made US labor a vocal advocate of Bolivian workers.[35] After the revolution, Robert Alexander provided his recommendation to neither 'break' nor 'brake' the revolution that opened this chapter. Alexander convinced Serefino Romualdi, head of the AF of L's Organización Regional Interamericano de Trabajadores (ORIT), that Bolivia's plan to nationalize the mines was not a blow against capitalism. Romualdi came out in support of the revolution at an AF of L convention in late May 1952; this was significant because ORIT and Romualdi were considered bastions of anti-communist unionism in Washington.[36]

Because there were so few competing voices on Bolivia, labor played a crucial role in legitimating and explaining the revolution back in the United States. Soon after they returned from Bolivia, Galarza and Jackson visited Washington to plead Bolivia's case. On Capitol Hill they distributed an eleven-page report to key Senate and House members. Beginning with the premise that the MNR needed and deserved help, their report stressed the need for time to allow the revolutionary government to put its economic development plans in place. The report then issued a challenge:

> The Bolivian situation presents a sharp choice to the State Department — a choice sharper than any forced on it in recent years by developments in Latin America. That choice lies between support of a clearly

> nationalist, home-grown force determined to pull the nation out of its feudal condition or benevolence toward an old and brutal power structure that has kept the country in that condition.[37]

State Department officials called the report 'a melodramatic oversimplification', but did not dispute the essential thrust of its message.

At an informal luncheon on 22 April with William Hudson, the State Department's Bolivia desk officer, Galarza and Jackson recommended that the USA reopen tin talks and pay a subsidized price for tin on condition that the Bolivian government use the subsidy to fund development projects. Hudson responded that a subsidy would create difficult precedents and would be virtually impossible to sell to Congress or the new administration. Hudson then added that he had a personal idea of how the USA could help Bolivia without subsidizing tin, though he had not yet taken up the matter with the Department. He thought that the USA might donate a two or three years supply of basic foodstuffs, which Bolivia normally imported, on the understanding that the government would use the local currency generated by the sale of these foods to fund economic development and diversification.[38]

On 30 April, Hudson sent a memo to his superiors that outlined an assistance plan for Bolivia. The plan included a three-year tin contract at market prices, a program of technical assistance and Hudson's idea to sell surplus food to raise investment capital. Paz's speech to workers the next day did not make selling the plan any easier. US Embassy officials called the tone of the president's speech 'demagogic, dishonest and malicious'.[39] But they also understood the political motives behind it. Paz was about to announce an austerity plan that froze wages and steeply devalued the *boliviano*. The economic measures came at considerable political peril and coincided with the decision to open talks on compensations with the former mine owners.[40]

On 10 May the State Department mentioned the possibility of an aid package to Ambassador Andrade for the first time. At the same time, Andrade was warned that it would be virtually impossible to get such a program past US administrative and congressional roadblocks unless the regime reached agreements on compensations with the Big Three and toned down its political rhetoric.[41] Immediately, the MNR government clamped a muzzle on official anti-Americanism and redoubled efforts to find a compromise compensation agreement. On 9 June, the Bolivians announced that an agreement had been struck with Patiño, the largest of the nationalized mining companies and the only one with US investors.[42] Now the Bolivians moved assiduously to reassure US officials in every way. Paz granted an interview to *US News and World Report* that allowed him to reaffirm his commitment to capitalism, and the Bolivians dropped plans to sell tin to the Czechs.[43]

Things moved more slowly in Washington. Low-level State Department officials who devised the aid plan found an important ally in Assistant Secretary of State for Inter-American Affairs John Moors Cabot. Cabot wished to increase the profile and significance of the part of the world he represented and used Cold War arguments to make his case. As a United Fruit Company shareholder and a convinced opponent of Arbenz, Cabot sought to clarify that the United States opposed communism, not reform. To Cabot, aid to Bolivia was an important alternative to policies pursued simultaneously in Guatemala and a clear indication that the United States would support authentic non-communist reform movements.[44]

Cabot, in turn, found an ally in Milton Eisenhower, who planned to visit Latin America with him in late June and early July of 1953. Jackson and Galarza again played a role, meeting with Dr Eisenhower in late April to make their case that Bolivia needed special assistance. Jackson then introduced Eisenhower to Ambassador Andrade at a family party at Jackson's home where the ambassador explained the goals and accomplishments of the MNR government. Dr Eisenhower (who described himself as a fiscal conservative who was liberal 'so far as problems of human value are concerned'), became sufficiently interested to meet Andrade again, the week before he and Cabot left for South America.[45] A blend of strategic thinking, American idealism and concern for his brother's mission to Latin America finally prompted President Eisenhower to become directly involved in the Bolivian aid negotiations in early July.[46]After a great deal of last-minute dickering and high-level politicking in Washington, the State Department finally provided an advanced text of a US offer of assistance on the eve of Milton Eisenhower's arrival in La Paz on 6 July. It announced a one-year tin contract at world market prices, a doubling of technical assistance and a promise to consider with the Bolivian government further steps toward a long-term solution to Bolivia's economic problems.[47] It was a less ambitious version of the plan Hudson had formulated back in April, but it nevertheless redefined US–Bolivian relations and the course of Bolivia's revolution.

The Paz government's shift from overt anti-Americanism in April and early May of 1953 to careful concern not to antagonize the USA by late May and June is striking. Equally so is the rapid shift from a foreign policy marking out an independent Third World position to an apparently docile acceptance of a place within a US-controlled hemisphere. But to MNR leaders, both were products of the same requirements of survival. If anti-Americanism had a certain internal political logic, coming to terms with the United States was deemed essential to the regime's economic and therefore long-term political survival by nearly all the revolution's leaders — even those on the labor-left. Lechín and the unionists attacked 'US imperialism' with relish in April and May, but ultimately they, too, were convinced that the nationalized mines could not survive without a US tin contract. Lechín later told a US official: 'Understand, I'm an anti-imperialist — naturally, because I'm Bolivian. But when it comes to a choice between Russia and the United States, I'm with the United States. Who do we think we are — a small and impoverished country — that we can afford to disregard the fact that we are a part of the American orbit?'[48]

Lechín was no Carranza, and neither was Paz. Nor was either a Villa who could engage American romance and idealism in the cause of revolution (though the sympathetic support US labor gave the revolution cannot be discounted). Paz was Bolivia's Madero who brought legitimacy to the revolution in US eyes — in part because of his constitutional claim to victory in the 1951 elections, but more because it became apparent that he was a liberal-developmentalist with whom officials in Washington felt quite comfortable. Lechín, like Zapata, became the conduit of revolutionary change and it was he and his followers who guaranteed that this would become a revolution. But Paz and Lechín shared Obregón's pragmatic penchant for consolidating and institutionalizing revolutionary gains through compromise and co-option. Like Obregón they also understood the need to come to terms with the United States. Bolivia's revolutionary leaders voluntarily braked their revolution and sought a patron in Washington.

Returning to the two factors Blasier believes determined US response, Blasier himself recognizes that the danger of interference by a foreign power was never credible in Bolivia. The important factor was the willingness of the MNR to seek mutually acceptable solutions to conflicts. However, accommodation seems rooted less in negotiation than in dependency. Bolivian revolutionary leaders believed that they needed not just US understanding, but US assistance, and they were willing to bend quite a bit in order to obtain it. The Bolivian Revolution was not broken because ultimately it proved too malleable to make that necessary. Malleability rooted in dependency is quite different from Mexico's flexibility rooted in diversity, though both eventually elicited US support. But for Bolivia, the patron-client dynamics that would ultimately limit its revolution had begun.

But Braked: Mexico and Bolivia.

Revolutions, by definition, destroy existing power relations and undermine the norms and institutions upon which previous political legitimacy was based. To a degree, every revolution must be braked if it is to complete its tasks to establish new power relations, to assure its survival or to develop the norms and institutions to reinforce the new order. The issue, then, is not the braking process itself, but who applies the brakes and to what end. Using the Mexican revolutionary leaders to allow a crude heuristic shortcut, it is clear that for good relations with the United States, a revolution in this hemisphere needs an Obregón. This becomes the more obvious when one adds Guatemala and Cuba (where there was no Obregón) to the analysis. The question remains, however, whether, in this hemisphere, a revolution can institutionalize itself as a revolution without a Carranza?

Turning first to Mexico, the US role in eliminating Madero was neither subtle nor indirect. Even Knight, who consistently downplays the influence of the United States on the revolution, observes that 'Ambassador Wilson, playing something of a freelance role, was an exception'.[49] But, if Ambassador Wilson's purpose was to apply the brakes, it was the accelerator that he inadvertently stepped on instead.[50] The influence of the United States during the Huerta interregnum was no subtler and the results were even less clear. If it was President Wilson's plan to guide Mexico toward constitutional legitimacy under US tutelage, he failed. If his purpose was to bring order to Mexico he failed again. But if he was willing to accept real change in Mexico, his opposition to Huerta made that possible.

According to Friedrich Katz, the influence of the United States on Villa was subtle, indirect and significant. Because Villa expropriated large landholdings in Chihuahua, rather than keeping them intact and taxing them as Carranza did, Villa was able to equip, arm and professionalize his army without forced contributions from foreigners.[51] But as he became the US favorite, Villa came to rely increasingly on fiat money backed by US interests.

> Suddenly, Villa had come into possession of Aladdin's lamp — all he had to do was print money, and the Americans and, as a result, Mexicans too would accept it. Why divide up land and cause dissension within his movement and weaken his army if he could attain an even greater degree of popularity by simply distributing the paper money he printed? As long as this expedient worked, it was a highly effective way of gaining support and popularity.[52]

Katz believes that if Villa had paid his soldiers with land, the quality of his support might have been more like Zapata's. Because he did not, he lost his ability to maintain a regular army once the United States swung against him, and this cost him a voice in institutionalizing the revolution.

The impact of the United States on Carranza was just as indirect and even more ironic. Katz argues that Carranza followed policies very similar to those of Porfirio Díaz in his early years: strengthening the state, playing local caudillos against each other, allowing them to enrich themselves so that they would not threaten him and, most of all, seeking the support of the landed class. If Katz is correct, then Carranza failed in part because he never got the US support that Diaz eventually did.[53] Thus, US policy effectively thwarted the conservative aims not only of Huerta, but also of Carranza. There is further irony in the fact that after Madero's death, Carranza and the *Carrancistas* — the man and faction most amenable to Wilson's image of revolution rooted in constitutional legitimacy and respect for property rights

— were the most stubbornly resistive to US meddling. But Carranza's real significance was the way he protected Mexico's revolution at its most vulnerable stage. As Katz points out, his greatest legacy to the revolution was 'to maintain his country's independence in the face of a rising tide of interventionism among the world's great powers'.[54]

The revolution ultimately tipped toward Carranza, not because he was the most revolutionary and certainly not because he was the US favorite. Rather, as Knight puts it, 'the strengths of Carrancismo ... lay in the shrewd opportunism of its leaders, their aptitude for national power and ability to transcend the narrower world of traditional relationships ... and to operate in the arena of mass impersonal associational politics'.[55] All those attributes, in addition to Carranza's consistent refusal to bow to US pressures, make the *Carrancistas* significant despite their limited commitment to reform. US influence, though considerable and usually aimed at slowing the revolution, often turned out to have precisely the opposite effect. Finally, it was the Sonorans who braked the revolution. Sons of the border, Obregón and Calles certainly understood the necessary restraints imposed by proximity to the United States. But if one examines the Mexican Revolution as a single long process, beginning with Madero and culminating (somewhat arbitrarily) with Obregón and Calles, then those who emerged on top — the Sonorans — largely braked the revolution on their own terms.

In Bolivia, the United States played a much more direct braking role, but on terms that initially might have been quite acceptable to party moderates.[56] There is evidence that leaders like Paz and his successor, Hernán Siles Zuazo, deliberately balanced the power of the labor-left with that of the United States under conditions where the traditional right and even the military had been severely weakened. Factoring the United States into the revolutionary equation certainly guaranteed that each reform step taken by the MNR was more cautious than the labor-left might have preferred. Aid gave MNR moderates considerable new leverage to use against labor and specifically the miners. But the problem with this conspiratorial theory is that Lechín and the general union rank-and-file — including miners — supported US aid and stayed loyal to the MNR until surprisingly late. Lechín and most of his followers shared the same conviction as MNR moderates, that their revolution needed outside assistance.

When the United States announced in March 1953 that it would buy no more tin, Lechín attacked US imperialism with gusto. But when the Eisenhower administration responded with offers of aid and a tin contract, the labor leader dutifully toned down his rhetoric and again worked with Paz to expedite agreements. In July, after communist leader Sergio Almaraz Paz criticized the agreements with Patiño and the government's drift toward the United States, Lechín explained to workers that both were economic necessities. In a direct rebuke to Almaraz, Lechín told workers that 'if Comrade Almaraz could prove that Comrade Malenkov' would purchase all the tin Bolivia had to sell without attaching political conditions, then the government would change course. Until then, there was no alternative to coming to terms with the United States.[57] To Lechín, as to MNR moderates, turning to the United States seemed both expedient and practical. In doing so, Lechín hoped that US tin contracts and aid would strengthen the newly nationalized tin mines and allow the country greater independence in the future.

Sixteen years later, in *Requiem para una república*, Almaraz issued an 'I told you so'. His succinct recapitulation of the dynamics set in motion by US aid is sufficiently accurate to merit quoting at length:

> The Bolivian revolution shrank and with it, its leaders, its projects, and its hopes. Its policies were based on concession and between concession and subjugation, the differences are subtle … In 1953 came the first North American food aid. In 1957 the monetary stabilization plan was imposed. A little later the army was reorganized. North American advisors were accepted into key administrative organizations. The petroleum code was passed. One thing led to another in this complicated game as surrender alternated with defense. It is not that there was no awareness of what was happening: 'we yield over here in order to hold firm over there'. 'This is more important than that.' Yet these choices, each the product of unique circumstances, led eventually to loss of control … One concession led to the next in a sequence that made it impossible to gauge the seriousness of each new step … The revolution did not crumble from a single blow, it fell bit by bit, piece by piece.[58]

Of course one could paraphrase Lechín to ask whether 'Comrade Almaraz' could assure that 'Comrade Malenkov' (or Khrushchev) would not write his own, somewhat different obituary for Bolivian independence. In light of the conditions confronting Bolivia's revolutionaries, was there an alternative to dependency of one form or another?

To phrase the question another way, would a Bolivian Carranza have made a difference? Perhaps not: Bolivia is not Mexico and perhaps, in its vulnerability, was more like Iran or Guatemala where Carranzas of sorts were effectively isolated and ousted while the Bolivian story was unfolding. The lessons the MNR drew from Iran were succinctly summarized in an August 1953 editorial in the semi-official newspaper, *La Nación*: 'In all areas of human action, one gains more by giving way than by rushing forward headlong. If Mossadegh had not been so obstinate and imperious, if he had been willing to momentarily concede in order eventually to win all, he might not have placed his triumph at risk nor endangered his cause.'[59] This was the MNR's approach to foreign policy. Without a driving or defining ideology beyond vague nationalism, the regime believed it must concede in order eventually to win all.

The 'all' that Bolivia's revolutionary nationalists eventually hoped to win was increased national autonomy, but to gain it they had to concede their dependency. Again, nationalization of the tin mines provides an example. Nationalization had been an act of national self-assertion. To again quote Almaraz (more quotable perhaps than he was politically astute), the events of 31 October 1952 helped Bolivians understand that they could make history.[60] But they could not make it just as they pleased, as Almaraz, a follower of Marx, would likely concur. Nationalization disrupted tin sales, frightened off potential investors and saddled the government with compensation payments in a worsening market. Such conditions led MNR leaders to believe that US development assistance was a potential solution to the imperialist threat posed by the tin baron's old system. As Whitehead comments in Chapter 2: 'the invocation of a "nationalist" justification for seizing power is not necessarily incompatible with a heavy resort to external support and protection'.

It was a pragmatic decision, but also one rooted in dependency. Once in place, Almaraz is correct; compliance resolved too easily into submission. It is precisely at this juncture that a Bolivian Carranza might have made a difference. Bolivia was not Mexico, but neither was it Guatemala or Iran. A leader who effectively fought for an independent nationalist position might have had an easier time in a country where the United States did not have the deep historical interests it had in Guatemala or with the economic and strategic importance of Iran. Bolivian revolutionaries excelled at bargaining from weakness. With no grand plan, the Paz government nationalized the mines despite strong US objections, then six months later convinced the Eisenhower State Department to buy tin and send aid. In between, it participated in an incipient non-aligned movement of developing nations at the very height of the bipolar Cold War. The originality of those policies and the broad support they drew is best illustrated by the successful UN resolution supporting nationalization and the enthusiastic first anniversary celebrations. Foreign policy independence actually seemed to encourage and expedite aid. Yet once aid was promised, the MNR gave up its bargaining strengths and fell quickly in line behind the United States.

By so quickly accepting Bolivia's dependency, the MNR forfeited strengths inherent in its pragmatic and non-ideological character, in the formidable bargaining and balancing skills of its key leaders and in the natural sympathy it drew from others in the hemisphere. Coming to terms with the United States ended the revolution's most dynamic phase of internal reform and its most innovative period of foreign relations. What could a Carranza have accomplished for Bolivia's revolution? The answer to that question would require another, far more speculative paper, but one suspects that such a leader, in a position of power, might have made this year's fiftieth anniversary register higher in the Bolivian consciousness as a point when Bolivians took control of history. As it was, in mid-1953 the regime found its patron but lost its initiative. To paraphrase José Fellman Velarde, aid in 1953 seemed the slender golden thread that could rescue the regime from economic ruin and give it hope for the future. Later it became a chain slowly constricting the regime, undermining party support and restricting national autonomy.[61] Like Jacob Marley's chains in *A Christmas Carol*, they were ones the Bolivian revolutionaries themselves helped forge.

Notes

1 Letter, Alexander to Miller, 16 May 1952, NA, Record Group 59, Office Files of the Assistant Secretary of State for Latin American Affairs (Edward G. Miller), 1949–53, Box 2, LOT 53 D 26.

2 Whitehead, chapter 2 of this volume, p. 40.

3 Lehman (1999), pp. ix–xiv.

4 Blasier (1985), especially pages 6, 68 and 216. In the revised edition to his 1976 book, Blasier added an extended postscript in which he applies his analytical model to Grenada and to US efforts to break revolutionary movements in Central America in the late 1970s and 1980s.

5 *Ibid.*, p. 6.

6 *Ibid.*, pp. 17-20; Katz (1981), pp. 25–26; Ulloa (1997), p. 159.

7 Blasier (1985), p. 38; Vázquez and Meyer (1985), pp. 106–7.

8 Both Friedrich Katz and Alan Knight agree that Ambassador Wilson played an important role in the fall of Madero, though they differ on the degree to which Wilson acted independently of Washington. See Knight (1986), pp. 485–90 and Katz (1981), pp. 94–5 and 112.

9 Nor did Zapata figure heavily in the calculations or objectives of US officials. Early agents sent by Wilson tended to disparage Zapata as little more than a brigand. One exception was Hubert L. Hall, who lived in Morelos and was impressed by Zapata and his agrarian message. Hall visited Washington and presented Zapata's position. He was made an agent to Zapata and reported faithfully from Morelos, but Larry Hill comments that the letters were apparently filed away and ignored. See Hill (1973), pp. 128, 244, 248, 250 and 300.

10 Katz (1998), pp. 217–18.

11 *Ibid.*, pp. 325–26.

12 Reed (1969); Hicks (1936), p. 117; Delpar (1992), p. 10; Katz (1998), pp. 318-21; Hill (1973), 189–91. On the meeting with Wilson, see Hicks, pp. 146–47.

13 US business leaders also drew comfort from Villa's hostility to the Partido Liberal Mexicano with its links to the International Workers

of the World and hoped that Villa would not tolerate strikes. Katz (1998), 313. That kind of business support led others on the American left to reject Villa as a tool of Wall Street. Both Lincoln Steffens and John Kenneth Turner preferred Carranza's authentic anti-American nationalism. Katz, op. cit., pp. 321–22.

14 Knight (1986), vol. II, p. 290.

15 Katz (1998), p. 541.

16 Hill (1973), p. 370.

17 Hall and Coerver (1988), pp. 76–77; Blasier (1985), p. 113; and Katz (1981), pp. 395 and 563.

18 Katz (1981), p. 563.

19 Grieb (1969), p. 40; Knight (1986), vol. II, pp. 68–69; and Gilderhus (1977), pp. ix–xi.

20 Katz (1981), p. 490; and Hill (1973), p. 357.

21 Rippy (1931), p. 368 and Vázquez and Meyer (1985), pp. 127–30.

22 See the thesis of Lehman (1997).

23 Telegram, Acheson to American Diplomatic Officers in Other American Republics except Bolivia, 17 April 1952, General Records of the Department of State, Record Group 59, Decimal Files (Hereafter NA) 724.02/4-1752; On Guatemalan responses, see Dispatch 1028 from Guatemala City, 15 April 1952, NA 724.00/4-1552 and Dispatch 1071 from Guatemala City, 25 April 1952, NA 724.02/4-2552.

24 Malloy (1970) and Mitchell (1977) both provide essential discussions of bargaining within the revolutionary coalition. Malloy observes that the results were filled with all the contradictions inherent in the party's multi-class and non-ideological nature. Mitchell agrees, but further argues that at each step the results tilted in favor of the more politically astute middle-class core of the party. For an internal US government assessment of the bargaining, see National Security Estimate, *Foreign Relations of the United States 1952–1954*, vol. IV (Hereafter *FRUS, 1952–1954*), pp. 547–57. All three of these sources, I believe, fail to see the broad areas of agreement between Lechín and labor, on one hand, and Paz and the *politicos,* on the other — most important their agreement that Bolivia would need outside assistance of one kind or another.

25 Lora (1977), p. 288; Office Memo, Hudson to Miller, 3 November 1952, NA 724.32/11-352, which includes a copy of the nationalization decree in Spanish and a summary in English. Dispatch 320 from La Paz, 3 November 1952, NA 724.11/11–352 and Joint Weeka, 7 November 1952, NA 724.00(W)/11–752.

26 Telegram 156, Andrade to Foreign Ministry in La Paz, 21 October 1952, Bolivian Ministry of Foreign Relations Archives (hereafter BMFRA), notebook CL–353.

27 Telegram 4, Guevara to Bolivian Embassy in Mexico, 22 November 1952, BMFRA, notebook CL–915 and 'Byfield Report,' by Robert S. Byfield, UN observer from the New York Stock Exchange, undated [late 1952] Dwight D. Eisenhower Library, Records, US President's Committee on International Information Activities, 1950–53, see especially pp. 25–30.

28 Eder (1968), p. 34; Joint Weeka, 12 December 1952, NA 724.00 (W)/12-1252 and Joint Weeka, 14 November 1952, NA 724.00 (W)/11–1452.

29 Telegram 223, Dulles to Embassy in Bolivia, 12 March 1953, *FRUS, 1952–1954*, vol. IV, pp. 522–3 and Telegram 53, Andrade to Foreign Ministry in La Paz, 12 March 1953, BMFRA CL–354.

30 *Ultima Hora*, 13 April 1953 carried Betancourt's statements; 15 April 1953, those by Galich; and 16 April 1953, those by Galarza. Joint Weeka, 17 April 1953, NA 724.00 (W)/4–1753 also gives summaries of the speeches. For the quote by Galarza see Memorandum of Conversation, Jackson, Galarza, Fishburn and Hudson, 23 April 1953, NA 824.00/4–2353. Paz's speech is covered in Joint Weeka, 10 April 1953, NA 724.00 (W) 4/1053.

31 Guatemalan relations are covered in *Ultima Hora*, 27 April 1953, p. 5. Hoz's visit is covered in despatch 516 from La Paz, 2 February 1953, NA 724.00/2–253.

32 *Ultima Hora*, 2 May 1953, p. 4 and editorial in *La Nación* of 3 May 1953 in Rodrigo (1955), pp. 210–11. See also the review of President Paz's May Day speech included in office memorandum, Hudson to Cabot, Mann and Atwood, 11 May 1953, NA 611.24/5–453. Telegram 300, Sparks to Secretary of State, 5/7/53, *FRUS, 1952–1954*, vol. IV, pp. 527–8.

33 Andrade (1976), p. 174.

34 Telegram 46, Guevara to Embassy in Washington, 20 March 1953, BMFRA, CL-354 and Telegram 66, Andrade to Foreign Ministry in La Paz, 26 March 1953, BMFRA, CL–354.

35 Berger (1966), pp. 215–19 and McConaughy (Second Secretary of Embassy) to Hull, 2 March 1943, *FRUS, 1943*, vol. V, p. 615.

36 Berger (1966), pp. 321—6; letter Schwarz to Miller, 6 May 1952, NA 724.00/5–652; and letter, Alexander to Miller, 16 May 1952, NA Miller LOT. COB issued a press release on the letter from ORIT indicating American labor support for the nationalization program. Dispatch from La Paz, 4 August 1952, NA 824.06/8–452.

37 Galarza and Jackson's report is attached to a letter from Senator Alexander Wiley, Chairman of Senate Committee on Foreign Relations to Assistant Secretary Cabot, 4 May 1953, NA 824.00/5–453.

38 Memorandum of Conversation, Jackson, Galarza, Fishburn and Hudson, 23 April 1953, NA 824.00/4–2353.
39 *Ultima Hora*, 3 May 1953 and commentary in Office Memorandum, Hudson to Cabot, Mann and Atwood, 11 May 1953, NA 611.24/5–1153.
40 Negotiations over tungsten contracts with the United States was a particularly sore point. When the US lost its mainland Chinese suppliers in 1949, it encouraged new investments in tungsten with long-term contracts at above market prices. Bolivian producers signed contracts through 1956, but after nationalization with tungsten again plentiful, the USA refused to honor its contract with the Bolivia's nationalized mining company. Finally, after selling no tungsten for more than five months, COMIBOL, in late April 1953, agreed to a formula discounting $10 dollars from each unit of tungsten to compensate the former owners. The USA then agreed to honor its contract so long as the tungsten was delivered under the label of the former owners. Telegram 104, Andrade to Foreign Ministry in La Paz, 18 August 1952, BMFRA notebook CL–353 and Telegram 88, Guevara to Embassy in Washington, 24 September 1952, BMFRA, notebook CL–352; Telegram 77, Guevara to Embassy in Washington, 27 April 1953, BMFRA notebook CL–354 and Andrade (1976), pp. 130, 153 and 163.
41 Telegram 87, Guevara to Embassy in Washington, 8 May 1953, BMFRA, notebook CL–354. Telegram 104, Andrade to Foreign Ministry in La Paz, 11 May 1953, BMFRA, notebook CL–354.
42 *Ultima Hora*, 13 June 1953; Telegram 96, Guevara to Embassy in Washington, 27 June 1953, BMFRA, CL–354; and Telegram 98, Guevara to Embassy in Washington, 9 June 1953, BMFRA, notebook CL–354.
43 'Bolivia Swings "Left" — How Far?' Interview with Víctor Paz Estenssoro, *US News and World Report*, 5 June 1953, pp. 68–72; and Telegram 132, Andrade to Foreign Ministry in La Paz, 12 June 1953, BMFRA, notebook CL–354. Other indications of Bolivia's decision to fall in line behind the United States during this crucial period can be found in Joint Weeka, 12 June 1953, NA 724.00 (W)/6–1253. Joint Weeka, 19 June 1953, NA 724.00 (W)/6–1953; Joint Weeka, 26 June 1953, NA 724.00(W)/6–2653; Joint Weeka, 3 July 1953, NA 724.00 (W)/7–353; and Joint Weeka, 18 September 1953, NA 724.00 (W)/9–1853.
44 See Cabot's comments on Bolivia and Guatemala: Cabot (1955), p. 86.
45 Memorandum of conversation, Jackson, Galarza and Hudson, 29 April 1953, NA 724.00/4–2953; memorandum of conversation, Milton Eisenhower, Andrade and Bennett, 17 June 1953, NA 611.24/6–1753; and Andrade (1976), pp. 171–2.

46 A fuller discussion of President Eisenhower's role and views concerning the Bolivian aid package can be found in Lehman (1997).
47 Press release 354 of 6 July 1953, reprinted in the *US Department of State Bulletin*, vol. 29, no. 734, 20 July 1953.
48 Dispatch 243, Memorandum of Conversation, 2 December 1954, NA 824.062/12–254.
49 Knight (1986), vol. I, p. 485.
50 Josefina Zoraida Vázquez and Lorenzo Meyer note the irony: 'To Ambassador Wilson, it was only natural for the Mexican government to be a dictatorship. This explains his initial optimism after the coup: everything in his opinion was back to normal. Wilson never realized that his efforts had not served to restore the status quo ante but that, to the contrary, they had hastened the arrival of the real revolution.' Vázquez and Meyer (1985), pp. 108–9.
51 Katz (1981), p. 152.
52 Katz (1998), p. 541.
53 Katz (1981), pp. 571–3.
54 *Ibid.*, pp. 577–8.
55 Knight (1986), vol. II, p. 449.
56 See, for example, Pike (1977), pp. 291–2.
57 Joint Weeka, 3 July 1953, NA 724.00 (W)/7–353.
58 Almaraz Paz (1988), pp. 17–18.
59 *La Nación*, editorial of 25 August 1953 in Rodrígo (1955), pp. 332–3.
60 Almaraz Paz (1987), p. 123.
61 Fellman Velarde (1981), pp. 353–4.

REVOLUTIONARY VISIONS AND ACTORS

CHAPTER 5

Revolutionary Memory in Bolivia: Anticolonial and National Projects from 1781 to 1952

Sinclair Thomson*

1781 … 1825 … 1899 … 1952 …[1] In 2002, if we look back over two and a half centuries of history in Bolivia, revolution may be the idea that most commonly frames collective imagination of the past. The mere recitation of dates is enough to summon up a spectral presence of leaders larger than life, insurgent masses and rampant militia, echoes of grandiose and incendiary discourse, scenes of destruction and renewal, triumphant climax and denouements of betrayal. Beyond their dramatic and symbolic resonances, the dates carry a set of abstract connotations: anticolonialism, race war, independence, republicanism, liberalism, federalism, nationalism, populism, class struggle. But does revolution provide the narrative for a coherent history of social struggle and transformation in Bolivia? Is there a long historical arc spanning from 1781 to 1952 and beyond — from the great anticolonial revolution that swept the southern Andes to the national revolution, whose fiftieth anniversary passed this year with remarkably little fanfare?[2] If we begin by looking back to the crisis and upheaval of the late-colonial era, is there a postcolonial history that helps elucidate the meaning of revolution and nationhood in Bolivia in the twentieth century?

These are questions that arise out of a nationalist imaginary and its dissolution. Fifty years after the 'national' revolution, a moment of presumed collective unity or at least profound social convergence, what strikes me as significant is, first of all, that we should ask such questions. Of course, because of its effects, the national revolution has come under fire from different camps for some time now. (1985 is another charged date that many would add to a list of counter-revolutionary moments.)[3] And of course many Bolivians would continue to defend the virtues and achievements of the national revolutionary tradition, drawing upon some of the historical symbols or analytical categories mentioned above in order to do so. Yet the nationalist narrative normally leaves out the single most important revolutionary moment in the history of the country's indigenous majority: 1781. When, more exceptionally, its exponents have included that moment, the history has been interpreted in such a way as to downplay or transpose its meaning. The questions noted above force us to rethink the history of colonialism and nationalism in Bolivia, to note the lapses in nationalist representations of history and to confront the contrasting forms of revolutionary memory past and present. As a historian of the revolutionary experience in the late-colonial Andes, I wish to focus in this essay on the relation between 1781 and 1952, in terms of this issue of collective imagination and remembrance.

My interpretation here is influenced by a small set of synthetic works, primarily political essays within Bolivian studies over the past 20 years that have in different ways offered an analytical perspective linking the eighteenth to the twentieth century. The authors I have in mind are Silvia Rivera Cusicanqui, René Zavaleta Mercado, Xavier Albó, Víctor Hugo Cárdenas and Florencia Mallon.[4] Building on their work, I want to examine historical representations of late-colonial Indian politics and uprising, especially as expressed in the nationalist moment of the mid-twentieth century. One of the findings of this chapter is that revolutionary political forces around mid-century shaped the particular contours of the historical awareness or neglect of 1781. I would suggest that the more recent interest in revolutionary dynamics of the late-colonial period, which these authors display, is likewise prompted by a new political cycle involving potential or real popular insurgency over the past 30 years.

The first point to note, however, is how often 1781 and 1952, the starting and end points for a long-term vision of revolution in Bolivia, have *not* been conceived of in conjunction with one another. If each stands for a powerful revolutionary experience, the two tend not to generate analogies or comparison, or indeed even inhabit a common historical frame. Where the two are commented upon together, and this more often than not only implicitly, they tend in fact to evoke antitheses. Let us consider some of the outlines and evidence for this disjuncture.

The revolutionary experience in the jurisdiction of Charcas or Upper Peru in 1780–81 was in fact complex and heterogeneous. Distinct regional movements emerged in different political and military theaters. Aymara communities headed by Tomás Katari combined judicial tactics with armed mobilization to overturn colonial political authority in the region of northern Potosí. Insurgent communities promoted a tentative alliance with creole elites to seize power in Oruro. Aymara communities under the leadership of Túpaj Katari joined forces with Quechua troops under *Tupamarista* command to sweep across the district surrounding Lake Titicaca and besiege the city of La Paz. Though overlapping and interconnected in certain respects, these movements retained substantial autonomy as regional movements. Each of these movements contained within itself diverse tendencies, rather than any single political project. The character of each movement also shifted over time, depending upon political and military conditions.

Despite this complexity, the experience in Upper Peru is often summed up in terms of several marked characteristics: radicalism, racial antagonism, violence and the power of base-level mobilization. These features are particularly associated with the regional theater of La Paz which became the crucial site for military conflict between insurgents and colonial forces in the second phase of the revolutionary war, once José Gabriel Túpaj Amaru had been captured and Cuzco secured by royalist forces in April of 1781. In Cuzco, the insurgent leadership was made up of Indian nobles, along with mestizos and creoles, that is to say a multiethnic sector of colonial society that possessed a relative degree of prosperity or honorable social standing. In Bolivia, by contrast, the revolutionary leadership and the revolutionary subject generally were of relatively more subaltern condition: that is, largely Indian and peasant.[5]

The Revolution of 1952 represents a sharp contrast. Again we could point to distinctive regional, ideological and temporal aspects present within the experience. Nonetheless, there emerges a conventional notion of the revolution that emphasizes its unitary national character as a multiethnic and multi-class alliance of workers, peasants and professionals under the direction of the Movimiento Nacional Revolucionario (MNR) cadre and leaders. The revolutionary leadership supplied by the party is that of a middle-class or petty bourgeois and a mestizo or creole intelligentsia, while the revolutionary subject in general is that of the 'people' defined in opposition to a seigneurial and oligarchic '*Rosca*'.

Continuing in these highly simplified terms, which are after all the nationalist historiographic inheritance, the result of comparison is a marked divergence between the two cases. 1952 to 1953 winds up not as the ultimate national fulfillment of the initial anticolonial impulse. Instead it represents a moment of racial and class convergence, whereas 1781 stands for antagonism and a parting of ways between creole elites and the indigenous majority that would have long-lasting implications. By this account, 1952 has more in common with the insurgent moment of 1825. The independence experience has often been treated as an intra-elite struggle upon which Indians looked with a detached gaze, or one in which they were manipulated from above and mobilized as cannon fodder. In fact, we know that popular participation was a reality of the Independence Wars, even if the political loyalties or alignments were diverse, including royalist military engagements as well as support for the 'little republics'. The outcome in any case would be a new republican polity with creole political leadership and the indigenous peasant majority assumed within a national community of 'Bolivians'. That is, colonized Indian subjects were conceded a putatively egalitarian and undiscriminating national identity, even as they were disenfranchized and excluded from the formal sphere of politics and citizenship. 1952 would in fact operate here as the fulfillment of 1825 insofar as it expanded the rights of citizens that were formerly restricted by the antidemocratic framework of the republic's institutions.

In the Bolivian historical imagination, the fulfillment of 1781, by contrast, goes unrealized in later revolutionary moments. Though elements of polarization and radicalism recur, the prospect of a revolutionary Indian subject and leadership, that is to say, indigenous political autonomy or hegemony, does not re-emerge forcefully until the late twentieth century, after the breakdown of the mid-century populist interpellations. This is evident in the *indianista* and *katarista* discourses employed by Aymara intellectuals and the peasant trade-union movement beginning in the 1970s.[6] If *indianismo* splintered into countless political particles, and *katarismo* waned as a self-conscious political movement, they generated effects that were widespread and warranted co-optation by the creole intelligentsia and political parties. The potency of the *altiplano* uprisings since 2000 testifies to the vigorous ramifications of these very seeds. Felipe Quispe at the head of the Bolivian Peasant Trade-Union Confederation (CSUTCB) reflects a new recombination of *indianista* and *katarista* ideological and political elements.[7] While 1781 is invoked both to condemn and to glorify Indian peasant mobilization today, these contrary interpretations both reaffirm the significance of the great anticolonial movement within present historical memory.

As noted above, the historical disjuncture between 1781 and 1952 is related to a geographical disjuncture in the southern Andes during the initial revolutionary moment. The previously indicated contrast between the regional experience in Cuzco and that of the southern Andes in the second phase of the insurrection is exemplified by the figures of Túpaj Amaru and Túpaj Katari who are commonly taken to be antithetical. José Gabriel Condorcanqui, who took the name 'Tupa Amaro' in claiming hereditary descent from the last Inka monarch, executed by Viceroy Toledo in 1572, governed over the towns of Tinta, Tungasuca and Surimana and maintained long-distance commercial relations throughout the southern Andes. He and his relatives were, if not the very wealthiest and most prestigious members of the Andean nobility in Cuzco, of legitimate Inka lineage and respected kuraka status. He and his commanders were educated, moved comfortably in upper strata of Cuzco society, and the peninsular generals who negotiated with them face to face were struck by their cultural refinement and self-confidence. Amaru himself emerges in the historiography, both academic and popular, as a dignified, honorable, stately character, bearing an enlightened protonational vision ('that creoles, mestizos, *zambos* and Indians live together like brothers in a single body and expelling the foreigners') and a coherent program for political reforms.

Túpaj Katari was a small-time muleteer of humble community origin, a *forastero* resident in the Indian town of Ayoayo whose suprising ascent to political power reflected the bottom-up surge of peasant community forces in the southern Andes in contrast to the Indian noble- and cacique-led mobilization in Cuzco and the district to the north of Lake Titicaca. In keeping with the contrast, he is represented in much historiography as fearsome, crude and violent, if not downright barbarous. Where Amaru was princely and diplomatic, Katari was a warrior, with little political vision and the brazen display of subaltern masculinity. Rather than the inter-ethnic alliance associated with Túpaj Amaru, he is associated with the agenda of race war. In contrast to the petty bourgeois and inter-ethnic profile in Cuzco, Katari represents an exclusively peasant and Indian revolutionary subject and leadership. While Amaru could stand in the refulgent light of national glory, Katari was banished to the dark netherworld of atavistic racial savagery.

René Zavaleta Mercado put the distinction this way:

> In effect, two wings or tendencies can be discerned in [the general movement]. On one hand, a political line that we might call peasant or ecumenical for all of colonial society (an *Inka* program for all Peru), incarnated by Condorcanqui himself but also by the Rodríguez brothers [in Oruro] and even their forerunner Tomás Katari [in Potosí]. On the other hand, a millenarian, militaristic and ethnocentric wing, which is expressed directly and rather ferociously in the figure of Julián Apasa… If Katari was more bloodthirsty, extremist and terrible than Amaru, the latter held a project for all, a utopia which was not merely utopian.[8]

The comparison with Peru is again instructive if we look at the twentieth-century political memory of 1780–81. The figure of Túpaj Amaru was sanitized and rehabilitated, beginning in the 1940s, to conform more closely to a nationalist vision — denying the radicalism, racial antagonism and violence of the civil war, or projecting it onto the later stage of the insurrection.[9] In the early 1940s, Peruvian scholars Francisco Loayza and Luis Eguiguren were publishing their volumes of primary source material collected in the archives of Peru, Spain and New York.[10] Peruvian historian Daniel Valcárcel believed that Amaru, while challenging misrule in Peru, had remained loyal to the king and therefore advanced only an underformed, protonationalist project. He was in other words a precursor of emancipation and could be inducted as a junior member into the pantheon of heroes of Independence. His historiographic rehabilitation was followed by a symbolic appropriation in nationalist political discourse, most notably in the Agrarian Reform instituted by the military regime of General Juan Velasco Alvarado (1968–75).

There was no equivalent appropriation of Túpaj Katari, however, in the nationalist historiography, political discourse, or arts and letters in mid-twentieth century Bolivia. Katari and his movement were largely absent from the intellectual and political panorama in Bolivia, but even when they were acknowledged, they remained marginal and awkward points of reference. The 'silence' or amnesia surrounding the late-eighteenth century Andean insurrection was initiated intentionally and immediately by colonial authorities in the aftermath of the revolt and was perpetuated by creole political leaders in the first century of 'national' political life.[11] Focusing on the region of La Paz, let us take a look at the way in which the late-colonial revolution was forgotten, trivialized, evaded or resignified in the period of the nationalist revolution.

For the first few decades of the twentieth century, the siege of La Paz was scarcely mentioned in public discourse. The single most important historical text of the time, the *Historia general de Bolivia* (1922), was the work of the conservative positivist Alcides Arguedas. His book never touched the topic of the Indian insurgency and began its actual chronology with creole revolution in the early nineteenth century. Arguedas's critical chapter on the Bolivian races portrayed Indians as feminized and domesticated subjects since the time of the Conquest.

This silence was not due to social order and tranquility, for Indian uprising was a stark reality in 1899, as well as in the 1910s and 1920s. At such moments, fear of an Indian attack could grip the minds of white urban and rural residents. Anxiety erupted, for example, in 1921 during the revolt in the town of Jesús de Machaca. One satirical journalist took the occasion to mock paranoia about Indian invasion of the city of La Paz and cannibal feasts.[12] Was his humor the trivializing flip-side to hysteria, in other words equal confirmation of elite preoccupation? The president of the Republic, Bautista Saavedra, whose troops sacked Jesús de Machaca in reprisal and massacred hundreds of Aymara community members, denied any legitimate political purpose to the uprising. Rebels, he declared, held on to an 'ancient hatred against the white race' and were irrationally seeking the 'restoration of Incaic communism'.[13] Here were the elements of a redeployed colonial discourse about Indians. Yet curiously enough, no explicit references to 1781 appeared. Was the parallel so obvious it needed no stating? Or was this the work of fierce psychic repression resulting from traumatic violence and fear? In the absence of any concrete explanation for the silence, we are left with only negative possibilities and shadowy psychological interpretations.[14]

This silence would obtain until after the Chaco War (1932–35), when Bolivian society was churning with political unrest. Networks linking hacienda peons, free communities, urban workers and leftist organizers had formed to challenge the seigneurial order. Socialist and radical *indigenista* currents were combining, both ideologically and practically, in fertile experiments. In such a climate of political polarization and popular mobilization, the late-colonial revolutionary experience finally began partially to resurface in public discourse. This was not a widespread phenomenon, occurring as it did mainly among intellectual and political sectors of the opposition. Yet its existence was revealing of emergent nationalist and radical outlooks at the time, and would have long-lasting effects.

In 1942, Gustavo Adolfo Otero published his *La vida social del coloniaje*, which made no mention whatsoever of the great Andean insurrection. Otero was a respected intellectual and 'independent' congressman only recently allied with the traditional parties. His omission was in keeping with a tradition of conservative amnesia. Yet that same year, other developments indicated a break from tradition.

The first was of an especially eccentric sort. Zacarías Monje Ortíz, a playwright of folkloric and *indigenista* bent, received a prize from the municipality of La Paz for his unprecedented biographical study of Túpaj Katari and his movement.[15] In it, the Aymara leader appears not only as a protomartyr of American freedom, but as a great and mystic soul, a solar man and telluric hero. Monje indulges in 'theological disquisitions', drawing for example from Mayan calendrics and esoteric Egyptian allegory, to portray Katari as a racial prototype reflecting a bizarre blend of metaphysics and evolutionary theory.

Monje was disturbed by the tendency of Bolivia's historians to downplay what he considered the truly revolutionary nature of 1781, and their tendency to dismiss the Aymara leader as a rude and vulgar character. These airs of intellectual superiority (*caciquismo*) towards the native population followed in the tracks of colonial historians and reflected a continuing creole vice of 'absenteeism', an originally European refusal to value and identify with America. The consequences of this were threatening: 'If we continue thinking and feeling like colonials, we contribute towards the growing European disdain for the Iberoamerican region.'[16]

Writing in 1941, Monje's nationalism was inflamed by world events. Two years after Franco's triumph and concurrent with Hitler's invasion of the Soviet Union, he warned of an impending threat of Hispanic recolonization of America, with phalangism as the mask for pan-Germanic expansion. At the same time, he denounced Soviet infiltration of trade unions and proclaimed democracy the only form of government suited for Ibero-America. But these more conjunctural concerns were laid out against a more sweeping visionary backdrop. For Monje confidently asserted that Ibero-America was poised to supersede the Anglo-American or Yankee civilization as the supreme race in the evolutionary development of mankind.

After establishing the grandeur of the Aymara caudillo, Monje's study proceeded to shift in tone. Katari's spiritual development was ultimately inadequate for the historical task, lacking above all in intellectual qualities, and the race he personified was in decline. Not fully possessed of his divine essence, his value lay in his aspirations for American freedom, yet he was unable to bring them to fruition. Katari was but an adolescent of Iberoamerican revolution, while Pedro Domingo Murillo and his creole compatriots of 1809 were the adults.

Monje's position here — that Katari transmitted the flame of liberty to Murillo — was quite awkward, for it obliged him to gloss over the overt and bloody conflict that existed between Indians and creoles in 1781.[17] Monje was forced to acknowledge this contradiction, yet he could offer no justification for it.[18] Indeed, at no point did he find fault with or question creole political conduct in 1781. While he began by challenging the colonial foundations of Bolivian historical memory and urged they be abandoned, he subscribed in the end to a teleological nationalism that evaded the problem of Indian/creole relations. In keeping with his broader vision of Iberoamerican racial-civilizational destiny, his idiosyncratic *indigenismo* yielded to an exaltation of creole leadership to fulfill Bolivia's spiritual mission.

Also in 1942, Augusto Guzmán fashioned the first portrait of Katari in the arts. A young intellectual from Cochabamba whose political involvements inclined to the left, Guzmán published his *Tupaj Katari*, a hybrid form of novelized historical biography, in Mexico two years later. His protagonist is an epic hero, an Aymara rebel following in a line of creole and mestizo insurgents who had dared to rise up against Spanish domination.[19] Katari's profile is burnished and embellished. Though Julián Apaza was in fact crippled, evidently by poliomyelitis, Guzmán presents him as virile and physically robust. Though his political status was never consolidated in his own community, where his low birth was well known, he appears as a respected cacique in the biographical novel. Similarly, the portrait of Katari's consort Bartolina Sisa, a *chola* who has taken up Indian customs, is sanitized to dispel potential doubts in the reader's mind: she is said never to chew coca to excess nor to neglect her physical hygiene.

Despite his charisma and perspicacity, Katari eventually succumbs to melancholy and obsession after the capture of Bartolina. Guzmán thus attributes the true political and intellectual direction of the movement to the Tupamaru command. Yet even the vision of the Inka commanders was limited, Guzmán asserts, since the Indians had essentially backward-looking, restorationist political aims. The French revolution, proclaiming the rights of man, had yet to occur, and only in the nineteenth century would mestizos and creoles be able to carry the anticolonial struggle through to successful completion.

The stark violence employed by insurgents is not excised from Guzmán's story, yet neither is it explained. The effect is one of shocking drama, yet little insight into the motives, strategy or psyche of the protagonist. Guzmán acknowledges that the larger confrontation was, as his lettered audience might expect, a war between the 'rival races'. Yet he goes on to add, adopting a Marxist idiom with sharp implications at the time he was writing, that the uprising was a case of class struggle provoked by economic exploitation: 'the first sign of the decomposition of feudalism, whose liquidation is still pending in certain respects'.[20] Guzmán fails however to recognize the implications of this. If indeed 1781 exposed such profound class and ethnic conflict, the Indian and peasant struggle cannot be comfortably fitted to a narrative of national unity in which creoles and mestizos fulfill the historic role of redeemers of 'the people'.

A more celebrated work, Carlos Montenegro's *Nacionalismo y coloniaje*, bears comparison here. Montenegro, like Guzmán, was a moderate and nationalist leftist of Cochabamba origin. He headed the important socialist (and pro-fascist) paper *La Calle* and played a major role in the founding and early leadership of the MNR. His essay, written in 1943 and published the following year, only slightly after the inception of the party, constitutes a foundational text of Bolivian nationalism.

Montenegro's powerful essay was, on one level, an inquiry into the history of print culture and journalism, and on another, a historical thesis about Bolivian national identity that reflected the political ideology and strategy of the MNR. In this account, Bolivian society was divided into two parts: the dominant colonialist and anti-Bolivian minority and the aspiring nationalist majority. At the root of the conflict was an attack perpetuated by colonialist historiography against the historical memory of the Bolivian people. This devastating force needed to be countered by a great defense of the national community, nothing less than the restoration of patriotic history (*historia patria*). The formation of national consciousness required an unprecedented historiographic project, 'oriented not only toward circumstances, but toward the future'. A unified scheme of the Bolivian past would be sustained by 'the national concept, as an affirmative and hence creative and perpetuating historical energy'.[21]

Montenegro's counter-narrative begins with a survey of late-colonial rebellion in Upper Peru. Yet it is an account in which Indian insurgency is closely identified with Túpaj Amaru and subsumed within a history of the multiethnic masses' common struggle against Spanish rule. The mestizo Alejo Calatayud, who led the Cochabamba plebian riot of 1730, and Sebastián Pagador, the creole firebrand during the uprising in Oruro in 1781, stand out as the exemplary protagonists of popular protest. Only passing mention is made of the 'brothers Katari', a blurry reference conflating the distinct regional insurgencies in the hinterlands of Potosí and La Paz.

Montenegro entirely skips over the disturbing aspect of ethnic and class polarization in 1780–81, in order to get to 1809 and the final phase of independence struggle. Here class analysis is explicitly rejected in order to justify a populist strategy for national revolution. As the unified efforts of creoles, mestizos and Indians in independence revealed, Montenegro argues, a revolutionary challenge to the upper classes is only guaranteed through an alliance between middle- and lower-class groups. In the final analysis, the significance of Montenegro's text is that his aggressive project to decolonize Bolivian historical memory in fact operated to recolonize it in new terms. It was now the creole and mestizo elites — refigured as 'popular' subjects by

Montenegro — who occupied the hegemonic position within a liberated 'national' community. In this rewriting of history, the actual anticolonial content of Indian struggles was erased and replaced by a nationalist narrative that would indeed have 'a perpetuating historical energy'.[22]

Enrique Finot's *Nueva historia de Bolivia*, published in 1946, offers another point of comparison for this discussion. Finot was an eminent and classical liberal intellectual from Santa Cruz aligned with more traditional political forces as well as an experienced diplomat. Writing in the mid-1940s, he did not ignore the late colonial struggles of native peoples altogether. Rather he adopted colonial discourse to describe the overall experience of the insurrection as a 'race war' in which Indian hordes engaged in criminal and bloody mayhem. Yet he also sought to point out some of the complexity of the experience, thereby rendering it more palatable for nationalist taste. There were understandable economic motives for Indians in Chayanta, valid political motives prompting creole involvement in Oruro and mestizo influences in Tupiza as well as La Paz. In the end, he maintained, these were the 'true preliminaries for the revolution of independence'.[23]

Guzmán, Montenegro and Finot took different tacks in the face of the uncomfortable features of Indian peasant politics in 1780–81. Guzmán sought to recast the figure of Katari but offered no coherent or revealing insight into the violence and social contradictions of his age. Montenegro preferred to look altogether elsewhere for the revolutionary subject. Finot's tone betrayed his distaste for the Indian role in the events. The three of them, however, shared an underlying assumption that coincided with that of contemporary Peruvian scholars, as noted above, as well as the great Argentine historian, Boleslao Lewin. The latter's magnum opus, *Túpac Amaru, el rebelde*, published in 1943, propounded the view that the eighteenth-century Andean rebellions were the precursors to Latin American Independence.

By the early 1940s, then, a teleological nationalist narrative had emerged and was circulating widely in neighboring South American countries. Indigenous struggle, especially in the southern Andean highlands, posed a central problem, but this was rather awkwardly resolved by treating it as one more current in the confluence of forces leading toward national independence. Insofar as Indians were considered in their own right, the rehabilitated figure of Túpaj Amaru cast an imposing shadow over Túpaj Katari and other peasant leaders in the south. These other regional figures attained only tentative and secondary status at best, and the colonial and class contradictions that they confronted in their own political struggles went downplayed in the nationalist historical narrative.

The most exceptional voice for the time was that of Alipio Valencia Vega who wrote *Julián Tupak Katari: Caudillo de la liberación india* in 1948 and saw it published in Buenos Aires in 1950. To situate Valencia Vega, we must begin by looking at his long-time political comrade Tristán Marof (the nom de guerre of Gustavo Navarro). Marof was a brilliant contemporary of José Carlos Mariátegui, and a foreign correspondent for Mariátegui's journal *Amauta*. Like the great Peruvian Marxist, Marof sought to root a socialist modernity in Andean soil, and he drew upon radical *indigenismo* in order to accomplish this. Marof did not simply imagine a glorious Inka past as a source of cultural inspiration. He also had first-hand experience of Indian community insurgency and had worked with urban radicals in Chuquisaca in order to back the *ayllus* of Chayanta during their rebellion in 1927.[24]

While in exile in Argentina after 1927, Valencia Vega teamed with Marof and other socialist revolutionaries to found the Grupo Túpac Amaru. The group organized opposition to successive oligarchic governments in Bolivia and against the country's involvement in the Chaco War. They were later joined by other Bolivian exiles in Chile and Peru to found the Partido Obrero Revolucionario (POR) in 1936. The POR subsequently divided between José Aguirre Gainsbourg, who sought to create an orthodox and doctrinaire Trotskyist vanguard, and Marof, who preferred a broad socialist front. After returning to Bolivia, Valencia Vega became a congressional deputy for Marof's Partido Socialista Obrero Boliviano (PSOB). In 1940, he also attended the First Inter-American Indigenista Congress in Pátzcuaro, Mexico, where he presented a paper on labor regimes and agrarian property in Bolivia. He held other ranking posts in the PSOB in the 1940s, including that of general secretary of the party.

Valencia Vega's study of the late-colonial insurrection focusing on La Paz thus merged revolutionary socialist analysis with a passionate *indigenista* commitment to Indian emancipation. In this, it must be seen as a final expression of the creative vision that Marof had developed in Bolivia since the 1920s. Today, Valencia Vega's book is more important as a document of radical political culture in the mid-twentieth-century Andes than as a contribution to eighteenth-century scholarship. Read in the historical context in which it was written, the book stands out for the originality of its analysis and for its politically charged passages. It is interesting above all for the way it stretched beyond the limitations of other nationalist and socialist analyses at the time. In fact, its underlying orientation suggests parallels with political and intellectual tendencies over 50 years later.

In spite of its limitations, the book is a substantive one. *Julián Tupak Katari* is the most fully elaborated account of 1781 by any Bolivian author prior to María Eugenia del Valle de Siles's account of 1990. Though he conducted no archival research for it, Valencia Vega did engage seriously with the finest scholarship of the day and with published primary sources. He wielded the 'tool' of Marxist analysis in rather awkward, self-conscious fashion and his discursive tone occasionally turned blunt in denunciation.

Yet there is coherence to his vision, rigor and depth to his presentation of historical material and brisk economy to the narrative.

Valencia Vega begins from a critique of elite thinking about the native population since the time of the first Spanish chroniclers. Since Indians never had historians of their own, their character and their past had been deliberately distorted, denigrated and covered over. Dialectical materialism was therefore needed to clear away the historical 'smoke screen'. The indigenous insurrections of the late eighteenth century, in particular, had been cast into shadows from which they never emerged. The founders of the republic never seriously examined the problem of Indian slavery and servitude, and colonial attitudes hostile toward Indians were solidly maintained by urban and provincial elites until the present.

Following from this analysis, Valencia Vega called for a new approach to history written from a non-Spanish and a non-colonial standpoint, and his own study aimed to fulfill this program: 'It is an inescapable task of socialist generations to eliminate the smoke-screen created by historical falsification, to tear down prejudices and to interpret the mass movements produced in colonial America, and especially among the great indigenous multitudes, in their true human and social content.' It was also an urgent task at the time he was writing. The land problem was inseparable from the Indian question, as Mariátegui had insisted, and racist sentiment — 'left over by colonialism as a pernicious inheritance' —blocked resolution of both. The late-colonial Indian revindications, he therefore affirmed, continued to be of 'palpable actuality'.[25]

Valencia Vega categorically rejected the common notion that the insurgency was a race war fought by hate-filled and bloodthirsty savages. The movement was a legitimate political struggle born of the internal economic conditions and social contradictions of the Spanish colonial order. Indians made up the agricultural and mining 'proletariat' that produced the wealth of colonial America, and they assumed the role of revolutionary subject due fundamentally to this exploitation. Túpaj Katari was not an 'impostor' who had placed himself at the head of the peasant insurgents through deceit, another common conception inherited from the counterinsurgent colonial officials. He was instead a revolutionary caudillo who knew from direct personal experience the contours of class domination and who naturally gave expression to the popular consciousness of the age. In contrast to Amaru, Katari was a man of the peasant masses and he shared and represented their more radical political aims. The movement throughout the southern *altiplano*, whose foremost leader came to be Túpaj Katari, constituted the left wing of the Indian insurrection generally. While Tomás Katari and Túpaj Amaru each brought their own strategic intelligence and political vision to the insurgent struggle, Katari's greatest contribution was a lucid awareness that the oppressed Indian majority could never achieve redemption under colonialism.

If creoles and mestizos did not heed the call of Túpaj Amaru, it was ultimately because their own class privileges were guaranteed by the colonial state. Neither group was willing to go along with a project, most evident among the Aymaras led by Túpaj Katari, that would have placed maximal political and economic power in Indian hands. While a few 'Indo-mestizos', imbued with an exceptional sense of social justice and humanity, took up the Indian cause, the greatest failing of the movement was the inability to forge a class alliance with poor laborers, mainly mestizo artisans, in the cities. This was not ultimately the fault of Indian leaders, yet it deprived them of access to military knowledge and firepower that were required for the war effort.[26]

What is strikingly different about Valencia Vega's account, compared to the others we have seen, is that the experience of 1781 is not subsumed within a nationalist teleology culminating in 1825. Creole and mestizo protagonists are not invoked to represent a mass, popular revolutionary subject in the late colonial period, and the gains of independence are seen as profoundly limited in social terms. In the mid-twentieth century, Bolivian society is marked by the ongoing legacies of colonial prejudice, exclusion and domination. While clearly influenced by radical *indigenismo*, he presents his own stance and interpretation as socialist. Yet it is also noteworthy that his conception of Indian emancipation does not require an enlightened (creole or mestizo) vanguard leadership. Nor does he rely on teleological certainties about the outcome of the class struggle, with peasants eventually realizing their rightful role as supporters of the (mestizo) urban/mining proletariat's dictatorship. His vision thus harkens back to the original Andean socialism of Mariátegui and Marof, and it anticipates the historical consciousness and political projects that would emerge a quarter century later in the form of Bolivian *katarismo*.

Conclusions

In the early twentieth century, there was an uncanny silence, a conspicuous absence of public historical discourse about the great insurrection and civil war that consumed the Andean highlands in the late-colonial period. This amnesia or lack of overt historical consciousness continued to mark Bolivia through the moment of national revolution. Yet this chapter has tried to show that a measure of historical reflection on the anticolonial movement of 1781, which we have been unaware of until now, did in fact emerge in the decade leading up to the national revolution of 1952.

In periods of social turmoil and potentially revolutionary change, contemporaries may become keenly aware of the revolutionary past and use it to work out their understandings of the present and future. The evidence presented here of overt historical awareness of 1781 in the mid-twentieth century is mainly associated with emergent radical and nationalist forces, rather than oligarchic counter-revolutionaries. Indeed, there was a stronger tendency towards silence on the part of more conservative or traditional intellectuals (from Arguedas to Otero), than towards vocal neocolonial discourse (though we get a subtle sense for Finot's hostility). Among those radicals and nationalists who did take up 1781 (from Monje Ortíz to Guzmán to Montenegro to Valencia Vega), engagement varied according to their own political and ideological agendas.

The case of Monje Ortíz is somewhat distinct. Unlike the other authors noted, he was apparently not aligned with organized political forces on the left. What preoccupied him were not so much the internal struggles involving class and state power in Bolivia, but the struggles in the international arena involving fascism, communism and Iberoamerican sovereignty. Thus, 1781 fired his imagination not because nationalism for him was bound up with the prospect of internal revolution, but rather with resistance to external neocolonialism. Yet in another respect, Monje Ortíz only anticipated subsequent historiographic expressions. His was the first to feature Túpaj Katari in a sustained modern interpretation of Bolivian history, and his peculiar effort showed that 1781 does not lend itself to a nationalist narrative.

Within revolutionary nationalist discourse, it was the creole independence movement that generated the most historical attention. Seventeen eighty-one, by contrast, was much more difficult to accommodate within nationalist memory and teleology. The great insurrection and civil war was a time of radical polarization and violence, in racial and class terms, and one in which Indians claimed the right to political autonomy and even leadership over potential allies. The late-colonial experience of Indian peasant community mobilization thus posed a challenge to the thesis of a populist multi-class and multiethnic alliance that mestizo and creole *movimentistas* would lead. The severed head of Túpaj Katari could find no convenient niche in the nationalist pantheon. Yet even if ethnic and class antagonism were downplayed, and popular mobilization were recast in the more appealing mold of Túpaj Amaru, as in Peru from the 1940s on, there was still the awkward problem of Indian rule, whether over themselves or over others. Ultimately then, despite the different strategic recourses available for historical representation, there was no natural and straightforward way to reconcile the anticolonialism of 1781 with the nationalism of 1952.

For revolutionary socialist narratives in the mid-twentieth century, 1781 also held upsetting implications. The teleology by which vanguard militancy would lead towards the dictatorship of a proletariat, backed by peasants, did not fit with ideas of Indian or communal autonomy. Only two years after this classic Marxist revolutionary scenario had been articulated for Bolivian miners in the Tesis de Pulacayo, written under strong Trotskyist influence, Alipio Valencia Vega was finishing his account of Túpaj Katari as a leader of Indian emancipation. The Andean socialist tradition of Marof, in other words, was the one radical tendency that could imagine a past and future at least partially in terms of Indian community struggle and political autonomy. Yet this was a marginal tendency on the left by mid-century, and the national revolution, with its peasantizing project and corporatist unionism, would make it difficult for any such tendency to grow.

In the aftermath of 1952, political mobilization and memory directed towards more autonomous aims would not begin to stir again for another twenty years. Out of this subsequent phase, associated explicitly with Túpaj Katari, in the form of *katarista* trade-unionism and the ideological critique of internal colonialism, 1781 would again be reimagined and on a new scale with fuller indigenous engagement and leadership. That this phase has not come to an end, despite the many premature pronouncements of the death of *katarismo* and the CSUTCB, is evident in the uprisings of April and September 2000. The ongoing conflicts in the countryside once again reflect aspirations for Andean self-determination at odds with internal colonial conditions, making 'Bolivian nationalism' an ever more questionable imaginary.

NOTES

* I would like to give special thanks to James Dunkerley, Laura Gotkowitz, Olivia Harris, Brooke Larson, Silvia Rivera and Seemin Qayum for stimulating exchanges involving the themes of this chapter and comments on an earlier draft of it.

1 1781 — The great Andean insurrection symbolically headed by Túpaj Amaru in Cuzco reached its culminating phase in current-day Bolivia. 1825 — Upper Peru achieved independence under the command of Bolivarian forces, liquidating the last royalist military opposition in South America. 1899 — The Federal War pitted southern conservatives against northern Lliberals, with a relatively autonomous insurgent force under Indian command erupting in its midst. 1952 — The Movimiento Nacional Revolucionario (MNR) comes to power after heading a popular uprising to overthrow the oligarchic old regime.

2 The MNR itself held only a perfunctory ceremony in the Plaza Murillo on 9 April. The lone academic event dedicated to the revolution was the II Congress of Bolivian Sociology held in May. Even media attention to the anniversary, in the form of editorial and opinion pieces, was minimal.

3 1985 — The MNR instituted an orthodox neoliberal economic model and began dismantling structural reforms, such as the nation-

alization of the tin mines, put into place in 1952.

4 Rivera Cusicanqui (1984, 1993); Zavaleta Mercado (1986); Albó (1987); Cárdenas (1987); Mallon (1992). I should also acknowledge here a set of references upon which I have heavily relied for biographical information throughout this essay: Abecia (1973); Klein (1969); Arze (1984); Finot (1975 [1944]).

5 There is a voluminous literature on the eighteenth-century rebellions in the Andes. For panoramic treatments, see Lewin (1967 [1943]); and O'Phelan (1985). A brief set of regional bibliographic references would include: Serulnikov (1998) on nothern Potosí; Walker (1999) on Cuzco; Cajías (1987) on Oruro; and Valle de Siles (1990) and Thomson (2003) on La Paz. For a recent discussion of historiography, and of the character of distinct regional movements, see Thomson (2003).

6 *Indianismo* and *katarismo* refer to two cultural and political movements headed by Indian intellectuals in Bolivia. These tendencies can be distinguished from the sorts of mestizo and creole *indigenismo* that developed in the Andes and Mexico in the first half of the twentieth century, both in aesthetic and official state spheres. *Indianismo* involves a unilateral emphasis on racial or ethnic antagonism of colonial derivation and has found expression in a multiplicity of political parties centered around charismatic individual leaders. *Katarismo* emphasizes both racial/cultural and class oppression and developed in tandem with peasant trade unionism.

7 Felipe Quispe Huanca, nicknamed 'El Mallku' (preconquest Aymara chieftain), was a longtime indianista party militant who founded the Túpak Katari Guerrilla Army. He emerged from political imprisonment and became elected as maximal representative of the CSUTCB. Under his leadership, the CSUTCB set up road blockades that paralyzed transportation and trade on the *altiplano* and isolated the capital city of La Paz in April and September of 2000.

8 Zavaleta (1986), pp. 87, 91.

9 I draw the notion of Túpaj Amaru's 'cleansing' from communication with Cecilia Mendes.

10 1942 was the 200th anniversary of the birth of José Gabriel Condorcanqui and of the opening salvos in the insurrectionary movement led by Juan Santos Atahuallpa, who also claimed Inka ancestry, in the central sierra and adjacent lowlands of Peru.

11 Even after the new resurgence of Amaru and Katari as symbolic figures in the twentieth-century Andes, the Andean insurrection has continued to be marginal at best within international literature on the Age of Revolution. This historiographic effect is similar to the 'silencing' of the Haitian Revolution discussed by Trouillot (1995).

While his argument is taken to an extreme — maintaining that slave emancipation was and has continued to be entirely 'unthinkable' — Trouillot's notion of the trivialization and banalization of the Haitian experience remains important and is quite applicable to much international scholarship to the present.

12 *La Ilustración*, vol. 1, no. 9, March 1921. I am grateful to Seemin Qayum for this reference.

13 Cited in Klein (1969), pp. 69–70.

14 The memory of 1781 among Indians themselves is even less evident in the early to mid-twentieth centuries. I have seen no evidence of it, for example, in the discourse of the *caciques-apoderados* who directed community legal struggles against hacienda encroachment, nor was it present in the *ayllu* educational experiment in Warisata (Carlos Salazar Mostajo, personal communication). I suspect that further investigation will ultimately yield new findings, however. Forrest Hylton (personal communication), conducting dissertation research into Indian involvement in the civil war of 1899, has found evidence that the memory of Túpac Amaru was in fact alive among Andean communities.

15 Monje Ortíz relied for his work on a sparse and somewhat antiquarian historiographic tradition in La Paz. Others in this tradition who had devoted some attention to the siege of 1781 were the bibliophile Manuel Vicente de Ballivián y Roxas (1977 [1872]); the geographer and folklorist Rigoberto Paredes (1973 [1897]); and the encyclopedist Nicanor Aranzaes (1915). Subsequent publications in this *paceño* tradition would include those of Imaña Castro (1971; 1973); Costa de la Torre (1974); Crespo Rodas (1974; 1982; 1987); and most importantly, María Eugenia del Valle de Siles. Her publications on the urban siege and the regional insurgency more generally are numerous, but for her foremost contribution, see Valle de Siles (1990). Just as I am arguing in this chapter that Túpaj Katari found no convenient niche within the nationalist pantheon, La Paz historians have been unable to treat the siege of 1781 as a glorious episode in regional/urban history, since it leads to no affirming regional/urban identity.

16 Monje Ortíz (1942), p. 37. The pejorative treatment of Katari or outright neglect of his project on the part of Bolivian historians resembles that of the famous counterinsurgent commander of royalist forces and chronicler of the siege: 'Our silence would be equal to that of [Sebastián] Segurola himself and of a hundred other authors on the topic, and this must not continue' (*Ibid*, p. 39).

17 Murillo not only benefited from the structures of colonial social and economic domination, but he had in fact personally participated in the repression of the insurgent movement. See Choque (1979).

18 '*Paradojas, sinrazones, contrasentidos que son inherentes a toda acción humana*' (Monje Ortíz, 1942, p. 187).

19 As Guzmán would add in an epigraph in 1972, at the time of the second edition of his work, the Indian race thereby offered its contribution as a 'nucleus of rebellious, hope-filled and enduring Bolivianness'.

20 Guzmán (1972 [1944]), pp. 95–6.

21 Montenegro (1993 [1944]), pp. 13–18.

22 The impressive staying power of MNRista historical discourse is best seen in José Fellman Velarde's later multi-volume *Historia de Bolivia* (1968–1970).

23 Finot ([1946] 1994), p. 126.

24 For the fullest account of the 1927 rebellion and the alliance between urban radicals and the *ayllus*, see Hylton (2000). On Mariátegui, see Flores Galindo (1989). On the diverse strands of *indigenismo* in Peru, see De la Cadena (2000); Salmón (1997).

25 Valencia Vega (1979 [1950]), pp. 342–3.

26 Valencia Vega did go on to suggest a 'lack of maturity' to the movement due less to internal failings than to the conditions of world history at the time. There had not yet been even a bourgeois revolution in the world, and hence the repercussions of the uprising were inevitably limited. Here we see one of the limitations of Valencia Vega's own analysis — a teleological notion of world historical development shared by other liberal and Marxist historians (as, for example, restated by Genovese (1979) in late-twentieth-century historiography). And yet, it was not a criticism that he seemed deeply committed to, or that would lead him to characterize the movement as backward looking. Nor did it cause him to diminish the aspirations or achievements of Andean insurgents.

Chapter 6

The Origins of the Bolivian Revolution in the Twentieth Century: Some Reflections

James Dunkerley

Mr Mann then referred to the fact that Bolivia is a one-economy country with the Government dependent upon the mining industry and particularly the tin industry, for a very large part of its tax revenues and virtually all of its foreign exchange. He recalled the income of the average Bolivian is about one-fortieth of the income of the average US citizen and there abounds in Bolivia not only economic misery but social strife which makes Bolivia one of the most unstable countries in the hemisphere ... [Mr Symington] stated that while he recognized that the cost of producing a portion of the Bolivian tin from the marginal-type mines was higher than it was in other countries, he thought that question of preventing a collapse of the Bolivian economy should be met by grants from Congress if they were needed rather than by subsidizing the economy through artificially high tin prices.

State Department memorandum, 15 June 1951.[1]

It is sheer incomprehension to assume that Bolivians will cause an upheaval against themselves. The United States and the American people have a substantial venture in Bolivia and I was sent here by the President of the United States, Harry S. Truman, to protect that venture. I therefore implore the Department of State to look for the roots of Bolivia's evils in countries other than Bolivia, for La Paz is as safe a city now as Norfolk, Virginia.

Ambassador Irving Florman, 2 August 1951.[2]

Hay que reconocer que el capitán Sanjinés, a la cabeza de la Escuela Militar de Ingeniería, subió por la Avenida Arce, decididamente. Cuando pasaba por la Belisario Salinas y Arce, desde un edificio en construcción donde estaban Alvaro Pérez del Castillo y otros, armados, hubiera sido matado como pajarito, pero Pérez del Castillo reconoció a Sanjinés y dijo a sus compañeros que no dispararan: era su amigo.

Mario Sanjinés Ugarte.[3]

This chapter reconsiders the two broad explanatory approaches to the origins of the 1952 Revolution. The first, sometimes termed 'the nationalist account', is largely associated with the MNR, cleaves strongly to the experience of the Chaco War (1932–35) and highlights the 'political logic' of a rising activism in almost teleological fashion over 17 years from armistice to revolt. The second perspective shares some features with the first but is more tightly focused on the political economy of the country's strategic tin industry. The tin industry and the mineworkers are centrally important in the chapters by Whitehead, Knight and Lehman. For some commentators, the industry was continuously managed to the prejudice of national interests and to the advantage of an imperialism directed by the British and the United States, as well as the oligarchic owners of the mines. For others, the often adverse conditions of production and world markets during the depression and the post-war years always complicated the sector's commercial viability. The matter was, then, not simply one of heroic mineworkers resisting superexploitation, but also of seeking the most practicable public policy for the industry on the part of an impoverished state.

The account that follows finds points of substance in both broad approaches. I argue, however, that they each need to be revised in the light of the other and to be stripped of the ideological motivations that often lie behind them and that obscure their linkages. It was, in short, neither the Chaco War nor the tin industry that in themselves explained 1952, but precisely their interaction and mutual aggravation. Accordingly, our analysis must simultaneously engage with cultural and economic history.

Points of Departure

Let's start at the end. Within the country there was very little public celebration of the 50th anniversary of the Bolivian Revolution. The MNR held a formal act of commemoration in the Plaza Murillo of the capital, and its *subjefe*, Guillermo Justiniano, produced a dutiful essay for *La Razón* that identified the insurrection of 9–11 April 1952 as opening 'the modern era of national integration, of social inclusion, of mining surplus recovery to reconstruct the country, of a development project'.[4] But there was rather more attention paid to the promise by the party's presidential candidates, Gonzalo Sánchez de Lozada and Carlos Mesa, to distribute hundreds of thousands of hectares of state land to 12,000 families in Santa Cruz: 'Carlos Mesa afirmó que en 1952 se avizoró a este departamento como el futuro, y ahora es el presente de Bolivia.'[5]

It is understandable that even in an election campaign as uninspiring as that of 2002, the concerns of the present and aspirations for the future should prevail over recall of the past. (It could also be that these lines, written in London immediately after the funeral of the Queen Mother, reflect a local approach to ritual and ceremonial commemoration that is poorly calibrated to international sensibilities.) However, I have the sense that what might be termed the 'low commemorative profile' of 1952 in 2002 has less to do with the pressures of actuality than with a misfit between its formal historical calendar and the life-cycles of its principal leaders and figureheads. Subsequent improvements in life expectancy mean that there are still tens of thousands who recall the uprising of three days and two moonlit nights in Holy Week half a century ago. Indeed, at the end of the millennium there were still drawing a pension some 7,500 veterans of the Chaco War, which began 20 years before the revolution and which is often deemed to be its principal cause.[6] This particular anniversary is not 'historical' in the sense that there is nobody alive who can remember its origin, as was the case with the centenary of the foundation of the republic in 1925. Nor does it possess exclusive claim upon a set of martyrs. The deaths of Germán Busch (23 August 1939) and Gualberto Villarroel (21 July 1946) are sensibly remembered as sacrifices on behalf of a process that *would become* the revolution, but even if both men drew on the services of Víctor Paz Estenssoro, neither of these soldiers could fully incarnate a memory that possesses only in part a military character. Juan José Torres, the third officer to be interred in the Museo de la Revolución, was arguably a better representative of the populist military tradition rooted in the Chaco and post-revolutionary armed forces than René Barrientos, who flew Paz in from Buenos Aires to take power in April 1952. However, Torres' own death (Buenos Aires, 2 June 1976) is much more associated with the ideological battles of the late Cold War.[7]

Now these three have been joined by the civilian remains of Juan Lechín Oquendo (27 August 2001, aet. 89), founder of the FSTMB and the COB, eternal champion of syndicalism whose blend of rousing rhetoric and glycerin opportunism infuriated and mollified by turn:

> I am exactly a Bolivian, and life has honored me with the most profound of our passions of the twentieth century: I am a soccer-lover, soldier and miner. I have lived according to the human values I believe in. I believe in goodness, courage and honesty. I have lived flirting with death as every miner in our country, and perhaps this flirting has prevented me from searching for comfort in power and home in money. I am not a judge. I want and will want not only a better Bolivia, but also better for all of us.[8]

Lechín was an essential foil to the enigmatic Paz Estenssoro, whose more provincial demise (Tarija; 7 June 2001, aet. 93) masked a longer and more decisive historical role. The passing of 'Doctor Paz' was of a person who had mutated in true family fashion into a genteel rural patriarch. Moreover, the politician who died was one who not only built and led the Revolution of 1952, but also played a big part in bringing it down in 1964, as well as reversing some of its core public policies when he returned to the presidency, for the fourth time, in 1985. Paz was the core figure of the revolution but never constrained by or fully symbolic of it.[9]

Had he lived another year, Víctor Paz might have provided the focus for a fuller, more energetic remembrance of 1952, but he was, of course, outside of the country, thousands of miles away, during the capture of power. The acknowledged leader of the uprising itself was Hernán Siles Zuazo, a less complex but equally controversial character whose final years were marked by public disappointment. Siles' death abroad (Montevideo; 6 August 1996, aet. 83) may have matched those of Jefferson and Adams by coinciding with national Independence Day. Yet he had generated much less historical respect than personal sympathy — as a man who reacted valiantly to circumstances rather than crafting events. Siles' was the 'human face' of 1952, but his own return to the presidency in 1982 was marked by economic and social chaos so profound that they have all but drowned out his Herculean efforts of the late 1950s to reconcile US pressure with popular expectations unleashed by the April uprising.

In keeping with republican and Bolivarian custom, we should mention the other recently departed presidents and vice-presidents around whom the memory of 1952 moved: Walter Guevara Arze (1996, aet. 84), who split from the MNR even before it fell and whose markedly *cochabambino* contribution remains under-valued, together with Ñuflo Chávez Ortiz (1996, aet. 73), the 'Lion of Inkahausi' in the civil war of 1949, *cruceño* proponent of an agrarian reform that barely touched the population of his own department, and a man more prepared even than Lechín to resign high office. Most particularly, we ought to note the passing of the oldest of the old guard, the writer Augusto Céspedes (11 May 1997, aet. 94), one of the first MNR militants to hold government office, only to lose it almost immediately (on 5 April 1944, just after Carlos Montenegro, who was removed on 11 February by the same US pressure). Céspedes' fierce, fluid prose acquired major book form once a decade — *Sangre de mestizos* (1936); *Metal del diablo* (1946); *El dictador suicida* (1956); and *El presidente colgado* (1966) — in a compelling combination of fiction, reportage, polemic and historical narrative.[10] These four titles — more than the writings and speeches of all those mentioned above — popularized and consolidated the MNR's vision of modern Bolivia and the role of the revolution for several generations at home and abroad.[11] Indeed, as we shall see, so successful has been this *óptica movimientista* that it is still a major target for academics, who are almost obliged to treat the *oeuvre* like the Bastille — a fortress that has to be stormed because it possesses such symbolic importance.

This does not apply to the only text which, in my view, competes with Céspedes' output — *Nacionalismo y coloniaje* by Carlos Montenegro. The reason is simple enough — this inspired interpretative essay was written in the immediate wake of the Catavi massacre of December 1942 and published in May 1944, within six months of the Villarroel government coming to power — the book forms part of the *ideológico*-intellectual origins of the revolution, not a subsequent defense or justificatory recasting thereof.

Although its effective rejection of a distinctive colonial identity, dismissal of class conflict in the independence struggle, narrowly dichotomous presentation of political life thereafter and celebration of the emancipatory power of the journalistic word are all legitimately open to critique, Montenegro's work is so palpably in and of its time that it has to be taken as an historical rather than critical subject. Few of those (many) who have a view on Montenegro argue that he is any less important because incorrect.

This might have been different had he continued to publish and polemicize what José Antonio Arze bluntly called his 'fundamentally nazi ideas'.[12] But Montenegro died within a year of the MNR reaching power, killed by a cancer of the bladder that limited his government service to a few weeks as ambassador in Santiago (New York; 11 March 1953, aet. 49). His was the first state funeral of the revolutionary era, but Montenegro could not be considered a martyr in the same way as, say, Vicente Alvarez Plata, who also died (15 November 1959, aet. 35) in the service of the MNR, but at the violent hands of others.[13]

Montenegro's intellectual legacy was most effectively carried forward by René Zavaleta Mercado, who never shook off this influence, nor that of Céspedes' pungent historical characterizations, nor the sobering experiences of official life (deputy 1962; minister of mines 1964) and exile (1971–84), even as he dug deep into new reserves of Marxist theory. Zavaleta belongs to the next generation — the mestizo who will consult the *yatiri* when the enlightenment runs out of puff; the nationalist who is sufficiently socialist to be published by Casa de las Américas; and the Marxist sensible enough to leave political parties before they became doctrinal, let alone sclerotic. His early death (Mexico; 23 December 1984, aet. 47) deprived us of a fully developed vision of that original historical sensibility already so distinct from that of his contemporaries, such as Fernando Baptista and Guillermo Bedregal.

Of course, historiography is never the exclusive property of the victors, and it is definitely not so when those victors spent a scant dozen years in power and retake it only 20 years later with many of their original policies reversed. Yet the MNR's effective 'move to the right' after 1964 – and certainly after 1985 — had the effect of limiting and softening a conservative criticism that had been so vitriolic in the 1940s and 1950s.[14] It may have been a higher democratic vocation that led Hugo Banzer to decorate the dying Lechín in May 2001, but such a public act would have been inconceivable in 1951 and 1961, let alone 1971 and 1981 (and Lechín had plenty of upper-class and right-wing mates). The MNR's exchanges with the orthodox right were almost always interesting, and they confused most US observers, whose own ideological outlook meant that when Paz returned to power in 1952, they could depict him as 'Communist of the Right' leading a 'blood-drenched comeback of the totalitarian MNR' whereas he had left office in 1946 directing a 'nazi-type tyranny'.[15]

The left, by contrast, was comprehensively split by the MNR, which after 1946 quickly recruited a good portion of those who preferred direct action to earnest reading groups.[16] The pro-Moscow current lost such ground in the late 1940s that the PIR dissolved itself in 1952 and the Young Communist Party (1950) ventured little beyond the provision of 'popular front criticism' and a stern invigilation of Lechín's FSTMB leadership. For these militants the MNR may well have been 'insufficiently radical', but the PCB was completely unprepared for the subsequent arrival of Che Guevara and the imposition of a Cuban 'praxis'. Proletarians with a narrow syndicalist history, they did not need the likes of Debray to instil confusion and humiliation, but they got him and a good deal else besides. Bolivian communism never acquired an authoritative historiographical voice, not even in Sergio Almaraz, whose critique of the tin oligarchy in *El poder y la caída* (1967) postdated his departure from the party, and whose critique of the MNR in *Requiem para una República* (1969) showed an even more marked shift from dialectical materialism to social psychology.

On the other hand, that sector of Trotskyism which had enjoyed a quite healthy existence in the 1940s preying on the 'Stalinist treason' of the PIR and the 'petty bourgeois opportunism' of the MNR did manage to elbow itself a distinctive interpretative niche. According to Zavaleta, Bolivian Trotskyism was akin to the Salvation Army, but the righteous distribution of paper and ink in pursuit of an heroically unattainable ideal was rarely accompanied by a charitable instrumentalism (operational or musical).[17] It was certainly predictable that Guillermo Lora (born Uncía, 1922, and still vocally very much in the quick) should remark, upon being informed of Lechín's death, that he had never represented the workers' movement — 'yo le dije a él que cabalgaba en dos potros, en la derecha e izquierda, y le advertí que desde ese momento sería mi enemigo y que lo combatiría …'[18]

Once exceptionally rich for its almost ethnographic attention to detail in the industrial relations of the mines, Trotskyism in general, and Lora's variety in particular, lost most of its interpretative authority with the collapse of the 1971 Asamblea Popular, which had fleetingly proffered a practical escape from the deadening hand of abstract formalism and the repudiation of all and any political creativity. Lora has reposed on his omniscient invective, and enough young people have followed this for it to have subsisted in sterility for at least two decades. It is, though, not so hard to see a productive Trotskyism tincture in the work of those who quietly slipped the corral — to feminism, *indigenismo*, critical theory, anthropology — in the mid-1980s, once 'resistance' palpably demanded intellectual risk and originality. It is not in the Trotskyist style and method of denunciation that the younger, archive-based generation of Bolivian historians are taking up the still daunting challenge of writing on 1952. Yet Trotskyist example has provided them with a species of critical precedent and a sturdy set of hypotheses.

Issues at Stake

At this point I should clarify that I am pragmatically treating the 'origins' in my title as inclusive of 'causes', the possibility of which even historians sometimes recognize when processes mutate into events and when synoptic presentation takes precedent over full narrative account.[19] Equally, I am sure that the 'twentieth century' endowed by world time has meaning for Bolivia and in terms that are chronologically about equidistant between the original and the Hobsbawmian 'shorter version' of 1914–89. This 'Bolivian twentieth century' would begin with the Federal Revolution of 1899, which established liberalism in office and La Paz as the seat of national power on the basis of a burgeoning tin industry, and it would end in 1985, with the collapse of the world tin price, the end of mining as a significant factor in national economic and cultural life and under Paz's final presidency, an enfolding of the nationalist tradition associated with 1952 back into liberalism.

On such a schematic basis the narrow causes of a revolution-as-event and the broader origins of a revolution-as-process must include the politics of the tin industry, which, as we can see from Table 6.1, was in continuous productive growth up to 1930, which contracted fiercely in 1930–33, but which continued to dominate the export economy thereafter, averaging 73.4 per cent of total exports in 1929–49.

Table 6.1: Tin Exports, 1900–30

Year	Metric tons (av. p.a.)	Index	Value (£)	Unit Price (£)	% total exports
1900	9,139	100	1,331,466	145.7	41.0
1901–5	13,163	144	1,483,941	112.7	58.7
1906–10	19,333	211	2,620,547	135.8	56.3
1911–15	23,282	254	4,013,239	172.4	51.3
1916–20	27,158	297	7,769,616	286.1	63.3
1921–25	29,129	318	4,984,102	170.6	70.5
1926–30	39,981	437	6,600,753	165.1	73.6

Source: CEPAL(1958), p. 7

Moreover, as can be seen from Table 6.2, Bolivia's place in the international tin market was such that it was often subject to direct global pressures as well as possessing a quite commanding position. The importance of mining, then, requires us to return to it specifically, but even on the most generous estimates of the labor force involved — the figure of

43,000 at the end of World War II is generally accepted — it was less than three per cent of the population, dwarfed in human terms by the agricultural sector and rural society (in which perhaps one third of all mineworkers in 1930 had begun their lives).[20]

Table 6.2: World Production of Tin, by country, 1900–52 (000 tons)

	1900	1929	1935	1940	1948	1952
Ger/Aus.	0.1	0.1	0.0	0.6	–	0.4
Port/Sp.	0.0	0.1	0.1	2.0	1.0	2.4
UK	3.9	3.3	2.0	1.6	1.3	0.9
Nigeria	–	10.7	7.0	12.0	9.2	8.5
S. Africa	–	1.2	0.6	0.6	0.5	1.0
Congo	–	0.1	6.5	12.3	12.9	12.3
USA	–	0.0	0.0	0.4	–	–
BOLIVIA	**9.1**	**47.1**	**27.1**	**42.1**	**37.3**	**33.0**
Burma	0.1	2.6	4.5	4.5	1.1	1.1
China	2.9	6.8	9.4	6.3	4.9	5.6
Indo-Chi.	–	0.8	1.4	1.5	0.0	0.2
Japan	0.0	0.9	2.2	1.8	0.1	0.7
Malaya	43.1	69.4	46.0	83.0	44.8	58.9
Thailand	3.9	9.9	9.8	17.1	4.2	9.7
Indonesia	17.6	35.7	24.7	41.3	30.6	36.2
Aus.	4.3	2.2	3.1	3.9	1.9	1.6
World	85.0	192.2	146.8	235.0	152.0	176.6
Bol %	11.2	24.5	19.7	16.1	24.6	18.7

Note: Columns do not tally exactly because of rounding.

Sources: all but last row: Thoburn (1994), Tables 2:1; 3:1; 4:1, pp. 48, 68, 88. Last row: Ayub and Hashimoto (1985), table SA.13, pp. 87–8.

On the eve of the revolution, agriculture accounted for a third of national GDP, against less than 15 per cent for mining. Thus, although the rural/*campesino* aspects of modern Bolivia are fully and expertly considered in other papers, their sheer and simple importance should be signaled here, not least because most comparative accounts depict the revolutionary role of the Bolivian *campesino* movement as subsequent to — and consolidatory of — that of the working class and urban middle class:

> Although *campesinos* did not officially take part in the Bolivian revolution as they did in Mexico, they in fact 'made' both revolutions. Those *campesinos* in Bolivia who seized land, facilitated by the breakdown of army and police authority in the provinces after 1952, helped undermine the political and economic power of the *hacendados* as a class. Had land not been redistributed, Bolivia at that time would have experienced little more than another coup. Labor already formally gained access to power in the 1930s and 1940s through its ability to name — directly or indirectly through political parties closely associated with labor — government ministries. However, the labor alliances with a segment of the petite bourgeoisie were not sufficiently forceful to displace 'la Rosca'.[21]

And just as we need to register the problems with neat sectoral frontiers, so is it necessary to recognize that international circumstances could rapidly and radically reverse approaches to the civilization versus barbarism dichotomy. The very same British diplomat who apologized to Foreign Secretary Eden for 'being wearisome' over the length to which he had expatiated in May 1945, at the end of World War II, on the Congreso Indigenal — 'an event fraught with great importance for the future history of Bolivia' — was two years later, in the depths of the Cold War, ready to declare, 'when the low mental state of the average Indian, his innate bestiality and his hatred of the white, or near-white, are borne in mind, it will be realized what dangerous consequences such propaganda is likely to engender, particularly with the help of alcoholic stimulants'.[22]

This is just the sentiment that, had he known of it, Augusto Céspedes might well have quoted in *El presidente colgado*, where the Congress is depicted as a 'superficial reform', even though its 'decretos abolicionistas sobresaltaron a los terratenientes feudales que engrosaron las filas de la contrarrevolución'.[23] For Céspedes only the victory of April 1952 would settle the essential social score. His later texts, like the less ebullient *movimientista* accounts, tend teleologically to depict a periodization of 'immediate origins' in which the deeper challenge of nation against colonialism etched by Montenegro is accelerated by the Chaco War (1932–35) and initial postbellum labor militancy (Tejada Sorzano, 1935–36); erratically expressed by the 'military socialist' regimes of Toro and Busch (1936–37 and 1937–39); repressed and rolled back under the *Concordancia* (Quintanilla and Peñaranda, 1939–43); revived in 1943–46 by the MNR in sub-optimal circumstances because of World War II, its own lack of experience and the need for an unreliable military alliance (RADEPA/Villarroel); and repressed anew (1946–52) but with enhanced ferocity because of the betrayal of the PIR and the Cold War.

Writing pretty much at the same time as Céspedes drafted his study of Villarroel, Herbert Klein argued persuasively for the strength of what we might term the 'nationalist interpretation' because the numbers for sustaining any explanation of the 1952 Revolution through economic immiseration and social mobilization did not, to put it bluntly, add up; or at least they did not do so until the late 1940s:

> To almost all Bolivians, the key to the understanding of the revolutionary process lies in the disastrous results of the Chaco War of 1932–35 … (Yet) while most commentators have assumed that the Chaco War created social discontent and economic dislocation, a careful examination of the post-war period reveals neither of these effects. The Indian peasant masses were easily reabsorbed into the feudal land system after the conflict, and the urban proletariat felt no unusual adverse effects or bitter hostility toward the system. As for the popularly accepted thesis of economic dislocation, that too is a myth. The national economy during and immediately after the war showed surprising resilience, and the immediate post-war years brought full employment, constantly rising imports and exports in a favorable balance of trade and at first only moderate inflation … The impact of the war must rather be seen in terms of political dislocations and basic changes in the political structure of national leadership and ideology.[24]

There can be little dispute over the impact of the Chaco War itself. The numbers, necessarily inexact, 'add up' simply by order of magnitude. The campaign of some 36 months — between April 1932 and June 1935 — was mostly fought hundreds of miles from established Bolivian settlements, in an environment thoroughly alien to the 250,000 men sent to the front — a very high per centage of all males aged between 17 and 50 in a population of some two million. Those sent to the front line in May 1934 had originally undertaken military service in 1915; the average age of the cohort demobilized that October was nearly 40, but their replacements included 17-year olds who would be under 40 in April 1952. (Lechín, who served in the Regimiento Abaroa and was wounded in action at Kilómetro Siete, was twice rejected for service because of his youth.)

Only from January 1935, when the Paraguayan offensive on Villamontes was repulsed, were Bolivian forces operating on remotely favorable logistical terms and in familiar terrain. Effective counter-attacks over the next four months led Asunción to seek a ceasefire. The fact, though, is that hitherto Bolivia had raised three entire armies and lost thousands of square kilometers of territory, 52,400 men dead (overwhelmingly through natural causes), 21,000 captured, 10,000 deserters, arms worth at least $4 million and any lingering claim to efficiency and legitimacy on the part of its high command and the old political order which had done much to provoke the conflict in the first place.[25]

In one sense it is remarkable that a state could fund a major international war conducted with the most modern weaponry when it had just declared inconvertibility and defaulted on its international debts in the wake of the Crash. On the other hand, the fact that between 1931 and 1935 the Bolivian government received some £2.5 million, or a quarter of the national budget, in direct loans from three companies — and some 78 per cent of that sum from Patiño Mines and Enterprises Consolidated (PMEC) — shows how starkly dependent it was upon a powerful industrial elite. In a way, the 5,000 new lorries, the tanks, flame-throwers, fighter and bomber aircraft, machineguns, howitzers and mortars bought from Europe and the USA may be viewed as offensive equivalents of the new extractive and concentration equipment installed by Patiño in his Llallagua operation, but all this weaponry proved to be entirely unproductive. It was not the capacity of the new cannon effectively used by Sergeant Víctor Paz's artillery unit in the defense of Villamontes that he recalled, so much as the shared experience of adversity (often fraternity) between men of distinct rank, class and race, as well as between all those of 'sangre mestiza'.

If the Paraguayans happened to be the enemy in the opposing trench — and, remarkably, the Chaco Boreal was contested as if it were a Flanders field — there had never been enduring animus between the two peoples, and the nationalism that emerged from the war was not narrowly xenophobic. For René Zavaleta,

> The country is right when it feels frustrated because, in the mobilization, in the conduct of War, in the everyday struggle, it discovers that it isn't truly a nation. When Bolivians conquer or defend the territorial Bolivia, they become aware of the need to conquer the historic Bolivia whose enemy is not, of course, Paraguay.[26]

The likes of Paz, Siles, Céspedes and Montenegro — all of whom saw front-line action — were quick to declare this baldly and boldly — Céspedes' spell as ambassador in Asunción in the '40s was famously successful. And it may well be, as once suggested by René Arze and increasingly supported by new scholarship, that the rural population was not quite so readily reincorporated into the established structures of power. Dissonant, if not yet dissident, energy was building up, less precipitately, volubly or directly — the timing is more distended than in what Zavaleta terms 'seigneurial space' — but the spark is shared.[27]

Reading Walter Guevara's *Manifiesto a los campesinos de Ayopaya* of May 1946, one is today struck by the incongruous addressing of a Marxist elite rhetoric to a rural audience. But one staccato passage tellingly combines nationalist zeal with the 'horse sense' of common folk:

> How can Americans of the North understand our problem of the indigenous, when they have never dealt with feudal servitude? Who had more democratic vocation, Busch or Peñaranda? The answer is simple for Bolivians, not for foreigners. Didn't Busch rehearse dictatorship? How can a democrat be more sincere than General Peñaranda? The superficial appearance, the only appearance seen from abroad, deceives easily. What is not known in the United States or Uruguay is that there is no poor home in Bolivia that doesn't have a portrait of Busch, while General Peñaranda has been kindly forgotten, even by those who took advantage of him.[28]

Busch it was who personally beat up the 70-year old Alcides Arguedas for writing a critical newspaper article, and he was only with difficulty persuaded not to shoot the tin magnate Mauricio Hochschild for failing immediately to comply with a decree requiring the tin companies to lodge all their foreign exchange with the Banco Central.[29] Yet Zavaleta has a point as strong as Guevara's when he tells that Busch, 'represents the heroic conception of the nation. Rational explanations of the defeat and frustration become insufficient, schematic, discredited, pale.'[30]

However whimsical one deems such a poetics of frustrated collectivity, it was rejected at great cost by the Marxist left, which, having largely gone into exile during the Chaco conflict, sought in the late 1930s and early 1940s to lay the bases for a new and radical syndicalist movement. World War II immensely complicated the challenge facing the militants of the PIR, but they were, after all, Bolivians, and so presumably had the choice between responding to local opinion and borrowing foreign categories, tactics and alliances. The twisting tale of their dilemma is too complex to bear even the briefest paraphrase here. I would, though, argue that it is precisely a failure to comprehend the sentimental and imaginative legacy of the Chaco — rather than their militant pacifism during the war itself — which lay behind the inability of the party leadership to hold onto a significant popular constituency built upon a radical social program and then lost to the MNR.

In Zavaleta's telling depiction, Busch – together with Villarroel and RADEPA five years later — sought to impose a military solution on an historical problem.[31] It was hardly in the nature of orthodox Marxists to sign up to such a proposal.[32] They could not grasp that although Busch, no less than Hochschild, possessed a bank account, his ultimate means for handling economic matters had to be the methods and kit in which he had been schooled and with which he had won fame as a patriot. Busch, however, is a hero because he eventually decided to kill himself and Villarroel because he effectively allowed himself to be killed.

The members of RADEPA responsible for the November 1944 executions at Chuspipata and Caracollo stand no higher than Luis Arze Gómez, responsible for the 1980 assassination of the MIR militants in the

Calle Harrington, and their murderous actions are, to my mind, direct precursors of the lynching of their comrade Villarroel and his aides in July 1946. By the time of the completely unnecessary elimination of Lt. Oblitas in September, a macabre kind of moral equivalence had been reached, and the customary rules of moral economy were restored. Thus, the repression of the protesting but unarmed Potosino miners in February 1947 — at the hands of forces directed by the baleful PIR — created great outrage, whilst the rebel casualties of the September 1949 Civil War, when both sides were armed and the question of power openly recognized to be at stake, were valiant casualties, not mere victims.

This, then, is not an entirely capricious ethical arena, but it is one that has to be respected for the purposes of making an appraisal of the fuzzy field of legitimation. That is the aspect that worries me about John Hillman's comments on Busch's decree of 7 June 1939 requiring all the large mining companies to lodge their foreign exchange with the Banco Central: 'The indispensable technical problem of just how the mining industry was to function under these new conditions was swept aside with a vacuous moral argument about the need to make amends for the past sins of capital flight.'[33]

This is a very good point — we shall have to return to it in a moment — but it is not the most important one. Even as late as June 1939, moral argument prevailed over technical policy. Capital flows were essential, but the Chaco was still the driver of the system. I reckon that Patiño and Aramayo — arriviste and aristocrat respectively, but savvy alike — intuited this and back-pedalled on protestations over profit margins and lesser desiderata of capitalist accountancy. The ever-calculating Hochschild, however, missed the indispensable point that there are markets in sentiment as well as commodities.

The crisis over the decree of June 1939 was certainly exceptional but still part of a pattern that is no longer presentable — whether from *nacionalista* or Marxist perspective — as a seamless, unproblematic and unchallenged class rule. This, I feel, is at the heart of Klein's original focus on the Chaco as historical driver, but it can be seen in other features too. Laurence Whitehead's careful analysis of the electoral record in the mining zones over the period 1923–51 reminds us of the importance of studying local conditions when testing headline hypotheses:

> What emerges is that the pre-1952 system of political representation shaped the process of social mobilization to a considerable extent. The image of unmediated political control exerted by the propertied classes over the disenfranchized masses requires substantial modification. Certainly the electoral system was narrowly based, and had been traditionally subject to manipulation by local elites. However, in the mining zone, such 'oligarchic' patterns of electoral control had started crum-

> bling as early as 1920 … Each brief interval of electoral freedom in the mining camps witnessed an upsurge of political and trade union activity, in which intransigent opposition to the mining management became the touchstone of electoral success.[34]

For our present purposes the key issue here is that of pacing. If, at least until 1946, it is the Chaco that dominates the 'strategic sphere' of political culture, this is hardly an evolutionary impulse; it cannot grow in its own terms alone. Indeed, in some senses, even when revivified by World War II, the Chaco is destined only to fade — to form part of historical memory, a moral marker and evocative index of agency and identity. Its momentum is expediently halted in the name of democracy upon the deaths of first Busch and then Villarroel; each time its revival is more diffuse and discursive. Yet underneath it, moving fitfully backwards and forwards, is a set of sociopolitical conflicts rooted in the mines. After 1946, those came to dominate the political dynamic, the dislocations caused by the Chaco now a familiar feature of the ideological landscape. Nevertheless, these class conflicts certainly began before the war and deserve consideration in their own terms, even if we do not expect to find in them a determining explanation of 1952.

Political Economies, Public Policies

It is much easier to assert the general existence of a tin oligarchy/*rosca minera*/*superestado minero* than it is to demonstrate in detail how such an elite secured its interests and enforced its rule. It is correspondingly tempting entirely to follow or comprehensively to reject the MNR account of the large tin enterprises as omnipotent, the principal bulwark against the attainment of national economic independence and the main conduit for imperialist interests in the country. In practice, as we have seen, there were plenty of ideological challenges at the top, and from the early 1920s progressive organization of the labor force in the mines meant that industrial relations became increasingly demanding. Labor costs could no longer be treated as entirely secondary to technical and financial issues, still less unproblematic items on the balance sheet.

The sparkling exchange between Laurence Whitehead and Herbert Klein of some 30 years ago over the nature of inter- and intra-class power at the time of the Depression yields an interpretative balance in which the big companies (Aramayo; Hoschschild; Patiño), while relatively well protected by their international ties and facing an uneven challenge from labor, still had to contend with significant local pressures with respect to rail rates, the demands of small and medium miners for devaluation and the financing of a state without other significant sources of internal revenue or, after 1931, the ability to borrow abroad. If, as Klein suggests, the companies were not unhappy with President Salamanca's belligerence towards Paraguay, then, as Whitehead indicates, the price of their own domestic belligerence was widespread resentment and sectoral opposition even before war broke out.[35]

More recently, Carmenza Gallo has provided a lucid review of the Bolivian state's dependence on the companies. Equally, Manuel Contreras has highlighted the previously undervalued role of the small and medium mining enterprises as well as revealing the extent to which, from the mid-1930s, the large companies were taxed through state control of their foreign exchange as much as by standard levies on exports and profits (Table 6.3).[34]

Table 6.3: Tax Burden of Patiño Mines, 1924–49

	Export Tax		Profit Tax		Exch. Tax		Others*	
	£000	%	£000	%	£000	%	£000	%
1924–29	205.1	50	119.8	30	–	–	90.3	20
1930–34	69.8	42	7.5	4	–	–	95.5	55
1935–39	74.6	19	19.3	5	216.4	54	84.5	22
1940–44	134.0	12	290.4	24	682.8	59	60.2	6
1945–49	137.6	11	120.8	9	808.1	66	164.8	13

* Import and municipal; universities; Potosí centenary; Cochabamba–Santa Cruz road.

Source: Derived from Manuel Contreras (1993), p. 43.

Table 6.4 relies on the statistics of Walter Gómez, whose numbers are at the core of Gallo's study and also used by Contreras. Here they show the official levels of tin company contributions to the national budget over the two decades before 1952. It can be seen that even before Busch's decree of June 1939, open mining taxes were increasing both absolutely and relative to revenue as a whole. It is, then, not so surprising that after the decree, Patiño, who was safely ensconced in Paris, should feel obliged to give Busch his unalloyed views of the matter:

> In a moderately organized country the burdens of a war and post-war period would have been equitably distributed, but in Bolivia this could not happen; all these burdens have weighed exclusively on mining ... with a tin price of about £160 per ton the mining industry has paid to the state practically 100 per cent of its profits.[37]

Table 6.4: Mining Taxes and State Revenue

	State Rev.	Mining Taxes	% Rev. from mines	Export Value	Taxes % Exports	Tin % Exports
1928	44.89	10.56	23.5	108.04	9.8	75.1
1930	34.83	4.18	12.0	87.67	4.8	76.2
1932	20.50	3.65	17.8	45.56	8.0	72.3
1934	32.40	13.55	41.8	165.44	8.2	79.5
1936	102.06	32.81	32.1	144.01	22.8	61.5
1938	274.27	142.84	52.1	647.30	22.1	63.3
1940	606.02	299.64	49.4	1,678.51	17.9	71.3
1942	976.35	606.83	62.2	3,082.63	19.7	66.8
1944	1,094.99	647.26	59.1	3,094.39	20.9	68.4
1946	1,037.64	491.17	47.3	2,772.05	17.7	70.6
1948	1,393.94	764.20	54.8	7,360.60	10.4	71.1
1950	1,755.44	853.97	48.6	8,253.19	10.3	70.8
1952	3,050.89	1,392.55	45.6	22,070.69	6.3	

Source: Gómez D'Angelo (1978), Table 12, p. 191.

In a series of detailed and energetic articles over the last 15 years, John Hillman has drawn attention to this position and gone beyond Patiño himself to challenge the *nacionalista* account of the social forces in the pre-revolutionary era. For Hillman, 'it is no longer feasible to see that weakness [of the state] as a function of the *superestado*, a power above the state, but rather as a result of the distinctive pattern of class and fiscal relations which makes it impossible for any group, including the large miners, to secure stable alliances'.[38]

In what is perhaps the most revisionist facet of his ongoing reappraisal of the large tin corporations, Hillman shows that it was not only ideologically unsympathetic regimes, such as those of Busch and Villarroel, that retained the 'exchange tax' on the companies (indeed, under Villarroel, Víctor Paz's management of the economy ministry was one of the more friendly): 'all governments, regardless of ideological persuasion, would … be compelled to continue to rely on exchange control', because of overbearing socioeconomic realities.[39] Moreover, this dependence constituted a paradoxical form of power on the part of an inefficient state over the technically efficient but politically and fiscally vulnerable enterprises:

> The companies were never able to reverse the fiscal policy of the state whereby they provided the major source of revenue, and they always had to recognize its power to allocate quotas ... While the state claimed authority over the mining industry, it lacked the administrative capacity with which to sustain it. Conceptualizing the weakness of the state as though it were a function of the large companies misses its internal source.[40]

Here the polemical qualities of the argument may be stretching somewhat too far ahead of its evidence, but Table 6.5 (based on information from Hillman, but an incomplete and amateur confection of my own) does at least suggest a consistency of behavior by the administrations of 1932–52 with respect to controls over the companies' foreign exchange holdings.

Table 6.5: Foreign Exchange Policies, 1932–52

Government	Foreign Exchange Control (%)	Concessions	Other Factors
Salamanca	65	Dividends excepted	Exchange rates of Bs 20 (necessities) and 80 per £
Tejada Sorzano	consolidated		
Toro	consolidated		13 exchange rates
Busch	100 (7/vi/39)	None	'impuesto adicional' of 41% for consolidation of exchange rates; 30% profits tax
Quintanilla	50 (1/x/39)	None	'impuesto adicional' set at 30%
Peñaranda	42 (15/v/40)	None	'impuesto adicional' cancelled
Villarroel	100 (13/iv/45)	40% retained for costs;15% profit remittance	
Hertzog			
Urriolagoitia	100(11/viii/50) 52 (21/x/50)	None	
Ballivián			Tin exports halted (x/51)

Let us follow Hillman through to the logical conclusion of his argument:

> The *superestado* thesis was a very convenient way of simplifying a very complex pattern of politics, but it came at considerable expense. In exag-

gerating the power of the large mines, it overlooked not only the significance of the struggle between Patiño and Hochschild but also the importance of the underlying features of the tin industry and the need to build the administrative capacity of the state with which to address them.[41]

Endgame

One senses here the next — unknown but much anticipated — step in Professor Hillman's project whereby the mines nationalized by the MNR will be shown to be much less effectively managed than under the private companies. This, of course, would hardly be an original position, but it has never been so fully analyzed with respect to the experience of the 1930s and 1940s, and it has rarely been discussed in non-partisan terms. At the same time, Hillman's emphasis upon competition between capitalist firms is a most welcome qualification to past insistence upon the unity of the corporate bloc. His distinction between Patiño's high-grade Llallagua ores and Hochschild's operation based on lower quality primary material at Unificada might carry less weight by the mid-1940s — as shown in Table 6.6 — but it is still germane to policy differences that extended well beyond national frontiers and, eventually, into international relations.[42]

Table 6.6: Tin Production by Firm (annual average; metric tonnes)

	Patiño		Hochschild	Aramayo	National
	Total	Llallagua			
1940–44	19,601	14,616	10,192	2,678	48,921
1945–49	16,022	12,118	9,666	2,607	36,571
(1945)					
grade %		1.9	2.6*		
Recovery %		74.5	71.4*		
Shifts/ton		208	303*		
$/ton					
Labor		444	405*		
Other		556	874*		
Depreciation		39	55		
Total		1,039	1,335		

* Colquiri

Source: derived from Hillman (2002), tables 3 and 4, pp. 60–1.

Hillman also picks up on Klein's early emphasis on the international nature of the large firms (although in the case of Aramayo this, to the best of my knowledge, extends little beyond company registration in Switzerland from 1915). Here the argument might be expected to play more directly towards the MNR's theses on 'imperialism'. Hillman, however, provides a plausible rebuttal of the notion that the enterprises — and indeed the governments alongside which they had to negotiate in an essentially regulated international market — 'sold out' to the USA for lower prices than they could have secured during World War II. Given that, in a way, he is up against Céspedes and Almaraz, Professor Hillman's prose is suitably pithy: 'the notion that the war created a special opportunity for the Bolivian government to secure a substantially greater transfer of real economic resources from the wealthy to the poor is … sheer fantasy'.[43]

This is an unusually complicated issue, but the layperson can make some progress through recognition that no 'free market' for world tin existed between 1931 and 1945, there first being a cartel set up as the International Tin Council (ITC), which administered three production quota agreements (1931–33; 1934–36; 1937–41, all of which treated the Bolivian firms quite favorably), and then a US government price, which, as Hillman convincingly shows, the British were effectively obliged to match. Secondly, Bolivia had never possessed a smelter and so could not achieve full vertical integration within her own borders, giving relatively technical issues of production a strong international projection. Thirdly, the USA neither produced tin itself nor smelted it until 1942.[44]

Until the World War, all the Bolivian companies sent their ore to be smelted in Europe, where Patiño owned a major stake in the large Williams Harvey smelter at Bootle (Liverpool). After the outbreak of hostilities in Europe, Washington built its first industrial facility at Texas City, and from early 1942 began to supplement its imports from the Belgian Congo by buying ore from Aramayo and Hochschild, who eagerly sought to exploit this unprecedented opportunity. Washington had earlier accepted the request from the Peñaranda government not to allow Patiño to build a second smelter of his own in the USA, even though this would have allowed optimal application of the expertise built up at Bootle, because it would also have strengthened the effective monopoly of the company. Equally, after the Catavi massacre Judge Magruder's report to the US government on labor conditions in the Patiño mines gave PMEC a particularly poor reputation within the Roosevelt administration. Nonetheless, in 1944 the USA did buy small quantities of Patiño ore, the high quality of which made a perfect 'sweetener' or catalyst for the smelter of lower-grade mineral.[45] However, there was no substantial shift of the Patiño trade from the UK, not least because London needed to replace the loss of its Malayan imports and also required a high-quality mix fully to exploit the processing of Nigerian ores. Accordingly (and after the requisite bluff-calling and hand-wringing), the British were prepared to match the higher prices offered by Washington. Indeed, they conceded relatively generous allocations of hard currency to both Patiño and Aramayo.

In sum, then, there did exist some margin for the Bolivian companies to negotiate, and Hillman suggests that the Allies only coordinated their tin pool with any real effectiveness in 1942, the first year of its full operation. As measured by import capacity, the companies, which palpably sought to improve their position on both sides of the North Atlantic, increased their real income to 50 per cent above that prevailing before the Crash.[46]Quite whether this chimes with the claim made above by Hillman, that any major transfer would be limited to the realm of fantasy, is a matter for discussion. It does, though, have an important link to the post-war position since, whatever the reasonableness of the price and efforts to secure it, increased production permitted the accumulation by the consumer states of buffer stocks, which were subsequently depicted — and not only by *nacionalistas* — as being vital to the capacity of the USA to 'fix' a notionally free world market price, and to do so at a time when demand was falling. It is this issue, and how it played through into the labor policies of the firms after the fall of Villarroel, when the ousted MNR needed desperately to secure a stronger working class alliance, that strikes me as more salient than charges over missed opportunities from 1941 to 1945.

Table 6.7: US and UK Tin Stocks, 1942–45 (long tons, metal content)

	Ore and metal		Weeks supply	
	USA	UK	USA	UK
1942	132,369	28,072	112	40
1943	135,043	23,335	121	42
1944	118,338	29,943	96	75
1945	100,808	32,600	88	87

Source: derived from Hillman (1990), p. 305.

We cannot know the precise extent of the US buffer stock after the war because this was a state secret. However, Table 6.7 provides a broad indication of the wartime position from which some sensible extrapolation can be undertaken. One should bear in mind that although tin is not a metal extensively used in the construction of armaments, demand would naturally have fallen after the end of the War. On the other hand, the return of supplies in south-east Asia was rapidly followed by the threat of their loss under a communist takeover, most directly, of course, in Malaya in the early 1950s. Under such circumstances, including the communist capture of power in North Vietnam (1946) and China (1949), these 'buffers' could have appeared to strategic planners as less generous than they might seem today.

In the event, of course, it was in Korea that war broke out, driving the open price of tin, which had fallen to around 80 cents per pound back up to $1.03. But that was in June 1950. The depressed market of the immediate post-war years meant that the Bolivian companies' production in 1947–52 was a fifth lower than in 1940–46, and they were now earning less in real terms than in the mid-1920s. Furthermore, the prospects looked worse: ore content was falling and whilst workers as a whole were not as militant as some suggest from the experience of Patiño mines in 1947 and 1949, the labor force was more pugnacious than 20 years earlier. Those laid off for commercial reasons or sacked as political agitators, particularly in 1947 and 1949, not only constituted the first substantial redundancies for a decade, but also took their ill-will back into a new inflationary environment — the level of 33 per cent in 1951 was the highest since 1939. Could the rise in tin price prompted by the war in Korea perhaps salvage the industry and stave off a wider economic crisis?

The irony is that the price rise brought the US government straight back into the market. When the level touched US$2 per pound in February 1951, Washington halted all purchases of metal for the buffer stock, reimposing a state monopoly on imports of the metal (through the RFC). Indeed, the North Americans now effectively drove the price down. Just as John Hillman doubts that the Bolivian companies could have secured a better deal in 1940–42, so I wonder whether by the first months of 1951 even the kind of price rise being sought by La Paz (US$1.50) could have held the crisis at bay. But the fact that the State Department was having problems pushing the RFC into an offer of even US$1.15 suggests that the numbers were very far from adding up. The issue had now taken on a directly political character, and although the traditional account properly stresses the cancellation of the MNR's victory in the presidential poll of May 1951 and the imposition of military rule, we should not lose sight of the enduring contradictions at the level of political economy.

So parlous was the state of the Bolivian economy at the outbreak of the Korean War that in August 1950 even the reactionary regime of Mamerto Urriolagoitia had felt obliged to emulate Busch and reimpose total state control over tin company foreign exchange earnings. A fierce debate with the firms ensued — Patiño had died in April 1947 and Aramayo took the lead protest role — and in October concessions were duly made on that front (Table 6.5), but within weeks, the tin price was again being forced back down. The junta which replaced Urriolagoitia in

May 1951 had no hope of resorting to full control of foreign exchange and was unable to persuade the US to improve the terms of even three-month contracts to purchase. It therefore resolved to cease export of tin altogether in a frankly desperate effort to force Washington's hand.

Aramayo, possibly recalling Víctor Paz's management of the economy in 1944–45, had already considered backing the MNR, whose victory at the polls he knew reflected much more than a protest vote.[47] At the same time, ex-President Hertzog, who had led the anti-MNR campaign of 1947–49, advised the junta itself to nationalize the mines so as to steal the thunder from the party, which had at its fifth congress in February 1951 settled on that policy, agrarian reform and universal suffrage as its platform.[48]

In Washington, the full consequences of this impasse were, by November 1951, beginning to be recognized:

> We understand that the RFC in its negotiations with the Bolivians has argued that the price should be based on the average cost of production in Bolivia. In order to keep the mines operating on this basis it would be necessary for the Bolivian government to control all tin revenues and to distribute them to individual producers so that the cost of each would be met. This is a very dangerous proposal to make to a foreign government. The United States is engaged in trying to protect the interests of American investors in underdeveloped countries against the strong desire of those countries to expropriate and nationalize. If other countries were to learn that the United States Government were proposing such action in the case of Bolivia it would be very difficult for us to protect the American owners of low cost mining properties in other countries. It would be an open invitation to the Chilean government, for example, to redistribute to locally owned copper mines the profits of Anaconda and Kennecott.[49]

The prophetic qualities of this reflection need no extra emphasis here, but it is worth reiterating the fact that six months before the revolution, the US government had contemplated a price arrangement which was a surrogate for nationalization, and that the Bolivian government — an anti-communist military dictatorship installed to keep the MNR out of power — felt it had no choice but to confront Washington by withholding supplies of a strategic commodity at a time of war. Moreover, a leading tin capitalist was considering collaboration with the party that depicted him as anathema to the economic interests of the nation. That same party, observing the deadlock from exile or conditions of domestic repression, was itself jettisoning the strategy of management through exchange control for one of outright expropriation, which at the very least could be conducted in openly nationalist language and draw directly on the legacy of the Chaco War rather than being mired in obscure financial formulae. In that sense, then, the MNR, rather than trimming its ideological sails, was actually reversing its prior economic conservatism. This obviously owed much to the FSTMB and pressure from the left, but it also had its own logic (just as would reversion to a deeper history in 1985).

The economic stalemate at the end of 1951 may well not be deemed a 'cause' of the Bolivian Revolution, but it was a decided mess within which the status quo was unraveling as fast as its opponents were consolidating. Few then or now had much sense of the finer strategic issues at stake, but one could apply to the years 1946–52 the comment made by Laurence Whitehead with respect to the period 1930–35: 'los bolivianos políticamente activos estaban escasamente interesados en un debate académico sobre si las compañías de estaño actuaron peor en la guerra o en la depresión'.[50]

The better known stories of the *sexenio* that we have not told here — of the strikes, repression, the thwarting of a democratic campaign and of the distillation of a partisan program into a common civic cause — all served to marginalize such academic debate. Yet, between the depression that followed a war (1946–52) and the war that followed a depression (1932–35) one finds rather more in common than the univocal account of either *nacionalismo* or political economy can comfortably handle.

Historians, of course, draw a salary for being wise after the event, but in recent years this relatively simple task has been made much more exciting by enthusiasm for counter-factual speculation (something to do with the micro-climates of the Isis and Cam?). In that spirit I should place all the above discussion under a final shadow of doubt. In December 1951, the Ballivián junta set about a task in which it possessed experience and about which it felt confident — the annual process of conscription of some 15,000 young men into military service. By mid-January 1952, these soldiers were in their barracks with the customary crew-cuts and rough uniforms. But their regime was rather different from those of previous cohorts because the regime, in an effort to improve its dire political position, had managed to secure from Chile agreement to repatriate the remains of Eduardo Abaroa, hero of the War of the Pacific. Accordingly, all the way through to the service of reinterment at the end of March, the conscripts exclusively drilled for the march-past. None of the six regiments stationed in and around La Paz had begun to provide their new troops with training in the shooting of a weapon when the uprising took place on 9 April. Perhaps, if they had, Alvaro Pérez del Castillo could have shot Julio Sanjinés and there would still have been no Bolivian Revolution?

Notes

1 National Archives (hereinafter NA) 824.2544/6-1551, reprinted in *Foreign Relations of the United States*, vol. II (1972), pp. 1152, 1154. Mann was Deputy Assistant Secretary of State for Inter-American Affairs. Symington had served six weeks as administrator of the Reconstruction Finance Corporation.

2 'Bolivian Political Psychosis', NA 724.00/8-251.

3 Quoted in Crespo (1996), pp. 134–5. Those who later identified Sanjinés as the 'intellectual author' of the coup of 4 November 1964 which overthrew the MNR might have preferred Pérez del Castillo to have shut up in 1952, but I am inclined to believe Julio Sanjinés' account that he was 'set up' by US air attaché Colonel Edward Fox, who certainly was the guiding hand behind Barrientos' revolt. Interview, La Paz, 24 August 1989.

4 *La Razón*, 10 April 2002. 'la era moderna, de la integración nacional, de la inclusión social, de la recuperación de los excedentes mineros para reconstruir el país, de un proyecto de desarrollo.'

5 *Ibid.*

6 8,603 *beneméritos* and 13,571 widows in 1997. *Hoy*, 9 March 1997.

7 I am here repeating a commonplace that needs refinement. Paz traveled from Ezeiza to El Alto in a meat cargo plane owned and piloted by Walter Lehm, who was suspicious of the military craft put on offer. Barrientos was the co-pilot.

8 Lechín Oquendo (2000), p. 9. 'Soy exáctamente un boliviano y la vida me ha honrado con lo más profundo de nuestras pasiones del siglo XX: futbolista, soldado y minero. He vivido de acuerdo con los valores humanos en que creo. Creo en la bondad, en el coraje y en la honradez. He vivido peinando a la muerte como todo minero de nuestra tierra y quizá este coqueteo me previno de buscar regazo en el poder y hogar en el dinero. Para muchos, estos fueron errores, para otros fueron aciertos. No lo sé. No soy juez. Quiero y querré una Bolivia no sólo mejor, sino buena para todos.'

9 'He was no populist rabble-rouser, but a pragmatic technocrat, committed to modernising Bolivia. It is given to few individuals to change the course of their country's history, let alone to do so twice. Yet that is what Víctor Paz Estenssoro achieved in Bolivia.' *The Economist*, 23 June 2001.

10 His robust approach to criticism and historiography is nowhere better exemplified than in this riposte to, 'un tal Roca, escritorcillo en vía de desarrollo … me refiero únicamente a sus dos premisas iniciales: *El presidente colgado* es un típico libro cespediano: historia indocumentada, escrita en primera persona … Si yo no hubiese sido iniciador de

un movimiento obrero en las minas; acusado en el putsch nazi; preso y confinado; luego ministro de Villarroel; más tarde diputado (como lo fuí también con Busch); si no hubiese sido uno de los fundadores del partido más grande de la historia de Bolivia; subdirector de *La Calle* y acusado en el juicio de responsabilidades contra el gobierno Villarroel — y fuera sólo un arribista silvestre venido a la capital — realmente no podría escribir en primera persona.' Céspedes (1975), p. 187.

11 Although they have acquired great fame, I confess to finding Paz's congressional speeches pretty pedestrian in their reliance upon statistics, quotation and rather labored irony. The competition, though, is rarely sharp, and, in the wake of the Catavi massacre it was surely only necessary to ask why, if the miners had attacked the army first, there were no injuries among the troops: 'Es la clásica fábula, sorprendentemente confirmada en nuestra política, de las palomas contra las escopetas'. *Discursos Parlamentarios* (1955), pp. 149–50.

12 Abecia López (1997), p. 187.

13 Alvarez Plata is generally accepted to have been killed on the orders of the 'cacique' of Achacachi, Toribio Salas ('Huila Saco'), denounced as a 'red' as assiduously as is his contemporary equivalent Felipe Quispe ('El Mallku'). For an interesting discussion of the background of the MNR leadership, see Mitchell (1977), pp. 18–26.

14 Compare, for example, Alfonso Crespo's *Hernán Siles* with the same author's *Enrique Hertzog: el hidalgo presidente* (1997). In 1979 the *falangista* Gonzalo Romero wrote a prologue to the fifth edition of *Nacionalismo y Coloniaje.*

15 *Time*, 21 April 1952, quoted in Lehman (1999), p. 99; Joseph Flack to Washington, 'Diary of a Successful Revolution,' 25 July 1946, NA 824.00/7–2546.

16 'Las diferencias básicas en el funcionamiento político del POR y el MNR, es decir, entre los marxistas ortodoxos y los nacionalistas revolucionarios, fundamentalmente, se resumían en lo siguiente: entre los primeros primaba la capacidad y la audacia doctrinal y teórica, y entre los segundos, la agresividad y la intrepidez práctica en la vida militante.' Moller Pacieri (2001), p. 32.

17 Zavaleta (1990), p. 89. Having a passing acquaintanceship with both Trotskyism and the Salvation Army, I can see the point of the analogy, but the latter certainly provides a much more congenial environment for those who are in a stable heterosexual union and enjoy brass band music.

18 *La Razón*, 11 August 2001. The diary of Juan Carlos Ríos relates a telling exchange from 1954: 'El otro día en una reunión del partido le pregunté al fiero: "El día que triunfe la revolución obera-campesina, camarada Lora, qué cargo ocupará usted, Comisario del Pueblo,

Presidente de la República o qué se llamara?" Me contestó: "No, yo no ambiciono nada; lucho por mis ideas. Con tal de abrir una librería yo estaré contento y seguiré trabajando." Esto me ha decepcionado — les dije a los dirigentes de la COB — yo luchaba para que mi Jefe por lo menos que sea Presidente; como no es así, algo anda mal. Quiero luchar junto a ustedes, aunque sea sin entrar el MNR. Usemos el poder para las masas.' *Hoy*, 6 September 1992.

19 If there were space for such a narrative account, I would probably follow the style of Donald Cameron Watt (1989).

20 Contreras (1993), pp. 4; 42. Ricardo Anaya cites the Banco Minero for a total figure of 57,000 in 1948 (Anaya, 1952, p. 85).

21 Eckstein (1976), pp. 42–3. Ian Roxborough and Alan Knight introduce similar depictions in wider comparisons designed to test the theories of Theda Skocpol, Barrington Moore and Eric Wolf: 'It is unlikely that [major transformations] would have happened if, in the months following the revolution, much of Bolivia's peasantry had not acted spontaneously to take over many of the country's landed estates.' Roxborough (1989), pp. 105–6. 'As the victorious MNR began to sponsor a (somewhat calculating and instrumental) agrarian reform, Indian peasants organised, rebelled and mobilised, breaking the traditional political and economic controls of the landlord class.' Knight (1990a), p. 189.

22 T. Ifor Rees to Eden, 16 May 1945, no. 38; Rees to Bevin, 11 June 1947, no. 68, in *British Documents on Foreign Affairs*, part III, section D, Latin America, vol. 11 (Bethesda, 2000), p. 106; *ibid.*, part IV, vol. 4, p. 183.

23 Céspedes (1975), pp. 196–7.

24 Klein (1969), p. xii. The Bolivian edition of this book, which rapidly became the standard account, is entitled *Los orígenes de la Revolución* (1968), which could, I feel, also have been employed for the original as it devotes 250 pages to the years 1880–1943 and only 40 to the period 1943–52, when the economic and social factors were arguably as sharp as those in the realm of ideas and ideology.

25 The loss of traditional values was, of course, an uneven process. In the aftermath of the Battle of Campo Via Paraguayan Captain Oscar Corrales reported, 'Una patrulla halló a 200 metros de nuestras posiciones, bajo un arbusto, en su catre de campaña, el cadáver del Tnt. Urriolagoitia, junto a él su fiel ordenanza, quien no quizo dejarlo abandonado. "Acaba de morir", nos dijo, "pertenece a una familia distinguida de Bolivia".' Quoted in Dunkerley (1988), p. 173.

26 Zavaleta (1990), p. 49. '… el país tiene razón cuando se siente frustrado porque, en la movilización, en la conducción de la Guerra, en la lucha de los días descubre que no es verdaderamente una nación. Los bolivianos van a conquistar o a defender el país territorial, descubren

que hay que conquistar el país histórico cuyo enemigo no es, desde luego, el Paraguay.'

27 Arze Aguirre (1987). Antonio Alvarez Mamani reminds us of the more obvious reasons why the immediate impact of the war was not uniform: 'la guerra fue un fracaso porque no se podía comunicar. Los campesinos no sabían manejar ninguna clase de armamentos, el clima no les favorecía y nadie era amigo de nadie. Todavía había mucho regionalismo, los aymaras se juntaban en un lado y los quechuas en otro, y se insultaban en sus dialectos … Pienso que el único aspecto de la guerra fue la toma de contacto entre campesinos de todo el país que nunca se habían encontrado'. Alvarez Mamani (1987), pp. 65–6.

28 In Guevara Arze (1988), p. 230. 'Cómo pueden los americanos del norte, que no conocieron jamás la servidumbre feudal, entender nuestro problema del indio? Quién tuvo mayor vocación democrática, Busch o Peñaranda? La respuesta es simple para los bolivianos, no lo es para los extranjeros. No ensayó Busch la dictadura? Cómo pudo entonces ser un demócrata más sincero que el General Peñaranda? La apariencia superficial, la única que se ve desde el extranjero, engaña fácilmente. Lo que no se sabe en Los Estados Unidos o en el Uruguay es que no hay hogar pobre en Bolivia en donde no hay un retrato de Busch mientras que el General Peñaranda ha sido piedosamente olvidado, incluso por los que se aprovecharon de él.'

29 'Entonces llegó a mí y con un gesto rápido me cogió por la solapa, me atrajo hacia sí y me dió un golpe violento sobre la ceja derecha con la mano cerrada y armada de un enorme anillo de oro … Repitió el golpe sobre el otro lado de la cara … Brotó la sangre a chorros por la ceja abierta, la nariz y la boca. Y el dolor, la sorpresa, la indignación, el estupor, el asco, la cólera me dejaron clavado en el suelo, suspenso, inmóvil. Aquello, era tan insólito, tan ordinario, tan bestial y tan salvaje, tan primitivo que hasta la noción de la defensa sentí anularse en mí. No acostumbro llevar armas ni nunca practiqué deporte alguno. Pertenezco, ay! a la casta, la pobre casta de estudiosos que viven en el aire confinado de las bibliotecas y descuidan cultivar el músculo de los brazos para únicamente la sustancia del cerebro.' Arguedas (1979), p. 203. Hochschild was a naturalized citizen of Argentina and probably owed his life to the petition for mercy from President Ortíz.

30 Zavaleta (1990) p. 60. 'representa la concepción heroica de la nación. Insuficientes resultan esquemáticas, menguadas, pálidas las explicaciones racionales de la derrota y de la frustración'.

31 *Ibid.*, p. 111.

32 '…un exceso de identificación con la mentalidad militarista le haría correr el riesgo de ver los hechos de la Vida Social muy "en militar"; sabido es que la psicología del militar es muy inclinada a admitir la

violencia como la ley suprema de la conducta colectiva, a despreciar a los hombres de pensamiento, a los predicadores de ideas pacifistas, etc., por considerarlos unos "ilusos", a juzgar con cinismo y frialdad los dolores físicos y morales de las masas sacrificadas en los planes belicistas.' Arze (1963), p. 119.

33 Hillman (2002), p. 64. At the time the decree was seen as enshrining rather more than 'vacuous moral argument': 'it fits in neatly with a general plan of coordination with Axis principles and in particular with those of Nazi Germany. There has been a disposition in many quarters to take the most favorable view of the decree and to see in it only a measure of the financial extremities of the Bolivian Government resulting in a more drastic control and further appropriation of the profits of the mining industry … there seems little justification for this optimism.' *Mining Journal*, 29 August 1939.

34 Whitehead (1981), pp. 344–5.

35 Klein (1969), pp. 153–4; (1968), pp. 103–8; Whitehead (1972), pp. 72–80.

36 Gallo (1991); Contreras (1993, 1990); Contreras and Pacheco (1989).

37 Quoted in Geddes (1972), p. 281.

38 Hillman (2002), p. 42.

39 *Ibid.*, p. 67. The corrective features of this work should be properly recognized by those, such as myself, who argued that after Busch's death his decree of June 1939 was 'left to collect dust on the statute books'. Dunkerley (1992), p. 34.

40 Hillman (2002), p. 68.

41 *Ibid.*, p. 69.

42 'Patiño worked established mines with high grade ores while Hochschild looked to the development of entirely new kinds of mines with low grade deposits that could only be worked profitably through extensive mechanization … Patiño's response [to the Depression] was defensive and he cooperated with the British and Dutch in forming the ITC to preserve the value of existing mines. Hochschild took the decline in prices as an incentive for cost reduction through mechanization and had no interest in production restriction … Patiño's position was ultimately based on the assumption that the past successes of Llallagua provided a reliable guide to its future. Hochschild's was based on the assumption that he could reinvigorate a declining mining complex at Unificada. Both were profoundly wrong and the criticism that each made of the other's position was therefore correct.' *Ibid.*, pp. 41; 1. *Sic transit gloria mundi.*

43 Hillman (1990), p. 313.

44 In 1903 the British had imposed a 40% tariff that saw off the burgeoning challenge to its world monopoly staged by the works at Bayonne, New Jersey.

45 Patiño tin was exported to the USA for the first time in March 1944. *Times*, 19 April 1944. The British ambassador in La Paz reported of Hochschild, 'He is very pro-United States and not sufficiently grateful for help which he has received in the past from the UK ... He is in continuous strife with the Patiño group of mines but the latter with their greater resources generally get the better of him.' Rees to Bevin, 16 August 1945, no. 71, in *British Documents on Foreign Affairs*, part III, series D, vol. 10, p. 43.

46 Hillman (1990), pp. 307, 313.

47 'Si el MNR hace, por su parte, honor a la legalidad y se somete a las normas de respeto a la dignidad humana, será *La Razón* la primera en reconocerlo'. *La Razón*, 11 May 1951. 'Víctor Paz Estenssoro the new Finance Minister, said the Government would not burden the mining industry, Bolivia's main source of wealth, with taxes beyond its capacity. He added, however, that the Finance Ministry would not be "a lawyer for the mining companies".' *Times*, 27 December 1943.

48 Crespo (1997), p. 181; Paz Estenssoro and O'Connor d'Arlach (1999), p. 104.

49 'Position Paper Prepared by the Acting Deputy Director of the Office of International Materials Policy (Evans),' 2 November 1951. NA 824,2544/11-251, reprinted in *Foreign Relations of the United States. American Republics. 1951*, vol. II, p. 1162.

50 Whitehead (1972), p. 80.

CHAPTER 7

Revisiting the Rural Roots of the Revolution

Laura Gotkowitz

Scholarship on the Bolivian Revolution marks a striking disjuncture: rural mobilization was central to the revolutionary process, yet peasants played a marginal role in the origins of the revolution. The commonly held view of the insurrection is three days of fighting protagonized by miners, workers, party militants and townspeople; the countryside played almost no part. The immediate revolutionary period evokes the antithetical image of a rural world turned upside down. Indeed, petitions demanding land, tax reductions, a labor code and schools poured forth from rural communities as soon as the revolution triumphed. Quickly, rural districts became the site of strikes, and by the final months of 1952, the countryside was enveloped in violence.

Bolivia's intense and extremely influential post-1952 rural ferment mirrored pre-revolutionary mobilization in fundamental respects. Yet scholars rarely emphasize the links between the two. To be sure, numerous works note the 1945 Indigenous Congress and 1947 uprisings as major turning points of the pre-revolutionary era. But they divorce those transformative events from the revolutionary origins and process. If rural mobilization lasted up to 1952, it was either dormant, minor or ineffective. The Ucureña peasantry's leading place in the roots of the revolution resonates as a remarkable exception.[1]

Some work certainly points to rural participation in the insurrection itself, without discounting the MNR's hesitancy. For example, Silvia Rivera notes the existence of *células campesinas* recruited among the independent leaders of the 1947 indigenous uprisings, who were jailed together with MNR militants following the party's defeat in the 1949 Civil War.[2] A crucial contribution of Rivera's work, more broadly, was to show that rural indigenous leaders pressed their communities' claims all the way up to 1952. James Kohl notes, additionally, that the mobilization of peasants was included in the MNR's contingency plan if the first urban uprising failed.[3] Kohl also records the strategic inclusion of some rural activists in the 1949 civil war and 1952 Revolution. Nevertheless, the connections — and disconnections — between rural movements, revolutionary action in the 1940s and the revolution itself are still not fully understood.[4]

At a most basic level, ignoring rural communities' wider role in the origins of the revolution makes it difficult to explain how and why such massive rural upheaval immediately followed the urban-based, three-day insurrection. Not seeing the rural roots of the revolution also impedes a fuller understanding of the revolutionary project itself, for the specific visions and expectations that rural communities and leaders invested in the triumph remain obscure. Although those alternative visions were largely suppressed, they were critical elements of the struggle to define the revolutionary project.

Focusing on the 1945 Indigenous Congress and 1947 unrest, this chapter argues that rural mobilization was central to the origins of the revolution. It suggests, further, that pre-revolutionary rural movements were closely, if tensely, intertwined with the sinuous process of populist state-making in the 1940s. The period of Gualberto Villarroel's short-lived military regime (1943–46) and its unwinding are central to understanding the rural roots of the revolution. Certainly a much deeper history of indigenous mobilization, state-making and agrarian change, and the social and political transformations wrought by the Chaco War, shaped rural encounters with Villarroel and, in turn, the roots of the revolution. The Villarroel era nevertheless constitutes a fundamental turning point, for the regime altered the dynamics of public representation by providing indigenous leaders with a national forum and a series of historic decrees.

The chapter first examines the origins and objectives of the 1945 Indigenous Congress and its relationship with rural political movements. While the 1945 assembly was closely linked with Villarroel–MNR reformism, it originated as a local indigenous project and was testimony to the force of those initiatives. The second section examines the protests that followed the Indigenous Congress. My discussion emphasizes a diversity of political practices; not just armed uprisings but petitions and other forms of peaceful agitation traversed the tumultuous years leading up to the revolution. Exploring this wider range of rural protest makes it possible to see that the countryside remained a site of active political mobilization all the way up to 1952. A close reading of four conflicts from 1947 reveals that the 1947 'cycle of rebellion' not only constituted an assault against landlord power, but was the product of a state-making process over which the state itself had incomplete control. In a most basic sense, the 1945 Indigenous Congress and subsequent unrest are strong evidence that indigenous mobilization remained a powerful political force on the very eve of the revolution. Just as Villarroel faced a highly mobilized countryside when he took power in December 1943, so too did the MNR face a highly mobilized countryside in April 1952. That rural upheaval — decades deep, interlinked with Villarroel populism and masked by three days of calm — was a fundamental source of the revolution.

Villarroel Populism and the 1945 Indigenous Congress

The 1945 Indigenous Congress was a massive, five-day meeting which brought together about 1,500 Indian representatives from large estates and communities of virtually every region in Bolivia. The Congress was undoubtedly influenced by indigenista congresses convened during the same period in Mexico and Peru. In contrast to those events, the principal impetus behind the Bolivian assembly was not the state but forceful indigenous movements. Indeed the regime was accused of convening the Indigenous Congress 'out of fear'.[5] Just before and after Villarroel came to power, a series of rural strikes rocked the countryside.[6] This precarious political situation led Villarroel's closest circle of advisors to convince him to sponsor a national congress of Indians.[7] Before the regime actually offered its sponsorship, however, local leaders grouped in the 'Bolivian Indigenous Committee' (Comité Indigenal Boliviano) had already begun to plan the event. Despite increasing government control, and the inclusion of two members of the Landowners Association (Sociedad Rural) on the organizing committee, 'with voice but no vote', the Villarroel regime could not fully suppress the more radical proposals endorsed by indigenous leaders.[8]

If the government's very participation was compelled by the pressures of rural mobilization, once committed, the Villarroel regime used the Congress to attract new political allies, counter inroads in the countryside by the leftist opposition and promote its own reform program. As for *indigenistas* in Mexico and Peru, education and the modernization of agriculture were crucial state projects for Villarroel and the MNR, the military president's principal ally.[9] Social wellbeing and the creation of a legal order were equally central goals. If any objective was paramount, it was to extend the state to a rural hinterland viewed as stateless. Above all, Villarroel sought to impose the law on an ostensibly lawless countryside.

Government support for the 1945 Indigenous Congress was fundamentally motivated by this concern with regulation and control. In practice, however, Villarroel–MNR backing for the event buttressed the autonomous agendas of local leaders. Two points should be stressed in this regard. First, the Villarroel regime considered indigenous authorities crucial for the very process of state regulation and control. In his inaugural speech to delegates at the Indigenous Congress, the president not only called *caciques* and *principales* (indigenous authorities) of 'haciendas, communities and *ayllus*' his representatives, he entrusted them to keep order and peace.[10] Second, although the Villarroel regime ultimately controlled the official agenda of the Indigenous Congress, it could not manage the *unofficial* agenda backed by local indigenous leaders. The government actually provided a forum where local leaders could publicize their demands.

The earliest concrete instance of preparations for the Indigenous Congress was a September 1944 meeting between Villarroel and members of the Bolivian Indigenous Committee. Comprised of 15 representatives from all over the country, this Committee emerged in late 1943. Although sponsored by the Villarroel regime, local leaders were responsible for organizing the group and its activities.[11] The committee's principal spokesperson was Luis Ramos Quevedo, son of a *piquero* (smallholder) from Cochabamba's Valle Bajo and a long-time rural organizer affiliated with Oruro's labor federation (Federación Obera Sindical — FOS).[12] Before the government had a chance to prepare and publicize its own program for the Congress, the Bolivian Indigenous Committee led by Ramos elaborated a 27-point agenda, which was reprinted in the national press. Of the many demands in this richly detailed plan, the most notable include: 'That the indian be free, secure in his life and work, and respected the same as everyone; that there be special laws and authorities for the indian; and that there be committees of lawyers paid by the government to defend the Indian.' Not coincidentally, the list begins and ends with the longstanding claim that all the land 'belong to the indians' — that it be 'returned to the Community' and belong to 'those who work it ... the indian'.[13]

As the date of the Indigenous Congress neared, rural unrest intensified and landlords' true and untrue denunciations of subversive activity got louder. In this increasingly tense context, government officials abandoned their support for Luis Ramos Quevedo and identified him as the principal agent of an elaborate anti-government program. By the end of April 1945, Ramos and five other 'agitators' were in jail. The approximately 1,500 rural delegates who attended the May Congress nevertheless arrived expecting a discussion of the demands endorsed and circulated by those jailed leaders. News articles published after the Indigenous Congress confirm that many of those items were in fact discussed, even though they no longer appeared in the government's official agenda.

Indeed the final organizing phases can be read as the government's unrelenting effort to reign in the meeting, to control the program and manage the composition of the delegates. With regard to the program, the Villarroel regime was successful; it created an official committee, comprised primarily of representatives from government ministries, which drafted and approved a formal agenda. This official program was embodied in four well-known decrees endorsed by the Villarroel government on the final day of the Congress. The measures called for the suppression or remuneration of free services that rural laborers were required to provide to landowners (mail delivery, weaving, *mukeo*, etc.); the abolition of *pongueaje* and *mitanaje* (forced turns of service in the landlords' home); the establishment of schools on rural properties (but with no reference to schools for Indian communities); and the preparation of an agrarian labor code.[14] The majority of the items listed in the Indigenous Committee's 27-point program no longer figured. Most notably, the items about land and community had been eliminated.

Given the demands and expectations of the delegates, the four formal decrees were fairly modest gains. There was, however, one significant shift. Delegates returned with the knowledge of more favorable decrees and the president's explicit backing. In at least one case, and probably in others, a *colono* was ordered by the minister of government to deliver duplicates of the new rulings to local authorities.[15] Of course making *colonos* direct conduits of the law wholly contradicted the institutionalizing mission of the Indigenous Congress. Rather than resolving a perceived crisis of the law by professionalizing, codifying and standardizing legal practice, the Indigenous Congress exacerbated the turmoil by empowering delegates themselves to be agents of a series of historic decrees.[16]

The 1947 Cycle of Unrest

Over the course of the year following the Indigenous Congress, sit-down strikes became common on haciendas in many regions, with hacienda *colonos* themselves trying to enforce compliance with the 1945 edicts.[17] Just as before the Congress, local leaders and 'outsiders' were accused of copying and distributing proposed laws and fraudulent land titles. As rural social conflict intensified in the months following the Indigenous Congress, police presence in the countryside was greatly augmented.[18] This period of acute political battles, violence and repression culminated in the brutal lynching of Villarroel, in July 1946. The ensuing government — led by Enrique Hertzog — insisted that peasants did not have the constitutional right to organize, but it did not rescind the murdered president's decrees. In some cases, post-Villarroel officials even publicized the 1945 measures. For example, in November 1946, the Prefect of La Paz ordered subprefects to inform the 'indigenous element' that the May 1945 decrees remained in place.[19]

Although the Hertzog government did not abrogate the Villarroel measures, landlords refused to heed them. In and of itself, this repudiation did not cause the rural uprisings that followed Villarroel's death, but the negation was a crucial source of the rebellions. Spanning the departments of Cochabamba, Chuquisaca, La Paz, Oruro and Tarija, and heterogeneous in their methods and demands, the 1947 uprisings were uniformly and aggressively repressed.[20] Much scholarship rightly views this 'rebellious cycle' as a critical turning point, given the extent and scope of the mobilization, the violence inflicted on landlords and the severity of the repression.

For all the truth it contains, this view of the rebellions nevertheless obscures significant continuity, both before and after 1947. In the aftermath of Villarroel's overthrow, attacks against landlord power did indeed take center stage. Insurgents destroyed hacienda houses and harvests. They assaulted landlords, their relatives and hacienda administrators, including the indigenous *hilacatas* or *mayordomos*. Along with hacienda personnel per se, hacienda schoolteachers were also victims of violence. Leaders of post-

1946 actions demanded education, just like their predecessors, but now they also attacked teachers, whom they considered accomplices of landlords. In two cases, Ayopaya and Caquiaviri, teachers and/or schools were attacked by rebels. In Caquiaviri the insurgents assaulted the teacher, dragged him to the plaza and yelled: 'What did you come here to teach, instead of educating you make sure everyone works.'[21] In Pucarani, the rebels not only demanded schools but the right to name the teachers themselves.[22]

Notwithstanding the heightened violence against landlords and their property, in many respects the 1947 unrest resembled the protests that preceded Villarroel's overthrow.[23] Protagonists of 1947 engaged in work stoppages, demanded land and education, called for official recognition of unions, insisted on enforcement of the 1945 decrees and denounced abuses by landlords and local authorities. They also employed a wealth of tactics, not only armed actions but petitions, strikes and mass gatherings on hillsides. In Cochabamba, the assault against haciendas by Ayopaya *colonos* stands out, but there were also less visible protests by a range of social actors. The Prefecture Archive contains mountains of petitions from the 1930s and '40s denouncing excessive *chicha* and muko taxes. Occasional and full-time chicha producers assailed the *licitadores* who levied these lucrative assessments. Likewise, *colonos* lodged complaints and pursued judicial action against landlords, administrators and police they accused of labor contract violations, rape and myriad forms of abuse.[24] 1947 certainly constituted a full-scale assault against landlord power, but armed action was not the only tactic and hacienda *colonos* were not the only actors, and the repression, for all its vigor, did not completely suppress rural political action.

The following pages look in detail at four 1947 conflicts. All are from Cochabamba, where the hacienda crisis was especially deep and where new middle sectors represented a burgeoning commercial counterpart to landlord hegemony. In many cases, *colonos* themselves were deeply immersed in market relations in this region, as buyers and sellers of goods, and even as buyers and sellers of land, land titles and — we will see — papers parading as land titles.[25] The four conflicts illustrate a broad range of motives, aims, actors and tactics, thus confirming that 1947 was a moment of outright rebellion, but not outright rebellion alone. The disputes also highlight some common aspects of the 1947 movements: large or small, the 1945 Indigenous Congress cast a shadow.

Of the many centers of rebellion, the Ayopaya uprising stands out for its magnitude and resonance. Ayopaya province, located in the department of Cochabamba, included a small number of Indian communities (*comunidades originarias*) but was essentially dominated by large estates.[26] Centered in the Hacienda Yayani, the February 1947 rebellion encompassed numerous other properties in the area and involved an estimated 10,000 individuals. In fundamental ways, the rebellion was linked with wider disputes over the law engaged by the Indigenous Congress. The Ayopaya rebels not only appropriated and redefined the state's rhetoric, they enacted their own vision of justice and the law.[27]

Over the course of a lengthy trial, witness after witness makes reference to laws and decrees. Many recall leaders traveling to La Paz in search of guarantees against *pongueaje* or authorizations to create schools and allude to Villarroel and the Indigenous Congress. They identify the leaders of the uprising as individuals who attended the Congress, or people who went to La Paz in search of 'guarantees'. Their references to the 'law' nevertheless center on a rather surprising and certainly implausible thing: a law passed by a revolutionary government that called for the murder of landlords, the redistribution of all the land and that everyone become *comunarios*. This 'law', many of the accused claimed, had been decreed by an existing government, usually the MNR, which was of course not in power.[28] Through loose inference and juxtaposition, the testimony of the accused connects the decrees against *pongueaje* with the demand that all the land be returned to the 'community'. It suggests that a very radical — unreal but palpable — edict to make everyone *comunarios* and all the land a community was one of the most important, albeit unintended, consequences of the 1945 Indigenous Congress.

Even before the uprising, communities in the Ayopaya region struggled to impose their views of the law. Local leaders not only insisted that Villarroel's measures be enforced by existing authorities. They implanted their own officials. One prominent leader apparently told the Indians of the area not to obey the landowners' orders nor any authority appointed by law. He said that they should heed only the *alcaldes*' commands, as the *alcaldes* were higher than any other authorities in Ayopaya.[29] An office of colonial origin, the indigenous *alcalde* was situated both to serve local government — primarily in a judicial capacity — and to represent the community before outside powers.[30] The meaning attributed by Ayopaya's 1940s rebels exceeded both roles: local leaders suggested that the *alcaldes* were both separate from and higher than officials appointed by the state. In their depositions to the court, landlords, foremen and the *corregidor* complained that the leaders not only enunciated such claims but enacted them. The rebels had appointed their own *alcaldes* and even the state's local representative, the *corregidor*. The 'real' *corregidor* was only so in name and title, apparently he no longer held any authority.[31]

Viewed together with this ritual of justice, the Ayopaya uprising not only represents a struggle against labor abuse and exploitation but a process of political empowerment and confrontation whereby the community substituted its own authorities for the state's local representatives.[32] Thus, the most threatening act may not have been the violent culmination of the rebellion, when landlords and their homes were attacked. Before the rebels of Ayopaya ever took up arms, they insisted on complete affirmation of the law and imposed their own authorities, *alcaldes*. In doing so, they not only took Villarroel's command to ensure order at its word. They exposed the state's absolute inability to control its own laws, institutions and lawmakers.

If the Ayopaya uprising was defined by collective action against landlords and local power, the 1947 agitation in Anzaldo — an area of haciendas and smallholdings in Tarata, Cochabamba —operated in the realm of individual exchange. For the plaintiffs, it was nothing more than a malicious swindle.[33] Like Ayopaya, Anzaldo involved a promise to restore or distribute land. It also entailed disputes over local authority. In addition, Anzaldo evoked a third characteristic element of the Villarroel-era mobilization: those ubiquitous forged land titles the government worried about. The defendants were accused of selling them to *colonos* on the Hacienda Churigua. A key witness, the administrator/teacher, charged that the 'instigator' of the rebellion, Virgilio Vargas, had distributed papers 'with the name of titles' and told *colonos* they were sufficient to make them 'absolute owners of the property'. Every *mozo* (*colono*) who wanted to own a small parcel of land would receive one such title in exchange for a contribution of one hundred bolivianos. Vargas also promised the *colonos* education: He was going to travel to La Paz and would return with a teacher who would show them how to read and write on typewriters. In fact he would bring 'typewriters instead of teachers because with typewriters alone it was possible to educate every child adequately, without the need of teachers'. The hacienda administrator's school was 'worthless', Vargas reportedly told the *colonos*.

Both the owner and the foreman seconded the teacher/administrator's accusations. Vargas was the 'intellectual author' of successive uprisings on the property. He had counseled the *mozos* to ignore customary obligations and persuaded two indígenas to collect *ramas* for Vargas's own enrichment. Vargas had tricked the *colonos* into thinking he was a kind of commissioner, authorized to distribute land. He told the *colonos* 'not to do any work for the owners of the property, that the *mozos* were exclusive owners of the land … all they needed to do was contribute some money for trips to La Paz so he could retrieve the titles, the government would give it [the land] to them'. Many other witnesses corroborated these declarations. A *colono* said that Vargas had sold them papers saying they were titles to land that would be distributed shortly. Two others said he 'sold them papers with seals' because the land was going to be turned into a community. Several other witnesses said the papers were linked with a land distribution the government (or revolutionary authorities) would soon carry out.

In elaborating a defense, Vargas asked witnesses to focus on his own social and moral standing. He was a hardworking tailor and smallholder; his wife owned some land in Tarata, which he worked independently. He earned enough to live 'decently'. As they attested to his good character, the witnesses also revealed that Vargas had deep roots in the region and was well known as a kind of local benefactor who assisted *colonos* when they were jailed. Apparently he also visited Churigua and adjacent haciendas to sell *aguardiente* and other goods. *Colonos* in turn frequented his house, perhaps in search of assistance or advice, to pay debts or maintain commercial ties.

Which story was true? Was Vargas a 'ringleader' as the landlords charged, who agitated against landowners and predicated imminent distributions of land? Or was he a more discrete, both loyal and self-interested ally, who quietly defended victims of local abuse while deepening ties of dependency and thus his own local power and authority? Or was he both? The fact that he was a locally known and legitimate defender of *colonos*' concerns makes it hard to see the title-selling as a mere ruse for self-enrichment. But it does not preclude the pursuit of personal interests, whether material or political. In distributing land titles and denouncing the 'schools of the *Rosca* (the rich)', as Vargas called the hacienda school, the artisan-smallholder-merchant perhaps fought two anti-landlord battles in one: the *colonos*' and his own.

The judge failed to note the 'illegible and incomprehensible' land titles in his final ruling against Vargas, but these curious papers were certainly the most compelling proof of the 'agitator's' presumed political intentions. They bear the seal of the Alcalde Mayor of Lechechoto (Mizque), Toribio Miranda. Miranda had been none other than the vice president of the 1945 Indigenous Congress and was a well-known rural leader. Whether or not Miranda or Vargas or both men together sought to pass off unreadable correspondence as property titles cannot be known. In either case, the papers bearing Miranda's seal suggest a link between Vargas, the agitation in Churigua, the Indigenous Congress and alcaldes *mayores*. There was no reversal of local power here, as in Ayopaya. But the correspondence from Toribio Miranda subtly links the Anzaldo agitation with broader disputes over local power unleashed by the Indigenous Congress and Villarroel's overthrow. The figure of the Indigenous Alcalde —although not actually present — represented higher powers here too, for it was Miranda's 'Alcalde Mayor' seal that lent the fake land titles government status. Without the seal, they would have been just papers, not official-looking titles.

Like the judge, the landlord neglected Vargas' connection with Miranda, but he did suggest that the 'instigator' had an ally: apparently Vargas led the *colonos* to believe he had an agreement with the juridical advisor (*asesor jurídico*) of the Security Police, Humberto Calvi. The juridical advisor appears to be a Villarroel-era figure, perhaps a transitional post established before two new institutions proposed at the Indigenous Congress could be installed: the Rural Police (apparently created by Hertzog in 1947) and the Court for Indigenous Affairs (never established).[34] Vargas seemingly persuaded the *colonos* that he had been authorized by Calvi to 'distribute land along with the relevant documents or receipts'.

Vargas flatly denied that he had ever 'raised the name of the juridical advisor'. Whether true or false, the accusation is revealing, for it points to the depth of the hacienda crisis and the growing gap between landlords and local political authorities. That Vargas said he was going to distribute hacienda land with the permission of the juridical advisor, or that *colonos* and landowners believed he said such things, indicates the extent to which landlords' authority had begun to erode. At very least, the allegation suggests that local actors did not unequivocally identify all local officials with the interests of landlords.

The juridical advisor's appearance in another 1947 case, from Vacas (Arani highlands), lends further weight to this interpretation. Here Calvi was referred to as the 'Chief of the Indigenous Department of the Police' and the 'Mediator for the Indigenous Class'. According to landlords, Calvi had intervened in defense of several Vacas 'cabecillas' taken prisoner by the prefect. Rather than being sent to the Chimoré, the indigenous leaders had been freed and were currently at large. Local landlords had charged them with usurping their land: the Indians had risen up, hurled rocks and prevented the landlords' associates from entering the property to inspect the fields.[35] Unless police action was taken, they intimated, there might be a rebellion as serious as the one in Yayani (Ayopaya). As far as the police were concerned, there had been no indigenous uprising. Instead the dispute concerned 'guarantees of possession', for the *colonos* of Vacas were also landowners, and they were involved in civil litigation with the non-Indian owners. The case was a matter for the courts. The landowners did not accuse the juridical advisor of wrongdoing, but they certainly viewed the official with skepticism — as an obstacle — since he refused to call the property-dispute a revolt and thus grounds for police intervention.

A fourth case, from Sacabamba (an extensive hacienda in Tarata), underscores aspects of the preceding examples: the growing autonomy of local authorities from landlords and the multiple meanings of the 1945 decrees. The grievances in a petition brought by two Sacabamba colonos were directed against the hacienda administrator, Fructuoso Ortuño, who also served as *corregidor*, *licitador* of the *chicha* tax, collector of municipal taxes and judge. Ortuño's monopoly of virtually all local offices left no other authority to hear complaints, the colonos said. Their petition accused him of numerous offenses ranging from excessive taxation to insults to seizure of animals and arbitrary detention. They opposed the excessive *chicha* tax Ortuño charged and demanded a substantial refund. They also complained that Ortuño had violated the Villarroel decrees by making the *colonos* sell chickens, lambs and eggs for insignificant prices. Their complaint fell under Decree 318, which explicitly prohibited landlords from demanding the delivery of such goods for miserable payments or nothing at all.[36] But Ortuño's most egregious offense, the petitioners said, was his treatment of itinerant vendors. With no legal right whatsoever, he had begun to tax the people who sold food occasionally in the Sacabamba train station, 'depriving all these poor people from earning a modest means to sustain themselves and their families'. The petition concludes with the demand that Ortuño be dismissed from the *corregidor* post and relieved of his duties as administrator; at a minimum, he should be compelled to cease committing abuse.

To justify the request, the petitioners noted the Villarroel decrees. Indeed the decree against *pongueaje* and *mitanaje* stipulated the dismissal of local authorities that required *colonos*, *comunarios* or residents of towns to provide services — such as the provision of goods — without payment.[37] The Sacabamba *colonos* nevertheless extended the significance of the decree to include myriad forms of abuse. Their petition thus underscores both the force of Villarroel's proclamations and their local significance. To the petitioners, the decrees meant redress against abuse or exaction and the right to punish or expel authorities who violated legal and moral norms in a most general sense. The Sacabamba colonos did not actually remove the *corregidor*, as the Ayopayeños had done, but they invoked the Villarroel edicts to achieve the same end.

Taken together, it is clear that one key source of the agitation in Ayopaya, Anzaldo and Sacabamba was the erosion of close ties between landlords and local authorities. In different ways, each case illustrates how new social actors — sometimes as allies of *colonos*, sometimes as new exploiters — contested landlords' domain. In Ayopaya, indigenous *alcaldes* not only attacked *hacendados* and their property but also expelled the local authorities that underpinned landlord power. In Anzaldo, a smallholder-artisan-merchant defended *colonos* and distributed land, apparently with the (phantom) backing of Mizque's indigenous *alcalde* and the police juridical advisor. In Vacas, the same police official refused to heed landlords' cries of rebellion and insisted on Indians' property rights. In Tapacarí, another important center of the 1947 mobilization, the *corregidores* were repeatedly accused of inciting subversion.[38] In Sacabamba, a *corregidor*/administrator/tax collector not only pursued his own interests but blamed the landlord for alleged abuse. Here, the *corregidor* certainly was not an ally of Indians — but nor was he a tool of landlords. Ortuño had a strong personal stake in local economic networks and had achieved certain autonomy. In response to the *colonos*' petition, he simply said they should take up their grievances with the *hacendado*.

A second common element of the unrest is the role the 1945 Indigenous Congress and the Villarroel decrees played in the construction of a 'language of contention'.[39] One recurring motif of the Villarroel and post-Villarroel protests was an association, direct or indirect, between the decrees, the government and the promise of land; sometimes that promise was combined with allusions to the 'community'. Ayopaya and Anzaldo are two especially striking examples, but other 1947 incidents include similar claims. For example, the leaders of an attack against the 'Botijilaca' property (La Paz) claimed to have the support of the government, which was going to 'return land to the indígenas'.[40] And those who assaulted the house of the Hacienda 'Quilloma' (also La Paz) told the landowners that they must 'leave the hacienda and never return', because they [the *colonos*] had formed a community which had been recognized by the government.[41] If land and government were persistent themes, another underlying element of the unrest was the idea that the Villarroel decrees had abolished *all* obligations to the hacienda. Of course, not all such claims for land or labor rights were rooted in the decrees. But it is striking to note that such 'misuse' of the decrees was anticipated by the government, for the law itself included a clause delineating punishments for those who 'deceitfully invoked' the decree against servitude to avoid their agricultural duties.[42]

The rural protests of the 1940s thus manifest fierce contests over the very meanings of the Villarroel decrees. Through peaceful and violent means, rural leaders insisted on compliance with the 1945 measures, or they insisted on adherence to their own interpretations of the decrees. At the same time, the government sought to impose its readings. In response to misuse or mis-interpretations, it seems that one of the Juridical Advisor's tasks was to inform Indians about the 'true' meaning of the Villarroel decrees, untouched by any local rendering, whether *colonos* or landlords'. Thus the juridical advisor Calvi was called to Capinota during a December 1945 *huelga de brazos caídos*, to clarify the actual scope of the laws and ensure that *colonos* fulfilled their obligations to the hacienda. And in May 1946, he traveled with a police commission to Ayopaya to 'explain to the peasants the true meaning of the agrarian-social laws promulgated … by the First Indigenous Congress'. The laws were being interpreted in an 'irregular manner' there, thus causing 'grave abnormalities in agricultural production'. And that July he journeyed to Aiquile, once again to adjudicate conflicts resulting from *colonos*' 'faulty interpretations' of the decrees.[43]

These misreadings, and the juridical advisor's role as interpreter, illustrate the close connection between rural mobilization and state-making in the Villarroel and post-Villarroel era. Was the 'chief of the Indigenous Department' of the police involved in deals with *colonos* and commercial middlemen? Did he defend Indians' property rights? The possibility that he might in and of itself is significant. Caught between local power networks and the rule of law, the juridical advisor post embodies the limits of Villarroel's attempt to take the state to what was considered a stateless rural hinterland. For this figure was at once a government delegate more autonomous of landlords, and one potentially beholden — or one who could be perceived to be beholden — to new local interests, whether merchants, smallholders or *colonos*. In short, the 1947 cycle of rebellion not only constituted an assault against landlord power, it was also the product of — and interconnected with — a state-making process over which the state itself had incomplete control.

It is thus inaccurate to say that the 1945 decrees were never implemented, as most studies do. The point, instead, is that the 'implementation' of the decrees was an eminently local matter, something the Villarroel government, and subsequent regimes, could not fully manage. Yet it would also be wrong to say that the laws were *only* a local matter, for the communities that molded the president's words against servitude to their own conditions and visions said, and could say: the government decreed.

Rural Unrest on the Eve of the Revolution

The 1947 cycle of rebellion comprised a full-scale assault against landlord power, with more direct aggression against landlords, their property and their agents than typified the Villarroel-era agitation. This scale and scope of unrest would not be repeated until after the revolution triumphed. But 1947 was not a year of outright rebellion alone. One key feature was the very same *huelgas de brazos caídos* of the late 1930s and early 1940s, through which *colonos* insisted on compliance with the Villarroel decrees, or through which they insisted on adherence to their interpretations of the decrees. In some places, 1947 meant de facto land occupations, as in Vacas, where the colonos considered themselves, and were considered, landowners. 1947 was also a time of verbal battles, petitions and juridical action against landlords, local authorities and tax collectors who were charged with a range of material and physical abuse by diverse social actors. Locating the range of rural political action that characterized this rebellious year underscores the role of the law and Villarroel's incipient state-making plan. It also alters our perspective on the succeeding years. For when 1947 is viewed in these more multivariegated terms, the contrast between the before and the after is not as stark.[44]

The repression unleashed against the 1947 rebels was virulent and almost unprecedented. Planes were employed against rural insurgency for the first time ever; in addition to the army, landlords called out their own civil guards. The growing disencounter between landlords and local officials partly explains the depth of the repression. Because landlords could no longer rely on local authorities to broker settlements to disputes, they appealed directly to prefects, who invariably dispatched troops.[45] In this context, even nonviolent protest could elicit the full power of the police and the army. The force of the repression also rested on the fact that it commenced not with the 1947 rebellions but with Villarroel. The Villarroel decrees provided a legal apparatus for the 1947 repression, for it was apparently Hertzog who operationalized the Indigenous Congress recommendation that a special rural police force be created. He made it 300 men strong and equipped it with horses and cars.[46] The 1945 decrees also included three articles delineating punishments for unruly *colonos* and agitators: instigators of unrest and others who shirked their obligations or prejudiced agricultural production would be sent to 'state colonies' organized by the Ministry of Agriculture.[47] Hundreds of individuals were detained by the Villarroel and Hertzog regimes on the basis of these and other legal provisions.

For all its intensity, the repression is best understood as a force that altered rural movements without fully suppressing political action in the countryside. Outright rebellion diminished, but the countryside was not quiet. Rural grievances, conflicts and political practices of the late 1940s, and their connections — and disconnections — with the MNR, have yet to be studied in depth. Antezana and Romero's survey of the press nevertheless provides an important starting point. The authors catalogue a total of 44 actions and rumored actions for the years 1948–52, ranging from rural strikes to land boundary disputes, to 'subversive' meetings and leafleting. Outright rebellion was less common after 1947, but there were some small uprisings on or against haciendas. Conflicts over boundaries between communities and ex-communities, and between communities and owners or *colonos* of contiguous properties, occurred repeatedly in Potosí and La Paz during these years. There were also collisions between landowners, who transformed their hacienda labor force into small armies. In 1950, small violent uprisings were noted, this time opposing the agricultural census. Houses were burned, census-takers expelled and the census itself postponed. Anti-landlord violence was also recorded at this juncture. In July 1951, a group of Indians armed with sticks and knives assaulted a Cochabamba landowner. Local inhabitants suspected the insurgents were followers of Anzaldo's Virgilio Vargas, now also known as the 'son of God'. If violent incidents transpired, the post-1947 period also witnessed peaceful political initiatives, including several regional meetings of 'indigenous agricultural workers', the distribution of false property titles and at least one attempt to form an agrarian union. As in 1947, the MNR and/or promises of land were sometimes identified as the source of the agitation.[48]

The triumph of the revolution resulted in three well-known reforms: nationalization of the tin mines, agrarian reform and universal suffrage. There was also a fourth sometimes overlooked measure, which was deeply linked with the pre-revolutionary era: after taking power, the MNR quickly labored to operationalize Villarroel's 1945 decrees via the newly established Ministerio de Asuntos Campesinos (MAC).[49] Above all, the revolutionary government tried to use the decrees to control and manage rural mobilization. As in the 1940s, the juridical advisor was dispatched to rural communities to 'correct' Indians' 'misinterpretations' of the decrees. In June 1952, for example, a commission led by Ñuflo Chavez, Director of the MAC, visited several highland haciendas to remind *colonos* and landowners to adhere to the terms of the 1945 measures. The Ministry also had plans to print the full text of the decrees in a pamphlet for wide distribution and to circulate a series of informational posters.[50] Once again, the police juridical advisor journeyed to rural properties to explain the decrees to both *colonos* and landlords. Prefects also sought to enforce the measures. In June 1952, Cochabamba's highest authority sent a memo to all sub-prefects and *corregidores* 'recommending that they strictly apply and correctly interpret' the decrees: *colonos* were right to insist on the abolition of 'humiliating services', but the decrees did not cancel their obligations to the hacienda.[51]

While the MNR made haste to promulgate the decrees, it was not the only entity with an interest: the Villarroel laws also played a key role in the rural mobilizations of the early revolutionary period, just as they played a role in pre-revolutionary movements. Of course some rural communities did not have vivid memories of the Indigenous Congress or the decrees. Some communities held negative recollections, or viewed the Villarroel reforms with skepticism. That said, there is no denying the profound influence of the Villarroel era for the rural mobilizations that immediately followed the revolution. Just as in the 1940s, some post-1952 leaders grabbed hold of the four historic laws; their struggles bear a striking resemblance to the 1940s rural agitation. *Huelgas de brazos caídos*, title-selling schemes and petitions all characterized the first phase of revolutionary mobilization, with claims for land and labor rights emerging forcefully and closely intertwined.

A December 1952 land recuperation campaign in Anzaldo reveals how ongoing disputes over the Villarroel decrees marked the tumultuous period before agrarian reform legislation was passed. Apparently the 'agitators' in this case persuaded *colonos* that 'the land was already theirs' and instigated a *huelga de brazos caídos* to make that promise a reality.[52] The refusal to work, they told the *colonos*, would effectively compel the government to expropriate the hacienda and give them the land. In addition, the 'agitators' advised that all labor must be 'based on remuneration agreed to by the patrón'. The second demand was certainly an allusion to the Villarroel decrees, but it exceeded their literal message: the decrees required 'prior consent' and 'just compensation' for services and tasks *other than* agricultural labor (my italics). In contrast, the Anzaldo 'agitators' linked the 1945 decrees with compensation for *all* work and with promises of land. Joining labor rights with land rights, the *colonos* seemed to suggest: either they be properly remunerated for the work or the hacienda was theirs.[53]

Conclusion

When rural political action is viewed from the dual perspective of persistence and transformation, the Villarroel decrees and the 1945 Indigenous Congress loom large. Traces of 1945 appear in 1947 and all the way through 1952. Of course the Villarroel era should not be divorced from its deeper historical context. A long-term history of agrarian change, state-making and rural mobilization, stretching back to the cacique networks of the 1920s and the late-nineteenth-century liberal reforms, itself shaped the encounter between indigenous leaders and Villarroel, and between the countryside and the 1952 Revolution.[54] The short-lived but influential 1940s attempt to take the state to what was considered a stateless rural hinterland nevertheless dispensed formidable legacies: empowerment, repression, decrees and the unintended promise of land and 'community'. The radical course that the revolution quickly took in the countryside surprised and disturbed the MNR. But the rural communities that lodged petitions, led *huelgas de brazos caídos* and carried out direct land invasions had every reason to expect that their land would be returned. From the perspective of some rural leaders, 'revolutionary authorities' or 'the government' had already once appeared to decree it.

The point, therefore, is not only that rural indigenous mobilization lasted all the way up to 1952. More importantly, those enduring movements for land, community, justice and education became entwined with a 'government' or 'revolutionary authorities' that seemed to validate their claims. At the very least, local leaders sometimes managed to make things look that way. In certain instances, indigenous leaders radicalized Villarroel's modest propositions. The populist regime's proclamations in turn granted unintended force to local leaders' actions.

Although the countryside remained a site of political mobilization all the way up to 1952, tactics, demands, leadership, local communities and the very scope of the unrest changed in fundamental ways that remain to be studied. Without doubt, those changes had enormous significance for the unfolding of revolutionary conflict. Yet it is also clear that there was no absolute rupture between 1947 — the height of rural mobilization — and the ensuing period of MNR-led revolutionary conspiracy. Not just conflict between *colonos* and haciendas persisted in particular regions during the years between the 1947 repression and the 1952 Revolution. In certain areas, discord within and between Indian communities and ex-communities also persevered. Those complex dynamics of internal strife are generally considered outside the scope of revolutionary ferment. Instead, we need to take them front and center. A closer look at the regionally-specific trajectories of alliance and conflict within and between communities — as well as the direct clashes against haciendas and landlords — would take us beyond MNR-centered views of the revolutionary project and its origins and shed new light on the course of Indian-state relations after 1952. The intricate (still unwritten) map of rural political engagement and 'disengagement' that culminated in an urban insurrection necessarily shaped the extremely contested phases of the initial revolutionary process.

Notes

1 On Ucureña's consequential role, see Dandler (1983).
2 Rivera Cusicanqui (1986), pp. 73–4.
3 Kohl (1978), pp. 239–42.
4 *Ibid.*, pp. 240–1. Antezana and Romero also note the failure to explore links between rural mobilization in the late 1940s and the coming of the revolution. Antezana E. and Romero B. (1973), pp. 195–6.
5 *El País*, 23 May 1945.
6 For a comprehensive study of rural uprisings both before and after Villarroel, see Antezana and Romero (1973). On the intensification of rural strikes in the early 1940s, see especially pp. 93–100.
7 Lehm and Rivera Cusicanqui (1988), p. 81.
8 Federación Rural de Cochabamba, *Memoria*, p. 29.
9 On the educational policies of the era see Larson's chapter in this volume.
10 *La Razón*, 11 May 1945.
11 Dandler and Torrico (1987), p. 344.
12 *Ibid.*, pp. 341–42; and Rivera Cusicanqui (1986), p. 63.
13 *El País*, 16 February 1945, p. 5.
14 'Primer Congreso Indígena Boliviano, Recomendaciones y Resoluciones. Acta de la Sesión Preparatoria, Apéndice,' La Paz, 10–15 May 1945, mimeograph, in USNA RG 59, 824.401/5-3045.
15 *Pregón*, 29 June 1945.
16 For a more detailed discussion of the relationship between 1940s rural mobilization and struggles over the law, see Gotkowitz (forthcoming).
17 Dandler and Torrico (1987), pp. 360–1.
18 Klein (1969), pp. 357–8, 360.
19 *El Diario*, 24 November 1946. Malloy (1970), p. 130.
20 Rivera Cusicanqui (1986), pp. 66–75; Dunkerley (1984), p. 34. On the character of the 1947 uprisings in diverse regions see also Antezana and Romero (1973), pp. 123–68; Harris and Albó (1986), pp. 71–2; Ponce Arauco (1989), pp. 107–128; Dandler and Torrico (1987); and Choque (1992).
21 *El Diario*, 5 June 1947.
22 On Pucarani, a center of the mobilization in La Paz, see *El Diario*, 11 January 1947; 12 January 1947; 22 January 1947; USNA, RG59 824.00/1–1447.
23 On similarities between rebellions before and after the Congress, see Gordillo (2000), pp. 194–209.

24 See, for example, Gordillo (2000), pp. 207–9; and Ponce Arauco (1989) pp. 113 and 122.

25 On agrarian change in colonial and post-colonial Cochabamba, see Larson (1998); Jackson (1994); and Rodríguez (1991b).

26 Alberto Rivera (1992), pp. 70–2. The most important study of the rebellion is Dandler and Torrico (1987).

27 My analysis draws much inspiration from Sergio Serulnikov's work on collective violence in Northern Potosí. See Serulnikov (1996 and forthcoming).

28 Margarita vda. de Coca vs. Hilarión Grájeda y otros, Archivo de la Corte Superior de Justicia de Cochabamba (ACSJC), AG# 1202, Segundo Partido Penal, Varios Delitos, 1947, Tercer Cuerpo, fols. 89–89v (incomplete trial record).

29 *Ibid.*, fols. 189v–190.

30 Thomson (1996), pp. 53–62; Rasnake (1988), pp. 76–80.

31 ACSJC, AG# 1202, fol. 192v.

32 Serulnikov (1996), p. 218. On juridical rituals see also Langer (1990) and Rivera Cusicanqui (1986). On the law as a key site of negotiations over culture and power see Harris (1996).

33 ACSJC, AG #791, Segundo Partido Penal. Oficio contra Virgilio Vargas y otros, Varios, 1947.

34 The 1945 decrees established that the 'Sección Jurídica Indigenal' (apparently an office within the Police) was to handle all 'indigenous issues'. See ACSJC, AG #3633, 2 IP, Augusto Iriarte Paz vs. Pedro Aquino, Agitador Indigenal, 1951. I have not been able to determine precisely when the juridical advisor post manned by Calvi was established, but it seems likely that he was the director of this 'Sección Jurídica Indigenal'; I have seen no signs of the juridical advisor post in documents from the pre-Villarroel years. On the Policia Rural see 'Primer Congreso Indígena Boliviano, Recomendaciones y Resoluciones,' pp. 7–8; 'Primer Congreso Indígena Boliviano, Principales Ponencias,' pp. 28–35 in USNA, RG 59, 824.401/7–1845; and Antezana and Romero (1973), p. 155. On the Court for Indigenous Affairs, see 'Primer Congreso Indígena Boliviano, Recomendaciones y Resoluciones,' p. 8.

35 Archivo de la Prefectura de Cochabamba (APC), Expedientes, Jaime Cavero, vecino de Punata ... una propiedad en la estancia de Muyoc-Chipa, Jurisdicción de Vacas, 1947.

36 See 'Primer Congreso Indígena Boliviano, Recomendaciones y Resoluciones,' Apendice, Decree 318, Article 6.

37 'Primer Congreso Indígena Boliviano, Recomendaciones y Resoluciones,' Apendice, Decree 319, Article 2.

38 Ponce Arauco (1989), p. 113.

39 Roseberry (1994), pp. 355–66.
40 *El Diario*, 5 June 1947.
41 *El Diario*, 2 February 1947. Political opponents of Villarroel also blamed his regime for promising that land would be returned and often identified Ramos Quevedo as a source of the promise. See *El Diario*, 11 September 1946; 21 September 1946; 16 February 1947; 6 February 1947; *El Imparcial*, 29 November 1945; 11 December 1945; *El País*, 1 March 1945; 18 March, 1945.
42 'Primer Congreso Indígena Boliviano, Recomendaciones y Resoluciones,' Apendice, Decree 318, Article 9.
43 *El País*, 29 December 1945 and 26 May 1946; and *El Diario*, 3 July 1946. Other instances of such faulty interpretations are noted in *Informe del Prefecto* (1945), p. 152.
44 On such scope of political action and vision in colonial Bolivia, see Thomson (1999).
45 Ponce Arauco (1989), p. 114.
46 Antezana and Romero (1973), p. 155.
47 'Primer Congreso Indígena Boliviano, Recomendaciones y Resoluciones,' Apéndice, Decree 318, Articles 9, 10 and 11.
48 Antezana and Romero (1973), pp. 169–202. See also Albó (1979), pp. 18 and 24–29; and, on Virgilio Vargas, ACSJC, AG #3633, 2 IP, Augusto Iriarte Paz vs. Pedro Aquino, Agitador Indigenal, 1951.
49 Gordillo (2000), pp. 44–45.
50 *El País*, 7 June 1952.
51 *El País*, 17, 19 and 26 June 1952.
52 Antezana and Romero (1973), p. 229.
53 Incidents like this one led landlords to abandon their previous opposition to the Villarroel decrees and to demand that *colonos* be required to comply with them. Gordillo (2000), p. 50. On the importance of the decrees after 1952 see also pp. 40 and 45; Dunkerley (1984), p. 67; and Kohl (1978), pp. 249–51.
54 On the caciques' *apoderados* networks see Rivera Cusicanqui (1986), pp. 36–65; Mamani Condori (1991), pp. 127–60; Ticona and Albó (1997), pp. 89–165; Albó (1999a), pp. 781–83; and Choque et al. (1992).

CHAPTER 8

Capturing Indian Bodies, Hearths and Minds: The Gendered Politics of Rural School Reform in Bolivia, 1910–52

Brooke Larson

For a good while now, cultural historians have illuminated the complicated gendered and racial processes that accompanied modern state-building and development policies in twentieth-century Latin America. Just as modernizing European nations devised social policies to cope with their emerging society of the masses, so, too, did Latin America's liberal and populist states develop educational, immigration and eugenic plans to manage their explosive demographic, social and political problems associated with all the opportunities and ills of modernity. In the era of World War I, Latin American reformers borrowed and adapted the latest biomedical, racial and social ideas to suit their own definitions of national need or racial heritage.

Needless to say, those interwar reforms assumed distinctive political and social significances and produced varied outcomes, in different national and regional settings. Brazil's reformism proved to be the vanguard of tropical medicine policies and sanitation sciences, whereas Argentina cast its fate with the eugenic process of 'whitening' through aggressive immigration policies and military violence against its interior Indian population. The Mexican Revolution, by contrast, made its development policies progressive compared with those of Argentina and Brazil. The revolutionary rupture of its oligarchic liberal state permanently altered the ideological landscape and transformed the national state, making it more beholden to the country's laboring classes and anxious to bring them into the ambit of the populist state. This, it largely accomplished through federal agencies of education, agrarian reform and health under Lázaro Cárdenas during the 1930s.[1]

In the Andes, modernizing and reformist elites confronted a more difficult task, as Sinclair Thomson has suggested in Chapter 5 of this volume. On the one hand, they lacked the institutional or ideological resources that neighboring nations enjoyed — Chile's relatively stable political system, Brazil's biomedical establishment, Argentina's immigration option or Mexico's unifying revolutionary state apparatus —in order to mobilize their own societies for purposes of social control and economic development in an increasingly competitive global economy. On the other, the *criol-*

lo reformers were deeply preoccupied with the 'dead weight' that their own racially heterogeneous, poor and illiterate populations placed on their modernizing and culturally homogenizing projects. As they gazed upon their interior landscapes of mountains, provincial potentates and Indians mired in feudal servitude or else erupting in episodic upheaval, *criollo* elites often turned pessimistic about their nation's racial unfitness or diseased body politic.[2] Anxiety about the future progress of Andean societies might then provoke deeper unease about modernity itself. Was Mexico's post-revolutionary paradigm of *mestizaje* to serve as the Andean prognosis of racial and cultural integration, or did race mixture hasten nineteenth century 'degenerative processes' of racial and republican decline? How might the Andean nation-state uplift and integrate its indigenous populations while pre-empting a Mexican-styled social revolution? Might Andean scientists and health workers manage to engineer sanitary cities and healthy bodies, purged of disease, alcoholism and other vices, without the kind of public health campaigns that Brazil boasted? No less urgent, if white European immigration was proving to be a colossal failure, how might public education be made to civilize, moralize and uplift the Andean nations? These questions vexed and divided *criollo* elites in Peru and Bolivia throughout the first half of the twentieth century. Furthermore, as Nancy Stepan notes, tropes of economic and cultural progress could easily be reversed as 'degeneration [became] the major metaphor of the day, with vice, crime, immigration, women's work and the urban environment variously blamed [on the racial and/or gendered victims] as its cause'.[3] At any historical moment or place, social policy-making might be motivated by a fragile calculus of optimism and pessimism, hope and fear — and never more so than in the Andes, where weak states and fractured elites competed with each other over regional/racial projects (as in the polarizing Lima–Cuzco regional rivalry in Peru), or where international conflicts or internal rural uprisings might suddenly alter internal political balances (as in Bolivia after the 1899 indigenous uprisings, the Chaco War of the early 1930s or the 1952 social revolution).

But sooner or later, modernizing states began to expand the notion of 'public interest' to encompass realms once thought of as 'private.' As patriarchal orders crumbled, rural peasants flooded into the cities and urban laboring groups mounted all sorts of democratizing challenges, Latin American states and social reformers sought new modes of 'population management', which could burrow into the intimate interior of the family. Nationalist ideologies quickly fastened on family, as they did on race, to promote cultural reforms designed to reproduce healthy, efficient, patriotic citizen-workers or peasants.[4] Brazil and Mexico in the 1930s offer striking historical examples of strong corporatist states taking aggressive measures to 'rationalize domesticity' in the service of broader political, economic and eugenic projects. As Mary Kay Vaughan writes, 'public appropriation of reproductive activities such as education, hygiene and healthcare demanded new interactions between households and the public sphere: [and] the appointed household actor was the woman, the mother'.[5] State policies therefore fastened onto gender as both a precept and a tool in their attempts to subordinate popular households to the interests of national development, social order and patriarchal power.[6]

Against this comparative backdrop, I seek to understand Bolivia's civilizing-schooling campaigns to bring Indians into the ambit of the state and remake them into a docile, moral and productive workforce over the course of the 1920s, '30s and '40s. Despite my emphasis on state-driven intrusions into indigenous communities and households, however, I am keenly aware of the empirical and methodological limitations of instrumentalist, top-down approaches — especially in the Bolivian case. In the first place, we have to recognize the long-term failure of the state to conquer illiteracy, especially in the countryside. In 1955, the very year that the new revolutionary regime launched its educational reform program, Bolivia's official rate of illiteracy hovered around 70 per cent and illiteracy rates among the indigenous population were estimated to be even higher (about 85 per cent). [7] Along with dismal poverty and low life-expectancy rates, Bolivia's pervasive problem of illiteracy was a stark indictment of past government policy, as Herbert Klein indicates in Chapter 10 of this volume. Indeed, it is tempting to toss off the whole pre-revolutionary era of reform as simply another Bolivian chronicle of failure, much in vogue with the pessimistic tenor of Bolivian social critics of an earlier era. But the point of this chapter is not to plot trends in literacy or schooling or to diagnose policy failures.[8] Instead, I want to grasp the changing social, political and cultural dynamics involved in the pre-revolutionary efforts to 'civilize' and educate the Indian masses, which composed about 63 per cent of the total population in 1955. It was during the 1910s and '20s that 'Indian education' took on its metaphoric currency in political debate, and the profusion of schemes bear witness to conflicting visions and agendas as to how best to instruct Indians in order to achieve their integration into the emerging hegemonic, Spanish-speaking culture. Throughout the first half of the twentieth century, rural schooling remained a highly charged issue around which elites tried to define the social utility of teaching literacy, modern farming methods, hygiene and/or morality to the rural masses. Even when reformers did manage to forge a consensus, they inevitably confronted a battery of obdurate landlords and entrenched regional elites who opposed the very idea that Indian children had the right to learn their letters or to attend a local school. In short, it is precisely in the *politics and cultural policies of Indian education*, where elite discourses, policies and practices became entangled, that I want to locate this story. For even if the pre-revolutionary state did not yet possess the political power or material means to enforce policies of rural education, it was already mapping the political and cultural parameters within which Indian men and women would be allowed to enter the future nation and western modernity.

To explore the cultural politics of rural school projects, it is necessary to follow a second line of inquiry. I want to take at least a passing glance at the grassroots struggle for *the right to popular education* that began to escalate throughout highland Bolivia in the 1920s and 1930s. New Bolivian-based historical scholarship has exploded the liberal myth that rural schooling was the sole project, or dubious achievement, of government, missionary or civilizing reformers. It documents the extraordinary escalation of indigenous petitions for the right to schools, as well as their communal-based initiatives to command Spanish literacy and law in order to defend title deeds and restore *ayllu* legitimacy.[9] This grassroots movement for rural schooling began to rearticulate the issue of *ayllu* restitution within the broader postwar project of popular citizenship and democracy, labor rights and economic justice that is explored by Laura Gotkowitz in the preceding chapter. This escalating wave of peasant politics and mobilization in the 1920s, 1930s and 1940s provides a crucial backdrop of my study because, as I argue below, Bolivian elites gradually turned the project of rural school reform into a weapon of class defense against the perceived threat of peasant politics and social revolution in the late 1930s and 1940s.

Here, a brief comparison to Mexico is instructive. Post-revolutionary Mexico, of course, launched an ambitious program of rural school reform in order to build a national 'mestizo' culture (in the 1920s) and to harness the peasant class to the corporatist state (in the 1930s). Under a relatively strong federal agency, the Secretariat of Public Education (founded in 1921), and later under Lázaro Cárdenas' heralded project of Socialist Education, the Mexican state inaugurated a whole complex of radical redistributive reforms. By contrast, Bolivian state-builders and reformers turned to rural school reform as perhaps their best means of domesticating the peasantry, containing unrest and pre-empting social revolution. Indeed, around 1940, the Bolivian Ministry of Instruction couched its school reform project precisely in those negative terms: to prevent a Mexican-styled revolution from erupting on the *altiplano* or in the Cochabamba valleys. This essay monitors the *reaction* of Bolivia's political and pedagogic forces to the rise of rural mass politics, as conservative statesmen began to transform *la escuela indigenal* into an arm of rural development, containment and counter-insurgency in alliance with emerging US imperial interests in the mid-to-late 1940s. Against this backdrop, the Bolivian government's effort to by-pass social revolution through the gradual introduction of educational and cultural reform becomes particularly ironic.[10]

Habits and Habitats: The Dilemmas of Rural School Reform

Around the year 1920, La Paz's *criollo* elites embarked on a remarkable campaign to remake the Aymara Indian into the nation's essential rural labor force. Wrestling with theories of *raza y medio,* the capital's civilizing vanguard rediscovered the 'purity' and 'authenticity' of Bolivia's pristine Aymara population, isolated in its mountainous habitat and splendidly adapted to the harsh climate of the *altiplano*. Beyond the romantic imagery of the pristine Indian and gentle critiques of feudal landlordism, the discovery of the utilitarian and telluric Aymara race had tangible implications. It fastened on the Aymara population, once the scourge of 'caste warfare' across the *altiplano*, as the nation's future rural labor force. The poet, politician and pedagogue, Franz Tamayo, declared in his newspaper column in 1910 that Bolivia's Indians supplied 'ninety per cent of the nation's energy', because they were born for only one destiny — 'to produce, to produce incessantly in whatever form, be it agricultural or mining labor, rustic manufacturing or manual service in the urban economy'.[11] It was dawning on the liberal vanguard that Bolivia needed to harness the 500,000 Indians who inhabited the *altiplano*, and who made up almost 25 per cent of the nation's entire population. Indeed, La Paz had already become the colonial metropolis of Bolivia's campaign to break-up remaining *ayllu* lands, advance the edge of rails and *latifundismo* and extend the reach of the federal bureaucracy and army into the outlying provinces.[12] But by 1920 it was clear that its principal eugenic project, that of white European immigration, was failing. Not only was Bolivia unable to inject white blood into its national veins, as Brazil and Argentina had done, but it could not even promote modern agriculture under its semi-feudal hacienda regime.[13] Yet highland agricultural development was crucial, if Bolivia was to feed its growing cities and diversify its mineral-skewed economy.

The solution? To turn the Aymara peasant into a productive yeoman and artisan — the rural counterpart producing for the domestic market of Bolivia's strategic mineworker producing wealth for export. No writer articulated this goal in quite such stark economic terms, but they deployed environmental determinism to accomplish three objectives: to identify the 'natural aptitudes' of the Indian (hardworking stoic agro-pastoralists; miners of great strength and endurance; and stoic, disciplined soldiers); to fix the Indian in his 'natural habitat' (the isolated high-country of the *altiplano*, where the air was as pure as the Indian's blood); and to map his destiny in the nation as the rural laboring force.

These new anthropological truths buttressed the pedagogic turn away from 'traditional schools' promoting the older imported European curriculum based on 'mere reading and writing', 'memorization', 'verbalism', 'scholasticism' and other forms of 'intellectualism'. The Liberal Party's earlier commitment to 'universal education', based on the ABCs plus a little scriptural study, came under harsh scrutiny after 1910, just about the time that La Paz's vanguard rediscovered the authentic Indian and heralded the new (anti-positivist) spirit of cultural nationalism.[14] Bolivian pedagogues decided around 1920 that they needed to do things their own way, adjusted carefully to Bolivian environment, history and race(s). That turn inward towards a 'national pedagogy' produced a crucial prescription, which was to undergird government policies on rural schooling for the next 50 years — the idea that Indians needed a separate, segregated system of rural education, geared to their 'racial aptitudes' and 'natural habitat'. In short, Indians needed special work-training schools (*escuelas de trabajo*), located in isolated rural settlements, far away from the corruption of the city and staffed by Indian teachers trained in special rural normals.

In 1919, the Ministry of Instruction issued a comprehensive school reform plan, calling for the reorganization of Bolivia's pioneering *escuelas normales rurales* (Umala, Puna and Sacaba). Government inspections had deemed them to have failed in their mission to create Indian teachers because, among many other shortcomings, they were located in towns and producing 'mestizo preceptors' who had refused to teach in rural indigenous primary schools and, worse, had ended up migrating to the cities and meddling in political life.[15] The new pedagogy would merge the *normal rural* with the new agricultural work-school so that the two institutions could calibrate their curricula to manual labor training and teaching. The new normal pedagogy would teach three subjects: practical knowledge in agriculture, new methods of soil preparation and methods to improve small industries (textiles, ceramics, brick making, hat making, carpentry and ironwork). Apprenticing in these agro-pastoral and artisan crafts, Indians would learn through 'active methods' of education, conducted in the Spanish-language. Thus conceived, the process of hispanization (*castellanización*) would be linked to hands-on knowledge rather than to literacy. In 1919, Minister Daniel Sánchez Bustamante, explained that '... all school lessons would have one material objective, manual labor, and one moral objective, to instill the value of socially useful labor'.[16]

The new pedagogy was also driven by an equally powerful concern about stabilizing the racial and spatial location of Aymara people, as they tried to gain access to literacy, knowledge and mobility. In a revealing 1918 report to the Congress, the Ministry stated unequivocally that the new work-school was designed to guard against Indians turning into *cholos* '... so they would not abandon their own domain, by converting themselves into extortionist *corregidores* or into electoral mobs; [with their newly acquired knowledge], they will know how to exploit the land and ... they will understand that the modest citizen should function only within the limits of his own sphere'.[17] These contradictory motives expressed a larger postcolonial dilemma — the ruling elite's need to promote economic progress (especially the formation of a disciplined rural labor force on the *altiplano*), while securing the internal borders of race, gender and class. This dilemma would not soon go away, and Bolivia's progressive reformers constantly felt themselves pulled between the promises of modernity and the imperatives of social order, between economic hope and racial fear.

'The education of the Indian in his medium' became the *grito* of rural school reform in 1920. But it posed another, perhaps deeper, dilemma for La Paz's colonizing pedagogues: namely, how simultaneously to preserve and alter Indians in their 'natural habitat'. This classic dilemma posed by cultural racism — the simultaneous need to construct socioracial difference in order to stabilize the social order in the aftermath of abolition (in this case, the abolition of Bolivia's enduring caste/tributary system, which was legally dismantled in 1874) *and* to eradicate it in the service of an homogenizing 'national race' and unifying culture — comes to light in an illuminating 1918 field report from two rural school teachers possessed of sharp ethnographic intuition. Mariaca and Peñaranda were director and teacher, respectively, in the rural normal school located in the tiny town of Umala, on the coast of Lake Titicaca. Already their school was plagued by problems, and would soon be judged an unmitigated failure. But these teachers used their bitter field experience to critique *indigenista* orthodoxies about race and environment because they did not draw a conceptual distinction between the Indian's *physical* and *social* environments. It was true, they argued, that highland Indians needed to be rooted, and instructed, in work-schools so they could take their place as highland rural laborers and artisans. But if the rural normal school had to mold indigenous laborers in harmony with the habitat, it had an equally powerful mandate to wrench the Indian from his social milieu, one which was '... saturated by prejudices and backward customs, the locus of alcoholism and demoralization'.[18]

But precisely *how* to manage the 'moralization' of the Indian pupil? Unhindered by practical matters, these teachers proposed a new kind of communitarian, agro-pastoral normal school for Indians, which would become a beacon radiating productivity and enlightenment into the dark rural hinterlands. This so-called 'school colony' (*colonia escolar*) was to revolve around the idea of the Indian boarding school (*el internado*), where teachers would be able to inculcate values and monitor routines of everyday life in classrooms, workshops and fields. The boarding schools complex would be housed in vast pavilions, surrounded by cultivated fields and pastures.[19] Not only would 'satellite' primary schools channel its most adept Indian pupils to the agro-normal, but the 'solar' normal school would become the axis of expanding agro-industrial colonies — attracting *padres de familia* and other 'healthy and hardworking elements' into their cultural orbit.

This brave new world, reminiscent of the totalizing utopian community of work, piety and civilization under the colonial Jesuit system of *reducción,* was certainly ahead of its time. But the Ministry of Instruction was also convinced that Bolivian rural school reform needed to refocus attention on the socialization of indigenous youth in newly established *internados.* In 1919, the Ministry called on the Congress to establish insulated boarding schools so as to promote middle class values — temperance, thrift, cleanliness and hard work — and 'instill an awareness [in Indians] of what it means to live like a civilized race, capable of continual improvement'.[20] Rural colonies of productivity, discipline and acculturation — the reformed rural normal thus was to reconcile the contradictory goals of reproducing and transforming the Aymara race without causing any fundamental social disturbance. Utopian yes, but the 1919 statute laid the conceptual groundwork for the state's intrusive cultural policies in the 1930s and 1940s, as I will discuss shortly.

The state's reorganization of rural schooling into a separate and unequal system in 1919 was in dialogue with an emerging *indigenista* canon, which began to explore the interior world of the Indian. Following in the footsteps of Bautista Saavedra's classic 1904 ethnography of the *ayllu*, these ethnographic studies raised troubling issues about the 'racial attributes' of the Aymara family: its fragility, instability, deprivation and ultimate dysfunction. [21] José Salmón's brief biography of an *alfaréz* was a meditation on the ways that the *ayllu*'s civil-religious rituals brought financial ruin, fragmentation and dispersion to the Indian family. Aymara men cast off from family and *ayllu* in search of livelihood, trade and wage work in distant mines, cities and haciendas; meanwhile, their women and children stayed back on the land, eking out a precarious existence in wretched isolation.[22] María Frontaura, in turn, worried about the destabilizing practices of domestic life, such as Aymara mothers abandoning their young children to go off into the *puna* to pasture their animals or to pursue long-distance trading activities in the cities.[23] Worse yet, Aymara daughters were socialized in ways that encouraged their mobility and absence from the home. For against proper female roles, young preadolescent daughters were sent off into the mountains to pasture sheep, and they sometimes accompanied their fathers on long llama-train treks to mines, markets, or into the fields.[24] Although they grew strong and agile from these journeys, Frontaura's Aymara girls continued to suffer isolation, physical abuse and deprivation in the confines of their own home. Thus, they came to embody a curious contradiction of resistance and resignation, strength and docility — the combustible elements that made up the Aymara 'woman of steel'. However these writers diagnosed the instability of the Indian family, they concurred that Aymara home life boded ill for the future regeneration of the race and the hope of forging an organic 'Bolivian family'.

Nationalizing the 'Indian Question'

But who exactly was paying attention? Certainly there was a flurry of *criollo* interest in the Indian problem after the 1927 indigenous uprising of Chayanta. Sucre's newspapers carried long diagnostic articles on the role that rural education should play in the redemption of the Indian race. But the public invariably lost interest in the Indian question until local rebellion or war forced it back into newspaper headlines and government fiats. More than any other event, it was the Chaco War (1932–35) that suddenly turned the Indian family from an exotic object of anthropological inquiry into a highly publicized national concern in the 1930s. First, because the nation suddenly needed to restore the 'Indian to the active life of the nation' (in the headlines of one news article) and second, because the war unleashed the miners, peasants and other popular sectors who clamored for reparations, citizenship and welfare rights in return for their horrific sacrifices in that disastrous war. In the late 1930s, Bolivia's postwar state had to attend to multiple mobilizing groups of ex-combatants, orphaned children and widows, whose welfare was suddenly deemed the responsibility of the Bolivian state. In particular, women invaded the public sphere to demand new social reforms. Bolivian feminist scholarship and, more recently, Marcia Stephenson have argued that both elite and popular organizations of women catalyzed social reforms which 'contested the public-private divide', brought urban working class women into the purview of the populist state and cast mothers as the new guardians of national peace and reconciliation.[25] Indigenous protests also began to take on more gendered significance. In 1935, for example, indigenous communal women organized a massive demonstration in the streets of La Paz to demand the return of community members from the Chaco, at the same time they petitioned for the restoration of communal land rights. Silvia Rivera writes that, although male *cacique-apoderados* helped organize the action and framed the language of the petition, 'the protest itself was organized around women's feelings; their anguish and suffering … gave force to the mobilization and rendered the … petitions more effective'.[26] It also represented a critical turning point in the political life of the nation because indigenous women began to define their own *gendered rights* as women — wives, mothers, widows of the disastrous war. Groping towards a new self-definition, the new 'military socialist' regimes of Toro and Busch began to intervene in all facets of society through newly created ministries of public health, welfare and labor. The government had no choice but to accommodate, and contain, these new social groups clamoring for public recognition and compensation.[27]

In this political climate, indigenous school reform made important advances. Under a semi-autonomous state organization, 16 *núcleos escolares* flourished during the 1930s as the tangible outcroppings of the earlier *imagined* school-colonies promoted by the Ministry of Instruction's 1919 Organic Statute and by progressive rural normal teachers.[28] New rural Indian normal schools were established to put into practice, in varied regional contexts, the notion of the integrated and insular Indian boarding work-school complex, designed 'to irradiate' knowledge and enlightenment to satellite primary schools and their surrounding peasant villages. And as envisaged by the earlier *indigenistas,* each of these communitarian schools aimed to train and civilize their male and female pupils, as well as the *padres de familia* who participated in the life and work of the boarding schools. In short, these rural schools remained faithful to many of the same principles and methods of teaching enunciated by the original communitarian school reform project of 1918 and 1919, discussed earlier. They were to mold Aymara and Quechua Indians into virtuous Indian laborers and consumers, stabilized in their own 'natural habitat' but wrenched from their backward cultural lifeways and reinstalled in these enlightened enclaves.[29]

Yet the wrenching experiences of the Chaco War and the growing radicalization of popular political forces in the mines, cities and countryside began to alter and polarize the pedagogical objectives of Indian school reform. The *núcleos escolare*s gradually became enclaves of leftist, syndicalist and nativist ideologies and social action, or so they were perceived in many political quarters. In 1936, the rural school of Vacas was born in the lap of the local syndicalist movement of peasants; Caquiaviri anchored itself in the volatile Aymara town, famous for its history of uprisings; and Warisata became a nucleus of nativism and resistance against *gamonal* landowners on its borders. It is true that all of Bolivia's initial *núcleos escolares* had to negotiate different relations to local indigenous communities, surrounding regional elites, leftist and syndicalist organizations and the federal bureaucracy. But as a whole, the *escuela indigenal* movement of the 1930s represented a potent multi-ethnic alliance among shifting factions of radical middle class teachers and intellectuals, a young bur-growing movement of peasant syndicalism and a radicalized *cacique-apoderado* movement across the *altiplano.*

Furthermore, indigenous people continued to take independent action to fight for their right to literacy, schooling and protection. All throughout the decades of the 1920s, 1930s and 1940s, peasant delegations carried their petitions to the Ministry of Instruction, the Congress and sympathetic politicians and newspaper editors in their growing demand for local schools or, at least, the redemption of state promises to protect and support peasant-based initiatives to found local primary schools in the villages or on the haciendas where they lived. In this, they paralleled the claims for land and justice explored by Gotkowitz in the preceding chapter. The official endorsement of *escuelas indigenales* obviously offered tremendous moral, if not material, encouragement to local peasant leaders, judging by the explosion of independent rural primary schools (*unitarias*) that sprang up after the Chaco War. This quasi-underground movement of rural schooling that emerged beyond the ambit of the official *núcleos escolares* merits a book unto itself.[30] But surely the explosive growth of autonomous village schools added intensity to the polarizing political forces in the countryside, as landlords and their political arm, the Sociedad Rural Boliviana, began to counter-attack 'subversive' schoolteachers and other agitators spreading sedition in the countryside. The state's effort to bring 16 'nucleated school districts' into the Ministry's orbit was a crucial means of monitoring the diffusion of dangerous political ideas. But as I have suggested, the new *núcleos escolares* themselves were increasingly shaped and mediated by varied syndicalist, nativist and leftist political agendas sweeping across Bolivia's landscape in the mid-to-late 1930s — the 'emancipation of the Indian', 'the *concienciząción de clase*', 'the restoration of the *ayllu*', 'the destruction of the old feudal order' and/or 'the advancement of citizen rights'. All these official communitarian schools promoted, to a greater or lesser degree, the direct participation of indigenous families in the cooperative labor and local governance of the rural school, and thus they brought the peasant family into the very center of building, debating and often co-governing communitarian school reform. Indeed, in some cases, the boarding school actually *became* the locus of a reconfigured community. As the 1930s progressed, however, polarizing political forces began to turn these experiments in communitarian school reform into local battlegrounds over the right of Bolivia's indigenous people to education and, more fundamentally, to land, citizenship and social justice in postwar Bolivia.[31]

The year 1940 marked the abrupt end of postwar populist era and the onset of a reactionary counterforce of imperialism, repression and what Josep Barnadas calls the 'feudal reaction'.[32] A new conservative group of reformers seized control of Indian education, redirecting its social purpose and methods towards the linked imperatives of economic modernization, social stability and counter-insurgency. Once more, only this time with teeth, the state fastened on *el hogar campesino* as a strategic point of cultural and political incursion.

The Resurgent Right, Mestizaje and Family Values

'If [the old] Warisata's slogan was "the community for the school and in the school", now we can say "the school [is] at the service of the community and in the peasant home".' In his speech to the Bolivian congress in 1947, the minister of education used this slogan to synthesize the government's critical pedagogic shift away from dangerous issues of land, literacy and justice towards issues of gender, family and the body. The minister explained:

> The 'Work School', eulogized by Warisata, retains its validity, but now it is directed towards the *improvement of the rural family*. If the dynamism

> which once flourished in Warisata were now to be redeployed for the benefit of the peasant household, Bolivia's rural living standards would soar to unimaginable heights; each material conquest would be irreversible and useful ...
>
> The rural school must also concern itself with the health of the campesino ... to ensure that he is imbued with the principles of a healthy life and that he practices the fundamental [routines] of personal cleanliness, good diet, good housing and systematic prophylaxis. To achieve such elementary success in the interior of the Indian household is the immediate imperative of the rural school.[33]

The Ministry's message to the Congress was stark: Bolivia's rural development pivoted on the intimate socialization of *campesino*. The 'new' rural work-school was to remake the peasant family and harness it to Bolivia's project of agricultural development. Capitalist development of the countryside, feeding the cities, the reproduction of the rural labor force and the self-sufficiency of the Bolivian economy all depended on forging, and monitoring, the nuclear farm family under the direct influence of federal bureaucrats, schoolteachers, agronomists and health and social workers.

To accomplish those goals, state agencies would have to destroy, or reverse, the dangerous *indigenista* school reforms of the 1930s. In fact, the whole ideological thrust of agrarian modernization after 1940 was to repudiate the *indigenistas'* aims and methods of Indian school reform during the earlier populist era, and Warisata became the favorite target of attack. The smear campaign began in 1940, marking the government's abrupt ideological shift towards work and hygiene, family farming and capitalist rural development. Under the conservative regime of Colonel Enrique Peñaranda, the Ministry of Education (via the newly formed Consejo Nacional de Educación) launched a massive attack on Bolivia's 16 *núcleos escolares* for having sowed the seeds of indigenous unrest, destabilized rural communities, neglected the health and welfare of rural families and deviated from the 'biological need' of the nation to create a segmented labor market of healthy productive peasants.[34] According to the 'tribunal of judges' commissioned to evaluate ten years of *indigenista* school reform, Warisata and the other *núcleos escolares* had failed to transform indigenous populations into modern agro-pastoralists, letting them practice their 'primitive' agricultural methods in communal work projects. More deviously, the communitarian schools had violated the national interest by destabilizing the rural Indian by teaching him industrial skills and awakening new economic aspirations and vocations, thus tempting him to abandon his natural sphere and migrate to the cities. The judges proclaimed 'the ultimate goal of the school is the making of great agriculturalists because

Indians are magnificently adapted to the harsh climate and thus irreplaceable ...'[35] This familiar axiom — to anchor the Indian in his 'natural habitat' — was magnified into a pan-Andean principle at the first joint Peruvian–Bolivian conference of indigenist educators in Arequipa. In 1945, the ministers reiterated the ultimate goal of the rural Indian school: 'to root the Indian in his natural environment, imparting morality and instruction oriented to that end, so as to avoid the depopulation of the countryside and the demographic congestion of the cities'.[36]

In Donoso's view, then, the peasantry's preparation for entry into the modernizing nation as propertied citizens was contingent upon the deep resocialization of the peasant family.[37] Ultimately, gender difference became the device through which rural schools might accomplish their dual ends: the stabilization of the rural peasant class (whose station in life would be narrowly confined to agriculture) and the incremental incorporation of normative values and hygienic routines into the peasant family, in ways that would not trigger urban migration or social revolution. To mold the *campesino* into Bolivia's modern (albeit still landless) farm producer was one aim; to fold the *campesina* into universal womanhood was its essential complement. It was this same educational philosopher, Vicente Donoso, who had the clarifying word on the issue of gender roles. Writing generally on 'the education of the Bolivian woman' in the mid-1940s, Donoso joined a chorus of populists, nationalists, social reformers and labor organizers eager to nationalize motherhood as the womb, nurturer and healer of the war-torn Bolivian nation. Donoso engendered a trans-racial discourse on the 'aptitudes' and 'indispensability' of the woman in building the 'Bolivian family' (both real and metaphorical). And he listed the gendered complementarity of biological traits. Women possess sweetness, patience, thrift, love and reconciliation; men boast valor, impulsiveness, profligacy, combativeness and intransigence. Such 'complementarities', of course, composed the organic basis of the nuclear family — regardless of geo-racial particularities. Naturalizing womanhood in bourgeois European terms, in vivid contrast to the stoic, strong, combative Aymara woman sketched in María Fontaura's 1932 ethnography, also rationalized the rigid sexual division of labor, sentencing all women (regardless of race, ethnic or class categories) to 'their fundamental responsibility ... the organization of the family, basis of the community, the *patria* and humanity. On this premise, the education of the woman should prepare her, above all, for the happiness of the home.'[38]

As far as cultivating conjugal bliss in the campesino family, however, Donoso and his colleagues had one primary prescription: hygiene. 'The new schoolhouses need supplies of drugs, DDT and soap because the educational question, as regarding peasants, must first deal with the extirpation of lice and filth.'[39] Indeed, the lack of hygienic reform had been one of the great sins of the earlier communitarian schools, according to the grand inquisitors of 1940. As we shall see shortly, by the late 1940s, rural school curricula would impose highly ritualized regimes to regulate and reform child rearing, food, clothing and fashion, sleeping arrangements, architecture and spatial layouts and modes of sociability in the interior of the peasant school and family.[40]

In the view of social reformers, the new rural work/hygiene regime of the 1940s responded to Bolivia's urgent development needs, especially the need to stabilize the farming family as the nucleus of agro-production/reproduction on the *altiplano*. Recurrent harvest failures, acute food shortages, labor migration and Bolivia's growing dependence on wheat importation from Argentina were factors that built up pressure for change in the early 1940s. But as I have already hinted, the Consejo's sharp reversal of leftist educational ideals of the 1930s also responded to shifting social anxieties under the converging pressures of rural labor unrest and leftist mobilizations across Bolivia. Indeed, I would argue that the overriding issue among reformers in the early 1940s was not the promotion of economic development, but the prevention of social revolution, Mexican-style. Vicente Donoso, himself, worried out loud that Bolivia was on a collision course in the race between development and social revolution: 'it is urgent to realize this peaceful evolution before it turns into a social revolution of the masses. It would be fatal for the nation, especially if it followed the path towards world communism, with its simplistic program to cure poverty by dissolving private property, without taking into account human and environmental difference.'[41] It was containment, more than any other factor, I would argue, that shaped social reform in rural Bolivia during the 1940s. In so far as Donoso and other *criollo* reformers could not conceive of indigenous men and women becoming proactive political subjects capable of mobilizing for land, labor laws, schools and citizenship rights, they heaped most blame on leftist parties, rural teachers and 'ex-*dirigentes*' of the communitarian schools. The 1940 council of educators, for example, warned that 'under the pretext of educating the Indian in his own *ayllu*, the [radical *indigenistas*] have crusaded unjustly and unpatriotically against whites and mestizos, turning countryside against city and using racist doctrines to wage a dangerous war against national unity'.[42]By the mid-1940s, conservatives thought Bolivia was caught in a spiral of violence and anarchy amid the brief Villarroel regime, the Indian Congress of 1945, the spreading rural sit-down strikes (*huelgas de brazos caídos*), the Ayopaya peasant uprising of 1947 and successive miner strikes in Catavi (see Gotkowitz's chapter in this volume). At the height of peasant unrest, one writer warned that 'professional political agitators, propagandists with new ideas and semi-literate *tinterillos*' were whipping up the rural Indian masses and plunging Bolivia into a state of internal warfare not seen since the end of the Chaco War.[43]

What could save Bolivia from the impending social cataclysm? Nothing less than the rapid bio-cultural conversion of Indians into mestizos — but 'cultural mestizos' still anchored in their fields and pastures, producing food for the cities. Vicente Donoso put it best: 'what we need to do is incorporate the elements of universal civilization into the life of the Indian, to benefit him in his own medium ... because the *end product of the Bolivian Indian has to be mestizaje*'.[44] Furthermore, *mestizaje* need not wait for biological race mixing to take effect. The state could regulate de-culturation by banishing 'ethnic clothing' (*lluchu, ponchos,* short *bayeta* pants, *ojotas* and *ckepi*), which has always stigmatized men as 'Indians' no matter that they knew how to read and write or spoke Spanish.[45] The reformed mestizo person and body were thus integral to the radical individuation accompanying Bolivian modernization. At the national scale, Donoso's critical redefinition of Bolivia's racial destiny as mestizo, in contrast to the earlier ideals of racial purity, marked an important ideological turning-point in Bolivian history — one which, of course, both borrowed from Mexican racial ideology and anticipated the MNRista project of aggressive national integration after 1952. But in the 1940s most reformers began to deploy the discourse of mestizaje to domesticate and channel indigenous and *cholo* people into the new rural laboring classes without unleashing social revolution. In 1940, the Consejo Nacional de Educación was already beginning to reformulate Bolivia's racial project: henceforth 'mestizaje would become the ethnic goal of Bolivia, instead of the formation of racial groups with their own languages, devoid of nationalist spirit and separated [from the rest of the nation] by hateful rivalries and incomprehension'.[46] The gendered nature of rural social policies (hygiene, development and schooling) would create out of Bolivia's unruly and heterogeneous populations, not only a disciplined and docile peasant class, but mestizo homogeneity on which a unifying Bolivian 'nationhood' ultimately might be erected. All they needed was a strong well-endowed partner to launch these reforms.

Empire, School, Home, Body: SCIDE Goes to the *Altiplano*

Enter the USA, with its hemispheric interest in promoting social order, capitalist development and friendly governments during World War II.[47] Under Lend-Lease, the State Department drew up a plan for massive economic aid to Bolivia in order to spur tin production under the new procurement plan.

But it would not be quite so easy. The US plan was immediately thrown into jeopardy by the onset of labor strife and the government's massacre of mine workers in the Catavi mines in December 1942, prompting the USA to send in a second team to investigate the incident and give recommendations as to how Bolivia and the USA could alleviate the problem of labor strife. Under the auspices of the newly-formed Institute of Inter-

American Affairs (IIAA), this Bolivian–US commission, headed by Calvert Magruder, produced a comprehensive study, the first bi-lateral report of its kind, diagnosing Bolivia's myriad social and economic problems — everything from the injurious conditions of mine work, use of child labor, inadequate housing, inflationary food prices, lack of health care and insurance and pervasive malnutrition in Bolivia's mining camps to the non-existence of a 'sound system of free public education'.[48] The International Labor Office (ILO), in turn, provided an appalling new set of statistics to support its indictment of Bolivia's failure to build public education: an official illiteracy rate of 75 per cent (and much higher in rural areas); less than one sixth of the nation's eligible school children were matriculated; 74 per cent of all primary school children lacked chairs and desk, and texts were almost completely lacking; and 70 per cent of all rural primary school teachers, themselves, had failed to complete six primary grades.[49] Thus, while this second commission set out to investigate the mining industry, it also began to refocus US attention on conditions of economic backwardness in the countryside, the potential for agrarian development and efficient food production and the urgent need for US economic, technical and educational aid — particularly in the areas of vocational training for the children of miners and rural Indians.[50] It urged a joint US–Bolivian effort to develop an ambitious long-term program in vocational training in Bolivia's cities and countryside. Thus, as Marten Brienen has recently argued, it was the Magruder Commission that set the stage for the rapid entry of the USA into the field of rural Indian education in the mid-1940s.[51]

But there were other, more alarming, messages converging on the US Department of State about the impending crisis of Bolivian agriculture in the early 1940s. Acute food shortages were fanning the fires of inflation and aggravating labor tensions, just at a moment of resurgent syndicalism, 'foreign subversion' and left political activity (among PIRistas and MNRistas). This volatile domestic situation was compounded by Bolivia's growing dependence on food imports (and attendant trade imbalances) from Brazil and, more importantly, Peronist Argentina — a pro-labor, pro-Axis influence the US State Department would rather neutralize as it forged this 'special relationship' with Bolivia.[52] What was the US diagnosis of Bolivia's agricultural crisis? In the flurry of embassy correspondence and reports, there emerged three explanations: the embedded 'structural' causes of economic backwardness (environmental constraints, primitive technology, low productivity, 'inefficient use of human capital'); the flight of rural labor to the booming mining cities and, across the border, into Argentina; and the spread of rural disturbances (Indian congresses and petitions, spreading *huelgas de brazos caídos*, and the ubiquitous 'agitators' and 'pettifoggers' 'preying on the ignorant Indian'.[53] It is the embassy's incipient fears of rural insurgency that most interests me here. In one 1942 account, an American vice-consul reported to Washington that there was 'considerable unrest among the Indians', especially among those who worked in 'farm areas' of Oruro. In particular, the embassy pointed to the Peasant Congress held a month earlier in Sucre, where hundreds of peasant delegates had convened to demand the abolition of *pongueaje,* including all forms of military, municipal or government obligations, and to enlist the alliance of mine workers. The embassy report worried about the intransigence of the government, noting that the peasants' petition had been shelved and that there was little hope that Bolivia would deal with the 'ancient system of land tenure' by breaking up feudal estates and redistributing land. As a result, agrarian relations were growing more tense and polarized, as Gotkowitz demonstrates (see Chapter 7 of this volume).

Bolivian landlords, in particular, had an apocalyptic view. They warned that 'the spread of the communal control of land by Indian communities' would set the country back by centuries, destroy the government's tax base and derail agricultural modernization just at a time when Bolivia was 'seeking to become more self-sufficient as regards food'.[54] In 1942, a regional Quechua congress, the nexus of the growing peasant strike organization, also provoked a violent reaction from much of the Bolivian press, which condemned peasant political activity as 'the work of [agitators] and Marxists ... seeking personal political power'. Reporting on the emerging public consensus, the vice-consul wrote, 'the newspapers said the Indian problem could be solved gradually by education without upsetting the national economy'.[55] It was this 'reactionary reading' of rural insurgency that the American embassy began to internalize and reproduce in its secret embassy reports.

By 1945, it was common knowledge that peasant labor agitation posed an intrinsic threat to US economic interests. As the US scenario went: Marxist agitators combed the countryside, stirring up the peasantry, whose political activities disrupted agricultural production and aggravated food shortages, which hurt mine workers and spurred labor agitation, which ultimately hurt the war effort. During the populist regime of Gaulberto Villarroel, and at the peak of peasant political organization for the historic National Peasant Congress, held in May 1945, the US embassy established a cottage industry which put out monthly dispatches, complete with a newspaper clipping service, on the escalating war in the countryside and its myriad threats to the Bolivian economy (and US political and ideological interests).[56] Although Villarroel never managed to take command of the nation's roiling domestic politics, it is no surprise that the USA worked furiously behind the scenes to purge the MNR from his government, to foreshorten his regime (ostensibly because of his fascist sympathies) and after July 1946, to realign itself with oligarchic forces with promises of ameliorative economic, cultural and technical aid.[57] The continued escalation of widespread peasant protests and miner strikes in 1947 pushed the

USA even farther into the arms of the resurgent right, while at the same time US policymakers advanced their interlocking goals for rural Bolivia: agro-modernization, cultural reform and containment, reform without revolution. This incipient cold war agenda for rural Bolivia had much affinity with the Ministry of Instruction's new conservative politics of Indian education, discussed earlier, and US embassy officials used that ministry to promote their objectives.

The Servicio Cooperativa Inter-Americano de Educación (SCIDE) was the instrument of choice. It began operating in 1944, ostensibly under the jurisdiction of the Bolivian Ministry of Instruction, but directed by Ernest Maes, a seasoned administrator in the US Bureau of Indian Affairs. Writing on the program for the American public, Maes extolled his program because it marked the first time that 'a powerful, rich and fortunate nation has seen fit to extend limited assistance to its less fortunate neighbors in fields which hitherto have not figured in the realm of international relations'.[58] Through this cooperative education program (now operated out of the State Department), he explained, the USA would work 'as a semi-autonomous authority within the framework of the Bolivian Ministry of Education' putting 'action programs' in the fields of rural, vocational and normal school education. But as Maes went on to explain, 'it soon became apparent to us that the problem of rural education was by far the most important of the three fields', and thus SCIDE was channeling most of its energies into the 'reorganization of the rural education system', particularly on the *altiplano*, where 57 per cent of Bolivia's total population lived.[59] SCIDE's educational innovations, which encompassed administration, curriculum and outreach, had one overarching goal: to 'greatly influence political thinking in favor of US political and economic models and the American way of life'.[60]

By 1948, only two years after it began operating, SCIDE had launched an extraordinary health, educational and propaganda campaign in the most densely populated Aymara and Quechua areas of Bolivia. In formal terms, SCIDE had direct control over only six strategic peasant school centers (the revamped *núcleos escolares*), including the famed Warisata, which now became a highly publicized showcase of American-styled school reform. But it magnified its ideological and institutional presence through other means. In 1948, the Americans had created a network of 70 Peasant School Centers (with their 1,026 satellite primary schools). In one way or another, all these rural schools were drawn into the expanding orbit of SCIDE — through the circulation of newly trained *maestros rurales,* an army of rural school inspectors, the dispatch of building materials, medicines, DDT, soap and other supplies; the organization of more than 350 4-H clubs, vaccine campaigns against typhus, typhoid and smallpox (reaching some 15,000 children in a two year period), cleaning brigades of fourth year normal students who built latrines and disinfected peasant schools and homes, hot lunch programs (provided by local parents' organizations) and not least, 'a rural cultural service' that took puppet shows, folk theater and movies into rural villages and schoolhouses.[61] This cultural crusade has yet to be fully explored, particularly from indigenous perspectives, but it is possible to capture SCIDE's vision of utopia on the *altiplano* in the first textbook on campesino education ever to be published in Bolivia. SCIDE's six-volume set of *Guías de instrucción para maestros rurales* covered every facet of health and hygiene, agriculture, morality and domesticity. By 1948 and 1949, SCIDE had distributed 4,000 published copies of the guides, which became mandatory reading in Bolivia's rural normal schools. Over the next decade, as education ministers came and went, and as the nation plunged into political chaos and revolution, these textbooks defined rural pedagogy and, implicitly, tried to chart the pathway to modernization without revolution.

To do so, SCIDE technicians needed a road map into the interior spaces of the rural 'peasant household'. For if Bolivia was to spread 'good living habits', it needed to domesticate the 'wild' Aymara woman, that liminal figure that once had inhabited the uneasy imaginings of *indigenista* writers like María Frontaura, and who now was an increasingly ubiquitous figure in the streets, retail marketplaces, trade guilds, antechambers of union offices and government ministries and kitchens of rich *criollo* families throughout the city of the La Paz. In 1948, the new Teacher's Guide defined its first objective: 'to form in the campesino good living habits with respect to diet, dress, house, personal health and civic, social and religious practices'.[62]

This is precisely what SCIDE's manual on 'home economics' sets out to do by inscribing gender difference onto the community, family and body of the modern *campesinado*. Through imagery, moral suasion and the codification of quotidian regimes, SCIDE's objective was to remake the Aymara woman into the ideal '*ama de casa*', situated in her own 'natural habitat' — the family and home — and eager to imbibe the new doctrine of domesticity. Recipes for peasant behavioral reform covered domestic and corporeal facets of bourgeois femininity, body management, child-raising and housekeeping — from infant care, food preparation, home remedies and vitamin supplements to techniques of ironing, setting the proper table, aesthetic combinations of colors and the choice of sewing patterns that were 'flattering to the slim figure'. Funny, absurd, trivial — the home economics guide was a combination of Doctor Spock and Martha Stewart, 1940s-style.

This textbook beautifully captures the salience of domestic and bodily reform in the process of inculcating western bourgeois values in the interior of the insurgent peasant world of Bolivia. Not only would the 'educated' (or, borrowing the Spanish connotation of the word, 'moralized') *campesina* breed a modern rural workforce for a developing Bolivia, but she would be schooled to stay off the streets, out of the cities and out of politics so as to fulfill her destiny as *ama de casa* in the safety of the countryside and the sanctity of the home, under her husband's patriarchal authority. Read against the grain, these textbooks also seem to target the nuclear family as a strategic entry point for colonizing Bolivia's internal market. For not only were rural schoolteachers to banish 'racial poisons' and vices (alcoholism, coca-consumption, prostitution, disease, filth, etc.), they also were to cultivate new habits of consumption. Although most peasant homes had no access to electricity or running water, SCIDE would propagate imperial norms of domesticity, comfort and feminine beauty through commodity fetishism. The desire for soap, irons, aprons and slim figures would become the opening wedge of Bolivia's internal commodity markets for imported goods.[63]

There is, of course, the terrible cultural cost to be paid for this form of western modernity. Anthropologists Jean and John Camaroff, writing on domesticity and colonialism in South Africa, note that 'social groups that seek to produce a new man through a process of "deculturation" and "reculturation" set great store on the redefinition of apparently insignificant bodily habits'.[64] The inverse is equally apparent: those interest groups that impose bodily reform as imperial practice set great store on projects of deculturation. Bolivia's new rural school regime, designed to make mestizos (according to the cultural blueprint of Vicente Donoso Torres) or campesinos (a la SCIDE project), was a blunt instrument of *ayllu* deculturation, disempowerment and silencing. Nowhere in the 100-page home economics text is there any reference to Aymara or Quechua cultural values, kinship ties or communal practices. The text is mute regarding indigenous women's aspirations or real life experiences of livelihood, migration or political struggle. Nowhere is the burden of poverty, patriarchy, domestic violence or illiteracy mentioned. Gone, too, are radical socialist perspectives on the 'socioeconomic question' of Indian oppression and backwardness. Instead, the new pedagogy inscribes an alternative set of middle-class (almost Victorian) values onto the body, behavior and desires of the 'educated' *ama de casa.* According to the new lesson plans, modernity would find its mimetic embodiment in the fastidious, svelte campesina housewife — no *chola* she! — who was becoming integral to the ultimate goal of remaking rural people into self-disciplined laborers in a developing, friendly, mestizo nation.

What did SCIDE's ten-year cultural and educational mission amount to? From a tangible point of view, not terribly much. A decade of SCIDE reforms barely made a dent in Bolivia's scandalous rates of rural illiteracy; its budget was meager, even by Bolivian standards; and it administered only six nuclear school districts. Indeed, SCIDE officials were the first to assess the severe limitations under which they were forced to operate.[65] But it turns out that SCIDE provided the vehicle through which the USA could impose a program of rural development and cultural control at a moment of political flux and transformation. SCIDE's presence in the Bolivian countryside during the late 1940s clearly positioned the USA to exert an extraordinary influence over the post-revolutionary regime, once the dust of insurgent action and radical reformism began to settle. Although the US embassy could not possibly contain the explosive forces of revolution, it might still use SCIDE to help shape post-revolutionary policy in the rural sector following the upheavals.[66]

Conclusions

Heralding agrarian reform, as well as universal education, suffrage and citizenship, the 1952 Revolution promised to rupture the neo-colonial order by bringing its massive indigenous peasantries into the cultural and political boundaries of the modernizing nation. As Laura Gotkowitz shows, its revolutionary intensity sprang from the trenches of local popular mobilization and politics, which stretched across the first half of the twentieth century. Pressing their claims for lands, schools and justice onto successive political regimes, Bolivia's indigenous masses forced their way into the center of elite debates over the role that state-directed educational and civilizing reforms should play in domesticating the Indian family and preparing it to enter the modern economy — if not the citizenship nation. In different historical moments, Bolivian elites turned the rural Indian school into a crucial symbolic site for articulating gender, race and class categories in the process of imagining a pastoral prospering countryside. In the 1920s, *indigenista* reformers fastened on race and habitat in the earliest state efforts to craft special 'Indian schools' on the *altiplano*. In the post-Chaco era, national unity and popular redemption called for radical experiments in communitarian schools and multi-ethnic coalitions. But in the 1940s, the specter of indigenous mobilization, mining strikes and communism jolted conservative reformers into rejecting those earlier experiments in favor of a new agenda of de-indianization, mestizaje and counter-insurgency. Even after the 1952 Revolution, Bolivian educational reformers were squeezed between two contradictory social forces — the mobilizing miners and peasants clamoring for lands, schools and justice, on the one hand, and the 'hovering giant' looking to the MNR to reimpose order in the mines and countryside and to discipline its left-wing cadres, on the other. Redeploying the rhetoric of class (*campesinización*) and cultural integration (*mestizaje*), the post-1952 educational reformers did not break with the past. Rather, they adhered to the ideal of administering and schooling the peasantry in isolation from the rest of the nation. Rural schooling would continue to promote work, hygiene and the colonization of *el hogar campesino*. As Bolivia's conservative pedagogues had discovered a decade earlier, gender and family proved to be crucial tools for turning unruly Aymara Indians into disciplined *campesinos* during the Thermidorian phase of the revolution.[67]

Notes

1 Stepan (1991); Helg (1990); Vaughan (1982, 1997).

2 The illness metaphor, borrowed from De Gobineau and other French race theorists, achieved apotheosis, of course, in Alcides Arguedas' celebrated *Pueblo enfermo* [1909], whose three editions circulated widely throughout Latin America and, interestingly, got progressively more fixated on degenerate hybridity. See especially the third edition (1936).

3 Stepan (1991), p. 24. See also Guy (1990).

4 Dore (2000).

5 Vaughan (1997), p. 196.

6 I draw inspiration from the growing historical literature on engendering inequality in processes of class formation and state building in Latin America. Aside from works already cited, a select sample of this scholarship includes: Besse (1996); Dore and Molyneux (eds.) (2000); Dore (1997); Klubock (1998); Alonso (1995); and McGee Deutsch (1991).

7 SCIDE (1955), p. 6.

8 In fact, there is no scholarly consensus on the magnitude of or reasons behind Bolivia's educational policy failure. Historical scholarship seems to be caught between two contradictory tropes: 1) the remarkable, if belated, achievement that the Bolivian government managed to carry out in spite of fiscal, political and structural obstacles it faced, if judged by the state's organization of an administrative apparatus of rural schooling and/or the number of rural primary, secondary and normal schools that were federalized between 1910 and 1950; 2) the dismal failure of rural education reforms over that period, if judged by official rates of illiteracy, rates of student matriculation and absenteeism, percentage of the national budget allocated to rural public schooling, severe material deprivation of rural schoolhouses, the continuing shortage of trained teachers and the gap between policy and implementation. It is not my intention here to assess the overall achievements, setbacks or failures of the rural educational system by a certain measurable set of standards, but rather to explore various political, social and cultural forces that shaped and mediated Bolivia's attempt to bend its 'national pedagogy' to the putative 'Indian Problem'. But I have drawn on many such studies, including the incomparable classic by Marcelo Sanginés Uriarte (1968); the path-breaking work of Roberto Choque, especially his 1996 piece; as well as Contreras (1999b) and Brienen (2001).

9 Roberto Choque (1992); Vitaliano Soria Choque (1992), pp. 41–78; Ticona Alejo (1992), pp. 99–108; Claure (1989); and Mamani Condori

(1991). More recently, see the extraordinary evidence that Brienen (2001) provides to argue that *the majority* of Bolivia's rural schools in the late 1940s were founded earlier by indigenous communities in *ayllus*, villages and haciendas, in his paper, 'The Clamor for Schools.'

10 However, it is arguably the case that, once the revolutionary upheaval subsided, the mines nationalized and the land redistributed in 1952 and 1953, Bolivia's MNR-led government fashioned its 1956 educational reform program around the fundamental precepts of rural educational reform that were worked out by conservative governments and their US allies a decade earlier during the 1940s (see chapter by Manuel Contreras in this volume).

11 Tamayo (1988), p. 64.

12 Rigoberto Paredes ([1914] 1965); Guillén Pinto (1919) Mamani Condori (1991); and Rivera (1986), chapters 1 and 2.

13 See the critical reappraisal of the so-called immigration solution in Guillén Pinto's influential book, *La educación del indio* (1919), pp. 116–19.

14 The construction of a 'national pedagogy, 'which was often a proxy for discourses on national authenticity and identity, was part of a larger movement of cultural nationalism (which included the reassertion of conservative hispanism and Catholicism against dominant western paradigms of liberal-positivism and universalism). The most celebrated expressions of this viewpoint came in the form of Franz Tamayo's newspaper editorials, which were bundled up and published as *Creación de una pedagogía nacional* in 1910.

15 Archivo Histórico Honorable de la Cámara de Diputados (hereafter AHHCD), Ministerio de Instrucción Pública y Agricultura (hereafter MIPA), *Memoria y anexo,* 1919, pp. 251–6.

16 *Ibid.*, p. 163.

17 AHHCD, MIPA, *Memoria y Anexo* (1918), pp. 57–58.

18 Mariaca and Peñaranda (1918).

19 Variant foreign models of boarding schools — from the famous monitorial schools of Lancaster, England, to the federal Indian boarding schools both on- and off-reservations in the US — were sources of inspiration for Bolivian school reformers. See Donald (1992), pp. 19–30; and Szasz (1974).

20 AHHCD, MIPA, *Memoria y anexo* (1919), p. 263.

21 Salmón Ballivian (1926). See also Saavedra ([1904] 1987).

22 Salmón Ballivián (1926), pp. 123–8.

23 Frontaura Argona (1932), pp. 36–8.

24 *Ibid.*, p. 42.

25 See Lehm and Rivera (1988, 1986) on the mobilization of La Paz's urban working class indigenous women in trade guilds and the mili-

tant Federación Obrera Feminina (FOF); and Marcia Stephenson's insightful analysis of changing ideologies of womanhood and the politics of resistance in La Paz before and after the Chaco War. Stephenson (1999), pp. 9–34.

26 Rivera and the Taller de Historia Oral Andina (THOA)(1990), quote on p. 165. *Cacique-apoderados* were indigenous authorities appointed by their communities to represent it before the Bolivian state.

27 The war also provoked deepening fears about the spread of venereal, typhoid, malaria and other contagious diseases, as well as the general unmooring of peasant conscripts, deserters, destitute women and orphans. In alliance with the medical establishment, the government began to crack down on public hygiene by targeting, in particular, working class and transient 'chola' women. See Stephenson (1999), pp. 141–6; and for an earlier period Zulawski (2000).

28 The *núcleo escolar* was Bolivia's most noted contribution to the *indigenista* educational movement in the hemisphere. Although there is still much controversy over its origins, founder and significance, the postwar indigenous school center clearly became a crucial source of solidarity, material support and cultural interaction with dispersed indigenous communities, vis-à-vis their rural primary school (or, *seccional*), under its jurisdiction. The creation of rural 'school districts' thus rendered the flagship Indian school a kind of multiplying effect.

29 These schools promoted an 'activist curriculum' which included new disciplines of 'sanitation, hygiene and sports'. See various *indigenista* memoirs on educator's efforts to introduce these modern subjects into the curriculum of rural schools: e.g., Pérez ([1962] 1992), pp. 110–11; and Claure (1989). See also Stephenson (1999).

30 The quasi-underground movement in rural schooling, promoted and financed by indigenous communities, is an extraordinary historical episode that is only beginning to emerge in the historical literature. Aymara historians have led the way in several pathbreaking studies, cited in note 9. Official documents rarely mention this, except to note in passing the 'admirable enthusiasm' that Indians showed towards the idea of schooling or the incredible number of petitions that government authorities continued to receive from peasant leaders trying to solicit the ministry's support for establishing a local primary school. The latter point is emphasized by Marten Brienen, who argues that the explosion in many, if not most, of the 898 indigenous schools newly registered with the state's centralizing Ministry of Public Instruction in 1948 were autonomous rural village schools, established, staffed and financed by indigenous communities over many years (Brienen, 2001, p. 3). That number (484) also encompassed, however, those private rural schools that had been founded by landlords, missionaries and

municipalities in prior years. In any event, the spread of communal schools in the face of violent landlord opposition, municipal monopolies and ambivalent state support was an amazing achievement under the circumstances.

31 Warisata's famed *escuela-ayllu* is the most dramatic case in point. Founded in 1931 by the young *normalista*, Elizardo Pérez, and a prominent Aymara educator, Avelino Sinani, the school was not a government creation but was built by indigenous families living in the shrunken *marka* of Warisata. The school's remarkable achievements over its nine years of existence (1931–40) have been chronicled in loving detail by Elizardo Pérez in his 1962 memoir and in various writings by the school's most notable teacher, Carlos Salaza. See Pérez ([1962] 1992) and Salazar Mostajo (1997). Warisata's iconic status was clinched by the MNR's proclamation of the Land Reform Act, on 2 August 1953, the nation's 'day of the Indian', which in turn honored the date of Warisata's founding, on 2 August 1931. Today, Warisata, *el día del indio* and the Agrarian Reform Act are inextricably linked in nationalist ceremonies and public memory.

32 Barnadas (1978).

33 AHHCD, *Redactores de Diputados* (1947), tomo 1, pp. 131–3; emphasis added.

34 Consejo Nacional de Educación (1940).

35 *Ibid.*, p. 140.

36 *Proyecto de Puno* (1945), quoted in Fell (1996), p. 219. Sponsored partially by the United States, this inter-Andean conference of teachers, *indigenistas* and administrators wanted to create a region-wide system of Andean rural education based on the Warisata 'núcleo' system of administration, but closely wedded to the work ethic of Adventist missionaries schools on the Peruvian *altiplano.*

37 On the issue of land reform, however, the new pedagogues equivocated. For example, Vicente Donoso Torres, the architect of *desarrollista* rural school polices, took a classically evolutionist stance. Agrarian reform, a la Mexico, was needed in Bolivia, but there should be no attack on the 'feudal regime of landholding' until Indians were prepared to enter into new forms of property relations. Bolivia's cultural revolution would have to carefully channeled through school reform before the peasantry was ready to take its place as property owners. Donoso Torres, (1946), pp. 180–1.

38 *Ibid.*, p. 168.

39 Consejo Nacional de Educación (1940), p. 5.

40 The politics of 'body management' is discussed Stephenson's (1999) literary study, chapters 3 and 4.

41 Donoso Torres, (1946), p. 181.

42 Consejo Nacional de Educación (1940), p. 105.
43 Jauregui Roquellas (1947), pp. 530–1.
44 Donoso Torres (1946), p. 179, emphasis in the original.
45 There is a long history of colonial and republican attempts to impose sumptuary laws, the most famous of which was the Bourbon repression of neo-Inca fashions, iconography and public rituals in the aftermath of the general uprisings of 1781. Under republican and liberal regimes, the Bolivian state periodically issued 'dress codes' outlawing women from wearing traditional Andean clothing or 'chola' fashions (*polleras*, etc.) in the cities. But as Marcia Stephenson points out, these impulses to regulate subaltern modes of dress were often opposed by other members of the elite, who preferred to sustain racial differences, 'requiring their maids to wear *polleras* rather than dresses' (1999, p. 113). On the politics of gender, sumptuary laws and indigenous dress in the late nineteenth century, see Barragán (1992), pp. 43–73.
46 Consejo Nacional de Educación (1940), p. 137. Marcia Stephenson notes that 'throughout the 1940s, this "narrative of progress" [which correlated *mestizaje* with modernization] was constructed in political tracts, educational textbooks and novels' (1999, pp. 36–7). The most salient example of the latter is Antonio Díaz Villamil's best-selling 1948 novel, *La niña de sus ojos*. It was the first novel to pose a mestiza (or more precisely, an upwardly mobile 'birlocha') as its main protagonist.
47 In 1940 President Roosevelt created the Office of the Coordinator of Inter-American Affairs (OCIA) under Nelson Rockefeller to coordinate US-Latin American relations during the war. Its goal was to promote complementary forms of economic development in Latin America so as to sustain the region after the end of the war. See Lehman (1999); and Siekmeyer (1999).
48 International Labor Office (ILO) (1943), p. 13.
49 *Ibid.*
50 Brienen (2000), pp. 38–9.
51 *Ibid.,* pp. 39–41.
52 National Archives and Records Administration (NARA) Record Group (RG) 166, Foreign Agricultural Service, Box 47, 'Annual Review of Commerce and Industry for Bolivia,' 1942; NARA RG 166, Box 48, Entry 5, 'Economic Background Report,' 3 June 1942; NARA, RG 166, Box 48, Entry 5, 'Economic Background Report for October 1942,' 6 November 1942; NARA RG 166, Box 3, NARS a_1, Entry 2B, 1940–54.
53 One intriguing sidelight of US imperial maneuvers surfaced in a 'strictly confidential' report on the 'possible resettlement of Puerto Rican agricultural laborers' (who were of the 'proper' and 'compatible' mixture of races) to Bolivia — particularly to work in new enter-

prises in the semi-tropical lowlands. See NARA, RG 166, Foreign Agricultural Service, Box 48, Entry 5, 1 August 1942.

54 NARA, RG 166, Foreign Agricultural Service, Box 48, Entry 5, 'Economic Background Report,' 7 September 1942, pp. 4–5.

55 *Ibid.*.

56 NARA, RG 59, Department of State, 824, 401, 'Government Sponsored Indian Congress. Condition of Bolivian Indians,' 15 February 1945; 'Unrest among Agricultural Indians,' 3 May 1945; *ibid.*, 'Indian Unrest in the Light of the Decrees resulting from the Indian Congress,' 24 May 1945; 'The Indian Congress and its Aftermath,' 29 May 1945; and appendices; etc. For insightful analyses of the indigenous congress of 1945, see Dandler and Torrico (1987), pp. 334–78; and Gotkowitz (1998), chapter 3.

57 Whitehead (1992), pp. 136–7.

58 NARA, RG 229, Institute of Inter-American Affairs (IIAA) Box 1175, Ernest Maes, 'An experiment in internationalism,' n.d. [1948], p. 5; SCIDE (1955).

59 *Ibid.,* p. 7.

60 SCIDE (1955), p. 8.

61 *Ibid.*

62 Min. of Education/SCIDE (1948), no. 1; Nelson (1949), p. 21.

63 Stephenson (1999), pp. 120–1; see also McClintock (1995), pp. 207–31; Stoler (1995), 2nd edition; and Suárez Findlay(1999).

64 Comaroff and Comaroff (1992), p. 70.

65 SCIDE (1955).

66 In 1953, the first post-revolutionary Bolivian Commission on Education Reform conducted a four-month study on the state of rural education. It concluded that the SCIDE model of nuclear peasant schools, showcased in the revamped nuclear school of Warisata, was the best exit from rural poverty, illiteracy, cultural backwardness and a half-century of failed educational policies. The commission's report is summarized and discussed in the 1955 SCIDE self-assessment, *Rural Education in Bolivia,* pp. 14–15. SCIDE was involved in policy discussions of the MNR educational reforms, codified in 1955 (Sanjines Uriarte, 1968, pp. 86–7).

67 How gender identities and inequalities played out under the impact of post-revolutionary educational, agrarian, military and syndical reforms is a topic that cries out for historical research. For suggestive studies, see Gordillo (2000) and Gill (1994).

REVOLUTIONARY CONSEQUENCES

Chapter 9

The National Revolution and its Legacy

Juan Antonio Morales

The purpose of this chapter is to assess the changes brought by the Revolution of 1952, through a contemporary lens and with the benefit of hindsight. There is no doubt that the revolution shaped the Bolivian economy and society in many ways. The current state of the country's economic and social development is path-dependent and pays tribute to history, especially to what happened in 1952 and its aftermath.

The social changes of the revolution are by now well known, but I want to reiterate them. Peasants in western Bolivia were freed from serfdom, a major feat indeed. Also, the participation of women and the peasantry in political life increased significantly after universal suffrage was promulgated. The oligarchic nature of Bolivian society, with its implications of racism and class superiority, was replaced by a society with more Popular Participation that became, at least in the beginning, more egalitarian. Bolivia's economy after the revolution was grossly inefficient and poorer than before, but more equal. In addition, the expansion of a new and vigorous middle class can be attributed to the National Revolution.[1] Under the old oligarchy, public education, the main channel of social mobility, was very limited; Manuel Contreras conjectures in another chapter that the oligarchy had a stake in not improving education.

On the whole, after the 1952 Revolution, Bolivia has treated its Indian population better than has been the case in neighboring countries. Now Bolivia prides itself in being an Indian country and has lost its shyness in the Latin American context. Before the end of the Cold War, the claim was made that the Bolivian (like the Mexican) Revolution vaccinated the country against communism. What is true, and more important, is that the revolution kept the rebellions of the masses within boundaries, hence sparing Bolivia the violence that neighboring countries suffered.

This volume focuses considerable attention on the Movimiento Nacionalista Revolucionario (MNR), the main architect of the National Revolution and a major actor in the past 50 years. It is somehow surprising that the MNR led the uprising of 1952 and the changes that followed, given its petty bourgeois origin and the generally conservative stance of its leaders. The revolution also engendered revolutions within the revolution and counter-revolutions, like those of 1957 and 1985, the latter with the adoption of neoliberal policies. Even so, after 1996, the policy of Popular

Participation that decentralized decisions to the municipalities was implemented. This policy brought forth grass-roots leaderships and the new local leaders have frequently opposed the neoliberal model. The development of Santa Cruz, the most dynamic region of the country in the past years, is a major development that needs to be credited to the MNR and the revolution.

The National Revolution was, however, unable to construct a modern economy. Social innovations were offset by very poor policies for the economy. A main theme through this chapter is that bad policies were more important than geography, topography, luck, the endowment of natural resources and initial conditions of the revolution to explain the poor economic outcomes. The lasting overemphasis on income and wealth redistribution, as well as political patronage, clientelism, the low quality of the bureaucracy in the aftermath of the revolution, corruption and paternalism towards domestic entrepreneurs killed the incentives to establish a vibrant private sector and a modern economy. The quality of economic policy somewhat improved with the counterrevolution of 1985, ironically by reneging some of the principles of the revolution.

More than a generation has passed since 1952. Many countries have experienced a doubling or tripling of per capita income over the same time period. This has unfortunately not been the case of Bolivia. In addition, and as Herbert Klein indicates in Chapter 10, the country still lags behind most Latin American countries — most of which did not experience a revolution — in many socioeconomic indicators.

While Alan Knight and others in this volume compare Bolivia's revolution to that of Mexico, the case of Colombia would provide a sharper counterfactual. Colombia, which did not undergo a revolution, has been governed by an enlightened oligarchy that has successfully managed the economy during most of the past 50 years, but that has miserably failed in creating a peaceful society. A main lesson drawn from this comparison is that revolutions, like the one of 1952, may be grossly inefficient in economic terms, yet they may bring needed social equilibrium.[2]

Bolivia's revolution has not led to a successful take-off of the economy, even allowing for a 50-year lag.[3] Economic diversification, a major economic aim of a revolution that tried to lessen dependency on tin and a handful of other exports, has been modest and it came late. Worse, diversification came unintentionally with the illegal coca traffic. Also, Bolivia has become highly dependent on foreign aid, although this is not entirely a consequence of the revolution; nor is this necessarily bad.

The argument can be made that bad economic policies themselves were the result of poverty and of a society highly polarized along class and ethnic lines. Poverty shortens the horizon of public policies, and they tend to be abandoned if the expected results do not appear rapidly. The revolution, despite its claims of class alliance, did very little to reduce the cleavages. In fact, it exacerbated the distributive issues in the beginning, although later a more consensus-based society emerged. Still, the very process of consensus-building led frequently to inefficient economic solutions.

What would have happened without the revolution? Had the oligarchic parties stayed in power, they probably would have applied policies leading towards a smaller government, a stronger judiciary, more enforcement of property rights and more private investment. On the other hand, they would have paid little attention to the demands of the workers and of the Indian peasants. Some of the elements in the list above would have contributed to modernization, while others would have reinforced exclusion, the opposite of modernization.

In section 2, the chapter surveys the ideological roots of the revolution. In section 3, there is a discussion of the unintended consequences of the revolution, with emphasis on the state-capitalism model that prevailed during most of the half-century. In section 4, there is a brief review of the counterrevolutions of 1957 and of the more important one of 1985. Section 5 gives some indicators of socioeconomic development in the past 50 years, in comparison with other Latin American countries and Latin America as a whole. Section 6, the main section of the chapter, addresses the question of why economic growth has been so low since the revolution. Some conclusions are drawn in section 7.

The Underpinnings of the Revolution

The National Revolution of 1952 was the result of a confluence of factors that were catalyzed by the extremely ambitious and opportunistic MNR.[4] Regarding the overall context, the mining-based economy had never truly recovered since the Great Depression. Also, the Chaco War had inflicted great demographic damage and altered the morale of the population.

As in all revolutions, international intellectual changes played a role. Around the mid-twentieth century, governments everywhere gave primacy to internal balance objectives (for example, full employment with decent wages and social safety nets). The new views on the role of the state and the welfare of the working classes had repercussions in Bolivia despite its isolation, and the domestic political parties aligned themselves with new international views.

At regional level, in the same epoch, a wave of populism swept Latin America, and the MNR was not immune to that trend. More pointedly, the MNR drew inspiration from the Mexican Revolution and from Mexico's PRI in the formation of its political platform. The MNR went further, borrowing many proposals of the radical left, co-opted some well-known leftists,[5] and concocted the theory of class alliance. It also tried to co-opt the labor movement, the army, the university and the judiciary. In this co-optation strategy, the MNR was, however, less successful than the PRI in Mexico.

The MNR cannot be understood without reference to its nationalist doctrine, especially of its left wing. Revolutionary nationalism was a dominant ideology in the MNR during the 1950s. Eventually this ideology was replaced by the 'developmental' (*desarrollista* in Spanish) tenets propounded by the right wing of the MNR. Many of the clashes within the MNR were between the revolutionary nationalists and the *desarrollistas*. The revolutionary nationalist doctrine was very popular with Bolivian intellectuals and the leftist governments (civil and military) between 1964 and 1985, and beyond; they preferred it to Marxism, considered too 'cosmopolitan' and, hence, too alien.[6]

The main changes of the revolution are well documented and I shall not dwell on them. Here I will focus on policies.[7] The MNR carried out the recommendations of the Bohan Mission of American Development experts that came to Bolivia in the 1940s. An important recommendation was to build a paved road to link Cochabamba and Santa Cruz, in other words to link the western with the eastern part of Bolivia. The completion of this project was a major accomplishment that produced large migratory movements and facilitated the development of a zone endowed with rich natural resources.

The MNR attempted a model of industrialization, with state-owned enterprises in the forefront of the process. Industrialization started with fuels and basic industrial commodities, like sugar and textiles. Import substitution in the manufacturing industries was very limited, the efforts were half-hearted, and with the wrong instruments, namely, a system of multiple exchange rates.[8] The Bolivian approach, in contrast to other Latin American countries, was to try to maximize the exploitation of its natural resources and add more value to them through some elementary industrial processing. Bolivian import tariffs remained low by Latin American standards. Indeed, topography and the geographic isolation of Bolivia provided the bulk of protection, with a limited role for tariffs or quantitative restrictions.

With the revolution, a model of state-led growth was put in place. Planning became fashionable and a ten-year development plan was launched in 1962. Other plans followed. Public investment became the most important component of investment; the use of price controls was pervasive; and job patronage became the dominant political currency. Access to foreign exchange was rationed and a system of multiple exchange rates was established, leading to exchange rate overvaluation for the exporting firms.

The Unintended Consequences of the Revolution

The revolution brought chaos to the economy: the usual sources of foreign exchange and taxes dried up with the nationalization of the mines and the system of multiple exchange rates; the agrarian reform produced a sharp drop in the supply of food; the government literally went into bankruptcy and its large deficits were financed by printing money (the most inefficient way to finance a government). Fiscal stress was compounded by the fact that the whole state-apparatus malfunctioned, staffed as it was by inexperienced and politically appointed bureaucrats. The main consequence of the fiscal disorder was high inflation, which, in combination with price controls on staples, produced food shortages. According to Zondag, per capita GDP fell 20 per cent in the five years from 1952 to 1957.[9] Famine was widespread, until the US food aid started in 1954. It is remarkable that Bolivia's GDP fell while its neighbors were growing at a fast pace, contrary to what would happen later, when periods of low growth were a uniform regional phenomenon.

In late 1956, the government, with US aid, launched a far-reaching stabilization plan (the Eder plan) that stopped inflation.[10] However, even after the successful stabilization of 1956, macroeconomic and political instability persisted. In particular, inflation was a permanent threat. When it was checked, it was largely due to foreign capital inflows that allowed exchange rate stability, which in turn stabilized prices. One can trace back the current high dollarization of the Bolivian economy to the high inflation of the 1950s and its continuing menace.

The mishandling of the state-owned mining corporation, the Corporación Minera de Bolivia (COMIBOL), illustrates well the problems with state-led growth after the Bolivian Revolution. COMIBOL was formed with the nationalized mines. The foreign exchange earned by COMIBOL was overtaxed, first through the complexity of multiple exchange rates and later with a systematically overvalued exchange rate. The 'revenue' from such 'taxes' was transferred to the Santa Cruz region and financed its development. The question is not whether resources should have been shifted to Santa Cruz, but whether alternative and more efficient ways existed for this financing, instead of having COMIBOL pay the whole bill. Because of the heavy overtaxation of its income and natural rents, COMIBOL could not meet the costs of depreciation and exhaustion of the mineral deposits, which led to a rapid de-capitalization of the corporation. The COMIBOL mines were limited for years to extracting the metal content of increasingly poorer ores, hoping for salvation in the workings of the price-fixing schemes of the International Tin Council.

The state was not the only culprit in COMIBOL's demise. The mining unions, enjoying benefits that other Bolivians did not have, eroded the income of the mining companies.[11] It is true that the working conditions in the mines were always hard, but the hardship in the COMIBOL mines was overcompensated, at the expense of the company and, ultimately, of the Bolivian economy.

The land reform became yet another facet of the failure of the model, notwithstanding its potential for modernization. The crucial titling of the distributed lands to give formal property rights to the peasants has not yet been completed. The required infrastructure of roads, irrigation, flood controls, commercialization and credit, as well as of technical assistance, has been deplorably inadequate.

Agricultural productivity continues to be very low. Moreover, the land reform was effected only in western Bolivia, with the large estates in the eastern lowlands and the southern territories left untouched. During the military governments, the publicly owned lands in the east were snapped up by privileged private groups. The incomplete land reform and the fiscal territories given away by the military governments have created great uncertainty over tenure rights in the east of the country.

After the National Revolution Bolivia became highly dependent on foreign resources, either through foreign assistance or through debt. The business cycles were shaped to a large extent by the capital inflows rather than by the terms of trade, as used to be the case in the pre-revolutionary years. In 1954, Bolivia started to receive food aid and financial cooperation, especially from the United States. The Alliance for Progress in the early 1960s gave a further impetus to the flows of foreign aid, financing most public investment expenditures and even budgetary current expenditures. The trend continued in the following decades. Official Development Assistance, that was 3.2 per cent of Bolivia's GDP in 1970, increased to ten per cent in 1990.[12] For a long while, the efficiency of the minister of finance was measured by the amount of foreign aid that he could garner.

After the first oil crisis in 1973, and the ensuing recycling of petrodollars, Bolivia, as other Latin-American countries, accumulated a large foreign debt. Indebtedness was not bad in itself. The problem lay with the misuses of the debt.[13] The foreign debt also caused the enrichment of the few who had access to it. Once foreign assistance and foreign debt started, claims to those resources were asserted by the military and, more broadly, by the middle classes.

It is interesting to compare Mexico's accumulation of debt with Bolivia's. Redistributive policies in both countries (followed by Echeverría and his predecessors in Mexico and Banzer in Bolivia) gave rise to large budget deficits. The fiscal expansion led to a devaluation in Mexico in 1976, while Bolivia had already devalued in 1972. The steep devaluations could have been the source of economic distress, but foreign credits came to the rescue of both countries. Foreign creditors were attracted by the prospects of oil discoveries in Mexico and the supposed oil deposits (that never materialized) in Bolivia, as well as by the high transitory prices for exports of the latter.

With these prospects, Bolivia and Mexico went on a spending spree. Mexico defaulted in August 1982, triggering the so-called Latin American debt crisis. Bolivia followed and ceased payments to its foreign creditors in September 1982, which went unnoticed because of the smallness of the

Bolivian economy. The fiscal and exchange rate crisis, itself explained by the debt crisis, led to high inflation in Mexico and hyperinflation in Bolivia.[14] Bolivia, however, stabilized its inflation before Mexico did. Also, unlike Mexico, Bolivia did not suffer any financial crisis of magnitude in the 1990s.

The Reversals of the Revolutionary Model

The main reforms in the aftermath of the Revolution of 1952 caused, as noted above, high inflation. The inflation stabilization of late 1956 involved a devaluation of the exchange rate that hit the real wages of the workers and tamed most of the revolutionary zeal. Foreign investment was again welcomed and liberal legislation to attract oil companies was enacted. The legislation to attract private investments in the hydrocarbons and mining sector met with some success that lasted a few years. Foreign direct investment went into oil and the (mostly) domestic investment went to mining, leading to the formation of an industry of medium-sized mines. The oil undertakings were unwisely nationalized in 1969. The performance of medium-sized mines starkly contrasted with that of the state-owned COMIBOL, but exchange rate overvaluation, heavy taxation and persistently low prices after the tin crash of 1985 took their toll on these undertakings. They barely survive now.

The state-led model reached a turning point within the revolution in the period 1960–64, that led to the beginning of the state-capitalism model. When Paz Estenssoro came back to power to serve a second term in 1960, he proposed a *desarrollista* agenda to the country, far from the revolutionary rhetoric of his first term. The main actors of the state-capitalism model were technocrats of the middle classes, although dependent on the political support of the coalition composed of the right wing of the MNR, the military and the peasantry.[15]

Sachs and Morales and Morales[16] further elaborate Malloy's diagnostic of the state-capitalism model, but more from the perspective of economics. In economic terms, the state-capitalism model was characterized by a high ratio of public investment to total investment, a large sector of state-owned enterprises, centralized planning and high levels of public expenditure and employment. The model also incorporated a system of rewards and sanctions for the private sector that often took the form of import tariffs, tax exemptions and heavily subsidized credit. In addition, most risks faced by urban households and enterprises were assumed by the government.[17] The document, *Bolivia 1971–1991, Socio-economic Strategy for National Development* (SSND), formulated in 1970, is probably the study that best reflects the official thinking on the state-led model.

The military government of 1964 and its successors were themselves the offshoot of the conflicts between right and left of the MNR.[18] The military did not dare to reverse the main revolutionary measures of 1952–57, but watered them down. In addition, they accentuated the state capitalism model propounded by the right wing of the MNR. This state-capitalism model reached a zenith during the government of General Hugo Banzer from 1971 to 1978. Banzer carried out the statist SSND, even though this platform for economic and social development was prepared by the populist military governments he had overthrown. Banzer's years in power were ones of high growth of the economy, largely explained by the temporarily high export prices and the disbursements of external debt. During Banzer's regime, a politically powerful middle class and a technocratic elite emerged.

Despite the obvious deficiencies of the state-capitalism model, the question remains whether it was a suitable (and opportune) response for a country heavily exposed to external risks.[19] The weak performance of the neoliberal model when facing external turbulences in the late 1990s lends some support to this hypothesis.

Democracy returned in 1982, with Siles Zuazo and the left wing of the MNR leading a coalition of small leftist parties.[20] Unfortunately Siles Zuazo inherited a severe economic crisis, and his handling of it was significantly less competent than during the 1950s. Opposition, led by the MNR in Congress and by labor unions in the streets, compounded the difficulties created by the international debt crisis.[21]

Shortly after being elected president in August 1985, Paz Estenssoro, in alliance with business groups, announced a sweeping stabilization plan coupled with structural reforms (Supreme Decree 21060).[22] SD 21060 was more than a stabilization plan insofar that it sought to re-establish the authority of the state through a better definition of its role. Neoliberal discourse replaced revolutionary rhetoric after SD 21060. Government minimalism became the order of the day and the market was to dictate the optimal allocation of scarce resources. This new conception of the economy and of politics was applauded by the international financial institutions, since it answered, prior to its announcement, the recommendations of the so-called Washington consensus.

Why did the MNR adopt such an extreme version of neoliberal economic policies? A tentative answer is given by the fact that the MNR was always a party of the petty bourgeoisie, a party of shopkeepers and of lower-echelon bureaucrats. Moreover, since the early 1960s, the MNR had felt more comfortable with a developmental agenda, as noted above, than with revolutionary transformations. The distribution of assets from the rich to the destitute was alien to its main constituencies after 1960. In Chapter 13, however, Merilee Grindle argues that the MNR was not actively involved in the design of the neoliberal revolution.

With the neoliberal policies, the economy improved significantly and the rate of growth hovered around four per cent per year until the international crisis of 1999. Four consecutive governments after 1985 followed the same neoliberal policies. Bolivia became an island of economic and political stability, to the surprise of many of its neighbors. As indicated by Rodrik, the importance of macroeconomic stability needs to be underscored and Bolivia's growth between 1985 and 1999 can be attributed to it.[23]

The Social Achievements of the Revolution in Numbers

Table 9.1 shows some surprising results. In terms of per capita GDP (measured in constant dollars and adjusted for purchasing power parity), Bolivia was better off in 1950 than in 1995; the same is true for Nicaragua.[24] By contrast, Mexico, Peru and Latin America as a whole improved their incomes over that period (see Table 9.2). It must be said from the outset that the national accounts of Bolivia are notoriously deficient in that they do not take into account the large informal sector. The data for 1950, when the national accounts were in an embryonic stage, are particularly subject to qualification.

Table 9.1: The Human Development Index and its Components for Selected Latin American Countries

	Life Expectancy		Literacy		Per capita GDP a)		HDI b)	
	1950	1995	1950	1995	1950	1995	1950	1995
Bolivia	40.4	60.5	32	83	1,844	1,744	0.284	0.593
Nicaragua	42.3	67.5	38	66	1,772	1,505	0.304	0.547
Mexico	50.7	72.1	57	90	2,085	4,979	0.418	0.855
Peru	43.9	67.7	41	89	2,263	3,000	0.363	0.729
Latin America	N.A.	N.A.	N.A.	N.A.	2,487	5,155	0.442	0.802

Notes: a) In 1990 US dollars adjusted by purchasing power parity.
b) Human Development Index as developed by the UNDP 1998 Human Development Report

Independently of the source of information and notwithstanding the difficulties encountered with the data, Bolivia seems to have done significantly less well than Latin America as a whole in terms of per capita GDP (Tables 9.1 and 9.2). Not only are the levels significantly lower in Bolivia than in Latin America as a whole, but the rates of growth (as shown by the column of indexes in Table 9.2) were much lower.

Unfortunately, I do not have data on the incidence of poverty nor on income distribution before the revolution. The oldest data are for 1976, when 80 per cent of the population was below the poverty line and the Gini coefficient (a measure of inequality) was 49.0 per cent. Twenty-one years later, in 1997, the figures were 60 per cent for poverty and 56.20 per cent for the Gini coefficient.[25] Further progress has been achieved since then. Indeed, the incidence of poverty has been reduced, but inequality has increased. The current Gini coefficient is similar to the coefficient for notoriously unequal Latin America (taken as a whole).

Table 9.2: Per capita Gross Domestic Product in Bolivia and Latin America

	GDP per capita		**Index of per capita GDP (1960 = 100)**	
Year	Bolivia	Latin America	Bolivia	Latin America
1960	606.2	1,497.3	100	100
1970	833.8	1,981.5	138	132
1980	961.7	2,672.6	159	178
1990	795.6	2,453.8	131	164
2000	910.5	2,869.3	150	192

Sources: *Anuario Estadístico de América Latina y el Caribe*, CEPAL, several numbers.
Cuentas Nacionales, no. 4, BCB. August 1983.
Boletín Estadístico, BCB, Several numbers.
Anuario, Instituto Nacional de Estadística, several numbers.
Dossier Estadístico, UDAPE, several numbers.
Notes. In constant 1990 dollars, not corrected by purchasing power parity.

GDP per capita is not the only, or best, measure of human development. As Crafts mentions, life expectancy at birth and literacy ratios are better indicators of living standards than per capita GDP.[26] A better indicator of living conditions is the Human Development Index (HDI) proposed by the United Nations Development Program. The HDI varies between 0 and 1, the closer to 1 the better the situation.

Many changes in living conditions would probably have occurred without the revolution. For instance, the remarkable expansion of education fits the general trend in Latin America, as indicated by Contreras and Klein in this volume. The same can be said of improvements in life expectancy and the drop in infant mortality. This has happened in most Latin American countries, whether they had a revolution or not. Yet, as the UNDP (2002) report reminds us, in 1950 Bolivia had one of the highest rates of illiteracy in the region, and in the world, and life expectancy was among the lowest. The narrowing of the gap in these indicators between

Bolivia and the rest of Latin America is truly remarkable. It is true that improvements in mortality rates, and even in literacy, resulting from advances in public health and more consciousness of the importance of education respectively, have been largely independent of the revolution, but their acceleration can be credited to the changes of 1952.

In terms of literacy rates, Bolivia has achieved more progress than Nicaragua, but still is well below Mexico or Peru. Still, the progress in education must not be underestimated. The revolution is behind the massive schooling of children, and the labor force is significantly better educated now than before 1952. We can make the conjecture that the old oligarchy did not have any interest in the promotion of education and health of the workers, especially if they were Indian, because what it could gain in terms of economic growth with a better and healthier population would not compensate what it was bound to lose in current resources (through taxation). Moreover, the oligarchy, highly concentrated in western Bolivia, lived in permanent fear that the Indians would reclaim their land that had been expropriated in the late nineteenth and early twentieth centuries. More education for the Indians would only cause, it was claimed, Indian unrest.

Life expectancy at birth (e_0) is probably the most important component of the HDI. In 1950, Bolivia had the lowest life expectancy among the four countries in Table 9.1; by 1995, it still had the lowest life expectancy, but showed considerable improvement. In 1995, Bolivia had a life expectancy similar to that of Argentina 45 years earlier (in 1950); and a literacy ratio slightly higher than Chile's in 1950. In terms of the HDI, Bolivia fared worse in 1950 than all the countries in the table; by 1995, Bolivia had a higher HDI than Nicaragua. By 1999, Bolivia's HDI was 0.648 that is to be compared with an HDI of 0.750 for Latin America as a whole. In terms of HDI, Bolivia was above only Nicaragua, Honduras, Guatemala and Haiti.[27]

Table 9.3: Infant Mortality Rates (per thousand) in Bolivia and Latin America

PERIOD	Infant Mortality Rate	
	Bolivia	Latin America
1950/1955	175.7	127.7
1960/1965	163.6	102.1
1970/1975	151.3	81.7
1980/1985	109.2	57.8
1990/1995	75.1	40.5
2000	67.0	35.0

Source: CELADE, 'América Latina: Fecundidad, 1950–2050,' *Boletín Demográfico* no. 68

In the 50-year period 1950–2000, the infant mortality rate dropped 108.7 points, while the same rate dropped 92.7 points in Latin America over the same period. However, starting levels do matter and Bolivia had the highest infant mortality rates in Latin America in 1950. Bolivia followed Latin American improvement in infant mortality rates and it seems safe to assert that they fell independently of the revolution.

The Revolution and Long Term Economic Growth

To what extent did the 1952 Revolution and the governments afterwards, almost all with a heavy influence of the MNR, modernize Bolivia? The answer is, unfortunately, only a little. In terms of sustained economic growth there is not much of a legacy, as shown in section 5. Post-revolutionary Bolivia has offered the opposite of what, in the view of North are considered important institutional developments for growth, like enforceable property rights and limits to opportunism and rent-seeking activities.[28] Indeed, the disregard for property rights, the unreliable legal system, the opportunism of the ruling parties (the MNR and the others) and the excessive growth of government probably impinged upon the long-term rate of growth of Bolivia. Most years in the past half-century have been ones of economic distress and when growth occurred, it was either modest or short-lived.

The Predominance of Redistributive Policies

Admittedly, Bolivia faced harsher conditions around 1952 than its neighbors. The land-locked country, due to a rugged topography, extremely poor transportation infrastructure, scarce land appropriate for agriculture (beset, moreover, by alternating cycles of droughts and floods) and a labor force with very low levels of education, faced tougher conditions to provoke economic growth than its better-endowed neighbors.

The extreme dependency on tin, and the vagaries of its international market, loomed large in Bolivia's economy well before the revolution, and their effects persisted after this event. Indeed, Bolivia has suffered a long trend of deteriorating terms of trade.[29]

Notwithstanding the importance of the factors mentioned, the dismal performance of the economy can be attributed mainly to bad policies, many of them originating with the revolution. These policies deterred private investment and were overly expansionary on the fiscal front. Even the land reform, the most daring reform, resulted only in modest progress and failed on many accounts.[30]

Powerful groups, labor on the one hand, high-income groups on the other, regularly vetoed the changes in the exchange rate and in income and wealth taxes needed to finance an outsized public sector. Even nowadays, there is a deep politicization of almost all instruments of economic policy. This has not changed with the neoliberal framework. There are few economic policy tools in Bolivia that are pledged mainly on the basis of efficiency rather than distribution.[31]

The weak policies themselves were the result of a society that was highly polarized along class and ethnic lines. Economic policies in a highly divided country tend to be feeble.[32] The extreme concentration of wealth in the hands of a few members of the white and mestizo elites before the revolution are likely to result in redistributive policies such as those of the 1950s. However, a more homogeneous society only emerged many decades later, still with unequal incomes and with better chances of adopting better policies.

At a deeper level, it may be that the economic policies were weak because the country was too poor to have long-term sensible policies. In the terminology of modern economics, poverty is a steady state, meaning that the social and political forces push the economy back to that state when it tries to move away.

The combination of an overemphasis on income and wealth redistribution in the design of economic policy, low quality bureaucracy during most of the half century, corruption and paternalism towards domestic entrepreneurs killed the incentives to establish a vibrant private sector and isolated the country from international trade and capital flows. Low growth ensued.

Since political muscle could determine a larger share in the country's resources for private benefit, political confrontations have been very acute since the revolution, some within the MNR itself. Nowhere are the costs of excessive politics as clear as in the allocation of fiscal budgets.

The Failure of the State

Kaufmann et al. and the World Bank attribute the poor policies and the low quality of the public services needed for growth to the shortcomings of the bureaucracy.[33] This is a narrow view and they may be only partially correct in their appraisal. In fact, the overall quality of the bureaucracy has improved over time, although possibly with results not commensurate with the resources invested. The more technical ministries and agencies of the Bolivian government and the upper-level civil servants are as good as their counterparts in any of the neighboring countries. Moreover, Bolivia has some of the best laws in the region on budgetary processes, taxation, banks, capital markets and social security. This has been largely the product of competent technocrats in the executive branch that prepared the work for Congress. This development, however, is recent. Along with the modern institutions co-exist very rudimentary public institutions, for instance the ones that provide schooling and health.

The state indeed has failed, but not on administration in the narrow sense. More important were the policy failures. Despite the early attempts at economic diversification through government policies, and that meant abandoning comparative advantage, Bolivia continued to depend on a handful of commodities for foreign exchange and fiscal revenues during almost four fifths of the period under consideration. Even within the realm of mining, there was little exploitation of the large deposits of minerals, besides tin, with which nature has endowed Bolivia.

Efforts at export diversification have met only limited success, with modest advances in soybeans. Unfortunately the most significant diversification of exports occurred in the late 1970s, when cocaine became a major source of foreign exchange and provided the livelihood for many poor peasants and displaced miners after the neoliberal changes of 1985. This trade has profoundly marked the contemporary history of Bolivia and its relations with the United States.

The Underdevelopment of the Private Sector

The most important failure in the economic development of Bolivia has been that of the private sector. The state capitalism model discouraged risk-taking and private investment in physical and human capital, as well as in technology. At the same time, misgovernance and hidden overtaxation blocked entrepreneurial development.[34] Excessive paternalism emanating from the state-led model, with the avowed goal to create a national bourgeoisie in the early years of the revolution, continued and provided incentives to the private sector to benefit more from the government than from its own entrepreneurship. State largesse with its subsidies to the privileged firms in the private sector was legendary. This does not contradict the fact that there was simultaneously (hidden) overtaxation of the private sector as a whole.

After the clumsy attempts to protect the private sector with import tariffs and privileged access to foreign exchange, some private entrepreneurs began to receive outright gifts. With a large state sector, contracts with the government for provisioning — from roads to shoes for the army — were very lucrative. Overpricing in contracts, a common practice, was tolerated. Grebe concurs: 'The private sector developed two different faces: in the west of the country it tended to play a rather parasitic role, chiefly supplying state contracts of one kind or another; in the *oriente*, a more dynamic business outlook less linked to the state prevailed.'[35] Still, regarding the development of the *oriente* Ladman observed that this was based on a massive transfer of wealth,[36] through heavily subsidized credit and the defaulting of loans owed to the state banks (Banco Agrícola and Banco del Estado).[37] Kaufmann et al. add 'influence became a key feature in the relationship of elite firms with the state, while the bulk of the enterprise sector — those without influence — were effectively shut off from the benefits of staying in the formal sector'.[38]

When the state capitalism model came to an end, the domestic private sector found itself at a loss. It did not know how to act in the new setting, a point emphasized by Grebe and Morales.[39] Grebe remarks that 'despite stabilization and new loans to favor investment, total investment in the years that followed [1985] was disappointedly low, although the proportion of foreign direct investment (FDI) rose somewhat'.[40]

Most of the true entrepreneurship was provided by foreign companies in the 1960s and in the latter part of the 1990s. Only a handful of Bolivian firms oriented to the export markets have shown business acumen: the medium sized mining companies in the 1960s and 1970s and firms in processed soybeans, wines, garments and furniture in the 1990s. The export-oriented industries have done systematically better than the rest.

The Ambiguities Bequeathed by the Revolution

After the revolution, clientelism and job patronage became permanent features of Bolivian society. Changes in government frequently implied big shifts in public sector employment. Political parties win elections by offering jobs in public administration to their voters. Bolivia stands out as an extreme case of this phenomenon in the Latin American region.[41]

The old oligarchy was insensitive and myopic but not corrupt, at least not to the extent of the governments after 1952. With the MNR, the practice of using the government as an accepted source of enrichment became usual, especially for the middle classes, and quick fortunes were made at the expense of taxpayers and foreign aid. This disturbing situation was most prevalent during the military regimes. The state-capitalism model provided great opportunities for corruption, but the neoliberal reforms which sought to dismantle these opportunities did not suffice to stop them. Cynics would claim that some of the reforms, especially the privatizations, actually increased it.

The revolution left other ambiguities. One of them is the relationship with foreign capital, private and official. On the one hand, the nationalist position, which was important in the early MNR and with some of the military, viewed all foreigners as the enemy. Planned or actual nationalizations were recurrent. On the other hand, there was the view that Bolivia could attract foreign capital only if it had very liberal laws, granting generous concessions to foreigners, especially regarding taxes. The alternation between the nationalist view and the submissive view has hampered Bolivia's relations in the international capital markets and with foreign direct investment. The nationalistic view obviously discouraged foreign investment, yet the submissive position created problems of credibility that also reduced the attractiveness for investment in Bolivia.

Also, as a legacy of the revolution and the shortages that followed, mendicity became an acceptable form of international behavior. Since the

1950s, Bolivia has permanently been seeking foreign aid and debt relief. Unfortunately, foreign resources, instead of becoming additional resources for the development of the country, to a large extent substituted domestic savings.[42] They did not amass in domestic investments as expected. Bolivia's heavy reliance on foreign aid has been unhealthy and probably counterproductive.[43] It has also been riddled with unwarranted conditionality that has led to a loss of independence in policy-making that is resented by the population.

Finally, Bolivia inherited from the revolution a very fragmented society. The lack of cohesion persisted after the return to democracy in 1982. Given that no leadership with a clear mandate emerged in the successive elections, governments were formed with coalitions. But governments of coalitions of parties with disparate programs, formed only with the purpose of distributing patronage among themselves, are bound to be weak and riddled with infighting.[44] Yet, they gave crucial congressional strength to the president and allowed governance albeit with little social participation. The feeling of exclusion produced by coalitions of vested political interests has led to a deep suspicion of representative democracy and to calls for a more participatory democracy and more voice for grass-roots organizations. The forms of this participatory democracy are still unfolding.

Concluding Remarks

The paucity of data does not allow a more complete quantitative review of the social and economic indicators covering the 50 years after the revolution. More importantly, we still lack a comprehensive theory to explain growth (or the lack of it) in countries that undergo a revolution of the depth of the Bolivian National Revolution of 1952.

This chapter leaves many unanswered questions. The main one is why Bolivia's performance regarding the economy and social development has been so poor on the whole, with its indicators lagging behind those of the neighboring countries. We have, at best, some tentative explanations and hypothesis. Our preferred one is that the poor economic policies spawned by the revolution affected outcomes. Yet, one has to admit that the object of the Revolution of 1952, as in most revolutions, was not to pave the road to economic progress and modernity but to redress social wrongs, real or imagined. It was only later, when the revolution was largely subdued, that economic considerations came to the fore. The revolution, however, unleashed forces that would determine Bolivia's economic fate, for better or worse. Was the revolution necessary for economic and social progress? For this question, there is no definitive answer.

Notes

1 Before 1952, Bolivia had an embryonic middle class of merchants — mainly in the import business — small traders; medium-sized farmers in the temperate valleys; clerical workers in the mining, banking, transportation and energy sectors; a small number in professions like law and medicine; and public sector employees. This middle class was largely destroyed by the revolution, but a new middle class emerged after 1952, with the help of government and grew to significance during the 1970s. Note that the expansion of the middle classes is a general phenomenon in Latin America.

2 I owe this point to Javier Comboni.

3 The Mexican economy took off after a time lag of 30 years.

4 The origins of the National Revolution are by now well studied, *inter alia* by Alexander (1958), Klein (1969), Malloy (1970) and Zondag (1966).

5 To the point of allowing the tiny Trotskyite movement to gain great influence with the leadership of the MNR.

6 The writings of Carlos Montenegro, Sergio Almaraz and René Zavaleta Mercado provided the intellectual basis of revolutionary nationalism. See Mayorga (2002) for a short but accurate account of the revolutionary nationalist doctrine.

7 The changes are documented, for instance by the authors cited in note 4.

8 In CEPAL's (1967) evaluation of the economic policies in the period 1952–64 the point is made that the MNR did not give much importance to industrialization, especially of the Latin American variety, based on import substitution. Grebe (2002) also criticizes the National Revolution for neglecting industrialization and, he adds, (regional) economic integration.

9 See Zondag (1966).

10 Eder (1968) gives a thorough and lively account of the inflation and the ensuing stabilization.

11 For a short while COMIBOL was co-administered with the union of miners.

12 See Orellana (1994).

13 On this point see Sachs and Morales (1988) and Morales (2001).

14 Sachs and Morales (1988) attribute the origin of the hyper-inflation that afflicted Bolivia between 1982 and 1985 to the accumulation of high fiscal deficits financed with foreign debt.

15 Malloy (1970).

16 Sachs and Morales (1988) and Morales (2001).

17 High public investment, rewards, sanctions and social insurance of privileged firms configured the 'Korean' model of development

(Rodrik, 1999). The Brazilians under the military also followed this model. The model worked well for Korea, but not for Bolivia (or Brazil).

18 José Ortiz-Mercado (2002) aptly brands the military governments between 1964 and 1982, as the military MNR. Barrientos, Banzer and, maybe, García-Mesa represented the military right wing of the MNR, while Ovando and Torrez were on the left wing.

19 Along the reasoning of Rodrik (1997).

20 Including the Communist Party of Bolivia. The coalition also encompassed the Movimiento de la Izquierda Revolucionaria (MIR) before it turned centrist.

21 Siles-Zuazo was obliged to call for anticipated elections. Congress, functioning as an electoral college, elected Paz-Estenssoro, who served a fourth term.

22 For details see, for example, Sachs and Morales (1988).

23 See Rodrik (1999).

24 For Bolivia, some other data show that per capita GDP increased slightly, by 19%, over the 45-year period. (UNDP, 2002).

25 These figures are drawn from R. Morales (2000).

26 See Crafts (2000).

27 UNDP (2002).

28 See North (1990).

29 The terms of trade remained stagnant or declined during most of 1960–2000, except for brief periods, the most notable being in 1975 (see Graph 2 in Kaufmann et al., 2001). There are no similar data for the 1950s. Still, the rates of growth of GDP are only weakly correlated with the terms of trade, except during the 1970s. This observation leads to the conjecture that the relationship between terms of trade and growth is non linear.

30 The main achievement is that, currently, most of the supply of food staples is provided by small peasant agriculture, which was not the case before 1952.

31 See Sachs and Morales (1988).

32 See Easterly (2001).

33 See Kaufmann et al. (2001) and The World Bank (2000).

34 See Kaufmann et al. (2001).

35 See Grebe (2001).

36 See Ladman (1982a).

37 See Ladman (1982a) for a thorough account of the income and wealth transfers to large landowners in Santa Cruz through these mechanisms during the 1970s. In all fairness it must also be said that credits from the Banco Minero in western Bolivia to small mine operators went largely unpaid.

38 See Kaufmann et al. (2001).

39 See Grebe (2001) and Morales (2001).
40 See Grebe (2001).
41 See Kaufmann et al. (2001).
42 Orellana (1994) in a careful econometric study shows that foreign aid substituted domestic savings in the period 1971–91.
43 The possible negative consequences of foreign aid in Bolivia were discussed as early as 1963. See Stokes (1963) cited by Zondag (1966).
44 Even in mature democratic societies, it is well known that coalition governments tend to define budget deficits that are larger than otherwise.

CHAPTER 10

Social Change in Bolivia since 1952

Herbert S. Klein

The aim of this chapter will be to define the major social changes that have occurred in Bolivia since 1952 and to compare them with the same changes that have occurred within the other countries of Latin America. By doing this I hope to delineate what was unique to the Bolivian experience and what was common to all such states. There is little question that the changes in Bolivia in the last 50 years have been profound, but it is difficult to determine which changes were due to continental-wide developments and which were due to the political and economic factors unleashed by the National Revolution of 1952.

Bolivia in 1952 was still a predominantly rural society, the majority of whose population was only marginally integrated into the national economy. Of all economically active persons listed in the census of 1950, fully 72 per cent were engaged in agriculture and allied industries.[1] Yet this workforce only produced some 33 per cent of the gross national product, a discrepancy that clearly indicates the serious economic retardation of this sector.[2] Although Bolivia had a modern, if aging, mining sector, it otherwise contained few national industries. Only a minority of workers participated in the modern wage sector. Most workers were agriculturalists producing traditional Andean highland crops. Largely rural and agricultural, Bolivia could not even feed its national population by the middle of the twentieth century. Through the constant expansion of the hacienda system, land distribution had become one of the most unjust in Latin America. The six per cent of the landowners who owned 1,000 hectares or more of land controlled fully 92 per cent of all cultivated land in the republic. Moreover, these large estates themselves were underutilized, with just 1.5 per cent of the lands on the 1,000-hectare estates under cultivation. At the opposite extreme were the 60 per cent of the landowners who owned five hectares or less, true *minifundias*, which accounted for just 0.2 per cent of all the land and were forced on average to put 54 per cent of their lands into cultivation (see Table 10.1).[3] The extreme inequality in the division of lands was essential in the control of rural labor. Owning the best lands in all the zones of the republic, the *hacendados* obtained their labor force by offering usufruct estate lands in exchange for labor. The Indians were required to supply seeds, tools and in some cases even animals for this work, which left the owner with few capital inputs to supply. The Indians were even required to transport the final crop to market. The *hacendado* also required personal service to himself, his family and his overseers. *Pongueaje* (personal service obligation) had been part of the work requirements of estate Indians since colonial times. But it did not make these obligations any less onerous. This system did not involve debt peonage or other means of force, and Indians tended to move on and off the *latifundia* with no restrictions, but the increasing pressures on land in the free community area, especially after the last great age of hacienda expansion from the 1880s to the 1920s, compelled the peasants to adapt themselves to the system.

Table 10.1: Distribution of Land in Bolivia in 1950

Hectáres*	Farms	Owned	Cultivated
< 1	24,747	10,880	5,715
1	18,130	31,962	18,031
3	8,321	31,036	16,282
5	8,790	59,086	25,953
10	5,881	76,959	26,015
20	3,441	85,764	21,247
35	1,391	56,651	13,164
50	1,881	107,711	19,352
75	895	75,466	15,373
100	2,238	295,114	41,366
200	2,494	756,073	70,462
500	1,539	1,049,332	64,329
1000	2,139	3,290,879	95,364
2500	1,861	5,433,897	71,642
5000	797	5,146,335	55,364
10000	615	16,233,954	85,851
	85,160	32,741,099	645,510
unk	1,217	8,750	8,748
	86,377	32,749,849	654,258

Source: INE, I Censo Agropecuario 1950 (La Paz, 1985), p. 25-26
Notes *In this and following tables hectares rounded to nearest whole number

Although self-governing and communal landowning Indian *comunidades* still existed up to the time of the Agrarian Reform of 1953, they owned only 22 per cent of the lands and their crops accounted for 26 per cent of the cultivated lands.[4] Moreover, the increasing subdivisions of the already small plots in the *comunidades* was rapidly reaching crisis proportions, so that more sons were forced to work either on the haciendas to obtain land to feed themselves and their families or migrate as a cheap labor force in the mines and towns.

Table 10.2: Land Ownership by Type of Unit, Bolivia 1950

		Number of Hectáres	
Type	Farms	Owned	Cultivated
Comunidades	3,779	717,844,857	17,010,644
Haciendas	8,137	1,270,107,657	29,016,469
Small Farms*	56,259	952,642,180	12,332,755
Others	18,202	334,390,256	7,065,941
Totals	86,377	3,274,984,950	65,425,809

Source: INE (1985), pp. 25-26

Notes: *Owner operator farms without *colonos* or *jornaleros*

With labor inexpensive, with seeds and even tools sometimes free or at minimal cost and with protected agricultural markets, the incentives for *hacendados* to invest in their holdings were minimal. In fact, absentee ownership was the dominant form in all the rural areas, and the majority of *hacendados* had urban professions. The result of this system was the use of rudimentary technology and poor quality seed with extremely low yields of foodstuffs. The agricultural sector was so backward that it was unable to meet the needs of the expanding population in the urban centers and of the nation as a whole. Whereas ten per cent of the imports in the 1920s were food, the figure was 19 per cent in the 1950–52 period and a good proportion of the imported food was traditional Andean root crops which were produced only in Bolivia and Peru.[5] Inefficient, unproductive and unjust, the Bolivian agricultural system also kept a large per centage of the national workforce out of the market by holding down its income in exploitive work and service obligations. This in turn restricted the market for manufactures to the small urban minority and the relatively few active agricultural centers such as the Cochabamba Valley.

In 1952, only a minority of Bolivia's population lived in towns or cities with populations over over 5,000. There had been some change since the first Bolivian census of 1900. The urban population, generously defined as those living in towns of 2,000 or more persons, had risen from 14 per cent to 23 per cent of the national population, and in each of the departments of the country, the major urban centers had grown faster than the department as a whole (see Table 10.3). There were only six cities with a population of over 20,000 and these represented 20 per cent of the total population, and the largest city, La Paz contained only ten per cent of the population.[6]

Table 10.3: Capital Cities According to the National Census, 1846-2001

Department	Capital	1900	1950	1976	1992	2001	Sq.Miles
LA PAZ		426,930	948,446	1,484,151	1,900,786	2,350,466	51,731
	La Paz*	52,697	321,073	654,713	1,118,870	1,487,248	
COCHABAMBA		326,163	490,475	730,358	1,110,205	1,455,711	21,479
	Cochabamba	21,881	80,795	205,002	397,171	778,422	
ORURO		86,081	210,260	311,245	340,114	391,870	20,690
	Oruro	13,575	62,975	124,121	183,422	202,010	
POTOSI		325,615	534,399	658,713	645,889	709,013	45,643
	Potosí	20,910	45,758	77,334	112,078	133,268	
CHUQUISACA		196,434	282,980	357,244	453,756	531,522	19,893
	Sucre	20,907	40,128	62,207	131,769	194,888	
SANTA CRUZ		171,592	286,145	715,072	1,364,389	2,033,739	143,096
	Santa Cruz	15,874	42,746	256,946	697,278	1,114,095	
TARIJA		67,887	126,752	188,655	291,407	391,226	14,526
	Tarija	6,980	16,869	39,087	66,900	135,651	
BENI		25,680	119,770	167,969	276,174	362,521	82,457
	Trinidad	2,556	10,759	27,583	57,328	75,285	
Pando**		7,228	19,804	34,409	38,072	52,525	24,647
	Cobija				10,001	20,987	
TOTAL COUNTRY		**1,633,610**	**3,019,031**	**4,647,816**	**6,420,792**	**8,274,325**	**424,162**

NOTES: * The figures for the city of La Paz include that for the newly established municipality of El Alto which only recently was separated from La Paz. In the census of 1992 the city of La Paz held 713,378 persons, and El Alto some 405,492. The census of 2001 listed the population of El Alto at 694,749 and that of La Paz at 792,499

** The province of Pando has had no significant urban centers before 1992. In 1976 Cobija had only 1,726 persons

Not only was the population mostly engaged in agriculture, mostly rural, it was also mostly non-Spanish speaking and over two thirds of Bolivians were illiterate in 1952. Although the level of literacy and the number of children attending school steadily increased in the first half of the twentieth century, literates in the period from 1900 to 1950 rose from only 13 per cent of the population to just 31 per cent of the population.[7] Quechua and Aymara at the time of the National Revolution still represented the majority languages spoken in the country and Spanish speakers made up only 36 per cent of the population.[8]

In terms of per capita income and health, Bolivia ranked with Haiti as the poorest nation in the hemisphere. That poverty in turn was reflected in mortality rates which were among the highest in the Americas. Infant mortality was estimated at 176 deaths per thousand live births in 1953,[9] and average life expectancy in the early 1950s was 38 years for men and 42 years for women,[10] a rate probably little different from nineteenth-century life expectancy levels. Yet, at the same time, Bolivians had among the very highest fertility rates in the hemisphere, with a total fertility rate of 6.7 children registered in 1953, which made for high crude birth rates of 48 per thousand resident population.[11] The impact of these high fertility rates on the potential growth of the population was, of course, reduced by the very high levels of mortality, which caused the population to grow at a slow pace. Between 1831 and 1900 it has been estimated that the population grew at just 0.51 per cent per annum. While slowly declining mortality rates permitted a more rapid growth from 1900 to 1950, the population still grew at only 1.1 per cent per annum for most of this period, a low rate given its very high fertility.[12] These high birth and death rates defined Bolivia at the time of the National Revolution as a classic pre-modern population, with some 40 per cent of both males and females under the age of 15,[13] and a mean age of 19 years (see Figure 10.1).[14]

There is little question that the National Revolution of 1952 had a profound impact on this population in both its intended and unintended consequences. Clearly the single most important intended consequence was the Agrarian Reform which was to have a profound effect on creating not only a much broader landed class, but a new political class and finally a new group of consumers as well. The 3 August 1953 Decree of Land Reform effectively confiscated all highland hacienda lands and granted these ex-hacienda lands to the Indian workers through their *sindicatos* and *comunidades*, with the proviso that such lands could not be individually sold. The government tried to salvage whatever modern sector remained in the rural area by excluding capital-intensive farms from being seized. In the highland Indian areas, almost all the lands were taken, and the Indians quickly stopped paying compensation, with the lands, in effect, being confiscated. The only exceptions were the relatively unpopulated Santa Cruz region; such southwestern medium-sized hacienda valley regions as Monteagudo, which had some modest capital-intensive agriculture and no resident Indian populations; and the smallholding vineyard region of the Cinti Valley. Everywhere else, the hacienda was abolished, the *hacendado* class destroyed and land now shifted predominately into the hands of the Indian peasants. By 1993 some 831,000 land titles had been issued for 44 million hectares — or some 40 per cent of the total land area of Bolivia — to some 626,998 persons.[15]

Figure 10.1: Age Pyramid by Sex, Bolivia 1950

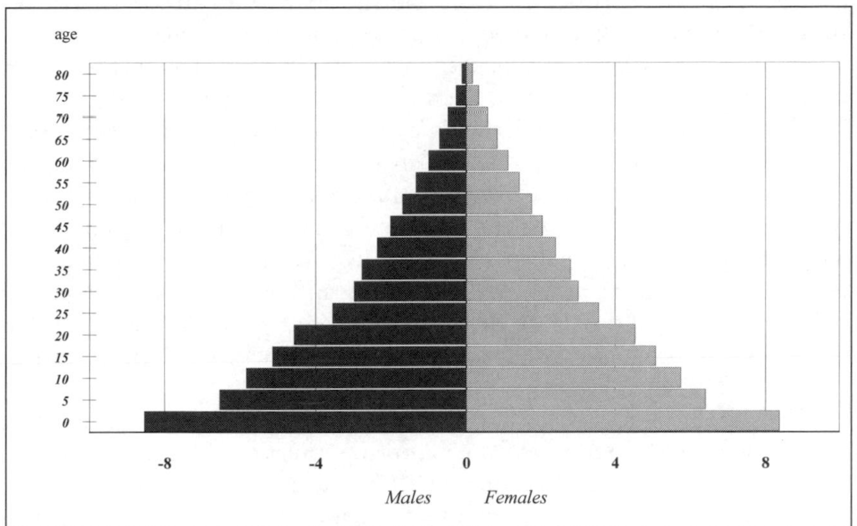

Source: CEPAL / CELADE – División de Población (2000).

Almost as important as land distribution in effecting rural change were the sharp periods of hyperinflation in the decade of the 1950s, which weakened and in many cases destroyed the traditional white hierarchies that had ruled over the small villages of the rural areas. These old elites were replaced everywhere by a new *cholo* class, that is Indians who adopted western cultural norms and became bilingual and moved into small towns and cities throughout the nation. These *cholos* now became the middlemen between the rural and metropolitan worlds evolving in Bolivia.[16]

Crucial as well in the long run was the enfranchizement of the Indian population.

One of the first acts of the new MNR regime of 1952 was to establish universal suffrage by eliminating the literacy requirements. In one stroke, the Indian peasant masses were enfranchized, and the voting population jumped from 200,000 to close to one million persons. Though the Indian masses would take several generations to find their independent political voice, every successive government, whether military or civilian, was required to make some gesture to satisfy their demands for schools, housing, electricity, sanitation and general economic support. Though the government was less than efficient in delivering this support, and the group's demands often shifted over time, the change to national political life was nevertheless profound.

The empowerment of the Indian and rural masses, however fragile and incomplete their participation, led to major social and even economic change. The active participation of the Indian peasant masses from the beginning in local unions and communal organization created support for common projects and an ability to make effective demands for better health and educational delivery, even if they were sometimes required to pay for it themselves. At the same time, the establishment of a viable road network and the opening up of rural areas to national markets brought in new wealth to the rural area and created more regional markets. Although national government investment was slow to arrive, major investment of international funding agencies directed a new wave of investment in the rural areas. Finally, the new road networks and the new labor freedom allowed for local and long distance migration on an ever more important scale, and the progressive shift of a majority of the population from the rural to the urban areas.

These political and economic changes appeared to be reflected in the health and mortality indices of the national population. By the time of the first post-revolution census, that of 1976, average life expectancy had increased from 1950 by over ten years for both men and women (reaching 48 and 52 years respectively) and the infant mortality had dropped to the 130s — still an extraordinarily high rate. Crude birth rates remained high at 41 per thousand resident population but crude death rates had dropped to 16 per thousand.[17] As the 1976 census revealed, Bolivia had finally begun to experience the effects of the arrival of modern medicine and education. The introduction of minimal medical care and the increasing literacy of the more mobile population meant that the death rates in Bolivia had finally dropped and stabilized at lower levels.

In contrast to the significant drop in mortality rates after 1952, the traditional high levels of fertility declined more slowly. These two factors guaranteed an explosive growth of population. From 1950 to 1960, the population grew at double the previous rates — or over 2.1 per cent per annum — and rose again to 2.3 per cent per annum in the following decade. By the late 1970s, it had climbed to 2.4 per cent per annum natural growth, a rate which meant that the population would double in 29 years.[18] From the census of 1950 to that of 1976, the total population increased by 1.6 million persons and then added another 1.7 million in 1992 and another 1.8 million in 2001 — in short, adding 5.2 million persons to the 1952 total of 3 million — increasing by 2.7 times over the pre-revolutionary population. This high fertility and declining mortality meant that the average age of the population actually decreased by almost a year, from 19 to 18 years of age, by the census of 1976.

The 1976 census thus captured the most dramatic effects of the demographic transition in Bolivia before the major decline in fertility. Completed family size had finally dropped below the six children level, but was still a very high 5.8 average for women who had completed their fertility.[19] The economic crisis and relative stagnation of the 1980s and early 1990s was not matched by any stagnation in the demographic indices. In the 1980s and 1990s, life expectancy rose ever more dramatically and infant mortality fell by an equal margin and total fertility rates continued to decline (see Figures 10.2, 10.3 and 10.4). By 1992, when the fourth national census was carried out, life expectancy had increased another ten years to 56.8 years and infant mortality had finally dropped by half to 75 deaths per thousand live births. Crude birth rates were dropping along with crude death rates (37 and 12 respectively). The population was up to 6.4 million or over double that of the 1950 census population.[20]

Figure 10.2: Changing Life Expectancy in Bolivia by Sex and by Decade 1949–2000

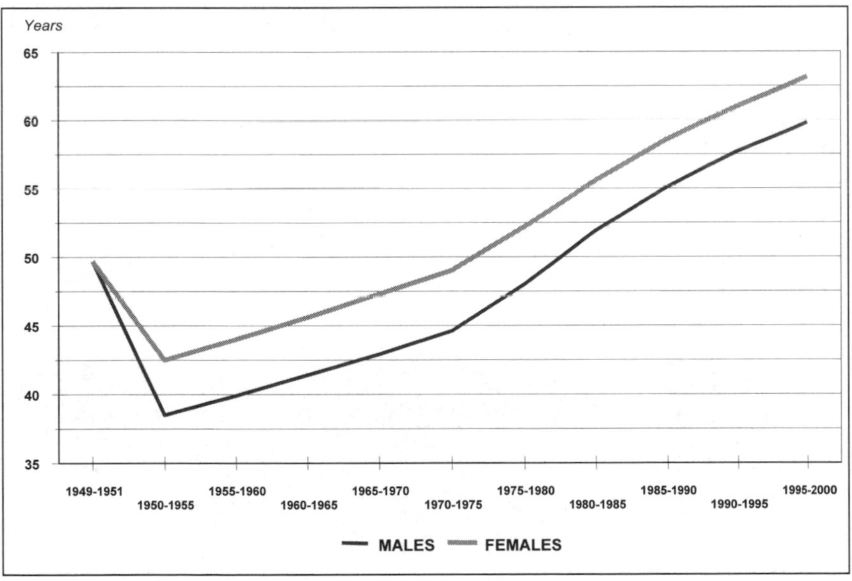

Source: United Nations: *Demographic Yearbook*, Historical supplement

Figure 10.3: Total Fertility and Infant Mortality in Bolivia, 1950–1995

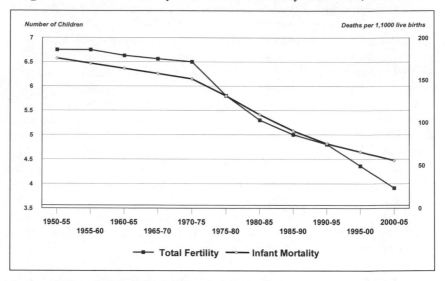

Source INE and CELADE (1995), cuadro 10.

Figure 10.4: Crude Birth, Death, Out-Migration and Growth Rates of the Bolivian Population, 1950-2005 (per 1,000 resident population)

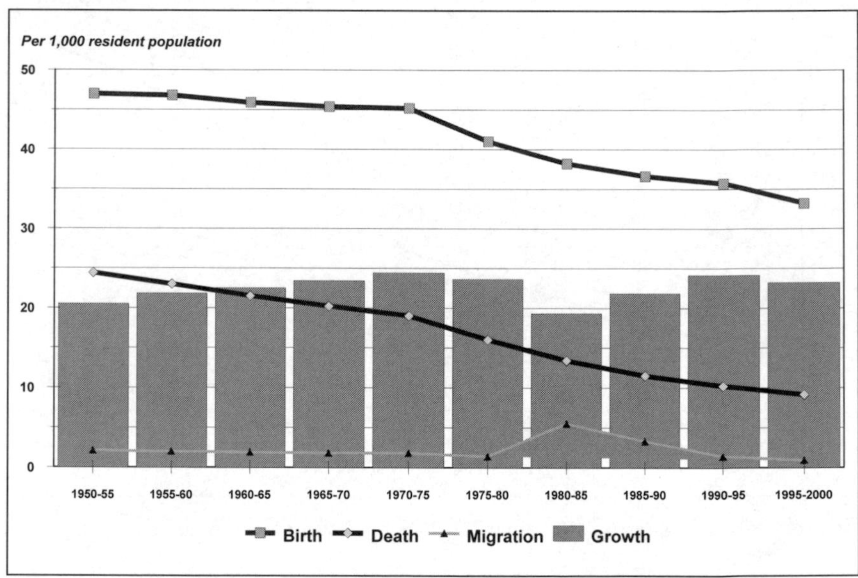

Source: CELADE - Population Division, Demographic Bulletin No. 66, July 2000

Though fertility continued to decline in the next decade, mortality declined even faster, so that growth rates remained well over two per cent per annum until the end of the census of 2001. By the beginning of the twenty-first century, the infant mortality rate was estimated to have dropped to 56 per thousand and the crude death rate was down to eight per thousand. Natality also declined — with total fertility now at 3.9 children — a bit less than half of the 1950s rate. Also by the first decade of the new century, it was estimated that the crude birth rate had dropped further to 30 per thousand although the natural growth rate still remained surprisingly high at 2.7 per cent.[21]

Increasing life expectancy and declining mortality of the population as a whole was primarily due to the major changes in child and infant mortality. The decline of child mortality was related to increasing medical assistance at births (up to 60 per cent of births had a medical person assisting by 2000),[22] which effectively aided in bringing down infant mortality and maternal mortality to 390 per 100,000 life births by the end of the 1990s.[23] Although these were still high rates by world standards, they were far better than had existed in previous decades. Direct governmental action was also fundamental in reducing child mortality. Whereas less than half the infants under one year of age were given the third DPT shot in 1990, by 1997, 78 per cent had been so vaccinated and by 2000 some 90 per cent of the children under three years had polio vaccines and 98 per cent had been vaccinated against measles.[24] Moreover, the differences between urban and rural rates of vaccination declined. Thus in 2000, 92 per cent of children under three years of age had the polio vaccination in the urban areas and 86 per cent of rural children had been so treated.[25] Finally, the increasing availability of potable water and sewerage in Bolivian homes clearly brought down the high rates of intestinal disorders which were the biggest killer of children. Although this will be examined in more detail below, the overall changes are impressive. Whereas two thirds of all Bolivian homes in 1976 had no potable water, this had declined to just over a quarter of the homes in this condition by 2000.[26] Rates of intestinal disorder and malnutrition among infants and children have also declined significantly. By the last decade of the twentieth century, cases of malnutrition had dropped to just ten per cent of the children under five years of age treated in health centers, though diarrhea and respiratory diseases — classic indices of poverty — still remained the biggest killer of children.[27] That most of the mortality decline over this entire period was in the younger ages can clearly be seen by the survival ratios by age of the Bolivian population in 1950 and in 2000 (see Figure 10.5).

In turn, fertility decline was greatly influenced by changing knowledge and attitudes of the female population. In fact, Bolivian women in various surveys have expressed one of the highest ratios — usually over two-thirds — for wanting to limit fertility and a high ratio of fertile women — usually in the range of three quarters — are using some method of contraception.[28] There is, though, still a major difference between urban and rural society and between monolingual speakers of Indian languages and bilingual and Spanish speakers. In 1994, it was estimated that 44 per cent of the decline in fertility in urban centers was due to the use of contraceptive methods, whereas it only represented 22 per cent of the decline in rural zones.[29] Moreover, monolingual Indian-speaking women had higher fertility rates than bilinguals and Spanish speakers.[30]

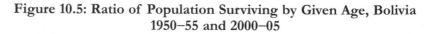

Figure 10.5: Ratio of Population Surviving by Given Age, Bolivia 1950–55 and 2000–05

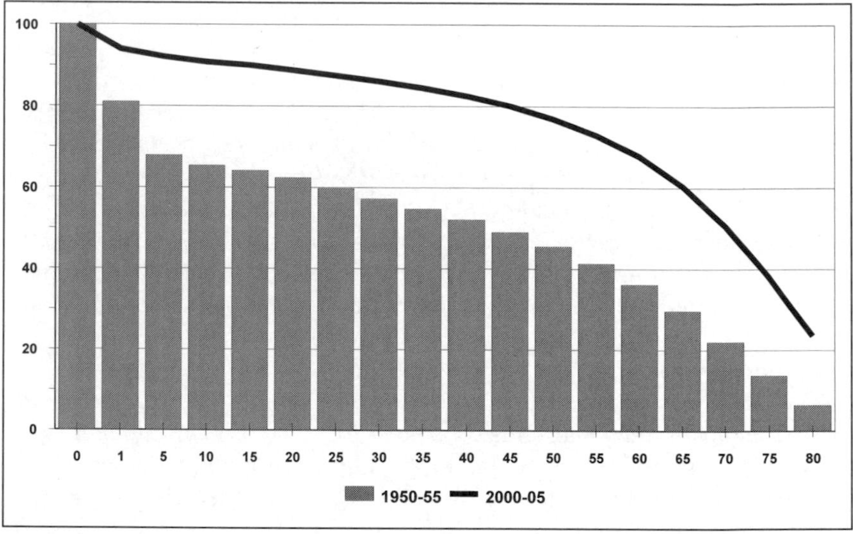

Source: CEPAL/CELADE, Model Life Tables

Though regional, class and cultural differences have been important in all these demographic changes there is little question that the direction of the secular trends in all regions and among all groups is the same. The question then arises as to how much of these changes are accounted for by the political, social and economic impact of the National Revolution and how much by general hemispheric changes that were affecting all nations in the hemisphere. The answer is that in some ways, both influences can be seen in comparable demographic statistics.

Despite very significant advances, Bolivia had not changed its rank position as the second worst in the Americas in terms of mortality or life expectancy, compared to all the other nations of the hemisphere. Nevertheless, the gap between the healthier and the higher mortality populations has declined consistently over time, at least for males. Thus in

1950 Argentine males lived on average 20 more years than Bolivian males, while in the year 2000 the gap was only ten years. The gap among females, however, has remained the same at roughly 12 to 13 years. Not only has Bolivia not changed its ranking in this half century of hemispheric change when everyone saw increasing life expectancy, but even compared to Haiti, the poorest nation in the Americas, it has changed very little for most of the period under study. From the 1950s until 1980, Bolivian trends in life expectancy for males actually followed behind the Haitian experience, though it was always far better for Bolivian women (see Figures 10.6 and 10.7). Even in terms of infant mortality, as can be seen in Figure 10.8, the decline in this mortality index in Haiti was even more precipitous than the decline in Bolivia, and by 2000–05 they both had reached the same lower level, despite the fact that Haiti has experienced no social revolution.

Other mortality and health rates for Haiti, however, did fall behind Bolivia after 1980, which after that date saw both Bolivian male and female life expectancy finally outpace Haitian trends. All this might suggest that the political and socioeconomic change that the National Revolution ushered in after 1952 made relatively little difference to demographic change, at least in terms of mortality, until the very last decades of the twentieth century. This suggests that the trends noted until 1980 were continental wide and common to even the poorest conservative states. But it would seem that after some 30 years of governmental reforms and peasant political activity brought on by the National Revolution, even some of the basic demographic indices were being influenced by unique Bolivian initiatives. As we will see below, the National Revolution, with its various intended and unintended consequences, would have a far more direct impact on education and literacy than on these demographic indices, but even these basic health and wellbeing indices were finally beginning to show unique patterns of evolution within Bolivia by the late 1980s, probably related to more coherent state policies on rural sanitation, housing, water supplies and other infrastructural activities. Bolivia after 1980 began to experience substantial changes in the health area that moved it ahead of general continental and world trends. As can be seen in Table 10.4, for life expectancy and all mortality indices, except that of child mortality, Bolivia in the 19-year period from 1980 to 1999 finally rose above the levels of the poorest nations in the world.

Although it has been suggested that increasing investments in education and rising student enrollments preceded the National Revolution,[31] there is little question that the most rapid changes which have occurred in the social area in Bolivia in the past 50 years are in education and literacy. From among the lowest indices of an educated population in the hemisphere in 1950, by 2000 Bolivia had finally achieved a level close to that of all its neighbors and ahead of most of the Central American republics. In fact the evolution of its educational and literacy indices compares favorably with that achieved by neighboring Brazil during this period.

Figure 10.6: Life Expectancy in Bolivia and Haiti, 1950–95 – Males

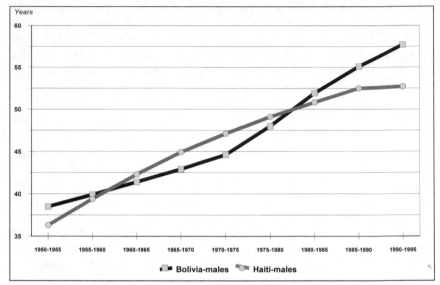

Source: United Nations, *Demographic Yearbook*, Historical supplement

Figure 10.7: Life Expectancy in Bolivia and Haiti, 1950–95 – Females

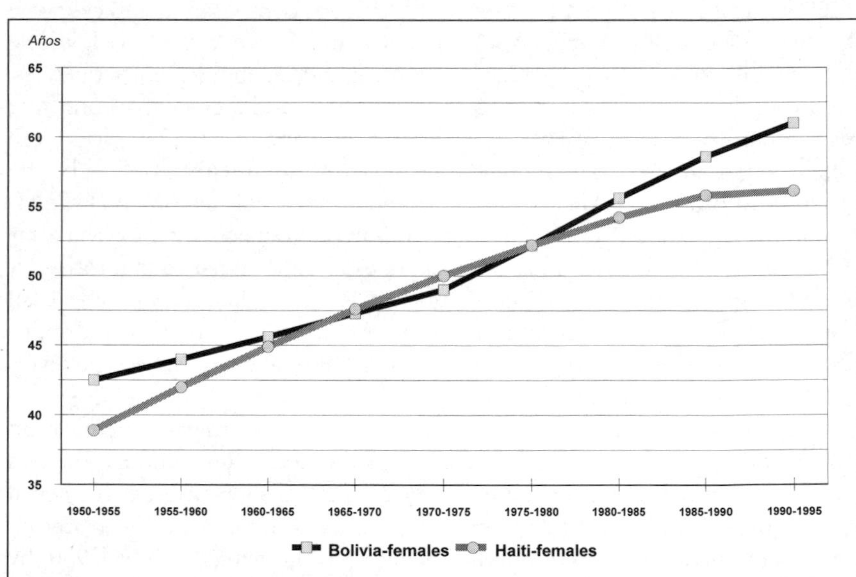

Source: United Nations, *Demographic Yearbook*, Historical supplement

Figure 10.8: Infant Mortality in Bolivia, Haiti and All Latin America, 1950–2000

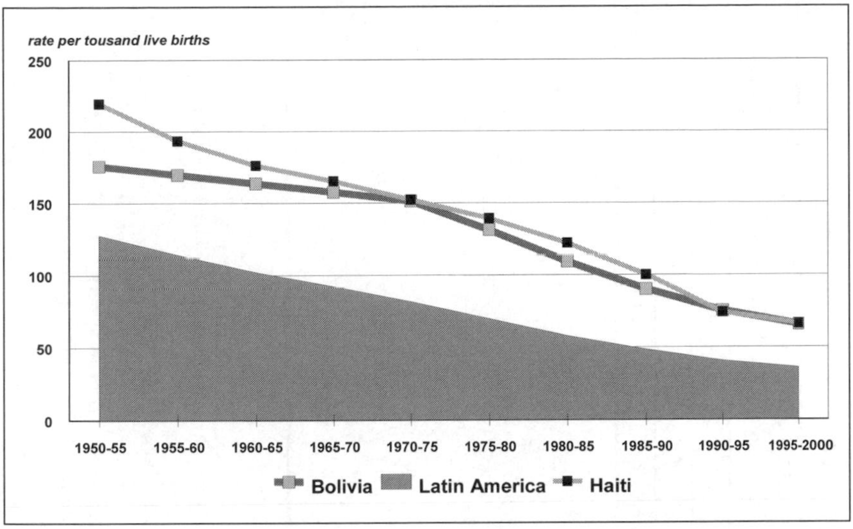

Source: CEPAL (2001), Table 16.

By the end of the century the government was spending more of its GDP (eight per cent) on education than most countries in the region.[32] In 1950, the country was still only educating a quarter of its children in primary schools, but by 1985, this ratio had risen to 84 per cent.[33] By 1999, the coverage had reached 87 per cent for primary school age children and 38 per cent for secondary school ages.[34] Though these extraordinary high ratios have been much debated, all recent studies suggest that they are correct.[35] But between high drop out rates and children retained over grades, the final completion rate is a relatively poor 60 per cent, with many leaving school after just four years. Bolivia does less well at the secondary school level, educating just 40 per cent of the boys and 34 per cent of the girls of this age group — rates that would place it below most Latin American countries. In 2000, there were 1.7 million students in primary and kindergarten schools and another 341,000 in secondary grades.[36]But whatever the current problems with the system, the trend of almost universal coverage is reaching completion, at least for the primary grades. At the same time the average number of years of schooling also has been climbing steadily in this period from four years toward six years. As could be expected, the more recent generations have much higher completed schooling years than the national average, with those born in 1980 completing nine years, according to the latest household surveys (see Figure 10.9). All this puts Bolivia in the middle levels of Latin American in terms of schooling by 2000 — despite the fact that its per capita income still puts it in rank of the poorest of nations (see Figure 10.10).

Table 10.4: Bolivia in Comparative Perspective – Life Expectancy and Mortality

	Life expectancy at birth		Infant mortality rate		Under-five mortality rate		Child mortality rate		Adult mortality rate		Survival to age 65	
							Male	Female	Male	Female		
	years		per 1,000 live births		per 1,000		per 1,000	per 1,000	per 1,000	per 1,000	per 1,000	cohort
Bolivia/Latin America	1980	1999	1980	1999	1980	1999	1988–99	1988–99	1999	1999	1999	1999
Bolivia	52	62	118	59	170	83	26	26	261	210	58	65
Latin Amer & Carib.	65	70	61	30	80	38	13	14	207	122	67	80
Bolivia/World												
Low Income	53	59	112	77	177	116	45	51	288	258	55	60
Middle Income	66	69	54	31	79	39	12	12	199	135	68	78
Lower Middle Income	66	69	55	32	84	40	12	13	191	133	69	78
Upper Middle Income	66	69	52	27	67	34	..	..	233	143	66	80
Low & Middle Income	60	64	86	59	135	85	32	35	239	190	62	69

Source: World Bank (2001), Table 2.19.

Notes **Definitions:**

- Life expectancy at birth is the number of years a newborn infant would live if prevailing patterns of mortality at the time of its birth were to stay the same throughout its life.
- Infant mortality rate is the number of infants dying before reaching the age of one year, per 1,000 live births in a given year.
- Under five mortality rate is the probability that a newborn baby will die before reaching age five, if subject to current age-specific mortality rates.
- Child mortality rate is the probability of dying between the ages of one and five, if subject to current age-specific mortality rates
- Adult mortality rate is the probability of dying between the ages of 15 and 60 — that is, the probability of a 15-year-old dying before reaching age 60, if subject to current age-specific mortality rates between ages 15 and 60.
- Survival to age 65 refers to the percentage of a cohort of newborn infants that would survive to age 65, if subject to current age-specific mortality rates.

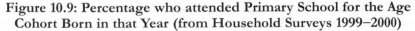

Figure 10.9: Percentage who attended Primary School for the Age Cohort Born in that Year (from Household Surveys 1999–2000)

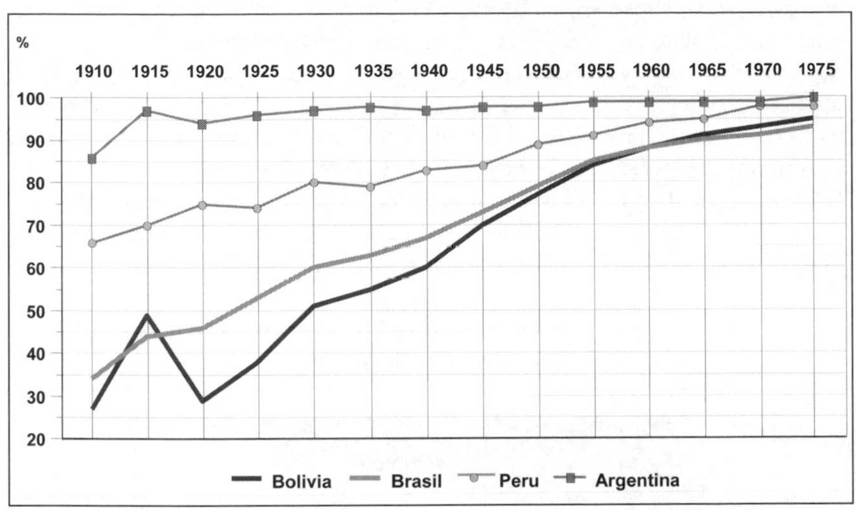

Source: BID, Servicio de Información Social, Departamento de Investigación

Figure 10.10: Average Years of Schooling Completed in 2000

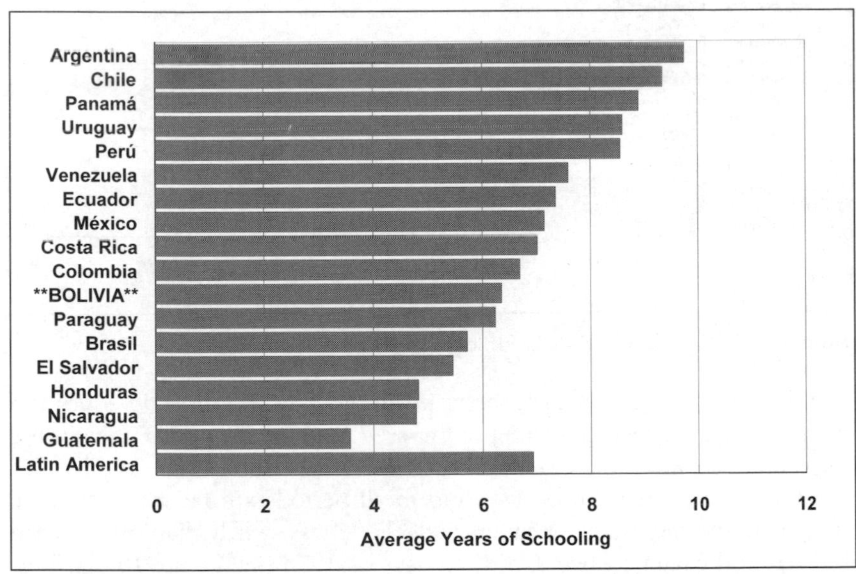

Source: BID, Servicio de Información Social, Departamento de Investigación

All of this had a direct impact on literacy. Given Bolivia's extraordinary language problems, with the fact that in 1950 the majority of the population did not even speak Spanish, let alone were literate in the language, the rapid reduction of illiteracy in Bolivia is truly impressive. Only 31 per cent of the population over 15 years of age was considered literate in 1950, but by 1976 the figure had climbed to 67 per cent; and by 2000 the figure was 86 per cent. In fact, Bolivia had moved in this period and from ranking as the sixth worst nation in the Americas to the eighth highest illiteracy rate and even had a better literacy rate than Brazil (see Figure 10.11).[37] Moreover, by world standards, this level of literacy placed Bolivia at the level of those countries listed as lower-middle income by world standards (see Table 10.5).

Figure 10.11: Level of Adult Illiteracy in Bolivia and Latin America in 2000

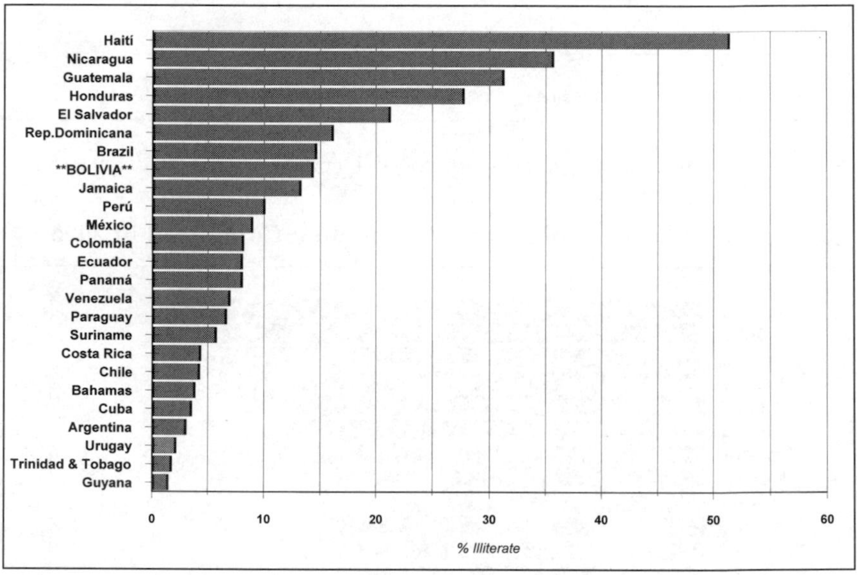

Source: CEPAL (2000), Part I, Table 33, p. 41

But the negative side of both the trends in literacy and those in education is the relative neglect of women compared to men. The difference in life expectancy in favor of women is reversed when we examine the literacy rates by sex. Women of all ages and in all periods are far more illiterate than men and their rates of illiteracy declined less swiftly than men, as can be seen in the data collected in the census of 1976 (see Figure 10.12). This is a reflection of the lower rates of female participation in education and the higher ratio of net rates of education of men versus women. But in fact, Bolivia was ranked around the middle of the Latin American states in this aspect. In a comparative study for 1995, it can be seen (Figure 10.13), that the net rates of attendance (number going to school of the age group at risk) was 97 per cent for boys and 93 per cent for girls — only four percentage points difference, and nothing like some of the quite pronounced variations even in Argentina, Venezuela and Colombia, all far wealthier than Bolivia.

Table 10.5: Bolivia in Comparative Perspective – Adult Illiteracy

	% of people 15 and above		% of people 15 and above		% of people 15 and above	
	Total		Male		Female	
Bolivia/Latin America	**1980**	**1999**	**1980**	**1999**	**1980**	**1999**
Bolivia	31	15	20	8	42	21
Brazil	25	15	23	15	27	15
Peru	21	10	12	6	29	15
Latin America & Caribbean	20	12	18	11	23	13
Bolivia/World						
Low Income	54	39	43	29	65	48
Middle Income	27	15	19	9	35	20
Lower Middle Income	30	16	20	9	39	22
Upper Middle Income	17	10	14	9	19	11
Low & Middle Income	38	25	29	18	48	32

Source: World Bank (2001)

Bolivia now educates almost all of its children at primary level and this has had a profound impact on all aspects of society, but most especially on the national language spoken. Spanish finally became the dominant language only by the census of 1992. As of this date, although 62 per cent of the total population was still listed as Amerindian, over 88 per cent of the population over the age of six years now spoke Spanish, though only 42 per cent of the population was monolingual in that language.[38] This meant that the Indian population, through education, has now become primarily bilingual and literate in the national language. Only eight per cent of the 1.7 million Quechua speakers over the age of six were monolinguals and only 15 per cent of the 1.1 million Aymara were not bilingual in Spanish — in fact only 19 per cent of the total national population remained monolingual speakers of any Indian language and only a quarter of the almost four million Indians were monolingual Indian language speakers.[39] This dramatic and continuing increase in bilingualism has not meant the loss of the major Indian languages, which have remained almost constant in the last three censuses (1950, 1976 and 1992) — with Quechua spoken by just over a third of the population and Aymara by another quarter of the population. It has been estimated that the 1.8 million indigenous language speakers in 1950 grew to four million in the census of 1992. Of those speakers whose mother tongue is an indigenous language, 2.5 million still live in the traditional rural Indian *comunidades*, a half million live in the eastern lowland colonies and one million in the cities.[40] By the year 2000, in fact, 49 per cent of the total population was still described as being of Indian extraction, no matter what language they spoke.[41] Monolingual Indian speakers, despite the growth of the rural population at unprecedented rates, nevertheless continued to decline. Quechua monolinguals had fallen from 988,000 to 438,000 and Aymara monolingual speakers from 664,000 to 168,000 between 1950 and 1992.[42] It is the growth of bilingual speakers that explains the majority position achieved by Spanish that was proof of the impact of the schools on the rural areas. Not only had the *cholo* population expanded enormously, as these figures imply, but even more important, rural Indian peasants were now using Spanish on a large scale, along with their traditional Indian languages.

Figure 10.12: Percentage Illiteracy by Age and Sex, Bolivia, 1976 Census

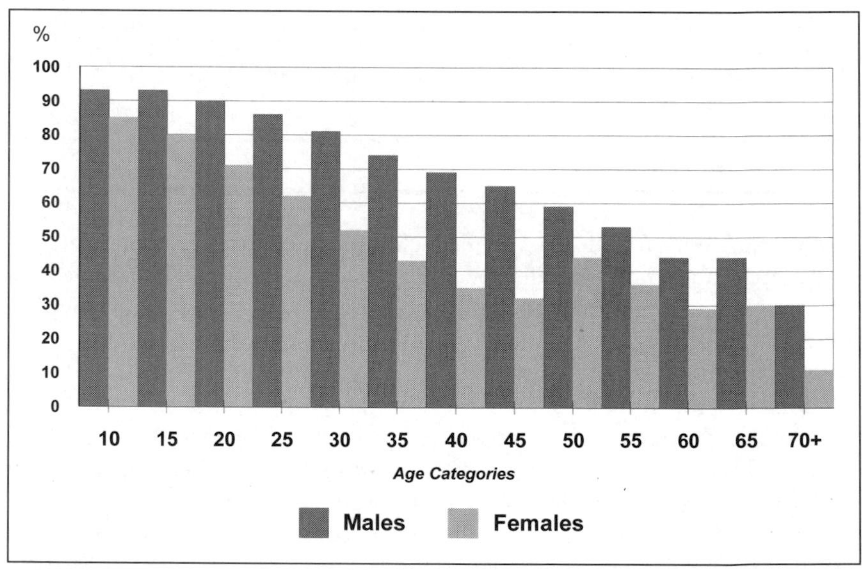

Source: INE (1976), vol. 10, cuadro pp- 7, pp. 52ff.

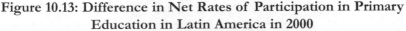

Figure 10.13: Difference in Net Rates of Participation in Primary Education in Latin America in 2000

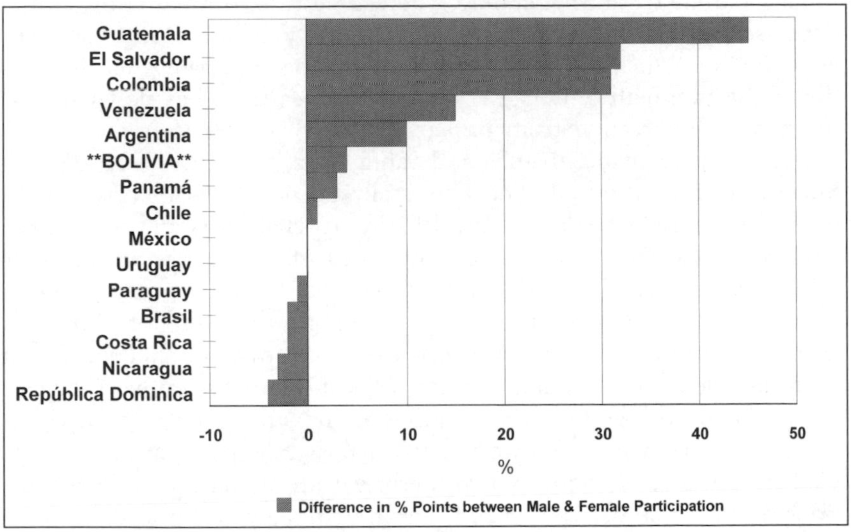

Source: CEPAL (2000a), Table 4.2

Many of the profound changes in fertility and mortality that the population experienced, as well as in language and literacy changes that occurred, were influenced by urban migration. From being a primarily rural society, the nation has moved toward a predominantly urban one in the 50-year period since the National Revolution. In 1950, only 20 per cent of the population lived in towns over 20,000 and by the census of 2001 the figure had risen to over half. The two cities of La Paz-El Alto and Santa Cruz alone, which in 1950 held just 364,000 persons and accounted for just 12 per cent of the national population, by the census of 2001 these held 2.6 million persons and accounted for just under a third of the national population. The increasing urbanization of the national population brought with it an improving standard of living. Every index of health, welfare and education shows a consistently better situation for the urban populations than for the rural ones. Thus, in 2000, the incidence of extreme poverty among national households was 24 per cent in the urban areas and 59 per cent in the rural ones. On the *altiplano*, 70 per cent of the rural population was listed as living in extreme poverty and only 35 per cent living in the highland cities experienced this below-subsistence income.[43]

Urbanization, as well as important rural-to-rural migrations and the opening of the eastern lowlands to colonization in the second half of the twentieth century, also brought about profound changes in the distribution of the national population. At the beginning of the twentieth century, the primary axis of the nation was La Paz-Oruro-Potosí, a north-south line, which was the dynamic heartland of the nation. Here was the center of mining, commerce and agriculture, whereas Santa Cruz was an isolated and depressed region and Cochabamba, a relatively enclosed and backward economy. With the progressive decline of mining, especially after the middle of the twentieth century, the commercial heartland has slowly moved in an easterly direction from La Paz and now encompasses the departments of La Paz, Cochabamba and Santa Cruz, while the Oruro-Potosí-Sucre axis has gone into decline. Essentially, the new NW-SE corridor connecting the three cities of La Paz-El Alto, Cochabamba and Santa Cruz and their respective provinces account for most of the economic activity of the nation. The three departments provided 92 per cent of state revenues in 1999,[44] and produced 71 per cent of the GDP of Bolivia in 2000.[45] The three provinces also had the most advanced and the fastest growing cities. The old mining centers of Potosí and Oruro have stagnated and their urban and rural populations are now the poorest in the country. The government recently estimated that over 80 per cent of the populations resident in these two formerly wealthy mining provinces were poor, and over 60 per cent were living in extreme poverty so that even a share of the urban populations were considerably poorer than the norm. Whereas Potosí, Chuquisaca and Cochabamba accounted for 34 per cent of the nation's population in 1950 — a figure quite similar to that in 1900 — by the census of 2001 these three provinces only accounted for 20 per cent of the population (see Table 3 above). Santa Cruz, which in 1950 held just ten per cent of the national population — almost identical to its importance in 1900 — by 2001 held a quarter of the residents of the country. Between them, the provinces of La Paz, Cochabamba and Santa Cruz went from containing just over half the population in 1950 to over 70 per cent in the latest census of 2001.

If the quality of health, the levels of literacy and the population attending school had all reached respectable levels by the end of the twentieth century, and a large part of the population had moved to rapidly expanding and relatively more wealthy urban centers and more fertile agricultural zones, the conditions for the rural population have remained extremely difficult. Change has occurred in housing and living conditions much more quickly in the urban areas than in the rural ones. As of the latest housing survey carried out in 1999, only 71 per cent of the homes had electricity (up 20 per cent from the previous census of 1992) and just 70 per cent had running water (again a major increase from just over half in 1992), with less than a fifth of the households having no access to potable water whatsoever and over a third with no indoor plumbing. Although the general situation had clearly improved over the last decade of the past century, the rural area was still profoundly impoverished. In 1999, less than one per cent of the rural homes had a telephone, 74 per cent cooked with firewood, two-thirds had no indoor plumbing and just 38 per cent had access to running water.[46] By the government's own measures, 52 per cent of the national population at the end of the 1990s could be judged as poor and 24 per cent as indigent. In the rural area, 82 per cent were poor and over half were indigent.

Even using the generous definition of urban (those living in communities of 2,000 persons or more), in the census of 1992, Bolivia still had 42 per cent of the national population living in rural areas. In these rural areas, people still worked in the most primitive of conditions. Although agriculture had dropped to 39 per cent of the economically active population in 2000,[47] farmers were not more efficient and farming only accounted for 14 per cent of the GDP.[48] Most of that agriculture remained traditional low productivity foodstuff farming. In 1950, something like 75 per cent of the foodstuffs sold in Bolivian markets were grown by peasants and only five per cent by agroindustry (the rest being imported). In 1981, peasants still produced 63 per cent of food sold in Bolivia, compared with only 15 per cent for agroindustry. Even as late as 1999, the largest crops in terms of acreage planted were devoted to soybeans — a new commercial crop — and maize and potatoes — two low productivity traditional food crops. Although the soybean farms in the Santa Cruz lowlands have an output close to world standards, maize productivity per hectare is still just a quarter of output per hectare achieved in the USA and potatoes yielded but 16 per cent per hectare of North American output levels. In fact, potato output in Bolivia was less than half the average of Latin America and was even a third less than potato productivity in neighboring Peru.[49] Much of this low productivity has to do with the fact that Bolivia spends less than any other country in Latin America on agricultural research and extension programs.[50] Despite major attempts by external funding agencies to improve seeds and deliver information, traditional agriculture remains the least affected. Change had clearly occurred in the Santa Cruz area with first sugar and cotton, then soybeans and sunflower seeds becoming highly productive commercial/industrial and competitive world crops. But traditional agriculture, which absorbed the bulk of the rural population, remained very much a low capitalized and backward production area. For all the recent agricultural transformations in Santa Cruz and some of the valley regions, rural Bolivia remains one of the poorest regions in the Americas. In the majority of Bolivia's rural areas, people still worked in the most primitive of conditions and workers in agriculture gained only a quarter of the low average national monthly salary in 2000. Although the percentage working in agriculture was consistently declining with the rise of the urban populations, the former peasants who migrated to the cities often only marginally increased their standard of living. Most were working in the informal service sector rather than manufacturing. In fact, the ratio of workers in manufacturing declined consistently in the last quarter of the twentieth century and accounted for only ten per cent of the EAP in 2000, nor was their income that extraordinary — being just 14 per cent above the national average and only a fifth of what the average salary was in mining.[51] All of which means that Bolivia still has one of the lowest per capita incomes in the hemisphere.

Although urban migration clearly does improve the life chances of rural migrants, the cities themselves are burdened by poor facilities and inadequate housing. Moreover, most cities have only moderately better conditions than the rural areas from which they draw their migrants. Thus in 2000, although the government estimates were that 91 per cent of the rural area population on the *altiplano* were living in poverty in terms of per capita consumption, 52 per cent of the population of the cities of the *altiplano* are listed as poor — with 23 per cent of the urban population living in extreme poverty (compared to 60 per cent in the rural areas). What is impressive is that while poverty changes in the rural areas by type of ecological zone, it varies little by such zones in the urban centers. Roughly half of all urban populations, whether located in the *altiplano*, the valley, or in the lowlands — are defined as poor. In contrast there is significant difference in rural poverty ratios by ecological zone, ranging from the 91 per cent rate in the rural highlands, to 80 per cent in the valleys and 68 per cent in the lowlands.[52]

The picture of Bolivia that emerges in this analysis of over a half century of social development is one of major social and economic change, combined with persistent poverty and economic backwardness. Education and health have seen the most dramatic progress. There has also been much better delivery of healthcare to children and expectant mothers so that some of the current statistics suggest that Bolivia is no longer among the worst countries in America in terms of mortality and morbidity statistics of its children under five years of age. But in most other indices, Bolivia still ranks alongside Haiti and the poorest Central American republics. Its per capita income was estimated by the World Bank to be US$990 in 1999, which placed it just ahead of Haiti, Honduras and Nicaragua as among the poorest in the continent.[53] Its economic growth rate has also been relatively low in the last decade and it continues to be heavily dependent on foreign aid. Bolivia ranked twelfth in the world in terms of per capita foreign assistance and was third in rank in the Western Hemisphere. This foreign aid has remained quite important to the government, with such aid being an extraordinary 41 per cent of central government expenditures in 1994 and still a high 30 per cent of such expenditures in 1999, when it still amounted to seven per cent of GNP.[54] Thus much of the change has been influenced by foreign funding, with the Bolivian government unable to carry out a large amount of welfare without that support.

Bolivia's continuing poverty and partial betterment of living standards, which is common to all the Americas, has occurred within the context of a radically changing social system. If the poor economic growth experienced in the past decades has not promoted much social mobility,[55] urban migration and the rise of rural peasant and urban *cholo* political power has made a profound difference in the response of all Bolivian governments to demands for improved social conditions for the poor. What can only be called the *choloization* of Bolivian society has become an important phenomenon after a half century of social revolution and two periods of hyperinflation, which have destroyed a great deal of the traditional white economic power. Although monolingual Aymara and Quechua speakers are disappearing, they are not being replaced by monolingual Spanish speakers. Rather, the traditional Indian languages are surviving with a surprising vigor, despite the lack of any systematic bilingual education until after the Education Reform of 1994. In the last decade the political power of the *cholo* population also has been finding expression, not only in traditional and radical parties and in the new municipal political arenas, but even with the transformation of a quintessential *cholo* town into the nation's third largest city. In 1988, the working-class suburb of El Alto on the outskirts of La Paz was finally incorporated as an independent city, whose administration was taken over by the new *cholo* elite. This high altitude town, which held some 307,000 persons, was half the size of La Paz and was overwhelmingly bilingual and very closely associated with the surrounding Aymara rural communities. The fourth largest city when it was created, by the census of 2001 it had 695,000 persons and had become Bolivia's third largest city, with the size difference lessening between itself and La Paz, which contained 792,000 persons. At the same time, the deterioration of the regional economies and the elimination of the old Spanish local *hacendado* elites in small towns, as the result of the events of 1952 and afterward, have created a more powerful *cholo* regional elite. It is from this elite and the upwardly mobile urban *cholo* population that a whole new generation of *cholo* merchants, truckers and university-trained professionals has emerged. While some *cholos* had obviously attended the university from the earliest times, they were a distinct minority and forced to abandon their language, culture and origins and adapt to the norms of 'white' culture. The new breed of educated *cholos* — far more numerous than ever before — now seems to have the option of retaining their ethnic ties, their traditional identities and original Indian languages along with Spanish, which many of them choose to do.

In reviewing the social changes which have occurred in Bolivia over the last half-century, it is evident that these macro-level social changes have followed trends quite similar to the nations of the hemisphere in terms of mortality and fertility, as the comparison with Haiti has shown. The decline of infant and mother's mortality, the mass vaccination of infants and children and the active intervention to prevent dehydration in early childhood, have occurred everywhere in Latin America and the Caribbean and cannot be exclusively tied to the impact of the National Revolution. The pace of these changes in Bolivia in the last two decades has been a bit more rapid than in the poorest of the nations of the hemisphere and has moved Bolivian into the higher end of the poorest countries in the world and ahead of several Central American republics. This more rapid pace of change in the most recent period may be due to a number of unique Bolivian factors, from government policies and foreign aid to a far more active lower class participation in national life, which is a direct result of the National Revolution. That far more was not accomplished in this long period may have more to do with the relatively slow growth of the national economy than with actions taken or not by the national government.

In terms of literacy and education, there is little question that Bolivia has moved farther and faster than comparable developments elsewhere and has achieved a higher level of literacy and arrived at a comparable level of net student enrollments at a faster pace than even neighboring Brazil, which had a per capita income over four times as large as Bolivia in 1999.[56] Despite chaotic delivery and often misplaced initiatives by the government in the area of education from the 1950s to the early 1990s, there is little question that profound changes have occurred beyond what has even been achieved in the areas of health and welfare. Clearly, the ability of the overwhelming majority of the population to become literate in Spanish, and to actively participate in education, are the results of both post-revolutionary government intervention and, even more, the Popular Participation in the whole literacy and educational enterprise, which has become a major demand of the formerly illiterate masses. The unleashing of that demand and the reception of the population to the changes which these developments imply, is due to the mass mobilization of the population, and it is in this unusual mobilization by Latin American standards, and in the raising of class and ethnic consciousness brought on by the post-1952 regimes, that we can see most dramatically the effects of the National Revolution.[57]

Notes

1 Dirección General de Estadística y Censos (DGE) (1955), pp. 42–3.
2 Wennergren and Whitaker (1975), p. 28.
3 INE (1985), p. 23–4.
4 *Ibid.*, p. ii.
5 Wennergren and Whitaker (1975), pp. 67ff.
6 DGE, cuadro 5, pp. 12–45.
7 DGE, cuadro 37 p. 112; and Oficina Nacional de Inmigración y Propaganda Geográfica (ONIPG) (1973), vol. II, p. 43.

8 DGE, cuadro 34, p. 103. In 1900 only 13% of the population were primarily Spanish speakers; fully 51% were listed as speaking an Indian language. See also ONIPG (1973), vol. II, p. 41.
9 INE and CELADE (1995), cuadro 2, p. 5.
10 United Nations (2000), table 9.
11 *Ibid.*, table 4.
12 Calculated from the estimated trend in mid-year populations given in Averanga Mollinedo (1998), pp. 30-3 in cuadro 3.
13 UN(2000), table 3.
14 INE and CELADE (1995), cuadro 10, p. 24.
15 Ministerio de Desarrollo Económico, Secretaria Nacional de Agricultura y Ganadería (1996), pp. 262–3. On the latest revisions of the Agrarian Reform Law and the attempt to rationalize and legitimize land titles in Santa Cruz and the Beni, see Muñoz and Lavadenz (1997).
16 For a fascinating analysis of the decline of a traditional small town white elite in the post-revolutionary period see Crandon-Malamud (1991).
17 [Victor Mezza Rosso] INE and CELADE (1995), cuadro 10, pp. 24–25.
18 CEPAL/CELADE (2000), table entitled 'Bolivia: Estimaciones y proyecciones de la poblacion de ambos sexos … 1950–2050'. Using their current population projections I calculated that the Bolivian population grew at 2.13 % in the decade of the 1950s, a figure that rose to 2.43 % per annum by the 1970s and was still estimated to be over 2 % per annum in the first decade of the twenty-first century.
19 [Rosso] INE and CELADE, p. 25, cuadro 10.
20 *Ibid.*, p. 25, cuadro 10.
21 The new finding announced in April 2002 of a 2.7% growth rate between the census of 1992 and that of 2001 suggests that many of the earlier projections of population growth were too low.
22 INE (2001), p. 129, cuadro 3.01.21 (for total births); and p. 157, cuadro 3.03.21 (for total assisted births).
23 Bolivia, Ministerio de Salud y Prevision Social, 'Salud de la Mujer … 1995' (http:///www.sns.gov.bo/salmuj.html), citing ENDSA (1994). This was the rate for the period 1989–94. These statistics cover deaths in pregnancy, birth and the puerperrium period just after birth.
24 *Ibid.*
25 INE (2001), p. 149, table 3.03.14.
26 INE (1993), p. 69; and INE (2001), p. 133, cuadro 3.02.04.
27 Bolivia, Ministerio de Salud y Previsión Social, Salud del Niño … 1995' (http://www.sns.gov.bo/salnin.html).
28 Westoff and Bankole (2000), p. 59, table 3.
29 INE (1997), p.29, cuadro 3.16.

30 *Ibid.*, p. 70, cuadro 3.17.
31 See Contreras (1999b); and chapter 11 of this volume.
32 CEPAL (2002), table 41, p. 49. Contreras claims that the Bolivian government figure is really just 5% of GNP.
33 Contreras (1999b), p. 484.
34 INE (2001) 'Indicadores de Educación, 1996-1999,' cuadro no. 7.1.14, based on data generated by the Unidad de Análisis de Políticas Sociales y Económicas (UDAPE)..
35 Urquiola (2000).
36 INE (2001), p.171 table 3.04.01.
37 CEPAL (2002), table 33, p. 42.
38 INE (1993), p. 131, table PP-12. There were 2.2 million monolingual speakers of Spanish and 2.4 million bilinguals. The Quechua monolinguals amounted to 428,000 and those of Aymara just 169,000.
39 Prada Alcoreza (1994), cuadros 38, 40, 44 and 46, pp. 69, 72, 79, 81.
40 Albó (1999b), p. 453.
41 INE (2001), p.128 table 3.01.20.
42 Censo demográfico 1950, cuadro 33, p. 102 for the 1950 data.
43 INE (2001), p. 212, cuadro 3.06.01.
44 Urquiola et al. (1999), p. 18, table 11.
45 INE (2001), pp. 291–2, cuadro 4.01.03,02.
46 These housing data come from the 1999 household survey carried out by MECOVI and are available online from INE.
47 INE (2001), p. 203, cuadro 3.05.03.
48 *Ibid.*, p. 270,cuadro 4.01.01.03.
49 Data on land sown to crops are found in INE (2001), p. 362, cuadro 4.01.04.01. The comparative Latin American, US and Bolivian yields per hectare data were taken from FAOSTAT, Current Statistics 2002. Even by Bolivian standards, the average output of potato production from La Paz was half a kilo per hectare below the national average in the period 1987–95. Grupo DRU (1996), p. 48, cuadro 10.
50 Godoy, de Franco and Echeverría (1993), pp. 6–7.
51 All the wage data will be found in INE (2001), p. 203, cuadro 3.05.03.
52 *Ibid.*, p.212, cuadro 3.06.010.
53 World Bank (2001), pp. 12–14, table 1.1.
54 *Ibid.*, pp. 348ff, table 6.10.
55 On the theme of social mobility in the post revolutionary period see Kelley and Klein (1981).
56 World Bank (2001), pp. 12–14, table 1.1.
57 For the very high level of rural and urban popular mobilization and participation in what are called 'organizaciones territoriales', that is 'sindicatos campesinos' and 'juntas de vecinos' and their demand for services, see the important study by Sandóval et al. (1998).

CHAPTER 11

A Comparative Perspective of Education Reforms in Bolivia: 1950–2000

Manuel E. Contreras*

In a period when education has been highlighted by development analysts and multilateral organizations as the cornerstone of economic and social development; when it is considered a key component to overcoming poverty and reducing inequality; and when Latin America is reforming its education systems, it is pertinent to analyze education reforms in historical and comparative perspective. Governments, policymakers and multilateral organizations have placed great expectations on the results of the education reforms currently in progress. The historical record would suggest that bringing about significant change in the education systems is more difficult than expected. Similarly, at least in the case of Bolivia, researchers, education specialists and the public at large have attributed more to previous education reforms than these reforms actually accomplished. Thus, comparing and contrasting them with experiences from other countries and with the current reform efforts will lead to a better understanding of past events.

This chapter analyzes the development of education in Bolivia in the second half of the twentieth century. In order to do so, it describes the Education Reform of 1955, carried out under the Bolivian Revolution (1952–64), highlighting its embodiment in an Educational Code. It then pursues comparisons with two other nations that underwent social revolutions in the twentieth century (Cuba and Mexico) and reformed their educational systems. First, it compares student enrollment growth rates before and after the Bolivian Revolution with the growth rates of student enrollment before and after the Cuban Revolution (1959–70). Second, it compares the growth in average years of education after the Mexican Revolution (1910–40) with the growth in average years of schooling after the Bolivian Revolution. By so doing, it shows how Bolivia's performance fared relative to other nations that also tried educational reforms. Subsequently, it briefly traces the development of education in Bolivia in the 1970s and '80s, highlighting the need for a comprehensive reform, because of the situation of the education sector. The chapter contrasts the Education Reform of 1955 with the current Education Reform (1994 to date), stressing the pedagogical emphasis and bilingual character of the latter. It seeks to identify continuities and contrasts in both efforts to modernize education in Bolivia in the twentieth century. The chapter concludes by highlighting the major challenges that the education sector faces at the start of the twenty-first century.

Education in Bolivia before the Revolution[1]

During the first half of the twentieth century, there were important advances in the Bolivian educational system. The foundations of a national educational system had been laid in the early part of the century with the first reform championed by the liberals. This reform set out to: (1) improve the administrative system of the education sector; (2) start teacher training programs in Bolivia; (3) give priority to primary education in urban areas; (4) develop the curriculum of both primary and secondary education; (5) strengthen indigenous education; (6) promote the provision of education for women; and (7) develop commercial and technical education. The education system was centralized and expanded as more resources were assigned to the sector. By 1950, the education budget represented 21.8 per cent of the national budget, up from 5.9 per cent in 1900. Similarly, the percentage of children in primary school increased from 2.0 per cent in 1900 to 25.8 per cent in 1951 and illiteracy was reduced from 81.5 per cent in 1900 to 67.9 per cent in 1950. Despite these advances, there is no doubt that much still remained to be done: only a quarter of the school-age population was in primary school and two thirds of the population was illiterate. The challenges faced in the rural areas were greater. Although there had been important advances in the 1930s and '40s, it was estimated that by 1950 rural schools enrolled only one fifth of the school age children. In order to give rural education more importance, the government placed it under the aegis of the Ministry of Peasant Affairs.

In addition to issues of school coverage and basic literacy, there was much discussion among the elite on the type of education that Bolivia required. There was an ongoing debate in the press about the basic philosophy of education: what type of society were Bolivians being educated for? The debate was more heated in the case of rural education, where the values underscoring Indian education were still widely contested, as is highlighted in the chapter by Brooke Larson in this volume.

In light of the above limitations, the National Revolution placed great expectations on the education sector.

Education Reform in the Bolivian Revolution

Of all the accomplishments of the Bolivian Revolution, the 1955 Education Reform is the least studied. Unlike universal suffrage (1952), the nationalization of the mines (1952) and the agrarian reform (1953), the education reform has yet to be extensively analyzed.[2] Those studies that do exist are partial.[3] Despite this, the 1955 Education Reform is widely credited with many things by politicians, education specialists and the public at large. For example, the Ministry of Education has recently stated that the 1955 Education Reform's main accomplishments were twofold. First, it credited the reform with expanding education for the indigenous population in rural areas previously excluded from education. According to the ministry, the reform accomplished this by broadening teacher training through the creation of normal schools while making it possible to hire teachers without training (known as *interinos*). Second, the Ministry of Education highlights the effort of this reform to turn Indians into Spanish speakers and change their identity by popularizing the use of the euphemism 'campesino'. Thus, the school became the central means of linguistically and culturally homogenizing the population. The ministry correctly stresses that the imposition of Spanish as the sole teaching language was one of the main reasons for the subsequent failing of indigenous children.[4] Indeed, research in the United States, Sweden, Mexico, Peru and more recently in Bolivia has shown that children first taught to read and write in their mother tongue (the language spoken at home: Quechua, Aymara or Guaraní in Bolivia) have greater fluency and literacy in the second language (Spanish in Bolivia) and do better in school generally.[5] The vast experience of bilingual and intercultural education in Latin America has also shown that bilingual education has a positive effect in self-worth, it increases the participation of children in their learning process, it helps mobilize the community and increases attendance and reduces drop-out rates and repetition. Thus, as López (1998) points out, we must not lose sight that this approach is eminently pedagogical.

Researchers have also argued that this reform reduced illiteracy and expanded access to education. Writing in 1982, Cariaga attributed the fall in illiteracy between 1950 and 1976 to the educational efforts of the MNR government. According to Cariaga, 'increased expenditures for education and better incentives for rural teachers' had 'been more effective than expected'.[6] More recently, using enrollment figures for 1951 and 1964 alone, Cajias (1998) concludes the revolution was responsible for increased enrollments. While recognizing that this expansion was not sufficient, she suggests that the other aspects of the reform (curricular and pedagogical change) could not be carried out because of the MNR's downfall. As I will show, a careful analysis of enrollment trends prior to and after the revolution permits a more subtle interpretation. Similarly, I will argue the reform had no pedagogical component to speak of and was unable to increase quality.

Only recently, celebrating the 50th anniversary of the revolution, the daily *La Razón* editorialized 'the current state of Bolivia can not be understood without the agrarian reform, the nationalization of the mines, universal suffrage, education reform (to mention only the most important measures undertaken since the 9 April 1952)'.[7] It is telling that the

Education Reform was the last to be implemented; it followed the Agrarian Reform and the nationalization of the mines. What exactly did it entail?

For President Paz Estenssoro, education had to be reformed to mesh with the new correlation of economic and social forces arising from the revolution. He made a strong call for the expansion of schooling to the masses not only in basic education but in intermediate and higher education as well. He was adamant in highlighting the need for technical education. He argued that technicians were needed to efficiently operate the recently nationalized mines, develop agriculture and build industry and infrastructure. He was critical of the current state of secondary education that only produced bureaucrats and called, instead, for technicians who would be able to make a living for themselves and become positive actors in the construction of a new Bolivia.[8]

The education reform materialized as a new Education Code, which organized the haphazard education legislation previously in existence. A commission of notable people associated with education wrote the code. The commission comprised a diverse group of twelve individuals: one representative from the president of the republic, two representatives from the Ministry of Education, two representatives from the Ministry of Peasant Affairs, three representatives from the teacher's union, one representative from the labor confederation (COB), two representatives from the universities and one representative from private schools. The code was drafted in 120 days. During this time the commission worked through a series of sub-commissions[9] that organized various round tables, conferences and lectures in order to inform itself and exchange views with interested parties. The reports of each sub-commission were discussed before presenting a draft of the code to the president in January 1954. It is significant that the code was not actually enacted until a year later, after there was pressure from the teacher's union for its promulgation.[10]

The code defined in 328 articles the bases and principles of the education sector, its organization and objectives, teacher training, adult literacy promotion, labor training and rural education. It enshrined the views of the teachers' union, the labor movement and the left of a liberating educational proposal. After its enactment, it was the major piece of legislation in education until it was repealed in 1994.

For our purposes, I shall highlight a few aspects of the code's contents. It characterized education as mainly the obligation of the state and as universal, free and obligatory. It also stressed education as democratic, collective, national, revolutionary, anti-imperialist and anti-feudal, active and work oriented, co-ed (giving both sexes equal opportunities), progressive and scientific. The code distinguished between urban education, under the aegis of the Ministry of Education and rural education under the Ministry of Peasant Affairs. In the case of rural education, it sought to:

1) Develop in the peasant good habits of life in relation to his nutrition, hygiene, health, living quarters, clothing and social and personal conduct…

3) Teach him to be a good agricultural worker through practical training in the usc of up-to-date systems of cultivation and animal rearing.[11]

Thus, the code sought to 'civilize' the Indians and convert them into 'peasant' farmers.

What were the effects of the Education Reform launched by the code? Given the low enrollment rates in Bolivia and the need to expand the system, I concentrate on flow and stock measures of the effects of the reform. To measure flow, I use enrollment data; and to measure the longer-term effects and gauge stock, I analyze the years of education of people of age 20 in 1999 from household survey data.

Historical data on education enrollment in Bolivia are difficult to come by, and I have used the UNESCO estimates for total primary school enrollment to analyze enrollment from 1942 to 1969. As Figure 11.1 indicates, there was a steady increase in enrollment during this period with no major increase in the 1950s. If one calculates the annual growth rate from 1942 to 1952 and compares it with the annual growth rate from 1952 to 1964, there was a slightly greater rate of growth in the decade prior to the revolution than during it (see Table 11.1). Thus, it appears the revolution did not have a major impact on total enrollment.

Figure 11.1: Primary School Enrollment in Bolivia and Cuba, 1942–69

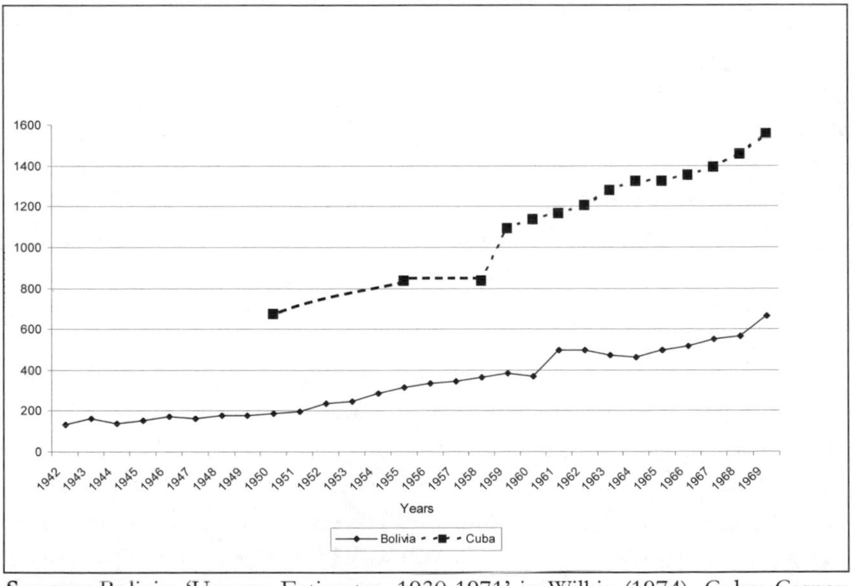

Source: Bolivia: 'Unesco Estimates, 1930-1971' in Wilkie (1974). Cuba: Carnoy and Wertheim (1979).

Table 11.1: Annual Growth Rates for Enrollment in Primary Education in Bolivia and Cuba for Selected Periods

Bolivia	**1942–1952**	**1952–1964**
Annual Growth rate (%)	5.97	5.87
Cuba	**1950–58**	**1958–69**
Annual Growth rate (%)	2.76	5.81

Source: Figure 11.1

Politicians and educational analysts have argued that the revolution's effect was greatest in the rural areas. Unfortunately, I was not able to obtain a time series for enrollment figures in rural areas to cover a significant period prior to and during the revolution. So, instead, I have used a proxy: the number of rural *núcleos educativos*.[12] As indicated in Figure 11.2, there was exponential growth of rural *núcleos* from 1935 to 1969. There is no doubt that rural enrollment increased, but it is worth noting that this increase did not take place in a vacuum. Rural education had been increasing since the 1930s, and by the 1940s there was some degree of institutional capacity to cater to this sector.[13] As demonstrated by Figure 11.2, once again there was no significant increase after 1955. What is certain is that as a result of the Agrarian Reform, peasants experienced greater freedom to migrate to urban areas where they had access to more (and hopefully also better) educational opportunities. In his comparative study of Peruvian haciendas and ex-haciendas in Bolivia in the Lake Titicaca district, Burke (1970) has argued that the Bolivian *campesino* no longer had to work for the landowner due to land reform. Since his own plot of land did not require full-time attention, there was more leisure time for families, especially children. Thus, children became more likely to attend school. Additionally, according to Carter (1964, cited by Burke) the expansion of rural *sindicatos* arising from the agrarian reform also promoted education.

Given the government's financial and organizational restrictions to satisfying the communities' demands, the Indian communities themselves established schools and paid the teachers. Thus, paradoxically, 'private' (non-publicly funded) education became prominent in the rural areas *after* the revolution. By 1966, there were 65,336 students in 1,424 community schools in rural areas. This represented 23 per cent of total enrollment![14]Because of this, the annual growth rate of rural *núcleos* in the 12 years prior to the revolution (1940–52) was 13.29 per cent and the annual rate of growth during the revolution (1952–64) was lower: 11.48 per cent. These results contrast with Kelley and Klein's (1983) estimate that the indigenous population received 40 per cent more education than they would have at the rates prior to the revolution.

Figure 11.2: Number of Rural Education *Núcleos*, 1935–68

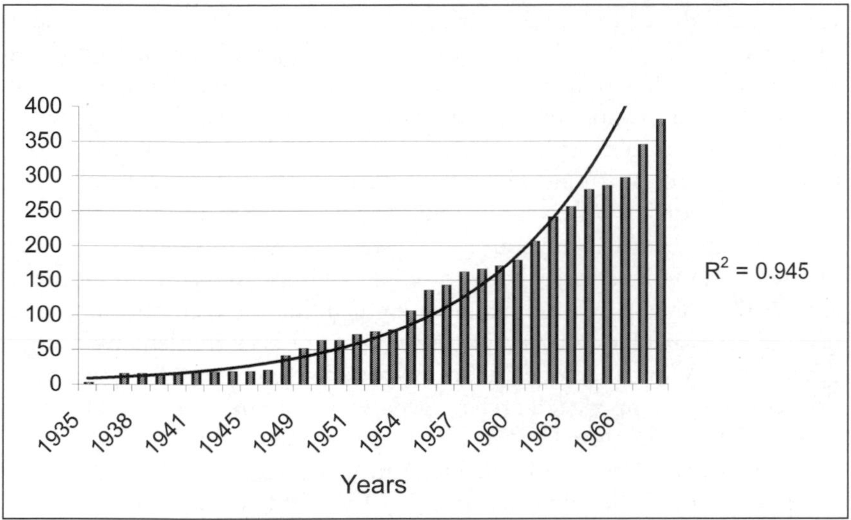

Source: Calculated from data in Sanjines Uriarte (1968).

Indians received more education, but there are great doubts as to the quality of this education. According to Comitas (1968), rural education during the revolution was a continuation of rural education before the revolution because it remained under the responsibility of the Ministry of Peasant Affairs. Comitas is critical of the curriculum's lack of pertinence and the dominant pedagogy, which was based on memorization and rote learning. He emphasizes the negative effects of the effort to teach Indian children in Spanish. This was compounded by the rural teachers' low level of training. Unlike those in the urban areas — who had four years post-secondary education in a normal school — rural teachers were only required to have a primary education and six months training in a rural normal school. Teachers were not well paid and their attendance was sporadic. Effective teaching time was further reduced by religious and national holidays, political crises that closed schools down, teachers' strikes and teacher absenteeism. Thus, Indian children received scarce preparation for modern life and had high drop out rates. Comitas therefore concludes that:

> … in education, the 1952 Revolution and the 14 years of MNR predominance did little to modify the hierarchical order of significant seg-

> ments of Bolivian society and did little, if anything, to provide new forms of institutionalized social articulation. It is obvious that whatever were the directives from the center of the system these were not revolutionary. The considerable social change that Bolivia experienced during the last 14 years, seems more like the result of a partial splintering of the traditional order that a comprehensive social reform.[15]

In urban education, Fernando Diez de Medina, the minister of education who headed the education reform commission, stated in 1958 that, due to insufficiency of financial resources, the education reform had not been able to change the appearance nor the essential features of the education system. He was aware of the limitations of the pedagogical practice in Bolivia whose main characteristics were using a verbose style, based on dictation and memorization. Thus, he argued, it limited critical judgment, reflexive thinking, a spirit of cooperation and self-regulation. He was also critical of the fact that the education system did not adequately recognize differences in individual aptitude to obtain an improved student performance.[16] The minister was not alone in highlighting the fact that the education reform, for all intents and purposes, had not been implemented at the school level. While the code advocated for an advanced pedagogical practice, in reality, there existed archaic pedagogy dominated by rote learning based solely on memory.[17]

What are unclear from the literature reviewed are the pedagogical underpinnings of the 1955 Reform. What would have been implemented had there been greater resources? This question remains unanswered. Another related issue is the absence of proposals for teacher training. Although there were efforts to expand teacher training, and the MNR government founded four new normal schools, there were no changes in the curriculum of urban teacher training schools. In rural normal schools, the reform sought to have graduating teachers become community level development promoters, but candidates still only had to have primary school completed to enter the rural normal schools.[18] Without more and better-trained teachers, there could not be changes at the classroom level and so education quality did not change.

What teachers' unions accomplished during the MNR government was to participate in running the Ministry of Education. Under *co-gestión* (worker participation) unions determined appointments from the director general down. Thus, the code legitimated a reciprocity pact between the state and teachers' unions. It marked the start of the interplay of the two actors that would dominate the realm of educational policy: the state and teachers' unions.[19]

Finally, what were the stock effects of the education reform? As seen in Figure 11.3, there was a gradual increase in the number of years of education within different birth cohorts from 1920 to 1975. This increase is very similar to the Latin American average. Bolivia's figures lagged behind those for Latin America until the 1970s, when they overtook the average for the region. If we analyze annual rates of growth for the birth cohorts before the revolution (1920–40), we see that their growth (1.83 per cent) is slightly lower than for those born during the period that benefited from the revolution (1945–60): 1.92 per cent. Thus, we could argue that the enrollment expansion during the revolution led to a generation of more educated people. The difference is slight, and there are no major discontinuities (breakthroughs) as a result of the revolution. So, to a large extent, the result is the outcome of the 'natural' growth of the education system and the intrinsic cumulative nature of a stock measurement. The type of discontinuity I have in mind are those similar to, for example, the Cuban Revolution, which I analyze below. Before this, however, I point out the evolution of the average years of education in Mexico in Figure 11.3. Note how the rate of growth increases in the second half of the 1930s and '40s, before it overtakes the Latin American average in 1945. I posit that it is this type of shift in the average age of education that can be expected from a significant expansion in the educational opportunities that took place in Mexico in the 1920s and '30s.

Figure 11.3: Bolivia, Mexico and Latin America: Average Years of Education by Birth Cohort, 1920–75

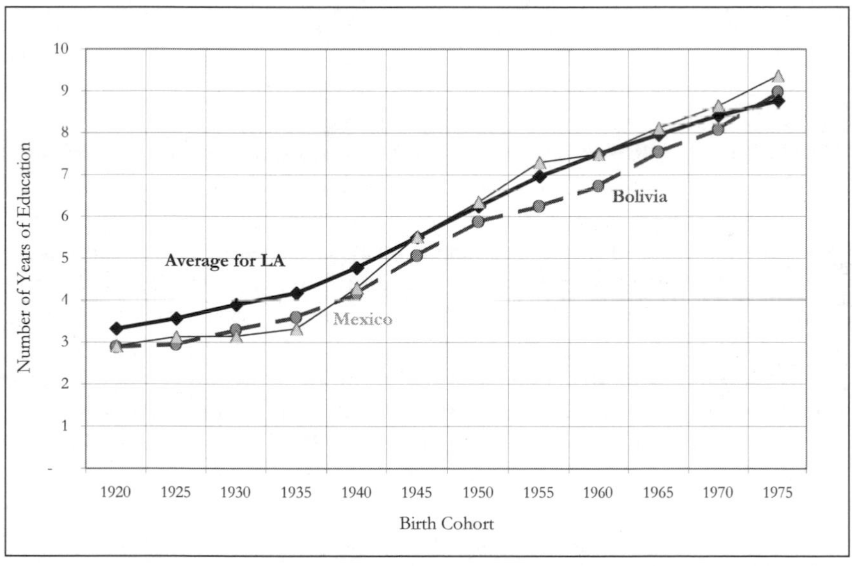

Source: Banco Interamericano de Desarrollo (2001). I gratefully acknowledge the help of Werner Hernani in processing the household surveys and facilitating me the final tables from which this graph is drawn.

Education in the Mexican and Cuban Revolutions

The Mexican and Cuban revolutions are the other two important social revolutions in the twentieth century with which the Bolivian Revolution has been compared. There have been comparisons of the US responses to the revolutions,[20] of their impact,[21] institutionalization and political parties[22] and restructuring of the national economies.[23] Surprisingly, there have been no comparisons of social accomplishments, such as access to education, which I deal with below.

After the first decade of civil war (1910–20), the Mexican Revolution made significant improvements and expanded education. It was under President Obregón that an enlightened minister of education, Vasconcelos, was able to overhaul the Mexican education system. The educational budget was doubled in the early 1920s, teachers were better paid, schools and libraries were built and books and newspapers published. These efforts were followed by those of President Calles, whose minister of education paid greater attention to rural education with an emphasis on practical instruction.[24] Educational expansion continued in the 1930s under President Cárdenas, who increased rural schools with a special emphasis on teacher training. The emphasis, however, was not so much on content or organization, but 'rather in the social and political context in which rural education was undertaken'. Unlike the Bolivian Revolution, rural teachers were expected to provide more than just basic literacy; they were counted upon to play a key leadership role in advocating for peasant rights and indeed did help organize agrarian protests.[25]

The Mexican Revolution centralized education, giving the federal government greater control over the education system after the establishment of the *Secretaría de Educación* in 1921. The federal government 'built and controlled schools in the states, especially in rural areas'[26] where there were no major efforts to foster bilingual education and *indigenista* education projects. Like the Bolivian Revolution, the emphasis was more on turning Indians into peasants, and class was given precedence over ethnicity.[27]

As in the case of the Bolivian Revolution, the Cuban Revolution is also credited with significant increases in enrollment in primary education, from 58 per cent in 1953 to 98.6 per cent in 1970, reduction of illiteracy and a decrease in the gap between rural and urban illiteracy rates.[28] Here also education was seen as key to transforming the structure of the Cuban economy and its political culture.[29] How was this accomplished?

Unlike Bolivia, one of the main approaches was to set up a massive adult education campaign. Over 34,000 teachers and 250,000 urban dwellers were mobilized from April to December of 1961 at a cost of over $52 million. This campaign is also credited with integrating Cuba, as it brought social services to the most remote regions and introduced the illiterate peasants to the urban educated classes and vice versa. A government led post-literacy adult education program to continue to expand the education of those originally alphabetized followed this campaign. Formal education enrollment increased by over 40 per cent between 1958 and 1959 and continued to grow steadily (see Figure 11.1). Expansion was particularly strong in the rural sector, where enrollment increased by seven per cent annually from 1959 to 1962. The emphasis of the reform was on primary and secondary education. The government emphasized technical education in the early 1960s, once a shortage of skilled labor resulted from industrialization efforts and the massive loss of technical personnel and professionals who left Cuba after the revolution (estimated at between 15,000 to 25,000). The budget for university education was initially reduced as enrollment declined and emphasis shifted towards vocational and technical education.[30]

Educational expansion was not free from problems in quality. The educational system was not able to retain students beyond primary school. Low promotion rates and high drop out rates reflected poor teaching quality in the early 1960s. There were teacher shortages, and by the mid-1970s 40 per cent of elementary-school teachers were not graduates from any teacher training school and had very little education. This led to what Domínguez (1978) skeptically refers to a 'primary-school-educated-people' led by 'junior-high-school graduates'.[31]

Significant financial resources account for the expansion of Cuban education at the primary level and in adult education. In 1965, Cuba's education budget was seven per cent of GNP, already very high by international standards. UNESCO set a target of four per cent for 1970 for developing countries. By 1975, education expenditure represented 12 per cent of GNP.[32]

In the Cuban case, in synthesis, 'educational reforms were a result of profound changes in the direction of economic and social policy on the island, not independent, ad hoc policies that emerged from imaginative people in the Ministry of Education or from Fidel himself. These changes were accompanied by a new concept of men's and women's relation to each other and the means of production.'[33] In Bolivia, changes in education attendance and attainment were more the result of greater social mobility after the revolution. The efforts to organize the legal aspects of the education system did not translate into either significantly more classrooms or better teaching or learning. Indeed, an analysis of Bolivia's educational system written by two Cubans in 1970 began with the anecdote that the Bolivian Education Code was supposedly considered 'the best and most modern' but was not put into effect. They concluded that true reform would only be possible once 'the people, under the direction of its vanguard, take power in its hands, wresting away from imperialism and the national oligarchy that detents it'.[34]

Education in the 1970s and 1980s in Bolivia

In this section, I briefly sketch the situation of education in Bolivia and present the rise and demise of the First Education and Vocation Training Project that synthesizes the problems in the education sector.

At the start of the 1970s, education analysts perceived that the resources allocated to the sector could not grow further. Education expenditure as a percentage of total government expenditure had increased from 29.4 per cent in 1960 to 43.3 per cent in 1970 and as a percentage of GDP it had actually doubled, from 1.58 per cent to 3.16 per cent. Further growth was not conceivable, so a more efficient use of available resources was required. There was a hodge-podge of educational interventions without central coordination and long term plans.[35]

Therefore, a major sector assessment was undertaken in 1973 in cooperation with UNESCO whose main recommendations for the ministry of education were to develop a series of long-term plans, which included administrative decentralization and merging of rural and urban education.

At the start of the decade, the World Bank summarized the tragic situation of education in Bolivia with impressive succinctness and pertinence, thus:

> Despite sizeable budgetary allocations to education, no significant improvements in access and quality have occurred. Some of the reasons for the low productivity of expenditures have been the following:
>
> a. Until recently, two subsystems, one for rural, one for urban education existed side by side — both with heavily over centralized inefficient administrations in La Paz.
>
> b. Drop out and repeat rates are high because children are taught in Spanish and not their native language, because they are malnourished and often cannot walk the long distances to get to a school and because they are taught an irrelevant and overly academic curriculum which bears little relation to future employment.
>
> c. Most of the expenditures go to salaries of untrained teachers. Few funds are available for expansion of the system and quality improvements such as distribution of learning materials or teacher supervision. [36]

Dissatisfaction with the educational system was not circumscribed or limited to technical documents such as the one cited above. A cross section of Bolivian society was frustrated with the educational system. They rejected the current system, felt an urgent need for change and perceived that education only served the dominant minority. Furthermore, Bolivians were critical of the alienation the system gave rise to, denounced its lack of practical opportunities and its monolithic and homogenizing character.[37]

In part to overcome this situation, the Bolivian government and the World Bank completed an educational project design that had begun in the late 1960s and early 1970s. It was finally signed in 1977. The project had a primary and community education component and a vocational training component. I refer to the former. The objectives of the project were to focus on the Aymara-speaking region through seeking cost-effective ways to (a) increase the access to education through expansion and improvement of basic and intermediate schools; (b) develop appropriate curricula, learning materials and teacher training programs; and (c) design a community education project for the non-school age population. The project sought to make better use of primary facilities and teachers and reorganize primary school administration and supervision. Total project costs were estimated at US$21.4 million and the World Bank's loan was for US$15 million.[38]

Ten years later, the project was brought to completion after only having disbursed three quarters of the loan amount, US$10.6 million. It had achieved the objective of expanding and strengthening basic education by constructing/furnishing and equipping 955 classrooms, ten new lower secondary schools, a teacher training college and 287 staff houses serving a total student population of 43,000. It took 9.5 years instead of the planned four in large part because of 'staff inexperience' and large administrative turnover (13 ministers of education and 18 project implementing unit directors!). The project also faced the economic crisis of the mid-1980s in Bolivia. The project was less successful in meeting objective (b) of developing curricula and training teachers. In the words of the appraisers: 'The Project as designed was a bold step in its effort to reform basic education. As in so many reform efforts the actual change achieved has turned out to be disappointingly limited.'[39]

There were legislative efforts to modify the education sector in the 1980s when President Paz Estenssoro presented a new General Education Law to Congress in 1986. This proposal was opposed by teachers' unions and popular organizations and was set aside. So too were the other efforts of the MNR government to make major changes in the education system in the late 1980s contained in the *Libro Blanco* and *Libro Rosado* produced by the ministry of education. The major changes proposed were to unify rural and urban education, to decentralize education and introduce curricular changes to develop a more reflexive and critical individual. All these efforts were seen as challenging the '*conquistas*' (hard won benefits) of the Education Code of 1955 and as an expedient way to accommodate the education sector to the New Economic Policy of the government.[40]

Education Reform in the 1990s

As in many other Latin American countries, Bolivia is presently implementing a profound educational reform. This is the third reform effort of the twentieth century. The liberals implemented the first reform in the early 1900s and the 1955 Education Code initiated the second one during the National Revolution. Of all the twentieth century reforms, the present one involves the most changes in the education system. A common feature of all three reforms is that they were initiated in moments of economic crisis, of changes in sociopolitical structures and of major transformations in the world system.[41]

The elaboration of the current proposal must be seen within the contextual framework of changes in the predominant views of development worldwide that privilege education as a key factor for development. These changes have been supported by international events such as the World Conference on Education for All held in Jomtien in 1990. It established the priorities of basic education and the basic needs for learning. Such conferences generated a wave of concern for education throughout the world and highlighted in academic circles the role of education as a means to development. In part, such events, along with support from political and multilateral international organizations, promoted a need for educational reform as well as influencing the contents of the reform itself.[42]

At the national level, there was increasing awareness in the various government administrations — as manifested in their development plans — of the need to strengthen human capital in order to achieve greater levels of economic growth. Education appeared to be the best way to increase the quality of life and to improve the distribution of income, making educational reform an attractive option for achieving these goals. With this in mind, it is important to note that during the formulation of the current education reform, it was the ex-minister of planning and coordination who provided the needed leadership, an aspect that will be later analyzed in more detail.

As stated, the deficiencies in the Bolivian educational system had been widely acknowledged for at least two decades yet, surprisingly, nothing was done to overcome them. By the 1990s the World Bank (1993) summarized the underlying problems of Bolivian education thus:

> The poor coverage and quality … stem partly from relatively low levels of spending on education overall during several decades (averaging 2.7 per cent of GDP between 1986 and 1991). Several other factors are also important in explaining its failings: (a) alienation and exclusion of primary beneficiaries — children, their parents and the society as a whole —from participating in the decision-making process and from the right to scrutinize operations and results; (b) weak administration of the system; (c) inappropriate and inefficient management of sector financing, including insufficient allocation of resources to primary education; (d) various barriers to access and obstacles to educational attainment, including materials, inadequate teacher training, inattention to the needs of non-Spanish-speaking populations and deficient infrastructure, which particularly affect girls and rural populations.[43]

It is under this scenario that the current education reform was designed.

The current Bolivian educational reform has several unique characteristics, one of which is that its preparation relied on a task force outside the Ministry of Education. In 1992, the Ministry of Planning, rather than the Ministry of Education, was selected to create this task force named the Technical Support Team for Education Reform (ETARE). The reason for this was that the ministry of education lacked the human resources required to carry out the reform and was not interested in assuming the responsibility for reforming a markedly deficient educational system because doing so meant clashing with the unions. Moreover, the control teachers unions had in naming authorities in the ministry of education hampered any real possibility of reforming the very structural problems that required modification, such as teacher training and hiring. Changes in the historical context and in the development model required an educational reform that would not only concentrate on the pedagogical aspects, but would also develop concrete actions and proposals to modernize the educational system, starting with the Ministry of Education. The reform proposals could no longer stagnate in abstract discussions about what type of society was to be built or how a 'new man' was to be formed as many proposals of the teachers' unions and the Catholic Church did. Instead, they had to effectively 'transcend diagnosis and definition of objectives in order to delineate policies, establish proposals and translate them into executable plans'.[44]

ETARE was set up as a pluralist and multidisciplinary team and received financial support and technical assistance from the World Bank. It worked in close coordination with the minister of planning and in many instances had to pursue the design of the reform despite government opposition. The Paz Zamora administration was not fully convinced of the full-scale reform that ETARE and the Ministry of Planning thought the education system needed, fearing opposition from teachers unions and the social unrest that might ensue.[45] Moreover, each new minister of education was suspicious of what ETARE was up to and, more often than not, placed obstacles in ETARE's way.

The process was not an easy one, and there were several disagreements between ETARE and the World Bank on issues of administrative and curricular emphasis. To what degree would the reform be an administrative effort at modernizing the Ministry of Education and the organization of the educational system and to what degree would it provide a new curriculum and pedagogy and seek changes in the classroom?[46] The reform set out to place education at the service of students. It considered the expansion and improvement of schooling as a means to further regional and national development. In the long term, the reform sought changes in four main areas: coverage, quality, equity and efficiency. First, it sought to increase total *coverage* in Bolivia, that is, the reform would encompass the educational systems within the entire country and not just certain privileged areas. Second, *quality* was important and it was expressed in terms of the social, cultural and linguistic relevance of education. A third goal, *equity*, refers to a leveling of opportunities for access to the same quality of education between men and women, rural and urban areas and between populations of Spanish-speakers and of vernacular language-speakers. The fourth goal was *efficiency* in the use of resources, whose assignment, moreover, must bear a direct relation to the priorities of national development. The new education policy also proposed to recover 'the main function of the education system which is to foster teaching and learning' and redefine the education system structure starting from the classroom and revalue 'the social function of the teacher'.[47]

As for teachers, the Education Reform Law allows access to teaching positions to all persons with four-year university degrees and for teachers who hold a normal school degree, but only after passing an aptitude test. These provisions effectively eliminated the monopoly within the teaching community that teachers have historically held. The law also excludes the teachers' unions from participating in the election of authorities such as the directors of education units. Likewise, it expanded teaching in national teaching colleges to all professionals with academic degrees — until then only graduates from the normal schools could teach. Through Supreme Decree 23968, the reform proposed free unionization by ending payroll reductions that formerly fed unions. According to Orozco (1997) this weakened the teachers' unions which by February of that year had been 14 months without a significant portion of their funds.

The execution strategy was based on two programs: transformation and improvement. The first, transformation, comprises 'the Reform itself inasmuch as it pursues profound changes both in the institutional dimension of the National Secretariat of Education and in the pedagogical dimension'.[48] From the pedagogical point of view, it is targeted and gradual. By 1996, the reform was being implemented in 2,200 schools that covered 16 per cent of primary school enrollment. This figure increased to 6,501 schools in 1997 and 9,308 schools, or two thirds of the total 13,981 schools, in 2000. In 2002, 12,214 of the 12,958 were in the process of transformation.[49]

The transformation program comprises a curricular transformation, through the design of a new curriculum with a common basis of intercultural character and the emphasis on modifying teachers' and students' roles to prioritize learning. Specially trained pedagogical advisors provide in-service training to teachers in the classroom to implement the reform's pedagogical and curricular changes. Transformation also seeks, among other goals, the development, production and distribution of educational material; the training of teachers and directors for centers and education units; a new school supervision subsystem; a new subsystem of teachers' education and training; and the establishment of a subsystem of quality education measurement.

In its institutional component, the transformation program includes the institutional reorganization-administrative unification of urban and rural education, the design of administration and information systems and the transfer of infrastructure to prefectures and municipalities. Moreover, it contemplates the creation of district and center schools, the training of non-teaching and administrative personnel and the physical reconditioning of certain administrative infrastructure.

The improvement program, on the other hand, was designed to cover educational deficits on a short-term basis, ensuring its universal coverage.[50] The program consists mainly of supplying school equipment and educational material for teachers and training them for their use. Under this program, 6.3 million books and teachers' guides were distributed among school libraries directly to teachers.

Due to the diversity and the wide range of the intervention areas, it has been correctly stated that executing the reform is a 'complex enterprise that does not have precedents in the Bolivian public sector'.[51] Therefore, its execution (covering both pedagogical and administrative aspects) requires 'extraordinary management skills and faculties'.[52] In the last eight years, the Ministry of Education has been able to set up a cadre of professional teams that have markedly strengthened its institutional capacity to a level never before attained.

What changes are taking place in the classrooms? After visiting more than 20 schools in several departments of the country, the second annual review mission of the reform, carried out between September and October 1996, had the following opinion:

> … the teaching imparted in the classroom is active, relevant and visibly interesting for the students. The directors and teachers expressed without reserves that students behave more inquisitively, more openly and creatively … this active methodology has an inductive effect in the rest of the courses — not yet included in this first stage of the Reform — which are progressively assimilating it.

Furthermore, the mission added that:

> … having spoken with teachers, directors, authorities and parents, they all said that there are notable changes in the children and that their level of communication, their participation in classwork and their enthusiasm for school have all increased. In the same way, we observed enthusiasm of teachers in their work and development of initiatives different to those offered by the Reform and oriented towards active and participatory learning in the children.[53]

These expressions synthesize the type of change the reform aims to accomplish and reflect the gradual modifications that have slowly taken place in thousands of classrooms all over the country.

Undoubtedly, a variation in attitude is significant, especially considering that the reform has been carried out for only a short time. However, an evaluation of whether changes in attitude are producin g changes in learning is necessary. The main problems in establishing the reform and the source of the most radical criticism arose from the sector most affected by the plans of the reform: the teachers. The most common a posteriori reaction was that ETARE and the government of the Acuerdo Patriótico, as well as the MNR, should have 'coordinated' efforts and criteria with the teachers, the Church, the COB and the university, among others, all of who showed their opposition to the reform. Several attempts were made to achieve this: meetings, seminars, congresses and the establishment of councils. Undoubtedly, many of these efforts were useful, although in my view, there are three reasons that explain why greater agreements were not reached.

First, as in other countries in Latin America, in Bolivia, the education reform proposals 'found fertile terrain, because, in effect, school systems did require modifications'. More importantly the 'insufficiency of reform plans presented from liberal, democratic positions and from an outdated left' did not present viable alternative options that could resolve structural problems in Bolivian education.[54] Instead, due to the 'predominance of ideological premises over the empirical reality of education' in Bolivia, the absence of education research by teachers and universities and the concentration of NGO research in popular education the country was left in a 'vacuum of social and educational theory to confront the challenges posed by a new education reform'.[55]

Second, 'education touches particularly the topic of power and how this is exercised in society. He who receives today the social codes and the adequate knowledge, benefits from them as trustee of this knowledge and this knowing.'[56] Thus, once the economic development model had been defined (as that of a market economy), and the political regime established (as that of democracy), it was fundamental to establish an education system that would be in accordance with the new economic and political system. Those who proposed the Education Reform knew which system to construct; those who criticized it did not have a clear idea of which system (political and economic) they favored; and, therefore, their proposals were weak.

Third, teachers' unions controlled by Trotskyite tendencies are particularly ideological in Bolivia. As I have shown elsewhere, there are major points of conflict between the government's position and the teacher's unions.[57] These include differing views on the objectives of education reform, the organization of the education sector, the teaching profession, the degree of parental participation, the pedagogical proposal and the process of implementation and immediate objectives of the reform. Many of these issues cannot be overcome through negotiation. For instance, while for the government education is a means to achieve development, for the unions its means to overturn the state. Opposition is greater at the leadership level. By way of illustration, the union leadership has unsuccessfully tried to prevent teachers from participating in the new training programs, especially those offered in private universities and in the courses for pedagogical advisors who are the facilitators of the reform implementers in the classroom. However, union opposition has not been uniform. There has been less opposition in eastern regions, somewhat more in the valleys and the most opposition has been in the highlands.[58] By 2002, the ministry of education had been able to develop a better working relationship with the rural unions, which by then had seen the benefits of the reform. Urban unions still presented much criticism and opposition.

Despite union opposition, there is evidence that the pedagogical proposals of the reform are being adopted and adapted to fit with current practices.[59] There will no doubt be greater changes once new teachers are trained with the new curricula developed for the reform in the reformed 16 normal schools currently being administered by the Ministry of Education and both public and private universities. Interest in becoming a teacher has increased significantly with applications to normal schools growing from 6,000 for academic year 1999–2000 to 20,000 for 2000–2001.[60] A major structural challenge is overcoming the apparent shortage of qualified teachers and the reduction of the number of *interinos*, which still represents a quarter of the total number of teachers and is more evident in rural areas.

In 2002, 17,585 new 'teacher-equivalent' positions had been assigned, making it the most important increase in the supply of teachers in the last decade. This incorporated 4,654 new teachers and increased the workload of 4,182 primary teachers. Over half of these new 'teacher-equivalent' positions were funded by resources from the Highly Indebted Poor Country initiative that Bolivia is part of.[61]

Contrary to popular belief, teacher's salaries in Bolivia have been increasing in real terms during the 1990s.[62] As in the case of other countries, recent research on the effect of teacher's salaries on quality of education in Bolivia is not strong. Namely, greater salaries do not account for better results. Similarly, if one compares teachers' salaries with other groups with the same level of education and in terms of income per hour worked, teachers do relatively well.[63] Since 2001, the reform has developed a series of incentives to primary school teachers, which have had interesting results. The incentives scheme for rural teachers awards US$100 a year and benefited over 23,000 teachers in 2002. The incentive for teachers involved in bilingual education awards US$200 a year and benefited 4,617 teachers in 2001. Finally, the institutional incentive is awarded to schools on a competitive basis to reward schools with good management practices with a monetary incentive for all school employees. In 2001 over 9,000 schools participated and 1,100 schools were awarded incentives.[64] The level of mobilization and participation in the institutional incentive competition is a good indication of the way parents and teachers are actively involved in the implementation of the reform.

Greater community and parental participation in the schools should also energize schools and improve both administrative and pedagogical aspects — a good example of which is the institutional incentive scheme highlighted above. Because of both Popular Participation and education reform, 11,500 *juntas escolares* (school boards) have been established to have oversight over the school and seek to improve both administrative and pedagogical issues. As a result of Popular Participation more resources haven been invested in education at the municipal level and there is evidence that local priorities are being better met.[65] What effect decentralization will have on educational attainment is still to be seen. There are no systematic studies of these aspects. The short-run effects appear to be greater clientelism at the local level that is hampering the establishment of a competent and professional regional and local level education system.[66]

The introduction of bilingual education is a important new and bold step of the education reform. The limitations of teaching in Spanish in rural areas had been highlighted since the 1960s and throughout the 1970s and '80s.[67] Building on pilot experiences from donor-funded projects in the 1970s and '80s, a UNICEF initiative in the 1990s and in response to long felt popular demands (rural teachers' union in 1984, the COB and the Peasant's Labor Organization in the early 1990s) that the education system should acknowledge the country's linguistic and cultural diversity, the reform introduced bilingual education to those populations that speak Aymara, Quechua or Guaraní in their households.[68] In 2000, 2,037 schools or 18.8 per cent of rural schools were bilingual schools. The introduction of bilingual education has presented significant challenges in developing appropriate educational materials and training teachers.[69] It has proven difficult to implement this part of the reform in certain regions due to parental opposition. They thought that their children were not going to be taught Spanish and, therefore would be excluded from the development process.[70] The use of bilingual education as a vehicle for obtaining more and better learning from indigenous students is also not fully understood by urban elites who have been critical of the whole process and question the effort.[71]

Finally, what about increases in coverage? There is no doubt that enrollment is increasing. According to the Ministry of Education, based on administrative data, net enrollment in primary schools increased from 74.3 per cent in 1990 to 96.6 per cent in 1999. The net effect of the reform on this increase cannot be gauged because of its gradual implementation and the short period since its commencement. But, according to the Ministry, retention has increased by 30 per cent from 1997 to 1999.[72] Bolivia still has many obstacles in achieving universal coverage in primary education (six to 14 years of age). Net enrollment rates are hampered by: (a) late entry into the school system, when children are eight or nine years old, rather than six; and (b) high drop out rates, at 11 years of age in rural areas and 12 or 13 in urban ones. Problems are concentrated in specific municipalities also; a well-targeted policy may be best to address these issues. In the light of the above, Urquiola (2000) estimates that at real GDP growth rates of five to six per cent per annum, Bolivia would attain full coverage of primary education in 2015. Recent evidence in four municipalities, where 18.4 per cent of households report that their 5 to 14 year old children do not attend school, would seem to support Urquiola's pessimistic estimate.[73]

According to recent estimates of the Ministry of Education, in 2002 there are approximately 320,00 children aged five to 15, representing 14 per cent of children in that age group, that are not in school. To overcome this, the Bolivian government is working on a program of school expansion, increase teacher availability and a new school attendance subsidy to stimulate demand. The program would require an additional $300 million as a grant from the international community to meet the Education for All goals by 2015. [74]

Figure 11.4. Education Expenditure as a Percentage of GDP

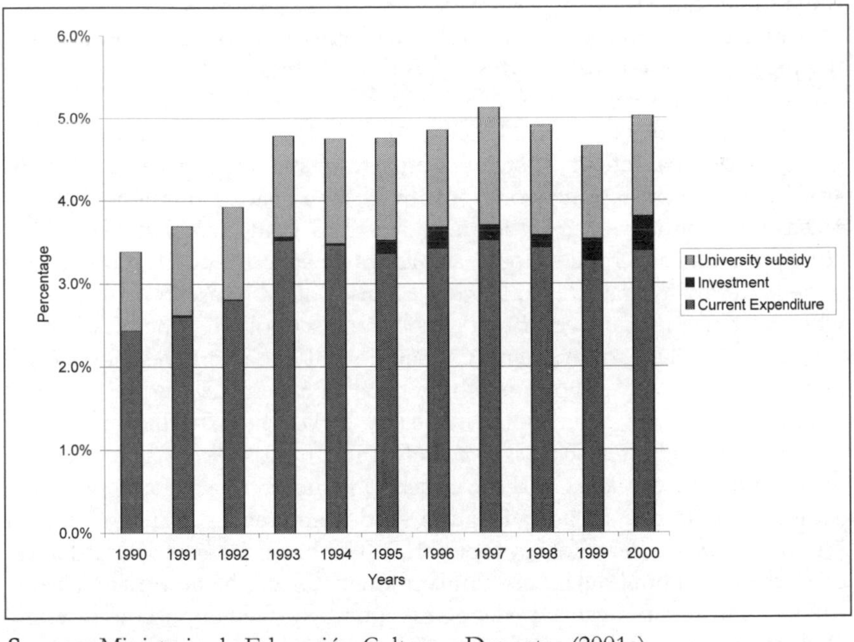

Source: Ministerio de Educación Cultura y Deportes (2001a).

This raises the issue of expenditures in the education sector. As can be seen in Figure 11.4, the education budget as a percentage of GDP increased in the first third of the 1990s. After 1994, it oscillated around 4.5 per cent to 5.0 per cent of GDP, well above the Latin American average of 3.9 per cent. Although this has been an improvement over previous decades, government officials pointed out that this was insufficient to maintain the reform effort and improve teachers' salaries.[75] There is no doubt, however, that the quality of the education sector's expenditure improved in the 1990s, as a greater fraction of resources were assigned to primary and secondary education. Also, there has been an increase in resources devoted to investments in the sector. Indeed, for the first time ever, schools have received classroom libraries, teaching materials, sports equipment and other pedagogical aids. In 2000 alone, schools received teaching material worth over US$14 million.[76] It is important to note that the current education reform has a total cost of approximately US$338 million. The World Bank and the Inter-American Development Bank loans account for US$192 million, grants from the Netherlands, Sweden and Germany for US$78 million and the national treasury has disbursed US$92 million. Given that there is now a need to expand initial education, reform secondary education and improve teacher's salaries, Bolivia will probably have to invest a similar amount to tackle these areas. The recurrent costs of these investments will require that significantly more resources be allocated to education.

Ultimately, an education reform has to improve children's learning. How has the reform been doing in this respect? The latest SIMECAL evaluations of language and mathematics achievement for third grade students in 2000 are shown in Tables 11.2 and 11.3. As shown in Table 11.2, in schools undergoing educational reform, there are better results in language than in mathematics. It is surprising and worrisome that over a quarter of students do not reach the minimum level of learning for third grade mathematics. If we compare urban and rural schools, as might be expected, urban schools perform better than rural ones in language. This is not the case in mathematics, where a greater percentage of students in rural schools (17.7 per cent) reach the highest level of achievement (C) than do children in urban schools (11.5 per cent). This is an important achievement in accomplishing the reform's objective of reducing educational inequality. If we contrast achievement levels between children in schools *under* reform with those *not under* reform the results are very similar. Children in schools under reform have a slightly greater success rate in both language and mathematics than children in schools not yet under reform (Table 11.3). The breakdown of those that do reach the minimum level is very similar though. Given the new materials distributed and the innovative pedagogical approach that supposedly is taking place in the schools under reform, one would have expected a greater percentage of students at higher achievement levels.

Table 11.2: Level of Achievement in Mathematics and Language by Third Grade Students in Urban and Rural Areas, 2000 (percentage of students at a given level)

Level of Achievement	Urban		Rural	
	Mathematics	Language	Mathematics	Language
Failure	27.1	4.7	27.9	8.5
A	44.6	22.0	38.5	28.3
B	16.8	51.7	15.9	46.2
C	11.5	21.6	17.7	17.0
Total	**100.0**	**100.0**	**100.0**	**100.0**

Note: Failure implies they did not reach the minimum required for the grade level. A is a lower level of achievement than C.
Source: SIMECAL (2001)

Table 11.3: Level of Achievement in Language and Mathematics by Third Grade Students *with* and *without* Education Reform (percentage of students at a given level)

Level of Achievement	Language		Mathematics	
	Under education Reform	Without education Reform	Under education Reform	Without education reform
Failure	6.2	7.7	27.4	31.6
A	24.6	25.9	42.1	41.8
B	49.5	49.9	16.5	14.1
C	19.7	16.5	14.0	12.5
Total	**100.0**	**100.0**	**100.0**	**99.3**

Note: As above
Source: As above

The reasons for the above results are not addressed in the literature consulted and no doubt constitute an area for further research. One reason is surely the need for more time to propagate and consolidate the results. But we must also continue to remind ourselves that changes in the educational systems are never uniform and consistent across schools. Moreover, according to McGinn (2002), 'Early research in the United States calculated that innovations on average take about 20 years to be adopted by half the schools.' Yet, despite all its travails and limitations there is no doubt that the education reform has established itself as a major public policy that has gained the respect of the media and the population at large. So much so that in a survey of July 2002, 59 per cent of the population thought that education had improved due to the education reform.[77]

Conclusion

Education Reform during the revolution accomplished little in terms of significantly increasing education enrollment. The widely held claim that the revolution changed education from the 'elites to the masses' is hollow. This chapter has shown that the rate of growth of enrollment in primary schools in the revolutionary period was not greater that the growth of the decade before the revolution. Similarly, the rate of growth of rural communal schools before the revolution is very similar to that after the revolution. What educational expansion took place in rural areas was more a result of the greater mobility of Indians after the Agrarian Reform. In terms of its effects, birth cohort analysis of years of education completed within the population aged 20 years or older in 1999 also shows no significant effect of a greater number of years of education between those born in 1940 and 1945 (who went to school before the revolution) and those born in 1950 and 1955 (who went to school during the revolution).

I have argued that what expansion of education occurred in the rural areas was of very low quality and the ideals of the revolution could not be accomplished because of a lack of resources and the impossibility of changing teaching conditions in schools. There was no effort to introduce new curricula, new teaching materials or teaching methods. There was no proposal or intent to change teacher training — as in Mexico where rural teachers became actors in the agrarian reform efforts. Thus, the revolution's major contribution to the development of the education sector was in ordering the sector's legal corpus in the form of the Education Code of 1955, which was, exactly that: a 'code'. This code enshrined a divided education sector (between urban and rural) with Spanish as the sole teaching language. It was the start of the State's and teachers union's monopoly over of education policy. All these aspects were very harmful for development of the education sector and would not change until the 1994 Education Reform abolished the code.

Unlike the Cuban Revolution, for all its educational rhetoric, the Bolivian Revolution was not able to mobilize society around education and make education an arena for reform and a contributing factor to change society. It is clear that unlike the Mexican and Cuban governments, the Bolivian government was unable to dedicate significant resources to the education reform effort. Indeed, in education — where the existing order was not destroyed — we would have to agree only with the latter part of Gómez-Martínez's (1988) conclusion on the 'tragic legacy' of the revolution: 'it destroyed an existing order, but was not able to construct a new one; it did not manage to formulate a national program in accordance with the country's reality and capable of immediately initiating progressive planning of its own resources'.[78]

The 1994 Education Reform still underway in Bolivia is the most significant long-term effort ever enacted to modify Bolivian education. It is noteworthy that it is the only reform of the social sector to date that has survived three administrations (Paz Zamora, Sánchez de Lozada and Banzer–Quiroga). And, for the first time in a five-year period there have only been two ministers of education in the Banzer-Quiroga administration. The first minister served for four continuous years and was succeeded in the last year by his vice-minister of initial, primary and secondary Education, ensuring complete continuity. This illustrates well that educational policy has become state policy and the importance attached to the current reform.

In contrast to the 1955 Reform, which was not able to modify education to the new demands of the social forces unleashed by the revolution, the present one is more in accordance with the new economic (neoliberalism) and political (democracy) reality of Bolivia. Unlike the 1955 Reform the current reform has a more participatory approach in its implementation and seeks to incorporate parents in the educational process. Thus, it has broken the monopoly over education policy that the state and the teacher's unions enjoyed since 1955. Another significant difference between the two is the amount of resources assigned to the current effort. As we have seen, it is an ambitious project to change the way children are educated which has developed a new curriculum, textbooks and teacher training. It has also modified the way the education sector is structured and has decentralized education to the departmental and municipal level. It has introduced bilingual and multicultural education. Not unlike other reforms in the region, its greatest challenge is to gradually incorporate a hostile teacher corps into its practice and effectively change what is going on in the classrooms. Only then will it be able to improve learning. This will be a gradual and long process; meanwhile the jury is still out on whether the education reform is effectively improving student learning and what will be its overall effect on the education system and society.

Notes

* I gratefully acknowledge the comments of Ricardo Godoy, Merilee Grindle, Wendy Hunter, Luis Enrique López, Okezi Otovo and an anonymous referee to earlier versions. All opinions and viewpoints expressed are my sole responsibility and in no way compromise the Inter-American Development Bank or its member countries

1 This section draws on Contreras (1999b, 2000).

2 It is noticeably absent from the standard references to the revolution e.g. Malloy's *Bolivia: The Uncompleted Revolution* (1970) and Malloy and Thorn's *Beyond the Revolution: Bolivia since 1952* (1971) as well as in later general works on Bolivia, e.g. Klein's *Bolivia. The Evolution of a Multi-Ethnic Society* (1982 and 1992). There is some limited reference to education issues in Jerry R. Ladman (ed.) *Modern-Day Bolivia. Legacy of the Revolution and Prospects for the Future* (1982b).

3 Comitas (1968); Contreras (1996, 1999b); Cajías (1998).

4 Ministerio de Educación y Cultura (2000).

5 McGinn and Borden (1995) are more skeptical and claim that transitional bilingual programs (such as the one in Bolivia) have 'mixed results'. 'About half the evaluations are positive as measured by achievement in basic subjects, the rest neutral or negative'. They underscore that 'one major factor is language ability of the teacher. It is often difficult to find teachers who are competent in minority … languages.' The latter point is particularly relevant to Bolivia. World Bank (1993).

6 Cariaga (1982), p. 160.

7 *La Razón* (2001).

8 Paz Estenssoro (1953).

9 Objectives and purposes of education, Administrative structure, Study plans, Programs and methods, Economics and statistics, Liaison with university education and Peasant and labor commissions

10 Cajías (1998).

11 Ministerio de Educación (1956), p. 136.

12 This is a cluster of a few schools (around six) that feed into a main school that provides the *núcleo* schools with pedagogical support.

13 Contreras (2000); Brienen (2001).

14 Calculated from tables 2 and 3 in Sanjines Uriarte (1968).

15 Comitas (1968), p. 649. Writing in 1988, the Spanish Guggenheim Scholar, José Luis Gómez Martínez, reached a similar conclusion: 'From the above, it is licit to conclude that the MNR ignored education progress in rural Bolivia, maintaining an attitude of indifference to its needs and the problems it faced' (1988, p. 339).

16 Ministerio de Educación y Bellas Artes (1958).

17 Ibañez Lopéz (1961).
18 Yapu (2002).
19 Martínez (1988).
20 Blasier (1976).
21 Eckstein (1976).
22 Domínguez and Mitchell (1977).
23 Eckstein (1985).
24 Meyer (1986).
25 Knight (1990), p. 31.
26 Vaughan (1982), p. 271.
27 Knight (1990b).
28 Mesa-Lago (1981).
29 Carnoy and Wertheim (1979).
30 *Ibid.*
31 Domínguez (1978).
32 Carnoy and Wertheim (1979).
33 *Ibid*, p. 121.
34 García Galló and Montero (1970), pp. 11 and 135.
35 Berry (1970).
36 World Bank (1983), p. 39.
37 Comisión Episcopal de Educación (1979).
38 World Bank (1977).
39 World Bank (1988), p. 26.
40 Martínez (1988).
41 Contreras (1996).
42 Martínez (1995).
43 World Bank (1993), p. v.
44 Anaya (1996).
45 Berríos Gosálvez (1995).
46 ETARE (1993).
47 *Ibid.*, p. 35.
48 Secretaría Nacional de Educación (1995).
49 Ministerio de Educación, Cultura y Deportes (2002a).
50 ETARE (1993).
51 Secretaría Nacional de Educación (1996).
52 Schülz-Heiss (1996).
53 Ministerio de Desarrollo Humano (1996).
54 Puiggrós (1996), p. 91.
55 Rivera (1992), pp. 28, 31.
56 Casassus (1995), pp. 17–18.
57 Contreras (1999a).
58 Orozco (1997).
59 Talavera (1999).

60 Ministerio de Educación, Cultura y Deportes (2002a).
61 *Ibid.*
62 Contreras (1999a); Urquiola et al. (2000).
63 Urquiola et al. (2000).
64 Ministerio de Educación, Cultura y Deportes (2002a).
65 Faguet (2001).
66 Ministerio de Educación, Cultura y Deportes (2000).
67 Comitas (1968); World Bank (1983, 1988).
68 López (1994).
69 For a more detailed discussion of the reform's bilingual proposal see Anaya and López (1993) and Comboni and Juárez (2000). On the origins of the proposal see López (1994); and for the wider comparative perspective see López and Kuper (2000) and Hornberger (2000).
70 See, for example, Widmark (2001).
71 See for example the discussion in *La Razón* in June 2000 regarding the usefulness of teaching in Aymara, Quechua and Guaraní in a globalized economy (Brockmann, 2000; Echalar, 2000; and Cárdenas, 2000).
72 Viceministerio de Educación Inicial, Primaria y Secundaria (VEIPS) (2000).
73 Grootaert and Narayan (2001).
74 Ministerio de Educación, Cultura y Deportes (2002b).
75 Ministerio de Educación Cultura y Deportes (2000).
76 VEIPS (2000).
77 Ministerio de Educación, Cultura y Deportes (2002a).
78 Gómez-Martínez (1988), p. 318.

UNFINISHED AGENDAS AND NEW INITIATIVES

Chapter 12

The Construction of Bolivia's Multiparty System

Eduardo A. Gamarra

Introduction

The 30 June 2002 elections in Bolivia were the first to occur since the death of Víctor Paz Estenssoro, Juan Lechín Oquendo, Hernán Siles Zuazo and Walter Guevara Arze, the great leaders of the Movimiento Nacionalista Revolucionario's (MNR) 1952 Revolution. With the death of General Hugo Banzer Suárez in May 2002 the entire generation of leaders who developed Bolivia's party system had expired. In 2002, the multiparty system that was constructed by these leaders was in serious trouble. Accused of corruption, mismanagement of the economy and of failing to establish credible and sustained links to the citizenry, in recent years traditional parties faced declining support and calls for an end to their constitutional monopoly over political representation. The surprising results, which included the dramatic showing by indigenous parties, headed by so called anti-systemic leaders such as Evo Morales and Felipe Quispe, added to the general view that Bolivia's party system was headed the way of its great founders.

The party system that emerged after 1952 resulted from a series of significant historical moments and political confrontations. Between 1952 and 1964, the MNR failed to institutionalize a single party system but at the same time designed an electoral legal framework that paved the way for the development of a multiparty system. The military governments that followed between 1964 and 1982 did little to change electoral mechanisms and paradoxically contributed to the development of Bolivia's fractious political party system. During the prolonged military experience, for example, one of the most significant parties, the Movimiento de Izquierda Revolucionaria (MIR), made its appearance in the early 1970s. The democratization experience that began in the late 1970s, but did not really take off until 1982, provided 20 years of experimentation with electoral law reform, constitutional change and profound structural reform that expanded the theatre where political parties in Bolivia act. This period also witnessed the appearance of many new parties including: Banzer's own Acción Democrática Nacionalista (ADN) in 1979 and a variety of smaller parties ranging from indigenous parties such as the Movimiento Revolucionario Túpac Katari (MRTK) to neopopulist groups such as Conciencia de Patria (CONDEPA) in 1988 and Unidad Cívica de Solidaridad in 1989.

In 1985, in the midst of the country's worst ever economic crisis, the political party system appeared to have found a way through 'democracia pactada', a system in which the three leading parties the MNR, ADN and MIR established and sustained a congressional majority to govern the country and pursue far-reaching structural reform. Through four different types of coalitions between these parties and other minority parties, these pacts gave Bolivia an unprecedented degree of political stability. In the same time period, Bolivia pursued significant transformations such as the administrative decentralization plan known as Popular Participation that has forced political parties to act at the municipal level. With the economic downturn of the last four years, however, the flaws in Bolivia's party system became evident once again.

The 2002 electoral process revealed the degree to which the pacted democracy in place since 1985 had reached its outer limits. ADN ran a weak candidate and virtually disappeared from the electoral landscape. The MIR barely placed fourth with its life long leader, former president Jaime Paz Zamora as the party's candidate. Gonzalo Sánchez de Lozada, another former president and his tired MNR barely won a plurality with 22 per cent of the votes. The big winners appeared to be candidates who ran against anti-party campaigns and who pledged to eradicate the major economic and political transformations achieved by the three principal parties. Manfred Reyes Villa, the former Mayor of Cochabamba, crafted a curious coalition of dissidents from other parties, regional leaders, business leaders and disaffected indigenous leaders to support his Nueva Fuerza Republicana (NFR). Reyes Villa, who led the polls until a few days before the election, placed third.

The major surprise in the contest was the dramatic showing of Evo Morales's Movimiento al Socialismo (MAS), which had simply borrowed a party label to run in the elections but was in essence a loose coalition of indigenous groups, unions, old timers from the Trotskyite labor left and coca growers. As a result, the MAS behaves more like a union than a party and draws much of its strength from attacking the party system it has now joined. The MAS obtained 20 per cent and 26 seats in Congress, including membership in the Senate.[1] A similar surprise showing was Felipe Flores' the Movimiento Indio Pachacuti (MIP), who were placed fifth, barely behind the MIR with six per cent of the vote and won six seats in the legislature. Together the MIP and the MAS controlled almost 30 per cent of the National Congress and insured that no matter who would emerge from the mandatory congressional second round, governing Bolivia would be a difficult task.

This dramatic presence of the MAS and the MIP was clearly evident in early August 2002 when the National Congress assembled to elect a new president. For the first time in history an indigenous person had a legitimate shot at becoming president of Bolivia. Evo Morales' second place showing, however, was not enough to secure control of the legislature as the MAS refused to reach across the aisle to form a coalition with parties and groups from Bolivia's political party establishment.

In this scenario, it was clear that only Gonzalo Sánchez de Lozada and the MNR could form a government. For weeks on end, the MNR negotiated with the Reyes Villa's NFR, which felt cheated out of second place and accused the National Electoral Court of hacking the computer system to favor the MNR. A deal with the NFR never materialized but at the eleventh hour when most Bolivians began to despair an arrangement typical of Bolivia's 15-year history of pacts was struck between the MNR and Paz Zamora's MIR. Described in the local press as a shotgun wedding crafted mainly by US ambassador Manuel Rocha, the MNR and MIR labeled their new arrangement Plan Bolivia. Rocha in turn claimed that the best outcome for Bolivia's democracy had materialized.[2]

While that may be the case for the survival of pacted democracy, the fact remained that unlike all previous pacts, the Plan Bolivia Pact assured Sánchez de Lozada a slim majority in the legislature but virtually no control over the country. The political costs to structure and maintain the Plan Bolivia have also been enormous. Perhaps more than any pact since 1985, the Plan Bolivia is fundamentally patronage driven with the MIR extorting a high price in cabinet posts, embassies and other coveted government jobs.[3] The irony has not been lost that while the elections of 2002 were precisely about ending these kinds of pacts, the Plan Bolivia is in fact an extreme case of party driven patronage. In sum, the weakened traditional parties retained control of the legislature and the executive branch but Evo Morales and the opposition forces retained effective control over the rest of the country. How Sánchez de Lozada will deal with this basic reality of politics will determine the future of Bolivian politics for at least the next decade.

Despite the outcome of the 2002 elections, Bolivia faced the apparent harsh reality that political parties are still both the cause of and the cure for the problems afflicting its fragile democracy. For most of Bolivia's recent experience with democratization, political parties and the politicians that make them up have been popularly perceived as the ones responsible for the current economic and political crisis. At the same time, in the absence of a more credible alternative, political parties are still the only ones capable of providing the way out of the crisis. The dramatic presence of the MAS and the MIP has not altered this fundamental reality.

Bolivian political parties have in fact never been popular. Political parties and other institutions of representative democracy have been under attack since at least the 1952 Revolution, which had a dramatic impact on the development of Bolivia's contemporary party system. Thus, the current moment of party unpopularity does not reflect only a tiring of political parties as a result of 17 years of neoliberal reform as many have argued.

It is more accurate perhaps to place this discontent within the confines of the long tradition in Bolivia of attempting to replace the institutions of representative democracy with ones that will presumably establish direct ties between state and society foregoing the intermediation link that parties are supposed to provide. Over the last 50 years, and in some measure beginning with the revolution, a recurrent trend has been that experiments aimed at abolishing political parties inevitably resulted in chaotic returns to a fragile representative democratic moment. These recurrent attempts at eliminating parties and establishing unmediated links between citizens and the state, which were generally done during authoritarian moments, inevitably affected the capacity of political parties to forge effective ties with civil society.[4]

The principal problem with the crisis of the party system is the fact that the political realignment that resulted from the 2002 elections produced a very weak government that has managed to do very little as it attempts to craft a policy that will satisfy all sides. Perception of the government's weakness is so palpable that some fear that President Sánchez de Lozada could face early retirement. The scenario of early recall, of course, is of great concern since no constitutional mechanisms exist for succession. A transition to Vice President Carlos Mesa is also not feasible, as he lacks the support of the political parties that make up the ruling coalition.

At issue are a vast number of urgent needs that Bolivia must face in the short term. The most pressing include launching some sort of an economic plan to address the spiraling economic crisis.[5] A plan was to be launched in early November; however, the government has been indecisive about the nature of the program. In October, for example, it announced a couple of tax measures but promptly retracted them when it sensed mounting public opposition. In an attempt to assure the electorate that it would pursue a social agenda, the government sent two bills to Congress: the first was an attempt to restore the so-called BonoSol, a popular yearly payment to senior citizens that was repealed by the Banzer government; the second involved establishing the Seguro Materno Infantil, a government insurance program for mothers and children.[6] President Sánchez de Lozada also announced that with foreign funding his government would invest nearly US$4 billion in job creation programs such as: highway and housing construction; irrigation projects; rural electrification; and the development of a service to deliver natural gas to homes.

The new government has also pursued a so-called fight against corruption. On the heels of a Transparency International report that Bolivia was still among the most corrupt nations in the world, the new plan was directed by Vice President Carlos Mesa, a former journalist and a strong critic of the corruption prevalent among political actors. Mesa's plan has yet to be properly unveiled but meek early attempts have been ineffective. Critics of Mesa's plan point out that attempts to root out corruption should begin with members of the ruling coalition. The same critics also point out that attempts to root out corruption will inevitably produce tensions within the already fragile MNR–MIR ruling coalition. Mesa and his collaborators have extensive public support, including the sympathy of groups such as Morales' that ran on an anti-corruption banner. He also has attempted to build on the previous World Bank funded anti-corruption efforts of former president Quiroga. Few believed that the Mesa program would be successful. Instead most feared that anti-corruption campaigns would only serve to weaken the ruling coalition.

The current government's most difficult decisions will involve natural gas and coca/cocaine, the country's best known exports. Because of the delicate nature of the decision to sell natural gas to the United States, the government has had to move very cautiously so as not to stir the wrath of the myriad groups that have expressed their opposition to building a pipeline to Chile and exporting Bolivian gas through Chilean ports. The most vocal opponents of the gas sales are groups such as those led by Morales and Quispe, although they have joined other groups that span the political spectrum. This issue is not clear-cut, however, as civic groups in Tarija, the department where most of the natural gas reserves are located, have expressed their view that Chile is the only export venue worth consideration. The complexity of this decision, which the government will have to make in the next few months, is perhaps one of the most serious sources of potential conflict in Bolivia.

Without a doubt, the coca/cocaine issue remains the most difficult issue facing the current Sánchez de Lozada government. Pressured on the one hand by the exigencies of US counter narcotics policies and Bolivia's own Plan Dignidad and threats by Morales's coca growers and other groups, the government has attempted to please both sides with hesitant moves in both directions.[7] It has publicly stated that it will continue to press ahead with eradication efforts under Plan Dignidad, while simultaneously negotiating an eradication 'pause' with Evo Morales and his followers. The results thus far have pleased neither the USA nor Morales, although the latter has at least held his protesters at bay. A visit by President Sánchez de Lozada to President George W. Bush did not produce a final decision between these two mutually exclusive approaches. No matter what the decision, Bolivia is likely to enter into a prolonged period of social conflict.

Bolivia's political party system is at a crossroads and its future shape is currently being decided. Its future is tied directly to the way in which the current government addresses the severe economic crisis, the coca/cocaine conflict and the sale of natural gas. To be successful the government will require both a strong executive branch and a very strong and stable congressional coalition. Given the current array of forces, the next five years are likely to be filled with severe tension and controversy.

Historical-Structural Factors that Affect the Arena where Parties Act

Any political analysis of contemporary Bolivian politics must begin with a glance at the tumultuous four final decades of the twentieth century.[8] During this period, Bolivian political dynamics were largely bounded by a number of factors that defined the behavior of the country's party system. This section attempts to interpret the contemporary crisis of the party system in Bolivia through an analysis of the legacies of the 1952 Revolution, the military-authoritarian period and the more recent democratization experience. In this section an analysis is provided of historical structural factors that contributed to the establishment of the current party system and the pattern of political behavior prevalent in the country.

The Legacy of the Revolution

The first factor is the legacy of the 1952 MNR Revolution that unleashed profound social and political changes, including the nationalization of the mining industry, agrarian reform and universal political suffrage. Apart from these well-known significant measures, the 1952 Revolution consolidated certain dynamics that have colored the behavior of political parties. These included corporatist notions of political representation, an attempt to establish a single party system, the role of the state in correcting social, political and economic inequality and a state centered development strategy.[9]

These dynamics unleashed by the revolution had the most dramatic impact on the behavior of the MNR over the past 50 years. The MNR's reliance on a corporatist scheme of representation that subsequently conditioned the way in which all contemporary political parties attempted to establish intermediation links with the electorate. The MNR's representation scheme included a logic aimed at co-opting functional groups (such as labor, *campesinos*, private sector, etc) into a single party structure. Any semblance of pluralism was evidenced solely through the distinct functional segments within the MNR and not through competing political parties, interest groups or other non-state organizations.

While corporatism was evident before the revolution, it was the National Revolution that consolidated corporatist representation in the country's political culture. One of the more difficult issues to overcome since the transition to democracy in the early 1980s has been precisely this characteristic, which paradoxically prevailed in Bolivia as a result of the internal structure of political parties, proportional representation electoral systems and the prevalence of 'single man' rule over these parties. Following attempts to control social mobilization by authoritarian governments, Bolivia's political leaders faced a serious contradiction. On the one hand they attempted to maintain internal party structures that facilitated control by a small group. To achieve this end, the principal way was to preserve functional lines of representation within the party.[10]

The corporatist logic of representation affected the development of Bolivia's civil society, whose principal institutions also organized along corporatist representational lines. Perhaps the most significant version of this type of representation was the relationship between the MNR and the Central Obrera Boliviana and the diverse sectors of the *campesinado*. These were precisely the sectors that during the democratization process of the 1980s and '90s posed serious challenges to the State as corporatist representational channels broke down.

This particular factor affected the process of party institutional development in post-revolutionary Bolivia. For example, the MNR and successive military authoritarian governments attempted in vain to design a legislative assembly to replace the old National Congress-based notions of representative democracy. In the 1950s the COB attempted to establish a worker's assembly. In 1971, as a rejection of the MNR and other traditional parties, the COB joined other groups including a faction of the armed forces in a fateful attempt at constructing a so-called Asamblea del Pueblo. In 1974, the de facto Banzer government attempted to create a corporatist assembly under a failed plan to design a new political party-less Bolivia. Finally in 1980 even the corrupt García Meza government attempted to replace Congress with a corporatist structure it called the Consejo Nacional de Legislación made up of 'apolitical notables'.

Despite the ideological differences all efforts coincided on two basic points: the need to eliminate traditional parties and the establishment of functional-corporatist representation schemes. In all cases appeals to so-called apolitical notables were also noteworthy. In each case, the failure to establish a new legislature was followed by a return to the old pre-revolutionary representative democracy structures introduced in Bolivia's 1880 Constitution. In any event, the contemporary dilemmas of Bolivia's representative democracy have much to do with the failure of the MNR and the subsequent military governments to replace the National Congress with another type of organic corporatist or functional system of representation.

The political expressions that today reject representative democracy are reminiscent of those that favored the dismantling of the National Congress and its replacement by a variety of assemblies. It is not surprising therefore to find high levels of rejection in a society that still has not fully opted for representative democracy and its maximum expression, the National Congress and the party system. The most probable scenario is that, at least in the medium term, this crisis of representation will continue.

This legacy explains partially the dilemma of political parties in contemporary Bolivia as they fail to break out of the logic of functioning mainly as vehicles to capture state resources to circulate among the dependent middle sectors. Elsewhere this conduct has been described as a fundamentally patrimonial dynamic. In this sense, political parties are ideologically permeable, party loyalty has been weak and the general motivation guiding political party conduct has been more to accede to state perks than to develop programmatically-based governments.

The Reaction to the Revolution and the Emergence of the MIR and ADN

The reaction to the revolution involved an 18-year period (1964–82) characterized mainly by intermittent military-based authoritarian rule. While military leaders did not modify the basic state-centered development strategy, this period was largely one of political institutional atrophy. Especially during the seven-year de facto Banzer government of General Hugo Banzer Suárez, key political parties such as the Movimiento de Izquierda Revolucionaria (MIR) and Acción Democrática Nacionalista (ADN), came into existence.

The MIR and ADN represent more than just the old left and the old right. They were also partners in the formation of Bolivia's pacted democracy and as such bear responsibility for the current party system crisis. The ADN experienced a generational shift from Banzer to Jorge 'Tuto' Quiroga, but the party appears to have all but disappeared following the death of the former, severe internal squabbles between *Banzeristas* and 'Tutistas' and the attempts of the latter to position himself for the 2007 elections. Its 2002 candidates (Ronald Maclean and Tito Hoz de Vila) achieved less than five per cent of the vote. While the only possibility for an ADN comeback may be for Quiroga to return to Bolivia to rebuild the party and run for office in 2007, the party is in absolute shambles as it has lost any semblance of what was once a powerful organization.[11]

In contrast, the MIR has yet to undergo a leadership shift and continues to rely on party founder Paz Zamora, who governed Bolivia between 1989 and 1993. Paz Zamora has barely held the MIR together despite rough times that included US charges that this party had financed its 1989 campaign with drugs proceeds. As a result, in the mid 1990s, the USA cancelled the visas of Paz Zamora and several other prominent MIR members. Following an extensive, expensive and successful lobbying campaign, in 2001 the US embassy announced that Paz Zamora's visa had been restored. With or without visa, the MIR fate hangs in the balance.[12] In 2002 the MIR is a deeply divided party, which has lost a great number of its old party stalwarts to other parties, including a few once prominent members who joined the NFR for the elections.

Realizing that the party's fate was on the balance, especially after its poor showing in the 2002 elections, Paz Zamora positioned the MIR within the Plan Bolivia coalition. The MIR lacks an electoral base outside Paz Zamora's home department of Tarija and it is unlikely that the party will be able to develop a broad based national following, especially because of its role in government.[13] Early in Bolivia's current administration perceptions are that the MIR represents the patronage wing of the coalition and that it is interested only in positioning Paz Zamora to again run for office in 2007. The MIR's long-term survival will depend on the party's ability to transcend the Paz Zamora era. This is a point that has yet to penetrate Paz Zamora's thinking about the MIR's future.

The Nature of Bolivia's Transition to Democracy and the Party System

The complex nature of the transition to democracy that began in the late 1970s and culminated with the election of a weak coalition government headed by Hernán Siles Zuazo, one of the four great leaders of the MNR Revolution, had a significant impact on the party system. The complexity of the transition was largely due to the culmination of the state development strategy, which was characterized mainly by the collapse of the tin mining industry that had been the mainstay of the Bolivian economy. The most telling outward sign, however, was a hyperinflation rate of historic proportions. (26,000 per cent between August 1984 and August 1985). Moreover, the transition was difficult because of the absence of political institutions capable of channeling the political forces demanding a role in the Bolivia's young democracy. The extremity of the three Siles Zuazo years triggered an aversion to political turmoil and in the current setting, no comparison draws greater emotion than those who deem today's crisis as severe. This time as in 1985, political parties appear as the culprits. Conditions are different and the prospects for the emergence of a Paz Estenssoro capable of forging a new regime-saving pact appear remote.

The Coca–Cocaine Complex and the Party System

A fourth critical element is the consolidation of a vast and complicated coca–cocaine complex that included coca farmers, displaced mineworkers, military officers, traffickers and political parties. Both the growth of the complex with its concomitant web of corruption and joint Bolivian–US efforts to combat its proliferation taxed Bolivia's weak political system. The coca–cocaine complex has profound ramifications in Bolivia that extend well beyond a simple law enforcement or national security perspective. Since at least the mid-1980s, Bolivia has pursued a strategy of crop eradication and interdiction efforts that have included a US funded alternative development strategy and military and law enforcement efforts. These efforts were largely ineffective until the launching in 1998 of Plan Dignidad, a plan that through forceful eradication claimed credit for eradicating all but 6,000 hectares in the coca-growing region of the Chapare and for expanding alternative development crops to 120,000 hectares in the same region. The Dignity Plan received enormous international accolades and earned former president Jorge Quiroga an international reputation. At the same time, however, the plan contributed to the development of a political movement and a political party (MAS) that achieved significant congressional representation and with its leader Evo Morales as a key national and international figure.[14]

To resolve the conflict with coca growers the former Quiroga government promised US$80 million in alternative development funds. Moreover, the government agreed to stop construction of military posts. In turn, the government claimed it would continue its fast paced eradication program. The government coca-growers agreement ended weeks of intense turmoil but it did not end the confrontation. In the aftermath of the government-coca growers' confrontation, the mutilated bodies of five policemen and the wife of one were discovered in the jungles of the Chapare region, apparently the victims of retaliation for government activities aimed at eradicating coca and lifting road blockades. The government arrested suspects in the case raising tensions with coca growers once again. It also did not pause the eradication of the estimated final 1,500 hectares of coca left in the Chapare.

The so called pause in the conflict that the Sánchez de Lozada government has experienced is only a temporary respite as the coca issue will surface again and will make governing Bolivia difficult. The problem is exacerbated by the fact that government negotiations with the MAS and Evo Morales in the first 90 days raised expectations that the pause in the conflict would also lead to a pause in eradication. These hopes were quickly dashed when Sánchez de Lozada received the message first hand from George W. Bush that the USA would consider a more participatory approach to alternative development only if eradication continued at the same rate as under Quiroga's Plan Dignidad.

Much has been written in the media about the emergence of Morales and his party. It is clear that he is more than simply a spokesperson for coca growers, as his movement reflected a broad-based national presence. The MAS is not a political party in the traditional sense of the term. It functions mainly as a union and Morales claims that any decision must be taken by a consultation with the 'bases'. As a result, the complaint is that apart from being a very significant presence, the MAS bench has done little legislating. To reiterate a point made earlier, the future of Bolivia's party system in some measure rests on the way in which the MAS will transcend its social movement unionism and become a real political party.[15]

The electoral results of 2002 consolidated the grip of the MAS on at least three provinces in the Chapare region, where most illegal coca is grown in Bolivia. Since at least 1997, when Evo Morales first became a single member district deputy, the MAS effectively used the structures of Bolivian representative democracy to increase its grip over the Chapare and to expand nationally and internationally. The MAS also swept the municipal elections in the

Chapare region. With a national presence in Congress and with total control over the Chapare, Evo Morales established a type of union-based government in the region. Critics charged that he had established dictatorial control in the Chapare, which ranged from determining the distribution of land to peasants to registering new births and marriages.

The key problem with the MAS in the Chapare is its overt confrontation with US efforts to control the expansion of coca and cocaine. The MAS's central reason for existence in the Chapare is to protect the right to plant coca. It has been excluded from receiving USAID Alternative Development funds and as a result, the MAS has been extremely critical of these programs, which it sees as ineffective and in place only to wipe out coca. Government officials and the US embassy point out that coca in the Chapare serves only the cocaine industry. While this may be true, the fact remains that unless a long-term viable alternative is provided, coca will continue to provide an income for at least 5,000 families in the Chapare.

The MAS realized that the coca issue and the Chapare are not enough to provide it with a national projection. Since 2000 the MAS has moved into other areas such as taking leadership over the anti-globalization movement in Bolivia and criticizing attempts to expand a free trade agenda. Morales also positioned the MAS to be the most critical voice against the sale of Bolivian natural gas to the United States, especially if it meant going through Chile. The 2002 elections reveal that the MAS has become more than just coca, although this issue is still the movement's core. The confrontation between the MAS and the government was placed on hold for the first 90 days of the new government and talks were initiated that might even produce a significant change in the way in which alternative development programs are implemented. It is unlikely, however, that the MAS will accept the continuation of eradication programs. Whether this will lead to confrontation is anyone's guess. Most Bolivians anxiously expected the renewal of severe confrontation after the Carnival holidays in early 2003.

Bolivia's Neoliberalism and Pacted Democracy

A fifth factor is the nature of the stabilization program imposed in 1985 and the characteristics of Bolivian democracy in the last 15 years. Bolivia successfully ended hyperinflation through a draconian austerity program dubbed Nueva Política Económica (New Economic Policy). Simultaneously, the country developed a significant capacity for coalition rule among and between the principal political parties. Between 1985 and 2000, Bolivian political parties formed significant coalitions that ensured support for executive branch initiatives, such as the NPE and other profound economic reform measures.

Political parties are a central element in Bolivian political life not only because they have served as recruitment mechanisms for future leaders but also because since 1985 they have become the principal vehicle for the implementation of governance schemes. In other words, and as stated earlier, political parties are the principal cause of the difficulties in governing Bolivia but at the same time they are the only real source for a solution.[16]

In this sense, parties have been crucial for the development of public life in modern Bolivia; especially in the formation and structure of the four governments that ruled the country between 1985 and 2002. While parties were the cornerstones of democratic governance they also lacked ideological coherence and clearly intelligible programs. At the same time, parties failed to articulate the interests of civil society at a time in which the old structures of corporatist representation were breaking down. Perhaps the most serious dimension was the concrete fact that the neoliberal strategy adopted after 1985 called first and foremost for the dismantling of the state resources that had been the base of the patrimonial dynamics of the party system.

In Bolivia, the sources of state wealth are extremely limited and these have not circulated with ease. Thus, despite the formal organic facade, the central political dynamic has been to circulate jobs, posts and perks among what is now a large dependent middle class that lacks access to other sources of wealth. The middle-class problem is exacerbated by the almost complete absence of a dynamic private sector capable of investing, competing and creating jobs in the new economic system.

This dynamic explains in part the constant need that parties have to expand the size of the Cartorial State, as Helio Jaguaribe labeled this pattern of political comportment by the political class in Latin America.[17] In Bolivia political parties always depended more on the State than on the resources and support ostensibly provided by developing linkages to civil society. So great has been the dependency of political parties on the State that to a certain extent they are indeed merely extensions of the State. Moreover, it is clear that in Bolivia political parties are so dependent on the State that without access to its sources of wealth, parties tend to disappear quickly.[18]

The principal problem of parties in Bolivia has been the inability to transform this fundamentally patrimonial dynamic within a context of neoliberal reforms.

One way of interpreting the process of reform is that it was an attempt to minimize patrimonialism, while simultaneously preserving its essence. In other words, parties sought a formula to preserve certain prerogatives ceding only where the reform process did not threaten their basic interests. In any event, in Bolivia, the key will rest on the ability of parties to establish a balance between the system's patrimonial dynamics and the realities of neoliberalism. Thus far they have failed dramatically, and the 2002 electoral results have made this goal even more elusive.

Bolivia's Informal Sector

A final factor concerns what might be called the quiet, yet forceful explosion of a huge 'informal civil society' that was largely excluded from the benefits of Bolivia's stabilization programs and which considered itself excluded from the formal political party mechanisms of interest representation. According to Inter-American Development Bank figures, nearly 70 per cent of Bolivia's population is involved in the informal economy, which ranges from the illicit coca-cocaine complex to the vast web of urban street vendors that dot the country's major cities. In Bolivia, this informal civil society — which is both rural and urban — is predominantly indigenous or mestizo and lives in extreme poverty. While this sector is an important 'informal' economic force in Bolivia, it is also evident that this sector will increasingly define electoral politics, and that political parties will have to find a formula to 'formalize' ties with this enormous component of the electorate.

In 2002, this sector determined the final outcome of the election as social discontent resulted in a vote for non-traditional party candidates, such as Morales and Quispe. By far the most serious challenge for Bolivia's party system is the plight of the indigenous and majoritarian population. Given the size of Bolivia's indigenous population, parties since 1952 have always grappled with the incorporation of this sector. Since 1952, and as a result of agrarian reform, universal suffrage, the 1994 Popular Participation Law and the 1995 Decentralization Law, Bolivians have been self-congratulatory for successfully incorporating indigenous sectors, thus averting the problems of other countries with large indigenous populations such as Ecuador, Guatemala, Peru and Mexico.[19]

The great tragedy of Bolivian democracy in the past few years is that despite sincere efforts to incorporate indigenous sectors into mainstream politics through both the election of indigenous leaders to Congress, the vice-presidency and municipal governments and the approval of important legislation, such as the Popular Participation Law (PPL), these appear to have not been enough. Critical poverty, unemployment and built-in exclusion have resulted in two separate Bolivias: one urban, white and the beneficiary of the process of democratization and economic reform and another indigenous or mestizo, poor, urban and rural and the indirect bearer of the costs of the economic development strategy.

The PPL and the process of decentralization that Bolivia embarked on in the mid 1980s is of extreme significance and could in the long run become the principal mechanism to achieve national oneness. But this is a long-term proposition, which assumes that decentralization and municipalization of the country will lead to the presence of the Bolivian state in even the most remote areas of the country. Furthermore, it assumes that these reforms will eventually result in citizen allegiance to the state rather than to the traditional community or 'patria chica'. Survey research, however, suggests that in the short tem, decentralization has led to a greater instability in the countryside; it has raised expectations among previously dormant sectors and has contributed to the emergence of the indigenous groups that are calling for autonomy from the 'país político'.[20]

The other challenge of political parties is to establish, renew or maintain, ties to organizations in civil society that since 1985 have borne the brunt of neoliberal. The most noteworthy is the coca grower's union (*cocaleros*), an arm of a much larger Confederación Sindical de Trabajadores Campesinos de Bolivia (CSTUTCB) that, in turn, forms part of a weakened Central Obrera Boliviana (COB). The COB, created by the MNR in the early 1950s, was once the country's largest and most powerful labor union capable of paralyzing the entire country through strikes and work stoppages. The most significant sector within the COB between 1944 and 1985 was the Federation of Miners (FSTMB), a reflection of the significance of mining for the Bolivian economy. Since 1985, the most significant sector within the COB has been the coca grower's unions headed by Evo Morales. This group is fundamentally organized around the resistance to crop eradication and military and/or law enforcement efforts in the Chapare Valley of Cochabamba.

Bolivia has also been characterized by the occasional burst of what was earlier termed *social movement unionism* around specific issues or, more explicitly, around sectors affected by government policy. In the 1990s, and as is evident in the current turmoil, social mobilization by local and national teachers unions — which are headed by Trotskyite leaders — was a common sight, especially following government attempts to reform the educational system. Similarly, former workers of privatized companies, or of companies targeted for such a move, have organized and periodically marched on the capital city. Where once parties had a presence in these organizations, today parties appear to have lost the ability to engage these sectors.

One significant movement is the Coordinadora del Agua y de la Vida, headed by Oscar Olivera.[21] Based in the central city of Cochabamba, this group was able to bring to a complete halt the current government's efforts to carry out a privatization plan for the water delivery system in the city. In April 2000, the Coordinadora, as it is popularly called, managed not only to paralyze the city of Cochabamba with demonstrations but nearly brought down the Banzer government. The Coordinadora established a very broad coalition of supporters that included the coca growers from the Chapare region who have been most affected by the Bolivian government's very successful strategy of coca crop eradication. In September 2000 it again called on its followers to march on Cochabamba to protest the high price of fuel and other goods. As a result, basic foodstuffs were prevented from reaching the city, roads were blocked preventing transport vehicles from hauling their wares freely and confrontation appeared inevitable with police and military troops mobilized into Cochabamba department.

The presence of a vast network of non-governmental organizations (NGOs) has been one of the most interesting characteristics of Bolivian democracy in the past 15 years. While European and Western sources fund many, an important number are nationally funded. Some NGOs are linked primarily to significant development efforts aimed at working with women and children. Their efforts are noteworthy, especially in terms of addressing poverty related issues in the remote areas of Bolivia's vast national territory. Some NGOs have political party linkages; however, with a few exceptions, the parties in question have fared poorly in electoral competition. Of greater concern perhaps is the completely antagonistic relationship that has emerged in Bolivia between political parties and civil society organizations. This issue will be addressed below.

In recent years, and in some measure associated with the Popular Participation Law, community development organizations have proliferated. These include long standing organizations such as *juntas vecinales*, *comités cívicos*, *comités de mejoras*, lions clubs, *grupos de mujeres*, church-related groups and other so-called *organizaciones territoriales de base* (OTBs). *Juntas vecinales* and *comités cívicos*, which today are more or less free from state or political party interference, were organizations created by the authoritarian governments of the past.

Notwithstanding the results of survey data that tell us that participation in civil society organizations (CSOs) is healthy, it is important to make an important observation about their anti-systemic bias, especially the prevalent anti-party sentiment. This has become particularly evident in the last few years and is evidenced by two broad trends. First, civil society organizations such as the CSTUCB, teachers unions, the Coordinadora and the Coca Growers Union, have primarily employed tactics that many claim do little to promote civic mindedness. On the contrary, through road blockades and the like, these civil society organizations have aimed to destroy infrastructure that serves the whole of Bolivian society. This is especially the case with the nearly complete destruction of Bolivia's road infrastructure during the road blockades of October 2000. Second, organizations have captured the attention of the press as they perform spectacular roadblocks. They have also publicly expressed rejection for political parties, the legislature and the judiciary, the principal institutions of Bolivian democracy. They are also more likely to endorse non-democratic mechanisms and avenues for political change.

To evaluate these actions as anti-systemic and therefore dangerous for democracy misses an important point. Given the inability of parties to represent the interests of the aforementioned groups and others, it is not surprising that civil society organizations resort to actions such as road blocks to demand government action. The pattern of road blockades, negotiation and conflict resolution is so widespread that it is not far fetched to argue that for these civil society organizations these 'uncivic' tactics are, in fact, the only strategies that produce results within the system.

In the Bolivia of the late 1990s and the early 2000s the undelivered promises to groups headed by Quispe and Evo Morales legitimated a free for all of demands. Perhaps the most serious threat was Quispe's calls for the establishment, presumably through violent means, of a worker-peasant government. But these threats were put on hold while Quispe and Morales, now congressional deputies, attempt to work within the system.

This raises a fundamental issue for contemporary Bolivia politics. Quispe and Morales both achieved significant electoral success and are, in fact, a major component of the system. It could even be argued that these two deputies have closer ties to their respective districts than any deputy or senator elected on the ticket of a traditional party. Quispe and Morales have pledged to donate their congressional salaries to their districts and their benches generally ask for direction from mass meetings back home. In other words, the MAS and the MIP deputies behave more along the lines of an ideal representative taking direction from home and holding these views in the National Congress. For this reason it is perhaps more important to examine their calls for improved delivery of services to their districts than the anti-American and anti-systemic rhetoric that catapulted them into office.

The question is whether Quispe and Morales and their respective parties can continue to deliver their anti-system message while they are inside the system. It is also clear that keeping both of these groups 'within the system' is crucial to the stability of the system. Thus, another irony of contemporary Bolivian politics is that the survival of the party system depends on the MAS and the MIP, two movements that reject the party label for themselves and which have repeatedly pledged that they will dismantle it. The long-term prospects of the party system then may be mortgaged on the possibility of transforming these union-like movements into parties with effective congressional agendas.

While the trend toward anti-systemic action has waned for the moment, the greatest demonstration that Bolivia is a long way from developing a stable party system is the high level of support for non-constitutional mechanisms to achieve political change. The empirical evidence for this claim can be found in survey research such as Mitchell Seligson's, which reveals that nearly one third (29 per cent) of his sample would support a coup because of high unemployment rates, too many strikes, or student unrest. Author interviews in Bolivia with the leadership of a number of civil society organization confirmed that support for non-constitutional political change is high. Finally, it is clear that the greatest challenge facing Bolivian civil society organizations is to find an effective way to relate to the principal institutions of democracy, especially parties and the legislature. Until the dichotomy that separates parties and civil society organizations is overcome, and at the moment the divide is wider than ever, the prospects for the consolidation of Bolivia's party system are weak.

Political Parties, Presidentialism and the Electoral System

In the early 1990s, Arturo Valenzuela and Juan Linz, two US university professors, swayed candidate Gonzalo Sánchez de Lozada to propose changing Bolivia's multi-party presidentialism into a parliamentary system. The proposal became part of the MNR's platform in 1993 but never progressed with the rest of the parties in Congress. Space restrictions do not allow for a complete discussion of the issues surrounding the proposal. Suffice to say that the concerns centered around four basic issues:

- Fixed terms for presidents either penalize a good and popular president with a short four or five-year term or unjustly rewards a bad and unpopular one with an entire term in office. Put another way, in Bolivia as elsewhere in the region, re-election has generally been banned, forcing good presidents to prematurely leave office. In contrast, a president who performs poorly during his first year in office is rewarded with an additional four or five years and presidential systems have no recall mechanisms to throw out the 'scoundrels' without having to wait until the term is over.
- Bolivia's hybrid brand of presidentialism has favored coalition formation to insure majority in the legislature, thus facilitating governance. These coalitions, however, are fragile and driven more by the logic of patronage than concrete programmatic needs.
- Since 1979, Bolivia's method for electing the chief executive has failed to produce a clear-cut winner in general elections and the National Congress has elected every president since 1982. Until 1994, the legislature elected the president from the top three candidates. As many congressional voting rounds as necessary were conducted until a president was elected. This method added to the uncertainty already generated by the need for a second round.
- Finally, advocates of parliamentarism argued that the inability of parties to represent constituent interests was rooted in the fact that Bolivia had a multiparty list-based electoral system that did not complement the basic nature of presidentialism. In other words, multiparty presidential systems are unstable by their very nature and more so in countries with weak institutions. Moreover, the list system of electing deputies lessened the possibility of developing significant legislator-constituent linkages.

While the MNR failed to convince the rest of the party system to adopt parliamentarism, it was able to push through three significant constitutional changes in 1994 that at least partially addressed the aforementioned concerns. The first involved the adoption of single member district representatives for 50 per cent of the lower house. This modification aimed to respond to criticisms that members of Congress lacked specific contact with their districts. Despite the sometimes justified and severe criticism leveled at political parties, with this modification Bolivia's electoral system fairly reflects the political interests at stake in every election. The electoral mechanisms which rely on a combination of proportional representation and single member district mechanisms to elect members of the lower house have dealt well with questions about the breadth of representation. As will be noted below, the election of Quispe and Morales are a significant reflection of this characteristic. On the other hand, proportional representation mechanisms have ensured the presence of minority political parties in the Chamber of Deputies. With 50 per cent of the lower chamber now elected by single member district norms, the aim is to both guarantee the formation of majorities that facilitate governance and improved contacts between representatives and their district. While some preliminary analyses are available of the 'home style' of single member district representatives, it is probably too early to reach any firm conclusions the effectiveness of these new representatives.[22]

A second change involved Article 90 of the Constitution, which was modified so that only the top two contenders are to be allowed to run in the congressional round. Moreover, if the congressional round yields no victor in two rounds of voting, in the third the candidate with the simple plurality is automatically granted the presidency. Finally, presidential terms were extended to five years so that popular presidents would not be tempted to modify the rules to stay longer. With no recall mechanism in place, however, it did nothing about unpopular presidents who face long years without support. These changes went into effect for the 1997 elections and the results were generally favorable.

The results of the 30 June 2002 elections revealed that the reforms in fact yielded the very results that were anticipated. Due largely to the single member district clause, indigenous parties around the country were able to win significant victories and send their own representatives to the National Congress. Evo Morales is perhaps the most important example. Already in 1997 he became the single most voted representative in the lower house with over 60 per cent of the vote in his district. The 2002 vote did the same for representatives throughout the country. Traditional political parties, however, failed to understand the significance of single member district voting. By focusing mainly on the patronage driven list system, they did not anticipate the local level response that was brewing largely under the coat tails of Evo Morales and Felipe Quispe.

Since the transition to democracy in the late 1970s, however, the most controversial dimension of the electoral system has been Article 90 of the Constitution that determines the method to elect the head of state. Until 1994, if no candidate secured 50 per cent plus one, it was up to the National Congress to elect a president from the top three candidates. After the 1994 constitutional reforms, the National Congress must select the head of state from the top two. The debate on Article 90 has heated up once again with many calling for a simple ballot, or second round run-off as in most of Latin America. Defenders of the current system note its impact on the formation of regime supporting coalitions and their role in the achievement of major political and economic reforms.

As expected the 30 June elections again tested Article 90 and renewed calls for its replacement. For nearly three weeks after the ballots were counted the degree of uncertainty produced a well-concealed run on the banks. The situation was exacerbated by the MNR's inability to put together a ruling coalition, by the NFR's refusal to accept the results, Morales's own unwillingness to give up his claim to the presidency and the calculated maneuvers by the MIR that eventually resulted in the Plan Bolivia government.

The electoral system at the municipal level is similar in that if the mayor is not elected in an absolute majority vote, it is up to the municipal council to determine to select the mayor of any given town or city. This system has proven to be much more complicated and unstable, as mechanisms are also built in that allow sitting mayors to be recalled after the first year. It has also led, however, to the formation of coalitions between parties that bode well for the development of a consensus-based democracy.

It is unlikely that Article 90 will be replaced in the next few years, as constitutional reform efforts have largely been stymied. The general sentiment favors the adoption of a second round between the top two contenders, as is currently the case in most of the Andean region and in Brazil. In any case, a second round system would do little to avert the atomization of the electorate and the problems that elected governments face in forming governments that can effectively govern. At the very least, Article 90 still has the merit of forcing parties to form coalitions and to propose long-term plans for governance. Even in the very tenuous first few months of the current Sánchez de Lozada administration, a weak Plan Bolivia is better than no plan at all.

The Representation Issue

The principal problem with the party-based electoral system is that it has developed few, if any stable and long-term ties with any civil society organization. As a result, and as noted earlier, parties and civil society organizations rarely interact and, for the most part, the latter are quick to criticize the role of parties and 'electoral' nature of democracy. It has not helped that parties have made few attempts to deepen and institutionalize ties with civil society and that many of their members have been involved in notorious cases of corruption. For democracy to ever take root in Bolivia, the linkage between parties and civil society will have to be fostered and developed.

It has also not helped that political parties have been a negligible presence in the recent political turmoil and have offered few constructive options to emerge out of the impasse between the government and the striking civil society organizations. Calls for 'direct and participatory' democracy are still heard widely and there are now those calling within the halls of the National Congress for such a democracy. As in Venezuela and Peru, a generalized sentiment appears to be taking root that a participatory democracy without the old corrupt traditional parties is possible.

The literature on Bolivian politics in the last decade convincingly argued that a minimal consensus had been achieved over the rules of the game.[23] This 'culture of consensus' was largely limited to a set of political pacts between the ruling party and the principal opposition party. The logic of Bolivia's pacted democracy was built around the need to provide the executive branch with decision-making space, especially in the economic area. As noted earlier, pacts were critical to the achievement of economic stabilization in the 1980s and the deepening of economic reform in the 1990s. These pacts were also crucial for the early- and mid-1990s constitutional, judicial and electoral reform.

Bolivia's pacted democracy, however, was not able to build an elite-mass consensus on the rules of the game. At the societal level, while parties pacted to achieve economic and political reform, they also imposed most policies on a society that had no alternative. In the early phases of Bolivia's pacted democracy, electoral results were used as evidence that most Bolivians supported economic reforms. Support for the MNR, ADN and MIR, the parties most closely associated with the reforms was proof that the Bolivian electorate preferred 'economic stability and minimal growth' over the turmoil of hyperinflation.

It is also evident, however, that every government since 1985 has resorted to states of siege to control labor unrest in the aftermath of economic restructuring. In the mid-1980s, states of siege were effective in basically dismantling the once all powerful COB. In the early and mid 1990s, governments used states of siege to control striking teachers, coca growers and other groups. In some measure, the current crisis is the culmination of mass discontent with the economic strategy and with what civil society organizations consider a minimal pacted democracy.

As things currently stand, the current crisis is systemic and to survive, fundamental change will have to occur. Change will have to necessarily address the issue of extending ruling pacts to civil society. To achieve this goal, perhaps the most serious challenge is faced by political parties, which will out of necessity be forced to develop serious ties with civil society organizations. How this will be achieved, however, is anyone's guess since it will involve fundamental shifts in policy-making mechanisms. In the future it will be difficult to govern by decree with the support only of a political party coalition. In the context of the current recession and economic crisis, this will be a most difficult task indeed.

This basic reality appears to have been understood somewhat by the Sánchez de Lozada government, which was all but paralyzed in its first few months in office as it attempted to figure out how to respond to multiple pressures. The situation for the government was made even more difficult by the fact that the president enjoyed no electoral mandate and held the highest negative ratings of any democratically elected president since 1982.

Two significant policy attempts are noteworthy, despite the new government's overall inaction. While publicly ratifying that it would not change the basic characteristics of the US funded counter drug efforts, Sánchez de Lozada initiated a round of conversations with Evo Morales that reduced tensions briefly with coca growers. At issue were calls by coca growers to halt eradication efforts or face large-scale demonstrations in Congress and throughout the country. What will come of these talks is anyone's guess as the message from Washington that it will not allow any regression on crop eradication is very clear. At the same time, Morales has done little to help the government's case with the USA. Since August he has become another key figure of the worldwide anti-free trade movement and he has become especially visible in anti-Free Trade Area of the Americas (FTAA) efforts. He has not helped matters either with recent declarations that a missile and not a commercial airliner had slammed into the Pentagon.

A second area of government action concerns social policy. In an attempt to stall criticisms that it would not respond to calls for greater social concern, President Sánchez de Lozada has worked on both producing an economic package that attempts to counteract the recession that has affected the country since at least 1999 and on jumpstarting some of the stalled social programs he attempted to develop before leaving office in 1997. While he has a slim majority in Congress to achieve passage of the basic laws, these will do little to prevent the reaction of Morales, Quispe and their constituents.

The current political impasse reveals that parties were able to achieve only a decade-long consensus but they did not fundamentally alter party behavior. In the near future the country is headed for another long period of bitter inter-party conflict. This is particularly serious because political party agreements were key to achieving significant reform.

The four ruling coalitions since 1985 worked well in terms of both providing support for government policy options and in providing perks to minority parties. The coalitions have been fundamentally different and each must be analyzed separately. Suffice it to note that the norm has been for at least two of the top three most voted parties to dominate a coalition. Depending on the need to obtain a majority in Congress (to elect a president or to pass a bill) majority parties have extended power-sharing arrangements to minority parties.

Until recently one of the most important and promising characteristics of Bolivia's party system was the willingness of larger parties to share power with smaller ones. While there were obvious cost/benefit choices that led to the formation of these coalitions, they were also important elements of a consensus building mechanism. In Bolivia as anywhere else context is everything. Since 1995, it is probably safe to argue that the principal opposition parties have generally exercised a sharpshooter approach to government policies. When the MNR was in office attempting to push through major pieces of legislation such as the Popular Participation Law, capitalization and pension reform, the ADN and MIR spearheaded an effort aimed at halting the efforts. Some critics also noted that these parties were conspiring to prematurely end the government of then president Gonzalo Sánchez de Lozada.

With the tables turned between 1997 and 2002, the MNR was extremely critical of the Banzer government. Because the government rolled back some reforms, the MNR had few incentives to collaborate with Banzer. In the context of the current crisis, for example, the MNR sat on the sidelines and, as was noted earlier, preferred to demand Banzer's resignation rather than to provide support that might ostensibly help end the crisis. Instead the MNR's actions were aimed more at the 2002 elections and less at dealing with a crisis that affects the state.

The notion of a loyal opposition refers not only to approval or rejection of government projects. Loyal opposition has to do with the extent to which the opposition supports the system above and beyond its disagreements with the current power holder. Political parties in Bolivia generally believe in and support democracy but are also not averse to violating its principles to expedite their immediate political needs.

Political debate in Bolivia since 1985 has been significantly substantive as the principal political parties engaged in discussions over specific policy issues. Thus, the debate was characterized by discussions over the merits of capitalization, pension reform and Popular Participation. Or the debate may have been over the logic of forcefully eradicating coca plantations.

Political parties have fundamentally abandoned ideological concerns, although the principal parties are completely taken over by the logic of trade integration and commitment to the free market. One of the critical elements facing Bolivian society today is that what might be termed the 'ideology of the NPE' has come to a dramatic end with the current revolts and turmoil.

At the same time as debate is substantive, the fact is that parties are still fundamentally dependent on a single leader. A cursory survey of the major parties reveals that they have a very difficult time abandoning their first generation of leaders. Even when they do, as in the case of the MNR, the succeeding figures also become life-long fixtures within the party and the system. For political parties to become truly modern and establish those essential civil society linkages, they will have to establish clear lines of succession for a party's leadership.

The previous discussion highlights one of the most significant issues in the Bolivian political economy. In the Bolivian case, the hybrid nature of presidentialism assigns a more significant oversight role to the legislature than might be expected. Moreover, the fact that Congress has elected every president since the transition to democracy has further strengthened the view that the legislature is important.

An ongoing analysis of the legislature's role in policy-making by Ivana Deheza reveals that, contrary to what might be expected, the National Congress has introduced the greatest number of bills. The key question, however, has less to do with quantity of bills than the types of bills introduced. A cursory review of major legislation over the last two decades suggests that the executive branch has generally introduced major reform bills. In fact, pacts have enabled the executive branch to control any serious opposition to reform. Moreover, if opposition was insurmountable, the executive branch has inevitably resorted to rule by decree.

Rule by decree also highlights an important trait in decision-making. Over the past decade, technocrats working closely with the cabinet have designed nearly every major policy ranging from the NPE to pension reform. Even political party participation was limited; thus, consultation with civil society organizations was virtually non- existent. This is a basic political reality in Bolivia as submitting significant measures for party or civil society consultation would have inevitably delayed and/or watered down any policy. Given this reality and the fact that Bolivia is again facing a major economic and political crisis, the design and implementation of more socially palatable policies will be a major task.

Bolivia did achieve a few important victories that altered the balance of power from the central to municipal governments. Despite attempts by the current government to roll back some features of the 1994 Popular Participation Law, the results are mildly encouraging especially in rural indigenous communities. The effective municipalization of the country (311 municipal governments were recognized) and the revenue-sharing scheme devised by the PPL, has shifted decision-making authority in a significant way. A number of important analyses of PP have noted key differences between large urban and small rural municipalities. Overall, however, they coincide that an important balance of power has occurred.

Conclusion: The Current Crisis and the Party System

In the past two years Bolivia faced the biggest challenge to democratic governance since the mid 1980s.[24] Following 15 years of steady economic growth, relative political tranquility and profound structural reform, the political stability that had come to characterize this Andean country bordered precariously on chaos. Calls abounded for interrupting the mandate of President Hugo Banzer Suárez, modifying the rules of democracy to strengthen anti-system options and destroying basic political institutions. Already in the early phases of the Sánchez de Lozada administration, predictions that he will not complete his term are rampant. Bolivia's democratic institutions, especially its party system, appeared too fragile to withstand the magnitude of the crisis.

These developments are extraordinary and surprising in a country seen until recently as the only Andean country unscathed by war, coups, or social turmoil. A few had even argued that the country was well on its way to democratic consolidation. Others compared Bolivia favorably to the rest of the Andes, noting that the party system was still virtually intact.[25] The pessimists pointed out that the fragility of political institutions, the high levels of intolerance that characterized Bolivia's political culture and the peculiar characteristics of the country's civil society did not bode well for the country's democratic future. However one examines the political turmoil of the last two years, the party system in Bolivia appears to be headed for serious trouble.

With Bolivia's democracy teetering on the brink of disaster, without a resolution of the conflict between 'el país profundo' and the political system in place since the mid-1980s no long-term prospects appear to exist. What were the lessons learned from Bolivia's recent conflicts? Was it the reflection of the inevitable confrontation between the 'país profundo' and the 'país politico?' Was the outcome of the 2002 election a reflection of a system that worked, that goes to the brink of disaster but that essentially resolves the problems it faces? Was Bolivia's political elite intelligent enough to learn the lessons of this experience and develop adequate responses that might avert future turmoil? Or, as one former minister of government asked: Was the current scenario a temporary time out in an insurmountable conflict with social forces whose demands cannot possibly be satisfied?

At the same time, Bolivia has shown a remarkable ability over the past decade and a half to resolve social conflict. While the magnitude of recent events is unlike any previous mobilization, the political system may yet be able to respond to minimize confrontation and maximize the gains of the democracy. With blame easily cast on parties for the crisis, it is also true that parties contributed to the resolution (or the postponement of the crisis). It is also true that in allowing new parties to enter the system, including ones like

Quispe's Pachacuti party that promises to do away with the system, the political party system has managed to thwart serious challenges to its survival.

This chapter has attempted to explain the critical situation of political parties in Bolivia. While the general picture that emerges is somber, the reality is that since 1985 political parties have presided over a very accelerated pace of reform but have failed to adequately construct institutions and political capacity. On the contrary, a paradoxical situation seems to have emerged: the very process of reform in the past decade has contributed to the very fragility of the party system and to its delegitimation. This leads to conclude again that democratization is not a linear process; instead it is characterized by constant progress and retreat.

Bolivia's party system experience reveals one of the more intense processes of reform in the Americas in the past decade. During this period parties attempted to modify norms, rules and regulations and new institutions were designed. The results of this process are still extremely uncertain, although it is noteworthy that the democratization process has not been interrupted and these reforms have already modified some changes in political behavior. These changes, however, are insufficient to conclude that a democratic political culture has been attained or that political institutions have managed to construct a greater capacity to represent civil society.

Bolivia's democracy still lacks a balance between institutions, representation and citizenship. In this sense it is noteworthy that Bolivian political parties attempted to respond to their own lack of legitimacy through the reform process. It is clear that political parties in Bolivia pursued reform in the 1990s in response to their own diagnosis of a severe crisis of representation. The reforms pursued two basic aims: to deepen the system's capacity to represent social interests while simultaneously preserving the privileges of the political parties. This dichotomy points out the severe disequilibria that exists in Bolivia between institutions, representation and citizenship. The central dilemma for Bolivia's party system has been how to continue to expand the Cartorial State while simultaneously pushing reforms that undermine the clientelistic basis upon which the system was constructed and which blocked both better citizen representation and the full exercise of democratic citizenship.

Improving the capacity of parties to represent citizen interests and to overcome the legacies of patrimonialism is the most difficult task facing the party system in Bolivia. Bolivia's recent experience shows clearly that reform destabilized the traditional party system but it failed to eradicate the patrimonial dynamics of the system. Put another way; in contemporary Bolivia reformers operate side by side with traditional patrimonial operators.

NOTES

1 Barely three days before the election US ambassador Manuel Rocha warned Bolivians about voting for candidates known to be associated with drug trafficking, terrorism and coca growing. Although Rocha did not mention Morales by name the average Bolivian clearly understood the message. Much has been made about the impact of the ambassador's statement, which was important for two reasons. First, it increased feelings of nationalism and stirred anti-US sentiment, thus increasing support for the MAS. Second, voters likely to vote for candidates such as Reyes Villa, Sánchez de Lozada and Jaime Paz opted to vote for the MAS to protest US intervention in the campaign. In the final analysis even by boosting a 2 or 3% increase in voting for the MAS, the statement was probably the main reason for the NFR's defeat. In the aftermath of the 30 June electoral round it became popular to call Rocha the campaign chief for Evo Morales. In fact, however, the MAS had experienced a dramatic growth since at least January 2001. Two US embassy-related reasons appear to have contributed to the increase in support for Morales: his expulsion from Congress to face charges against him that he was behind the murder of several policemen in the Chapare region; and, the signing of a decree in January that prohibited coca markets in the Chapare region.

2 According to his own account, Ambassador Rocha played a very significant role in convincing Jaime Paz Zamora and the MIR to support the MNR. Rocha also met with Reyes Villa several times in an attempt to help broker a deal with the MNR. The US ambassador claimed that as a result of the final MNR–MIR deal his admiration for Sánchez de Lozada and Paz Zamora had grown because both men had swallowed a lot of pride for the welfare of Bolivia. Considering Paz Zamora's troubled relationship with previous US ambassadors and the less than flattering statements that Rocha made about Sánchez de Lozada in previous interviews with the author, this was indeed a significant description of the arrangement. Personal e-mail communication and multiple interviews in La Paz, Bolivia with Ambassador Rocha.

3 As late as November 2002, Plan Bolivia was still in the design phase. This is a notable contrast to Sánchez de Lozada's first term in office when the *Plan de Todos*, which introduced most of the significant reforms of the 1990s, was already fully designed before he even assumed office.

4 The rejection of parties is not unique to Bolivia as has been evident from recent trends in the Andean region as a whole. In Peru and Venezuela, for example, attempts to construct direct linkages

between state and society have resulted in the collapse of traditional institutions. In Peru's case the failure of Fujimori to construct political institutions led to the institutional crisis still facing that country.

5 One of the most significant discussions in Bolivia in the early phases of the Sánchez de Lozada–Mesa administration was over the health of the economy inherited from the Banzer–Quiroga period. Quiroga argued that the fiscal deficit he left was only 5% of GDP, a figure acceptable to the IMF and which would indicate that things were not that bad. The new government argued that the fiscal deficit was 8.6%, a figure that would place the economy near bankruptcy. Additionally, nearly 600 million left the banking system in the aftermath of the June 30 election. Claiming that confidence in the banking system had returned, the new government argued that over $300 million had returned to Bolivia between August and November 2002.

6 In the first 90 days, the coalition held together to pass the BonoSol and the Seguro Materno Infantil.

7 After the visit with Bush in November, Sánchez de Lozada announced that eradication would continue at the same pace as under the Plan Dignidad. The government also noted, however, that the USA had agreed to the Bolivian government's petition to modify alternative development programs. The exact nature of the proposal was still in the works at the time of writing.

8 See Dunkerley (1984) and Malloy and Gamarra (1988) for an in-depth treatment of this period.

9 For a theoretical treatment of the revolution, see James M. Malloy's classic text *Bolivia: The Uncompleted Revolution* (1970).

10 An expansion of this analysis can be found in Gamarra (1987). In revolutionary Bolivia, the State created several organizations that today form part of civil society, including labor unions, civic committees, neighborhood associations and the like. In some countries, a fusion between corporatist and representative forms of representation has occurred. In the long run, to overcome the representational deficit in Bolivia a similar fusion will have to occur. See for example, Lijphart (1999), chapter 9; Schmitter (1974), pp. 85–129.

11 In a number of interviews with the author since his departure from office, former president Quiroga made it clear that a return to office in 2007 is his goal but not necessarily through the ADN, which in his view simply requires too much work to rebuild. The key for Quiroga will be what kind of a party mechanism he can join or create to make the run for office. Quiroga, who left office with very high polling figures, is spending a year at the Wilson Center in Washington, DC and has assumed the role of consultant for conservative parties in the hemisphere.

12 The returning of the visas to the MIR raises a number of questions about US policy in general. In September 2002, Otto Reich, the assistant secretary for Inter-American Affairs announced with great fanfare a new approach to deny visas to corrupt Latin Americans. Yet at the same time, the USA returned a visa to Oscar Eid Franco, who was credited with having crafted the Plan Bolivia. Eid Franco spent four years in prison in the mid-1990s after being sentenced for crafting the MIR's relations with a prominent drug trafficking organization. Upon receiving his visa, Eid Franco flew to New York where he attended ceremonies honoring the September 11 victims. The irony of this situation is that also in 1997, Peter Romero, then Assistant Secretary of State for Inter-American Affairs and US Ambassador Curtis Kamman both warned President Banzer that the USA would not look kindly on the presence of Paz Zamora and his party in the governing coalition. In interviews with Ambassador Rocha, who left Bolivia in August 2001, it became clear that the decision to return the visas to MIR politicians was based on the incorrect assessment that Paz Zamora was the only one capable of preventing the emergence of Evo Morales.

13 The only new faces of note in the MIR in 2002 were Paz Zamora's two sons who were elected to the lower house from single member districts.

14 The government held Morales responsible for the deaths of several police officers murdered by rioting coca growers and attempted to prosecute him. To that end, Morales's congressional immunity was lifted and arrest warrants were issued. Government actions appeared to strengthen his appeal in the Chapare region, his electoral district where during the 1997 elections he commanded of the 69% for his single member district lower house seat.

15 Interviews with Evo Morales and others in the MAS suggest that this movement has no intention at the moment of organizing like a political party. In his view, the MAS is an instrument of the union movement and its representatives in Congress, including himself, are subordinate to the union. An analysis of the structure of the MAS, however, reveals a corporatist hierarchy that is more in line with the way in which Bolivia's traditional parties structured themselves. In sum, the MAS looks more like the MNR of the 1950s than its leaders care to admit.

16 For a similar argument see Gamarra and Malloy (1996).

17 Jaguaribe (1972), p. 7, defines the Cartorial State as one in which in exchange for support, the public bureaucracy orients itself less towards the effective delivery of public service and more towards the delivery of jobs for the clientele of governing sectors. The Jaguaribe definition appears to describe the current Plan Bolivia very well, especially in its overwhelming need to dole out patronage to sectors of the MIR.

18 This Cartorial characteristic extends and reproduces itself at the municipal level, where despite the modern logic of reforms linked to Popular Participation, patrimonial dynamics appear to prevail, see, 'Superar el clientelismo y ampliar la cultura institucional,' in PNUD (1998), chapter 6 for a similar line of analysis.

19 The literature on popular participation in Bolivia is vast. The most representative include the following books and articles: Grindle (2000); Booth, Clisby and Widmark (1997); Gray-Molina (1997); Gray-Molina and Molina (1997); Tuchschneider (1996).

20 See Seligson surveys cited earlier. Gray Molina discusses Popular Participation in greater detail in chapter 14 of this volume.

21 Olivera has become Bolivia's poster boy for the anti-globalization movement. Since his dramatic arrival on the Bolivian scene he has been paraded around the world at events in several US cities.

22 The Senate, which is comprised of 27 senators, is elected by a simpler proportional formula that guarantees the party lists that win the most votes in each of the country's nine-departments two senators. The second place party automatically wins one senator.

23 James Malloy once noted that politics in this country was essentially a zero-sum game between ins and outs. Since 1985, however, many analysts argued that Bolivia had transformed into a culture of bargaining and compromise. A few described the polity as a 'consensus based democracy'. The latter view is a product of the examination of the coalitional nature of Bolivian democracy over the last 15 years.

24 For a good analysis of events in the year, see 2000 Fundación Milenio (2000).

25 Gamarra (2001).

CHAPTER 13

Shadowing the Past? Policy Reform in Bolivia, 1985–2002*

Merilee S. Grindle

Bolivia — poor, decidedly underdeveloped, and often forgotten among Latin America's larger and richer countries — set a model for neoliberal policy reform during the 1980s and 1990s. In the face of a severe economic crisis, it adopted and implemented a far-reaching orthodox stabilization and structural adjustment program in 1985, with reforms that were sustained across changes in administrations and party alliances. The country's social adjustment program, introduced in 1986, was one of the earliest experiments of its kind in the world and was widely emulated in other countries. In the 1990s, Bolivia adopted a creative approach to pension reform, successfully introduced an innovative program to privatize state enterprises, legislated an extensive education reform and significantly altered political and fiscal structures through a radical municipalization policy. Health reform, significant efforts to eradicate coca and improved transparency in public fiscal management were other changes introduced during a decade and a half of policy reform.

The most important of the policies that made Bolivia a showpiece of neoliberal reformism in the 1980s and 1990s were introduced when the party of the 1952 Revolution, the Movimiento Revolucionario Nacional (MNR), controlled the executive branch of government. This party, whose revolutionary vision was statist, nationalist and protectionist, thus ushered in policies that were market-oriented and internationalist. Like the PRI in Mexico under Presidents de la Madrid and Salinas, the Peronist party in Argentina under President Menem and Venezuela's Acción Democrática under President Pérez, the MNR turned its back on its past in order to undertake economic, social and political policy reform. Or is this what happened?

This chapter considers the policy reform process in Bolivia during the 1980s and 1990s to assess how the MNR became a party of neoliberal reform and to what extent its support of change required the party to reinvent itself. I suggest that while the party was clearly important in marshalling electoral support for MNR candidates and it continued to make successful patronage claims on its standard-bearers, it was not responsible for the content of reformist initiatives. Rather, the party served as a vehicle for reformists with a distinct vision of Bolivia's future, who drew on its traditional base of support to introduce this vision. At the same time, however, the party that made reform possible was acting in ways consistent with its past. Like the Mexican PRI, the Peronists in Argentina and the AD in Venezuela — other Latin American parties whose traditions were statist and nationalist — the MNR drew on its traditions of 'big tent' membership, coalition building and patronage-based loyalties to enable reformists to pursue their goals.

In the following section, I review the policy reforms put in place by MNR presidents in the 1980s and 1990s. Although Juan Antonio Morales argues in Chapter 9 that these reforms were not enough to set the bases for growth in the economy, there is no question that the policies were a striking departure from the MNR's past. The second section of the chapter demonstrates the extent to which neoliberal policy changes emerged from think tanks and executive policy units that had little connection to the MNR party apparatus or membership. In the subsequent section, I consider the extent to which the party, while not much engaged in designing the reforms, participated in their approval and implementation. I conclude, as does Eduardo Gamarra in Chapter 12, that the MNR was important to the process of reform, but not in framing the content of change. Throughout, I use the term 'reform' to imply deliberate changes in policies and institutions; it is not meant to imply a normative judgment about the appropriateness or the social or economic consequences of change.

The Policy Revolution

Bolivia's record of policy reform during the 1980s and 1990s was impressive. Table 1 indicates the broad range of changes adopted in the five administrations in office between 1985 and 2002. The most profound policy changes were introduced between 1985 and 1989 under the Víctor Paz Estenssoro administration and between 1993 and 1997 when Gonzalo Sánchez de Lozada was president. Both presidents were voted into power under the banner of the MNR and both put together governing coalitions with the MNR as the lead party. Their policy reforms amounted to a neoliberal revolution in the country. Indeed, Bolivia was the first formal democracy in Latin America to adopt this fundamental shift in its national development policies and strategy. That it did so primarily under the MNR is notable.

Table 13.1: Policy Reform in Bolivia 1985–2002

President and Party	Governing Coalition	Significant Policy Actions	Year of Decree or Law	Description
Víctor Paz Estenssoro 1985–89 MNR	Pacto por la Democracia (MNR–ADN)	Supreme Decree 21066 (Nueva Política Económica, NPE)	1985	Package of economic stabilization and structural adjustment policies
		State of Siege	1985, 1987	Extraordinary executive powers to respond to political protest and violence
		Supreme Decree 21137	1985	Austerity and public sector downsizing
		Supreme Decree 21456 (Social Emergency Fund)	1986	Mechanism and funds for local projects and public works
		Supreme Decree 21660	1987	Economic Reactivation Package including banking, foreign trade, and foreign debt policies
Jaime Paz Zamora 1989–93 MIR	Acuerdo Patriótico (MIR–ADN)	Supreme Decree 22407	1990	Continuation and, in some cases, deepening of NPE
		State of Siege	1989	Extraordinary powers to respond to political protest and violence
		SAFCO Law	1990	Administrative and fiscal reform; accountability of public service; independence of Central Bank
		Law 1330 (Privatization)	1992	Enabling legislation for privatization of the majority of state-owned enterprises

Table 13.1 continued

President and Party	Governing Coalition	Significant Policy Actions	Year of Decree or Law	Description
Gonzalo Sánchez de Lozada 1993–97 MNR	Pacto por el Cambio (MNR–MRTKL–MBL–UCS)	Law 1544 (Capitalization)	1994	Partial privatization of state enterprises with injection of private capital and capitalization of a collective benefit pension plan
		Law 1551 (Popular Participation)	1994	Creation of municipalities throughout the country as basic level of public authority, direct election of municipal councils and mayors, assignment of 20 per cent of government revenue to municipalities
		Law 1565 (Education Reform)	1994	Comprehensive reform including bilingual education, teacher training, merit hiring, ministry capacity-building, teacher and student testing, local councils
		Constitution	1994	New rules of the game for electoral competition
		Law 1654 (Administrative Decentralization)	1995	Elimination of Regional Development Corporations, administrative powers assigned to departments, and establishment of formal relationships among municipal, departmental and national governments

Table 13.1 continued

President and Party	Governing Coalition	Significant Policy Actions	Year of Decree or Law	Description
		State of Siege	1995	Extraordinary powers to respond to political protest and violence
		Law 1732 (Capitalization)	1996	Introduction of an individual contributory system of pensions, privately administered, and collective benefit fund
Hugo Banzer Suárez 1997–2001 ADN	ADN–UCS–Condepa–NFR–MIR (Mega–coalition)	Plan Dignity	1997	Multifaceted effort to eradicate illegal coca production by 2002
		Economic Recovery and Social Development Plan	2000	Tax, public investment, and public procurement initiatives
		State of Siege	2000	Extraordinary powers to respond to political protest and violence
Jorge Quiroga 2001–02 ADN	ADN–UCS–MIR	Proposals	2002	Measures to generate growth, create jobs, deal with extreme poverty, attack public sector corruption

ADN: Acción Democrática Nacionalista
Condepa: Conciencia de Patria
MBL: Movimiento Bolivia Libre
MIR: Movimiento de Izquierda Revolucionario
MNR: Movimiento Nacional Revolucionario
NFR: Nueva Fuerza Republicana
UCS: Unión Cívica de Solidaridad

The policy revolution was initiated by Víctor Paz Estenssoro, who assumed the presidency in the midst of an economic crisis of epic proportions. This crisis had been building since the 1970s and was a consequence of a complex of problems involving extensive and mismanaged state intervention in the economy, the collapse of the international tin market, an international recession and extensive corruption and political instability.[1] By 1985, the economy was in a perilous state. The GNP growth rate fell six per cent in 1982, a further three per cent in 1983, showed no growth in 1984 and then declined three per cent in 1985. Inflation mounted from 32 per cent in 1981 to 11,750 per cent in 1985.[2] The external debt stood at almost US$5 billion in 1985. Per capita GNP declined from US$590 in 1981 to US$440 in 1985. Paz Estenssoro's predecessor, Hernán Siles Zuazo, was forced to end his administration early in the face of the political upheaval that accompanied this downward economic trajectory.

In response to the crisis, the new government's economic team quickly put together a package of reforms. Paz Estenssoro announced them on 29 August 1985, just 23 days after taking office. Supreme Decree 21060, known as the Nueva Política Económica (NPE), introduced an orthodox shock program to end hyperinflation and put the foundations of a market-oriented economy in place. Devaluation, liberalization, a freeze on wages and salaries and public sector downsizing were at the heart of this reform, whose longer-term purpose was to open the economy to international capital and trade.[3] On the heels of this policy package, the government introduced one of the earliest social emergency programs, an innovative and rapidly instrumented initiative that reached some 1.2 million people through the creation of jobs and public works.[4]

Decree 21060 meant a radical reversal of the fundamental strategy for economic development that Bolivia had followed since the 1950s. Clearly, the NPE needs to be understood from the perspective of hyperinflation — a situation so painful that many politically relevant groups, as well as the population more generally, agreed that 'something must be done' and were willing to give government latitude and support to do it. Indubitably, an underground economy fueled by coca production increased the sustainability of households, many of which also benefited from the social emergency program. Nevertheless, against the backdrop of the extreme political instability in the period leading up to the Paz Estenssoro government and the previous incapacity to deal with the mounting economic crisis, the NPE was an important moment in Bolivian history.

While the NPE and the social emergency program were the most notable policy innovations of the Paz Estenssoro government, other important changes were also introduced. In the same year that the economic package was introduced, another decree tackled the problem of state reform by introducing public sector downsizing, including severe reductions in the state enterprise sector and a series of austerity measures. Between 1985 and 1986, public sector employment dropped by 24,600 people; by 1987, a further 8,550 people had been dismissed; and by 1988, public sector employment had dropped by 17 per cent over 1985.[5] In 1987, banking, foreign trade and foreign debt policies were significantly altered.

These reforms were successful on two fronts. First, the economy stabilized rapidly. By 1987 inflation had been reduced to 14.5 per cent, GNP growth was 4.7 per cent and per capita income had risen to US$620. Politically, the ability to produce quick results helped sustain the government in power as well as keep the policies in place. Moreover, the social emergency program helped cushion many poor communities from the worst impact of the draconian measures that were adopted. Just as important, a state of siege declared by the president in September 1985 enabled the government to arrest and send labor leaders into internal exile and to manage the protests that followed the dismissal of as many as 23,000 workers from the state mining company, the Corporación Minera de Bolivia.[6] Two years later, Paz declared another state of siege to deal with massive public protests against the new policies. These repressive actions help explain the ability of the government to maintain a series of policies that imposed significant burdens on large sectors of the population.

In 1989, Jaime Paz Zamora of the Movimiento de Izquierda Revolucionaria (MIR) assumed the presidency. In short order, his government committed itself to the policies of the NPE through Supreme Decree 22407. Like his predecessor, he relied on a state of siege to manage ongoing political protests and to sustain the reforms. In addition, this administration sought to push the neoliberal agenda further through privatization of state-owned enterprises.[7] As a first step in this direction in 1990, it introduced performance contracts that allowed for the restructuring of the country's most important enterprises.[8] In 1992, enabling legislation allowed the sale of over 100 (of a total of 159) state-owned enterprises. Implementation was another matter, however, and the Paz Zamora administration only managed the divestiture of a few small and medium-sized enterprises, and of none of those that were most responsible for draining the public budget.[9] This government also adopted the SAFCO law, a comprehensive effort to improve administrative and fiscal accountability in government by setting up a series of procedures for decision-making in the public sector; this law also established the independence of the Central Bank.[10]

The Paz Zamora administration was notable for its ability to commit the government to the continuation of the NPE policies of the preceding government, a significant feat in Latin America. In other ways, however, its reformism was checked by the difficulties of managing the political relationships within the governing coalition. In addition, tensions within the MIR and the Acción Democrática Nacionalista (ADN) parties made it difficult to ensure that congressional votes would be forthcoming for major pieces of legislation.[11] As the 1993 elections approached, the MIR was engulfed in accusations of corruption and cronyism. To add to the government's troubles, the economic advances of the Paz Estenssoro years began to falter. While overall growth continued, inflation rose to 21 per cent by 1991, the budget deficit increased and the public debt mounted; in 1990 and 1991, per capita income fell slightly. Public sector employment began to grow again.[12]

The elections of 1993 brought the MNR back to the presidency with Gonzalo Sánchez de Lozada as its standard bearer. 1994 was a banner year for the introduction of new policies in Bolivia. An innovative 'capitalization' law provided for the sale of 50 per cent of the shares of government enterprises in exchange for infusions of capital into these firms. Shares for the remaining 50 per cent were distributed to Bolivians and vested in a new pension program.[13] In the same year, the Law for Popular Participation created municipalities throughout the country, gave them funds and significant autonomy to invest in health, education and infrastructure development and enabled local citizens to vote for local officials and hold them accountable for their actions.[14] Shortly after this major local government initiative, a law for decentralization reconfigured the relationship of the country's departments to the national government, shifting more power to municipalities, while maintaining departmental dependence on the center.[15]

A broad and innovative education reform law was also introduced in 1994. As described by Manuel Contreras in Chapter 11, it provided for bilingual and intercultural education, improved teacher training and compensation based on performance, brought changes in teacher qualifications, a strengthened ministry of education, merit hiring of school supervisors, special attention to girls' education, national testing of students and teachers and local school councils, among other measures.[16] The constitution was also significantly altered, increasing the number of legislators voted into office through a simple plurality system, changing the way presidents were selected by congress, aligning the timing of the election of executives and legislators and lengthening the term of office of presidents, legislators and mayors to five years.[17] In 1996, a major pension reform, tied to the capitalization program, introduced private management of funds and individual contributory accounts. Dividends from the pension accounts provided for the BonoSol, a program of annual payments to Bolivians over the age of 65.[18]

In 1997, the MNR lost the election to the ADN presidential candidate, Hugo Banzer Suárez. His presidency was rife with confrontation over the neoliberal policy agenda and noted for dissent within the governing coalition.[19] Nevertheless, he introduced a comprehensive initiative to eliminate the illegal production of cocaine in the country. Under strong pressure from the United States government, and with significant funds from the same source, this effort included infrastructure, direct eradication and alternative employment programs, and reaped strong protest from coca farmers and regions. The administration's efforts to introduce new economic policies in 2000, however, were little noted and effectively stymied by conflict within a large and unstable governing coalition.

While not notable for the introduction of new policies, Banzer's government was committed to maintaining the economic reforms introduced in the 1980s. In addition, it provided significant impetus to the implementation of the 1994 education reform and pushed for more privatization of state enterprises, often in the face of considerable protest.[20] At the same time, this administration sought to undermine other reforms of the Sánchez de Lozada administration by diminishing support for Popular Participation and curtailing the BonoSol program.[21]

When Banzer resigned in 2000, his more reform-minded vice president, Jorge Quiroga, took over the executive. The new president also sustained the market-oriented economic policies of previous administrations and provided significant additional impetus to the education reform. He proposed a series of measures to strengthen the economy and deal with the deep and massive problem of poverty in the country, but had little success in introducing major reform initiatives. Nevertheless, Quiroga was successful in calming some of the political upheaval that had become an everyday event under Banzer. Like Banzer, however, he was constrained by the lack of an effective governing coalition.

Overall, the period from 1985 to 2002 was remarkable for the extent to which basic policy commitments of the past were overturned. A statist economic development strategy was firmly replaced by a market-oriented one, protectionism was replaced by much liberalized domestic and international markets, a highly centralized state became much less so and state-controlled social services were significantly transformed in terms of how they were organized and administered.[22] And the MNR, which had created the structures of the past, was the party identified with the introduction of the neoliberal measures that destroyed them.

Designing Change: The MNR as Bystander

The MNR provided political space for the introduction of significant reforms that challenged most of what was embedded in MNR ideology and rhetoric. However, it is difficult to argue that the policies emerged from the party in other than the most perfunctory way. Indeed, the major reforms of the Paz Estenssoro and Sánchez de Lozada administrations were developed by small groups of technocrats and politically astute presidential advisors who had few links to the traditional MNR political machine. Indeed, the traditional party leadership was generally outside the room when the major decisions were made. Moreover, party leaders and voters often distrusted and deeply disagreed with the new policy broom wielded by the presidents that represented them.

The Neoliberal Beachhead

Víctor Paz Estenssoro, of course, could easily have been reckoned an MNR 'dinosaur' as he entered the electoral campaign in 1985. He had been at the helm between 1952 and 1956, when the new structures and policies of the revolution were first put in place. He led the country again between 1960 and 1964 and was re-elected in 1964 for a third term of office. Under his guidance, the MNR led the country toward statist and nationalist development. During the 1985 electoral campaign, it was unclear to most voters that he no longer held true to the party's old revolutionary mission. He expressed commitment to a mixed economy, even while he recognized the importance of bringing change to state enterprises and economic policies more generally.[23] He presented few specifics about what he would do if he were to win the presidency and his speeches were peppered with traditional MNR rhetoric.

Despite the ambiguity of the campaign debate, within weeks of assuming office, President Paz introduced the policies that were radically to restructure the relationship between the state and the economy in Bolivia. But the plan for this policy revolution was only distantly an MNR plan. Much of it, in fact, originated in the rival ADN party, which emerged in the late 1970s as the electoral vehicle of Hugo Banzer Suárez. And Banzer's 1985 program was only distantly related to his own party apparatus. It was instead the product of extensive reliance on technocrats and special advisors.

In preparation for the 1985 electoral campaign, Banzer's advisors for economic policy, Ronald McLean and David Blanco, arranged for a group of young economists and entrepreneurs to travel to Cambridge, Massachusetts to discuss the country's economic problems with Harvard faculty members Jeffrey Sachs, Lawrence Summers, Jorge Domínguez, Oliver Oldham and others.[24] Among them was Juan Cariaga, then the manager of the Bank of Santa Cruz and a political independent. The team returned from this meeting and, with Cariaga in the lead and Sachs providing additional advice, prepared the economic reform program the ADN would introduce if it won the elections.[25] The program stressed changes in the exchange rate, deregulation of prices of gasoline and public utilities, the end to a large number of subsidies, a wage freeze and a temporary moratorium on debt owed to private international banks.[26]

The ADN won the popular vote, but without the required 51 per cent to ensure the presidency. As a consequence, the presidential decision was thrown into the Congress, where an alliance between the MNR and the

MIR brought Paz Estenssoro to power.[27] Shortly thereafter, Paz assembled a small group to develop a program to deal with the country's severe economic crisis. Among the new team were Juan Cariaga and MNR Senator Gonzalo Sánchez de Lozada, president of the Senate and a wealthy businessman from Cochabamba. In addition, the group included an MNR stalwart, Guillermo Bedregal, as minister of planning and coordination, Fernando Romero, a well-known businessman, several technocrats and Antonio Sánchez de Lozada.[28] Adopting the groundwork originally prepared by the ADN group, this team also received advice originally sent to Banzer from Sachs.[29] The resulting NPE adopted much of the Banzer program and added tax reform, trade liberalization and the reorganization of the Central Bank to the policy package.

During the three weeks in which the economic plan was being developed, Gonzalo Sánchez de Lozada was in charge of the working group. Sachs, now active in providing advice to Paz and Sánchez, encouraged the former to name Sánchez de Lozada as his minister of planning and coordination, from which position he could coordinate the Economic Policy Group. In short order, planning minister Bedregal, an old guard MNRista, was consigned to foreign affairs. Then Cariaga, the independent economist who had emerged from the Banzer planning exercise, became minister of finance when the incumbent was moved to the ministry of industry. Although Sánchez de Lozada represented the MNR, he was part of a reform movement within the party that was seeking to push it toward a market-oriented perspective on economic development.[30] In distinction to Bedregal, he did not emerge from the old guard of the party.

In addition, Paz divided the cabinet so that the economic ministries were less tied to the political ministries that were headed by MNR politicians.[31] To further strengthen the hand of the reformers, Paz asked Bedregal to assume the vice-presidency of the stabilization commission he headed, undercutting his ability to speak out against the reforms.[32] Clearly, then, the traditional *movimientistas* of the MNR were sidelined from the design of the program; just as clearly, their power to resist the neoliberal package was undermined. And, although the NPE would bear the label of an MNR program, the party was largely absent at its creation.

The social emergency program followed a similar dynamic. Extensive public protests followed the announcement of the NPE. Highly organized miners, in particular, were of great concern to the government because the restructuring of the state mining company, COMIBOL, had thrown thousands of miners out of work. In the fall of 1986, Paz asked Fernando Romero, a businessman who had been part of the team that put the NPE together, to head up an agency that would provide an immediate response to the social and political consequences of the economic reforms.[33] The outlines of the program and its administration were developed rapidly, with extensive input from World Bank officials in La Paz and Washington, largely *in camera* and largely without input from the party apparatus.[34] The program was also remarkable for the extent to which it was rapidly implemented, often relying on the talents of bright young people drawn into the public sector for the first time. Many of them came from the private sector, while others had become politically engaged in small left-leaning parties focused on the demands and rights of indigenous people.[35] Again, the distance between the MNR party and its leadership and the formation of policy was great. Nevertheless, the program was implemented in ways that were sensitive to the party's base of support and its interest in securing that base and attracting additional electoral support.[36]

The 'Three Damned Laws'

Gonzalo Sánchez de Lozada, the architect of the NPE, became a national political figure in its wake.[37] As a reformer, he represented a new entrepreneurial and technocratic elite in the country and, importantly, within the MNR.[38] He had strong backing among the modernizing entrepreneurs of the country, new technocratic elites in the public and private sectors and both technocrats and leftist intellectuals who had been part of the social adjustment program experience. Although he faced internal opposition, notably from Guillermo Bedregal and others who represented the statist and populist core of the party, Sánchez de Lozada had strong support from Paz Estenssoro and the party's reformist wing; he emerged as the MNR standard-bearer for the 1989 elections.[39] Although he won the popular election by a small margin, a congressional alliance between the MIR and the ADN brought Jaime Paz to the presidency and left Sánchez de Lozada angry, thoughtful and eventually determined to have another try at the presidency in 1993.

In the aftermath of the 1989 elections, Sánchez de Lozada and several close associates created a think thank, the Fundación Milenio, to carry out studies and make recommendations in a variety of areas of concern. The ex-candidate wanted help in considering the economic, social and political situation of the country and in developing a vision of 'what ought to be' in considering a second presidential bid. He was particularly interested in issues of political reform, the reform of the state and sustainable development. With Sánchez de Lozada as its president, the foundation assembled an international board of advisors and began an intensive period of study, discussion and debate.[40] By all accounts, the technocrats and modernizing politicians brought together in the foundation fundamentally challenged the central beliefs of Bolivia's post-revolutionary politics — a centralized state, a statist development strategy, a paternalist approach to the country's indigenous population and rural hinterlands and nationalist protection of industry.[41]

According to one central participant in these discussions,

> There were two or three areas in which we were particularly interested. We believed that the government should completely cease being a producer of goods and services and that this activity should be carried out by the private sector. We also wanted to open up the country to the rest of the world and make Bolivia part of the modern trend toward globalization. The third thing we wanted to do was to redesign the state, to increase its efficiency and organize it along efficiency grounds rather than functional ones. We wanted to get away from the rigid centralized system that had been in place. The state in Bolivia suffers from a paradox. On the one hand, it is very paternalistic in terms of taking on problems, but on the other hand it is very limited in its capacity to respond to real problems.[42]

Eventually, discussions at the foundation resulted in an electoral platform for the MNR in 1993. The *Plan de Todos* outlined three strategic pillars for a future government. First, it promised a solution to unemployment, low salaries and corruption through the privatization of a large number of state-owned enterprises. This was to be carried out with a process dubbed 'capitalization', a term chosen to counter nationalist concerns about selling what many regarded as the national patrimony. Second, the capitalization of these enterprises would generate funds for a social development foundation to introduce improvements in education, health and social services, particularly in the poorest areas of the country. At the same time, distributing shares of the enterprises to the population would redistribute wealth in the country. Third, the plan called for Popular Participation of communities in their own development planning.

The *Plan de Todos* introduced these ideas, but was vague about how they would be achieved. Moreover, much of the debate throughout the campaign involved personalities and exchanges of vituperation among the candidates of the major parties, the MNR, the ADN and the MIR. Thus, when Sánchez de Lozada entered the presidential office in August 1993, it was still not clear what his main policy goals would be, other than the general intention to continue the neoliberal economic reformism that had guided Paz Estenssoro and Jaime Paz. In generating the ideas and policies that would mark his presidency, Sánchez de Lozada clearly followed in Víctor Paz's policy development footsteps. Small design teams were appointed by the president, given assignments by him and sent off to deliberate, plan and draft detailed legislation in isolation from public discussion or debate.

One design team was appointed to consider how the *Plan de Todos* commitment to capitalization would work.[43] The original idea for this variant of privatization came from Sánchez de Lozada. It was 'inspired by the kinds of capitalization contracts that he had used in the mining sector for many years. Goni had many mining properties but he didn't have capital, so for many years he put in the property and external investors put in the capital.'[44] After the election, several advisors to the president-elect were given the task of working out the details of this idea. Team members had been part of the Fundación Milenio experience and had participated in a series of seminars organized by the foundation on privatization. Of particular interest in this series was understanding the privatization experiences of the post-communist Eastern European countries; indeed, some of the team had visited these countries to gain first hand knowledge of how the process was managed.

The team, which included primarily economists — among them Juan Cariaga and Juan Antonio Morales — and lawyers who were not affiliated with any political party, met in closed door sessions to design the capitalization program.[45] While some international advisors were part of this group, the World Bank and other international financial institutions were not engaged in the design effort.[46] After the policy was designed and approved, members of this team were put in charge of a new Secretariat and then Ministry of Capitalization, with team member Alfonso Revollo as minister.

No one from the MNR was directly involved in the initial design of the program. After its content had been set, however, party officials criticized the idea and warned against its consequences. Those designing the new program fully anticipated that they would face significant opposition from the country's labor unions. For example, in considering the capitalization of the state oil company, YPFB, the team anticipated the 'mother of all battles' with the unions.[47] The inability of the MNR leadership to help explain and defend the policy did nothing to allay union reaction or the ideological backlash against it more generally. Capitalization was roundly denounced as one of the 'three damned laws' of the Sánchez de Lozada administration. In the absence of a blessing from the party, an MNR government set about dismantling many of the state enterprises the MNR government had created after the revolution. Indeed, not engaging the MNR more in early discussions of the policy was later recognized by Sánchez de Lozada as having been a strategic error.[48]

Another team was set to work thinking about how the idea of engaging local communities in their own development could be made practicable. Those selected included a young academic from the Santa Cruz region, Carlos Hugo Molina, who was an advocate of strong municipal — rather than departmental — governments and a critic of the MNR. He was asked to head up the group. In addition, modernizing elites of two small political parties, the MBL and the MRTKL, were asked to join the group. Under Molina's guidance, and often with the president participating, the group quickly developed the outlines of Popular Participation, which would create municipalities throughout the country and empower mayors and local councils to make decisions about much expanded resources.

Municipalization was an idea brought to the table and promoted by Molina; initially, the president favored community-level participation, and at the same time he was under considerable political pressure to decentralize to the departmental level.[49]

The leadership of the MNR was not involved in the closed door meetings that developed Popular Participation. Even ministers were denied access to them.[50] Of course, an important objective of the reform was to build a Bolivian state that was strong and capable of managing development, a theme reminiscent of the goals of the MNR on the verge of the Revolution of 1952.[51] But the original MNR national state was centralized and directive, not dispersed throughout 311 municipalities making their own decisions about development expenditures and objectives. To be sure, the designers of the reform wanted rural Bolivia, a traditional base of MNR support, to gain power vis-à-vis urban areas. But the reform actually put the party at some risk because expanded local elections increased the chances that other parties might become active challengers to MNR's long-standing role in the countryside. Moreover, the reasoning of the designers had less to do with the rural support base of the party than with curtailing the growing power of regional elites at the departmental level who were increasingly demanding more regional autonomy.[52] Further, the powerful national peasants' union, the Confederación Sindical Unica de Trabajadores Campesinos de Bolivia (CSUTCB), traditionally supportive of the MNR, was opposed to Popular Participation, fearing that the new system would displace much of its local power.[53] The COB, an MNR ally from the past, also branded this initiative another of the 'three damned laws'.

The Education Reform was the third of these laws. It evolved differently from capitalization and Popular Participation, but in a way that was equally distant from the MNR. The 'apasionada' of education reform in Bolivia was Amalia Anaya, who began her reformist career as a MIR activist. In 1987, she was put in charge of formulating the party's social policy platform for the elections of 1989. When the MIR's candidate, Jaime Paz Zamora, became president in 1989, Anaya was named under secretary of social policy in the powerful Ministry of Planning and Coordination. She was convinced of the importance of 'building human capital in the country in order to achieve higher levels of economic development' and of education reform as 'the best way to improve the quality of life and to correct the inequitable distribution of income'.[54] When World Bank officials came to Bolivia to assess the country's social fund, Anaya managed to interest them in her proposal to set up a technical design unit to put together an education reform.

By November 1992, a comprehensive reform plan was ready, but the MIR government was divided about its merits. While the plan had strong support from the planning and finance ministries, several powerful ministers, including the minister of education, believed that the reform would ignite too much political opposition, particularly from the teachers' unions. National elections were fast approaching, increasing the caution with which politicians viewed policy proposals that would be met by protests in the streets. As a consequence, the legislative proposal developed by Anaya was put on the shelf by Paz Zamora.

Meanwhile, education reform was an important part of the *Plan de Todos*. When Sánchez de Lozada became president, he surprised many by deciding not to start from scratch on a new reform plan but to adopt the work of Anaya and her team. This team became part of the new government and the president often attended its planning meetings.[55] Frequently, he referred to education as the much loved 'adopted child' of his administration.[56] The education reform, then, was born under the MIR. The MNR was little involved when it was further developed during the Sánchez de Lozada administration. Of course, the MNR had, in 1955, sponsored the Comprehensive Education Law that expanded education throughout the country and particularly to indigenous people. The 1994 reform included bold new measures to introduce bilingual and multicultural education. But the 1955 education reform law envisioned one national school, one national language and one national curriculum for all citizens. Guillermo Bedregal, among others, dismissed the new reform for resurrecting 'dead languages' as a teaching mechanism in indigenous communities. Moreover, while the 1955 reform sought to expand access to education and was popular with teachers' unions, the 1994 reform sought many goals that were strongly opposed by the unions. The education reform was, perhaps, an 'adopted child' of Sánchez de Lozada, but it was not at all loved by the MNR.

Reformism from Above

Reforms introduced by Paz Estenssoro and Sánchez de Lozada were carried out through centralized executive decision-making. This was most clear in the government of Víctor Paz Estenssoro, when a small group of technocrats designed and implemented the major policies for stabilization and the initial efforts to replace the state-centered development strategy of the past with a more market-oriented strategy. Indeed, those designing the program believed that solutions to the economic problems were technical and should not be subject to political negotiations.[57] These programs were put in place by presidential decree, not through legislation. Under Sánchez de Lozada, the major reforms were legislated, but they were still developed by small groups of people unaffiliated with the major political parties. In this process, the party was a bystander.

Popular dissent, particularly from organized groups of workers and peasants, greeted the policy changes and surrounded their approval and implementation. Each government that supported the neoliberal reforms declared states of siege to deal with massive popular dissent and protest against the governments and their policies. Uninvolved in discussions that led to the policies, the groups that were major supporters of the traditional parties had little scope for anything more than protest. Indeed, one common description of the Popular Participation Law was that it was neither popular nor participatory. The political lessons that could be drawn from the experience of the NPE and the major reforms of the next MNR government were stark: centralization of power, technocratic decision-making and repression of opposition were important ingredients of neoliberal policy change.[58]

Facilitating Change: The MNR as Participant

While not engaged in the design of new policies, the MNR was not irrelevant to the reform experience. Reformers who promoted the NPE and the three damned laws, as well as other policies adopted during the Paz Estenssoro and Sánchez de Lozada administrations, drew on some of the most traditional aspects of the party in order to make their policies possible. The party had long had a 'big tent' philosophy about its support base and its development over time showed it to be highly flexible in terms of who was in the tent. It was also a party skilled in the arts of coalition-building, a factor that was important in gaining approval for the new policies. Further, it was a party built on state patronage; reformers were able to use this traditional political mechanism to their advantage.

At its founding in 1941, the Movimiento Nacionalista Revolucionario, like other Bolivian political parties that emerged in the 1930s and 1940s, was a party whose objectives were both nationalist and socialist. It was committed to the broad and vague goal of 'affirming and defending the Bolivian nation'.[59] Initially, the party was reluctant to mobilize a mass base beyond the periodic need to rally votes to its cause.[60] Nevertheless, as rival parties emerged and began mobilizing support from among those who had been largely excluded from politics in the past, the MNR turned to wider publics to gain support for its cause and to mobilize displays of power. This search for support was a characteristic that came to define the party.

A Big Tent

Historically, the MNR was many parties. Periodically, it sought new bases of support, purged itself of others or found itself mired in debates that could only be resolved by splitting the party. Initially a party of urban middle class intellectuals, it was at various times a party that flirted with fascism and with radical populism. It was a party that had generated support from leftist workers' organizations, conservative peasant organizations in the *altiplano* and emerging business elites and technocrats from the major cities. It was, in fact, a party capable of reinventing itself as times and politics encouraged.[61]

In its infancy, the MNR focused on the political mobilization of urban middle and lower middle class groups — artisans, merchants, professionals, students — as well as workers and peasants.[62] Soon, it became active in encouraging organizations representing the interests of mine workers. Thus, it supported the creation of the Federación Sindical de Trabajadores Mineros de Bolivia (FSTMB) and gave encouragement to its legendary leader, Juan Lechín Oquendo. At the same time, the party was an available vehicle for the political aspirations of military officers attracted to national socialism. The party joined in the coup that brought the military government of Gualberto Villarroel to power in 1943 and then became part of an administration that was increasingly noted for its repressiveness against political activists of the left.[63] Simultaneously, this new party participated in the government's efforts to draw peasant leaders into national politics. But by the late 1940s, the MNR had eschewed its fascist wing and, in the face of extensive persecution, was advocating armed struggle against the established authorities and in the interests of radical worker organizations and urban groups that had not been previously organized.[64] This was indeed a flexible party.

In the early 1950s, the MNR had become a radical party of the left with an active middle class base pulling it to the center.[65] Government repression at the hands of the military strengthened this coalition and increased the extent to which party militants anticipated that only through armed struggle could their goals be achieved. Nevertheless, its support coalition was never fully secure because, from the beginning, labor organizations resisted the control of the MNR, seeking instead the capacity to negotiate independently on issues as they emerged. The awkward relationship between the party and its support base was also characteristic of the revolution and its immediate aftermath. The party captured political leadership of the insurrection, but the rapid pace with which armed worker and (later) peasant militias emerged meant that the foot soldiers of the revolution were the organizations representing these groups, not the party cadres. In fact, the mining unions were far in advance of the MNR in taking control of the mines and forcing their nationalization and the rural unions were far in advance of the MNR in taking over land and forcing the agrarian reform by fiat.

When the MNR took over the government in April 1952, the peak labor organization, the Central Obrera Boliviana (COB), acknowledging affiliation but not union with the party, was able to demand control of several ministries and dictate the terms for the relationship of labor to the nationalized industries. Asserting the principle of co-government, the COB insisted on naming labor ministers and others for the cabinet and the right to representation in the leadership ranks of the party.[66] Similarly, it demanded worker control in the mines. In rural areas, regional and local *caciques* (bosses) were forces to be reckoned with and, by the late 1950s, national political figures were required to court their support and at times needed invitations to 'intrude' into the areas they controlled.[67]

Certainly, the MNR's effort to build an enduring base of support was part and parcel of its revolutionary objectives. Giving strong support to the COB was one such initiative. Eliminating the literacy requirement for voting and then promulgating a comprehensive agrarian reform law were other strategies that engendered a strong presence in rural areas that persisted over decades. At the same time, however, MNR policies in favor of workers and peasants created significant economic instability — high inflation, diminished production in mines and farms and much increased public spending — that worked to undermine its urban middle class support.[68]

Indeed, the pull of various constituencies — radical labor, increasingly conservative peasant syndicates, the urban middle class — was a leitmotif that kept the party a flexible organization. Its leaders, perhaps most comfortable with a center-left position that allowed the party to maintain the support of the urban middle class, helped pull it away from its more radical and conservative supporters in the years after the revolution. In the midst of a major economic crisis, it traded 'sensible' economic policies for US assistance and, later, IMF support. While this stance was acceptable to the peasant population — largely withdrawn from national politics after the agrarian reform except during elections — it caused the party's left to align itself with the more progressive elements in the leadership. This alliance eventually led to the creation of the MNRI (MNR Izquierda) and contributed to the emergence of the MIR in the 1970s. Foreshadowing these events, in the early 1960s, the party was restructured by Paz Estenssoro to empower the center and the right; the left wing of the party, joined by the workers' movement, broke with it, leaving Paz with support from the army and the peasantry.

Patronage and Coalitions

At the same time that it was juggling left, right and center supporters, the MNR was also developing political forms that were important in its reemergence as a significant political party in the late 1970s. While in power, the party became skilled at responding to specific needs of specific groups and at distributing jobs and resources to supporters in an effort to establish and maintain internal order. Over time, this response became more embedded in the dynamics of everyday politics, and eventually much support for the MNR reflected response to the particularistic needs of organized groups rather than identification with a program or even a leadership group.[69] This dynamic held the seeds of the systematic weakening of the party over time as its power became increasingly dependent on spoils and parceling out policy areas to its supporters.

When Paz was re-elected in 1964, his government was overthrown by a military that was confident that it could dispense with civilian politicians and wield power in its own right.[70] Almost two decades of military rule ensued, during which the MNR saw its rural base undermined by the famous 'military-peasant pact' in which the government ensured that rural areas would be recipients of more education, social spending, agrarian reform and development programs. By the end of the 1970s, many parties had emerged to contest for power and the MNR, like these others, found that it needed to appeal to a broad sector of the electorate for support — both labor and peasant voters were much less likely to cast their ballots with a single voice.[71] In the elections of 1985, 1989, 1993 and 1997, the electoral base of the MNR had become similar to that of many other parties — a cross-class coalition of the center held together by electoral appeals and clientelism and the liberal application of state patronage. The other two relatively well-established parties, the MIR and the ADN, flanked the party on the left and right.[72]

In 1985, Paz Estenssoro pioneered a new kind of governing coalition in Bolivia. Based in part on common perspectives about economic policy reforms, the governing agreement signed with the ADN, the Pacto por la Democracia, joined the two parties in an executive-led initiative to support government policy in the legislature. Through this pact, the parties pledged to support the reforms and a state of siege that enabled the government to control and repress opposition. This pact provided representation in government ministries and the cabinet in exchange for a green light on executive-initiated policy.[73] The Pacto por la Democracia was a firm one, maintained until 1989, when the ADN threw its support to Jaime Paz Zamora. Although it was not called on to provide legislative approval of the NPE and other policies, the pact created enough political stability to see them implemented consistently during the Paz administration.

The alliance with the ADN during the Paz Estenssoro administration set a model for how such a coalition could be put together and why it was important to sustain it. Each succeeding administration reinvented the model more or less successfully. The Pacto Patriótico underpinned the Jaime Paz government. Sánchez de Lozada followed suit with his own Pacto por el Cambio in 1993, which legitimated the three damned laws and his other policy reforms. That he was able to corral the necessary congressional votes for highly controversial laws was remarkable, the fact that most were passed with little debate was even more so. The MNR and its coalition allies were essential to the approval and sustainability of the reforms, even though, as we saw, they were largely excluded from the policy decision process.

But in the 1980s and 1990s the MNR was no stranger to the arts of coalition formation.[74] Indeed, throughout its history, it was active in seeking electoral coalitions with particular interests and governing coalitions with other parties or the military. Until the 1980s, for example, the relationship with the labor unions was characterized more by negotiation and pact-making than by incorporation and control. Mobilizing the vote involved bargains, horse-trading and promises about public policy and spoils. Moreover, the party had been actively engaged in governing coalition making as far back as the Villarroel government in the 1940s.[75] Those experiences involved using positions in government as a currency for gaining support from sectoral leaders and trading government largesse for votes through clientelism.

In the 1980s and 1990s, the mechanism that made the MNR's governing coalitions work so well was the exchange of acquiescence to policy for patronage positions in government.[76] The pacts ensured that congressional input into economic policy would be limited to approving the plans of the executive and that there would be little debate.[77] The traditional politics of patronage were thus put to use in the service of economic reform and helped marginalize the party from participation in decision making, affirming that, as one observer noted, 'power in countries like Bolivia is the power to appoint people and provide jobs'.[78]

As Eduardo Gamarra aptly shows in Chapter 12, however, the shortcoming of the governing pacts in which the MNR participated was that neoliberal policies conspired to do away with the political resources that cemented agreements among politicians — public sector jobs and an activist state that created positions, contracts, projects and programs that could be exchanged for political support. By the late 1990s, the capacity to form patronage-based pacts had diminished through state retrenchment and decentralization, the 'dismantling of the state resources that had been the base of the patrimonial dynamics of the party system'.[79] At the same time, these pacts made all kinds of reforms possible, save the centrally important reform of state institutions, because control over them, and opportunities for corruption through them, were the glue essential to the maintenance of the political peace.[80]

Conclusions: Form and Content

The reformism of the 1980s and 1990s did not emerge from the belly of the revolutionary party. Indeed, for the leadership of the party and much of its electoral constituency, the policies introduced under Paz Estenssoro and Sánchez de Lozada were anathema, deeply resisted by many of the party faithful. Yet the MNR facilitated the introduction of these reforms and, in some cases, even came to champion them after they had demonstrated some success and political utility. Its contributions to the neoliberal revolution were a result of a party that had learned to survive through tumultuous political and economic times in the past, that had learned the arts of building and sustaining political coalitions and that managed to extract a patronage price from its reformist standard bearers. That it had to stand by and watch MNR governments move against some of its traditional support bases in order to do this was part of that bargain with the neoliberal devil. It did not contribute content to the reforms; it did contribute form.

The MNR can be likened to many other major national parties in Latin America — the PRI in Mexico, the Peronists in Argentina, AD in Venezuela — that helped usher in neoliberal policies in the 1980s and 1990s. That is, it was primarily a party whose purpose it was to mobilize votes and whose goal it was to share in state largesse. Its value to those who set the agenda and designed the policies was high, however, as it was the party that helped introduce and sustain these policies once they had been decided upon by presidents and advisors. More simply, the pacts that were so effective in aiding MNR presidents helped maintain some level of political peace and government legitimacy through some very difficult years. Thus, according to two participants in policy making under Sánchez de Lozada, 'To the extent that political stability provided policy room to design and implement ambitious reforms, the Bolivian reform program owes as much to politicians and political parties, as to technocrats and economic policy-makers.'[81]

Notes

* Portions of this chapter are adapted from Grindle (2000). I would like to thank Aaron Jette of the Kennedy School of Government, Harvard University, for research assistance.

1 See Cariaga (1996); Morales (1995); Sachs (1987).

2 Statements about the extent of hyperinflation vary from this World Bank (1997) annualized rate to those that cite 24,000 per cent at its highest point that year. Throughout, I use World Bank figures for consistency across time and measurement.

3 For discussions of the NPE, see Morales (1994) (1995); Sachs (1987); Cariaga (1982); Conaghan and Malloy (1994).

4 Graham (1994); Jorgensen, Grosh and Schacter (1992).

5 Morales (1994), p. 159. Decreases in public sector employment were most notable in the public enterprise sector.

6 Grindle (2000), p. 110.

7 Morales (1994), pp. 140–1.

8 Mallon (1994), p. 928.

9 Mallon (1994).

10 See Sánchez de Lozada (2001).

11 See Gamarra (1994a).

12 Morales (1994), p. 159.

13 See Graham (1997); Grebe López (2001).

14 Grindle (2000), chapter 5; see also Gray-Molina (2001).

15 Grindle (2000), chapter 5.
16 Grindle (forthcoming); see also Ruiz-Mier (2001).
17 Mayorga (1997a), p. 152.
18 Graham (1997)
19 This administration put together a governing pact of five parties and was hamstrung from the beginning by the factiousness inherent in an unwieldy grouping of parties. Within a year, one of the larger of the parties, Condepa (Conciencia de Patria), dropped out of the coalition.
20 Among these initiatives, the most well known was a decision to sell water concessions to private firms. The public resistance in Cochabamba was particularly strong and the government had to rescind its original policy. On the education reform, see Grindle (forthcoming).
21 The BonoSol Program was replaced by a much more modest program known as Bolivida.
22 On the development model of the revolutionary state, see Toranzo Roca (1999); Mayorga (1999); Klein (1992); Dunkerley (1984); Malloy (1970).
23 Conaghan and Malloy (1994), p. 127.
24 Both McLean and Blanco had strong ties to the Kennedy School of Government at Harvard. Others included in the group were Carlos Iturralde, Willy Vargas Vacaflor, Jorge Balcázar, Mauro Bertero, Carlos Morales Landívar and Alvaro Ugalde. Cariaga (1996), p. 92.
25 Sachs reviewed the proposal and recommended harsher measures to tame the fiscal deficit. He wrote a confidential memorandum to Banzer and promised to be available to advise the government if the party won the elections. See Cariaga (1996), pp. 92–3.
26 Cariaga (1996), p. 92. The moratorium had been put in place by then President Siles Zuazo.
27 In accordance with the constitution, the Congress was to choose the president and the vice president from among the three candidates who won the highest proportion of the popular vote. In 1994, this provision was altered so that the choice had to be made between the top two vote winners in the popular election.
28 Carriaga (1996), pp. 95–7. The team included Juan Cristóbal Urioste, Francisco Muñoz, Raúl España and Fernando Prado, head of the economic policy analysis unit (UDAPE). Antonio Sánchez de Lozada was the brother of Gonzalo Sánchez de Lozada and an expert in public management.
29 Drosdoff (1997), pp. 2–4.
30 Mayorga U. (1996). Sánchez de Lozada was a member of the influential business council, Confederación de Empresarios Privados, that had been actively engaged in demanding the return of democracy to the country in 1982.

31 According to Conaghan and Malloy (1994), p. 190, Paz was sensitive to the need to engage some of the *movimientista* leadership and to provide some opportunities for patronage to the party as a way of gaining its acquiescence in the new economic policy measures.
32 Conaghan and Malloy (1994), pp. 190–1.
33 Graham (1992) pp. 1234–6); Marshall (1992), pp. 26–7.
34 Marshall (1992).
35 *Ibid.*, pp. 31–2.
36 See Graham (1992), pp. 1238–42.
37 He was referred to as a 'prime minister' in the Paz Estenssoro government. Interview, 26 February 1997, La Paz.
38 Sánchez de Lozada owned and managed COMSUR, a large mining company in Bolivia. In the 1970s he had become active in representing business groups through the Confederación de Empresarios Privados de Bolivia (CEPB). This and the follwoing three paragraphs draw on Grindle (2000), pp. 111–16
39 The maintenance of the NPE was particularly important to Paz Estenssoro and his support of Sánchez de Lozada was not only an effort to strengthen the modernizing wing of the party but also to see his economic program carried out in the future. On the internal party conflicts between the modernizers and technocrats on one hand and the traditional populist leaders on the other, see Mayorga U. (1996). The former claimed the traditional politicians were an anachronism while they in turn called the modernizers anti-nationalists (Mayorga U. (1996), pp. 109–10, 139.
40 The international advisory board included Juan Linz of Yale University, Arturo Valenzuela of Notre Dame University, Carlos Nino of Argentina and Bolívar Lamunier of Brazil. See Grindle (2000), pp. 113–15.
41 According to Carlos Hugo Molina, architect of the Popular Participation Law, 'the participation of Goni … was always relevant and positive. When he didn't have in-depth knowledge of a particular theme, he asked questions and listened. His open and receptive attitude allowed him to gain much from the discussions and from people like I, who didn't agree much with neoliberal propositions. We worked with pleasure, without political pressures or party annoyances. In fact, because of the varied professional backgrounds and experiences of the members of the group, we all learned.' Personal correspondence, 2 September 1998, author's translation. The experience of the foundation is discussed in Molina Monasterios (1997).
42 Interview, 4 March 1997, La Paz, cited in Grindle (2000), pp. 114–15.
43 I am grateful to Gonzalo Chávez, in personal communication of 19 March 2002, for insight into the development of the capitalization program.

44 Gonzalo Chávez, personal correspondence, 18 March 2002, author's translation.

45 In addition, the group included Fernando Candia, Edgar Saravia, Alfonso Revollo, Carlos Miranda, Gonzalo Chávez and a few others.

46 'In fact, the World Bank was the institution that was most resistant to the idea of capitalization, especially in the first four or five months of the government. Goni had to talk to people at the highest level of the WB in order for there to be a better understanding of what his government wanted to achieve.' Gonzalo Chávez, personal correspondence, 18 March 2002, author's translation.

47 *Ibid.*

48 *Ibid.*

49 This and the following paragraph draw on Grindle (2000), pp. 116–22.

50 Molina Monasterios (1997), p. 205.

51 Of considerable concern to this group was the role of the Bolivian state in economic and social development. According to a participant in these discussions, 'In the early 1990s, it was essential to lessen the demands and pressure on the central state. It was also imperative to get the presence of the state known and understood throughout the country. This was not so much a concern for security in the traditional sense, but because of a concern for political security.' (Interview, 4 March 1997, La Paz, cited in Grindle, 2000, p. 118). In addition, the president encouraged the group to think hard about how to deal with the level of corruption that characterized government in Bolivia. A tradition of clientelism had created a prebendal system in which jobs, contracts, favors and bribes constituted the normal business of government. In the perspective of the president, centralized power was threatened by a weak central state and by incomplete nationalism, extensive corruption and resulting loss of legitimacy for government. See Grindle (2000), chapter 5.

52 *Ibid.*, pp. 116–22.

53 The CSUTCB, which provided the only governance structure for many rural communities in the highland areas of western Bolivia, was particularly concerned that Popular Participation's structure for granting representation to local organizations would not include local unions. Moreover, the rural union had long benefited from un-official local autonomy that was the product of a weak state. They believed that if they were not part of the new structure, the organizations that did end up representing the communities would be hand-picked by government or would be dominated by the political parties. Grindle (2000), pp. 120–1; Urioste and Baldomar (1996), pp. 30–5.

54 Contreras (1999b), pp. 491–2; see also Contreras (1998a).

55 This decision owes much to the influence of Victor Hugo Cardenas, vice-president elect, who headed the in-coming government's team on the transition commission established by the Jaime Paz government.

56 Nevertheless, the child seemed to have been less loved than capitalization and Popular Participation. Once the law was approved in July 1994, the reformers found it difficult to move ahead decisively with the reform. The government had other priorities, the unions were vociferously opposed to it and the Ministry of Education and the Superministry of Human Resources began to suffer the kind of leadership instability often endemic to social sector ministries. Thus, between 1995 and mid-1997, when Sánchez de Lozada left the presidency, education reform was implemented very tentatively. This task was given higher priority by Hugo Banzer's government.

57 Morales (1994), p. 131. See also Cariaga (1996) and Conaghan, Malloy and Abugattas (1990).

58 So was external support. While international financial institutions were initially cautious of the NPE, they soon pledged their support to the stabilization and structural adjustment measures. The World Bank was a major supporter of the Social Emergency Fund, and between 1989 and 1999 the government received almost US$7 billion of Official Development Assistance and close to another US$2 billion in technical assistance funding (Gray-Molina and Chávez, 2001, p. 7, based on DAC dataset).

59 On political parties in Bolivia, see Partidos Políticos en Bolivia (1998) and CIDES-PNUD (1997).

60 Malloy (1970), p. 115.

61 See particularly Klein (1992), chapter 8.

62 Malloy (1970), p. 116.

63 *Ibid.,* pp. 120–6.

64 *Ibid.,* pp. 127–35.

65 Klein (1992), chapter 7; Dunkerley (1984), chapter 2.

66 See Malloy (1970), pp. 185–6.

67 Whitehead (1974–75), p. 98; Malloy (1970), p. 291.

68 Klein (1992), pp. 236–7.

69 See Whitehead (1974–75), p. 75.

70 Early on a participant in this government, the more conservative wing of the party was soon ejected as unimportant and Paz Estenssoro was sent into exile (Klein, 1992, p. 244).

71 In its relationship to the military, it failed a significant revolutionary test — despite considerable effort, the party never managed to take control of the armed forces. Malloy (1970), pp. 179–82.

72 Domingo (2001), p. 144.

73 See especially Gamarra (1994a). In the pact that supported the policies of the Jaime Paz Zamora government, the exchange of positions for political support became more explicit, including quotas and specific distributions based on control over ministry leadership. Gray-Molina and Chávez (2001).

74 Malloy (1970).

75 Klein (1992), p. 218.

76 Gamarra (1994a, 1996); Domingo (2001).

77 Gamarra (1994a, p. 116) points out that an important difference between the Pacto por la Democracia and the Acuerdo Patriótico is that the former is an agreement between a governing party and the principal party in opposition, while the latter is an agreement about sharing government between two parties that are relatively equal in power.

78 Interview, La Paz, 28 February 1997.

79 See Gamarra in this volume, chapter 12, page 300.

80 This is a major point made by Gamarra (1994a). Gray Molina and Chávez (2001, p. 10) make reference to 'coalition politics that create space for innovative reform, but lessen the possibility of sustaining reform through non-clientelistic or matrimonial means'.

81 Gray Molina and Chávez (2001), p. 5.

Chapter 14

The Offspring of 1952: Poverty, Exclusion and the Promise of Popular Participation

George Gray Molina[1]

No sentirse como los que se sienten clase,
en vez de sentirse nación.[2]

Introduction

From a political perspective, the history of the Bolivian National Revolution can be described as a continuous but contested process of social and political inclusion. Carlos Montenegro, intellectual leader of the MNR, conceptualized the aims of the revolution in terms of a struggle between *nación* and *anti-nación*, 'in order not to be like those who feel a class, but those who feel a nation'. The key tenets of the revolution revolved around staples of twentieth century state- and nation-building: universal suffrage, agrarian reform and nationalization of industry. The inclusive reforms of the revolution had a tangible material impact through the 1960s and a lasting symbolic impact over the development of national identity and political citizenry well into the new century. Although those born before 1952 account for only 13.3 per cent of the present-day population, much of the revolutionary discourse lives on through a strong legacy of popular mobilization and state reform.

This chapter discusses changing forms of social and political inclusion from the standpoint of the offspring of 1952: first- and second-generation heirs of the National Revolution. The cohorts born before and during the National Revolution lived through a period of ambitious state-led inclusion under agrarian reform, unionization and corporate political intermediation. Their offspring, the first generation born after the revolution, however, experienced the fragmentation of this political project in the 1970s and the atomization of worker and peasant unions in the 1980s. New forms of social mobility and political integration arose after the democratic transition of 1982 and the economic reforms of 1985. Educational attainment, urbanization and formal labor insertion were then perceived to be more effective vehicles of social mobility and integration for the second-generation cohort born after the revolution.

Despite these shifts, a legacy of popular mobilization and state-led inclusion continues to set the political agenda in Bolivia. New demands for social and political integration translate into skepticism over the effectiveness of trickle-down economics, coalition democracy and the promise of a pluri-cultural and multi-ethnic society, all of which sustained reform efforts during the 1980s and 1990s. New forms of state-led inclusion, in particular the 1994 Popular Participation Reform, continue to articulate a vision of collective integration, citizenship and multi-ethnic national identity. The divide between new and old forms of social inclusion accelerated as state-led reforms were substituted by market-led ones, sorting along educational, labor and income lines.

In this chapter, the terms social 'inclusion' and 'exclusion' are used to describe relative changes in social status across time. This contextual usage is meant to accommodate to the changing scenarios of social change observed after the National Revolution. Where collective bargaining, negotiation and clientelist politics once led state-sponsored vehicles of social mobility, today, educational achievement, urbanization and formal labor skills provide new — yet more precarious — forms of social opportunity. The chapter is divided in four parts: first, a stylized description of social change across three generations; second, a discussion of social and political fragmentation of collective forms of inclusion, mediated through worker and *campesino* unions as well as the hegemonic MNR; third, an analysis of Bolivia's most recent effort at state-led inclusion, the Popular Participation Reform of 1994, as well as disillusion and disenchantment with this reform since April and September 2000. The final section surveys new forms of social and political inclusion, 50 years after the National Revolution.

The Offspring of the Revolution: 1952–2002

The offspring of the revolution can be sorted into three demographic groups: (i) a 'revolutionary cohort' comprised of those citizens born before and during the 1952 Revolution; (ii) a 'first generation' cohort born after 1952 but before 1972; and (iii) a 'second generation' cohort born after 1972. The revolutionary cohort accounted for 13.3 per cent of the population at the turn of the century, the first-generation group for 22.3 per cent and the second-generation group for 64.4 per cent of the population. The distribution of cohorts provides a preliminary snapshot of the demographic weight of the offspring of the revolution. The dominant demographic group comprises second-generation grandsons and granddaughters of the revolutionary cohort. Table 14.1 shows population growth since 1950. The demographic transition that bridges the three generations is marked by three distinctive shifts: first, a move from a predominantly rural society in 1950 (74 per cent) to a predominantly urban one in 2001 (69 per cent); second, a significant regional shift toward the eastern lowlands. The department of Santa Cruz exceeded a population growth rate of four per cent for over 50 years and continued to be the fastest growing department in Bolivia; third, the move from a predominantly indigenous-speaking population to a predominantly bilingual population. In 1950 63 per cent of the population spoke an indigenous language at home, in 2001, approximately 62 per cent was bilingual in Spanish and indigenous languages.

Table 14.1: Population Growth 1950–2001

	1950 Pop. (000s)	1976 Pop. (000s)	1992 Pop. (000s)	2001 Pop. (000s)	1950–76 Growth Rate	1976–92 Growth Rate	1976–2001 Growth Rate
La Paz	854	1,465	1,900	2,351	2.07	1.66	2.30
Oruro	192	310	340	392	1.84	0.58	1.54
Potosí	509	658	645	709	0.98	(-0.12)	1.00
Cochabamba	452	721	1,110	1,457	1.79	2.75	2.94
Chuquisaca	260	359	454	529	1.23	1.50	1.66
Tarija	103	187	291	391	2.28	2.82	3.17
Santa Cruz	245	711	1,364	2,034	4.09	4.16	4.30
Beni	72	168	276	365	3.28	3.16	3.08
Pando	16	34	38	52	2.88	0.63	3.38

Source: Instituto Nacional de Estadísticas (2002).

Table 14.2 shows schooling attainment by cohorts. Schooling increased threefold over 70 years and almost sixfold in rural areas. Significant increases in schooling can be tracked to post-revolutionary cohorts. Rural schooling was almost non-existent prior to the revolution and this can be seen in the educational attainment of those born prior to 1952 (0.82 for 70 year olds, 1.28 for 60–69 year olds and 2.17 for 50–59 years olds. Urban schooling attainment, on the other hand, made a significant leap in the 1960s and stabilized for two generations. Second-generation youth reached and surpassed the Latin American average in schooling (11 years of schooling for 20–29 year olds). Overall the gap between urban and rural schooling attainment remains significant, almost equivalent to the 50-year gap between pre- and post-revolutionary age groups. While schooling attainment statistics provide a long-run snapshot of potential social mobility, income and consumption data offer a more short-run evaluation of current welfare, as measured by standardized poverty lines.

Table 14.2: Schooling by Age Cohorts

	Urban	Rural	Total
Second Generation			
20–29 years	10.95	5.71	9.70
First Generation			
30–39 years	9.99	4.22	8.13
40–49 years	9.03	2.93	6.83
Revolution cohort			
50–59 years	7.49	2.17	5.31
60–69 years	5.98	1.28	3.72
70+ years	5.22	0.82	2.73
Total	**9.42**	**3.31**	**7.33**

Source: Instituto Nacional de Estadísticas (2001), based on MECOVI 1999 surveys.

Table 14.3 estimates the exit time for poor households living under the poverty line, at four per cent and six per cent GDP growth rates, given unchanged distributional patterns. The MECOVI survey of 1999 estimated that 63 per cent of the population lives below the national poverty line, 47 per cent in urban areas and 82 per cent in rural areas. At four per cent growth it would take 131 years for the poorest rural household to escape poverty, 99 years for the poorest urban household. The dismal figures are largely explained by a highly unequal distribution of income, steadily worsening during the 1990s. The 1999 survey estimates a Gini income concentration coefficient of 0.59, one of the highest in Latin America, only surpassed by Brazil and Colombia. Under a more optimistic scenario of six per cent GDP growth, the poorest rural household would escape poverty in 63 years, the poorest urban household in 48 years. Under both scenarios many generations will live under poverty despite high and sustained economic growth rates. The explicit move from discussing 'poverty' in the 1990s to discussing 'exclusion' in the 2000s largely mirrors this reality. Inequality has overtaken poverty as a matter of policy concern in Bolivia and was the object of political debate during the 2002 electoral campaign.

Table 14.3: Poverty Exit Time

	4 % Annual GDP Growth /b		6 % Annual GDP Growth	
	Rural	**Urban**	**Rural**	**Urban**
1st decile (+ poor) /a	131 years	99 years	63 years	48 years
2nd decile	105	57	50	27
3rd decile	89	39	43	19
4th decile	76	24	36	12
5th decile	65	11	32	6
6th decile	53	0	26	0
7th decile	40	0	19	0
8th decile	28	0	13	0
9th decile	10	0	5	0
10th decile (+ wealthy)	0	0	0	0

Source: Own source, based on INE (2002) and Mecovi (1999).

a/ The growth line taken for this table is the same as that used in EBRP (2001): Bs. 328/month, equivalent to US$50/month or US$1.6 a day, close to the international poverty line of US$2 a day.

b/ The projected rate of population growth is 2.2% per annum. Under this assumption, a rate of growth of 4% translates in 1.8% per capita and a rate of 6% translates in 3.8% per capita.

Fragmentation after the National Revolution

1952–1964: Agrarian Reform

The National Revolution of 1952 cast the rural and urban poor, at least by official discourse, as key protagonists of vast social and political change. Universal suffrage, nationalization of mines, agrarian reform and education reform were the hallmarks of a revolution driven by mass mobilization and characterized by political contestation.[3] The agrarian reform, in particular, was to be regarded as one of the most comprehensive land redistribution initiatives carried out in the region.[4] The expropriation of hacienda land and redistribution to tenant farmers, smallholders and *campesino* communities was accompanied by a continuous process of state-led rural mobilization. The creation of thousands of new agrarian unions promoted and supported by the ascendant MNR, would set the grounds for a long period of corporatist state-building and political clientelism. By 1956–60, the objectives of popular mobilization had shifted from land reclamation to political negotiation with a highly dispersed network of state patronage. Public works and food subsidization schemes managed through line ministries and departmental prefectures were channeled through networks of party sympathizers and militants, inducing atomization within the national peasant movement. By the early 1960s the zeal of the initial period of revolution and reform had abated and given way to a more pragmatic realignment with the emerging developmental state.

1964–78: Corporatist State-Building

A second, and quite contrasting, period of policy-making arose with corporatist and clientelist politics. After 12 years of MNR rule, the 1964 military coup initiated an 18-year period of military rule, marked by interim periods of civilian government.[5] The diminished political power of MNR patrons and the political containment strategy of the military vis-à-vis radicalized miner and worker movements led to the establishment of a military-*campesino* pact (Pacto Militar Campesino), which endured through the mid-1970s. The pact thus substituted the MNR-union clientelistic ties, secured the continuity of land reform gains and laid the foundations of a new corporatist and clientelistic political relationship.[6] The rural poor lost their organizational autonomy and although they still exercised some capacity for political expression, this was subject to a series of vertical controls organized through local garrison commands. The demobilization of the *campesino* union movement was to last only a few years. By 1968 calls for an independent and unaligned union leadership emerged after the Barrientos administration floated a new policy proposal aimed at consolidating a single rural land tax.[7] The Banzer coup d'etat of 1971 contained the splintered *campesino* movement and restored the Military Campesino Pact until the mid-1970s. Price hikes decreed in 1974, however, fueled a bloody confrontation between military troops and *campesino* protesters in Tolata, reigniting a more radical mobilization period aimed at opposing the authoritarian regime and pushing toward a popular and democratic transition. The creation of a unified agrarian union confederation (CSUTCB) marked a political shift in the *campesino* movement in 1979, leading to a three-year stretch of active popular mobilization through the democratic transition of 1982.

1993–2000: Popular Participation

A third scenario emerged from a period of democratizing state reforms. First generation reforms that focused on economic stabilization and fiscal balance in the 1980s were followed by second generation reforms focusing on decentralization, capitalization, pensions, education and judicial reform in the 1990s. These initiatives aimed to reintroduce the poor as agents of public policy. The Popular Participation Reform is perhaps the most salient of the reforms for its local political and institutional effects. Close to 200 new municipalities were created and rural areas were included within municipal jurisdiction for the first time. Initially rejected by the *campesino* and indigenous leadership, Popular Participation was to gain momentum with the municipal elections of 1995, which for the first time included open and direct rural municipal elections.[8] Close to one fourth of municipal councilors in 311 municipalities were self-identified *campesino* or indigenous candidates.[9] More important for the grass-roots movement, however, was the institutionalization of participatory planning procedures involving some 16,000 *campesino*, indigenous and neighborhood organizations.[10] While the development of the Popular Participation is widely regarded as being marked by an equal measure of 'success' and 'failure', the emphasis on territorially based grass-roots organizations restructured the rules of the game for political intermediation and policy-making in rural areas. State patronage and political clientelism, which had relied on national-to-local networks of redistribution and reciprocity, increasingly competed with newly established local networks — some building upon the political capabilities of a previous era — and some newly adapted to the changed rules of political engagement.

Political Fragmentation

Political fragmentation largely mirrors underlying patterns of social or regional political integration. The Bolivian political system consistently moved toward greater political fragmentation since democratic transition in the early 1980s, particularly at the local level of government. Six local elections held in 1987, 1989, 1991, 1993, 1995 and 1999 frame the trajectory of local politics before and immediately after the adoption of the Popular Participation Reform. Four of these were held in non-national election years: 1987, 1991, 1995 and 1999. A number of changes in electoral rules, voter age, voter registries and party inscription occurred over this period. The first, and in many senses foundational, was local election independence from national elections. The 1987 elections were the first to be held in between national election years. The 1989 and 1993 local elections, however, took place six months after national elections. This pattern made for awkward comparisons, most evident in the swift upturn (in non-national election years) and downturn (in national election years) in local electoral participation rates. The 1991 local elections were the first to introduce a computerized voter registry, managed by a newly independent National Electoral Court (CNE) rather than by political parties, as had been the norm in previous elections.[11] The 1991 registry also provided a relatively reliable geographic baseline for successive comparisons. The 1995 elections, following 1994 constitutional reform, expanded the franchise to citizens over the age of 18, from 21, but included new restrictions on registration documents. Only a *cédula de identidad* (ID card), rather than birth certificate or military conscription booklet, could be used for registration.[12] A number of characteristics can be highlighted during the 1987–99 electoral period.

The first is a steady increase in local electoral participation. Voter registration peaked at 3.5 million in 1999. The peak was most significant in urban areas, where registered voters numbered more than twice those in 1987. The 1991 elections show an exceptional decline in registered voters, which most analysts attribute to the new registry system put in place following the 1991 Electoral Code Reform. Given this discontinuity, perhaps the most accurate figures for electoral participation are given by actual voting participation (which includes valid, null and blank votes). Voter participation increased from 1.2 million in 1987 to 2.1 million in 1999, adding nearly 0.9 million new voters to the local elections. Most new voters were from urban areas. Rural voter participation picked up significantly after the adoption of the Popular Participation Reform. The rural vote almost doubled between 1993 (0.3 million) and 1995 (0.7 million). The increase can be attributed to a number of factors, including the extension of rural council elections, the extension of identification documents in rural areas and the grass-roots mobilization that followed the initial wait-and-see period between 1994 and 1995.

Local electoral turnout is difficult to estimate. Although official figures suggest rates anywhere from 28 per cent in 1987 to 40 per cent in 1999, the shifting denominators driving these figures do not allow direct comparisons across years. The number of 'registered' voters accumulates two types of errors. The first can be traced back to the discontinuity posed by the introduction of a comprehensive and independently monitored electoral registry in 1991; the second, and more persistent error, is that the 1993, 1995 and 1999 elections carry accumulated deceased, migrant and other 'absent' voters on the registry. Double counting, by counting voters that moved and registered in a different electoral district as different voters, is a pervasive problem that called attention to the need for a comprehensive review. While the 1991 discontinuity had the temporary effect of driving the abstention level down, the accumulation of registry errors subsequently drove it up. An alternative turnout ratio can be estimated using the potential voting population, as proxied by the over-18 population estimated for 1990, 1995 and 2000 based on projections from the 1992 census. Under this proxy turnout formula, local turnout rates are higher everywhere but more stable over time.

A second characteristic of local elections between 1987 and 1999 is the large number of parties that competed for the vote. The 1987, 1993 and 1995 elections each fielded 13 political parties; the 1999 elections fielded 18 parties. The effective number of parties (ENVP), which indicates the number of parties weighted by share of the electorate, shows the degree of political party fragmentation within the political system.[13] In a perfect two-party system, for example, with the vote split 50-50, the ENVP equals 2; in a four party system (25-25-25-25) it equals 4. If some parties are larger than others, however, the effective number of parties is usually some fraction of the intuitively expected number of parties. In the Bolivian case, the ENVP for local elections in 1987 is 7.2; for 1989, 5.7; 1991, 5.4; 1993, 5.7; 1995, 8.5; in 1999 it was 9.5. Electoral fragmentation increased significantly after the adoption of Popular Participation. Not only did more political parties compete for the local vote but more parties were voted on to local councils around the country. The degree of electoral fragmentation varies sharply from one region to another. Electoral fragmentation was highest in highland municipalities and lowest in the lowlands.

A third characteristic of local elections between 1987–99 is the degree of volatility in electoral preference. The standard volatility index (V) measures the percentage of the vote that shifts among parties, on aggregate, between elections.[14] As with electoral fragmentation, volatility was unevenly distributed between regions. The highland departments of La Paz, Oruro and Potosí were consistently more volatile than the lowland departments of Santa Cruz, Beni and Pando. Between 1987 and 1999 the average degree of local electoral volatility, as measured by (V) was 26.2 per cent. This is the average proportion of the vote that shifted from one party to another throughout the period. An alternative way of visualizing political party volatility is to track the share of traditional MNR/ADN/MIR votes through the local elections. Inasmuch as the traditional parties are associated with long-run loyalties, the non-traditional vote tends to represent the extent of party machinery instability or volatility. In 1987, the traditional parties received 42 per cent of the popular vote; 25 per cent in 1989; 42 per cent in 1991; 26 per cent in 1993; 25 per cent in 1995; and 28 per cent in 1999.

Table 14.4: Municipal Election Results 1987–99

	1987	1989	1991	1993	1995	1999
Total Bolivian						
Registered	1,812,288	1,844,984	1,614,984	2,231,945	2,828,526	3,573,851
Voters	1,288,933	1,003,520	1,398,045	1,189,896	1,797,526	2,124,509
Votes Cast	28.9 %	45.6 %				
Official						
Abstention						
Urban Areas						
Registered	838,576	899,768	1,023,672	1,361,411	1,609,015	
Voters	702,492	637,227	902,081	798,015	1,074,362	
Votes Cast	16.2 %	29.2 %				
Voter						
Abstention						
Rural Areas						
Registered	973,712	945,216	591,308	870,534	1,219,511	
Voters	586,441	366,293	495,964	391,881	723,164	
Votes Cast	39.8 %					
Voter						
Abstention						
MNR	146,627	172,714	321,444	391,029	365,854	408,824
ADN/AP	326,855	300,325	369,744	87,885	196,159	292,803
MIR	298,439			105,826	159,512	319,399
MBL	86,485		74,561	131,545	227,801	89,505
CONDEPA		168,038	163,533	219,303	265,533	80,857
UCS		147,530	297,318	94,001	229,460	237,094
IU/MAS		73,539	51,982	9,095	51,458	65,425
FRI	22,770	13,829		25,099	53,540	37,833
VR–9	71,458	5,468		2,604	8,587	43,713
FSB	22,824			23,526		43,364
MFD	18,985	2,704				
AP	68,193					
PS–1/PS	45,313					55,823
MIN	16,584					
ID	9,582					
PDC	9,511					7,538
MST		6,858				
VS–B		3,219				
ASD				20,551		
Eje Pachacuti				7,132	31,263	
MRTKL				2,258	20,446	1,473
MPP					32,386	4,607
MKN/KND					3,989	8,216
NFR						166,173
MSM						116,652
PCB						21,502

Source: Author's own processing, based on Corte Nacional Electoral data.

The Promise of Popular Participation

Pluri-Multi Nation-Building

The 'national question' debated by liberals and conservatives late in the nineteenth century recurred throughout the twentieth century and was the cornerstone of the Bolivian National Revolution of 1952. Throughout this period, conceptions of nation and nationality changed, as did the importance of regional, ethnic and national cleavages in democratic politics. A key aspect of the Popular Participation Reform, adopted in April 1994, was its effectiveness in forwarding an array of multicultural and pluriethnic policies, recognizing customary political authorities and base organizations within a common framework of decentralization and citizen participation. As with past initiatives of state-building, Popular Participation also framed a new debate on nationality and nationalist claims.

The recent literature on nationality and ethnicity suggests a convergence upon historical explanations of nation-building and the consequences of modern state-building in the twentieth century.[15] Kymlicka, in particular, argues that nation-building is often accompanied by the diffusion of a 'societal culture', a set of understandings over the content and forms of citizenship within the nation-state. Societal culture often revolves around the adoption of a common language, but also extends to multiple arenas of nationhood. Standardized public education, common standards of law and democratic practices are each valuable forms of diffusion of a shared societal culture, a common denominator across regions, ethnicity and locality. In the course of constructing a societal culture, however, disputes arise over what types of claims should inform common norms, identity and nationality. In recent cases of state and nation-building, in the former Soviet republics and Eastern Europe, civic-minded nationalists vie with ethnic-minded nationalists and liberals and socialists of various stripes. What is verifiable, argues Kymlicka, is that the diffusion of societal culture dispute is not neutral among competing visions of nationality.

Framing the Pluri-Multi Nation

'Pluri-multi' politics entered the mainstream political arena in the early 1990s. A book sponsored by ILDIS, and edited by Carlos Toranzo in 1991 (*Lo pluri-multi*), forwarded some of these views to a broader audience. Among the key challenges facing Bolivia was a need to reconcile the *Bolivia profunda* of Bolivian sociological jargon with the modern Bolivia in ways that would both affirm a shared national identity but also recognize multiculturality and pluriethnicity as key sources of a new national identity. Paradoxically, the emphasis on *pluri-multi* supposed a civic, rather than an ethnic or culturally distinct, conception of nationhood. In this view, what stitched together the Bolivian nation was a commitment to respect and promote unity in diversity. A number of historical events ended up placing the *pluri-multi* conception on the national agenda.

The first event was the election of Víctor Hugo Cárdenas as vice-presidential candidate of Gonzalo Sánchez de Lozada. As noted by Xavier Albó, the story of indigenous contestation to homogeneous nation-building had come full circle with the 'audacious pact between neoliberals and Aymaras'. Cárdenas had risen as leader of the *katarista* current within the Confederación Sindical Unica de Trabajadores Campesinos de Bolivia and was the co-founder of the Movimiento Revolucionario Túpac Katari (MRTK–L), an indigenous *katarista* party that emerged in the 1980s and allied with the MNR for the 1993 presidential race.[16] Defeating 'internal colonialism' as manifested in subtle and not-so-subtle forms of discrimination, segregation and subaltern strategies of indigenous contestation was at the core of Cardenas' political platform. The appeal to reveal and expel internal colonialism cut across the left-right political spectrum and through barriers of class and ethnicity. Only a country founded on 'unity in diversity' was likely to bury the paternalism of leftist politics and the discomfort of traditional nationalist politics.

The second event that coincided with *pluri-multi* agenda setting was the opportunity for constitutional reform, begun by Congress during the Paz Zamora period and ratified under the Sánchez de Lozada administration. The opening article of the reformed Constitution spelled out the importance of the new *pluri-multi* ideal: 'Artículo 1ro. Bolivia, libre, independiente, soberana, multiétnica y pluricultural, constituida en República unitaria, adopta para su gobierno la forma democrática representativa, fundada en la unión y la solidaridad de todos los bolivianos.' The reformed Constitution thus canonized 'multi-ethnicity' and 'pluri-culturality' as founding principles of the Bolivian state. The struggle over the precise wording of the first article pitted traditionally liberal constitutionalists against those, including indigenous and left-left political parties, who defended the change as a natural consequence of the National Revolution.

A third determining factor was the fact that something similar to the recognition of territorial base organizations, in the form of 'indigenous' or '*campesino* communities', had been on the political agenda long before the Popular Participation Law. The proposal of a Ley de Comunidades, forwarded by the CSTUCB and backed by the MBL in the early 1990s, spelled out in basic form many of the articles and clauses included in the Popular Participation legislation. A common denominator in both pre- and post Popular Participation proposals was an explicit recognition of 'communities' as the key bearers of social and political rights and not merely individuals of one or other ethnic or cultural identity. The group rights aspect of Popular Participation marks, in many ways, a departure from a traditionally liberal or neoliberal conception of constitutionalism in Bolivia and Latin America.

The construction of a shared conception of a *pluri-multi* nation is backed by a paradox in Bolivia's demographic and urban transition since the 1970s: as indigenous language loss has increased throughout the 1980s and 1990s, so has the self-perception of being indigenous or ethnic. As 'societal culture' spread, so has 'ethnic culture'. The 1999 MECOVI household survey, which is the first urban and rurally representative in-depth household survey, maps out this contrast quite clearly. A little over 11 per cent of men and women in urban areas spoke an indigenous language at home and nearly 68 per cent in rural areas. Language conservation is strongest amongst Quechua speakers, and stronger among women than men. Xavier Albó's pioneering comparison of language loss in the 1976–92 period largely confirms this basic pattern.[17] In contrast, ethnic self-perception has increased over the past two decades. The MECOVI survey reports that approximately 40 per cent of urban men and women perceived themselves as being indigenous, four times the rate of indigenous languages spoken at home. In rural areas, self-perception reached almost 80 per cent of the population. Indigenous self-perception was strongest among Aymaras in urban areas and among Quechuas in rural areas. Ethnic self-perception was stronger for women than for men.

As indigenous languages decline and ethnic self-perception increases, the construction of a common societal culture hinges on more traditionally political determinants of inclusion such as electoral participation, running for public office and participation in the formal political system. Popular Participation clearly had a positive impact in each of these arenas, where the participation of indigenous and *campesino* voters, elected officials and communities surged with respect to the immediate past, but was still far from representing the indigenous share of the population. As with other forms of identity, ethnicity can move from being largely invisible in the political arena, to being highly politicized, particularly with regard to key contested issues such as land, taxation and access to natural resources. The language/perception paradox is therefore contingent on particular times and spaces where ethnicity comes to the fore of public affairs of *campesino*-indigenous communities.

As Popular Participation moved from design to implementation, the 'nation-building' aspects of the reform became more visible. In municipalities such as Pocoata in the north of Potosí, the very terms of political participation under *vecino*-led political parties were perceived as threatening and ultimately as mechanisms designed to empower mestizo political brokers. To the extent that this was actually how events played out with the active participation of NGO members and rural teachers, perceived sympathetically as 'inside/outsiders', the reform became a self-fulfilling prophecy for many *campesino*-indigenous communities. The *pluri-multi* character of OTB recognition and the promotion of indigenous districts quickly faded away in favor of a more traditional perception of urban/rural cleavages that worked to the advantage of entrenched local bosses and urban elites.

Beyond Pluri-Multi

Social mobilization and unrest in September 2000 marked a turning point for state-society relations in general, but more specifically for the *pluri-multi* conception of politics promoted by the Popular Participation Reform. Felipe Quispe, the secretary general of the CSUTCB and Aymara leader, amplified *campesino* perceptions that Popular Participation was not a pro-*campesino* or indigenous reform. Rather, it 'introduced the political system into the ayllu'.[18] Although the September/October movements trace back to a long tradition of social contestation, many of its tenets were crafted in the wake of Popular Participation. The decentralization reforms exacerbated state control over political and economic development in the northern *altiplano* and revived mestizo and *vecino* political power throughout the *altiplano*. The shift of power toward local councils weakened the corporate *campesino* negotiations of a previous era and reminded community organizations that the new sources of power lay in the hands of local politicians, NGOs and development agencies.

Road blockades in September tipped the scale back to old-style corporatist negotiations between the CSTUCB and the central government. Between 2000 and 2002, the list of demands grew from an initial agrarian petition to a 90-point manifesto, negotiated and renegotiated on separate occasions in August 2001 and February 2002.[19] An immediate effect of the September protests was a significant change in discourse concerning national politics and nationality. In Quispe's words, heatedly debated in the Bolivian media, 'two Bolivias, one Indian, one k'ara (white)' were pitted against each other since colonial times. The 'two Bolivias' conception broke with the more hopeful *pluri-multi* ideas of the previous five years. The 'two Bolivias' speech also triggered a backlash against multicultural politics from public opinion leaders of the urban media. The notion of easy coexistence and unity in diversity were perceived to be naïve and distorting of the true shape of power relations, which favored definite moves toward a modern and liberal, or at least formally liberal, state.

Two books written by Bolivian academics after September 2000 crystallized the shortcomings of the *pluri-multi* period. In *Retorno de la Bolivia Plebeya* and *Tiempos de Rebelión*, García Linera et al. argue for a new beginning in multi-ethnic relations: 'la plebe aymara dispersa y congregada en sus comunidades, desparramada y aglutinada en la furia de los siglos, retorna ahora comenzando un nuevo tiempo y reinventando el mundo'.[20] Luis Tapia best expresses this approach in his analysis of 'societal conflict in the democratic underground'.[21] Tapia suggests that much of the conflict observed in the formal/popular dynamics of reform and contestation can be attributed to societal differences — as opposed to merely social, regional or ethnic difference — between traditional and modern sectors of the Bolivian polity. Societal differences dig deep into pre-revolution and pre-republican conflicts expressed in continuous dispute over remnants of colonial relations between indigenous and non-indigenous groups. Although this tension is longstanding, Tapia argues that episodes of state reform and new state-society relations trigger movement at the societal level, in this case triggered by the institutional reforms enacted during the Sánchez de Lozada administration. Much of Tapia's discussion revolves around somewhat reified conceptions of 'societal difference', which nevertheless provide perhaps the most lucid and provocative reading of the unraveling of *pluri-multi* politics from a long-term historical perspective.

The 'two Bolivias' discourse reveals an additional fault line in the Bolivian political debate, between those who value the idea of nation as a normative political goal and those who perceive talk of nationhood or nationality to be arcane. In a sense, the idea of 'nation' as a shared set of secular or non-ethnic doctrines, as hinted by the *pluri-multi* conception, never did exist. The National Revolution of 1952 set forth a relatively clear vision of a national bourgeoisie, committed to mestizo cultural ideals and middle-class political values. The 'alliance of class' promoted by the MNR in the wake of nationalization of mines and agrarian reform, was highly effective in defining the nation in contrast to a paradigmatic 'anti-nation' — the tin barons, foreign oil companies and bourgeois politics. The *pluri-multi* discourse on nationality struck a chord with opinion leaders and intellectuals who advocated the predominant language of liberal and democratic politics, while it alienated traditionally nationalist advocates, who understood nationalism, ethnicity and class relations in urban mestizo terms.[22]

Conclusions: Patterns of Inclusion

We return to the initial paradox considered in the introduction. Despite changing forms of social and political inclusion, particularly a shift toward non-collective and non-corporate forms of social mobility (education, labor and urban skills), Bolivian society faces recurring demands for collective, mobilized and state-led processes of social integration. State-led inclusion after the National Revolution can be likened to a process of political layering, where practices and institutions of corporatism overlay institutions and practices of clientelist politics and these, in turn, overlay the institutions and practices of new state reforms. Popular Participation and contestation over Popular Participation illustrate this paradox well. While the Popular Participation Reform shares with other state reforms some of the foundational features of state-building reminiscent of the National Revolution, it developed over a complex fabric of social and political relations of a different chronological era. Some of the most effective critiques of Popular Participation are that it is not *sufficiently* corporatist or collectively inclusive, rather than its failing to deliver the means for individual social mobility.

The study of multilayered politics has long been a backbone of scholarly work in Bolivia. René Zavaleta's (1980) account of *abigarramiento*, Silvia Rivera's (1984) analysis of long-run and short-run 'memories' and Luis Tapia's (2001) most recent discussion of societal change in the 'democratic underground' all recall a process of modern political construction upon remnants of past social practices and institutions. It is thus unsurprising that scholars studying Bolivian history are accustomed to viewing fragments of the past influencing and molding practices of the present and future. When *campesino* mayors under Popular Participation follow the *sindicato* tradition of rotating posts for office or local clienteles capture public office in the tradition of corporatist politics, we encounter the legacy of multilayered state-building in its starkest form. The process of political construction that follows this formal/popular logic is not necessarily bereft of structure. The crises of April and September 2000 translated into very precise legal claims over land, water rights or other arenas of political contestation. The disillusion with democratic rule expressed by public opinion polls also translated into demands for a Constitutional Assembly, in what might be regarded a highly legalistic form of popular protest.

Three aspects of formal/popular politics help to frame how the 50-year period between National Reform and Popular Participation initiated a new cycle of state-led inclusion in Bolivia. The first was the highly territorial nature of the 1990 reforms, which created localized and geographically identifiable forms of participation and decision-making. The recognition of OTBs and the empowerment of local elites moved power away from traditionally functional and corporatist vehicles of social mobilization, such as labor and peasant unions, in favor of territorial forms of collective action. The cycles of state reform and contestation observed at the polity-wide level were reproduced on a smaller scale at the local level. This made for a heterogeneous process of political construction and offers clues to why some regions of the country witnessed the politicization of ethnicity (Achacachi) and others did not (northern Potosí). To the extent that Popular Participation 'succeeded' in extending legal and bureaucratic presence across municipalities formerly governed through local clienteles and *campesino* mobilization, the weak-state covenant that enables relatively frictionless power sharing largely breaks down. New rules of the game that favor some elites over others, particularly close to the traditional political parties and the NGOs, made friction over scarce resources more apparent and sparked a new cycle of local political contestation.

Second, Popular Participation displaced sources of state patronage from national to local levels. This had unforeseen consequences over national coalition politics as observed in the disintegration of the *mega-coalición* during the Banzer–Quiroga administration (1997–2002) and the heightened struggle over patronage and employment. The construction of local clienteles linked to local sources of patronage put a premium on local politics. Traditional forms of clientelism exercised via investment funds, prefectures and decentralized government bodies yielded to new triangles of power brokerage — local government, local elites and local NGOs — that enhanced a distancing from traditional political parties, long a source of patronage and power. At the aggregate level, Popular Participation resulted in a larger payroll for public employees and increased local opportunities for graft and petty corruption.[23] The reforms also resulted in the creation of more short-term employment through decentralized public works. From the perspective of formal/popular politics, to the extent that the decentralization reforms relocated one of the most important sources of intra-party stability, they accentuate fissures, splinters and non-party vehicles of political collective action.

Third, Popular Participation also displaced union politics in favor of party politics at the local level. To the extent that election to local councils is restricted by party adscription, it induced the *partidización* of union politics, which have long stood as a parallel circuit of political intermediation. The move toward party politics was first observed within the *cocalero* movement in Cochabamba, which swept the 1995 elections in the Chapare district. It was followed by rural teacher unions in Potosí, which ran under the Eje Pachacuti in two elections and was later observed with the political entry of the Movimiento Indígena Pachacuti, Felipe Quispe's political party. The formalization of *sindicato* politics also multiplied fissures within grass-roots movements themselves, which participated in political as well as civil society as vehicles for contestative collective action. Far from having a stabilizing effect, party politics was increasingly a key site for contestative politics.

A significant feature of the recurring demand for state-led social and political inclusion is that practices or conditions that seem antithetical to social integration in the short run — weak and uneven state reach, weak political authority — are often conducive to longer-run processes of resilient political change. In this view, the continuous process of state reform and social protest that characterizes Bolivian lawmaking and policy-making is an integral part of a larger equilibrium. Popular mobilization, contestation and rebellion thus often drive social change, while constitutionalism and reformism internalize changes and prepare the ground for further distributional struggles that play out over long periods of time. The withering of a system of corporate inclusion is one such struggle, supplanted by a more fragmented and open-ended system of territorial representation. The move from functional to territorial representation involved the exclusion of many time-tested means of social mobility and political inclusion, including the transformation of the military, political parties and popular organizations.

First and second generation heirs of the National Revolution continue to use practices and institutions of social mobility and integration constituted after 1952. The present day 'promise of Popular Participation' lies precisely in its capacity to revive collective vehicles of social and political inclusion, under forms of territorial democratic politics. Contestation to Popular Participation and the *pluri-multi* conception of nationality that informed state reforms in the 1990s deem these very vehicles to be insufficient and ineffective. The expansion of new spheres of Popular Participation to land, water and natural resources, as proposed by Felipe Quispe in 2000, reaffirmed demands over state-led vehicles of social integration and suggests that first and second generation heirs to the National Revolution have not discarded notions of nationality and collective citizenship. After September 2000, those who 'think nation', in Montenegro's terms, are likely to outweigh those who 'think class' across the generations.

Notes

1 Maestrías para el Desarrollo, Universidad Católica Boliviana..
2 Montenegro (1953).
3 Early assessments of the National Revolution were made by Alexander (1958); Peñaloza (1963); Zondag (1966); and Malloy (1970).
4 Assessments of the agrarian reform include Heath (1959); Carter (1965); Antezana and Romero (1968); Heath, Erasmus and Buechler (1969); Dandler (1969); and Calderon and Dandler (1986).
5 See Whitehead (1986); Malloy and Gamarra (1988); and Dunkerley (1984) for political and historical accounts of this period.
6 See Rivera Cusicanqui (1984) and Calderon and Dandler (1986).
7 See Lavaud (1986), pp. 283–4. The 'Proyecto de Impuesto Unico' proposal was revived through USAID technical assistance by the Inter-American Committee on Development and the University of Wisconsin Land Tenure Center.
8 See Molina (1997) for an account of the policy-making process behind the Popular Participation Reform. See also Gray-Molina, Perez and Yañez (1999); Graham (1998); and Grindle (2000).
9 See Albó (1997) and Ayo (1997) on the emergence of indigenous candidacies and Calla and Calla (1996) and Rojas and Zuazo (1996) on the municipal elections of 1995.
10 On participatory planning, budgeting and oversight, see Medina (1997a) and Gray-Molina (1997).

11 Since 1991, and following perceptions of fraud in the 1989 elections, the National Electoral Court has been led by five 'notables', one of whom is appointed by the executive and four by a two thirds congressional majority from a list of three. The 'depoliticisation' of the CNE is regularly cited as a significant factor behind the relatively wide acceptance and legitimacy of the electoral process.

12 According to 1992 census data, only 38% of voting age women and 53% of voting age men had a *carnet de identidad* (cited in Albó, 1997, p. 25).

13 The ENVP indicator is summarized by: ENVP = 1/å p2. See Mainwaring and Scully (1995), p. 29, based on Laakso and Taagepera (1979).

14 The V indicator is summarized by: V = 0.5 å | pt+1 – pt |. See Coppedge (1998), p. 564), based on Pedersen (1979).

15 See Kymlicka (2000) and Miller (1995).

16 See Yashar (1999) and Van Cott (2000).

17 Albó (1995).

18 *Pulso*, October 2000.

19 Víctor Orduna, 'Dos años y un día negociando lo mismo,' *Semanario Pulso*, February 2002.

20 García Linera et al. (2000a).

21 Tapia (2001).

22 See García Linera et al. (2000b).

23 See Gray Molina, Pérez de Rada and Yañez (1999).

CHAPTER 15

Revolution and the Unfinished Business of Nation and State-Building

Pilar Domingo

The chapters in this book have examined the Bolivian Revolution of 1952 from a diverse range of perspectives. Historical and structural, political and ideological, social, economic and international dimensions have been explored in an attempt to revisit a landmark moment of political, social and economic change in twentieth century Bolivia. In this concluding chapter the aim is less to summarize the findings of preceding chapters and more to reflect on certain recurrent themes with regard to the state-building process that was triggered by the experience of revolution and the impact of this upon subsequent patterns of state reform and policy implementation.

The Bolivian Revolution of 1952

The 50th anniversary of the revolution took place in an electoral year, which threw up many of the unresolved problems of exclusion, underdevelopment and conflict that continue to shape Bolivia's political and social landscape. The death of key revolutionary figures in recent years seems to have led to a, perhaps, premature closure of the legacy and memory of the 1952 Revolution. In contrast to other major social revolutions, there is little by way of commemoration — either in the form of official iconography or indeed in the popular culture and memory of contemporary Bolivians. Nonetheless, the fact that only 13 per cent of Bolivia's population today was alive in 1952 is not sufficient to explain the speed with which the legacy of 1952 fades into a distant memory. In France, Bastille Day, and all it stood for, remains as the singular most important national holiday. In Bolivia it is difficult to imagine that 9 April will ever be resurrected as a day of national commemoration to the same extent.

In part this difficulty with finding what aspects of the revolution to celebrate inevitably reflects the incomplete nature of its achievements — many of these discussed in the preceding chapters. In some cases there have been outright reversals of the revolutionary legacy. The reality of unfulfilled expectations and the experience of counter-revolutionary, if you will, policy directions, which have been reinforced paradoxically even more so under democratic rule than under earlier periods of authoritarianism, have further served to undermine the significance of 1952. This in part explains the apparent popular indifference towards the revolution in Bolivia today. It is worth recalling, on the other hand, the comparative absence of widespread violence surrounding the events of 9 April and the installation of an MNR revolutionary government, so that at least the memory of 1952 is not tarnished by images of violence on a scale similar to the loss of life that ensued in Mexico or the USSR, or indeed, in France — albeit in different ways and in each case with very different consequences for the preservation (or not) of a revolutionary memory in the popular culture. Specifically in the case of Bolivia, the failure to commemorate 1952 seems to be less a matter of public, or indeed, ethically constructed rejection of the past. Instead what prevails is more a sense of the irrelevance that the revolutionary memory holds to contemporary Bolivian society. This is at least the sentiment that prevails in the political culture of Bolivia at the beginning of the twenty-first century.

Academic revisionism in fact seems also to be less about passing judgment on the revolution and more about fine-tuning our understanding of the events and processes that led to 1952, of the political, social and economic developments that resulted from this transformative process and of the scale of its impact and long-term historical relevance. On the whole the chapters in this book take as given that 1952 was indeed a revolutionary and transformative moment, whatever its origins, the scale and outreach of its achievements or the longevity of its legacy. Moreover, what emerges from the analyses developed in this volume is a measure of the complexity of interacting processes that culminated in the Revolution of 1952 and its aftermath. Social revolutions are inevitably complex processes. They have no clear beginning nor end. They are the culmination of long-term structural factors, but are also propelled by short-term developments. They unleash processes of social and political transformation with unforeseen consequences, but also, more often than not, unfulfilled expectations. They express the conflict of mutually exclusive ideas about social and political organization and culminate in sufficiently irreversible systemic shifts. They respond to national dynamics, but are also forged out of global processes of domination.

Whitehead reminds us in his chapter that in theoretical terms 1952 does meet the criteria that places it within that exclusive family of great revolutions as a sufficiently transformative process of social, political and economic structures. For Whitehead, revolution must be seen, moreover, as an extended process of confrontation of ideas over time. Outcomes are uncertain and the durability of revolutionary projects unpredictable. Furthermore, interpretations of revolutionary processes will inevitably evolve over time, colored not only by historical conjuncture but also by shifting ideological ascendancies. This is a theme that is developed further in the chapter by Thomson which places 1952 in the long-term perspective alongside such dates as 1781 and 1825. Here Thomson points to the complex construction of historical narrative and political interpretation, which reflects particular configurations of ascendant social and political forces at key moments of popular insurgency and political change. Finally, Dunkerley alerts us to the importance of seeing revolutionary processes as the result of the complex interaction between structure and conjuncture.

1952 was a major revolution of the 'nationalist' and also 'bourgeois' variety, but this categorization only very loosely tells us about the specific processes that combined to culminate in its realization, the degree to which the revolutionary project — in as much as it projected a coherent view of state-building and national integration — became embedded in Bolivian society at the local level, both in rural and urban terms, or the extent of its impact on subsequent patterns of social, political and economic development. Nonetheless, taking the National Revolution of 1952 as the point of departure helps us work through the confrontation of ideas that preceded it, the processes of change that it both reflected and accelerated, the structural constraints that limited its consequences and outreach and finally its long-term legacy.

State-Building and National Integration

A recurrent issue throughout the chapters is the question of locating the relevance of structural factors and state development in understanding the events leading up to 1952, as well as the unfolding of a revolutionary project and the complex reconstitution of political and social forces into the twenty-first century. Characteristic of almost any point in Bolivia's development is the gap between the state-building aspirations of successive regimes and dominant ideological orientations and the reality of dramatically weak or inefficient state structures and weak state presence in large areas of the country. Much has been written elsewhere about the revolutionary state, and it is not the intention of this concluding chapter to go over the characteristics of state corporatism as it unfolded and evolved after 1952. Here I wish merely to reflect on some of the consequences over time of the *weakness of state structures* with regard to the issues of state-society relations, state 'embeddedness' throughout the national territory, integrative processes of nation-building and the construction of citizenship.

The Chaco War drew instant attention in a dramatic way to the structural weaknesses of an oligarchic regime that, as subsequent challenges to its authority unfolded, would ultimately be incapable of reinventing itself to accommodate the growing pressures for political and social change. The revolutionary project after 1952 was ultimately thwarted in its attempt to replicate the Mexican model of dominant party rule, in part by the structural limitations of weak state structures. Whilst the Revolution of 1952 marked a transformative change in the role of the state in the economy and as facilitator of social change, in many important respects continuity with a past legacy of weak societal embeddedness and outreach of state institutions would undermine the nationalist agenda in terms of consolidating an effective and lasting nation-building project. Democratization since 1982 has also been undermined by structural constraints and institutional inefficiencies. This section aims to reflect on the problematic question of state capacity and nation-building in a socially fragmented, regionally diverse and culturally pluralistic society.

State capacity of the modern nation state typically depends on the extent of authoritative state presence across the national territory, of minimally effective administration of state institutions and public resources and of state control over the legitimate use of violence — so claims modernization theory drawing on a Weberian tradition of social theory. But state embeddedness is also about the degree to which state authority is constituted through a positive connection between state and society, based on a relationship of legal accountability, responsive government, minimum levels of protection of rights and entitlements that facilitate citizenship and enable the development of civil society.[1] At the dawn of the twenty-first century the balance sheet on many of these aspects of state-development in Bolivia is still fragile — despite considerable and indeed transformative changes on most fronts during the twentieth century — with important consequences for the integrative and legitimizing capacity of nation-building. The tortuous process of state-building in Bolivia has been neither even nor linear, nor does it amount to a cumulative process with a clear end point in mind.[2] The goal posts have constantly shifted, as have the ideological and nation-building aspirations that have driven it. Moreover, the basis of regime legitimacy that ultimately binds state and society together has changed over time and continues to be in some crucial respects a contested matter.[3]

What prevails in the history of Bolivian state-formation — before and after 1952 and into the current context of democratic politics, and despite quantum leaps in the administrative capacity and territorial presence of the state — is a sense of weak state embeddedness and a fragile connection between state and civil society.[4] This is compounded in current times by the sense of exclusion and marginality that the experience of market rule and state 'shrinking', albeit in the context of democratic politics, has reinforced for large sectors of society. It is not only a case of 'low-intensity' and 'delegative' democracy, using O'Donnell's well known terms, despite efforts to bring policy-making to the grass-roots level through such measures as Participación Popular, but also of the weakness of the state in terms of minimally providing both the institutional space within which citizenship (whether conceived in liberal, or communitarian terms) can be protected and advanced, as well as adequate mechanisms of public accountability and responsive government.

Before unraveling the question of state capacity and nation-building, it is worth stressing firstly that for all the structural weaknesses of the Bolivian state and its (continued) problematic insertion in society, the picture at the beginning of the twenty-first century is hugely different from the image of statelessness that prevailed a century ago — or indeed, half a century ago. Secondly, there is no doubt as to the significance of 1952 in terms of changing state structures and propelling new forms of social and political exchange and state and society relations. Thirdly, Bolivia's state-building experience is not at odds with the general trend of developmental options and dilemmas in the region, although the particular circumstances of the drive towards nation-building that culminated in the Revolution of 1952 and subsequent patterns of political and structural accommodation have led to a specifically Bolivian experience of conflict and consensus, exclusion and participation, growth and marginality.

The 'Weak State' and Revolutionary Nationalism

As various of the authors remind us, the formidable challenges of state-building and national integration have concerned policy-makers, statesmen, ideologues and insurgency leaders since Independence. Parallel and competing worldviews and ideological beliefs have underpinned a range of nation and state-building aspirations, at the same time that successive hegemonic systems, reflecting the interests of dominant ruling coalitions, have largely failed to overcome structural obstacles to ensure the long-term viability and endurance of their respective nation-building projects. By the early decades of the twentieth century, limited oligarchic rule, claiming a narrowly based constitutional legitimacy which by 1952 had lost all credibility, was giving way to a new vision of state and nation, resulting in the formula of corporatist revolutionary nationalism. This, in turn, following an extended period of military authoritarianism, transformed its aspirational direction more explicitly towards the establishment of a constitutional liberal democracy of sorts — still fragile and incomplete in many respects.

The 'weak state' throughout this period appears as a recurrent explanatory factor that both undermined successive political systems and fueled ideological debate over alternative developmental options. Typically, the revolution is seen as the product of the moral bankruptcy and collapse of a weak oligarchic state subsumed by the *rosca minera*. The chapters by Dunkerley, Gotkowitz and Larson, however, provide a more nuanced picture, from different perspectives, of the complexities of change and transformation in state, economy and societal structures that took place in the decades before 1952. The Chaco War galvanized a process of rethinking and recreating new political projects concerned with nation-building and national identity. The intellectual debates of the time — amply discussed in the chapters by Thomson and Dunkerley — focused on the problem of state-building and reconstituting the nation. The concern with the problem of weak state presence was also shared by governing elites. Gotkowitz documents the concern in this regard expressed by Villarroel. The education initiatives examined by Larson also point to the growing public policy preoccupation in the first half of the century with using state resources as an instrument of both social control and top-down modernization efforts. Finally, as Dunkerley illustrates in his chapter, the critical relationship between the state and the *rosca minera* was undergoing a complex process of redefinition long before 1952.

If concerns about state- and nation-building were a matter of debate and discussion for urban intellectual circles, and amongst emerging political forces such as the MNR, this was also a process propelled by bottom-up pressures. Political activism in the mining sector has been documented at length elsewhere.[5] In this volume, Gotkowitz develops a telling assessment of rural mobilization around issues of community, land, education and political change. Here the relevance of 'stateness' and the potential usefulness of state institutions as a way of advancing specific social grievances was becoming a part of bottom-up mobilization. The *indigenista* subtext of rural mobilization would be suppressed under the rhetoric of mestizo revolutionary nationalism — only to re-emerge in the 1980s. But changes in rural activism and engagement in public life had begun to highlight the relevance and perceived potential benefits of strengthening state presence in rural society. Larson's examination of the education policy initiatives from the 1920s also points to a two-way flow of ideas about nationhood and identity. The modernizing view from above would not translate into an unfettered implementation of education directives, but instead would be countered by subaltern views of identity and community at the local level, as witnessed by the experience of the Warisata schools. Thus rural mobilization from below, and increasing engagement with public life in rural society — albeit in a fragmented and uneven manner — were also informing the emergence of new ways of thinking about state-building, social reform and national integration.

The incomplete and partial nation-building attempts leading up to the revolution, combined with societal demands for change — however diffuse or fragmented — and a changing geopolitical environment had sufficient cumulative effect to have prepared the stage for the events of 1952. The format of revolutionary nationalism, with its radical components, was rooted in this patchwork of shifting economic and political alliances, changing social landscape and new emerging political forces for change that followed the Chaco War and the disintegration of oligarchic rule. The Bolivian Revolution was clearly of the nationalist variety. Moreover, it had deep nationalist roots that stretched out into the past — unlike the Mexican Revolution, which was borne of a liberal legacy and tradition. Nationalism in Mexico as a unifying ideology, combined with radical measures of social reform, would be thrashed out through civil war and drawn-out violence and conflict. In Bolivia, by contrast, the discourse of nationalism was firmly in place by 1952 — and the implementation of a radical agenda was less a matter of discussion and more a matter of whether the first MNR government had sufficient structural and political resources to see it through.

Paradoxically, though, as the chapter by Knight shows, the sense of national identity and cultural integration was far less developed in Bolivia by 1952 than in Mexico in 1910. State presence and territorial outreach were also considerably stronger in Mexico at the start of the twentieth century than in Bolivia on the eve of the revolution. Knight's chapter is important in signaling the explanatory relevance of the structural differences between Mexico and Bolivia. While the nationalist rhetoric was core to the integrative discourse of the revolutionary forces by 1952, the reality of weak state structures made consolidating the MNR project a highly problematic venture. This was not helped by the fragility of the revolutionary coalition. Ultimately, according to Knight's analysis, the Bolivian Revolution lacked the 'tested' quality of the Mexican revolutionary family, forged over decades of conflict and had, moreover, a far weaker pool of state capacity and structural resources to draw from.

The chapter by Whitehead makes note of the implications of a highly fragmented sense of national identity for the pursuit of any nation-building aspiration. Echoing the analysis by Gotkowitz in this regard, the interface between local, regional and national levels of political engagement was particularly problematic precisely because of the weak, fragmented and uneven nature of state presence throughout the national territory. Events at the national level — both before and after 1952 — played out in a very diverse and fragmented manner at the local level interacting in different and complex ways with specifically local political conflicts and social dynamics. Thus, the manner in which the revolutionary process was filtered down into the local experience was varied and uneven and by no means represented a homogenous implementation of a coherent national project. Instead, more often than not, it was probably absorbed by local power structures and subsumed to the logic of local power struggles. While much has been written on the nationalist revolutionary project at the national level, there are far fewer studies that examine the manner, the extent and the degree to which nation-building efforts at the center were replicated at the local and rural level. Without a more informed understanding of the disjuncture between local and national political dynamics, we still have an incomplete and patchy picture about the way in which state authority after 1952 was constituted at a societal level, across regions and social sectors, and the impact this would have on state-society relations and the construction over time of notions of citizenship, political inclusion and participation and, ultimately, of regime legitimacy.

The nationalist revolutionary state ultimately failed to constitute a durable and integrative project of nationhood. The combination of structural limitations, contradictory policy directions, the reality of a regionally diverse and fragmented society in which class and ethnicity remained forceful determinants of marginality and exclusion and a geopolitical context in which Bolivia's national sovereignty would be critically compromised, weakened the prospects for nation-building. The scope for authoritative state embeddedness remained limited and citizenship remained a remote concept, which would only serve to undermine the possibility of positive connection between state and society. The years of military rule further weakened the integrative aspects of state development. It was not until the return to democracy in the 1980s that issues of inclusion and nation-building would once again resurface as a matter of public policy — though now subsumed to a very different logic of state shrinkage and economic liberalization.

Participación Popular in the 1990s marked a turning point in the history of public policy in terms of attempting to extend 'stateness' in an innovative way to the very local level. This combined moreover with a constitutionally formalized recognition of the 'multi-ethnic and pluri-cultural' nature of the Bolivian society. In his study of the development of Participación Popular, Gray-Molina also underlines the heterogenous way in which state structures have operated at the local level, both at the height of state-corporatism and subsequently. Echoing the work by Bolivian scholars, Gray-Molina develops a nuanced analysis of state-building as a complex process in which modern institutions of political engagement are layered in a cumulative and uneven manner upon past practices and structures. These in themselves are a combination of previous ventures of state-building or constitutive moments and traditional or community forms of social organization. New institutions are absorbed into the local political practice, but are themselves reshaped to reflect existing local social, political and cultural constructs. Yet new institutions can also open up opportunities for new forms of political engagement and inclusion. It may well be that Participación Popular, at a time of indigenous mobilization, facilitates new channels of political contestation from below, which will in turn impact upon state-society relations and upon how notions of citizenship are reclaimed. As yet, the results are mixed and there remains a prevalent sense of fragile state embeddedness at the local level.[6]

The recurrent theme throughout the chapters of the negative impact of weak state structures over time should not obscure the significant expansion of the role of the state that came with the National Revolution. The establishment of a nationalist state and eventual consolidation of a state-led model of growth was a foundational legacy of 1952. The expansion of a large state bureaucratic apparatus did bring with it important aspects of state- and nation-building capacity, despite the tremendous inefficiencies that characterized the new developmental model. Moreover, it opened up in important structural ways new opportunities for social mobility, a change in the nature of state-society relations and new rules of political engagement. It is to these issues that I now turn.

The State as Facilitator of Economic Growth and Social Transformation

The chapters by Morales, Klein and Contreras from different perspectives raise the pressing question — to which a negative response can only invoke a hypothetical counterfactual argument tested against the comparative experience of other countries in the region — as to whether Bolivians are better or worse off in terms of economic growth and social progress as a result of the Revolution of 1952. All three shed a critical light on the achievements of the revolutionary state.

In terms of social indicators Klein acknowledges important accomplishments in the years following the revolution. Given Bolivia's starting point these gains are far from negligible. From a comparative perspective, though, Bolivia's performance is comparable to other countries in the region that did not undergo revolutionary processes. Moreover, Bolivia is still ranked at the bottom of the list of countries in the region, alongside Haiti, in terms of social indicators. Similarly, Contreras' analysis of education policy signals important progress in the 1950s, although not necessarily as a result of a specifically revolutionary impetus on the issue. Ultimately, education reform was undermined by structural weaknesses, insufficient resources and a weak political commitment to education innovation.

Morales' chapter is particularly critical of the revolutionary legacy in terms of economic growth, placing the blame clearly at the door of mistaken policy decisions, shoddy economic management and an over-inflated, yet ultimately weak and inefficient state bureaucracy. The model of state-led growth that evolved into state-led capitalism undercut entrepreneurial initiative and stifled economic innovation. The trappings of economic dependency around a narrow range of products were never seriously addressed, and Bolivia's economic development became increasingly tied to a heavy and unhealthy reliance on foreign aid. Overall, according to Morales, the state structures set up in 1952 and subsequent economic policy directions did more harm than good to the developmental prospects of Bolivia.

What permeates, then, from the analyses on the developmental and social accomplishments of the 1952 Revolution is that in comparative terms Bolivia is not really better off as a direct result of the revolutionary experience. However, the three authors concur, in different ways, with the view that 1952 opened up important valves of political and social opportunity. The National Revolution represented a critical distributional moment in as much as it created a seismic shift in power structures and social relations that was much more than purely symbolic or cosmetic. Morales, moreover, draws attention to the counterfactual example of Colombia, where the absence of a constitutive moment of social and political reform has severely undermined long-term social equilibrium. The relative stability and social peace of contemporary Bolivia may well be rooted in the distributional and empowering experience of revolution, despite persistently high levels of poverty and economic exclusion, a retrenchment of inequality and gradually increasing levels of political violence and social polarization.

The balance sheet on the developmental and social legacy of 1952 is overall disappointing. Again, what prevails is a picture of a state apparatus weakened by structural constraints, but also by the lack of political direction in which nation-building aspirations were obscured by the inefficiencies of an over-bloated, patrimonial state structure.

The Patrimonial State

The patrimonial character of the Bolivian state since 1952 is one of the most pervasive and lasting legacies of the revolution. Much has been written about the vicissitudes of a political culture of clientelism and graft that became one of the dominant features of public office in Bolivia. State-society relations within the corporatist structures that were put into place after 1952 were mediated by a logic of state patronage and political favor, benefiting mostly those middle sectors of urban society that became empowered with the revolution. Changing social and political alliances at the top would lead to a constant reconfiguration of how the benefits of state patronage were shared out.

A culture of state patronage did indeed pre-date 1952 — only the pie was much smaller and the locus of control over public resources lay more evidently outside the state bureaucracy. The patrimonial state that emerged with the revolution would also outlast the corporatist structures of both the first three MNR administrations and later military governments. Military authoritarianism after 1964 in its different guises very naturally reproduced what had become established patterns of state patronage and clientelism. Finally, the eventual stabilization of democratic rule around rotating congressional coalitions after 1985 would settle into a system of political accommodation in which the lure of public office continues to overshadow any sense of the representational or ideological attributes of elective office.

With democratization, political parties have become the key vehicles for the passage and implementation of policy through the institutions of representative government. Yet, as Gamarra argues in his chapter and also elsewhere they are also first and foremost channels of state patronage and the perpetrators of a culture of graft and personal enrichment. Grindle further develops this analysis of the dual functionality of political parties. In her chapter she argues that the MNR governments of 1985 and 1993 used the political machinery of the party structure, precisely with the promise of state patronage, to ensure the passage of a succession of sweeping reforms. But the reality, as well as the public perception, is that policy-making is predominantly the result of top-down technocratic decision-making processes that take place behind closed doors and with very limited sense of broader public or political consultation. While the intention may be that both governability and technocratic neatness are thus ensured, this form of government reinforces the image of corrupt, unresponsive and unreliable institutions of representation.

The patrimonial state is thus perpetuated in contemporary democratic politics in Bolivia, adding to the fragility of state embeddedness in society and the weakness of state authority. Moreover, it undercuts the promise of accountable and legally bounded public office that is intrinsic to the discourse of rule of law of liberal democracy. Regime legitimacy is thus gradually eroded in the face of ineffectual mechanisms of accountability. At the same time, it is important to stress that the full impact of the recent state reforms is yet to be seen, some of which precisely seek to address issues of accountability, weak rule of law and weak state presence in civil society.

The end of state corporatism and the establishment of democratic rule and market economics have not shifted clientelist practices of state patronage nor diminished the scale of corruption in public office. However, while this represents a major limitation in state capacity that ultimately undermines the reconstitution of state authority over time, it is hardly a problem that is exclusive to a revolutionary legacy.

The 'Weak State' and National Sovereignty

A final manifestation of state weakness that is intrinsic to the story of the 1952 Revolution is the relationship between the Bolivian State and an external world dominated by the USA. Writing shortly after the US embassy in the La Paz actively discouraged voter support for Evo Morales during the electoral campaign of 2002 and subsequently undertook to facilitate and encourage the MNR–MIR coalition — among other things by inexplicably revoking an earlier decision to deny a US visa entry to Oscar Eid from the MIR — it is difficult to imagine any real scope for sovereign decision-making by the Bolivian state.

Nationalism is defined not only by how notions of national identity are constructed within a territorially bounded community, but also in relation to the outer world. Clearly revolutionary nationalism in 1952 was defined not only by the quest for internal integration, but also articulated an anti-imperialist position promoted by the radical elements of the revolutionary alliance. Lehman's chapter explores the evolution of the relationship between the USA and Bolivia during the revolutionary period, looking at both the Bolivian perspective in how a discourse of nationalism unfolded in the negotiations with the USA and also at the US side of the equation. He suggests that nationalism was perhaps less an expression of anti-US sentiment than in Mexico, inevitably more dramatically threatened by its neighboring 'hovering giant'. The point here is that for significant sectors of the Bolivian population the USA was probably not part of the popular imagination in 1952, precisely because of the very fragmented and weak sense of national integration at this time. Although the discourse of revolutionary nationalism, at least in the initial radical phase, had a clear international intentionality behind it, used ably by Paz Estenssoro to maneuver between the limited spaces afforded to Bolivia in its relations with the USA (and beyond), this international dimension had possibly only limited impact at the local rural level.

Lehman's chapter alerts us also to the complexities of US foreign policy, driven not only by hegemonic design, but also by a variety of competing views and interests. This provided a range of limited opportunities and spaces within which revolutionary actors — Mexican and Bolivian — could maneuver in their relationship with the USA. The US decision to tolerate Bolivia's brand of revolutionary radicalism had probably less to do with Bolivian pressure on Washington in the end than with a reasonable calculation based on the relative remoteness and the absence of direct threat to US interests of the revolutionary process. Moreover, this did not entail a passive acceptance of 1952, as very soon US pressure began to exert a highly visible moderating pressure on the developmental and political options available to a structurally weak and financially bankrupt state.

Ultimately the Bolivian State has had very little leverage in influencing US foreign policy, or in asserting a meaningful sense of national sovereignty either in the Cold War context or in the sobering experience of post-Cold War years of coca eradication.[7] The US role in 'braking' the revolution unsurprisingly led to the consolidation of a relationship of dependency and political and economic subordination. This has changed tack over the decades, as the geopolitical context moved beyond the Cold War context and new concerns in the form of counter-narcotics strategies and programs have taken shape, but US presence and policy priorities have remained a prominent and constant factor in public policy choices and in the political economy of Bolivia.

The Political Legacy of 1952

It is perhaps in the realm of political contestation and political participation that the legacy of the revolution is most noteworthy, albeit in a complex and contradictory manner. Whitehead signals the establishment of universal suffrage as a major radical contribution of the revolutionary agenda. Electoral legitimacy provided the possibility for the long-term reconstitution of state authority. Although this would not prove to be the case in the short run, as it was not really until 1985 that access to political power would be determined primarily by electoral outcomes, the impact of universal suffrage was tremendously important in terms of underlining the instant enfranchizement of a previously excluded majority of the adult population. The empowering effect of electoral inclusion was more than purely symbolic, even at the height of state corporatism when political power was brokered less through elective office than through sectoral, corporatist and also personalist structures of negotiation.

Ultimately the forces unleashed by 1952 culminated in a zero-sum conflict of irreconcilable ideological positions, the extreme expressions of which would be the Asamblea Popular of 1971 and the subsequent counter-reaction of General Banzer's repressive dictatorship. The tortuous path of democratization would smooth out historical positions of mutual exclusion, more through the experience of adversity (the brutality of the García Meza dictatorship and the extreme instability of hyperinflation) than through any meaningful reconciliation of conflicting worldviews. By 1985 state authority would be reconstituted primarily through institutions of democratic representation. As political parties founded around the revolutionary matrix of the MNR have resurfaced, electoral politics seem to have settled around a pluralist democracy of sorts in which there is some room for the inclusion and participation of newly emerging political forces, in some cases articulating the demands of traditionally marginalized social sectors that have been excluded from the benefits of economic stabilization.

Moreover, by the 1980s and 1990s the ideological references had shifted. The geopolitical context was changing in a post-Cold War world, pushing forward an agenda of liberal democracy and market economics. At the national level, elite preferences also moved in this direction at the same time that changing dynamics within old corporatist sectors and at the grass-roots level were beginning to reframe and construct new visions of national identity and citizenship. An emerging indigenous movement reclaimed a discourse of cultural and ethnic diversity, which not only challenged the revolutionary legacy of *mestizo* nationalism but also questioned the basic premises of liberal democracy. To a certain extent, the constitutional formalization of a pluri-cultural national identity and the Participación Popular Law reflect some concession extended to demands articulated from below.

Although democratization has dislodged to some extent old corporatist actors, and consensus politics became the name of the game, this has neither displaced nor neutralized an underlying culture of contestation and political mobilization from below. Popular protest has remained a vibrant challenge to what are perceived as top-down and exclusionary policy directions, and has in some measure also served to alter and inform the dominant political (if not economic) agenda from below. The revolution was perhaps the most forceful expression of the power of protest politics in twentieth century Bolivia. In many ways, then, the revolutionary process of 1952 crystallized and consolidated a much older tradition of popular insurgency, which has survived into the politics of democratic rule since 1985. The MAS movement, with its strong community-based roots, and the resilience of recent peasant-led protest politics is a forceful reminder of this legacy. At the same time, its integration into the formal institutions of democratic representation signals the possibility of political inclusion of marginalized social sectors, as well as the potential for a degree of political renovation.

The Bolivian political heritage, reflected in and perpetuated by the 1952 Revolution, is characterized by cyclical processes of zero-sum conflict and consensual political pacting. Equally there seems to be a cyclical dynamic of constitutional formalization of nation-building projects articulated from above, which are also informed by the forces of popular mobilization from below. Thus, it would seem, contemporary channels of political contestation and articulation of social demands, and indeed of competing visions of nationhood and state, are rooted in the empowering experience of revolution.

While this suggests that an important long-term political legacy of the revolution has been to facilitate the articulation of conflict and competing visions of nation-building, it is important to recall that by no means is this comfortably contained within the formal institutions of democratic representation. It is significant that the sweeping range of state reforms — in economic, political and social terms — instigated primarily by the MNR, but upheld by all other governing coalitions since 1985, have been imposed through recurrent recourse to states of emergency and repressive means. At the same time the political system, ultimately still dominated by the MNR, has proved to be sufficiently resilient in terms of absorbing what are viewed as 'anti-systemic' challenges. Nonetheless, the escalation of social protest and the increase in politically motivated violence and human rights violations at the hands of security forces in the last two administrations is particularly telling of an atrophied system of political representation in which state authority is questioned — and questionable — and regime legitimacy is weakened. The political discourse of alarm across urban-based elites following the electoral gains of Evo Morales in the recent electoral contest, if anything, reflects precisely the degree of social and ethnic polarization that continues to characterize Bolivian society. Gamarra highlights the gravity of what he sees as a fundamental systemic crisis in which the current fragile 'pacted democracy' has yet to find credible and sustainable forms of extending state authority and resources to an excluded majority of civil society.

By Way of Conclusion

The Revolution of 1952 and its aftermath does not in general terms set the Bolivian experience of political and economic development significantly apart from other countries in the region which, with the exception of Mexico (and later Cuba and Nicaragua), did not experience the phenomenon of social revolution. The emergence of nationalist mobilization founded on a multi-class alliance and promoting inward -looking economic growth around an interventionist state system describes the political phenomena of various neighboring countries. The passage through military authoritarianism and subsequent incursion into liberal democracy and economic liberalization tells a familiar story. Other than the MNR's desire to emulate the longevity of the PRI experience in Mexico, a broad brush view would suggest that the events of April 1952 did not significantly affect Bolivia's vantage point in terms of establishing a more developed sense of state-society relations and state embeddedness, a more rooted and credible political system of demand articulation and political representation, legal accountability and rights based citizenship, or significantly better indicators of social progress and economic development.

Nonetheless, the dramatically transformative experience in social and political terms of the early years of revolutionary radicalism should not be underestimated. Long-term patterns of state development and indicators of economic growth may not be telling signs of change. Yet the cycles of conflict and consensus politics that have come to characterize the dynamics of political and social exchange in Bolivia may signal an underlying capacity of the state to accommodate and absorb change and demands from below, albeit in a piecemeal and deficient manner, but with sufficient impact so as to deflect a collapse of the system as witnessed in some neighboring countries. Whether this underlying resilience of what is to all appearances a fragile democratic state is attributable or not to a revolutionary legacy is highly debatable. But it would seem in hindsight that contemporary forms of political contestation and articulation of demands are rooted in the experience of revolution.

NOTES

1 O'Donnell's (1993) discussion of the different levels of state presence is a useful framework of analysis for thinking about the relationship between state and society, about issues of citizenship and about levels of accountability of state institutions.

2 In a compelling study of the Geographic Society of La Paz, Qayun

(2002) traces the nation-building efforts of the oligarchic elites at the turn of the twentieth century, ultimately frustrated by the weakness of state-structures and by the unbridgeable gap between the inevitably exclusionary vision of modernity that these efforts represented and the reality of structures of internal colonialism which served to perpetuate class and ethnic divisions. Nonetheless, the foundations of the administrative, cognitive and territorial capacity of the state were gradually being laid out, however flawed. Whitehead's (1998) useful historical reconstruction of the tale of state-building in Latin America stresses the uneven and patchy and, at times, even reversible nature of this process, but also draws attention to the important and transformative — in political, social and economic terms — material and institutional changes that shaped state-formation in the second half of the twentieth century.

3 At the end of the twentieth century, the historiography of Bolivia's political and social development is being rethought through new interpretative spaces that suggest also different visions of nationhood, national identity and political power rooted in the experience of marginality of traditionally excluded sectors of society. See, for instance, Stephenson (2002).

4 See Tapia (2002) for an insightful discussion of the limitations of the Bolivian state in terms of fostering a sense of integrative nationhood and societal ownership of public spaces and institutions. This weakness, in turn, contributed to undermining national sovereignty in relation to the outer world.

5 Whitehead, (1981).

6 Albó (2002a).

7 Rodas (1996).

Bibliography

Abecia, Valentín (1973) *Historiografía boliviana* [1965] (La Paz: Juventud).

Abecia López, Valentín (1997) *Montenegro:homenaje del Honorable Senado Nacional, a los 44 años de su muerte* (La Paz: Honorable Senado Nacional).

AHHCD, *Redactores de Diputados* (1947), tomo 1.

Aikman, Sheila (2000) 'Bolivia,' in David Coulby, Robert Cowen and Crispin Jones (eds.), *Education in Times of Transition* (London: Kogan Page).

Albó, Xavier (1979) *Achacachi: medio siglo de lucha campesina* (La Paz: CIPCA).

Albó, Xavier (1985) 'De MNRistas a kataristas: campesinado, estado y partidos (1953–83),' *Historia Boliviana*, vol. V, nos. 1–2, pp. 87–127.

Albó, Xavier (1987) 'From MNRistas to Kataristas to Katari,' in Steve Stern (ed.), *Resistance, Rebellion, and Consciousness in the Andean Peasant World, 18th to 20th Centuries* (Madison: University of Wisconsin Press).

Albó, Xavier (1995) *Bolivia plurilingüe: guía para planificadores y educadores, 3 vols.* (La Paz: UNICEF, CIPCA).

Albó, Xavier (1997) 'Alcaldes y concejales campesinos/indígenas: la lógica tras las cifras,' in *Indígenas en el poder local* (La Paz: Ministerio de Desarrollo Humano, Secretaría Nacional de Participación Popular), pp. 7–26.

Albó, Xavier (1999a) 'Andean People in the Twentieth Century,' in Frank Salomon and Stuart B. Schwartz (eds.), *The Cambridge History of the Native Peoples of the Americas, Vol. III, South America*, Part 2 (Cambridge: Cambridge University Press), pp. 781–83.

Albó, Xavier (1999b) 'Etnias y pueblos originarios: diversidad étnica, cultural y lingüística,' in Fernando Campero Prudencio (ed.), *Bolivia en el siglo XX. La formación de la Bolivia contemporánea* (La Paz: Harvard Club de Bolivia).

Albó, Xavier (1999c) *Ojotas en el poder local: cuatro años despues*, CIPCA no. 53 (La Paz: CIPCA).

Albó, Xavier (2002a) 'Bolivia: From Indian and Campesino Leaders to Councillors and Parliamentary Deputies,' in Rachel Sieder (ed.), *Multiculturalism in Latin America: Indigenous Rights, Diversity and Democracy* (London: Palgrave), pp. 74–102.

Albó, Xavier (2002a) 'Todos ellos Aymaras y tan distintos,' *Cuarto Intermedio*, vol. 62, pp. 48–86.

Alexander, R..J. (1958) *The Bolivian National Revolution* (New Brunswick: Rutgers University Press).

Almaraz Paz, Sergio (1987) *El poder y la caída*, 5th edition, originally published in 1967 (La Paz: Editorial 'Los Amigos del Libro').

Almaraz Paz, Sergio (1988) *Bolivia, Requiem para una república*, 2nd edition, originally published in 1969 (La Paz: Universidad Mayor de San Andrés).

Alonso, Ana María (1995) 'Rationalizing Patriarchy: Gender, Domestic Violence, and Law in Mexico,' *Identities*, vol. 2, pp. 29–47.

Alvarez Mamani, Antonio (1987) *El camino perdido* (La Paz: Unidad de Comunicación y Capacitación, SEMTA).

Anaya, Amalia (1996) 'Proceso de formulación de la reforma educativa,' Documento de Trabajo 01/95, Maestrías para el Desarrollo (La Paz), mimeo.

Anaya, Amalia and López, Luis Enrique (1993) 'Protagonismo del aprendizaje, interculturalidad y participación social: calves para la reforma educativa,' *Revista UNITAS*, no. 11 (September).

Anaya, Ricardo (1952) *Nacionalización de las minas de Bolivia* (Cochabamba: Imprenta Universitaria).

Anderson, Rodney (1976), *Outcasts in Their Own Land. Mexican Industrial Workers, 1906-11* (De Kalb: Northern Illinois University Press).

Andrade, Víctor (1976) *My Missions for Revolutionary Bolivia* (Pittsburgh: University of Pittsburgh Press).

Ankerson, Dudley (1984) *Agrarian Warlord: Saturnino Cedillo and the Mexican Revolution in San Luis Potosí* (De Kalb: Northern Illinois University Press).

Antezana E., Luis (1988) *Historia secreta del Movimiento Nacionalista Revolucionario: La Revolucion del 9 de Abril de 1952* (La Paz: Editorial Juventud).

Antezana, Luis and Romero, Hugo (1968) 'Origen, desarrollo y situacion actual del sindicalismo campesino en Bolivia' (La Paz: CIDA, University of Wisconsin), mimeo.

Antezana E., Luis and Romero B., Hugo (1973) *Los sindicatos campesinos. Un proceso de integración nacional en Bolivia* (La Paz: Consejo Nacional de Reforma Agraria, Departamento de Investigaciones Sociales).

Aranzaes, Nicanor (1915) *Diccionario histórico biográfico de La Paz* (La Paz: Editorial Gráfica La Prensa).

Archondo, Rafael (1997) *Tres años de participación popular: memorias de un proceso* (La Paz: Ministerio de Desarrollo Humano, Secretaría Nacional de Participación Popular).

Ardaya, Gloria (1992) *Política sin rostro: mujeres en Bolivia* (Caracas: Nueva Sociedad).

Ardaya, Rubén (1995) *La construcción municipal de Bolivia* (La Paz: Strategies for International Development).

Arguedas, Alcides (1936) *Pueblo enfermo* [1909] third edition (La Paz: Puerta del Sol).

Arguedas, Alcides (1979) *Cartas a los presidentes de Bolivia* (La Paz: Última Hora).

Arguedas, Alcides (1992) *Historia general de Bolivia* [1922] (La Paz: Juventud).

Arze Aguirre, René Danilo (1987) *Guerra y conflictos sociales. El caso boliviano durante la campaña del Chaco* (La Paz: Centro de Estudios de la Realidad Económica y Social).

Arze, José Antonio (1963) *Sociología Marxista* (Oruro: Universidad Tecnica).

Arze, José Roberto (1984) *Figuras bolivianas en las ciencias sociales. Diccionario biográfico boliviano* (La Paz: Amigos del Libro).

Averanga Mollinedo, Asthenio (1998) *Aspectos generales de la población boliviana* (La Paz: Librería Editorial Juventud), 3rd edition.

Ayo, Diego (1997) 'La elección del tres de diciembre de 1995: análisis de las 464 autoridades indígenas y campesinas elegidas,' in *Indígenas en el poder local* (La Paz: Ministerio de Desarrollo Humano, Secretaría Nacional de Participación Popular), pp. 27–40.

Ayub, Mahmood Ali and Hashimoto, Hideo (1985) The Economics of Tin Mining in Bolivia (Washington, DC: World Bank).

Ballivián y Roxas, Manuel Vicente de (1977) *Archivo boliviano. Colección de documentos relativos a la historia de Bolivia durante la época colonial* [1872] (La Paz: Casa de la Cultura Franz Tamayo).

Banco Interamericano de Desarrollo (BID) (2001) Planilla Educativa de las Encuestas Integrada de Hogares, Servicio de Informacion Social. Departamento de Investigación.

Bantjes, Adrian (1998) *As If Jesus Walked on Earth. Cardenismo, Sonora and the Mexican Revolution* (Wilmington, Del.: Scholarly Resources).

Barnadas, Josep (1978) 'Apuntes para una historia aymara,' *CIPCA Cuadernos de investigación*, vol. 6, 2nd. edition.

Barragán, Rossana (1992) 'Entre polleras, nanacas y lliqllas: los mestizos y cholas en la conformación de la "tercera república",' in H. Urbano, *Tradición y modernidad en los Andes* (Cusco: Centro Bartolomé de las Casas), pp. 43–73.

Basurto, José (1983) *Cárdenas y el poder sindical* (Mexico City: Ediciones Era).

Benjamin, Thomas (1989) *A Rich Land, A Poor People. Politics and Society in Modern Chiapas* (Albuquerque: University of New Mexico Press).

Berger, Henry Weinberg (1966) 'Union Diplomacy: American Labor's Foreign Policy in Latin America, 1932–1955', PhD thesis (University of Wisconsin).

Bernstein, Marvin D. (1965) *The Mexican Mining Industry, 1890–1950: A Study of the Interaction of Politics, Economics, and Technology* (Albany: State University of New York).

Berríos Gosálvez, Marlene (1995) *¿Quién le teme a la reforma educativa?* (La Paz: CEDOIN).

Berry, L.A. (1971) 'La educación en Bolivia. Análisis del sector' (La Paz), mimeo.

Besse, Susan (1996) *Restructuring Patriarchy. The Modernization of Gender Inequality in Brazil, 1914–1940* (Chapel Hill: University of North Carolina Press).

Bethell, Leslie (1992) *Cambridge History of Latin America,* vol. VIII (Cambridge: Cambridge University Press).

Bethell, Leslie (1995) *Cambridge History of Latin America*, vol. XI (Cambridge: Cambridge University Press), bibliographical essays.

Blair, Harry (1997) *Democratic Local Governance in Bolivia* (USAID: Evaluation, Number 6).

Blanes, Jose and Ayo, Diego (1998) 'Participación social y modernización del estado: la sociedad boliviana y la oferta de participación estatal' (La Paz: CEBEM), unpublished.

Blasier, Cole (1976) *The Hovering Giant* (Pittsburgh: University of Pittsburgh Press).

Blasier, Cole (1985) *Hovering Giant*, revised edition (Pittsburgh: University of Pittsburgh Press).

Blasier, Cole (1971) 'The United States and the Revolution,' James M. Malloy and Richard S. Thorn (eds.), *Beyond the Revolution. Bolivia since 1952* (Pittsburgh: University of Pittsburgh Press).

Bolivia, Dirección General de Estadística y Censos (1955) *Censo demográfico 1950* (La Paz: Dirección General de Estadística y Censos).

Bolivia, Ministry of Planning (1970) *Bolivia 1971–1991, Socio-economic Strategy for National Development* (La Paz: Ministry of Planning).

Booth, David, Clisby, Suzanne and Widmark, Charlotta (1997) 'Popular Participation: Democratising the State in Rural Bolivia,' Report to SIDA, commissioned through the Development Studies Unit, Department of Social Anthropology, Stockholm University.

Booth, John and Seligson, Mitchell A. (1993) 'Paths to Democracy and the Political Culture of Costa Rica, Mexico, and Nicaragua,' in Larry Diamond (ed..) *Political Culture and Democracy in Developing Countries* (Boulder: Lynne. Rienner Publishers), pp. 115–24.

Boyer, Christopher R. (1994) '*Coyotes y nopales: Caciquismo*, Popular Movements and State Consolidation in Michoacán, Mexico, 1917–34,' paper given at the Latin American Studies Association Congress, March.

Brading, D.A. (1985) *The Origins of Mexican Nationalism* (Cambridge: Centre of Latin American Studies, University of Cambridge).

Brading, D.A. and Cross, Harry E. (1972) 'Colonial Silver Mining: Mexico and Peru,' *Hispanic American Historical Review*, vol. 52, no. 4.

Brewster, Keith (1996) 'Caciquismo in Rural Mexico during the 1920s: The Case of Gabriel Barrios,' *Journal of Latin American Studies*, vol. 28, no. 1 (February), pp. 105–28.

Brienen, Marten (2000) 'Histoire secrete d'une présence étrangere dans l'e-ducation rurales bolivienne, 1944–1956,' *Histoire et Sociétés de l'Amérique latine*, vol. 12.

Brienen, Marten (2001) 'The Clamor for Schools. Rural Education and the Development of State-Community Contact in Highland Bolivia, 1930–1952,' Paper presented at the 2001 meeting of the Latin American Studies Association, Washington DC, September 6–8.

Brockmann, Robert (2000) 'Lenguas globales, mentes locales,' *La Razón*, 14 June.

Burke, Melvin (1971) 'Land Reform in the Lake Titicaca Region,' in James M. Malloy and Richard S. Thorn (eds.), *Beyond the Revolution. Bolivia since 1952* (Pittsburgh: University of Pittsburgh Press).

Cabot, John Moors (1955) 'The Political Basis for Continental Solidarity,' *Toward Our Common American Destiny: Speeches and Interviews on Latin American Problems* (Medford, Mass.: Fletcher School of Law and Diplomacy).

Cajías, Beatríz (1998) '1995: de una educación de castas a una educación de masas,' *Ciencia y Cultura. Revista de la Universidad Católica Boliviana*, no. 3 (July), pp. 42–53.

Cajías, Fernando (1987) 'La sublevación tupacamarista de 1781 en Oruro y las provincias aledañas: sublevación de indios y revuelta criolla,' Doctoral Thesis, Universidad de Sevilla.

Calderón, Fernando and Dandler, Jorge (eds.)(1986) *Bolivia: la fuerza histórica del campesinado* (La Paz and Geneva: CERES and UNRISD).

Calla, Ricardo and Calla, Hernando (1996) *Partidos políticos y municipios: las elecciones de 1995*, Debate Político 2 (La Paz: Instituto Latinoamericano de Investigaciones Sociales).

Calla, Ricardo, Pinelo, José and Urioste, Miguel (1989) *CSUTCB: Debates sobre documentos políticos y asamblea de nacionalidades* (La Paz: CEDLA).

Camacho Romero, Juan Carlos (1989) *Un combatiente: Luis Sandoval Moron* (Santa Cruz), mimeo.

Cárdenas, Victor Hugo (1987) 'La CSUTCB: elementos para entender su crisis de crecimiento (1979–87),' in *Crisis del sindicalismo en Bolivia* (La Paz: ILDIS and FLACSO).

Cárdenas, Víctor Hugo (1988) 'La lucha de un pueblo,' in Xavier Albó (ed.) *Raíces de América: el mundo aymara* (Madrid: Alianza Edictorial).

Cárdenas, Víctor Hugo (2000) 'Prejuicios sobre lenguas y educación,' *La Razón* (23 June).

Cariaga, Juan (1982) 'The Economic Structure of Bolivia After 1964,' in Jerry R. Ladman (ed.), *Modern-Day Bolivia. Legacy of the Revolution and Prospects for the Future* (Tempe, Arizona: Center for Latin American Studies, Arizona State University).

Cariaga, Juan I. (1996) *Estabilización y desarrollo* (La Paz: Los Amigos del Libro).

Carnoy, Martin and Wertheim, Jorge (1979) *Cuba: Economic Change and Education Reform, 1955–1974*, World Bank Staff Working Paper no. 317 (Washington, DC: World Bank).

Carranza Fernández, Mario (1972) *Estudio de caso en el Valle Bajo de Cochabamba: Caramarca, Parotani e Itapaya* (La Paz: Servicio Nacional de Reforma Agraria).

Carter, William (1965) 'Aymara Communities and Agrarian Reform in Bolivia,' *Monograph in Social Science* 24 (Gainesville).

Casassus, Juan (1995) 'Concertación y alianzas en educación,' in FLACSO et al. (1995) *Es posible concertar las políticas educativas? La concertación de políticas educativas en Argentina y América Latina* (Buenos Aires: Miño y Dávila Editores).

CEBIAE (1996) 'La reforma educativa boliviana y el Foro Educativo,' Editorial de *Nuevas Palabras. Carta Informativa del CEBIAE*, año 3 no. 29–30 (November–December).

CELADE — Population Division (2000), *Demographic Bulletin*, no. 66 (July).

CEPAL (1958), *El desarrollo económico de Bolivia* (Mexico).

CEPAL (2000) *Indicators of Social and Economic Development in Latin America.*

CEPAL (2000a) *Statistical Yearbook of Latin America, 2000.*

CEPAL (2001) *Boletín Demográfico*, no. 68 (July).

CEPAL (2002) *Statistical Yearbook, 2001* (Santiago de Chile).

CEPAL/CELADE — División de Población (2000) *Boletín demográfico*, no. 66 (July).

Céspedes, Augusto (1975) *El presidente colgado*, 2nd edition (Buenos Aires: Editorial Universitaria de Buenos Aires).

Chalmers, Douglas, Vilas, Carlos, Hite, Katherine, Martin, Scott, Piester, Kerianne and Segarra, Monique (1997) *The New Politics of Inequality in Latin America: Rethinking Participation and Representation* (Oxford: Oxford University Press).

Chávez, Gonzalo (2002) E-mail correspondence, 18 March.

Checci and Company Consulting, Inc. (1994) *Final Report: Evaluation of Democratic Institutions Project (511–0610)* (Washington: Checci and Company Consulting, Inc.)

Choque, Roberto (1979) 'Situación social y económica de los revolucionarios del 16 de Julio de 1809,' thesis in History, Universidad Mayor de San Andrés.

Choque, Roberto (1992) 'Las rebeliones indígenas de la post-guerra del Chaco. Reivindicaciones indígenas durante la prerevolución,' *DATA 3*, pp. 37–53.

Choque, Roberto (1996) 'La educación indigenal boliviana. El proceso educativo indígeno-rural,' *Estudios Andinos*, vol. 2, pp. 125–82.

Choque, Roberto et al. (1992) *Educación indígena: ¿Ciudadanía o colonización?* (La Paz: Aruwiyiri).

CIDES-PNUD (1997) *Gobernabildad y partidos politicos* (La Paz: CIDES–PNUD).

Claure, Karen (1989) *Las escuelas indigenales: otra forma de resistencia comunaria* (La Paz: Hisbol).

Claure, Toribio (1949) *Una escuela rural en Vacas* (La Paz: n.p.).

Collier, Ruth Berins and Collier, David (1991) *Shaping the Political Arena. Critical Junctures, The Labor Movement, and Regime Dynamics in Latin America* (Princeton: Princeton University Press).

Comaroff, Jean and Comaroff, John (1992) *Ethnography and the Historical Imagination* (Boulder: Westview Press.

Comboni, Sonia and Juárez, José Manuel (2000) 'Education, Culture and Indigeneous Rights: The Case of Educational Reform in Bolivia,' *Prospects*, vol. XXX, no. 1 (March).

Comisión Económica para América Latina (CEPAL) (1967) *Boletín Económico.*

Comisión Episcopal de Educación (1979) *Si la educación surgiera del pueblo* (La Paz), mimeo.

Comitas, Lambros (1968) 'Educación y estratificación social en Bolivia,' *América Indígena,* vol. XXVIII, no. 3 (July).

Conaghan, Catherine M. and Malloy, James M. (1994) *Unsettling Statecraft: Democracy and Neoliberalism in the Central Andes* (Pittsburgh: Pittsburgh University Press).

Conaghan, Catherine M., Malloy, James M. and Abugattas, Luis A. (1990) 'Business and the "Boys": The Politics of Neoliberalism in the Central Andes,' *Latin American Research Review*, vol. 25, no. 2, pp. 3–30.

Consejo Nacional de Educación (1940), *El estado de la educación indigenal en el pais* (La Paz: n.p.).

Contreras, Manuel E. (1990) 'Debts, Taxes and War. The Political Economy of Bolivia, c. 1920–1935,' *Journal of Latin American Studies*, vol. 22, no. 2 (May).

Contreras, Manuel (1993) *The Bolivian Tin Mining Industry in the First Half of the Twentieth Century* (London: Institute of Latin American Studies).

Contreras, Manuel (1996) 'Análisis comparativo de tres reformas educativas en Bolivia en el siglo XX,' paper presented to the III Congreso Iberoamericano de Historia de la Educación Latinoamericana, 10–14 June (Caracas), mimeo.

Contreras, Manuel (1998a) 'El conflicto entre los maestros/as y el gobierno a la luz de la reforma educative,' *Conflictos*, vol. 2, no. 23, pp. 9–12.

Contreras, Manuel (1998b) 'Formulación, implementación y avance de la reforma educativa en Bolivia,' *Ciencia y Cultura. Revista de la Universidad Católica Boliviana*, no. 3 (July), pp. 55–76.

Contreras, Manuel (1999a) 'El conflicto entre maestros/as y gobierno,' *Tinkazos. Revista Boliviana de Ciencias Sociales*, no. 4 (August).

Contreras, Manuel (1999b) 'Reformas y desafíos de la educación,' in Fernando Campero Prudencio (coord.), *Bolivia en el siglo XX. La formación de la Bolivia contemporánea* (La Paz: Harvard Club de Bolivia), pp. 483–507.

Contreras, Manuel (2000) 'Bolivia, 1930–1939: Mining, Railways and Education,' in Enrique Cárdenas, José Antonio Ocampo and Rosemary Thorp (eds.), *An Economic History of Twentieth-Century Latin America*, vol. 1: *The Export Age* (London: Palgrave).

Contreras, Manuel E. and Pacheco, Marco Napoleón (1989) *Medio siglo de minería mediana en Bolivia, 1939–1989* (La Paz: Biblioteca Minera Boliviana).

Coppedge, Michael (1998) 'The Dynamic Diversity of Latin American Party Systems,' *Party Politics*, vol. 4, no. 4 (October), pp. 547–68.

Costa de la Torre, Arturo (1974) *Episodios históricos de la rebelión indígena de 1781* (La Paz: Ediciones Camarlinghi).

Crabtree, John and Whitehead, Laurence (2001) *Toward Democratic Viability: The Bolivian Experience* (Oxford: Palgrave).

Crafts, Nicholas (2000) 'Globalization and Growth in the Twentieth Century,' IMF Working Paper (Washington, DC: International Monetary Fund).

Crandon-Malamud, Libbet (1991) *From the Fat of Our Souls Social Change, Political Process, and Medical Pluralism in Bolivia* (Berkeley: University of California Press).

Crespo, Alfonso (1996) *Hernán Siles. El hombre de abril* (La Paz: Plural Editores)

Crespo, Alfonso and Lara, Mario (1997) *Enrique Hertzog: el hidalgo presidente* (Lima: Didi de Arteta).

Crespo Rodas, Alberto (1974) 'Los coroneles de Túpac Catari,' *Presencia Literaria* (April).

Crespo Rodas, Alberto (1982) 'Las armas de los rebeldes,' in ACI, *Tupac*

Amaru y su tiempo (Lima: Comisión Nacional del Bicentenario de la Rebelión Emancipadora de Túpac Amaru).

Crespo Rodas, Alberto (1987) 'Pedro Obaya, el Rey chiquito,' *Historia y Cultura*, vol. 11, pp. 41–72.

Dandler, Jorge (1969) *El sindicalismo campesino en Bolivia: los cambios estructurales en Ucureña (1935–1952)* (Mexico: Instituto Indigenista Interamericano).

Dandler, Jorge (1983) *El sindicalismo campesino en Bolivia: los cambios estructurales en Ucureña* (Cochabamba: CERES).

Dandler, Jorge and Torrico, Juan (1986) 'El congreso nacional indígena de 1945 y la rebelión de Ayopaya (1947),' in Fernando Calderón and Jorge Dandler (1986), *Bolivia: La fuerza histórica del campesinado* (La Paz: CERES and United Nations), pp. 135–205.

Dandler, Jorge and Torrico, Juan (1987) 'From the National Indigenous Congress to the Ayopaya Rebellion: Bolivia, 1945–1947,' in Steve Stern (ed.), *Resistance, Rebellion, and Consciousness in the Andean Peasant World, 18th to 20th centuries* (Madison: University of Wisconsin Press), pp. 334–78.

Davies, James C. (1969) 'The J-Curve of Rising and Declining Satisfaction as a Cause of some Great Revolutions and a Contained Rebellion,' in H.D. Graham and T.R. Gurr (eds.), *Violence in America* (New York: Bantam), pp. 671–709.

De la Cadena, Marisol (2000) *Indigenous Mestizos: The Politics of Race and Culture in Cuzco, Peru, 1919–1991* (Durham, NC: Duke University Press).

Deheza, Grace Ivana (2000) '¿Inestabilidad contínua en el sistema de partidos de Bolivia? Los Efectos de las leyes electorales,' *Umbrales* no. 7 (Julio)

Delpar, Helen (1992) *The Enormous Vogue of Things Mexican: Cultural Relations between the United States and Mexico, 1920–1935* (Tuscaloosa: University of Alabama Press)

Deutsch, Sandra McGee (1991) 'Gender and Sociopolitical Change in Twentieth-Century Latin America,' *Hispanic American Historical Review*, vol. 71, pp. 257–306.

Development Associates Inc. (1997) *Strategic Assessment of Bolivian Democracy* (Washington: Development Associates).

Discursos Parlamentarios (La Paz, 1955).

Domingo, Pilar (2001) 'Party Politics, Intermediation and Representation,' in John Crabtree and Laurence Whitehead (eds.), *Towards Democratic Viability: The Bolivian Experience* (Oxford: Palgrave), pp. 141–59.

Domínguez, Jorge and Mitchell, Christopher N. (1977) 'The Roads not Taken: Institutionalization and Political Parties in Cuba and Bolivia,' *Comparative Politics*, vol. 9, pp. 173–95.

Domínguez, Jorge I. (1978) *Cuba. Order and Revolution* (Cambridge, MA: Harvard University Press).

Donald, James (1992) *Sentimental Education. Schooling, Popular Culture, and the Regulation of Liberty* (London: Verso).

Donoso Torres, Vicente (1946) *Filosofía de la educación boliviana* (Buenos Aires: Ed. Atlantida), pp. 180–1.

Dore, Elizabeth (1997) '"The 'Holy Family"': Imagined Households in Latin American History,' in Elizabeth Dore (ed.), *Gender Politics in Latin America. Debates in Theory and Practice* (New York: Monthly Review Press), pp. 101–17.

Dore, Elizabeth (2000) 'One Step Forward, Two Steps Back: Gender and the State in the Long Nineteenth Century,' in Elizabeth Dore and Maxine Molyneux (eds.), *Hidden Histories of Gender and the State in Latin America* (Durham, NC: Duke University Press).

Dore, Elizabeth and Molyneux, Maxine (eds.) (2000) *Hidden Histories of Gender and the State in Latin America* (Durham, NC: Duke University Press).

Drosdoff, Daniel (1997) 'Night Dive, Head First, into a Swimming Pool. Political Risk and Bolivian Stabilization (1985–1997): The Actors Tell the Story,' unpublished manuscript, November.

Dunkerley, James (1984) *Rebellion in the Veins: Political Struggle in Bolivia, 1952–82* (London: Verso).

Dunkerley, James (1988) *Orígenes del poder militar en Bolivia: historia política e institucional del Ejército Boliviano hasta 1935* (La Paz: Quipus).

Dunkerley, James (1992) *Political Suicide in Latin America* (London: Verso).

Dunkerley, James (ed.) (2002) *Studies in the Formation of the Nation State in Latin America* (London: Institute of Latin American Studies).

Easterly, William (2001) *The Elusive Quest for Growth* (Cambridge, MA: The MIT Press).

Echalar, Augustín (2000) 'Lenguas locales, mentes globales,' *La Razón*, 16 June.

Eckstein, Susan (1976) *The Impact of Revolution: A Comparative Analysis of México and Bolivia* (Beverly Hills: Sage Publications).

Eckstein, Susan (1985) 'Revolutions and the Restructuring of National Economies: The Latin American Experience,' *Comparative Politics*, vol. 17, pp. 473–94.

Eder, O.J. (1968) *Inflation and Development in Latin America: A Case History of Inflation and Stabilisation in Bolivia* (Michigan: University of Michigan Press).

ETARE (1993) *Reforma Educativa. Propuesta*, Cuadernos de La Reforma (La Paz: Papiro).

Faguet, Jean Paul (2001) 'Does Decentralization Increase Responsiveness to Local Needs? Evidence from Bolivia,' Policy Research Working Paper 2516 (Washington, DC: World Bank).

Farber, Samuel (1976) *Revolution and Reaction in Cuba, 1933–60* (Middletown, Conn.: Wesleyan University Press).

Federación Rural de Cochabamba (1946) *Memoria de la tercera conferencia nacional de agricultura, ganadería e industrias derivadas realizada en Cochabamba* (Cochabamba: Editorial Atlantic).

Fell, Eva Marie (1996) 'Warisata y la irradiación del núcleo escolar campesino en los Andes,' Pilar Gonzalbo(ed.), *Educación rural e indígena en Iberoamérica*, (Mexico City: El Colegio de México-UNED), pp. 209–23.

Fellman Velarde, José (1981) *Historia de Bolivia, tomo III La bolivianidad semi-colonial* (La Paz: Editorial 'Los Amigos del Libro').

Finkler, Kaja (1974) *Estudio comparativo de la economía de dos comunidades de México* (Mexico: Instituto Nacional Indigenista y Secretaría de Educación Pública).

Finot, Enrique (1974) *Historia de la literatura boliviana* [1944] (La Paz: Gisbert & Cia).

Finot, Enrique (1994) *Nueva historia de bolivia* (*ensayo de interpretación sociológica*) [1946] (La Paz: Juventud).

Flores Galindo, Alberto (1989) *La agonía de Mariátegui* (Lima: Instituto de Apoyo Agrario).

Foreign Relations of the United States, American Republics, 1951, vol. II, (Washington, 1972).

Fox, David J. (1970) *Tin and the Bolivian Economy* (London: Latin American Publications Fund).

Friedrich, Paul (1986) *The Princes of Naranja: An Essay in Anthrohistorical Method* (Austin: University of Texas Press).

Frontaura Argona, María (1932) *Hacia el futuro indio* (La Paz: Intendencia de Guerra).

Fundación Milenio (2000) *Informe Político de Coyuntura* (La Paz: Milenio).

Galindo, Mario (1998) 'La participacion popular y la descentralizacion administrative,' in *Las reformas estructurales en Bolivia* (La Paz: Fundación Milenio).

Gallo, Carmenza (1991) *Taxes and State Power. Political Instability in Bolivia, 1900–1950* (Philadelphia: Temple University Press).

Gamarra, Eduardo A. (1987) 'Political Stability, Democratization and the Bolivian National Congress,' PhD Dissertation (University of Pittsburgh).

Gamarra, Eduardo A. (1994a) 'Crafting Political Support for Stabilization: Political Pacts and the New Economic Policy in Bolivia,' in William C. Smith, Carlos H. Acuña and Eduardo A. Gamarra (eds.), *Democracy, Markets, and Structural Reform in Latin* America (New Brunswick, N.J.: Transaction Publishers), pp. 105–27.

Gamarra, Eduardo A. (1994b) 'Market Oriented Reforms and Democratization in Bolivia,' in Joan M. Nelson (ed.), *A Precarious Balance, Democracy and Economic Reforms in Latin America* (San Francisco: International Center for Economic Growth and Overseas Development)

Gamarra, Eduardo A. (1996) 'Bolivia: Managing Democracy in the 1990s,' in Jorge I. Domínguez and Abraham F. Lowenthal (eds.), *Constructing Democratic Government in South America in the 1990s* (Baltimore: The Johns Hopkins University Press), pp. 72–98.

Gamarra, Eduardo A. (1997a) 'Superar el clientelismo y ampliar la cultura institucional,' in *Desarrollo Humano en Bolivia, 1998* (Programa para el Desarrollo de las Naciones Unidas)

Gamarra, Eduardo A. (1997b) 'Neoliberalism Reconsidered: The Politics of Privatization and Capitalization in Bolivia,' in *Capitalization: The Bolivian Model of Social and Economic Reform* (World Bank).

Gamarra, Eduardo A. (1998) 'Bolivia: Managing Democracy in the 1990s,' in Jorge I. Dominguez and Abraham F. Lowenthal (eds.), *Constructing Democratic Governance, South America in the 1990s* (Baltimore: Johns Hopkins University Press)

Gamarra, Eduardo A. (1999) 'Municipal Elections in Bolivia,' in Henry E. Dietz and Gil Shidlo (eds.), *Urban Elections in Democratic Latin America* (Wilmington, Del.: Scholarly Resources Books).

Gamarra, Eduardo (2001) 'The Andean Region and US Policy: Beyond the Plan Colombia' (Washington: Interamerican Dialogue)

Gamarra, Eduardo and Malloy, James M. (1996) 'The Patrimonial Dynamics of Party Politics in Bolivia,' in Scott Mainwaring and Timothy Scully (eds.), *Building Democratic Institutions* (Stanford: Stanford University Press).

García Linera, Alvaro, Gutierrez, Raquel, Prada, Raúl and Tapia, Luis (2000a), *El retorno de la Bolivia plebeya* (La Paz: Editorial Muela del Diablo).

García Linera, Alvaro, Gutierrez, Raquel, Prada, Raúl and Tapia, Luis (2001), *Tiempos de rebelión* (La Paz: Editorial Muela del Diablo).

García Galló, Aspar J. and Montero, René J. (1970) *El sistema educacional en Bolivia* (Habana: Casa de la Américas).

Garciadiego Dantan, Javier (1996) *Rudos contra científicos: la Universidad Nacional durante la Revolución Mexicana* (Mexico City: Colegio de México, Centro de Estudios Históricos).

Garner, Paul (2001) *Porfirio Díaz* (Harlow: Longman).

Geddes, Charles (1972) *Patiño. The Tin King* (London: Hale).

Genovese, Eugene (1979) *From Rebellion to Revolution: Afro-American Slave Revolts in the Making of the Modern World* (Baton Rouge: Louisiana State University Press).

Gilderhus, Mark T. (1977) *Diplomacy and Revolution* (Tucson: University of Arizona Press).

Gill, Lesley (1994) *Precarious Dependencies. Gender, Class, and Domestic Service in Bolivia* (New York: Columbia).

Gobierno de Bolivia (1997) El pulso de la democracia: participacion ciudadana y descentralizacion en Bolivia (Caracas: Nueva Sociedad).

Godoy, Ricardo, de Franco, Mario and Echeverria, Ruben G. (1993) 'A Brief History of Agricultural Research in Bolivia: Potatoes, Maize, Soybeans and Wheat Compared,' Development Discussion Paper Series, no. 460 (Cambridge, MA: HIID, July).

Gómez D'Angelo, Walter (1978) *La minería en el desarrollo económico de Bolivia* (La Paz: Los Amigos del Libro)

Gómez Martínez, José Luis (1988) *Bolivia: un pueblo en busca de su identidad* (La Paz: Los Amigos del Libro).

Goodwin, Jeff (2001) *No Other Way Out: States and Revolutionary Movements, 1945-91* (Cambridge: Cambridge University Press).

Gordillo, José M. (2000) *Campesinos revolucionarios en Bolivia. Identidad, territorio y sexualidad en el Valle Alto de Cochabamba, 1952–1964* (La Paz: Plural).

Gotkowitz, Laura (1998) 'Within the Boundaries of Equality: Race, Gender and Citizenship in Bolivia, Cochabamba, 1880–1953,' PhD dissertation, University of Chicago.

Gotkowitz, Laura (forthcoming) '"Under the Dominion of the Indian": Rural Mobilization, the Law, and Revolutionary Nationalism in Bolivia, 1940s,' in Nils Jacobsen and Cristóbal Aljovín (eds.), *Political Cultures in the Andes, 1750–1950* (Durham, NC: Duke University Press).

Graham, Carol. (1992) 'The Politics of Protecting the Poor During Adjustment: Bolivia's Emergency Social Fund,' *World Development*, vol. 20, no. 9, pp. 1233–51.

Graham, Carol (1994) *Safety Nets, Politics, and the Poor. Transitions to Market Economies* (Washington, DC: The Brookings Institution).

Graham, Carol (1997) *Building Support for Market Reforms in Bolivia: The Capitalization and Popular Participation Programs* (Washington, DC: The Brookings Institution).

Graham, Carol (1998) *Private Markets for Public Goods: Raising the Stakes in Economic Reform* (Washington, DC: Brookings Institution Press).

Gray-Molina, George (1997) *Participación popular: construyendo políticas públicas locales en Bolivia* (La Paz: Unidad de Análisis de Políticas Sociales –UDAPSO).

Gray-Molina, George (2000) 'Three Reform Pathways,' chapter 3, DPhil dissertation, Nuffield College, Oxford University.

Gray-Molina, George (2001) 'Exclusion, Participation and Democratic State-building,' in John Crabtree and Laurence Whitehead (eds.), *Towards Democratic Viability: The Bolivian Experience* (Oxford: Palgrave), pp. 63–82.

Gray-Molina, George (2002) 'The Politics of Popular Participation in Bolivia, 1994–1999,' DPhil Dissertation, Nuffield College, Oxford University.

Gray-Molina, George and Chávez, Gonzalo (2001) *Technical Cooperation and Capacity Development: Bolivian Case Study* (La Paz: Catholic University of Bolivia).

Gray-Molina, George and Molina, Carlos Hugo (1997) 'Popular Participacion and Decentralization in Bolivia: Building Accountability from the Grassroots' (La Paz: Harvard Institute for International Development-HIID).

Gray-Molina, George, Pérez de Rada, Ernesto and Yañez, Ernesto (1999) 'Economía política de reformas institucionales en Bolivia,' *IDB Research Network Paper R350*.

Grebe López, Horst (2001) 'The Private Sector and Democratization,' in John Crabtree and Laurence Whitehead (eds.), *Towards Democratic Viability: The Bolivian Experience* (Oxford: Palgrave), pp. 160–78.

Grebe, H. (2002) personal communication.

Grieb, Kenneth J. (1969) *The United States and Huerta* (Lincoln: University of Nebraska Press).

Grindle, Merilee (1999) 'In Quest of the Political: The Political Economy of Development Policymaking,' Working Paper no. 17 (Cambridge, MA: Harvard University, Center for International Development).

Grindle, Merilee S. (2000) *Audacious Reforms: Institutional Invention and Democracy in Latin America* (Baltimore: Johns Hopkins University Press).

Grindle, Merilee S. (forthcoming) *Against the Odds: Education Policy Reform in Latin America in the 1990s*.

Grootaert, Christiaan and Narayan, Deepa (2001) 'Local Institutions, Poverty and Household Welfare in Bolivia' (Washington, DC: World Bank), mimeo.

Grupo de Estudios Históricos (2002) *Diccionario histórico de Bolivia* (Sucre: Grupo de Estudios Históricos).

Grupo DRU (1996), *Bolivia: anuario estadístico del sector rural 1995–1996* (La Paz).

Guevara Arze, Walter (1988) *Bases para replantear la Revolución Nacional* (La Paz: Librería Editorial 'Juventud').

Guillén Pinto, Alfredo (1919) *La educación del indio. Contribución a la pedagogía nacional* (La Paz: González y Medina).

Guy, Donna (1990) *Sex and Danger in Buenos Aires. Prostitution, Family and Nation in Argentina* (Lincoln: University of Nebraska Press).

Guzmán, Augusto (1972) *Túpaj Katari* [1944] (La Paz: Juventud).

Hall, Linda B. and Coerver, Don M. (1988) *Revolution on the Border* (Albuquerque: University of New Mexico Press).

Hamilton, Nora (1982) *The Limits of State Autonomy: Post-Revolutionary Mexico* (Princeton: Princeton University Press).

Harris, Olivia (1996) 'Introduction: Inside and Outside the Law,' in Olivia Harris (ed.), *Inside and Outside the Law* (London: Routledge).

Harris, Olivia and Albó, Xavier (1975) *Monteras y guardatojos: campesinos y mineros en el Norte de Potosí* (La Paz: Cuadernos CIPCA, Centro de Investigación y Promoción del Campesinado).

Harris, Olivia and Albó, Xavier (1986) *Monteras y guardatojos: Campesinos y mineros en el norte de Potosí* (La Paz: CIPCA).

Harrison, Lawrence (1985) *Underdevelopment is a State of Mind: The Latin American Case* (Cambridge: Center for International Affairs, Harvard University and Madison Books).

Heath, Dwight (1959) 'Land Reform in Bolivia,' *Inter-American Economic Affairs,* vol. 12, no. 4, pp. 3–27.

Heath, Dwight B. (1969) 'Bolivia: Peasant Syndicates among the Aymara of the Yungas: A View from the Grass Roots,' in H.A. Landsberger (ed.), *Latin American Peasant Movements* (Ithaca: Cornell University Press).

Heath, Dwight B., Erasmus, Charles J. and Buechler, Hans C. (1969) *Land Reform and Social Revolution in Bolivia* (New York: Praeger,).

Helg, Aline (1990) 'Race in Argentina and Cuba, 1880–1930: Theory, Policies, and Popular Reaction,' in Richard Graham (ed.), *The Idea of Race in Latin America, 1870–1940* (Austin: University of Texas Press), pp. 37–70.

Hicks, Granville (1936) *John Reed: The Making of a Revolutionary* (New York).

Hill, Larry D. (1973) *Emissaries to a Revolution* (Baton Rouge: Louisiana State University Press).

Hillman, John (1990) 'Bolivia and British Tin Policy, 1939–1945,' *Journal of Latin American Studies*, vol. 22, no. 2 (May).

Hillman, John (2002) The Mining Industry and the State: The Politics of Tin Restriction in Bolivia, 1936–1939,' *Bulletin of Latin American Research*, vol. 21, no. 1 (January).

Hobsbawm, E.J. (1959) *Primitive Rebels* (Manchester, 1959).

Hornberger, Nancy (2000) 'Bilingual Education Policy and Practice in the Andes: Ideological Paradox and Intercultural Possibility,' *Anthropological & Education Quarterly*, vol. 31, no. 2.

Hylton, Forrest (2000) 'Common Ground: Indian Caciques, Urban Radicals, and the Chayanta Rebellion,' unpublished MA thesis, University of Pittsburg.

Ibañez López, Mario (1961) *Fundamentos para un regimen autónomo de la educación pública en Bolivia* (Santa Cruz: Universidad Gabriel René Moreno).

Imaña Castro, Teodosio (1971) 'Katari y la acción pre-emancipadora,' *Presencia Literaria* (Mar.ch).

Imaña Castro, Teodosio (1973) 'De lo pasional en la vida de los caudillos indígenas de 1780,' *Historia y Cultura: Revista del Instituto de Estudios Bolivianos*, vol. 1, pp. 125–42.

INE (Instituto Nacional de Estadística)(1976) *Resultados del Censo Naconal de Población y Vivienda, 1976*, vol. 10.

INE (1985) *I Censo Agropecuario 1950* (La Paz).

INE (1993) *Censo nacional de población y vivienda 1992, resultados finales* (La Paz).

INE (1997), *La transición de la fecundidad en Bolivia y sus determinantes (1965–1995)* (La Paz).

INE (2001), *Anuario estadístico, 2000* (La Paz).

INE and CELADE (Instituto Nacional de Estadística and United Nations, Centro Latinoamericano y Caribeño de Demografía) (1995), 'Bolivia. Estimaciones y proyecciones de la población 1950-2050' (La Paz: Instituto Nacional de Estadística).

Informe del Prefecto, Superintendente de Hacienda y Minas del Departamento, Cnl. Alberto Arauz (Cochabamba: Editorial América, 1945).

International Labor Office (ILO) (1943) *Los problemas del trabajo en Bolivia/Labour Problems in Bolivia* (Montreal: n.p.).

Jackson, Robert (1994) *Regional Markets and Agrarian Transformation in Bolivia: Cochabamba, 1539–1960* (Albuquerque: University of New Mexico Press).

Jaguaribe, Helio (1972) *Political Development: A General Theory and a Latin American Case Study* (New York: Harper and Row).

Jauregui Roquellas, Alfredo (1947) 'Reflecciones sobre la cuestión indigenal. Sublevaciones y levantamientos,' *Boletín de la Sociedad Geográfica Sucre*, vol. 62.

Johnson, J.J. (1958) *Political Change in Latin America: The Emergence of the Middle Sectors* (Stanford, 1958).

Jorgensen, Steen, Grosh, Margaret and Schacter, Mark (1992) *Bolivia's Answer to Poverty, Economic Crisis, and Adjustment: The Emergency Social Fund* (Washington, DC: World Bank).

Joseph, Gilbert M. and Nugent, Daniel (eds.) (1994) *Everyday Forms of State Formation. Revolution and the Negotiation of Rule in Modern Mexico* (Durham, NC: Duke University Press)

Katz, Friedrich (1981) *The Secret War in Mexico* (Chicago: University of Chicago Press).

Katz, Friedrich (1988) 'Introduction: Rural Revolts in Mexico,' in Friedrich Katz (ed.), *Riot, Rebellion and Revolution: Rural Social Conflict in Mexico* (Princeton: Princeton University Press).

Katz, Friedrich (1998) *Pancho Villa* (México: Ediciones Era).

Kaufmann, D., Mastruzzi, M. and Zavaleta, D. (2001) 'Sustained Macroeconomic Reforms, Tepid Growth: A Governance Puzzle for Bolivia?,' mimeo (Washington, DC: World Bank).

Kelley, Jonathan and Klein, Herbert S. (1981) *Revolution and the Rebirth of Inequality. A Theory Applied the National Revolution in Bolivia* (Berkeley: University of California Press).

Klein, Herbert (1968) 'The Crisis of Legitimacy and the Origins of Social Revolution – the Bolivian Experience,' *The Journal of Inter-American Studies*, vol. X, no. 1 (January).

Klein, Herbert (1969) *Parties and Political Change in Bolivia, 1880–1952* (Cambridge: Cambridge University Press).

Klein, Herbert (1971) 'Prelude to the Revolution,' in James M. Malloy and Richard S. Thorn (eds.), *Beyond the Revolution. Bolivia since 1952* (Pittsburgh: University of Pittsburgh Press).

Klein, Herbert S. (1982) *Bolivia: The Evolution of a Multi-Ethnic Society* (Oxford: Oxford University Press).

Klein, Herbert S. (1992) *Bolivia: The Evolution of a Multi-Ethnic Society* (Oxford, New York: Oxford University Press).

Klubock, Thomas (1998) *Contested Communities. Class, Gender and Politics in Chile's El Teniente Copper Mine, 1904–1951* (Durham, NC: Duke University Press).

Knight, Alan (1985) 'The Mexican Revolution: "Bourgeois", "Nationalist", or Just a "Great Rebellion"?,' *Bulletin of Latin American Research*, vol. 4, pp. 1–37

Knight, Alan (1986) *The Mexican Revolution*, vol. 1 (Cambridge: Cambridge University Press).

Knight, Alan (1987) *US–Mexican Relations, 1910–40: An Interpretation* (San Diego: University of California, Center for US–Mexican Relations).

Knight, Alan (1990a) 'Social Revolution: A Latin American Perspective,' *Bulletin of Latin American Research*, vol. 9, no. 2.

Knight, Alan (1990b) 'Mexico, *c.* 1930–46,' in Leslie Bethell (ed.), *The Cambridge History of Latin America*, vol. VII *1930 to the Present* (Cambridge: Cambridge University Press).

Knight, Alan (1991) 'Land and Society in Revolutionary Mexico: The Destruction of the Great Haciendas,' *Mexican Studies/Estudios Mexicanos*, vol. 7, no. 1 (Winter), pp. 73–104.

Knight, Alan (1992) 'The Politics of the Expropriation,' in Jonathan Brown and Alan Knight (eds.), *The Mexican Petroleum Industry in the Twentieth Century* (Austin: University of Texas Press).

Knight, Alan (1994) 'Cardenismo: Juggernaut or Jalopy?,' *Journal of Latin American Studies*, vol. 26.

Knight, Alan (1997) 'Habitus and Homicide: Political Culture in Revolutionary Mexico,' in Wil G. Pansters (ed.), *Citizens of the Pyramid. Essays on Mexican Political Culture* (Amsterdam: Thela Publishers), pp. 107–30.

Knight, Alan (2000) 'The Mexican Revolution: Five Counter-Factuals,' in Jaime Bailón Corres, Carlos Martínez Assad and Pablo Serrano Alvarez (eds.), *El siglo de la Revolución Mexicana*, 2 vols. (Mexico: Instituto Nacional de Estudios Históricos de la Revolución Mexicana, Secretaría de Gobernación).

Knight, Alan (forthcoming) 'The Agrarian Origins and Character of the Mexican Revolution (Reconsidered),' in Friedrich Katz. (ed.), *The Agrarian Origins of the Mexican Revolution* (provisional title).

Knudson, Jerry W. (1986) *Bolivia: Press and Revolution 1932–1964* (Lanham, Maryland: University Press of America).

Kohl, James V. (1978) 'Peasant and Revolution in Bolivia, April 9, 1952–August 2, 1953,' *Hispanic American Historical Review*, vol. 58, no. 2.

Kohl, James V. (1982) 'The Cliza and Ucureña War: Syndical Violence and National Revolution in Bolivia,' *Hispanic American Historical Review*, vol. 62, no. 4, pp. 607–28.

Kymlicka, Will (2000) *Politics in the Vernacular: Nationalism, Multiculturalism and Citizenship* (Oxford: Oxford University Press).

Laakso, Markku and Taagepera, Rein (1979) 'Effective Number of Parties: A Measure with Application to Western Europe', *Comparative Political Studies*, vol. 12 , p. 3–27.

Ladd, Doris (1988) *The Making of a Strike, Mexican Silver Workers' Struggles in Real del Monte, 1766-75* (Lincoln, NE: University of Nebraska Press).

Ladman, J. (1982a) 'The Political Economy and the "Economic Miracle" of the Banzer Regime,' in *Modern-Day Bolivia* (Tempe, AZ: Center for Latin American Studies, Arizona State University), pp. 321–43.

Ladman, Jerry (ed.) (1982b) *Modern-Day Bolivia. Legacy of the Revolution and Prospects for the Future* (Tempe, Arizona: Center for Latin American Studies, Arizona State University).

Landsberger, Henry A. (1967) 'The Labor Elite: Is It Revolutionary?,' in Seymour Martin Lipset and Aldo Solari (eds.), *Elites in Latin America* (New York: Oxford University Press), chapter 8.

Langer, Erick D. (1989) *Economic Change and Rural Resistance in Southern Bolivia, 1880–1930* (Stanford: Stanford University Press).

Langer, Erick D. (1990) 'Andean Rituals of Revolt: the Chayanta Rebellion of 1927,' *Ethnohistory*, vol. 37, no. 3, pp. 227–53.

Larson, Brooke (1998) *Cochabamba, 1550–1900: Colonialism and Agrarian Transformation in Bolivia*, Expanded edition (Durham, NC: Duke University Press).

Lavaud, Jean Pierre (1986) 'Los campesinos frente al estado,' in Fernando Calderón and Jorge Dandler (eds.), *Bolivia: La fuerza historica del campesinado* (La Paz: CERES and United Nations), pp. 277–313.

Lazarte, Jorge (1985) 'Cogestión y participación: ideología y práctica del movimiento obrero,' *Estado y Sociedad*, no. 1 (La Paz: FLACSO).

Lechín Oquendo, Juan (2000) *Memorias* (La Paz: Litexsa Boliviana).

Lehm, Zulema and Rivera, Silvia (1986) *Polleras libertarias: Federación Obrera Feminina, 1927–1964* (La Paz: TAHIPAMU).

Lehm, Zulema A. and Rivera Cusicanqui, Silvia (1988) *Los artesanos libertarios y la ética del trabajo* (La Paz: THOA).

Lehman, Kenneth D. (1997) 'Revolutions and Attributions: Making Sense of Eisenhower Administration Policies in Bolivia and Guatemala,' *Diplomatic History*, vol. 22, no. 2 (Spring).

Lehman, Kenneth (1999) *Bolivia and the United States: A Limited Partnership* (Athens: University of Georgia Press).

Leons, Madeline Barbara (1984) 'Political Penetration and Conflict Resolution in the Bolivian Yungas,' *Journal of Developing Areas*, vol. 18, no. 4.

Leons, Madeline and Leons, William (1971) 'Land Reform and Economic Change in the Yungas,' in James M. Malloy and Richard S. Thorn (eds.), *Beyond the Revolution. Bolivia Since 1952* (Pittsburgh: University of Pittsburgh Press).

Lijphart, Arend (1999) *Patterns of Democracy: Government Forms and Performance in Thirty-Six Countries* (New Haven: Yale University Press, 1999).

Lloyd Mecham, J. (1966) *Church and State in Latin America* (Chapel Hill: University of North Carolina Press).

López, Luis Enrique (1994) 'La educación intercultural bilingue en Bolivia: ámbitos para el ejercicio de los derechos linguisticos y culturales indígenas,' *Data. Revista del Instituto de Estudios Andinos y Amazónicos*, no. 5.

López, Luis Enrique (1998) 'La eficacia y validez de lo obvio: lecciones aprendidas desde la evaluación de procesos educativos bilingues,' *Revista Iberoamericana de Educación*, no. 17 (May–August).

López, Luís Enrique and Kuper, Wolfgang (2000) 'La educación intercultural bilingue en América Latina: Balance y perspectives,' mimeo.

Lora, Guillermo (1977) *A History of the Bolivian Labour Movement* (Cambridge: Cambridge University Press).

Lynch, John (1986) 'The Catholic Church,' in Leslie Bethell (ed.), *Cambridge History of Latin America*, vol. IV (Cambridge: Cambridge University Press).

Machicado, F. (1964) *La Política Económica de Bolivia en el Periodo 1952–64*, mimeo (La Paz).

Mainwaring, Scott, and Scully, Timothy R. (eds.) (1995) *Building Democratic Institutions: Party Systems in Latin America* (Stanford, Calif.: Stanford University Press).

Mahoney, James and Rueschemeyer, Dietrich (eds.) (2003) *Comparative Historical Analysis* (Cambridge: Cambridge University Press).

Mallon, Florencia (1992) 'Indian Communities, Political Cultures, and the State in Latin-America, 1780–1900,' *Journal of Latin American Studies*, vol. 24, pp. 35–53.

Mallon, Florencia (1995) *Peasant and Nation. The Making of Postcolonial Mexico and Peru* (Berkeley: University of California Press).

Mallon, Richard D. (1994) 'State-Owned Enterprise Reform Through Performance Contracts: The Bolivian Experiment,' *World Development*, vol. 22, no. 6, pp. 925–34.

Malloy, James M. (1970) *Bolivia: The Uncompleted Revolution* (Pittsburg, PA: University of Pittsburgh Press).

Malloy, James M. and Gamarra, Eduardo A. (1988) *Revolution and Reaction: Bolivia 1964–1984* (New Brunswick: Transaction Publishers).

Malloy, James M. and Thorn, Richard (eds.) (1971) *Beyond the Revolution: Bolivia since 1952* (Pittsburgh: University of Pittsburgh Press).

Mamani Condori, Carlos B. (1991) *Taraqu, 1866–1935: Masacre, guerra y 'Renovación' en la biografía de Eduardo L. Nina Qhispi* (La Paz: Aruwiyiri).

Mariaca, Juvenal and Peñaranda, Arturo (1918) *Proyecto de organización de una escuela normal agrícola de indígenas en el altiplano* (La Paz: Boliviana).

Marshall, Katherine (1992) 'The Genesis and Early Debates,' in Steen Jorgensen, Margaret Grosh and Mark Schacter (eds.), *Bolivia's Answer to Poverty, Economic Crisis, and Adjustment: The Emergency Social Fund* (Washington, DC: World Bank), pp. 25–32.

Martin, Cheryl English (1996) *Governance and Society in Colonial Mexico. Chihuahua in the Eighteenth Century* (Stanford).

Martínez P., Juan Luis (1988) *Políticas educativas en Bolivia 1950–1988 (Estado de arte)* (La Paz: CEBIAE).

Martínez P., Juan Luis (1995) *Reformas educativas comparadas. Bolivia, México, Chile, España Estado del arte* (La Paz: CEBIAE).

Mayorga U., J. Antonio (1996) *Gonismo: Discurso y poder* (Cochabamba, Bolivia: UMSS).

Mayorga, F. (2002) 'El discurso nacionalista,' in Tiempo Político (La Paz: La Razón).

Mayorga, René Antonio (1997a) 'Bolivia's Silent Revolution,' *Journal of Democracy*, vol. 8, no. 1, pp. 142–56.

Mayorga, René Antonio (1997b) 'Presidencialismo parlamentarizado y procesos de decision en Bolivia,' *Revista Paraguaya de Sociología*, año 34, no. 100 (September–December).

Mayorga, René Antonio (1999) 'La democracia o el desafío de la modernización política,' in Fernando Campero Prudencio (ed.), *Bolivia en el Siglo XX* (La Paz: Harvard Club de Bolivia), pp. 329–58.

McCaa, Robert (forthcoming) 'Missing Millions: The Demographic Costs of the Mexican Revolution', *Mexican Studies/Estudios Mexicanos.*

McClintock, Anne (1995) *Imperial Leather. Race, Gender and Sexuality in the Colonial Contest* (New York: Routledge).

McEwen, William J. (1975) *Changing Rural Bolivia. A Study of Communities in Bolivia* (New York: Oxford University Press).

McGinn, Noel (2002) 'Why We Should End Reforms in Education,' paper presented to the Inter-American Developent Bank's Regional Policy Dialogue Education Network, 4–5 April, Washington, DC, mimeo.

McGinn, Noel and Borden, Allison M. (1995) *Framing Questions, Constructing Answers. Linking Research with Educational Policy for Developing Countries* (Cambridge, Mass.: Harvard Institute for International Development).

McIntyre, Alistair (1971) *Against the Self-Images of the Age* (New York).

Medina, Javier (1997a) *Poderes locales: implementando la Bolivia del próximo milenio* (La Paz: Fondo Editorial FIA/Semilla/CEBIAE).

Medina, Javier (1997b) 'La participación popular como fruto de las luchas socials,' in *El pulso de la democracia: participación ciudadana y descentralización en Bolivia* (República de Bolivia, Caracas: Nueva Sociedad).

Mesa-Lago, Carmelo (1981) *The Economy of Socialist Cuba. A Two-Decade Appraisal* (Albuquerque: University of New Mexico Press).

Meyer, Jean (1986) 'Mexico: Revolution and Reconstruction in the 1920s,' in Leslie Bethell (editor), *The Cambridge History of Latin America, vol. V c. 1970–1930* (Cambridge: Cambridge University Press).

Miller, David (1995), *On Nationality* (Oxford: Oxford University Press).

Ministerio de Desarrollo Económico, Secretaría Nacional de Agricultura y Ganadería (1996) *El agro boliviano: estadísticas agropecuarios 1990–1995* (La Paz), pp. 262–3.

Ministerio de Desarrollo Humano (1995) 'Misión de revisión anual. Proyecto de Reforma Educativa. Ayuda memoria,' La Paz, 5 –13 October, mimeo.

Ministerio de Desarrollo Humano (1996) 'Misión de revisión anual. Proyecto de Reforma Educativa. Ayuda memoria,' La Paz, 23 September –4 October, mimeo.

Ministerio de Educación (1956) *Código de la educación boliviana* (La Paz: Emp. Ind. Gráfica Burillo).

Ministerio de Educación y Bellas Artes (1958) *Plan de fomento de la Educación Nacional* (La Paz: Ministerio de Educación).

Ministerio de Educación, Cultura y Deportes (2000) *Evaluación para todos en el año 2000. Informe de evaluación* (La Paz).

Ministerio de Educación, Cultura y Deportes (2001a) *Información estadística e indicadores escolares, 1996–2000* (La Paz, CD–ROM).

Ministerio de Educación, Cultura y Deportes (2001b) *Logros escolares y factores asociados. 3er año de educación primaria. Resumen* (La Paz).

Ministerio de Educación, Cultura y Deportes (2002a) *Memoria de actividades* (La Paz).

Ministerio de Educación, Cultura y Deportes (2002b) 'Bolivia: Educación para Todos – Fast Track Initiative,' mimeo, September (La Paz).

Ministerio de Salud y Prevision Social, 'Salud de la Mujer … 1995'

Ministry of Education/SCIDE (1948) *Guía de instrucción para maestros rurales* (La Paz, n.p.), no. 1.

Mitchell, Christopher (1977) *The Legacy of Populism in Bolivia. From the MNR to Military Rule* (New York: Praeger).

Molina Monasterios, Fernando (1997) *Historia de la participación popular* (La Paz: Ministerio de Desarrollo Humano, Secretaría Nacional de Participación Popular).

Molina, Sergio and Arias, Iván (1996) *De la nación clandestina a la participación popular* (La Paz: Centro de Documentación e Información).

Moller Pacieri, Edwin (2001) *El Dios desnudo de mi conciencia revolucionaria* (La Paz: Plural Editores).

Monje Ortíz, Zacarías (1942) *Sucasuca mallku* (La Paz: Ed. Universo).

Montenegro, Carlos (1953) *Nacionalismo y coloniaje* (La Paz: Editorial Los Amigos del Libro).

Montenegro, Carlos (1993) *Nacionalismo y coloniaje* (La Paz: Juventud).

Morales, J.A. (1993) 'Bolivian Trade and Development, 1957–87,' in R. Dornbusch (ed.), *Policymaking in the Open Economy*, EDI Series in Economic Development (New York: Oxford University Press), pp. 321–43.

Morales, Juan Antonio (1994) 'Democracy, Economic Liberalism, and Structural Reform in Bolivia,' in William C. Smith, Carlos H. Acuña and Eduardo A. Gamarra (eds.), *Democracy, Markets, and Structural Reform in Latin America* (New Brunswick: Transaction Publishers), pp. 129–48.

Morales, Juan Antonio (1995) *Bolivia and the Slowdown of the Reform Process* (Washington, DC: World Bank).

Morales, Juan Antonio (2001) 'Economic Vulnerability in Bolivia,' in J. Crabtree and L. Whitehead (eds.), *Towards Democratic Viability. The Bolivian Experience*, St. Antony's Series (Oxford: Palgrave), pp. 41–60.

Morales, Juan Antonio and Pacheco, Napoleon (1999) 'Economía. El retorno de los liberales,' in Fernando Campero Prudencio (coord.), *Bolivia en el siglo XX. La formación de la Bolivia contemporánea* (La Paz: Harvard Club de Bolivia), pp. 160–1.

Morales, R. (2000) *Bolivia, política económica, geografía y pobreza* (La Paz: Universidad Andina Simón Bolivar).

Muñoz, Jorge A. and Lavadenz, Isabel (1997) 'Reforming the Agrarian Reform in Bolivia,' Development Discussion Paper no. 589 (Cambridge, MA: Harvard Institute for International Development).

Nash, June (1979) *We Eat the Mines and the Mines Eat Us. Dependency and Exploitation in Bolivian Tin Mines* (New York: Columbia University Press).

Nelson, Raymond (1949) 'Education in Bolivia,' *US Office of Education Bulletin*, vol. 1, p. 21.

Niblo, Stephen R. (1995) *War, Diplomacy and Development. The United States and Mexico, 1938–54* (Wilmington, Del.: Scholarly Resources).

North, D.C. (1990) *Institutions, Institutional Change and Economic Performance* (Cambridge: Cambridge University Press).

O'Donnell, Guillermo (1993) 'On the State, Democratization and Some Conceptual Problems: A Latin American View with Glances at Some Post-Communist Countries,' *World Development* (Special Issue)(1993), vol. 21, no. 8, pp. 1355–70.

O'Donnell, G. (1994) 'Delegative Deomocracy,' *Journal of Democracy*, vol. 5 no. 11, pp. 55–69.

Oficina Nacional de Inmigración y Propaganda Geográfica (ONIPG) (1973), *Censo general de la población de la República de Bolivia...1900,* 2nd edition (Cochabamba), vol. II.

O'Phelan Godoy, Scarlett (1985) *Rebellions and Revolts in Eighteenth-Century Peru and Upper Peru*, Lateinamerikanische Forschungen 14 (Köln: Böhlau).

Orellana, W. (1994) 'El impacto macroeconómico de la ayuda externa,' MA dissertation (La Paz: Universidad Católica Boliviana).

Orozco, Noel (1997) 'La reforma educativa como crisis,' *Revista UNITAS*, no. 17 (February).

Ortiz-Mercado, José (2002), personal communication.

Paige, Jeffrey M. (1978) *Agrarian Revolution: Social Movements and Export Agriculture in the Underdeveloped World* (New York: Free Press).

Paredes M., Rigoberto (1965 [1914]) *La altiplanicie. Anotaciones etnográficas, geográficas, y socials de la comunidad Aymara* (La Paz: ISLA).

Paredes, Rigoberto (1973) *Tupac Catari: apuntes biográficos* [1897] (La Paz: Ediciones ISLA).

Partidos Políticos en Bolivia (1998) *Opiniones y Análisis,* Special Issue (La Paz).

Paz Estenssoro, Victor (1953) 'Discurso del Excelentísimo Señor Presidente de la República … al posesionar a los miembros de la Comisión,' in Ministerio de Educación (1956) (1956) *Código de la educación boliviana* (La Paz: Emp. Ind. Gráfica Burillo).

Paz Estenssoro, Victor and O'Connor d'Arlach, Eduardo Trigo (1999) *Conversaciones con Víctor Paz Estenssoro* (La Paz; Comunicaciones del País).

Pearse, Andrew (1975) *The Latin American Peasant* (London: Cass).

Pedersen, Mogens N. (1979) 'The Dynamics of European Party Systems: Changing Patterns of Electoral Volatility,' *European Journal of Political Research*, vol. 7, p.1-26.

Peñaloza, Luis (1963) *Historia del Movimiento Nacionalista Revolucionario, 1941–1952* (La Paz: Editorial Los Amigos del Libro).

Pérez, Elizardo ([1962] 1992) *Warisata. La escuela-ayllu* (La Paz: HISBOL).

Pike, Frederick (1977) *The United States and the Andean Republics* (Cambridge, MA: Harvard University Pres).

Platt, Tristan (1982) *Estado boliviano y ayllu andino: tierra y tributo en el Norte de Potosí* (Lima: Instituto de Estudios Peruanos).

PNUD (1998), *Desarrollo humano en Bolivia 1998* (La Paz).

Ponce Arauco, Gabriel (1989) 'Los alzamientos campesinos de 1947,' *Busqueda*, vol. 1, no. 1 (March), pp. 107–28.

Prada Alcoreza, Raul (1994) *Análisis sociodemográfico: poblaciones nativas* (La Paz: INE).

Prado Salmon, General Gary (1984) *Poder y fuerzas armadas 1949–82* (Cochabamba: Los Amigos del Libro).

Puiggrós, Adriana (1996) 'Educación neoliberal y quiebre educativo,' *Nueva Sociedad*, no. 146 (November–December).

Qayum, Seemin (2002) 'Nationalism, Internal Colonialism and the Spatial Imagination: The Geographical Society of La Paz in Turn-of-the Century Bolivia,' in James Dunkerley (ed), *Studies in the Formation of the Nation State in Latin America* (London: Institute of Latin American Studies), pp. 275–98.

Rasnake, Roger (1988) *Domination and Cultural Resistance: Authority and Power among an Andean People* (Durham, NC: Duke University Press).

Reed, John (1969) *Insurgent Mexico* (New York: Greenwood Press).

Republica de Bolivia (1950) *Censo demografico de 1950* (La Paz: Ministerio de Hacienda y Estadística, Dirección General de Estadísticas y Censo).

Rippy, J. Fred (1931) *The United States and Mexico* (New York: F.S. Crofts and Co).

Rivera, Alberto (1992) *Los terratenientes de Cochabamba* (Cochabamba: CERES/FACES).

Rivera Cusicanqui, Silvia (1984) *'Oprimidos pero no vencidos': luchas del campesinado aymara y quechwa, 1900–1980* (La Paz: UNRISD, HISBOL, CSTUCB).

Rivera Cusicanqui, Silvia (1986) *Oprimidos pero no vencidos: luchas del campesinado aymara y qhechwa, 1900–1980* (La Paz: UNRISD).

Rivera Cusicanqui, Silvia (1993) 'El raíz: colonizadores y colonizados,' in Xavier Albó and Raúl Barrios (eds.), *Violencias encubiertas en Bolivia 1* (La Paz: CIPCA and Aruwiyiri).

Rivera C., Silvia and the Taller de Historia Oral Andina (THOA) (1990) 'Indigenous Women and Community Resistance: History and Memory,' in Elizabeth Jelín (ed.), *Women and Social Change in Latin America* (London: Ded), pp. 151–83.

Rivera P., Jorge (1992) 'Bolivia: Society, State, and Education in Crisis,' in Daniel A. Morales-Gómez and Carlos Alberto Torres (eds.), *Education, Policy, and Social Change. Experiences from Latin America* (Westport, Conn.: Praeger).

Roca, Jose Luis (1979) *Fisonomia del regionalismo boliviano* (Cochabamba: Los Amigos del Libro).

Rodas, Hugo (1996) *Huanchaca: modelo político empresarial de la cocaina en Bolivia* (La Paz: Plural Editores).

Rodrigo, Saturnino (1955) *Diário de la revolución* (La Paz: Libería Editorial 'Juventud').

Rodríguez Ostria, Gustavo (1991a) *El socavón y el sindicato: ensayos historicas sobre las trabajadores mineros* (La Paz: Ildis).

Rodríguez, Gustavo (1991b) 'Entre reformas y contrareformas: las comunidades indígenas en el Valle Bajo cochabambino (1825–1900),' in Heraclio Bonilla (ed.), *Los Andes en la encrucijada: indios, comunidades y Estado en el siglo XIX* (Quito: Flacso).

Rodrik, D. (1997) *Has Globalization Gone Too Far?* (Washington, DC: Institute For International Economics).

Rodrik, D. (1999) *The New Global Economy and Developing Countries: Making Openness Work* (Washington, DC: Overseas Development Council).

Rojas, Gonzalo and Zuazo, Moira (1996) *Los problemas de representatividad del sistema democrático boliviano: bajo el signo de la reforma del Estado*, Debate Político 1 (La Paz: Instituto Latinoamericano de Investigaciones Sociales).

Roseberry, William (1994) 'Hegemony and the Language of Contention,' in Gilbert M. Joseph and Daniel Nugent (eds.), *Everyday Forms of State Formation: Revolution and the Negotiation of Rule in Modern Mexico* (Durham, NC: Duke University Press, 1994), pp. 355–66.

Rouquié, Alain (1987) *The Military and the State in Latin America* (Berkeley: University of California Press).

Roxborough, Ian (1989) 'Theories of Revolution: The Evidence from Latin America,' *LSE Quarterly*, vol. 3, no. 2 (Spring).

Ruiz-Mier, Fernando (2001) 'Human Development in a Multi-ethnic Society,' in John Crabtree and Laurence Whitehead (eds.) *Towards Democratic Viability: The Bolivian Experience* (Oxford: Palgrave), pp. 120–137.

Saavedra, Bautista (1987 [1904]) *El ayllu. Estudios sociológicos* (La Paz: Juventud).

Sachs, Jeffrey (1987) 'The Bolivian Hyperinflation and Stabilization,' *American Economic Review*, vol. 77, no. 2, pp. 279–83.

Sachs J., and Morales, J.A. (1988) *Bolivia 1952–1986,* Country Studies 6 (San Francisco: International Center for Economic Growth).

Salazar Mostajo, Carlos (1997) *Warisata mía* (La Paz: Juventud), 3rd edition.

Salmón Ballivian, José (1926) 'El indio íntimo. Contribución al estudio biológico social del indio,' in, *Ideario aimara* (La Paz: Salesiana), pp. 105–163.

Salmón, Josefa (1997) *El espejo indígena: El discurso indigenista en Bolivia, 1900–1956* (La Paz: Plural).

Sánchez de Lozada, Antonio (2001) 'Accountability in the Transition to Democracy,' in John Crabtree and Laurence Whitehead (eds.), *Towards Democratic Viability: The Bolivian Experience* (Oxford: Palgrave).

Sandoval Morón family, *Bolivia: Revolucion y Contrarevolución en el Oriente* (1952–1964) (unpublished).

Sandóval, Godofredo et al. (1998) *Organizaciones de base y desarrollo local en Bolivia: estudio de los municipios de Tiahuanaco, Mizque, Villa Serrano y Charagua,* Working Paper no. 4 (Washington, DC: World Bank, Local Level Institutions).

Sanjines Uriarte, Marcelo (1968) *Educación rural y desarrollo en Bolivia* (La Paz: Editorial Don Bosco).

Santos, Gonzalo N. (1984) *Memorias* (Mexico: Grijalbo)

Saragoza, Alex (1988) *The Monterrey Elite and the Mexican State, 1880–1940* (Austin: University of Texas Press).

Schmitter, Philippe (1974) 'Still the Century of Corporatism?,' in Frederick Pike and Thomas Stritch (eds.), *The New Corporatism: Social-Political Structures in the Iberian World* (Notre Dame: University of Notre Dame Press).

Schülz Heiss, Gunther (1996) 'Revisión del diseño del Programa de la Reforma Educativa. Hacia un plan de ejecución del programa para los años 1997 a 1002,' documento presentado a la Subsecretaría de Educación Preescolar, Primaria y Secundaria. La Paz, mimeo.

SCIDE (1955) *Rural Education in Bolivia. A Study in Technical Cooperation* (La Paz: IIAA).

Scott, James C. (1976) *The Moral Economy of the Peasant* (New Haven: Yale University Press).

Secretaría Nacional de Educación (1995) 'Informe de avance de ejecución, febrero 1994–agosto 1995,' Misión de evaluación 5–15 de octubre de 1995, La Paz, Ministerio de Desarrollo Humano, UNAS, UNSTP.

Secretaría Nacional de Educación (1996) 'Programa de Reforma Educativa. Informe de avance período septiembre 1995–julio 1996,' La Paz, Ministerio de Desarrollo Humano, Subsecretaría de Educación Preescolar, Primaria y Secundaria.

Seligson, Mitchell (1999a) 'Bolivia's DDCP Program: An Audit of Citizen Impact, 1999' (Pittsburgh: University of Pittsburgh), unpublished paper.

Seligson, Mitchell (1999b) *La cultura politica de la democracia boliviana* (La Paz: Encuestas y Estudios, Asi piensan los bolivianos), no. 60.

Serulnikov, Sergio (1996) 'Disputed Images of Colonialism: Spanish Rule and Indian Subversion in Northern Potosí, 1777–1780,' *Hispanic American Historical Review*, vol. 76, no. 2, pp. 189–226.

Serulnikov, Sergio (forthcoming) 'Andean Political Imagination in the Late Eighteenth Century,' in Nils Jacobsen and Cristóbal Aljovín (eds.), *Political Cultures in the Andes, 1750–1950* (Durham, NC: Duke University Press).

Siekmeyer, James (1999) *Aid, Nationalism, and Inter-American Relations. Guatemala, Bolivia and the United States, 1945–1961* (Lewiston: Edwin Mellen Press).

Solís, Leopoldo (1971) *La realidad económica mexicana: retrovisión y perspectivas* (Mexico: Siglo Veintiuno).

Soria Choque, Vitaliano (1992) 'Los caciques-apoderados y la lucha por la escuela, 1900–1952,' Roberto Choque et al. (eds.), *Educación indígena: ¿ciudadanía o colonización?* (La Paz: Aruwiyiri), pp. 41–78.

Stepan, Nancy (1991) *The 'Hour of Eugenics.' Race, Gender and Nation in Latin America* (Ithaca: Cornell University Press).

Stephenson, Marcia (1999) *Gender and Modernity in Andean Bolivia* (Austin: University of Texas).

Stephenson, Marcia (2002) 'Forging an Indigenous Counterpublic Sphere: The Taller de Historia Oral Andina in Bolivia,' in *Latin American Research Review*, vol. 31, pp. 99–118.

Stokes, J.W. (1963) 'The Counterproductive Consequences of the Foreign Aid in Bolivia,' in H. Shoeck and J. Wiggins (eds.) *The New Argument in Economics: The Public versus the Private Sector* (New York: Van Nostrand Company), pp. 145–85.

Stoler, Ann Laura (1995) *Race and the Education of Desire. Foucault's History of Sexuality and the Colonial Order of Things* (Durham, NC: Duke University Press), 2nd edition.

Suárez Findlay, Eileen (1999) *Imposing Decency: The Politics of Sexuality and Race in Puerto Rico, 1870–1920* (Durham, NC: Duke University Press).

Szasz, Margaret (1974) *Education and the American Indian. The Road to Self-Determination, 1928–1973* (Albuquerque: University of New Mexico).

Talavera, Maria (1999) *Otras voces, otros maestros: aproximación a los procesos de innovación y resisitencia en tres escuelas del Programa de Reforma Educativa, ciudad de La Paz, 1997–1998* (La Paz: PIEB).

Tamayo, Franz (1988 [1910]) *Creación de una pedagogía nacional* (La Paz: Juventud).

Tapia, Luis (2001) 'Movimiento societal,' in *Pluriverso: teoría política boliviana* (La Paz: Editorial Muela del Diablo).

Tapia, Luis (2002) *La producción del conocimiento local: historia y política en la obra de René Zavaleta* (La Paz: Muela del Diablo Editores).

Taussig, Michael T. (1980) *The Devil and Commodity Fetishism in South America* (Chapel Hill: University of North Carolina Press).

Thoburn, John (1994) Tin in the World Economy (Edinburgh: Edinburgh University Press).

Thomas, Hugh (1967) 'Middle-Class Politics and the Cuban Revolution,' in Claudio Véliz (ed.), *The Politics of Conformity in Latin America* (London: Oxford University Press for the Royal Institute of International Affairs).

Thomson, Sinclair (1996) 'Colonial Crisis, Community, and Andean Self-Rule: Aymara Politics in the Age of Insurgency (Eighteenth-Century La Paz),' PhD dissertation (University of Wisconsin-Madison).

Thomson, Sinclair (1999) '"We Alone Will Rule...": Recovering the Range of Anticolonial Projects among Andean Peasants (La Paz, 1740s to 1781),' *Colonial Latin American Review*, vol. 8, no. 2, pp. 275–99.

Thomson, Sinclair (2003) *We Alone Will Rule: Native Andean Politics in the Age of Insurgency* (Madison: University of Wisconsin Press).

Thorn, Richard (1971) 'The Economic Transformation,' in James M. Malloy and Richard S. Thorn (eds.), *Beyond the Revolution. Bolivia since 1952* (Pittsburgh: University of Pittsburgh Press).

Ticona Alejo, Estaban (1992) 'Conceptualización de la educación y alfabetización en Eduardo Leandro Nina Qhispi,' Roberto Choque et al. (eds.), *Educación indígena: ¿ciudadanía o colonización?* (La Paz: Aruwiyiri), pp. 99–108.

Ticona, Esteban and Albó, Xavier (1997) *Jesús de Machaqa: la marka rebelde, 3. La lucha por el poder comunal* (La Paz: CIPCA/CEDOIN, 1997).

Ticona, Esteban, Rojas, Gonzalo and Albó, Xavier (1995) *Votos y whipalas: campesinos y pueblos originarios en democracia* (La Paz: Fundación Milenio [Serie Temas de Modernización] and Centro de Investigación y Promoción del Campesinado [Cuadernos de Investigación 43]).

Toranzo Roca, Carlos (1999) 'Introducción,' in Fernando Campero Prudencio (ed.), *Bolivia en el Siglo XX* (La Paz: Harvard Club de Bolivia), pp. 1–19.

Toranzo, Carlos (1998) 'Banzer un Año Despues,' *Cuarto Intermedio* (August)

Trouillot, Michel-Rolph (1995) *Silencing the Past: Power and the Production of History* (Boston: Beacon Press).

Tuchschneider, David (1996) *La participación popular: avances y obstáculos* (La Paz: Unidad de Investigación y Análisis, Secretaría Nacional de Participación Popular, Plural Editores, CID, UDAPE).

UDAPE (2000) 'Estrategia para la reduccion de la pobreza' (La Paz: Unidad de Analisis de Política Económica).

Ulloa, Berta (1997) 'The US Government versus the Mexican Revolution, 1910–1917,' in Jaime E. Rodriguez O. and Kathryn Vincent (eds.), *Myths, Misdeeds and Misunderstandings* (Wilmington: SR Books).

United Nations (2000) *Demographic Yearbook, Historical Supplement* [1948/1997] (New York: United Nations).

United Nations Development Program (UNDP) (1998) *Human Development Report.*

United Nations Development Program (UNDP) (2002) *Informe de Desarrollo Humano en Bolivia* (La Paz: UNDP).

Uriarte, Marcelo Sanginés (1968) *Educación rural y desarrollo en Bolivia* (La Paz: Ed. Don Bosco).

Urioste, Miguel (1987) *Segunda reforma agraria* (La Paz: CEDLA).

Urioste, Miguel and Baldomar, Luis (1996) 'Ley de Participación Popular: seguimiento crítico,' in Gonzalo Rojas Ortuste (ed.), *La Participación Popular: avances y obstáculos* (La Paz: Grupo DRU/SNPP).

Urquiola, Miguel (2000) 'Educación primaria universal,' in *Remontando la pobreza. Ocho cimas a la vez* (La Paz: EDOBOL).

Urquiola, Miguel et al. (1999) 'Geography and Development in Bolivia: Migration, Urban and Industrial Concentration, Welfare, and Convergence: 1950–1992' (La Paz: Universidad Cátolica Boliviana).

Urquiola, Miguel et al. (2001) *Los maestros en Bolivia. Impacto, incentivos, y desempeño* (La Paz: Sierpe).

Valencia Vega, Alipio (1979 [1950]) *Julián Tupak Katari: Caudillo de la liberación india* (La Paz: Juventud).

Valle de Siles, María Eugenia del (1990) *Historia de la rebelión de Tupac Catari, 1781-1782* (La Paz: Editorial Don Bosco).

Van Cott, Donna Lee (ed.) (1994) *Indigenous Peoples and Democracy in Latin America* (Washington, DC: Inter-American Dialogue).

Van Cott, Donna Lee (2000) *The Friendly Liquidation of the Past: The Politics of Diversity in Latin America* (Pittsburgh: University of Pittsburgh Press).

Vaughan, Mary Kay (1982) *The State, Education, and Social Class in Mexico, 1880–1928* (DeKalb: Northern Illinois University Press).

Vaughn, Mary Kay (1997) *Cultural Politics of Revolution. Teachers, Peasants, and Schools in Mexico, 1930–1940* (Tucson: University of Arizona).

Vázquez, Josefina Zoraida and Meyer, Lorenzo (1985) *The United States and Mexico* (Chicago: University of Chicago Press).

Viceministerio de Educación Inicial, Primaria y Secundaria (2000) 'La reforma educativa: una realidad indiscutible en las escuelas,' *Nuevas Palabras*, epoca 2, no. 28. http://www.cebiae.edu.bo/nuevo28.html.

Watt, Donald Cameron (1989) *How War Came. The Immediate Origins of the Second World War 1938–1939* (London: Heinemann).

Wells, Allen (1985) *Yucatán's Gilded Age. Haciendas, Henequen and International Harvester, 1860–1915* (Albuquerque: University of New Mexico Press), chapter 6.

Wennergren, E. Boyd and Whitaker, Morris D. (1975) *The Status of Bolivian Agriculture* (New York: Praeger).

Westoff, Charles and Bankole, Akinrinola (2000) 'Trends in the Demand for Family Limitation in Developing Countries,' *International Family Planning Perspectives*, vol. 26, no. 2 (June).

Whitehead, Laurence (1972) 'El impacto de la gran depresión en Bolivia,' *Desarrollo Económico*, no. 45 (April–June 1972).

Whitehead, Laurence (1973) 'National Power and Local Power: The Case of Santa Cruz de la Sierra, Bolivia,' in Francine F. Rabinowitz and Felicity M. Trueblood (eds.), *Latin American Urban Research*, vol. III (Beverly Hills: Sage).

Whitehead, Laurence (1974–75), 'El estado y los intereses seccionales: el caso Boliviano,' *Estudios Andinos*, vol. 4, no. 1.

Whitehead, Laurence (1981) 'Miners as Voters: The Electoral Process in Bolivia's Mining Camps,' *Journal of Latin American Studies*, vol. 13, no. 2 (November).

Whitehead, Laurence (1986) 'Bolivia's Frustrated Democratic Transition 1977–1980,' in Guillermo O'Donnell, P. Schmitter and L. Whitehead, *Transitions from Authoritarian Rule: Prospects for Democracy* (Baltimore: Johns Hopkins University Press).

Whitehead, Laurence (1991), 'Bolivia since 1930,' in Leslie Bethell (ed.)., *The Cambridge History of Latin America*, vol.. VIII (Cambridge: Cambridge University Press).

Whitehead, Laurence (1992) 'Bolivia,' in Leslie Bethell and Ian Roxborough (eds.), *Latin America between the Second World War and the Cold War, 1944–1948* (Cambridge: Cambridge University Press)

Whitehead, Laurence (1998) 'State Organization in Latin America since 1930,' in Leslie Bethell (ed.), *Latin America: Economy and Society since 1930* (Cambridge: Cambridge University Press), pp. 381–411.

Widmark, Charlotta (2001) 'Education as Expanding Freedoms for the Poor in Bolivia,' a contribution to the Poverty Conference, 18 October, Sida, Stockholm, mimeo.

Wilkie, James (1974) *Statistics and National Policy*, Supplement 3, *UCLA Statistical Abstract of Latin America* (Los Angeles: UCLA Latin American Center Publications).

Womack Jr, John (1969) *Zapata and the Mexican Revolution* (London: Thames and Hudson).

World Bank (1972) *Current Economic Position and Prospects of Bolivia*, Report No. WH–213 (a) (Washington, DC: The World Bank).

World Bank (1977) *Staff Project Report. First Education and Vocational Training Project in Bolivia,* Report No. 1367a–BO (Washington, DC: The World Bank).

World Bank (1983) *Bolivia. Structural Constraints and Development Prospects*, Report No. 4194–BO (Washington, DC: The World Bank).

World Bank (1988) *Project Completion Report. Bolivia First Education and Vocational Training Project (Loan 1404–BO)* (Washington, DC: The World Bank).

World Bank (1993) *Bolivia. Education Sector: A Proposed Strategy for Sector Development and International Assistance*, Report No. 12042–BO (Washington, DC: The World Bank).

World Bank (1997) *World Tables* (Washington, DC: World Bank).

World Bank (2000) 'From Patronage to a Professional State: Bolivia Institutional and Governance Review,' Report No. 201115 – BO, PREM, Latin America and the Caribbean Region, Wash. D.C.

World Bank (2001), *World Development Indicators* (Washington, DC: World Bank).

Yapu, Mario (2002) 'Evolución y prácticas de formación docente en Bolivia,' *Tinkazos. Revista Boliviana de Ciencias Sociales*, no. 11 (February).

Yashar, Deborah (1998) 'Contesting Citizenship: Indigenous Movements and Democracy in Latin America,' *Comparative Politics,* vol. 31 (October).

Yashar, Deborah (1999) 'Democracy, Indigenous Movements and the Post-Liberal Challenge,' *World Politics*, vol. 52 (October).

Zavaleta Mercado, René (1986) *Lo nacional-popular en Bolivia* (Mexico City: Siglo XX).

Zavaleta, René (1990 [1967]) *La formación de la conciencia nacional* (Cochabamba: Editorial Los Amigos del Libro).

Zondag, Cornelius (1966) *The Bolivian Economy 1952–1965* (New York: Frederick Praeger).

Zulawski, Ann (2000) 'Hygiene and the "Indian Problem": Ethnicity and Medicine in Bolivia, 1910–1920,' *Latin American Research Review*, vol. 35, pp. 107–129.

Index

Abaroa, Eduardo, remains repatriated, 157
Acción Democrática Nacionalista (ADN), 2, 289–90, 296, 308, 310, 315, 320, 322, 324–30, 337, 353
Achacachi, 35, 159, 360
agrarian reform, 1–3, 5, 9, 14, 16, 18–20, 26, 29, 31, 58, 156, 177, 203, 261, 294, 301, 349-50, 359
  Decree of Land Reform (1953), 236
  gives peasant freedom to migrate to cities, 264, 282
  gives MNR strong presence in rural areas, 336
  in Mexico, 59, 183, 282
  in Peru, 121
  Mexican experts employed, 73
  produces drop in food supply, 216
Alexander, Robert, 91, 101
Allende, Salvador, 43, 69
Alliance for Progress, *see* USA
Almaraz, Sergio, 106–108, 140, 153
American Federation of Labor (AF of L), 91, 101
Anaya, Amalia, 332–3
Aramayo, 147–8, 152–6
Argentina, 27, 64, 186–7, 223, 243
  Bolivia imports wheat from, 196
  Perón, 27, 198
  Peronists, 318–19, 339
  universal suffrage in, 32
  'whitening' of, 183, 187
Asamblea del Pueblo/Popular (1971), 41, 44, 140, 295, 376
Aymara, 2, 11, 118, 121, 129, 189, 192, 200, 236, 249–50
  Aymara women, 190, 201
Ayopaya, 145, 169-75, 196

Ballivián Rojas, Hugo (General), 66, 151, 157
Banzer Suárez, Hugo (General), 139, 218, 220, 283, 289, 295, 310, 312, 322, 326, 327, 361, 376
Barrientos, René (General), 34, 68, 74–5, 78, 137, 350
Bogotazo, 32
Brazil, 27, 183, 184, 185, 186, 187, 198, 256, 348
  Bolivia has better literacy rate than 245
  universal suffrage in, 32
  Vargas, 27
Busch, Germán, 27, 66, 137, 143, 146–50, 155, 191
  beats up Alcides Arguedas, 146
  decree of 7 June 1939, 147
Bush, George W., 293, 298

Cabot, John Moors, 103
Calvi, Humberto, 172
Cananea, 62, 63
Caquiaviri, 169

Cárdenas, Lázaro, 63, 65, 68, 70–1, 73–5, 77, 183, 186, 268
Cárdenas, Víctor Hugo, 118, 356
Castro, Rubén Julio, 75
Catavi massacre, 101, 138, 153, 196–7
Catholic Church, 33, 38, 56–7, 72, 74, 273, 276
Central Intelligence Agency (CIA), 27
Central Obrera Boliviana (COB), 5, 27, 29–31, 34–7, 44–5, 98, 137, 262, 332, 335–6
coca growers' increased influence, 302
escapes control of MNR, 71
factions emerge, 8
influence in 1952 government, 335
opposition to education reform, 276, 278
participates in Asamblea del Pueblo, 295
strength beyond unions, 45
weakened in 1980s, 308
Céspedes, Augusto, 138, 143–4
ambassador in Asunción, 145
Chaco War, 11, 12, 30, 58, 66, 121, 136–7, 143–4, 147–8, 156, 167–8, 185, 192, 215, 368–9
highlights weakness of state, 366
impact on perception of Indians, 191
sharpens nationalism, 27, 41
surviving veterans, 137
Chávez Ortiz, Ñuflo, 138, 177
Chile, 27, 32, 41, 183, 223
universal suffrage in, 32
China, 3, 7, 25, 26, 27, 42, 43, 55, 66
Chuquisaca, 35
Cliza, 35, 36
coca-cocaine, 293, 297–8, 302
Cochabamba, 2, 70, 75, 167, 169, 171, 178, 185, 234, 302
Chapare Valley, 297-99, 302, 314, 316, 361
mass mobilization in 2000, 44
connecting road with Santa Cruz, 216
Cold War, 25, 97, 98, 108, 137, 143–4, 213, 375
Colombia, 25, 27, 214, 348
Comité Indigenal Boliviano, 166–7
Conciencia de Patria (CONDEPA), 290
Condorcanqui, José Gabriel, *see* Túpac Amaru
Confederación Sindical Unica de Trabajadores Campesinos de Bolivia (CSUTCB), 34, 120, 302–3, 332, 350, 358
Congress of Industrial Organizations (CIO), 101
Constitutional Convention (1938), 42
contraception, 242
Corporación Minera de Bolivia (COMIBOL), 217, 219, 328
Cuba, 1–2, 6–7, 9, 2–6, 34, 37–8, 40, 42, 47, 63, 67, 93, 105, 259, 267–9, 282, 378
Batista coup, 27
Bay of Pigs, 37, 39
education campaign, 268
iconography of revolution, 2
Soviet client, 78

Díaz, Porfirio, 68, 76, 105
Donoso Torres, Vicente, 195–7, 202

Ecuador, 300
universal suffrage in, 32
education reform, 16, 185, 245, 261, 262, 263
1955 reform, 16, 259, 333
1994 reform, 16, 17, 259, 283, 333
Eid Franco, Oscar, 374
Eisenhower, Dwight D., *see* USA
Eisenhower, Milton, 103
elections, 40, 306
(1951), 4–5, 28, 32, 67, 104
(1978), 6
(1979), 6
(1980), 6
(1985), 337
(1989), 329, 332
(1993), 325, 327
(1997), 306, 325, 327
(2002), 136, 289, 291–2, 296, 299, 301, 306, 312
local, decline in voters, 352–3

Falange Socialista Boliviano (FSB), 28, 41, 65
Federación Sindical de Trabajadores de Bolivia, 5, 37
Federación Sindical de Trabajadores Mineros de Bolivia (FSTMB), 71, 137, 302, 335
Flores, Felipe, 290
France, 3, 7, 25, 42, 55, 365

Galarza, Ernesto, 101, 102
García Meza, 295, 376
Guaraní, 2, 261, 278
Guatemala, 9, 43, 77, 93, 98, 100, 105, 107, 223, 301
overthrow of Arbenz, 27
universal suffrage in, 32
Guevara Arze, Walter, 1, 99, 138, 145–6, 289
Guevara de la Serna, Ernesto (Che), 44, 140

Haiti, 15, 223, 243, 254–5, 372
Hertzog, Enrique, 151, 156, 168, 172, 176
Hochschild, 146–7, 153, 163
Honduras, 223, 254
Hoz de Vila, Tito, 296
hyperinflation, 297

Ibáñez, Carlos, 27
indianismo, 120
Indigenous Congress (1945), 12, 164-178
infant mortality, 236
Inter-American Development Bank, 280
International Labor Office, 198
International Monetary Fund (IMF), 5, 29, 33, 38, 336
Iran, 27, 107
overthrow of Mossadeq government, 27

Jalisco, 70
Jesús de Machaca, 121
Juárez, Benito, 57, 58, 64

Kami, 35
Katari, Tomás, 108, 118, 128
katarismo, 120, 131, 356

Korean War, 27, 98, 154
Kornilov, Lavr Georgiyevich, 69

La Paz, 2, 186, 188, 189, 191
land reform, *see* agrarian reform
Land Tenure Center at Madison Wisconsin, 34
Lechín Oquendo, Juan, 11, 29, 40, 44, 73, 98–9, 103–6, 137, 140, 289, 335
 controls power on street in 1952, 30
 entrista policies, 99
 decorated by Banzer, 139
 expelled from MNR, 78
 in center-left coalition, 74, 98
 leads COB, 5, 27
 leads PRIN, 37
 USA dubious about, 37, 39, 99–100, 106
 vice-president, 34
 wounded in Chaco War, 144
life expectancy, 223, 238–43
literacy, 15, 223, 236, 248
 lower levels for women, 248
Llallagua,, 62
Lora, Guillermo, 140

Maclean (McLean), Ronald, 296, 327
Mariano Melgarejo, 57
Mariátegui, José Carlos, 127, 128
Marxism, 45
 in exile, 145
 considered too 'cosmopolitan', 216
McCarthyism, 27
Mesa Gisbert, Carlos Diego, 1, 132, 292, 293
 anti-corruption plan, 293
Mexico, 1–9, 25–27, 37, 41–2, 46, 55–8, 63, 183–5, 213–15, 218, 259, 282, 301, 365, 375, 378
 Amaro, Joaquín, 68–9
 Ávila Camacho, Manuel, 68
 Calles, Plutarco Elías (and *Callismo*), 67–9, 72–3, 75, 105, 268
 Carranza, Venustiano (and *Carrancismo*), 57, 67, 69, 77, 93, 95–6, 104–6, 108
 Confederación Regional Obrera Mexicana (CROM), 71, 74
 Confederación de Trabajadores de México (CTM), 71
 Cristeros, 69
 Huerta, Victoriano, 69, 73, 77, 105
 Madero, Francisco (and *Maderismo*), 57, 61–9, 93–6
 Magaña, Gildardo, 75
 Maximato, 70
 Obregón, Alvaro, 67–9, 75, 95–6, 104–5, 268
 Porfirian state, 57–8
 Partido Nacional Revolucionario (PNR), 66
 Partido de la Revolución Mexicana (PRM), 66
 Partido Revolucionario Institucional (PRI), 9, 45–7, 54, 64, 66, 318–19, 339
 students become political force, 64
 universal suffrage in, 32
 Villa, Pancho (and *Villismo*), 57, 95, 105

Zapata, Emiliano (and *Zapatismo*), 57, 68, 75, 95, 104–5
migration, 15, 195–6, 238, 240, 251, 254–5
military, 4–9, 12, 20, 27–31, 34, 165, 373
1964 coup, 25, 54, 78, 219, 289, 295–6, 350
Pacto Militar Campesino, 350
relations with Paz Estenssoro, 39
mining, 5, 11, 14, 30, 35, 37, 56, 61–2, 102, 125, 217, 219, 226, 232, 252, 254, 302, 335
Catavi/Siglo XX *sindicato*, 35–6, 59–60
collapse of tin mining, 297
Huanuni *sindicato*, 36
loss of significance, 141–2
nationalized, 294
Miranda, Toribio, 172
Monje Ortíz, Zacarías, 122, 130
Montenegro, Carlos, 138–9, 345
Morales, Evo, 289, 291, 300, 304–9, 374, 377
controls Chapare, 299
opposition to gas sales to USA, 293, 299
surprise performance at 2002 presidential elections, 290
Morón, Salvador, 75
Movimiento al Socialismo (MAS), 290, 304, 377
Movimiento de la Izquierda Revolucionaria (MIR), 42, 289, 296, 324, 353
lacks electoral base, 296
survival will depend on ability to transcend the Paz Zamora era, 297
Movimiento Indio Pachacuti (MIP), 290, 304
Movimiento Nacional Revolucionario (MNR), 1–9, 11-12, 14, 17-18, 20, 25–47, 54–5, 60, 63–78, 225, 261
adopts developmentalist strategy, 14
banned in 1974, 6
becomes party of neoliberal reform, 20, 220, 318–339
commemorates 50th anniversary of Revolution, 136
corruption, 227, 293
dealings with USA, 97–108, 199, 374
education, 266, 271
electoral framework, 289, 305–6
establishes universal suffreage, 237
implements Villarroel decrees, 177–8
inspired by PRI, 215
katarista alliance, 356
left marginalized, 5
moves to the right, 139
nationalist doctrine, 216, 359
origins, 4
urban, educated, middle-class, 63, 219
Movimiento Nacionalista Revolucionario Auténtico (MNRA), 65, 74
MNR Izquierda, 336
Movimiento Revolucionario

Túpac Katari (MRTK), 290, 356

nationalization, 1, 5, 14, 16, 18–20, 31, 100, 108, 177, 261
neoliberalism, 20, 323, 327
Nicaragua, 2–3, 6, 9, 25, 40–2, 47, 221, 254, 378
non-governmental organizations (NGOs), 17, 276, 303, 357–61
Nor Yungas, 35
Norte de Potosí, 35
Nueva Fuerza Republicana, 290–1, 306, 322, 354
Nueva Política Económica, 18, 299, 323, 328

Olivera, Oscar, 302
Ortuño, Fructuoso, 172–3
Oruro, 2
Ovando, 74

Pacto Militar-Campesino, 33, 350
Paraguay, 144–5, 149, 161
Partido de la Izquierda Revolucionaria (PIR), 28, 140, 144, 146–7, 198
Partido Obrero Revolucionario (POR), 127
Partido Revolucionario de la Izquierda Nacionalista (PRIN), 37
Partido Socialista Obrero Boliviano (PSOB), 127
Patiño Mines and Enterprises Consolidated, 35, 60, 102, 105, 145, 147–8, 152, 155
Paz Estenssoro, Víctor, 1, 8, 29, 30–31, 37–8, 40, 44, 65, 78, 98– 105, 137–8, 145, 150, 156, 219, 262, 271, 289, 319, 323, 326–7, 330, 333–8
1980s' reversal of 1950s' policies, 31
alliance with AND, 337
break with COB, 37
center-left coalition, 74, 98–9
complicit in demise of revolution, 8
constructs nationalist project, 31
education, 262, 271
elected to third term (1964), 6, 327
fourth term, 327 (1985)
MNR recognized by USA, 91
nationalizes mines, 108
reliance on army, 78
returns from exile, 5, 137
returns to presidency in 1985, 6
second administration (1960), 37–8, 219, 327
states of siege, 324
Supreme Decree 21060 (Nueva Política Económica), 220, 323
Triangular Plan, 34, 71
US support, 10, 78, 99–102
Paz Zamora, Jaime, 273, 283, 291, 296–8, 320, 324, 329, 332–3, 337
assumes presidency (1989), 324, 332
fourth in 2002 presidential elections, 290
struggles to hold MIR together, 296–7
supported by AND, 337
USA cancels visa, 296

Peñaranda, Enrique (General) 143, 146, 151, 153, 161, 189, 193
Peru, 27, 57, 63, 221, 234, 253, 301, 308
agrarian reform of Velasco Alvarado, 121
Peruvian–Bolivian conference of indigenist educators in Arequipa, 195
Pinochet, Augusto (General), 69
Plan Bolivia, 291, 307
Plan Dignidad, 293, 297–8
Popular Participation Law (1993), 19, 301, 303, 310, 311, 325–6, 330, 334, 346, 351, 353, 355, 356–7, 359–62, 371
Partido Revolucionario Institucional (PRI), *see* Mexico
Prieto Laurens, Jorge, 72
Pro-Santa Cruz Committee, 38

Quechua, 2, 11, 33, 192, 199, 200, 236, 249, 250, 357
Quintana Roo insurrection, 57
Quintanilla Quiroga, Carlos (General), 143, 151
Quiroga, Jorge 'Tuto', 283, 293, 296, 315, 322, 326, 361
Quispe, Felipe, 289, 300, 304–7, 309, 313, 358, 361
opposition to gas sales to USA, 293

Ramos Quevedo, Luis, 167
Razón de Patria (RADEPA), 143, 146
Reed, John, 95
Reyes Villa, Manfred, 290, 291
Rosca, La, 31, 45, 65–7, 69, 119
rural schools, 12
Warisata experiment, 12
Russia, 3, 7, 25, 26, 27, 41–2, 55, 59, 107, 365
disintegration of Soviet bloc, 43
Stalinism, 71

Salamanca, Daniel, 151
San Pedro, 35
San Román, Claudio (Colonel), 30
Sánchez Bustamante, Daniel, 189
Sánchez de Lozada, Gonzalo, 1, 17, 136, 283, 298, 307, 309, 312, 319–21, 325–6, 328, 330, 333–4, 337, 339, 356
architect of NPE, 329
poor performance in 2002 presidential elections, 290
forms weak government, 291–2
proposes parliamentary system, 305
Sandoval Morón, Luis, 36
Sanjinés, Julio, 74, 135, 157
Santa Cruz, 35
Santa Cruz–Cochabamba highway, 35
Seleme, General Antonio, 5, 32
Servicio Cooperativa Inter-Americano de Educación (SCIDE), 200–2
Siles Zuazo, Hernán, 1, 6, 29, 30, 34, 36, 38, 40, 44, 74, 100, 105, 138, 145, 220, 289, 297
dies in Montevideo (1996), 138
'human face' of 1952, 138
leads 1952 uprising, 5
president (1956–60), 34
president (1982), 22, 220

Stabilization Plan, 71
stands down (1985), 323
vice-president (1952), 30
weak administration (1956–60), 33

Tamayo, Franz, 186
Tarija, 35
Tejada Sorzano, Luis, 151
Tesis de Pulacayo, 59, 130
Titicaca, Lake, 70, 108, 118, 189, 264
Toro, José David, Colonel, 143, 151
Trotskyism, 48, 60, 99, 127, 130, 140, 159, 229, 276, 290, 302
Túpaj (Túpac) Amaru, 10, 119, 120–8, 130
Túpaj Katari (1781), 10, 108, 118–131

Ucureña; 35, 36
Unidad Cívica de Solidaridad, 290
Unidad Democrática Popular, 6
United Nations, 100
universal suffrage, 1, 5, 14, 31–3, 177, 237, 261
1950s rise in electorate, 32
urbanization, 251–253, 254
Urriolagoitia, Mamerto, 151, 155
Uruguay, 41
USA, 5–6, 8–10, 12, 27, 30–1, 34, 38, 47, 62–4, 76–8, 91, 153–4, 185, 197–9, 253, 297, 309, 374–5
Alliance for Progress, 37–8, 218
conflict with MAS in Chapare, 299
counter narcotics policies, 293
Eder plan, 217
Eisenhower, Dwight D. 99–100, 103
influence on Villa, 105
Kennedy assassinated, 39
Kennedy elected president, 37
Mann Doctrine, 39
Triangular Plan, 34

Vargas, Virgilio, 171–2
Venezuela, 27, 100, 308, 318–19, 339
Villarroel, Gualberto, 4, 12–13, 27–8, 31, 41, 66–7, 137, 146, 148, 150–1, 165–6, 168–70, 196, 199, 335, 338
lynched in 1946, 147
Villarroel decrees (1945), 172–9

Wilson, Woodrow, 95–96, 105
women, 14, 213
birth rate, 239, 241
educational neglect, 248
enter public sphere, 191
ethnic self-perception, 357
granting of vote to, 33
World Bank, 224, 254, 270–3, 280, 293, 329, 331
World War I, 8, 95, 183
World War II, 28, 66, 142-3, 145–6, 148, 153, 197

Yaqui insurrection, 57

Zapatismo, *see* under Mexico
Zavaleta Mercado, René, 139, 146